BOZEAT 2000

BOZEAT INDEX TO STREETS

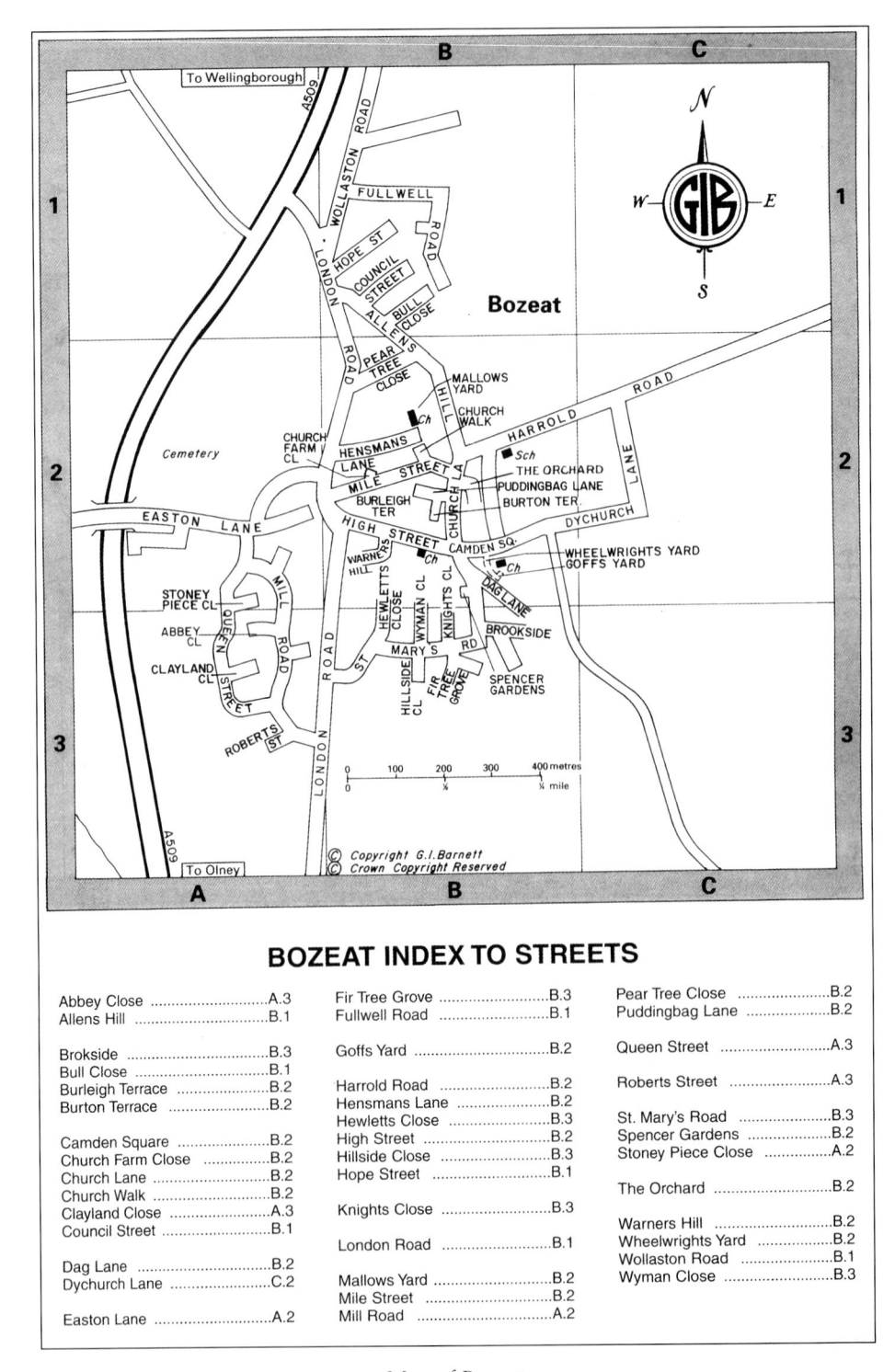

Abbey Close A.3	Fir Tree Grove B.3	Pear Tree Close B.2
Allens Hill B.1	Fullwell Road B.1	Puddingbag Lane B.2
Brokside B.3	Goffs Yard B.2	Queen Street A.3
Bull Close B.1		
Burleigh Terrace B.2	Harrold Road B.2	Roberts Street A.3
Burton Terrace B.2	Hensmans Lane B.2	
	Hewletts Close B.3	St. Mary's Road B.3
Camden Square B.2	High Street B.2	Spencer Gardens B.2
Church Farm Close B.2	Hillside Close B.3	Stoney Piece Close A.2
Church Lane B.2	Hope Street B.1	
Church Walk B.2		The Orchard B.2
Clayland Close A.3	Knights Close B.3	
Council Street B.1		Warners Hill B.2
	London Road B.1	Wheelwrights Yard B.2
Dag Lane B.2		Wollaston Road B.1
Dychurch Lane C.2	Mallows Yard B.2	Wyman Close B.3
	Mile Street B.2	
Easton Lane A.2	Mill Road A.2	

Map of Bozeat
(Reproduced from 'Northants Street Atlas' by kind permission of the publishers, G. I. Barnett & Son Ltd)

BOZEAT 2000

The Story of a Northamptonshire Village

Compiled by Philip Bligh

W. D. WHARTON
Wellingborough

Dedicated to my wife Audrey
and our children Stuart, Rachel, Judi, Sarah and Jon and their families
and the good people of Bozeat

First published in 2003 by
W. D. Wharton
37 Sheep Street
Wellingborough
Northamptonshire NN8 1BX
Tel: 01933 222690

© Philip Bligh 2003

Philip Bligh asserts his moral right to be identified as the author of this work.

ISBN 1-899597-13-1

All rights reserved. No part of this publication may be reproduced, stored in a retrieval system, or transmitted, in any form or by any means, electronic or mechanical, photocopying, recording or otherwise, without the prior permission of the publisher.

Typeset by John Hardaker
Wollaston, Northamptonshire

Printed and bound in Great Britain by
Impress Print, Corby, Northamptonshire

Contents

Preface	6
Introduction	7
Frontispiece	9
What's in a Name?	10
Memory Lane	**11**
1. The Land of Our Fathers – Victorian and Edwardian Bozeat	12
2. The Years of The Great War – 1914-18	23
3. The Years Between the Wars – 1920s and 1930s	26
4. Battle for Britain – 1939-45	42
5. After the War was Over – 1945-80	61
6. Bozeat Today – 1980-99	81
Boot and Shoe	**95**
7. Northamptonshire and the Rise of the Shoe Trade	96
8. Shoemaking in Bozeat	100
9. The Botterills – the History of W. Botterill & Son	115
10. Boot and Shoe from a Personal Point of View – Philip Boswell	120
Livelihoods	**125**
11. Farms and Farmers	126
12. Inns, Innkeepers and Beer	145
13. Business and Trade	165
14. Shops and Shopkeepers	183
15. The History of the Co-op in Bozeat	195
16. Buildings and Builders of Bozeat	203
Infrastructure	**233**
17. Education	234
18. Health	251
19. Roads and Travellers	259
20. Fire!	275
Religion	**283**
21. Methodism and Nonconformity in Bozeat	284
22. The Church of St Mary, Bozeat	299
23. Bells and Bell-ringers	311
24. Vicars of Bozeat 1220-2000	320
25. Closure of the Parish Churchyard	340
The Arts	**343**
26. Music	344
27. Spencelayh	350
Appendices	**361**
Bozeat Home Guard – 200 Years Ago	362
The Bogs	364
Village Diary	365
Field Names	406
Place Names of the Past	409
Honest John's catalogue (1921) – a selection of pages	419
Bozeat in Springtime – a poem by William Harold Drage (1945)	436
Bibliography	437
Index	438

Preface

The year was 1990; Sue and I had attended yet another induction of a new vicar in the Borough of Wellingborough.

Afterwards I said to the then Rural Dean, Rev. Haydn Smart, "It's been a most enjoyable service, but when will Bozeat have a new vicar?" We had been without one for a while. His reply was interesting: "Don't say anything, but we have the very man, his name is Philip Hamilton Bligh. He's an evangelical, with three university degrees." "Is Bozeat ready for him, or more to the point – is he ready for Bozeat?" I asked jokingly.

The years that followed were a joy to everyone in the parish. It didn't matter if you were church or chapel, believer or non-believer, old or young, Philip related to all.

One day Philip arrived at our house in Mill Road riding his Honda motorcycle, it was a familiar sight in the village. But where was his helmet? I asked him of its whereabouts. It transpired that while he was on his way he had stopped to play football with some village children; the helmet had been used as one of the goalposts. He was so keen to play with the youngsters that a minor detail like a helmet was unimportant. His boundless energy and unbridled enthusiasm left most of us standing. I never saw him walking, he was always breaking into a canter.

Truly – a man of God who has the unique ability to make everyone feel important and loved.

We not only gained a vicar, but also a vicar's wife, Audrey. She came from priestly stock and knew the art of being a vicar's wife, and very well you could say. Although Philip held the title of Vicar, it was very much a joint ministry. People of the parish would feel comfortable in going to the vicarage for help, advice, guidance and comfort; the door was ever open and there was always a welcome, with the kettle on.

The people of Bozeat were delighted when they heard that Philip was going to write a book on the history and day-to-day activity of the village. Philip began to interview anyone who could tell him a tale of yesteryear.

Copious amounts of tea and coffee, and many gallons of midnight oil later – here we have it, and, may I say, what a wonderful book it is.

If you thought Bozeat was a sleepy little village in the middle of England with no tale to tell, then you would be very wrong, for within the pages of this excellent book you will find accounts of murder and intrigue. You will read of the rise and fall of the British shoe industry, matters of national, cultural, religious and social history and much more.

It is with great pleasure I commend this book to you. I hope you spend many happy hours reading it.

May I also take this opportunity to thank Philip and Audrey Bligh for sharing their lives with us here in Bozeat. We can all see Christ more clearly as a result of your ministry among us.

God bless you both.
Tom Partridge-Underwood

Introduction

I can claim little more than to be the Compiler of the following history. It truly is the work of others who know far more than me about Bozeat's past, for they have delved more deeply into it; or they know more of its present for they have spend more of their lives living in the village.

The publication in 1936 of *The History of Bozeat Village* written by Rev. J. H. Marlow, Vicar of Bozeat from 1929 to 1944, was a milestone because it was until now the only known published record of its life. It is an important work as it arises out of his own research into original historic documents and his own unique acquaintance with the village. He was also meticulous in keeping a record of village events given to him by others of the recent past, as well as keeping a log of those of his own time. His findings were first published in his church magazine started after he became Vicar in 1929, and these articles have recently been republished as a book *Bozeat: Your Village History* by Bozeat Historical and Archaeological Society. I have quoted and drawn from both these works liberally as they are so important in gaining an understanding of the life of the village and how it evolved.

Norman Palmer was for 20 years my predecessor as Vicar of Bozeat and gave considerable time and skill to researching original documents on the life of the village, particularly in relation to its character in the 19th century, but also back to its roots in the 17th century (where most of our available documents begin) and earlier still. He published several articles in the village magazine *About Bozeat* which were the result of his meticulous work, and several of these I have used in their original form as he gave them to me, together with other interesting and careful studies which he carried out. In these cases, I have shown his name in the chapters concerned in this book.

Acknowledgement must be made to the village magazine *About Bozeat* which since its inception in 1980 has been a mouthpiece for much of the village history as remembered by villagers themselves, and was the product of sterling and faithful work by such people as Penny Brannon, Diane West and Lynne Ward. We owe them and all who have worked with them a debt of gratitude. The use of information from *About Bozeat* in this book is appropriately and gratefully acknowledged.

In the early 1990s, two publications of *A Pictorial History of Bozeat* were published by a group mainly associated with Bozeat Methodist Church, with photographs and other visual and verbal information. I gratefully acknowledge information used from these publications.

I am also indebted to local historian David Hall for information both from his publications and from tape recordings of talks he gave to the Bozeat Historical and Archaeological Society.

My indebtedness to Trevelyan's *History of England* which has inspired in me a love of 'real' history – that of ordinary people – is clear from repeated quotations from this beautifully written masterpiece.

I wish to express my gratitude to:

Judith Line for reading the complete text with meticulous care and attention to detail, and advising me on errors and suggesting amendments.

Tom Partridge-Underwood, with his outstanding knowledge of Bozeat and its people, who has in his usual cheerful way looked over the text, for which I give my appreciation.

Those who have contributed the photographs and drawings which illustrate this book.

The Headteacher and Governors of Bozeat Primary School for access to the Coronation Scrapbook.

Robert Wharton, who for many years had the bookshop in Wellingborough, for his enthusiasm and punctilious attention to detail. His willingness to publish this history will win a debt of gratitude both from Bozeat and myself.

Finally my thanks go to so many villagers themselves who have become such good friends and shared so much of their life story with me. Here I have tried to communicate their precious memories and words as faithfully as I can. Inevitably, however hard I have tried not to do so, I must at times have misrepresented them or misunderstood them, or been insensitive to little details. For this I must ask their forgiveness. To have done nothing and preserved nothing of their precious memories would, I believe, have been the greater offence as their story might then have been lost for ever. In order not to lose the vitality of these stories, I have retold them wherever possible in the first person, in the way that I have received them orally in the first place through many conversations. This I have done to capture as much of the flavour, character and mood of friends, some sadly no longer with us, who shared themselves as much as their memories with me and left this precious human archive for others to enjoy.

I have had to firmly limit the amount that I could record from information given me, or otherwise the book would have been at least ten times longer than it is. My hope is that it will build up a picture in the minds of its readers of quite a remarkable village – a village of which I have been privileged to be its Vicar for nine years – from 1990 to 1999. It will be apparent that whilst it would be ideal to take this 'picture' of the village at one point in time, the book has been written from anecdotes related to me over a period of years; further, it has taken some time to see the book in print, to the extent that items written as 'now' are already history. I hope that any time lapses in the story I have told will be understood.

In one sense Bozeat remained cut off from the modern world until the Second World War and remained an integral community within itself until its boot and shoe industry, which was its life and economy, suddenly collapsed and disappeared at the end of the 1970s. This, together with the influx of newcomers during the 1960s to the 1980s which doubled the village's population, has meant that we are in danger of losing for ever the soul of a village that has kept its character and mentality with little change for some 800 years. This is a piece of human history – indeed of Northamptonshire and English village life – that we must not forget.

To preserve this precious story between the covers of one book is my way of thanking a village that has been such an important part of my life.

Philip Bligh

Frontispiece

On a dark cold Friday night in early February 1995, fifty Bozeat men sat down to dinner together in the church hall to enjoy an evening of good food and good company.

Then, well fed, Derek Taylor, the local butcher's boy for 40 years, kept us spellbound for a full hour with his tales of his experiences – so full of mischief and humour that we laughed until we cried! I had never tasted good company such as this until I became vicar of the village of Bozeat.

Early next morning I drove my wife and daughter to catch the London train from Bedford. I came back through Turvey and then on to Carlton and Harrold following the River Ouse.

The River lay flat and swollen in its broad valley moving easily through the wide green fields on either side, stretching as far as the eye could see and marked out by leafless hedgerows and a scattering of bare trees. And the entire pastoral scene was warmed to life by the bright yellow rays of the low morning sun.

I compared this idyllic experience with the inferno of endless queues of traffic – the fumes and the noise and the miles of brick and concrete and litter in downtown London to which my wife and daughter were returning and where we had lived for 17 years before coming to Bozeat!

As I looked at the flooded valley and thought of the rains of these past weeks, I remembered Mrs Gertrude King, then aged 94, at our village lunch club for senior citizens the previous Wednesday who gave me the benefit of her country wisdom: *"Well you know what they say – 'February fills the dyke, black or white.'"*

I drove back to the vicarage up Hensmans Lane and shuddered as I saw the rooks pairing up in the tall limes in the glebe alongside our house and heard their first loud rasping 'caws' for 1995 as they gathered to think about building their large clumsy nests. *"Crows get married on Valentine's Day,"* village folk tell me – and I think they are right. It takes these ingenuous birds two weeks to make up their minds to get started – and then no peace for four months! *"If they nest high 'twill be a fine summer"* – comes more of that wisdom from the soil.

There is a country spirituality with ancient laws and gentle reverence which I, from downtown South London, knew nothing about.

What's in a name?

Bozeat Millennium Village Sign.

One possible explanation of what Bozeat means has received a lot of attention lately. However, in his original book *The History of Bozeat Village*, published in 1936, the Rev. J. H. Marlow gave two alternatives:

1. Bozeat probably existed in Saxon times – Saxon coins have been found – and an early spelling of Bozeat was Bosgate suggesting Bozeat may have meant bosa's gate. Bosa was a common Saxon name and a Saxon Earl Bosa held land here. In a similar way Strixton is named after the Saxon Thane *Strix*.

In old English *gear/gaet*, and in Middle English *yatt* and *zett* are all recognised as meaning gate, opening or entrance to woods or land. All the various spellings of Bozeat over the years show some link to both Bosa and gate.

The Oxford Dictionary of Place-names quotes written records held in the British Museum which show Bozeat spelt:

1066	BOSIETE
1154	BOZEYATE
1150-60	BOSEGATE
1180s	BOSGIETA
1200s	BOSEGATE
1255	BOSYATE
1350	BOSGATE

Our possible French influence is shown in the *Domesday Book* (1066) spelling BOZIETE and it is possible that the Normans slightly altered the name to make it more French. There may even be a link with the French BOSQUET (small wood) or Latin BOSCUS (wood).

With all the vagaries of spelling and spoken English over the centuries it is not likely that BOZEAT is still pronounced in the same way it was originally.

2. The second explanation of the name Bozeat – that it means beautiful spring from the French Beau-jet – does assume that the pronunciation of Bozeat was the same centuries ago as it is now. So although this theory is very appealing it does not have the same historical credibility as the first – BOSA'S GATE.

Christine Downey, *About Bozeat*, March 1994

Memory Lane

A personal journey through the century

Mem'ries
Light the corners of my mind.
Misty water coloured mem'ries of the way we were.

Alan and Marilyn Bergman

Drawing by Michael Pollard from an aerial photo dated 1964. Note that the two vicarages are in the picture, also Church Farm Yard. *(M. Pollard)*

CHAPTER 1

The Land of Our Fathers – Victorian and Edwardian Bozeat

Where past and present meet
Until Don's death in October 1998, Don and Dolly Roberts lived at 55 London Road. Their home is one of two attached stone cottages built by the Manor Estate of Bozeat in 1857 together with a church school building which still stands alongside them at the bottom of Mile Street. The cottage adjacent to the school was built for the school teacher, the other for the doctor. Harry Edmunds who died in 1969 at the age of 100 was the last surviving pupil of the old school. He remembered the thick frosted windows in the school which were high up the wall to prevent pupils looking out and being distracted from their lessons. Don kept a piece of this glass as a memento!

In June of 1857 the Estate was sold by Archdeacon Cotton to Mr Thomas Revis, and it appears that Mr Revis bought it largely by mortgage. (However, the advowson, or right of presentation to the Vicarage of Bozeat, remained with Earl Spencer, whose family inherited the estate through marriage in 1744. The advowson was handed over to the Bishop of Peterborough in 1922.) The tragic story of the only son, Thomas Henry Revis, is preserved for us in the East Window of the church.

The story goes that he committed suicide at the age of 36 on 11th February 1869 because his parents refused to allow him to marry a common village girl with whom he had fallen in love (*The History of Bozeat Village* by Rev. J. H. Marlow, 1936, p.8). This matches the tragic death of Diana Princess of Wales, famous daughter of Earl Spencer, in a car accident in Paris with her boyfriend, Dodi Fayed (whose father owns Harrods) just hours before we celebrated the Bozeat Feast Day on Sunday 31st August 1997 with a live-link between St Mary's, Bozeat and Holy Cross Anglican Church, Canberra, Australia whose Rector Archdeacon Allan Huggins was on a vicar exchange with myself. I sat in silence with the congregation in Holy Cross as the sound of the Bozeat tenor bell came clearly over the P/A system as it solemnly tolled her death – ringing as clearly as though it were above us. How curious are the coincidences that link human lives and families over the centuries – the tragic deaths of Thomas Revis and Diana Spencer whose families both owned the village of Bozeat.

It is interesting to note that thirty miles from Canberra is the town of Yass where the mother of Lady Di had a farm at Broomfield (since sold to Rupert Murdoch I believe). Shortly after Diana's engagement to the Prince of Wales she visited her mother and had a drink with the locals in the bar of the Club House Hotel on the High Street and there was erected a plaque on the wall of the bar to commemorate the occasion:

THIS PLAQUE COMMEMORATES THE TIME ON 10th DAY OF FEBRUARY 1981 WHEN LADY DIANA SPENCER THE PRINCESS OF WALES HONOURED THE MENNO BAR OF THE CLUB HOUSE HOTEL WITH HER CUSTOM.

Licensee: P. Tracey, Tooth Hotels Pty Ltd

Easton Maudit
Directly opposite the Roberts' cottage, the old road from Castle Ashby enters the

THE LAND OF OUR FATHERS – VICTORIAN AND EDWARDIAN BOZEAT

This thatched building became the Post Office in 1900. The previous Post Office was in High Street in the first Co-op shop (Mrs Sarrington's Buildings). John Partridge married Miss Hardwick, the postmistress, and moved the Post Office here, 70 London Road. *(Bozeat School Scrapbook)*

The thatched building housing the Post Office was demolished and rebuilt c.1900 with W. J. Hayes, drapers, also in the property. Mr Hayes was also Sunday School superintendent, and took over the running of the Post Office on the retirement of Mrs Partridge. This is now a private house named 'The Post House'. *(Bozeat School Scrapbook)*

London Road. It ran straight along the present Easton Lane to Easton Maudit, then on across what is now called the golf links and then continued directly across farmer Richard Allebone's fields, making a beeline for Castle Ashby House, the home of the Marquis of Northampton, Lord Compton, and a broken line of trees still betrays this old route. Villagers now in their eighties remember how as children in the 1920s they would spend a profitable morning opening the gate near Easton Maudit for the carriages to pass through for the reward of a halfpenny. There were two gates at Easton Maudit at either side of The Park, where Park House is now situated and where up until the end of the 18th century was to be found the magnificent Manor and Park of the Yelverton Family. This was sold to the Comptons of Castle Ashby and demolished in 1799, its priceless library being parcelled up by dealers and sold for virtually nothing, so it is said. The gate nearest Bozeat where the old wall to the Park ended was operated by the Bozeat children and the gate near the church was taken charge of by the Easton Maudit children and there were often quarrels between them!

Ten yards to the right of this junction still stands the Post House, 70 London Road, in 1995 occupied by Dennis and

Mr B. Morris, postman in 1912, who came to the village each day from Wellingborough, outside the Lord Nelson, with Nelson Yard to the left.
(Bozeat School Scrapbook)

Sue Evans. In fact the actual stopping place for the London Coach, for mail and passengers, was the Red Lion Inn across the road. John Partridge and W. J. Hayes who were 'big' (i.e. Methodist) chapel colleagues had the two stone cottages (the one now called the Post House adjacent to the Co-op and the one next to it) in 1900. John Partridge opened the first Post Office at number 70 and Mr Hayes opened a drapery next door. Incidentally Mr Hayes' daughter Dorothy gave Marjorie Drage her Victorian aspidistra which in 1995 was 130 years old and very much alive at 13 Wyman Close and which got a special mention on BBC Gardeners' Question Time!

Don and Dolly Roberts' forebears

Don was born on the 4th May 1911. His grandfather, Amos Roberts, married to Priscilla, came to Bozeat from Great Doddington and was a shoemaker by trade. He had built a house which is now number 10 Wollaston Road presently occupied by Bernard Line. Bernard married Ivy, one of the 120 evacuee children from London who came to the village during the Second World War in 1939. Ivy became a lively leader of the Wesleyan Chapel and Sunday School. The injection of new life into the village by such outsiders particularly in the second half of the twentieth century is a story with much interest.

If you enter Bernard's house there is evidence of how Amos' workshop was incorporated into the building, where he made shoes for the local factory of John Drage, consolidated in a building at the bottom of Hope Street presently used by Knapp Tools. Prior to this the Drage Shoe Company business was scattered in various buildings around the village. Amos had three children, one being Percy the father of Don. Don was born in Hope Street, one of six children, and the family soon moved to a cottage (now demolished) behind the Working Men's Club. Percy worked in John Drage's factory from the time he left school until 1929. He retired in 1947 at the age of 67.

The third building from the right along Wollaston Road is No. 10, once the house of Don Roberts' father. Also in this picture are houses occupied by Miss Laura Bettles, schoolteacher, and Bernard and Gladys Line.

Dolly was born at what is now 6 Burton Terrace, adjacent to Pudding Bag Lane and now the home of Derek and Pat Taylor. Up until 1990 Derek had worked for 40 years for the village butchers owned by Olive and her brother Sam Garrett, a business that began in the last decade of the 19th century. Derek, a lad from Podington, became their butcher's boy in 1950 at the age of 15. In fact this was Dolly's grandparents' house. Her grandfather, Fred Tompkins was also a shoemaker and his workshop is still to be seen in the barn or shed across the yard. One lady in the village remembers how as children they were frightened of Dolly's grandfather as "he hadn't got a nose – just two holes!" This was due to an abscess which had eaten it away, a consequence of the malnutrition and poor hygiene of his childhood in the middle and late nineteenth century. "I will not have him ridiculed," said Dolly hotly, as she remembered how "he had to put up with many taunts of ignorant people who made fun of his disabilities, especially youngsters."

Fred Tompkins and his wife (Dolly Roberts' grandparents) outside 6 Burton Terrace in c.1938. (D. Roberts)

A childhood view of life at 6 Burton Terrace at this time is recalled by Winifred Corby. "As a child I remember sitting ... by an old black-leaded grate with a fire burning leather bits which we bought by the sack from Corby's leather factory. For lighting we had an oil lamp on the table. We had no hot water, only a drop in the 'boiler', which was a cavity in the grate, with a lid on, by the side of the fire. In the oven on the other side we dried the sticks to light the fire." (*About Bozeat*, March 1982)

Fred Tompkins was born not long after the potato famine of the 'hungry forties' 1845-1849 which spread over Europe killing millions (over a million in Ireland alone) and was followed by typhus and other diseases. "In Bozeat burials increased from 12 in 1847 to 38 in 1848. In 1849 these dropped back to 21 and then to 13 in 1850" (Norman Palmer, *About Bozeat*, September 1995). Much of his right foot particularly toward the toes had also been rotted away by gangrene and Dolly remembers how as children they would sometimes help their father pack his boot with lamb's wool so he could walk. The gangrene set in after a horse stamped on his foot and there was not enough money to pay the doctor's fees for treatment. From a photograph of Fred in later years one can see that apart from these two features he has the small finger missing from his left hand which was cut badly, possibly using a shoe knife. Such accidents were not an uncommon occurrence. "He had so much to endure with his gangrenous leg," remembers Dolly, "He could only hobble about, not walk at all. He always rode a bicycle if he went to his allotment and had to fall off to get off.... I know he endured much pain but no amount of pain could tempt him to be anything

Church Farm. *(Bozeat School Scrapbook)*

but a strict teetotaller as he belonged to the Band of Hope.... His brother Jack, a builder by trade, took to drink and was well known in the village – seldom sober and thoroughly earned his nickname as 'Happy Jack'!" Don remembers how when Jack was taking down a wall in their house some of the rubble which was used to fill the wall cavity poured out with clouds of dust. "You should have heard the string of swear words he uttered" – colourful but shocking to Don's Chapel ears!

Fred Tompkins must have been born some years before 1877 as he told Dolly how as a lad he helped dig and move stones for the building of the Methodist Church which opened that year. He died in 1949. Fred, or Bamp as Dolly called her grandfather, had a good ear for music. Self taught, he played the trombone in the Bozeat Brass Band (see Chapter 26) which was formed about 1887 (Queen Victoria's Golden Jubilee Year). He could play the mouth organ and Dolly remembers him tinkering on their piano which they were given in 1930. Dolly herself must have inherited some of his musical gifts for she became a fine pianist and in 1995 still plays the organ at the Methodist Chapel. Her grandparents rented 6 Burton Terrace from Cephas Drage, the baker, who lived across the yard at No. 1, what is now called The Old Bakery. "When we visited, Bamp wanted to know all the Chapel news. Bamp talked a lot about the Band of Hope and drink and I signed the Pledge at seven years of age," – one of the many childhood memories Dolly has of her grandfather.

Dolly's father, also born in Jubilee Year, 1887, was Herbert Tompkins, or Bert, as he was known. For many years he worked for George Knight who owned Church Farm and lived at Church Farm House adjacent to Hensmans Lane. The stone houses in Church Farm Close built in 1987 are (see Michael Pollard's drawing) where the farmyard and barns used to be, but the old house, parts of which date back at least to the 17th century, still stands. (My predecessor, Norman Palmer, was seen wheeling

Looking up Allens Hill, where Dolly Roberts' family moved in 1926. No. 5 is just off to the left.

barrow-loads of muck from the old yard to fertilize our kitchen garden before the builders moved in!)

When Dolly was born in 1923, Bert worked for the Knights for 28 shillings (£1.40) a week. He and his wife lived at Shepherds Lodge across the fields, Strixton way, by the 'Tin Pits'. When Dolly was three her parents moved into the first council house to be built in the village at what is now 5 Allens Hill in 1926. This experience formed one of her earliest memories. "We came to the village in a dray cart pulled by two horses, Nimble and Diamond. We three children were under five years of age and we all sat under our big round table clinging to its legs as the road track was very bumpy! Dad stopped half way, just past the blackberry hedge leading into the avenue of sixteen elm trees on the north edge of Bozeat, to adjust the tablecloth so that the rain did not come in. I remember the cloth was green and rust in colour. It was a dull miserable day but Joyce and I were excited about living in a new house with a bathroom!"

Marjorie Drage remembers

Marjorie Drage was born at Town Farm in December 1909 having an older brother Dick and a younger one Ted, whose skill as a carpenter is apparent in chapel, church and village. The family lived there until 1930 when their father Harry Drage retired. Harry married Sarah Emma Cave, sister of Tom Cave's father, Uncle Bert, who was the undertaker. They rented the farm from Mr Blunt of Rushden just before they were married in about 1903. Harry died eight years after retirement in 1938 at the age of 70. Mr Threadgold took over Town Farm after Harry but the land was gradually sold off to the Browns at Manor Farm on one side and the Greens at White House Farm towards Olney on the other.

In 1996 there is only one field left owned by Malcolm Threadgold (landscape gardener) living in Goffs Yard and used for the annual village fireworks display on 5th November. Paul and Fiona Mason, who have an osteopath practice in Olney, live

John Drage's Arch Villa factory 1885. (*Bozeat School Scrapbook*)

High Street with London Road and the Co-op in the distance, Arch Villa straight ahead, the building which housed Laughton's furniture shop on the right, and behind it four old cottages, now demolished, where the Colecloughs lived. On the left is the 1878 Co-op building.

at Town Farm House. Ted Drage, Harry's son, is in 1996 still making superb furniture in the small wooden shed in the garden of his bungalow at the top of Allens Hill overlooking the Glebe field, and teaching the children carpentry at the village school at the age of 81!

Marjorie's great-grandfather was born in 1835 and died on 1st April 1906 at the age of 72. His wife Emma was born in 1830 and died only two months before him on 4th February 1906 at the age of 76.

Marjorie's grandfather William was in the shoe trade as was his brother John and together they founded the business which was to bear their name, Drage's Shoes. It developed as one of the most flourishing businesses in the village. John Drage gained the nickname 'Honest John' and lived with his family in the house which is now the Paper Shop at the west end of the High Street in what is called Arch Villa. The original factory buildings are still there adjacent to the house in an L shape, the fish and chip shop (run by a young couple from Vietnam and Hong Kong) and the publishing and publicity company of Rachel Mallows which occupies the other part. Rachel's father David Mallows owns the whole Arch Villa site.

Uncle William, Honest John's son, married Marjorie's father's sister, Polly. As the eldest son he took over the family business and lived at Arch Villa. William was a devout and leading Chapel man and Marjorie remembers going to Sunday lunch there when often they would also entertain the preacher after the service. Ted did not go so often because he would not eat up his vegetables! After lunch you had to be absolutely quiet whilst Uncle Will had his sleep. Then you would have to tiptoe to the toilet and out to Sunday School at 3 o'clock. Ted remembers the abject boredom that filled a young boy's mind on these occasions!

THE LAND OF OUR FATHERS – VICTORIAN AND EDWARDIAN BOZEAT

Marjorie's father's mother – her grandmother Christina – lived with her daughter (after her husband had died) at 105 London Road, now called Spencelayh House after the famous painter of that name who lived there from 1941 to 1958. As a little girl Marjorie often spent Sunday evenings with her grandmother and she remembers her showing her the pair of white gloves and cotton stockings and embroidered night dress threaded with black ribbon in which she was to be buried – along with all her membership tickets issued annually by the Methodist Church, tied up with a black ribbon – and she had been a member "all my life"! She also asked that four workmen from the factory be bearers of her coffin, "But if they don't do it that way I shan't interfere!"

Water, water, everywhere!

Bozeat could not be further from the sea but water is its life blood, thanks to its peculiar geology and strange geography, full as it is of ups and downs and clay and gravel beds. Finding water is not a problem – there are wells and springs everywhere. As has been commented before, even the name 'Bozeat' may come from the Norman-French meaning of the word 'beautiful jet' which some believe refers to the Town Well where a jet of clean water sprang out from the side of the meadow adjacent to Dychurch Lane into a stone walled pool, which had disappeared through neglect, where once cattle drank and horses were watered. For the year 2000, the Parish Council has refurbished the pool and water now flows again.

It was from the high ground above Dychurch (meaning ditch) on either side but especially from up towards Harrold that water flowed down into the lane and along it into the High Street, once as an open brook. In the 19th century, the High Street was called Brook Street with the so-called 'brook' acting as an open drain for the

Bozeat has always been prone to flooding, here on 2nd June 1924 in Camden Square.
(Bozeat School Scrapbook)

This shows the Lord Nelson, and beyond, the building that housed the Fish & Chip Shop of Mr and Mrs Yorke, now demolished.
(Bozeat School Scrapbook)

village. When it reached the London Road it turned along it northward towards Grendon, eventually to empty itself into the River Nene. Water also joined it from the high ground above Dag Lane reaching the High Street at Camden Square. Sid Jones, who was born in 1901 and lived for over 50 years opposite the arch in Dychurch, where the water goes underground, wrote in 1980: "Years ago nearly every field had a pond, until the end of the 20s and beginning of the 30s when piped water was laid in the village. It was then that the farmers filled in the ponds as water was now piped on to their farms. One of the deepest ponds was where the new school is built (in Harrold Road)."

And Winifred Corby remembers: "In the winter in The Rookery there was a very deep pit which filled with water and was grand for sliding on, as it froze over very quickly – now the new school is built over it. Now all the ponds are gone, the water has got to run somewhere so it all comes down the fields to the brook. But that's not all. Problems and mischief lay at the arch where now the brook goes underground as far as the London Road and where all the rubbish collects and blocks it. Years ago we had a resident roadman who always saw that the arch was kept clear, especially if we had a lot of rain. We have always had floods but not so bad as we have these last few years." (*About Bozeat*, March 1982).

The filling in of the ponds may help to explain the terrible flood in May 1952, for example, when two inches of rain fell in an hour on Bozeat. Water poured off the high ground all around Dychurch and the High Street, causing a six foot deep torrent to sweep down through the heart of the village, pouring into Cake Walk (or Fish Alley) and on down the London Road causing havoc as it went. After this disaster, massive pipes were laid to make sure that such devastation never happened again.

But as Sid said, "There have always been floods in Bozeat". In November 1894, for example, there are repeated references to floods and blocked drains. An inclusion in the school log for that month reads: "No school in afternoon. The water was knee deep all down street and round the school"! And an entry in the log for Nov. 22nd, 1912 reminds us of conditions in wet weather: "… cannot attend school on account of the mud they have to go through to get there …"

As a footnote to his recollections in *About Bozeat* for December 1980, Sid Jones writes: "By the way, I left school when I was 12 years old (1913) and started work in the local shoe factory for an old penny an hour. We worked 52 hours a week before the trade unions got it down to its present 40 hours."

The village stocks

These do not figure prominently in the history of Bozeat. Indeed, it has been difficult to discover precisely where they were located. Perhaps Bozeat was more law-abiding than some villages where they still remain as a tourist attraction on the village green; perhaps it was that, until the demolition of the Cross Keys Inn, there was no obvious village green in Bozeat.

Their location was in the High Street, to the left of the Methodist Church, or to be precise, to the left where it was to be built. On the site now is the house named Stonebank.

Marlow lists from the Constable's Accounts of 1688: For a new part of Stocks and Whipping Post, 13/4d Paid to Goody Dodson for ironwork for ye said Stocks and Whipping Post 4/-.

They are known to have been on Stonebank High Street as late as 1850.

Bozeat fayre

Bozeat Feast which celebrates the dedication of our Church in c.1130 to St Mary has been celebrated annually on the first Sunday after 26th August, the Feast of the Annunciation of the Virgin Mary (depicted on our Rood Screen) according to the old Julian calendar. Ever since it has been, apart from Christmas, the most important festival of the village.

Floss Tivey recalls how it was in about 1912 when an extra week of holiday was given to the children for the Bozeat Feast. In 1912, of the fields that were used for the fair – Windmill Field (owned by Mr Knight of Church Farm), 'Little Gains', 'The Lime Kiln', and 'The Chequers Field', the last was chosen. "I can remember quite clearly after weeks of anticipation seeing the caravans turning the corner by the factory and so up Allens Hill which was so steep for the poor horses (some 30 of them) to drag such a heavy load … the children ran in all directions to meet them, trying to peep into the caravans, and in their excitement tumbling over into the muddy road." On arrival, the boys unharnessed the horses after a wooden scotch was placed at the rear wheel. Often as not they would stampede down the hill to Windmill Field which was "… their haven of peace for the whole week with plenty of green grass and water from the Windmill pond. Then the showmen soon proceeded to 'set up' the stalls and were mostly in a bad temper."

"Bozeat Feast Sunday was such an important day. Most parishioners attended the Parish Church or the two Wesleyan Chapels. Relatives and friends came from far and near on bicycles or horses and carts or walking! Special fare was provided and our local bakers were kept very busy in coping with larger Yorkshire puddings." Most households had a receptacle called a 'ponshon' in which marigold wine and diadrink (a cure for all ills!) was made.

"After a hurried tea of real bread (not sliced) and dairy butter, fruit cake and other niceties, everyone would make their way to Camden Square to hear the Wollaston Silver Band play a selection of popular tunes. Meanwhile many organisations from nearby villages arrived in waggonettes dressed in full uniform to parade to either the Parish Church or the Methodist Chapel. Amongst the organisations which were headed by the band were our St John Ambulance Brigade, Nursing Sisters, Girl Guides, Boy Scouts and several others….

It made an imposing sight for such a small community …" the Square crowded with onlookers "busily chatting with friends they had not seen for many years" and hard working mothers of large families "having time to stand and watch from their front doorsteps in their best clothes … after the Service, another band concert was given on the Red Lion Hill where more crowds of people congregated along by the Cross Keys Inn and the row of stone cottages. Miss Rice's shop window had its blue blinds lowered, being the Sabbath Day, and dear Mrs Allebone's paper shop was also closed. Gradually the crowds dispersed and we children looked forward to Feast Monday!"

The celebrations and the Fayre lasted the whole week with its roundabouts and stalls and coconut shies and "the organ of the flying horse … set in the centre of the circle of horses and the almost-concealed steam engine provided the power needed" – a real show piece with its models, ladies in Grecian gowns and their hair in ringlets with men smartly dressed with doublet and hose, all moving slightly to the music – and the 'Try Your Strength' where young men could show off their muscular ability to the crowd!

Not until the evening did the thrills of the feast come alive with the bright oil lamps and the colour and music and excitement. Then the young men and maidens entered the show ground, all looking very smart, the men "with short hair heavily brilliantined" and girls "with long hair neatly brushed and tied up with a large black ribbon bow at the back of the neck" – no cosmetics or expensive hairdos in those days but "lovely to look at and I've heard many a romance started at Bozeat Feast!" Saturday night was the climax of the week and everyone was in a happy frame of mind ... and maybe even some children stayed awake until the Parish Church clock chimed midnight, the flying horses organ played 'God be with you till we meet again' followed by the national anthem and groups of happy young people made their way home and 'Bozeat Feast' – like the years – moved on." (*About Bozeat*, December 1980)

As a postscript, we should add Winifred Corby's memories of the Feast and those years. "On Bozeat Feast Sunday the Working Men's Club held a flower show and we had to go and see the fruits, flowers and vegetables with an uncle or cousin.... Then in the evening Wollaston Town Band used to play lovely music on the Square for an hour.... Mr Strudwick's Fair would also arrive about Bozeat Feast in Chequer's field – a family affair with swing boats, coconut shy, roundabouts, toffee apples and rock. Another lovely time was when there was an election and men walked about with huge red or blue ribbons on, but we kept well away from the pubs and the clubs that night."

Epilogue

As Norman Palmer and I sat in the coach together touring Israel in February 2000 and reflecting on Bozeat and its history, Norman turned to me and said: "You know the story of the East Window, how young Revis took his life because his father refused to allow him to marry a local girl. Well that was probably wrong. It was Don Roberts' grandfather who told him that the boy wanted to marry an auctioneer's daughter from Bedford. He must have been a very proud man," reflected Norman as we looked back to those Victorian times. "Of course what finished Revis was the poor harvests of the 1880s – and it finished others too – three years of heavy rain, and cheap imports of grain from abroad," continued Norman. "I gather from Don Roberts that old Revis used to come into the village in his pony-and-trap down from the Grange. But the poor harvests made him a bankrupt."

CHAPTER 2

The Years of the Great War (1914-1918)

Where have all the young men gone?

Old school days

Don's earliest memories are of his first day at Bozeat School – by then moved to what is now the old school house in Camden Square. It was 1916 and the five-year-old, frightened by the stern face of the headmistress, Mrs Bennell, had run the hundred yards down the High Street back home to their cottage behind the Working Men's Club.

There is an interesting entry in the School Log for 26th May 1916: "We celebrated Empire Day on Wednesday with a special lesson on the Flag and the Empire. We sang Patriotic songs with older scholars in the school yard and saluted the Flag."

Marjorie Drage went to school two years earlier than Don in 1914, the year war was declared. "Every winter the village flooded", remembers Marjorie (as did Sid Jones) for the water poured off the high ground towards Harrold, rushed down Dychurch Lane causing the little stream that flowed along the High Street, and then along London Road towards Grendon and the River Nene to turn into a flood. Marjorie and her friends on that side of the High Street would come to the high ground where the Post Office now is, alongside the blacksmith's, and look across the flood waters to the school on the other side, and loved it as they could not get to school! "We felt sorry for the children on the other side who still had to go! When they piped the stream underground we would throw rubbish in the stream up Dychurch to block the grill to the entrance to the pipe to, hopefully, bring the floods back, until the policeman or the roadman chased us away!"

Mr Wallace was the blacksmith and had his smithy in Wheelwrights Yard. Sid Jones remembers, as a lad, watching the blacksmith and his mate "getting the red hot (metal) tyres out with long tongs and hammering them on the wooden wheels and then they would throw cold water over them and make such a steam" (*About Bozeat*, June 1980) – hence the name, Wheelwrights Yard.

Mr Wallace was very fond of Marjorie and she of him and she spent many hours watching him at work shoeing the horses and he sometimes let her blow the bellows for him. He even wanted to adopt Marjorie but her parents weren't too keen! He would tease Marjorie about going to chapel; "We will now sing hymn two hundred and two-tee-two!" he would say laughingly. "Just in front of the blacksmith's, where the Post Office now is, was Mrs Robinson's where we children used to spend our Saturday pocket money of half a penny."

"Mr Lack was headmaster when I first went to school at the age of five. The previous head was Mr Kirby (appointed 1894). Mr Lack, headmaster from 1909 to 1946, taught the seniors with Mrs Lack and Miss Smith, and the infants were taught

Percy Roberts, Don's Dad. (*D. Roberts*)

by Mrs Bennell (Head of Infants) and Miss Bettles." Miss Bettles joined the staff as a young assistant teacher on 15th January 1915 and was to become one of the great characters of the village for most of the century, living as she eventually did in the attractive double-fronted house at 4 Wollaston Road. Mrs Bennell lived at 17 Bull Close.

A terrible war
In 1918 there were the Peace Celebrations in Warner's Field (which is now Hewlett's Close). Don remembers dancing around the maypole on this occasion and the other boys teasing him as he had to partner arm-in-arm one of the girls in his class! Some things never change! We have to remember that, in that terrible war, 210 Bozeat young men joined up and 38 never returned. Terry Drage is the son of Mrs Ada Drage (a devout member of St Mary's) who was sister of Hollingsworth (Hol) Smith, headmaster of Wollaston School and organist of St Mary's for many years between the wars. In 1994 Terry went to look for the grave of his uncle Percy Drage who was one of the 38 and no-one knew where he had fallen. Terry found his remains at last in the Military Cemetery at Meaulte, a village and commune in the Department of the Somme. There on a white stone amongst hundreds of rows of white stones stretching majestically and tragically across the countryside he found the words:

DRAGE, Pte. P.W. 331101
1st/1st Bn. Cambridgeshire Regt.
27th Aug., 1918.
F.31.

His death was part of the appalling loss of life along the Western Front in the Battle of the Somme where 60,000 fell on the first day. Incidentally, Terry Drage's father owned the bakery in Church Lane and before him his father Cephas Drage, who was also the money lender "… before the days of building societies – and he used to give out gold sovereigns!" remembers Arnold Dobbs.

Don's father, Percy, was in the army stationed at Sheringham on the north Norfolk coast with the Royal Engineers during part of the war. The family planned to go and stay with him during the summer holidays for five weeks and there was great excitement amongst the five children at the prospect of a holiday by the seaside. But soon after mother arrived there with the children, a German Zeppelin dropped a bomb on Sheringham (there is still a plaque marking the spot saying that it was the first bomb to be dropped on Britain in the War, at 8.30 pm on 19th February 1915 in Whitehall Yard) and mother promptly took the family back home again to the safety of Bozeat!

The war years and those prior to them were hard, except perhaps for the shoe trade which thrived on the need to provide the British army with boots (Drage's factory was enlarged at this time). We should not forget that several of Don's schoolmates died of diphtheria and measles in those years just prior to the First World War. Don's mother, married in 1903, lost two of her children in this way and the three surviving children all had diphtheria at the same time over one Christmas during the war, so she could easily have lost her three remaining children as well. A blanket soaked in disinfectant was hung across the door to minimise the spread of infection and Don remembers Dr Selby, who lived at Greenwood across the road from Peter and Rose Drage's House,

91 London Road (previously occupied by Dr Baxter and before him William Botterill, the shoe manufacturer) came and gave them an injection. "Do you want horrible medicine or an injection?" said the doctor and Don remembers having to roll over and have it in his backside! "He said it like that so we would choose the injection as the medicine would do us no good," said Don reflectively. What he also remembers of this visit was that we children peeped round the curtain and saw Dr Selby come up the path in the uniform of an army officer. He had obviously come and visited his patients while on leave. His wife was an army nurse ("I could tell you stories about her!" said Don with a twinkle in his eye!) The doctor in the village at that time was Dr Baxter from Wollaston who, as we have seen, lived opposite the Selbys, and stood in for Dr Selby while he was away at war.

Winifred Corby remembers Don's father from her childhood days. "We didn't have all the organisations that you have now, only the 'Band of Hope' which met once a week in the Wesley (i.e. Methodist) Chapel where we had singing and games, and sometimes Mr Percy Roberts came with his magic lantern and showed us films. That was a great night and it cost one halfpenny, a whole week's spending money. Once a year at the Independent Chapel we had a 'tea drinking'. We put on our best dress and took, each of us, a cup and saucer and plate, tied up in a big handkerchief, to a tea of jelly and custard and cake, and afterwards we went up to Warner's Field and had races. We talked of it for days afterwards. Now Warner's Field has a lot of neat houses on it (i.e. Hewlett's Close)." (*About Bozeat*, March 1984)

Dolly's father, Bert Tompkins, volunteered for the Great War at the age of 17 and was accepted. (The minimum allowed age was 18!). "With the glamour and low casualties of the Boer War still in recent memory, these boys eagerly volunteered with no idea how appallingly different this terrible war was to be," Don remembers. Bert was trained as a gunner and was in the trenches in France. "He had nightmares for years when we girls were small," remembers Dolly. "War widened the horizons but was terribly frightening, even exciting at times. Many of his mates were killed. He felt he was saved for a purpose."

The enormous premature loss of life in that terrible ordeal was to leave a cruel wound on the nation's history as heard in the poetry of Wilfrid Owen, but also seen in our village in the list to those 210 names on the memorial board under the organ loft in St Mary's Church of those young men who went to war and of whom 39 never returned. As we look at them we realise that virtually all the young men of the village must have gone to war. I had two aunts who never married primarily because there were not enough young men after the war to go round.

Spiritualism was popular after the war as mothers sought to contact the spirits of their departed sons, a belief that found support from such famous men as Sir Oliver Lodge and Sir Arthur Conan Doyle. The Toc H movement, founded behind the Allied lines in 1915 in Poperinge, Belgium for all servicemen to find rest and a place to talk and make friends in a quasi spiritual society, had a group formed in Bozeat in March 1932, becoming a fully fledged branch on 15th September 1937 and closing in October 1955. As a final commemoration to these young men of Bozeat we remember Ernest Hamilton Drage who was awarded The Distinguished Conduct Medal. The citation stated that he stayed at his post while under enemy gunfire.

Note: The names of those who fell are given towards the end of Chapter 4.

CHAPTER 3

The Years between the Wars – 1920s and 1930s

In this quiet little world of our own.

Building Booms and Population Explosions

We have told already how Dolly Roberts (Tompkins as was), at the age of three, came to live in the first council house to be built at 5 Allens Hill in 1926. In 1930, twelve new council houses were built in what was Bennes Field which adjoined the Tompkins garden and is now Council Street. "We children missed talking to the horses over the fence. I remember the road was very rough (Bill Silsby with the milk cart could hardly get up it!) – like Hope Street, Peartree and Bull Close were for years. Bull Close was such a rough messy road. We had to use it each day as Bamp, Uncle Sid, Dad and Uncle Alf had allotments there. They grew all kinds of vegetables. Bamp had a lovely Golden Drop plum tree and Uncle Sid a red apple tree. Dad and Bamp had the corner piece of the Lime Kiln (there is still evidence of the quarry behind the present allotments) and a huge hen run. The hens had to be fed, watered and cleaned out each day and so two daily visits were necessary. We had to work hard and the eggs had to be collected. And there were rat holes galore! Spot our terrier was the best rat catcher anywhere. His mother was Gibson's dog. He killed rats like lightning and my sister used to cut the tails off and the rat man gave us a penny for each tail."

These were the years of the First Labour Government formed in the General Election of 1924 which "created something like an apocalyptic atmosphere in many areas ... where socialism was a force to be reckoned with and had claimed the allegiance of many former chapel-goers." (Stuart Mews in *A History of Religion in Britain*, Blackwell, 1994 p.457). In 1926 the TUC called a National Strike. The post-war economic boom reached its peak in 1920. In the decade ending 1924, the average earning of full time workers rose by 94%. But this boom was quickly followed by the bust of The Depression which haunted the nation in the late 20s and 30s – the slump, mass unemployment and the cost-cutting national government.

George Old from Somerset went to Canada in 1929 aged 19 looking for work, joined the forces in Canada when war broke out, came to England and met Evelyn Bird in Northampton before they came to live in Easton Maudit to work for farmer William Penn, moving finally to 2 Queen Street, Bozeat when the council house estate here was built in 1952.

Bert and Emily Tompkins, parents of Dolly Roberts, both aged 21 in 1918.   (*D. Roberts*)

Cyril Garbett, Bishop of Southwark, among others drew attention to the inadequacies of housing in both town and country. Indeed overcrowding was much reduced in the inter-war years and by 1939 over a million new houses had been built in Britain. Overcrowding was also reduced by the fact that the family size shrank from an average of 5 to 6 children before the First World War to an average of 3.2 in 1939. Compare this with 1.8 in 1994 and typically 10 or more in the Victorian period – see the testimony on Thomas and Mary Hensman's large gravestone in our churchyard where it is inscribed, thankfully, with the words: 'Their (13!) children all survived her' – all having been born between 1799 and 1821.

We must not forget the huge explosion in population in England and Wales, which increased five-fold from 9 million in 1800 to 37 million in 1900 and only doubled in the 20th century to some 70 million. So housing was an even greater problem in the 19th century for Dolly's grandfather's generation and his parents.

To reflect back for a moment to the 19th century; in 1821 there were 148 houses in Bozeat compared with the 736 or so in 1995, which gives you some idea of the comparative size of the village then, which is only one-fifth of its present size in terms of houses. But in terms of overcrowding there were then some 199 families which meant at least 51 families having to double up in houses which may have only had two rooms. In one house in Dychurch in 1851 for example lived; Frances Partridge aged 70, Samuel Drage aged 40, possibly the son-in-law, Hannah aged 40, Samuel's wife, Mary aged 16, Sarah 14, Joseph 12, John 11, Thomas 9, Hannah 7, Ann 5 and Ruth at 9 months! Typically all the girls slept in one bed, the boys in another, and the infant with her parents. Fred Tompkins (Dolly's bamp) was one of 10 children living together with their parents in a one-up one-down house in Spangle Row up Dag Lane. "Bamp was a weakling – always ill as his mother suckled him with an abscess in her breast.... His sister Polly died and had to be laid out on the table until burial which shocked and devastated him.... The family was very close," writes Dolly.

Small wonder that in these crowded conditions disease flourished, such as smallpox which had been a killer for centuries until arrested by inoculation in the 1830s, and epidemics in Bozeat of such diseases as typhus in 1858 and scarlet fever in 1885, not to speak of diphtheria. We get some idea of the dangers in the first few years of life from the fact that in the ten year period 1860-1870, the Parish Registers for Bozeat record nearly half (49%) of those buried were under 10 years of age, the greater number being less than a year old with only a fifth of those buried over 60. A sad reminder of these days is to be found in our churchyard where, next to the memorial stone of their great-grandparents, Thomas and Mary Hensman, is the memorial stone to Thomas Capell Hensman who died at the age of 2 years and 11 months on 26th July 1864 and his little sister Emma Capell who died 7 days later, only 22 months old. What a tragic loss for their young parents.

The population in Bozeat was 680 in 1801 (having been some 400 in 1671 – see *Marlow*) and it had risen to 812 by 1831 compared with a population of some 1784 in 1995. So the population has only trebled in two centuries, and today almost a third of that population is over 60!) In the twenty years from 1801 to 1921 however only seven houses were built (much of this information is provided by Norman Palmer in *About Bozeat* for September 1995). In contrast, our new council estate in Allens Hill and Council Street may well be a result of the inter-war years' house building policy. These issues are discussed further in Chapters 16 and 18.

Falling on hard times

But the boom of the early '20s had little effect on the miserable wage of farm labourers. Dolly's father Bert Tompkins bought home his 28 shillings a week which was hardly sufficient to provide for his family of three (later four) daughters. He could have worked for John Drage in his shoe factory for double that pay. As it was, Bert kept on with George Knight at Church Farm and in winter months supplemented his meagre earnings by stoking the huge coke Robin Hood boiler which helped keep the workers warm in Drage's factory next door to their house at 5 Allens Hill. Bert remained with George Knight because he loved the outdoor life and working with the animals. "Mr and Mrs Knight were most generous to us as a family," Dolly remembers, "but in the slump of the 1930s Dad, as did many others, had to turn his hand to other sources of income. He harvested for four different farmers as the time came round, Garrett being one ("we all joined!") so we were seldom short of offal meat or flour. He also, as we have seen, helped Frank 'Wassie' Tompkins who was the engineer-cum-boiler-stoker in Drage's factory.

Wassie was also a road sweeper for many years and when he died the job came to Bert. He worked in the stuffy atmosphere of the factory for many years until he cut his finger badly and so moved in 1933 to Odell Leather. Most of the evenings were spent in helping the farmers, Garrett, Hedges, Drage at Spring Vale Farm and Phipps at Low Farm and at the Grange and Stocken Hollow, mostly at harvest time. His final job was at John Whites, Higham Ferrers where he was made redundant."

But he had his recreation too. He loved singing and sang in choirs all his life. He joined the Rushden Adult School Male Voice Choir, also the Wollaston Co-op Choir and the Methodist and Independent Wesleyan Chapel Choirs (an important link between the two). "He had an excellent tenor voice and was always singing regardless of anyone else even in bus queues – much to mother's annoyance as people stared! He knew so many people in the district as he was in the many concerts that were frequently performed. He made many friends and singing meant so much to him.

After he retired he travelled the last nine years of his life with Shelton Coaches from Wollaston on trips abroad. He had a wonderful time seeing so many of the sights and relating them to us on his return. Mother died in 1952. Dad lived for a further 27 years which he enjoyed but they were often lonely ones and he would come to see Don and me every day, and his granddaughter Myra whom he adored," remembers Dolly, as we talk in her sitting room at 55 London Road.

Bert and Emily Tompkins, with their three children, Dorothy, Joyce and Margaret. *(D. Roberts)*

Bert, like many of his contemporaries in the first third of the 20th century, had a hard life. Like them, he had to look for work wherever he could find it. At six years of age he would run in the dark of the early morning to Wollaston taking shoes his father (crippled by his gangrenous foot) had made and would queue with other boys in the dark and cold outside one of the factories to sell them and collect more uppers and soles for his father to work on. Then he would run back to Bozeat, hopefully in time for school. The roads were little more than rough cart tracks in those days (about 1906) and as he ran, often because he was frightened, behind the milk float for protection (then a two wheeled horse-drawn cart) he would become plastered with mud if wet and choked with dust in dry weather. And the reward for his labours on arrival at school, often late, dirty and untidy, would be a caning on the hand from Mr Kirby! Experiences like this may explain why "he resented injustice so strongly all his life." (Dolly).

1921 was one of the driest summers and all the wells, save the Town Well, dried up. This being the only source of water, folk also had to walk with their buckets out towards Grendon to Sandwell Springs which never ran dry. Don remembers how Mr Lack, the teacher, lectured to them, presumably after the fall of the first Labour government after only nine months in office in 1924, on how the Zinoviev letter, which claimed that once Labour was in power the Russians would take over control, was a fraud. Most of the children did not understand what he was talking about except that his sympathies were with Labour and Socialism.

When men came back from the war, there was no work for them so they became Jack-of-all-trades. Everyone was a keen gardener – they had to be to grow food. Don remembers Grandma Drage and his mother going gleaning. They would take the grain to the windmill, the old base of which can still be seen in the back garden of the Minney's house at 5 Roberts Street, where it would be made into enough flour to last winter. His mother went flax-pulling in farmer Britten's field (Manor Farm) opposite the James's farm up Harrold Road which provided linen and linseed oil. Yellow fields of rape are a more familiar sight today although blue linseed is not uncommon.

Life in a close-knit community

The village was still a close-knit community – especially up to the Second World War – after which the motor car, increased mobility, and the tremendous advances in technology, many spurred on through the war effort, were to produce a rapid transformation in village life. Up till then the whole of your life was lived in the village. You were born there. As a child you found your pleasure roaming the fields and hedgerows looking for flowers and eggs and fishing and playing in the ponds and streams, trapping rabbits, harvesting or gleaning fields. "And we played so many games as children," remembers Dolly. "Practically all of the children this side of Peartree Close played together on The Triangle (at the bottom of Allens Hill). Many memories are awakened as we pass today."

Marjorie Drage also has some vivid memories of her childhood in these years:

"Our special day was 24th May, Empire Day, which was the anniversary of Queen Victoria's birthday but, far more important to me (as I never knew Queen Victoria!) it was my Dad's birthday.

Silver Jubilee Celebrations in Warners Field in 1935. (*D. Edmunds*)

Silver Jubilee celebrations in Camden Square (with the Lord Nelson on the right) on 7th May 1935, with church services, sport on the Windmill Field, a fancy dress parade, tea, fireworks, and a dance in the church hall.
(*Bozeat School Scrapbook*)

THE YEARS BETWEEN THE WARS – 1920s AND 1930s

Silver Jubilee Celebrations in Camden Square in 1935 'Here's Health unto their Majesties'. This RAOB entry has in the bowler hat Winnie Wyman's father, Fred Wyman, the village postman; second from left, Ron Coles' father, Arthur; 2nd from right, Don Roberts' father, Percy; with accordion, Dick Edmunds; with guns, George Pettit's father; in front of car with moustache, J. P. Hewlett. (*D. Edmunds*)

The parade comes up Allens Hill passing Bull Close. (*Bozeat School Scrapbook*)

The old Church Hall which opened in 1929. (*Vicars' Logbook*)

"For several weeks we would have been practising patriotic songs and hymns and learning dances. I remember especially when I was in Miss Ada Smith's class and she, being very artistic and musical, would choose a piece of classical music and arrange a dance to fit the music, a good choreographer! One favourite which we danced for several years Miss Smith called 'Spring Awakening the Flowers'. There were three snowdrops, three daffodils and three crocuses. Our mothers made simple dresses of dainty muslin, in appropriate colours, and the year I was chosen to be Spring I wore green muslin.

"The younger children danced round the maypole, using some traditional and, to me, very complicated patterns, the girls in pretty dresses and the boys in sailor suits or knickerbockers and jerseys.

"All this was performed before parents and friends in the girls' playground, and afterwards we would assemble in the boys' playground ... there we would sing our patriotic songs and, with a word from Mr Lack our headmaster, we would stand at attention to salute the Union Jack which would be flying from the bell tower. After this, to great cheers, Mr Lack would announce a half-day holiday."

Winifred Corby (Aunt of Olive Underwood, Tom Partridge-Underwood's mother) also has happy memories of these childhood years:

"We did lots of jobs for people in order to earn a halfpenny; we would go down by the side of the cemetery and over 'White Wall', then down the 'Long Meadow' as far as 'Watsons Hole' to gather watercress and sell it for a penny a bunch to housewives.

It was safe to wander anywhere in my younger days." (*About Bozeat*, March 1982)

Marjorie continues: "Each of our fields had some special features, beautiful blue chicory flowers grew in the ditches of 'Top Field', and I never knew them to grow elsewhere. Specially large blackberries grew in 'Hungry Hill'. In the pond in 'Second Field' were tadpoles and newts, with many gorgeous dragonflies darting round. A brook meandered through most fields and gave us endless hours of delight, sailing our little boats made of rushes and bark through the little tunnels, often getting shoes and socks soaked and muddy, then trying to dry them in the sun before going home."

Winifred: "I remember the hours that a dozen of us played in Pit Field at the bottom of New Road (i.e. Harrold Road) – it was all hills and hollows."

Marjorie: "Hay time and harvest meant lots of fun as well as hard work for everyone. If at school, we would dash home at 4 o'clock to pick up large cans of tea, baskets of cups, and thick slices of cut-me-and-come-again plum cake, to have a picnic with the farm helpers. The prickly stalks of the cut corn scratched our legs as we helped stand up the sheaves into stooks, praying that there would be no rain until all was safely gathered in. Looking back, one imagines that it rarely did, unless a short sharp thunderstorm."

Winifred: "At harvest time, when we came out of school we went in the fields gleaning corn, for which the people who kept hens would pay us a penny for a sack."

Then nearly everyone worked in the village and shopped in the village – the 30 or so shops and the Co-op sold everything! Many families had a garden or allotment where they grew food to live on – and flowers as well – and most families had their own pig and chickens and you had to trade in kind. There were the mean and the generous in this kind of trade as you would soon learn from village gossip! And, of course, your social life was found in the life of the churches, their seasons and festivals, and around the five pubs and the Working Men's Club and concerts and dances at the old Church Hall in Allens Hill and elsewhere.

The village cinema

And we should not forget the village cinema. It was a 100 foot long wooden shed between Corby's bungalow and Cave's the Undertakers in the London Road. It was also known as the Brownie Hall. It was a First War barrack hut (there is a similar one in Hope Street behind the factory, bought at the same time and still there! – 1996) purchased in the mid-'30s by W. Botterill and used in later years to store football boots, leather, etc. until the late '70s. Then it was sold as a building site and the house built on it in the early '80s is number 85 London Road.

The cinema must have been a fire safety officer's nightmare, made entirely of wood with a cast iron stove whose chimney went straight up through the roof. The projectionist was Mick Corby's uncle, Bert Johnson, and it was owned by the Drage Shoe Company. Throughout the '20s and '30s it showed silent films, with Iris Smith on the piano to add audible excitement to pursuits across the deserts, etc! The entrance fee was one penny (latterly 3d in front, better seats 6d and 9d) and you can imagine the children sitting wide-eyed with anticipation in the warm, smoke-filled darkness and adults enjoying a night out with the latest technology! I can still remember the sheer magic of the cinema before television stole the show.

Winifred Corby remembers that when she was about thirteen, "they opened a cinema in Wollaston and called it 'The Gaff'. Miss Rice and Mrs Hewlett used to have a bill in their shop to say what was showing. With the bill went two free tickets and it was a great race to get to the shop first to see if they wanted any jobs doing, hoping to get a ticket. If we didn't have a ticket, about a dozen of us used to walk to Wollaston and back to see a film. It cost us three old pence for the pictures and one penny for a bag of chips."

Sunday was special

Sunday was a special day. Women would make the Yorkshire pudding for Sunday lunch. We have to remember that Northamptonshire Yorkshire pudding was baked with the meat inside the batter! "Our only means of having a Yorkshire pudding was to take it to one of the bakehouses. On a Sunday there would be about forty pans of different sizes, all with a name on and a small joint of meat, which had to be fetched away at twelve. This facility cost a penny ha'penny ... for ½d the baker would bake you a bread pudding, by leaving it all night in the warm oven. A crusty fresh cottage loaf cost 2d." (Winifred Corby, *About Bozeat*, March 1982). Men would take it to one of the five bakehouses and visit the pub for a lunch time drink whilst it was cooking. This may partly explain why not infrequently they came home with the wrong lunch – usually a better one (although all the trays were marked!) and why to the annoyance of the baker, such as Dick and Emily Squires' father at the bakehouse (still visible as such) at 21 London Road, some men turned up for their family dinner when they themselves had at last sat down to their own! ("That's when you heard Dad swear," Dick remembers!).

Of course all the rights of passage were part of village life. The five bells of St Mary's would ring out for weddings and Sunday services and festivals, toll for the passing of a life (three for a man two for a woman), and the old Church clock, probably dating from the last decade of the 17th century, told out the hours of night and day for the labourers in field and factory and those staggering home late at night. And the village gossip would add spice to life – folk who could not be sure who their father was, "whose cat ran up our alley!" – and poaching was not an unfamiliar trade!

But it was a tight knit community where vagrants and vagabonds, Tom, Dick and Harry, parson, doctor and school teacher, labourer and landlord, manager and farmer and factory worker all had their place, and in a curious way cared for and respected each other. Of course you had good and bad farmers, managers, and workers, petty and more serious crime as well as violent and happy family life, but this was all part and parcel of the rich tapestry of village life. Even if it was rather narrow and petty and dull at times it had its many compensations, and an endless series of stories to tell and only those who have been immersed in its life for a lifetime – nay for generations – can tell them and tell them well in that lilting Northamptonshire drawl and with a twinkle and a smile that is Northamptonshire through and through! Monochromatic suburbia knows little of the community life where plumber, roofer, farmer, labourer, doctor, teacher, poacher, butcher, baker, lacemaker, seamstress and clothier, thatcher, undertaker, potman, road man, factory worker, builder ... "tinker, tailor, soldier, sailor, rich man, poor man, beggar man thief" ... live cheek by jowl, where the cross-fertilisation of life in pub and church, factory and field produces its own unique fabric of human experience.

A sample of village life – its institutions and characters

In the '20s and '30s there were, in the village, almost 40 shops selling 'everything', three bakehouses, five pubs (the Lord Nelson in the High Street, The Chequers and The Red Lion on the London Road, Cross Keys on the Village Green and The Engineer up Mile Street), the Working Men's Club, four churches or chapels (Anglican, Baptist, Methodist, Wesleyan) and three factories (Hooton & Barnes up Easton Lane, Botterills up London Road and Drages at Hope Street) where most men worked if not working on the land in the ten farms in the village (Town Farm, Manor Farm, Home Farm, Glebe Farm, Church Farm, Grange Farm, Red House Farm, White House Farm, Newlands Farm and Slype Farm).

Mrs Lucy Jones, a child in the late '20s and '30s, gives us a glimpse of the shops and the village characters in those days. There was Miss Cave and her grocery shop where the present Post Office is. On the corner opposite was Mr Strange the butcher. "He was tall and thin and always wore drainpipe trousers." Then in Dag Lane there was Mrs Smith's bakehouse where "now and then" Lucy's mother "would take the Sunday roast." Opposite Mrs Smith's "was a small thatched cottage where lived Jim Roper, a hurdler, and his wife. Humour has it that when he had a bad back she thought to ironing him…. Mr Drage (John Laddie to us) had a sweet shop at the bottom of Church Lane on the corner, where one could buy a great variety of sweets, sherbet, or broken biscuits for a halfpenny, and along the High Street, where Mrs Owen lived until recently was Mrs Hewlett's (Mrs Baycock's) shop. She made the best coconut ice I've ever tasted."

"Also along the High Street, where the Club car park now is, was John Farey, the barber. We used to sit in a row at the back of his shop and wait to be scalped."

"When we came out of school, old Edwin Robinson was always standing at the bottom of Wheelwright's Yard, and we all used to ask him the time, just to see him take out his big pocket watch. There was also Mr Partridge living up Wheelwright's Yard. He had a fluffy white cat that followed him everywhere. His wife was very deaf and used an old-fashioned ear trumpet."

"In the row of cottages next to the school in Dychurch Lane lived two elderly gentlemen, 'Pepper' Moore and 'Major'. If walking past 'Peppers' door one had to watch out for the flying contents of his chamber pot."

"We had a resident policeman who patrolled the village on his bicycle, PC Willie, I think, but I only remember PC Forth, a very nice man." (*About Bozeat*, June 1982)

Visitors

And there were visitors to the village who came to sell their wares. There was for example the pot stall which Marjorie Drage remembers, "we used to have in the village every spring and autumn when I was a child. A few days before this important evening the village crier would announce all around the village that the Potman would be setting up his stall on the Square, outside the Lord Nelson Inn, on the following evening.

"The Potman would borrow a trestle table from the Lord Nelson and older children would be allowed to help him unpack his wares from straw-filled crates and baskets. These he would arrange on the table and in a wide circle on the ground then, ringing his bell and clashing a few basins, business would begin.

"There would be basins of all types and sizes, plates, cups and saucers, jugs large enough to hold half a gallon of milk, as well as many other sizes, hot-water bottles, chamber pots, meat dishes, brown stew jars ("We still have some!" – Dolly Roberts, 1996), pancheons of many sizes. Somehow these always fascinated me, with their brown rough outsides, and highly glazed insides.

"In the very big ones, clothes would be soaked overnight before wash day, and some would be used for winemaking. Very many people in those days made dandelion, cowslip, elderberry wines and a specially refreshing drink made from herbs of many kinds, and stored in large pottery jars, also from the potman, in readiness for hay time and harvest. This was known as Dyer drink, and Mrs Maria Tompkins, who lived in the High Street, had a very closely guarded secret recipe for making this. We children would bring along an apple or a few sugar lumps for the Potman's horse, patiently waiting for the end of the sale, and by dusk the stall would be nearly empty – housewives would have stocked up, replaced their former breakages, and ordered any item which was not available. This would be bought on the next journey, probably in six months time."

Winifred Corby continues: "Marriott's pot stall came to the village ... once every month.... He would spread out straw on the road outside the Nelson Inn on Camden Square and cover it with every kind of plate and utensil you could buy. He would lay six plates up his arm; these cost one shilling. It was great fun!" (*About Bozeat*, March 1982)

"Having let my mind wander back to the Potman, I then began to think of the scissor-grinder, another well known character who used to visit the village more frequently than the Potman. "His name was George and he lived in the hedge bottom in Blackmile Lane, Grendon. He had cross-eyes and would come in our house to drink a cup of tea in a big enamel jug, dirty white edged with blue. He was quite nice really, quiet and shy." He was a tall, wiry, weather-beaten old man, wearing ancient brown cord trousers, tied at the knee with sack string, an old tweed jacket and slouch hat well pulled down over his beetling eyebrows.

"During spring, summer and autumn he would push his queer contraption from village to village sharpening scissors, knives, hatchets, etc., each for a few coppers. It was quite fascinating to watch him prepare to sharpen them. Sitting on the little seat, putting his foot on the pedal, the wheel would whirl around making a high pitched whining sound."

There was another visitor who came when Marjorie was very young and she remembers him coming only once, "although I am told he came several times. On the Square [Camden Square] was a tree, surrounded by a tall spiked railing. One afternoon when we came out of school, a man was standing there and, tied to the railing, standing on its hind legs, was a big brown bear. The man told us to hurry home, each to bring back a ha'penny, or a few jam jars, and he would make the bear dance. It was to me a sad sight to see the poor moth-eaten looking creature slowly dancing round a pole. I think the man played some kind of instrument, but I soon ran home crying bitterly."

Dolly Roberts also remembers "the hurdy-gurdy man with his tiny monkey in a red jacket who visited frequently and played outside the school gate," and the "rag man who gave out goldfish for rags was a regular visitor also."

Work was hard and manual

If work was hard and manual for men it was no less so for women housekeeping. The roads were of rough loose stones or just tracks, either muddy or dusty, and with wood and/or coal fires, old decaying buildings and clothing of thick natural materials, it was almost impossible to keep homes clean and tidy. And they would be cluttered up with the commodities of home industry whether it be of the boot and shoe or of the building trade or the shop, often a converted front room. (Spencelayh's pictures beautifully capture the atmosphere of such tiny homes.) And of course there were larger families then and more crowding in their unspacious cottages.

Monday is washing day,
Mother has a busy day …

And indeed she had, with no labour-saving devices and everything having to be done by hand, washing would take a whole day. And Tuesday is ironing day … yes a whole day and evening for darning and mending, and a day for cooking and cleaning, not to forget helping with the shoemaking, feeding the chickens and so on. Small wonder Sunday played such a significant part in a life in which there was little leisure to relax and reflect, no annual holidays with pay (legislation for these came in 1938 but was not implemented until after the war) and only the Church Festivals to help break the monotony along with the weekly Sabbath to give a breather in the relentless routine.

Electricity arrives in Bozeat

We should not underestimate the effect on domestic life of the establishment of the National Grid in 1926 and the arrival of electricity into home and workplace. It was the advent of the 'electric house' – clean and bright with spacious square rooms and large windows, to be followed in the 1930s with an increasing range of electric home 'labour-saving appliances' from the washing machine to the carpet cleaner – that was to transform the life of women. The green and white Hoover factory on Western Avenue at Southall, built in the 1930s and now a listed building, is a symbol of this New Age. It produced a new generation of women with time on their hands who looked increasingly outside the home to find work to do, until today there are parts of the country where there are more women out at work than men.

Philip Boswell remembers the giant electricity pylons being erected in the early 1930s around Bozeat. As a boy of 12 in 1931 he and his friends would clamber up the framework and, with a handkerchief to protect their hands, slide to the ground down the huge metal cables (yet to be hoisted into their final position). In retirement he was to live in the house of his father-in-law, Jack Walker, at 35 Easton Lane. This is a good example of the first generation of 'electric' houses (wired for the labour-saving world of electricity), with its curved corners to the bay windows and its airy, light simple square rooms with large metal-framed windows.

Jack would have had the house built in 1938 but rumours of war with Germany made him hesitate. However, when Neville Chamberlain came back from Munich and Hitler with the famous piece of paper in his hand with its promise of 'Peace for our Time', Jack told Alfie Underwood, the Wollaston builder, to go ahead and so the house was built in 1939 just as war was to break out.

Prior to this there had been no electricity or piped gas in the village. Gas wasn't to arrive until 1991! Drage's shoe factory had to make its own gas out of white spirit –

it was needed to melt the wax used in stitching and finishing. And a 70 horse-power turbine with a huge 7-foot flywheel generated the electricity as well as driving the machines by joining them to the engine with thick driving bands which splayed out across the factory in all directions – a safety nightmare I should imagine!

Mrs Lucy Jones of 40 Mile Street remembers how, as a child in the 1930s, they moved into a cottage in Camden Square (where the council houses now stand). "... we were fortunate in having electric light, and instead of a pokey little grate we had a large square black stove with a round chimney going straight through the roof.... Our back garden was a cobbled yard with a 'loo' up one corner, consisting of a wooden seat with a hole in it and, under that hole, a bucket. This was emptied by Mr Frost, who came round the village with a horse and cart in the dead of night – and I don't remember him ever going on strike.... Our water had to be carried in a bucket from the tap on the pavement across the road outside the present Post Office, which was then a grocery shop owned by Mrs Cave...." So, having electricity could not alleviate the limitations of no sewage system or piped water." (*About Bozeat,* June 1982)

Boot and show business blossoms and ...

The boot and shoe industry began to develop rapidly in the closing decades of the 19th century and in the first decades of the twentieth, and it boomed around the time of the Great War. At the turn of that century, the Parish Council offered a piece of land to anyone who would build a factory on it. William Botterill from Wollaston (father of Flo, George and Alf) accepted the offer, moved to Bozeat about 1903, and built a factory just above 115 London Road where Margaret Elliot (née Howard) now lives. The original factory was built at right angles to the road with the front part adjacent to the road being the house in which the family lived. George was Don Roberts' wife's cousin and he remembers visiting the house when the Botterills lived there. William made a modest 'fortune' out of those boom years so he could retire. He then bought 99 London Road from Mr Ward. The factory ceased to make shoes in 1974 and was bought by Spiers (and is still owned by them). Until 1994 it was used to assemble pine furniture for Olney Galleries.

Looking north from the south end of London Road with a horse and cart outside Botterills' house and shoe factory. To the left is Tennyson Terrace.

THE YEARS BETWEEN THE WARS – 1920s AND 1930s

The Drage Shoe factory in 1953, with some Coronation decorations. (Bozeat School Scrapbook)

Arch Mallows, son of a boot and shoe man, worked at Botterills shoe factory only 50 yards up the road from where he lived at 111 London Road for 60 years, serving four generations of the Botterill family. Arch was actually born in London Road in 1906, in the middle one of the three cottages (now number 88) at right angles to the road behind the Co-op and opposite The Red Lion, where Dennis Perkins was born 16 years later in 1922, so he spent all his life in the same road, was born there, worked there, lived and eventually died there in December 1991 at the age of 85. Although he worked in the boot factory, he was a great gardener and in his substantial garden (100 feet by 60 feet), with its barn and greenhouses, he grew vegetables not to speak of bedding plants and his prize-winning chrysanthemums, azaleas and carnations.

In his time he kept chickens and even pigs, and he could repair anything from wooden handles on tea pots to chairs. "He kept everything to repair everything in his barn – yes, everything!" said his sons smiling grimly at the prospect of clearing it all out! But Arch also had a thirst for adventure. He was the third person in the village to own a motor car in 1933 and in retirement he travelled Europe. Arch was always dressed well. He was never seen without a tie and earned the nickname, 'The Duke of York!' A modest man with an inventive mind and warm ability, careful of his appearance he was much like his father whose personality is captured in the portrait of him by the painter Spencelayh, seated behind the table, his hands resting on the large leather-bound family Bible. Arch stands for much of what is typical and what is best of Bozeat life in much of the last hundred years.

Another factory that opened just before the Great War was Hooton & Barnes up Easton Lane. It is now Electrosite (UK) Ltd. Don Roberts worked there until 1927 when it became bankrupt through lack of work – after the boom years of the war the depression was beginning to bite. "All they owed was £600 and they could not pay it back," said Don. Then Don went to work for Drage's in their enlarged factory at the bottom of Hope Street. Marjorie Drage left school when she was 12 years old in

Painting of John Bull/Honest John (Drage) on the end of the Hope Street factory.

1921 and started to work in the Drage factory on a penny an hour. "We worked 52 hours a week then, before the trade unions got it down to the present (i.e. 1988) 40 hours." Don remembers that, "Factory work was boring but that's where the money was. But trade was so bad (late twenties/early thirties) I only worked for one day a week for 2 shillings and 4 pence! I didn't mind though. It gave me five days holiday a week and I went off on my bike into the countryside! My father wasn't pleased and insisted I found another job. 'Your trouble is you don't like work!' he said.

"But I stayed on another two years until I was 'stood off' as I was too old, too old at 22 (in 1932)! – and I'm still 'stood off' without pay or compensation for I was never taken back! So I took up gardening and worked for Mrs Selby, Flo Botterill, Mrs Lack – those who'd got a bit of money! Philip Boswell who was then manager at Drage's (we take up his story later) said I'd made a good decision to leave and look for work elsewhere." Incidentally Don was a saver (and hoarder!) rather than, like his brother, a spender! "I always saved my money," he said as we sat together and as he spoke he smiled and drew from his jacket pocket a book of National Savings certificates from the First War looking as new as if printed yesterday, much to my, and his wife's, surprise!

It was about this time (1932) the Drages decided to sell direct to the public in an attempt to improve trade under the name of Honest John. On Feast Monday, Jack Walker painted the outline of a huge boot on the west brick wall of the Hope Street factory adjacent to the London Road and inside it a picture of Honest John with a bulldog, perhaps suggesting that it is was meant to represent John Bull and not merely the founder of the business? (The picture was still visible with the name Drage still showing beneath – even though an attempt had been made to obliterate it with black paint, and for the year 2000 it has been repainted by Steve Linnell.) But the decision to sell did not have the hoped for benefits as in the process Drage's lost all their wholesale customers.

These were hard times for the shoe industry – one that has existed for hundreds of years in this part of Northamptonshire proudly (we imagine) making boots for Cromwell's soldiers in the mid 1600s. Alf Botterill told Don once that he could lose an order by pricing a pair of shoes, typically selling at 4 shillings and eleven pence, one farthing (quarter of a penny) too much. (There were 20 shillings to a pound and 12 pence to a shilling remember!)

Religion and village life
Religion still played a large part in the life of our village in those years between the wars. Reflecting on the life of the Drages who founded and ran their family shoe business in the village, and of which she was a member, Marjorie Drage said, "Uncle Will and Auntie Polly were great chapel people. But my father went to church and his

father played the church organ for 30 years. Then Uncle George (Dolly Line's father) played it and then my father played it for 10 years – and then they all left St Mary's and went over to the chapel!" One would love to know why. Marjorie remembers going to the Primary Sunday School on Sunday mornings at the chapel when Mr Percy Roberts was superintendent (Don Roberts' father). "You started in the church (i.e. chapel) with the adults and after a hymn, a prayer and the children's talk you went out to your lessons. The senior Sunday School was in the afternoon and the superintendent was Mr Hayes who owned the draper's. I started going at four-years-old and when I was in the seniors I would go to chapel three times on Sunday, morning and evening services with our parents and Sunday school in the afternoon. Sunday was a happy day. Everything we did was concentrated on the Bible. We remembered all the idiosyncrasies of the lay preachers who came to lead the services. 'It's Mr Panther's turn today'. He had a speech impediment which made it more interesting and we knew which favourite hymns each would choose. Another local preacher in his prayers would always say, 'going down the variegated pathway.'"

Besides the chapels and church, there were other small religious groups in the 1930s. Loreen Drage née Line – Ted Drage's wife remembers 'the Black Stocking Brigade' as they called them which met at 'Georgie' Dick Drages up Dychurch. They were the Mormons (founded in the U.S. in 1830 by Josiah Smith) from Olney and were always dressed in smart black apparel. Then there was a Baptist Chapel half way up Church Lane on the left – where the two Tanyard Cottages now stand. Sam Garrett's father went there. (The Skevingtons were the butchers but the Garretts took over from them in 1895.) Bill Silsby remembers how you could rent a pew at the Baptists and how, on one occasion, his two lively sisters Ada and Freda went once out of curiosity but found it too boring! Then Mrs Swinn the butcher's wife at 46 Mile Street used to hold séances. The story goes that Ada and Freda also went there on one occasion and spoilt the spiritual atmosphere by passing wind at the crucial moment and were promptly told to leave! Mabel Line (née Pettit), when 81 in 1996, remembered how as girls in the 1920s they would tap on the window during a séance and then run away! "If you brought Mrs Swinn any wild flowers, like primroses, she would give us children a bag of sweets. And she'd give you money for wild orchids!"

In those days George Everest was Undertaker and Carpenter. He lived on the left just as you go out from the main gate to the churchyard, 'Burnt Cottage' as it is now called (in memory of the 1729 fire). He also had the land on the other side of the churchyard gate where now stands a row of small cottages (built in 1960) where he kept a cow and had pigsties. George was also superintendent and sick visitor for the Independent Wesleyan Chapel ("Who'd want a visit from a sick visitor who was your undertaker!" said Tom Partridge-Underwood with that chuckle of his) and his daughter Miriam was organist there ("If you wanted to know anything going on in the village, you asked Miriam." – Mabel Line). Loreen Drage still had the bill from George Everest for her father's funeral in 1923 – 12 shillings and 6 pence. Ted, Loreen's husband, who made coffins for Tom Cave, the later undertaker and carpenter said, "George only planed the outside of the coffins so you got splinters if you were inside!"

CHAPTER 4

Battle for Britain 1939-1945

*Pack up your troubles in your old kit bag
And smile, smile, smile.*

The village Co-operative
In September 1939, the month the Second World War with Germany was declared, Robert Yates installed his splendid new organ in St Mary's Church and Dolly Roberts joined the Co-op staff in Bozeat and worked there for five and a half years. She left because it was too cold! The cold affected her badly because she had had rheumatic fever when she was younger. To improve her health she went to work at Abergele in Wales. After 12 months there she went as a childcare worker in 1946 to Hinwick Hall, opened in about 1938. It is still a successful home for the care and training of those with physical disabilities (many of us locals buy our potting plants from their well-stocked nursery). Dolly then went as a child companion to Birmingham followed by 6 months in a National Children's Home and finally she worked in a similar capacity for the County Council in Raunds until she married Don in 1955.

When Dolly joined the Co-op, the manager was Mr Wright of Dungee (Danger!) Corner, and he was the manager during those war years. The Co-op was a major village institution then as it had been for most of the century. (We shall look at its history in more detail later.) "He [Mr Wright] wore spats up to here," remembered John Darnell pointing to his knees, reflecting on those boyhood days during the war. John was born at 9 Allens Hill, was one of those village boys who passed the 'Eleven-Plus' and went to Wellingborough Grammar School and was seven years old when the war broke out. He was a choirboy at St Mary's, learned to play the organ and still plays for us each Sunday at Easton Maudit. Before retirement, he was a director of Pioneer Sand and Gravel. "Mr Wright was high up in the village pecking order as manager of the Co-op, just below the Parson and above the Policeman. Everyone knew their place in the village hierarchy in those days," John continued reflectively. Mr Wright built the splendid house that stands at Dungee Corner with its fine mature orchard and its famous meadow of orchids, which form a carpet of purple when in bloom, and is designated an SSSI (Site of Special Scientific Interest). Gordon James grazes his sheep on it for part of the year to fertilize the fungi which nourish the orchids, sheep being light enough of foot not to damage these delicate organisms.

In 1914, the Wollaston Co-op opened a branch shop in Bozeat opposite the Paper Shop in the High Street (the house still has the appearance of a shop front). Before World War I, the Bozeat Co-operative Society had had a shop opposite the Methodist Church in the High Street. Don remembers as a little boy running next door to the Co-op to get his mother's groceries, etc. The manager at this time was Mr Chapman. He was followed by Mrs Rivett. About this time (1920) the Co-op bought the grocery shop opposite the Red Lion in London Road owned by Mr Barker of Olney, together with the adjacent houses.

When Dolly joined the staff, it consisted of Mr Wright the manager, Miss Esther Dobbs, the drapery manageress, Dolly, Cliff Drage the shop boy and Bernard Neil from Wollaston to help with weighing the rations. In wartime "it was a full time job weighing out and sorting the rations and unit cards for members. There were many dissatisfied customers, also queues for everything that was in short supply. People bought whether they needed it or not and would pass it on to their neighbours.... Cliff Drage was employed when Bernard joined the Navy. As we were so busy Laura Tompkins joined the staff then Enid Tompkins and Edgar Geeves, an evacuee. Cliff is Don's cousin and was a bundle of laughter through those dark and cloudy days. He was usually standing on his head, in between wrapping large parcels of lard, etc and was an excellent mimic of village characters which brightened up a monotonous task .... One of my first jobs was demaggoting a huge bin of rice. Mother made so many rice puddings that I completely went off them until recently!" (Dolly Roberts)

Dolly had the task of carrying the weekly takings on Friday evening to the office in Wollaston for banking on her bicycle. Her Dad, believing she should not go alone, went with her. She never knew how much she took except, one week in 1944, the manager told her to go carefully as they had had a good week, taking over £300. Dolly's dad was annoyed at having to go with her and with the Co-op putting on a young girl to undertake this task ("He thought it ought to be taken by the milkman on his early morning round") so he persuaded her to leave. Her last wage packet in 1944 was two pounds, ten shillings and seven pence.

Harold Drage, the father of Philip Drage, worked at the bakery at the Wollaston Co-op for 38 years. When it closed and moved to Wellingborough, Harold didn't move with it. "Wellingborough's too far," he said, so he went to work in Botterill's shoe factory in the village instead! Harold joined up in the First War, as did virtually all the young men in the village, and baked for the army at Stafford. His son Philip, who retired in 1994 at the age of 65, worked all his life in boot and shoe and lived his whole life in the house where he was born at 13 Allens Hill (next door to Nona Darnell – Philip died in 1999). He 'joined up' at the end of the war in 1945 in the Queen's Own Regiment and spent 18 months abroad "at Her Majesty's expense!" I have a photograph of Phil aged seven in 1936 looking angelic in his choirboy's surplice and cassock and he has remained a faithful server in the Church all his life (made a Eucharistic assistant in 1993) and never lost his boyish looks or boyish grin!

Fred Tivey was born in Wollaston on 30th May 1903 where his father was manager of the Co-op, so he would have been in his prime (36) when war broke out. He had one brother Len and his sister Elsie became an actress. He remembers as a boy helping his dad take milk to Strixton on bitterly cold mornings. His father was a fine pianist and choirmaster at St Mary's, Wollaston and he got little Fred singing solos in church from an early age as a boy soprano. An official from Peterborough Cathedral offered him a place in the choir school but he was too shy to accept! He enrolled in Wollaston Co-operative choir and continued to sing with them after moving to Grendon.

When he moved to Bozeat, he took over as Church secretary from Fred Wyman in 1963. He was Churchwarden first with Mr Denton and then with Mr Marriott. Following his resignation as Churchwarden he joined the Church choir until he retired in 1983. I can still hear his fine tenor voice which even at the age of 87 rose from his pew in St Mary's, Bozeat. Fred died two days before his 88th birthday in 1991. His life truly spanned the century and embraced with his family the whole history of the Co-op in these parts. He sang in church choirs all his life. His father died when he was 11 years old and he went into the shoe trade but left because he "didn't like dipping leather in water" as his wife Floss remembers.

He seemed destined for a life in the Co-op and became manager of the Grendon branch where he met and married Floss on 5th August 1929 – a double marriage with Floss' sister! Fred was chorister for 32 years, vicar's warden and treasurer at Grendon church and secretary of the well-known Grendon Cricket Club, for he loved sport. And he loved gardening too – everyone in Grendon had one of his famous marrows – and when retired he would be seen in Bozeat with his barrow full of vegetables. In the war he was in the Home Guard and ran the St John Ambulance. When in a quandary about which uniform to wear at Church Parades, he solved the problem by alternating between the two!

Their home in Grendon was almost a medical centre where mothers brought their children to Fred to be bandaged and for advice, and wide-eyed children came to gaze at his 'instruments of torture'! He had motorbikes all his life – never a car, for he loved the fresh air. With Margaret their only daughter on the pillion and Floss in the sidecar they would go to Hunstanton on Bank Holidays and even to Wales. He was in every sense a gentle man. The last word I ever hear him say, lying ill in hospital, was "Thank you." "We went along together. We couldn't bear arguments," was Floss's testimony to her husband.

Interestingly, when Fred was manager of the Co-op, a young girl joined the staff in 1956 at the age of 15. Her name was Glenda Drage. She stayed and worked for the Co-op for 40 years. Eventually she became manager at Bozeat in 1989/90 and when this branch closed in 1991 she moved to be a manager at their branch in Olney. Glenda has lived all her life at the family home at number 2 Hope Street from which her father once ran the Drage Coach Company.

Briefly to complete the Co-op story (to be told in more detail later), the new Co-operative building in Bozeat came after Fred had retired under the managership of Bernard Neil. By the time Glenda Drage became manager in 1990 there were only two full-time staff and five part-timers. In those earlier days they sold everything – heating oil, clothes, buttons, bread, nails, drawing pins, pens and paperbacks. When the Co-op closed down in 1991 M&M Superstores took it over, being run by the Singh family from Bedford (Mohan Singh and his wife Mohinder moved to Bedford from the Punjab in about 1970). But there was not enough trade for both them and the Spar up the other end of the High Street run by Keith and Carol Cullip and so it closed in 1995 leaving only one food shop in the village. As a lasting memory to the life of the Co-op Mr and Mrs Wright lie buried in our village cemetery.

Joining up

While the Battle of Britain was raging, Don was taken seriously ill with typhoid. He had registered for military service in June 1940 and his medical call up papers came in that month (when Frank Hewlett was our local Justice of the Peace). He was classed unfit to go to war so after six months convalescence he started gardening again. These war years held many memories for the village and in many ways changed its life as they did the life of the nation. Dolly's father, Bert Tompkins, and Mr Woolnough, director of the leather company in Harrold, who lived in the large stone house up Allens Hill called Stoneleigh (converted from three cottages during the First War by the shoe manufacturer, Mr Taylor), were in charge of the Home Guard. There are many tales to tell of the Dad's Army of those days.

Don and Dolly remember the shock on hearing that Don's sister's young man, who had been so proud of getting into the Grenadier Guards, was killed in Italy. Some, like Max Laughton and Stan Dunmore, joined the RAF at RAF Cardington, where the R101 and R100 airships were built in the 1920s, and returned safely. Max was in Iraq and remembered how they had a fine choir at the Anglican church out there. When Max was a boy in Bozeat Church choir, Vicar Marlow wrote of him: "Max Laughton aged 13 has in the last two years developed a very good solo voice. It is a pity it was not 'discovered' earlier in his life and made use of in a choir school." Max was demobbed on 24th April 1946.

And we should not forget young women like Betty Line (born 1923) of 21 Harrold Road who joined the WAAF (Women's Auxiliary Air Force) and was stationed at Rutland Water with the Lancaster Bomber Squadron. Betty's father, Bert, spent all his working life at the Drage Shoe Company. Her two younger brothers, Bernard and Ron, followed Dad into the shoe trade (Bernard retired in 1995) and William her older brother was a butcher working for Garretts the village butcher and trained Derek Taylor when he joined the business as a 15-year old boy in 1951.

The Yanks are here!
And there were the dances in the Old Church Hall up Allens Hill to raise money for the Parcel Fund to send food to the troops overseas. And the young American boys, members of the United States 379th Bomb Group stationed at the air base at Podington who flew the flying fortresses – the massive B29 bombers – over Europe and Germany, not only brought a new kind of life and excitement to the dances but to the village altogether. Several carried their GI brides back from Bozeat to America. Dolly remembers her mother refusing to allow her to go to more than one dance. "We don't want you going off with those American airmen," she warned her daughter! Dolly's best friend was Winsome Drage from Red Gables Farm, up towards Wollaston, the eldest of a family of two sets of twins, Kath and Malcolm and then Alison and Ian, and the youngest Graham. Winsome was going out with one airman, Eddie Brown, and was eventually to marry him. And there were others who were swept off their feet by these dashing young airmen, many only 19 years old, who took the locals by storm with their cheeky and outgoing ways. Richard Zang's mother was bought up by an aunt in Strixton, as her mother died when she was young. She met and married a young airman on the ground staff at Podington but partly under pressure from her aunt, who did not wish to lose her, did not return with their two young children with her husband to America. One of those young children, Richard, a successful local electrician, living with his wife Sue (néc Bayes) and their 21-year-old son Andre (1996) at 18a Fullwell Road, has since then met his American half-brothers and is amazed how similar they are to him in profession and personality.

Richard Zang's mother (néc Ellis) told him how 'The Marquis' in Wollaston was a popular meeting place for the pilots. They would come by bike or in jeeps from Podington. When she entered the pub with her husband she remembered how these boys, some only 18 or 19 with their boyish complexions, would stand up and salute her husband. She developed a real concern for them and remembered how on one evening when she asked one of them what he did, he said: "They all say they are pilots," but this boy insisted, "I really am a pilot – I fly them!" She remembered him vividly, sitting there in the pub looking gloomily at the floor and saying, "I'm flying tomorrow. I don't know where we're going but I know I won't come back."

And he didn't. The procedure used was to get these boys up at six in the morning and give them all a stiff drink. They would then load up the planes with fuel and bombs until they could hardly fly and send them off. The bombers would assemble over East Anglia and then climb continuously to their targets – Dresden or whatever – many of them never to return. One highly secret mission from Podington was the Disney Bomb which was dropped from 1,600 feet and then at 1,000 feet a rocket ignited driving the bomb downward at enormous speed to penetrate the concrete bunkers of the German submarine fleet. The Germans wanted to find Podington and often dropped flares to locate it – and spies too – one was captured at Easton Maudit "and spoke perfect English" remembers Richard Allebone, then in the Home Guard there – but they never found it for Podington was too small and was surrounded by trees.

The village barber
John Farey remembered these young airmen coming for their short haircuts to his little barber's shop just across the pavement from the Paper Shop. (It is now used by Bozaid, the village charity shop.) John was born in Wellingborough on 30th May 1911 in Nene View Cottages opposite the 'Dog and Duck'. His father apprenticed all his children in different trades and John was apprenticed to Alex Thorneycroft in Midland Road beginning as a lather boy and progressing to cutting and perming (called Marcel waving in those days!).

In 1929 his father gave him five pounds and a cash box and he cycled to Bozeat and set up business in a little shop in what became the Working Men's Club car park as the village hairdresser, tobacconist, toilet requisites, etc. He married Grace Marriott in 1935 (in the time of Vicar Marlow) and lived in the bungalow at 95 London Road. John had to pump water for the bungalow either from Mr Spencelayh's pump or from Miss Botterill's well at 21 London Road where Peter and Rose Drage now live. About this time John moved to the present shop at 29 High Street (when the lease ran out). He was a real character and had a lively sense of humour.

Smith's Buildings in High Street in 1923 (left), opposite the Methodist Chapel, These two shops are a mixture of Cody Craxton's garage and bicycle shop, S. Drage baker and also hairdresser, which in 1929 became John Farey's barbers. These shops, shown here (right) in 1953, were demolished for the Working Men's Club car park. (*Bozeat School Scrapbook*)

John Farey standing outside his barbers and tobacconists in Smith's Buildings in 1929.
(Bozeat School Scrapbook)

John Farey later moved to this shop next to the Paper Shop, now BOZAID.
(Bozeat School Scrapbook)

He called himself a tonsorial artist but Arnold Dobbs, just a boy in those days, remembers that it didn't matter what artistic style of hair you asked John to create to impress your peers it always came out as the same uniform short back and sides! ("... if he thought a lad was requesting a haircut out of line with parent's wishes, he would temper what he did with caution," writes his daughter Joy in his defence! – *About Bozeat*, March 1993). And customers shuddered as he sharpened his cut throat razor on the leather ready to shave, for he would sing the lines of the harvest hymn "... first the blade and then the ear"! – and, allegedly, he did occasionally nick an ear or two in the process!

Charles Spencelayh, the famous artist, who came to live in Bozeat at the age of 75 in 1941 having been bombed out of his house in Lee, London, narrowly escaping with his life, bought his cigarettes (and borrowed some of his props!) from John. (At nearly 90 years of age, Spencelayh would say that he had kept John Players cigarettes in business!) John appears in one of his paintings as a slightly 'butched up' soldier, dolled out in his Home Guard uniform! John remembers being sent with his great friend Clarry Drage up to the fields near White House Farm to look for enemy aircraft as members of the wartime Home Guard.

Spencelayh's wife was godmother to John's only child, Joy, who became a primary school teacher and owns the bungalow and shop. Joy writes of her father: "Spencelayh's house was not strange to him.... If only John had bought *The Scything Reapers* hanging in the hallway, the corn catching the light through the stained glass, or *Girl Asleep on the Raft*, sea washing over her, he would have been a rich man instead of struggling against angina and the fashion of long hair .... Actually John went about his trade with great good humour and even commented on the fun they had in the days of the depression when village lads would congregate in the shop ...."

Life was not always easy and Joy remembers seeing bank statements quite literally 'in the red' being printed in red ink. "The year of the great Bozeat cloudburst and floods in 1952 when someone banged on the bungalow door to say, 'John, your shop's floating,' was a time of hardship. Stock spoiled by layers of mud was thrown away and John was not insured for such an eventuality." There is a picture in *Pictorial Bozeat* of Barry Drage waist-deep in water outside John's shop with the blind clearly marked 'Wills Gold Flake' pulled down over the shop window.

"John loved cars", writes Joy, "and in 1950 acquired a 1936 Austin 7. Although only able to afford a few days' holiday each year, from then on he chose somewhere different to stay each time. In ten years he had seen a large part of England, Wales and eventually went as far as Scotland. He was 17 before he had seen the sea, so he had a lot of time to make up! ... When driving was no longer an option, he was delighted to buy Mr Fred Tivey's old Batricar when Fred bought a newer vehicle." One of my last memories of John was shooting out of the church at Easton Maudit in his electric car and then driving it rather precariously back to Bozeat. John's funeral was at St Mary's, Bozeat on 21st January 1993. Afterwards many old friends crowded into his little bungalow for tea and I remember Richard Allebone greeting one of them with the words, "Hallo – nice to see you again. We always seem to meet at funerals these days. We must be getting near the front of the queue!" John would have appreciated the joke! For as his daughter Joy put it, "with his death, another link with Bozeat's past is severed." (*About Bozeat*, March 1993)

So, to return to those far off wartime days, we must try and catch the atmosphere in this tiny shop thick with cigarette smoke selling all the intimate things that men need, and John on home guard duty by night and, in the cosy chaos of his little shop, cutting the hair of village boys and men by day. And business was boosted by these fresh-faced American boys who gave a new dimension to the life of our little village.

Podington air base
They did the same for other villages around, especially at Podington. Derek Taylor, butcher's 'boy' for 40 years, spent his childhood days at Podington and grew up there. He remembers how these young airmen would come up to the local boys and ask, "Say, boys, have you got an older sister you could introduce me to?" If you said yes they would give you a packet of American chewing gum and ask for an introduction! Derek even at that early age had an eye for business for when an airman approached him with the question, he replied, "Yes I've got three older sisters!" – and received three packets of gum for his exaggeration! Derek and his young friends would play around the perimeter fencing of the aerodrome, watching the giant bombers come and go – now the drag-racing strip of Santa Pod situated on the high ground out of Podington in the direction of Harrold. They used to watch the guards at the entrance and the airman coming in and out. Just at the entrance was a cardboard box on which were written the words "Help yourselves guys." Derek and his mates crept up and looked in the box one day and to their surprise it was full of little white balloons! They took some home and tried, unsuccessfully, to blow them up. Derek remembers that, when his father caught him doing this, "He gave me such a thrashing!"

The loss of life among these young airmen was frightening. At the dance one week you could meet one of them and dance with him and the next week he would not be there. They had to live for the present moment for this is all many of them had left. Newman Darnell, the son of a drover and a man of the countryside and country ways, with his ferrets and his vast knowledge of the wild life and local animals and plants, worked on the aerodrome during the war and remembers seeing these huge planes loaded up with bombs and taking off in a continual procession day after day. They would then assemble like a huge flock of rooks, their wing tips almost touching, ready to fly across Europe and drop their deadly load. He remembers how as every plane prepared to take off the Padre would say a prayer for the crew and their safety and then pray that "God would forgive them for what they had to do." "It stirred in me a faith in God," said Newman to me, over fifty years later.

At this time Nancy Pettitt (née Bayes) was working in the canteen at Podington air base together with Newman Darnell. Nancy went to live with her stepfather Mr Summerlin in his two cottages in Mile Street just up from Fish Alley in 1915 when she was 8 years old. Mr Summerlin was a carrier. He had a horse-and-cart which he kept in the yard at the back and went to Wellingborough three times a week. "He would carry anything. If you wanted eggs carried, or a pound of sausages from Wellingborough, he'd bring them," remembers Nancy.

Of her memories of Podington she writes: "They flew in the daytime. The English bombers flew at night. They came back at night, the English in the morning. Once one of these young pilots gave me his wristwatch and said: 'If I don't come back send my watch to my mum.' That night he didn't come back. One of the American girls on the base said to me: 'Don't send it back yet – I'm sure he'll come back.' A week later the door opened and he walked into the canteen. He'd been shot down but had been picked up and brought home. 'Where's my watch then?' he asked, and I gave it to him. 'Why didn't you send it to my mum?' 'Because we knew you'd come back,' I replied."

A young hero
Bozeat folk to this day still tell the story of the young pilot who saved their village. There is a plaque in the church in memory of this event and each Easter Sunday there is an Easter Lily in the church to remember the young man. We still have Americans visiting us who ask to see the memorial. The actual citation in the Church reads: A few days before Christmas 1944, during the Second World War, Lt. John Ahern, 22-year-old US Air Force pilot, found his plane had got into difficulties. He directed his crew to bale out saying he would follow them when the plane was past the houses in Bozeat. He was never to follow his crew, for after clearing the houses of Bozeat he was killed when the machine crashed. It came down in a field behind Red Gables Farm occupied by Cyril Drage. The farm buildings were damaged by the blast, but the farmer's family were unharmed.

In gratitude to Lt. John Ahern, who thus gave his life for Bozeat, the villagers made a house-to-collection for his mother in America. Woman of the W.V.S. organised this. The American Air Force showed their appreciation of the village's act by presenting a plaque to the Church in memory of this episode of the war. 400 people gathered in the Church when the plaque was handed over by an American Air Force Chaplain. The Chaplain took part in the service, which was conducted by the vicar Rev. S. F. W. Powell and the lesson read by Rev. E. Hardwick, the Methodist Minister.

Bill Silsby was working with his brother Harry for Mr Knight of Church Farm at the time and remembers the day clearly. I will try to paraphrase his words as he told me about it in 1994 aged 76. "It was a foggy morning. I was out in Church Farm meadow when it came over – it was about eleven in the morning. You could hear the plane but could not see it for fog. It was very low by the sound of it. From our house up Easton Lane you could see these large bombers landing and taking off at Podington. They took a battering they did – came back all in pieces. Something was wrong with this one. It was coming back with one bomb still on board trying to get

> A few days before Christmas 1944, during the second World War, Lieut. John Ahern, a 22 year old U.S. Air Force pilot, found his plane had got into difficulties.
>
> He directed his crew to bale out, saying he would follow them when the plane was past the houses in Bozeat.
>
> He was never to follow his crew, for after clearing the houses of Bozeat, he was killed when the machine crashed. It came down in a field behind Red Gables Farm occupied by Mr Cyril Drage. The farm buildings were damaged by the blast but the farmer's family were unharmed.
>
> In gratitude to Lieut. John Ahern, who thus gave his life for Bozeat, the villagers made a house-to-house collection for his mother in America, organised by the women of the W.V.S.
>
> The American Air Force showed their appreciation of the village's act by presenting a plaque to the Church in memory of this episode of the war.
>
> 400 people gathered in the Church when the plaque was handed over by an American Air Force chaplain. The Chaplain took part in the service, which was conducted by the Vicar, the Rev. S.F.W. Powell and the lesson was read by Rev E Hardwick, the Methodist Minister.

Close up of Citation in memory of Lt. John Ahern.

Close-up of plaque in memory of Lt. John Ahern.

Presentation of plaque in memory of Lt. John Ahern on 8th March 1945. (*Vicars' Log Book*)

to Podington (in fact this one came from Kimbolton – see later) but didn't make it. Two men parachuted out and came down in the paddock to the left of the London Road just before it meets the bypass at the Wollaston end.

They jumped out when it was too low to the ground. One man's knee hit his nose and made a bit of a mess and the other damaged his leg. One engine also fell near them. They said it was white hot when it hit the ground. The pilot told them to jump. He'd have to jump off last of course but didn't make it. The plane hit the ground just beyond Malcolm and Graham Drage's, exploded and made a huge crater. They said he tried to avoid the village. No one can tell really. The fog was so thick he probably couldn't see it – except the church spire perhaps! When he saw he could not make Podington he told his crew to bale out. That's all we know." Whatever the whole story, our memorial is a testimony to those brave young men in their flying machines. Nancy Pettitt also remembers the day well over 50 years later. "I worked seven days a week, even Sundays. On one Sunday morning an officer rushed into the canteen and shouted, 'Quick open all the windows. It was winter but we did as he said. Suddenly there was a big bang that would have broken all the windows if they were closed. It was the bomber that crashed behind Red House Farm and its bombs exploding." It was a mercy no-one in the farm itself was injured.

Alison Botterill (née Drage) was a child at Red House Farm when it crashed, as were her brothers and sisters. Talking together at their brother Malcolm's funeral (March 1998) they remembered how their mother shouted out, "There's a plane on fire coming this way. Quick, get into the house and lie down on the floor." They all said it was a miracle none of them was hurt what with flying shrapnel and glass (all the windows were blown out) and bombs exploding – the house must have suffered some structural damage. But if so nothing was done about it and it is still standing!

Prisoners of war

There are other memories of the war. Don reflected that hatred of Germans and everything German (e.g. dachshunds) was not so obvious as it had been in the First War. He remembers how in that war Mrs Selby had had a German housekeeper and, being patriotic, had given her the sack, such was the public feeling against her because of her nationality. That story could be repeated many times over around the country as my mother, a Londoner, born in 1908, well remembers.

In contrast, I think of Bill Ormsby, a German prisoner of war in the Second War who stayed on and who lived and worked on as a farm hand at Easton Maudit. A friendship was built up with him and his family back in East Germany until he died in 1993, especially by the family of Elizabeth Saving with whom he lived the last years of his life in her cottage at 15 Easton Maudit, eventually becoming blind.

And other prisoners of war stayed and became part of our village. There was Max who had a house at 2 St Mary's Road and who fed the village with eggs from his chickens. And at the top of Hope Street lived Salvatori Bovenzi with his eight children until sadly he died on 30th June 1998, cutting his grass on a Tuesday afternoon. He was an Italian prisoner of war and married Sheila Drage in 1949, the sister of Barry Drage and they lived at Arch Villa (now the Paper Shop).

Salvatori was remembered as a very jolly and sociable man, popular in the village. "I wanted twelve bambinos," he would say jovially, as one villager remembers. Derek Taylor remembers how as a prisoner during the war Salvatori worked on the Garrett's Farm at Dungee Corner (Garrett's the butchers – Derek's old employers). "There was no piped water at Dungee Farm so Mr Bovenzi had to get water with his water wagon from Hinwick. And that was no joke if you had 80 head of cattle to get water for as well as yourself! That's how I remember him, going with his wagon from Dungee to Hinwick getting water."

Don remembers too how, early on in the war in 1940, two small English planes – "they seemed to be larking about to me" – were flying above the fields at the top end of the village towards Olney, touched wings and crashed in the field bursting into

The house named 'Canada', now demolished, was in St Mary's Road. During the war, it was occupied by German prisoners of war, who ran a chicken farm. *(D. Roberts)*

flames and killing all three people in each plane. This event stunned the village and Don remembers running down the London Road and telling Mr Cooper in Easton Lane factory what had happened. He remembers too how all the tall glass windows in the Methodist church were painted over with black paint – as all buildings had to be blacked out. "It looked horrible and took years to scrape off. It was done in haste and anyway we decided to worship in the hall behind!"

Mavis Holman (née Line) has childhood memories of those war years (born 1936) when, at this time, they lived at Glebe Farm up the Harrold Road. "I can still remember the huge explosion that shook the earth when six planes loaded with bombs collided on the runway at Podington and blew up. I remember the ammunition dumps along the Harrold Road ("There seemed to be piles of ammunition everywhere," said Arnold Dobbs) and one lone German bomber probably returning home from a raid on Coventry dropped its bombs on Wellingborough, destroying buildings in the town centre. But apart from Podington and the occasional incident, the war never really reached us, and certainly never reached a child like me who was only four when it began and ten when it ended."

The evacuees
Almost as profound as the impact of the American airmen on the village was the arrival of the evacuees. About 120 came from London in 1940 and were under the responsibility of Mr Cooper from Cuffley, Herts. The children lived with different families in the village and went to school and met together in the factory building up Easton Lane. The building was originally a shoe factory and is now occupied by Electrosite (UK) Ltd. Mr Cooper was the headteacher and other staff came with him to run a separate school from the village school where Mr Lack was head. At first they had to share the village school, evacuees and village children each using the

building for half a day. The School Log for 11th September 1939 reads: "Opened School – War with Germany – Children evacuated from London, 120 at Bozeat. Working shifts."

And of course the evacuee children swelled the Sunday Schools of church and chapels. One evacuee, Ivy Burgess, was to marry Bernard Line and become a most lively leader of the Independent Wesleyan Chapel (as I remember her in 1991).

There was also an AYPA – Anglican Young People's Association at St Mary's which met in the Church Hall. "My best friend Winsome Drage of Red Gables Farm was allowed to go but, being a Methodist, I wasn't!" remembers Dolly Roberts ruefully. It was in 1946 that Winsome's brother, Malcolm, as a member of the AYPA was persuaded by the vicar to join the Church Council at the tender age of 19 and remained a member for 52 years till he died in 1998, still farming Red Gables Farm with his brother Graham.

Dolly's mum, Emily, with an evacuee in front of a Dutch barn by Cow Lane, close to the family home, Shepherd's Lodge, in July 1950.
(D. Roberts)

One heartening development amidst such divisions was the formation in 1940 of a village choir. Hollingsworth 'Hol' Smith (head of Wollaston School), the organist at St Mary's, had a choir of boys and men. Mr Cooper, a Methodist Lay Preacher had formed one at the Methodists and Mr Lack (head of Bozeat School) likewise at the Independent Wesleyans. In 1940 they united and Dolly remembers how together they sang the Easter cantatas for several years. When they sang in St Mary's, Vicar Marlow would not allow Mr Cooper to conduct from the front, so the choir had to stand at the back of the church by the tower and sing to the backs of the congregation! If the choir sang at the church on Palm Sunday they would sing at the Methodist Church at Easter (from the front!) – "and they always sang better at the Methodists!" Dolly believed. The favourite cantatas were Olivet to Calvary and Stainer's Crucifixion.

Dolly also remembers how Mr Cooper was a cellist and his wife a violinist and, with others in the village, such as Cyril Tompkins on his violin, they made a good little orchestra – a memory of the good old days when, before the Victorians installed an organ in the church, such a group of musicians would perform for worship from the minstrel's gallery attached to the tower. And perhaps that is the best place perhaps to sing and play from in the church, from the back where the organ pipes are situated.

"Hol Smith, whose full name was Henry Hollingsworth Smith was son of J. H. (John Henry) Smith who lived at Eaglesmere at the back of Hope Street. J. H. Smith used to watch us children playing in the Triangle at the bottom of Allens Hill and would separate us when we quarrelled! He was very nice and polite but could speak sharply and to the point. He sold vinegar and paraffin. He had four children, Ada, Madge, Hollingsworth and Florence. The last three became schoolteachers being all similar in character. Ada married Sid 'Cephas' Drage of the Bakehouse in Church Lane and Madge had a bungalow built in Chequer's field, now occupied by George Pettit at 3 London Road. (The Triangle was built on in spring 1998.) Hol with his wife Olive and daughter Mary came to live opposite the Squires in what is now 19

London Road. Evan Drage, one of the famous five Drage brothers, was Olive's father and he had the fine house at the top of Bull Close built for himself."

"Hol fascinated me. He was a fine musician and orator – words flowed freely (big ones). He was very knowledgeable about all things, could relate easily, and was most profound in his convictions. He loved to expound his theories to any listening ear. He always wore gaiters in the cold weather and a hard hat later in life. He loved visiting churches and cathedrals and claimed to have been in practically all the cathedrals in the country. He loved architecture and history and his talks made everything come to life. He and my uncle Harold were both excellent musicians keen on singing (choir), organ and piano playing. Whereas Hol always had a lot to say (like his father), Uncle Harold was quiet, shy and conscientious. They both were cricketers, musicians and teachers." (Dolly Roberts)

Lil Williams was an evacuee from Hackney but she came towards the end of the war in 1944. When the doodlebugs began to fall on London during that year, Lil's mum had had enough. They had been bombed out twice already so she left for Bozeat with Lil – Bozeat because Lil's auntie had come with the main group of evacuees in 1939. And they never went back! Lil was 18 when she came and they first went to live at one of the cottages up the Olney Road at Northey Farm – half in Northants, half in Bucks! Her Dad and her elder brother Jim had jobs in London and stayed there at first but Jim had TB so could not go to war (he was in the ACT and had hoped to go into the RAF). He was so ill that the doctor advised their mum to bring him to Bozeat as he would not live very long.

The Howkins who owned the next farm along towards Bozeat (Grange Farm) allowed the family to live in one of their cottages on the main road and there Lil's mum nursed Jim back to health. Jim married a local girl, Norah Drage whose grandfather was 'Rocker' Drage, subject of a fine painting by Spencelayh. Their daughter, now Sue Woods, is in 1996 training as a Methodist Local Preacher. Lil's parents eventually settled more permanently at 32/34 Mile Street.

In 1945 Lil met a local lad Dennis Berrill Perkins (Berrill being the family name on his mother's side, a family which built Bozeat), while he was still in the army, and they were married in St Mary's in 1948. Dennis was born in 1922 in the middle of the three cottages at right angles to the London Road and opposite the Red Lion (where Arch Mallows was born 16 years earlier). His dad was in the Great War, was gassed and died, while his son was in the army in the Second War. Dennis joined the Northants Regiment in 1940 but transferred to the Tank Regiment "to see more of the world". He served in North Africa and in Italy, "I was there when they needed them not feeded them!" he liked to say. He was posted to Yugoslavia at the time of Marshal Tito and so was not demobbed until 1946. He then worked for 20 years in the boot and shoe trade for Jack Whites of Rushden, because they could pay a better wage than the factories in the village!

Another villager who served in the Tank Regiment in North Africa was Sue Zang's father, Alec Bayes, who in now lives at 9 Mill Road. Alec drove lorries carrying munitions and fuel to the tanks chasing Rommel's army. It was Rommel's defeat by the Allied Forces pushing him eastwards across the North African desert that was a turning point in the war. Alec and his group were not to share in the victory as they were surrounded and captured by the Germans at Tobruk. Knowing they would be captured, they decided to hide their munitions, etc. and then go for a swim in the sea, which is where the German soldiers found them! Alec spent four years in prison in

Germany during which time he managed to keep up his hobby of collecting butterflies, which on liberation he handed to the guard with whom he had struck up a friendship.

Alec's father came from Harrold to live in the yard up Mile Street (where Christine Line now lives) which backed onto the farmyard of Church Farm, now a smart collection of six stone houses called Church Farm Close built in 1988. Alec was one of 13 children and they occupied two cottages, the boys sleeping in one and the girls in the other! Alec was the youngest (born 1919). His two eldest brothers, Charlie and Percy, he never knew as they were killed in the trenches of the First World War. His father was a shoemaker making shoes in the workshop or barn at the back of the house for a firm in Wollaston while his son Jack kept his racing pigeons in the loft above!

It was one afternoon, when Alec was watching out of the window for his brother's pigeons to return that he saw lightning strike the Church steeple. The incident is recorded in Vicar Knight's notes so we know the exact time and date! It was 2.15 pm on 18th July 1953, just as the funeral of Mrs Annie Bryant was to begin. It caused minor damage to the spire, stonework round the clock was dislodged and the lightning conductor was burnt to a frazzle like a blown fuse. The clock was stopped and not until Nov 4th did Messrs Elliotts of Higham come to repair it (staying at Joshua Partridge's house in Mile Street) and get it going again. The notes continue: "Praise is due to Mr J. Partridge [tower captain], Mr Dick Edmunds [14 Hope Street] and his friend and fellow worker from Wellingborough Mr A. White for their work in repairing, making a new cog wheel for our old clock." [brackets mine]

Incidentally, Alec's uncle was Jack Bayes, nicknamed 'Johnny Bundlehead', the character painted by Spencelayh in those war years – and a character he was as his nickname indicates. His family remember him as a dirty and scruffy man, an embarrassment to the family who lived in a tiny cottage Little Thatch (beautifully restored in 1999 by Chris Sanders) by the Town Well. Johnny often took round the night cart on which was a large metal container into which households emptied their toilet buckets. Max Laughton remembers how as lads, coming back late at night from the pub, they would try to avoid an encounter with the cart and its stench. Spencelayh's painting captures not only something of the character of Jack but also the nature of village life.

Alec loved his sport. He was a member of the football team and also of the cricket team which played in the meadow beyond Windmill Field towards Grendon. He was a member of the cricket club and also remembers playing on Vicar Marlow's tennis court and on the court at Farmer Knight's at Church Farm. Dennis Perkins was also a sports enthusiast and in the years before and after the war was also a member of Bozeat football team. They were often near the top of the league then, and on his sideboard there is a Runners-Up cup for the 1951/52 season. Dennis (and Lil) were members of the carpet bowls club in the church hall from its very beginning. His membership card is No. 10, the 10th person to join, and the first meeting is recorded as 9th January 1989. The club started with the help of Comsport run by the Northamptonshire Leisure and Libraries to encourage recreational activities.

A great buddy of Dennis from those years was Ernie Dilley who struggled all his life with injuries incurred in Italy during the war until he died in 1995 at the age of 78. Amy and Ernie lived at 2 Pudding Bag Lane. Dennis died later in the same year as Ernie aged 73. Such men knew a comradeship which bonded them together and they were never happier than in pub or club or just at home recalling those impressionable years as they relived their vivid memories of active service. As Peg Price said of her husband Kit, another old soldier from London now handicapped by several strokes, "Somehow those memories get more vivid to him the older he gets."

Other organisations

In 1940 the Girls' Life Brigade was formed at the Methodist Church and 60 girls joined with three officers, Norma Hayes as captain and Joyce Partridge, Winnie Wyman and later Doreen Dimmock as lieutenants. "Norma Hayes, sister of Dorothy (of aspidistra fame!) was my dearest friend, one of the mainstays of our chapel, and of the village life," writes Marjorie Drage. "The Brigade was open to all girls who belonged to a Sunday School, Anglican, Independent Wesleyan or Methodist. Before long, younger girls wanted to join so a cadet section of 40 girls was formed under the leadership of Lt. Doreen Dimmock and pioneer Pauline Nichols. They carried on during the war years, despite the blackout, and many of the evacuees joined them. A letter was sent to the London Company and a dozen girls came and shared a peaceful time of fellowship and hospitality in the village. Apart from the serious work of badge-collecting the girls gave a variety of entertainment, including several pantomimes. It was a great occasion when, in 1956, four trophies were won by the 1st Bozeat Company.

"The Wesley Guild was formed in Bozeat in 1927 and during the war years combined to include both Methodists and Anglicans. The Guild had four sections, Christian Service, Literary, Devotional and Social – the 4 'C's, Comradeship, Consecration, Culture and Christian Service. During the war years over 100 (including some 30 men) came to the meetings. There was also the Wesley Institute particularly for young men and women, and the additional room at the back of the Methodist school hall was built (by Berrills) in around 1900 for their use. Methodism from its beginnings offered the opportunity for working people to better themselves and the Wesley Guild was attractive to men for the political and social opportunities it afforded as much as for the spiritual ones. It offered a social centre alongside the Pub and the Working Men's Club which until recently were almost exclusively for men only.

The Guild was still active in 1983, meeting on Thursdays, and the names of the ladies who have served as its officers span the century since its inception – Marjorie Drage, Dollie Line, Flos Tivey, Miss G. Dunmore and Dolly Roberts.

It seems that between the wars the Guild also had a tennis club in Windmill Field with a pavilion to hold mowers, balls and court marker. There was also a cricket pitch there but cricket was also played in the field (called Hop Ground) opposite the Chequers belonging to Springfield Farm. Bill Silsby remembered one occasion when a cricket ball went clean through one of the Chequers windows!

Dorothy (Dolly) Roberts when Cadet Leader (with Doreen Dimmock) of the Girls Life Brigade in the 1940s. (D. Roberts)

We will remember them

Each year the Remembrance Service, organised by the Bozeat branch of the British Legion in the village, is a particularly moving occasion. The names of the Dead of two World Wars are read out whilst a Scout and a Guide place a cross in a tray of sand for each one of them. "We will remember them" – for they are our village and its past and we should not forget them. There were 15 who fell in the 1939-45 war and they are:

Roy Candy	James Healey
Fred Dobbs	Jack Line
Clifton Drage	Stanley Mabbutt
Cyril Drage	Edward Patrick
Sidney Drage	Leslie Partridge
Arthur Dunmore	Frank Taylor
Fred Furr	Horace Wilson
Jack Goodman	

Our War Memorial in the village cemetery was erected in 1920 and engraved on it are the names of these men. In the Great War of 1914-18, out of the 210 young men who went to war, virtually all the young men of the village, 39 men fell, and these names are engraved on the Memorial:

Arthur E. Abbott	Charles Hooton
Frederick C. Bradshaw	Herbert E. Hooton
James W. Bayes	W. Cuthbert Jones
Frank A. Botterill	Alfred C. Johnson
Sidney Church	A. Reginald Luck
Samuel Corby	Bertie Mallows
Charles W. Craxton	Alfred Page
Sidney R. Dobbs	Bertram Partridge
Abraham Drage	John W. Partridge
Archie B. Drage	William G. Pettit
Frederick T. Drage	William Robinson
Jack Drage	Albert O. Ross
Percy W. Drage	Harry Ross
Thos. Edward Drage	John A. Silby
Edward Driver	Albert S. Silsby
Thomas Ealy	Ralph H. Tompkins
Bernard Eden	William Tyler
H. Bryant Goodman	Frederick W. Wallis
Edwin Harris	Reuben T. Warner
Edward Harrison	

POSTSCRIPTS

A village tale – evacuees
(Told to me by Tom Partridge-Underwood, 13th February 1997)

Miss Hayes, the Big Methodist lady who ran the drapery shop in London Road next to the Co-op, went to see Mr Summerlin who lived up Easton Lane where Joyce Wesley now lives (1996).

"I've come to inspect your house Mr Summerlin to see how many evacuee children you can take," said Miss Hayes officiously.

"I'm taking none of those London children in my house," he replied.

"Oh yes you are Mr Summerlin. It's your duty," replied Miss Hayes and she entered the house with some determination and began inspecting the rooms.

"Where is your toilet Mr Summerlin?"

"At the bottom of the garden," he replied, upon which Miss Hayes went out the back to inspect.

"You've got no padlock on the toilet Mr Summerlin. You'll have to get one."

Mr Summerlin looked rather sourly at the well-meaning woman and replied: "There's no need for a padlock on my toilet Miss Hayes. I've been using it for 40 years and no one has ever taken anything from it up to now!"

2nd Lt. John J. Ahern Jr.
Research (completed in 1999) by George Hanger and George White regarding the events relating to the Incident over Bozeat on 16th December 1944.

To give an overall picture of the day's action, it would appear each Bombardment Division was scheduled to contribute one Combat Wing in an operation targeting of German Marshalling Yards. The plan required the First Division to send the 41st Combat Wing to ULM and involved 116 aircraft. The 303rd, 379th and 384th Bomb Groups each provided 39 aircraft, but obviously there was an abort. This wing abandoned the mission over England during assembly at about 1000 hours due to deteriorating weather. The 379th diverted to RAF Kirmington and did not return to Kimbolton until the next day. The 2nd Division launched 72 B23s but these were also recalled due to the weather. The only successful aspect of the day's mission was an attack by 124 aircraft from the 3rd Division on the Marshalling Yard at Kornwestheim which is north of Stuttgart. All this on the day the Germans launched their Ardennes offensive.

The 525th Bomb Squadron diary shows the following times for the Crews of the 379th who participated:

Crews awakened	0445 hrs
Breakfast	0515 "
Briefing	0615 "
Stations	0745 "
Taxi Time	0845 "
Take-off Time	0900 "
Estimate Return	1611 "

Because the mission was scrubbed at 1000 hrs during assembly over England the Group did not count this operation as one of its missions.

Amongst the 12 crews from the 537th Bomb Squadron taking off on this day was that of 2nd Lt. John A. Ahern flying in 44-8275 (FO-p). This aircraft had arrived in the UK on or around 18th September 1944, and, after theatre modifications at Burtonwood Base Air Depot, had been sent to Kimbolton as a replacement aircraft on 26th September. Now almost three months after its arrival in the UK, aircraft #275 was assembling for its 24th operational sortie. It was during this time the aircraft developed engine trouble and Lt. Ahern ordered his crew to bale out. Reports suggest Lt. Ahern attempted to land his Vega-built B17G near Bozeat, but sadly the aircraft cracked up and exploded during the landing, killing the brave pilot. The other eight crew members parachuted to safely. The explosion also caused damage to properties in the village of Bozeat. The crew comprised:

Pilot	2nd Lt. John J. Ahern Jr.	KIA
Co-Pilot	2nd Lt. Frederick W. Barley	Safe
Navigator	F/O Thomas N. Ramsey	Safe
Nose gnr	Sgt. Whitney J. Reese	Safe
Radio op	Sgt. Fred F. Estlinbaum	Safe
Top Turret gnr	S/Sgt. Warren G. Barlow	Safe
Ball Turret gnr	Sgt. Saul L. Ancelet	Safe
Waist gnr	Sgt. John W. Cox	Safe
Tail gnr	Sgt. William J. Watkins	Safe

The survivors were returned to combat on 10th January 1945 and were dispatched on a mission to Bonn/Hangalar airfield with Major Raymond E. Davis as their skipper. Sadly luck ran out for the survivors of Bozeat when their aircraft, 43-38237 collided with 43-38955 of the group near the target. Only Watkins and Ancelet survived. (Barlow was not flying with this crew.)

I speculate that 2nd Lt. Ahern and his crew arrived at Kimbolton as replacements during 1944. It would appear Lt. Ahern flew his first mission as a Co-Pilot with Lt. Miller's crew (526th BS) on 2nd Dec in an aircraft called 'White Lightning'. On 4th Dec. John Ahern and crew flew their first mission as a new crew and they borrowed 43-37677 (WA-A). They were airborne again on 9th December in 44-8275 and then again on 11th in 44-6507. Their next operation came on 16th with the fateful consequences described above. It must have been a testing time for the crew, as they had to cope with bad weather as well as adjusting to flying in combat.

The operational history for 44-8275 is as follows:

27-9-44	Rhodes crew (525BS)
2-10-44	Hayfield crew
3-10-44	Tarken crew
5-10-44	Anderson crew (525BS)
6-10-44	Schlesinger crew
7-10-44	S. Thomas crew
9-10-44	Teichman crew
14-10-44	Schlesinger crew

15-10-44	Ryland crew
17-10-44	Schlesinger crew
18-10-44	Breda crew (526BS)
19-10-44	Schlesinger crew
22-10-44	Conroy crew
30-10-44	Schlesinger crew
1-11-44	" "
6-11-44	" "
10-11-44	Lafferty crew
11-11-44	Schlesinger crew
16-11-44	" "
20-11-44	" "
21-11-44	" "
29-11-44	" "
9-12-44	" "
16-12-44	" "

The above crews belonged to the 527th BS except where stated. It is interesting to see how frequently other Squadrons borrowed the aircraft. This was a common practice. It would be interesting to know if the aircraft ever received a name in view of the fact Schlesinger and his crew flew the aircraft fairly regularly. This crew was lost on the notorious Zitz mission of 30th November 1944.

This shows the Chequers public house with land from Spring Vale Farm in the foreground.

CHAPTER 5

After the War was Over – 1945-1980

Oh I believe in Yesterday ...

Looking for work

Just before the Second World War, Don Roberts bought from Mr Deverill the equipment to make ice creams, for £7. This included the 'truck' to make wafers at three thicknesses to sell at 1, 2 or 3 (old) pence and also cornets for a halfpenny. These he sold around the village for two or three seasons. Being rather retiring in nature he found this hard but, waiting outside the school yard every day for the children as they left school to sell them ice creams, he soon "improved my standing" with them! All the children came to know him as 'Don'. He sold ice creams to make money in order to realise a dream – of having his own market garden. He also grew produce and sold it. He rented the old church school at the bottom of Mile Street in the 1940s to carry out his business and eventually he was able to buy it and opened a shop there in 1950.

Mr Cave put a large shop window in the building and over it for all to see the words, 'Don Roberts'! He grew produce in the greenhouses in the garden of his house and on allotments in Stoneypiece. It opened as a fruit, flower and vegetable shop and all produce was home-grown. But he was also an agent for garden implements Sowman Hardware of Olney, conifers from Staughtons of Northampton and hardware from Harris' and groceries as well. Don and Dolly ran the shop for 30 years until it closed in 1980 – and he remembered when he was selling his prized tomatoes for two shillings and sixpence a pound! Don couldn't forget how one week they cut and bunched and sold 3,600 daffodils for a shilling a bunch!

Improvisation

Those early years after the war were not easy in many ways and improvisation was necessary to get Britain on its feet again. "During an early post-war fuel crisis when factories were not allowed to use electricity on certain days except for lighting, Botterills managed to keep going by connecting up their machinery, mostly still driven by shafts, pulleys and belts, to two tractors loaned by local farmers, I think Browns and Howkins, who had largish tractors with a drive-pulley to run threshing floor machines. Some time later Botterills were able to return the help

Don Roberts' shop in London Road, in the Old School House building.
(*D. Roberts*)

Part of the wreckage of the old post mill which had been blown down in the severe gales which swept the country at the end of February in 1949. This is the gearwheel demonstrated by young Lionel Drage.

to Browns by making up a special shoe for one of their prize cows that had a foot problem. Hedley or Cyril (Brown) will remember this." (Dick Botterill, 1996)

A foot in the past

It must be remembered too that, in many ways, Bozeat still had its feet still firmly planted in the past. For, although electricity had come to the village in the thirties, there was still no piped water and no sewage system, and drainage still had much to be desired.

Symbolic of the passing of the sheltered seclusion of yesterday was an event that happened on the last night of February 1949 when terrible gales whipped across England. The old post mill which stood as a landmark at the end of Mill Road at the top of the village, one of the last windmills of its kind in England and the only one remaining in Northamptonshire, came crashing to the ground. All that was left in the morning was a heap of broken woodwork and twisted metal exposing the massive giant millstones in the centre. Although it stopped operating in 1921, it stood boldly as a memorial to the past. In Arthur Mee's *Northampton* it is written: "... the people of three counties look out on one of the last windmills of England on a massive post as sound as the day it was fixed." Miss Little who lived at Mill House only 20 yards from its long sails, and whose father was the last miller of Bozeat, reported that it was, "because there was so much noise from the wind that we did not notice anything unusual and did not know it was down till this morning." (*Northamptonshire Evening Telegraph* for 1st March 1949)

Mr Little had continued to work the steam mill until the Second World War. This was demolished in 1955, and the former mill house in 1956.

A village of wells

Other reminders of 'yesterday' are the wells of Bozeat. The village's peculiar geology means there were wells everywhere. Many still exist as a reminder of days when they were the main source of water for home, farm and factory. As has already been speculated, a possible origin for the name of our village could be 'Beautiful Jet' from the Norman French "Beau", beautiful or fine and "Jetter", to throw or jet, i.e. a fine jet of water. Beaujet it close to the pronunciation used today although its spelling has varied with the centuries (see page 10). What does seem likely and natural is that a hamlet, perhaps Saxon in origin, should have grown around the beautiful well known as the Town Well. And this most accurately fits the description Beaujet for it "is not a well but a jet or throw of water coming out of the side of a bank in the Dyches (or ditches) near Marshes Manor. As far back as can be traced, there has been land, the income from which is for the upkeep of the Town Well. Tradition says it has never

AFTER THE WAR WAS OVER – 1945-1980

A prolonged drought in 1947 had Bozeat's wells all but dried up (left), in contrast to the picture on the right, taken in January 1983, which shows James Case, a Trustee of the Town Well, who then lived in Little Thatch, the cottage next to it. *(Evening Telegraph)*

The refurbishment of the Town Well, a Millennium project. Picture shows Lyndis Payne, Tom Partridge-Underwood, Andrew Underwood (Parish Council chairman), Len Drage (builder) and Linda Blenkharn (monumental masons).

been known to run dry: but 1934 was too great a strain and spoilt its record." (*Marlow*, p.1)

A further reminder of the precarious dependency on wells for water came in September 1947 when after a long period of drought the wells had all but dried up. I quote from the *Wellingborough News* for 5th September: "Most of the wells are now dried up or out of action. We had to go to six different wells before we could get any water." These words, spoken by a Bozeat resident on the Monday, came as the water crisis in this village of 1,200 folk became really acute. As early as four o'clock in the morning villagers with buckets and baths had been lining up at Bozeat 'Town Well' to start pumping for water.

"First there, first served," is the cry, but soon the supply gives out. The position is so serious that if the dry spell continues the whole village will be threatened. "We are 100 years behind the times at Bozeat where water is concerned," said one housewife, as she left with her buckets in search of water. The paper gives photographs of some of these antiquated providers of water, like the 'Zinc Square' well with the words 'THIS Pump Belongs TO This yard' scored on its wooden box surround, providers that were now empty. The Town Well had only dried up once in living memory (1934). Bozeat's third oldest resident, 90 year old Ellen Perkins says of its water, "It has all other water beaten. It's the best I have ever tasted." But a resident 'hooking' water, with a bucket lowered by a wooden rod with a hook into the water, from the supply in Burleigh Terrace described it as "sewage water"!

One begins to realise the vast amount of human time and energy that had to be expended in obtaining water and the enormous saving in these precious human commodities that piped water was to bring.

Loreen Drage (née Line) remembered how, when her brothers rented Glebe Farm about this time, they hired a water diviner to look for water in the two Church fields adjacent to the farm further up Harrold Road. "I remember how we had to go to the vicarage with the rent," Loreen recalled. The man with the divining gift in the village was 'Seppy' (Septimus) Drage who lived at the top of London Road – No. 142. "He found it all right," said Loreen.

Farms were particularly dependent on water. "We could get some water from Dag Lane brook, but that often dried up. There were water butts everywhere to collect water, and ponds of course, but it came mostly from wells, the deeper ones using pumps and others using buckets," Loreen's husband Ted remembers from his days as a boy at Town Farm.

Nursery rhymes remind us how much human life was centred around the well.

> *Ding, dong, bell*
> *Pussy's in the well*
> *Who put her in? Little Tommy thin*
> *Who pulled her out? Little Tommy stout*
> *What a naughty boy was he to drown poor pussy cat*
> *Who never did any harm but killed all the mice*
> *In the farmer's barn.*

Old Mr Bowyer, Helen Ingram's father, born at Sherrington in 1905 (died 1995), had a favourite tale of how at the age of four he fell down the well, how the soft mud broke his fall and mercifully saved his life and how he was brought up again in a bucket – an experience retold in his eighties as vividly as if it had happened yesterday. Many such tales were told, including that of labourer William Bettles aged 63 who, in 1891, took his own life by throwing himself down a disused well into seven feet of stagnant water. There are also similar stories of the ponds, most of which have now been filled in.

This aspect of village life was swiftly relegated to the past when piped water came to the village in 1949, as was the night soil cart, and the tales that were told about its nocturnal journey, when Bozeat acquired its own sewage system in 1950.

But a memory of these days was relived when, in 1992, George Line brought his JCB into the vicarage garden and dug a trench from the church to the vicarage, seven feet deep in places, so that the Church could have mains water and a soil pipe for a toilet. But could we find the mains water pipe where it entered the vicarage? Eventually we called in Anglian Water who came from Kettering with a van full of the latest technology but they tried in vain to find it. Finally, in desperation, one of these experts said to the other, "Right George we'll have to use the wires," whereupon George went to the van and returned walking slowly down the vicarage path with a wire in each hand until the wires uncannily swung round towards each other at a particular spot along the path. Suddenly I realised these modern water experts were water divining! "There it is," they said with conviction, and with that they packed up their equipment and went home!

And it was nice to walk into the garden of Jim Jarvis in July 1996 in the middle of another dry summer and to be shown the working well round the back of his bungalow half way up Allens Hill. "In 1976 the drought was so severe that Pitsford Reservoir completely dried up. Newspapers showed pictures of a dried-out basin of cracked clay. So I dug a well nine feet deep, fitted a hand-pump, and still use it for the garden today." And as he spoke, Jim worked the pump and up came clear cool fresh water from the bowels of the earth. Jim's bungalow is built in what was Chequer's Field, in which in earlier days was situated the fayre ground at Bozeat Feast – an event already so vividly described for us by Floss Tivey. And it was in June 1999 that Irene Collins, living in what was the old Workhouse in Mallows Yard adjacent to the Churchyard, showed me the well they had just opened up. Its circular wall, beautifully and geometrically built in curved stones, descended into the water whose surface lay some seven feet below us – long ago having served as a source of supply to the inmates.

Life at 'The Mount' – Andrew and Sydney Gillitt

Frank Sydney Gillitt (relative of Robert Wharton, publisher) was the 9th child (born 29th March 1887) of a family of nine boys and two girls whose father Thomas farmed land on both sides of the road between Wilby and Wellingborough and between 1885 and 1914 had a butchery at 1 Oxford Street, Wellingborough.

All the boys went to Wellingborough School and in 1903 Frank became an engineering pupil; in 1912 he decided to chance his luck, went to Buenos Aires, and made a successful career working on the railways of South America. In 1914 Phyllis Turnell from Harrowden joined him. They married and had four sons Andrew, Jim, Frank and Bill.

At the age of 59 Frank decided to return to England to retire and in 1947 bought 'The Mount', 46 Mile Street from the village carpenter, joiner and undertaker Mr Cave who had bought it as an investment.

Frank's son Andrew describes the house and life in Bozeat at that time.

"We think the house originally consisted of 2 or 3 thatched cottages and legend says it was once used as the Manse, perhaps after the great fire of 1729. There was clear evidence that the cottage forming the upper end of the house was a

'Doll' Gillitt washing vegetables under the water pump which was later sealed off as polluted. The Gillitts had a garden party every year for the WRVS. (S. Gillitt)

The former slaughter-house which was turned into a hen run. (S. Gillitt)

butcher's shop for there was a semi-cellar at the side containing the remains of an ice tank and shelving, a cold stone slab etc, and a storeroom above, which gave access to the bedroom above the former shop. My Mother, known to everyone as 'Doll' on account of her small stature, used the cellar as a larder for years before she had a fridge. The house, outbuildings, side gate and some of the stone walling around the garden were in a poor state of repair. One of the stone-built out-buildings had been used as a slaughter-house, and the area between the house and slaughterhouse was used as a cattle yard, surfaced with limestone. There was a well but the water was found to be unfit for human consumption so it had to be boiled. There was a large rainwater tank which served for domestic requirements. There was not as yet any piped water or sewerage in the village but these services were shortly provided. It was perhaps fortunate that my parents had lived for many years in countries where conditions for some are similarly primitive and therefore knew how to cope!

My Father immediately set to work building an indoor toilet and bathroom assisted by my brother Bill and at weekends by myself. We dug up the cattle yard and used the stone for making garden paths, bringing the displaced soil back to make a lawn. Father turned the outbuildings into deep litter hen runs and sold the eggs to the Packing Station. He also cultivated vegetables in the large garden and sold the surplus to the village greengrocer Don Roberts. At one time he had two allotments and again Don Roberts bought what he required.

The house contained some interesting features. Built of limestone, like all the old houses in the village, the end wall at the lower end was 6 feet or more thick and the upstairs room contained walk-in cupboards each side of the fireplace. The only wooden downstairs floor was in the end room, the rest were tiled. The wall separating what had been the shop from the middle room was also very thick, some 5 feet or so. The thatched roof was replaced by tiles when rain started coming through.

My Mother took an active part in village life. Having been abroad throughout the war she felt she was doing her bit for the country by cycling round the village every Saturday morning selling National Savings stamps to anyone wishing to save that way. My Father was devoted to his garden and allotments and took part in village gardening competitions. He died on 15th December 1969 at the age of 82. He got up early one morning, went out to inspect his garden as he always did; felt unwell, went back to bed and died there. Mother died in 1980 four days before her 92nd birthday.

My brother Bill remembers that the roof was tile, supported by a structure made of tree trunks and branches. It sagged dramatically. The only heat was from small grates in a couple of the rooms. There was no plumbing in the house, a well in the back yard and a one-holer around the back of the shed. We had water jugs and basins in the bedrooms in which the water froze at night in winter. Water shortage was a constant problem. We used a large metal tank from the butcher's shop to collect rainwater for watering the garden. All other water had to be hand pumped from the well into a bucket and carried indoors. When it had been used it had to be carried out again. We used the copper (used for scalding the bristles off the slaughtered pigs) to heat water for an occasional slipper bath in the same shed that housed the copper, a cold and uncomfortable process in winter since the door fitted very badly. Later it was discovered that our well and others in the village were polluted and we were supplied with water from a tanker truck which parked at the top of the hill from time to time. The water had to be fetched in buckets and jugs. Every drop was used at least three times, ending up eventually on the garden. This crisis was solved by the extension of piped water up Mile Street. The piped water made it possible for a tap in the kitchen and for me and my dad to build a bathroom and toilet inside the house on the lower floor and to add a water heater. My father turned the cattle yard into a beautiful garden."

Frank Gillitt digging in a new flower bed in the former cattle yard. He later replaced the thatched roof of 'The Mount' with a tiled one. The house has now been rebuilt as the home of Robert and Pam Fenn. (S. Gillitt)

Floods and torrents

Another incident which was a reminder of the past and of the vulnerability of village life to the whims of the elements was the floods of 1952. At about 9.00 pm on the Monday night of 19th May, a freak storm hit Bozeat and within minutes a raging torrent swept along the High Street reaching a depth of six feet at its peak. In just over one hour, 2 inches of rain fell on Bozeat. Mr S. Underwood of 8 Camden Square reported that he "actually saw a large cloud open and a sheet of rain descend." (*Northamptonshire Advertiser* 22nd May 1952)

This compared with only 0.66 inches in Wellingborough and 0.122 inches at Kettering. The water poured off the high ground to the south and east of the village and then was channelled along the High Street westwards turning right before the Paper Shop and just past John Farey's little barber shop and down narrow Fish Alley (then Cake Walk) into the bottom of Mile Street. It then plunged into the brook along London Road, flowing northwards to the Nene valley.

As it swept down the Alley it took down the wall on the one side and the fence on the other. At the far end were a corrugated garage and a six-foot wall which were both carried by the strength of the water into Mile Street, and another wall was demolished and strewn across the London Road. In its progress down the High Street huge slabs of pavement and tarmac were torn up and 40 houses were flooded, furniture was ruined and foodstuffs contaminated. At Frank Laughton's furniture shop hundreds of pounds worth of damage was done as carpets and lino and suites were submerged. A car was carried 30 yards down the High Street, its lights still burning brightly in the dark under the flood water. Chickens were drowned in their coops which were carried away by the water and the police rescued half-drowned pigs from a floating sty. Some folk lost ration books and supplies and 100 people had to be given a meal in the Ambulance Room the next day. Mr J. H. Cole, the oldest inhabitant at 90 said he had never seen a storm like it in his whole life.

Barry Drage was a teenager at the time. A photograph of Barry appeared in the local paper waist deep in water outside John Farey's shop. "The water wasn't waist deep," confessed Barry when I visited his radio and TV repair shop in Wollaston in 1996. "But in the photo it came up to your waist!" I objected. "That's because I was kneeling down. Look as the door to John Farey's shop. It's all visible above the water! It was up to my waist but by the time the photographer arrived two hours later the water had gone down and so he told me to kneel to show how it was!"

Barry lived in Arch Villa (the Paper Shop since 1960) from which his father ran a taxi business. When the flood waters were at their highest it was over three foot deep in their sitting room. "Dad told me to stand on the table but when he stood on the other end it tipped up and Dad disappeared under the water!"

It was as bad for John Tompkins in a cottage just upstreet from John Farey's. He saw the dividing wall in his house collapse as the water rushed in the front door and out the back one. The water was up to his chin before he managed to clamber upstairs.

It was even worse for John and Gertie Coleclough, next door to both him and John's shop – clearly visible in the photograph of Barry. Bedridden for a year John, aged 65, was trapped downstairs. Gertie, unable to lift him, cried for help and Frank Laughton's son Max fortunately heard her and carried the sick man upstairs to safety. Tom Partridge-Underwood was only a boy at the time (the son of the Mr Underwood who "saw the heavens open") and Gertie Coleclough was his Sunday School teacher at the Wesleyan Chapel. "She was such a wonderful spiritual woman," said Tom in 1996. "She had a great influence on me spiritually. She had a little cottage in Fish Alley where Mary Wallace now lives in her bungalow and on the night of the great flood she was at home with her invalid husband confined to bed. As the floods rose rapidly, it was dead of night and there was little or no chance that anyone would

Newspaper pictures of the great flood of 1952, on the right showing Barry Drage in front of John Farey's barber's shop.
(*Evening Telegraph*)

know of their plight. She could have left her husband to try to raise help but he might well be drowned in bed in the meantime. So, pious woman as she was, she decided to die with him and knelt down by his bed in prayer so they could end their lives together."

As it happened Max Laughton, whose home was just up the High Street from theirs, suddenly remembered the Colecloughs and wondered if they were all right. He forced his way into the house as the water was rising to its peak and found the couple just in time." Max told me (July 1996) that he was in the Working Men's Club that night when the heavens opened, just a stone's throw up the High Street from where he lived with his wife Eta and 18 month old son Stephen, sharing the house with his parents. Suddenly water like a tidal wave poured down the High Street and began filling their home and it was then he heard screams from Mrs Coleclough only a few doors away. "I put on my Wellingtons and waded down the High Street. There were four cottages between us and John Farey and theirs was the third along. You went down a few steps to the front door which opened into their front room. By the time I got there Mrs Coleclough had somehow managed to get her invalid husband onto the small table in the front room. I got there just in time for the water was already up to the top of the table and still rising. I don't know where I got the strength to carry him up those narrow stairs, sodden and heavy with water both of us, but, thankfully, I did! The next day there was mud everywhere and the fireman came and hosed it all down ("They did a wonderful job," added Eta).

If the wall along the brook in London Road at the bottom of Church Farm paddock had not burst, the water would have remained high much longer. As it was it burst with the force of the water hurling the bricks into the London Road and the water level suddenly went down. Next morning I walked down the London Road towards the cricket field and Grendon and there, hanging along the hedges like a washing line, were people's clothing and personal belongings …"

"They improved the drainage after that – but not enough. There was another flood in about 1976 but this time the water only rose just above floor level in our house, and ruined our carpets! ("Max rushed in and shouted, 'It's 1952 again mi gal!'" said

Old junction between Easton Lane and London Road with Don and Dolly Roberts' house straight ahead.

Eta). Then in 1982 they put in really big pipes, ones you could easily crawl along. One of the workmen said to me, "You'll never get another flood with these." I'm not so sure. Nothing would ever stop the water in a storm like the one in 1952!"

Don remembered the night well. The storm as he remembers it came from Harrold way falling on the high ground above and between the two villages (Harrold High Street was flooded to a depth of four feet) as well as on the villages themselves. Remember that Don's garden with his two greenhouses sloped down towards Fish Alley. Being May they were full of bedding plants ready to sell. But the water came up to the eaves of the greenhouses and ruined them all. The only plants saved were those he had already moved into the shop (the old school) which like their house was just too high for the flood waters to reach. Being a Monday night he would normally have gone to the Guild meeting at the Methodist Church but decided not to. Those who did were stranded and had to escape via the back of the church to get home.

The plight of the small shopkeeper
Until the fifties there were few cars about and the roads were still quite empty. The majority of people still shopped in the village for most of what they needed, although the regular bus services, such as Drage Buses, made weekly shopping in Northampton and Wellingborough more and more popular. As a result the little village shops became the 'mother forgot shops' as Don called them. They provided, as village shops do today, the convenience shopping for the inhabitants. Don did quite well as the bus stopped outside their shop and folk would pop in for items they forgot to buy in Wellingborough or things they thought of whilst waiting for the bus. When they 'straightened' the corner of the road to Easton Maudit in 1979 and the bus stop moved to its present site, business dropped noticeably. Little shops did well from the factories but again as these closed (most by 1979), so the little shops suffered. In the sixties frozen foods started to come in and eventually Don saved enough to buy a big

fridge from Fred Hawkes of Rushden. But again he lost out because people went and brought their frozen foods across the road at the Co-op with its bigger range of products. "We had to give away samples to get people to buy," remembers Dolly ruefully.

The building of the new private estates in the late sixties and seventies produced an improvement in trade but by now many families had cars and much convenience shopping could be done further afield where there was a wider range of products. There was also the problem that when the allotment in Stoneypiece was sold for housing Don lost land on which to grow his vegetables.

Another problem was that more and more of Don's time was taken up with commercial travellers. They were everywhere in the sixties! In the early days, leather travellers came every Wednesday packed into the early morning bus from Wellingborough, – the modern equivalent of the ancient pedlar's way! – and they spent the day invading the factories trying to sell the products of their companies. By the fifties they were coming by car. "And they took up a lot of your time – there could be seven a day, all from different companies. There were six different varieties of biscuits, for example, sold by six different companies! And they came just when Don should be out growing his vegetables!" Dolly remembers one traveller being quite stroppy with her because Don was on the allotment and he had to do business with her. "I only deal with men not women!" he said rudely. "I left him in the shop to fetch Don. The man was very persistent, and when I told him Don did not want anything he replied, 'I can see I'm dealing with a hen-pecked husband here!' – and he shut his case and went!"

At the end of each Wednesday the travellers would pile onto the bus and leave the village in peace for another week. One is reminded of the itinerant traders of earlier years, like the pot man, the main difference being that he brought his goods with him, the others only promises! Commercial travellers never completely disappeared but mergers and bigger trading companies and chain stores like Spar and the other methods of placing orders brought about their virtual demise by the end of the 1970s.

But all this could not save Don or the 30 or more other little shops that had served the village so well from the earliest years of that century. "Trade had moved so much to the towns that is was not worth continuing," said Don ruefully. In one year their profits were only £13 – for the whole year! This was mainly because they bought too much stock and so had to live on their savings. Towards the end, in the late 1970s, they typically took only £20 a week to live on, and when they sold off the stock in 1980 (when the shop closed) it amounted to £700.

Life had not been easy in those busy years of working life. They had bought a quarter of Don's parents house at 55 London Road, two doors away from the shop, and a good sized garden with greenhouses to grow produce in – Don being one of four brothers. The house was partitioned off to accommodate them and their daughter Myra, born in the 1960s. Eventually Don had to buy the rest of the house from his brothers. In that hard year, when the profits were only £13, he was asked to be Chapel Steward at the Methodist Church but declined because of his business difficulties. In consequence some were critical of him for this decision and went to the Co-op instead!

Don felt very bitter about this and shared his feelings with the Methodist minister at the time, the Revd Michael Allen (c.1970). Don remembers them praying together about it in the back room of the house. There were also problems with their accountant – particularly when they applied for a grant for Myra to go to take her B.Ed at Reading University in 1975. He was a devout Baptist from Rushden but had been lax about the accounts which were three years behind so Don could not complete the tax statement on the grant application form! In 1976 when VAT came in Don was only taking a little over £100 a month! Dolly throughout this time gave piano lessons to supplement their modest income (she remembers teaching the Botterill girls) – and she is still giving lessons today! (1995).

Today we can see the results of the decimation of retail life in the village. Even the mighty Co-op closed at last in 1991, and the M&M Supermarket – Happy Shopper – which took over the shop, lasted only three years until 1995. The village garage run by Mike from Sri Lanka closed in 1993 (it opened again in June 1998 but only for a year) and what we have left today (1998) is the Post Office and its store, part of the Spar supermarket chain run by Keith and Carol Cullip and Robert and Pat Driver at the Paper Shop which was once Arch Villa at the other end of the High Street. Tucked behind it as part of what was the original Drage Shoe factory is a ladies hairdresser and round the High Street side of the same factory block a take-away run by a young Chinese man from Hong Kong and his Siamese wife. John Farey's men's hairdressers is now a shop for the village charity Bozaid led by our roofer Eric Green. The biggest of the out-of-town superstores in Wellingborough, Tesco's and Sainsbury's, have won the day, thanks to the motor car. Our village of 1,780 souls can only be thankful for this remaining and invaluable retail enterprise – not forgetting the travelling family butcher Mick Gell who lives in the village.

The allotments
A feature of the village which has all but disappeared is the allotment. It played a vital role in the two world wars to enable people to grow their own food and has links with a past where most people grew their own food anyway. It is the remaining memory of the days before tidy gardens when villagers had a strip of land which they not only worked for the landowner but on which they could grow their livelihood. With the Enclosure Act (Bozeat Enclosure Act was granted in 1799) larger areas of land came under the management of tenant farmers who employed farm labourers to work for them. The Act also gives interesting details of private and public roads allowed in the village and of allotments, plots of land 'allotted' or awarded to different people, e.g. "an allotment awarded to William Whittingham whereon a windmill now stands." An allotment was also awarded to Baroness Lucas to the south of the village for use of her agents, tenants, servants and workfolk (see *Marlow*, p.75). Lucas, now a large electronics company, sold their remaining land at Stocken Hollow when its idiosyncratic living-in tenant, an ardent beekeeper, died in 1995 (see also Chapter 16). And that has been the situation up to recent times until mechanisation brought an end to labour-intensive farming. Since the sale of the Bozeat Estate in 1909, more and more farmers have been able to buy their own farms and the farmer with his family with only one or two employed workers can run the entire farm. The fields are all but void of human life and labour and all we see now are crops, sheep and cattle and the occasional horse, horse-riding being an increasingly popular leisure activity. (Glebe Farm is now an Equestrian Centre.)

There is only one allotment left in Bozeat – up Allens Hill alongside Bull Close. All the rest of the land in the village has been built upon. The Harrold Road Council Estate was built at the end of the 1930s soon after Council Street which in turn was built after the council houses in Allens Hill in 1926. The Rural District Council built homes soon after the Second World War as well, such as those in Roberts Street first, and then at the top of Queen Street. Gerald and Dorothy Corby got the keys for their new council house at 11 Queen Street the day before they were married in 1956 and have lived there ever since, for 39 years in 1995. In 1980 these houses were valued at £12,500.

The land up from Easton Lane towards Olney was called Stoneypiece and was owned by the Botterills. Don remembers Mrs Botterill coming to him for the rent each month for his allotment. One day she came up to him rather apologetically in 1964/5 and asked him, "Would you be upset if we sold the allotment land for building?" Not long afterwards, the land was sold and the first houses, nearly all bungalows, were built in Queen Street. This was the first phase. Then in 1967 the first two houses were built in Mill Road, number 47 owned by Cliff and Eileen Fenn which were then selling for around £3,700 and next to them, number 49 bought by Jo and Bettie Watson.

The building company was Abbey Homesteads. The other allotments were also privately owned. The Oddfellows owned Backside and stretched from Dag Lane brook as far as Wyman Close. It was bought by the builder Alfie Underwood from Wollaston ("He builds good houses" – is the local opinion!) and who, though 'retired' in 1996, is still building. He built Brookside, the private houses in St Mary's Road, and Firtree Grove in the sixties and early seventies. The Rural District Council placed a compulsory purchase order on Warner's field and built the council houses in the top half of St Mary's Road and Hewlett's Close in the fifties, the first to be built after the war. Walter (Tumpy) Drage owned the allotments up Dock Hill and Alfie Underwood brought this as well and built Fullwell Road in 1966. The rest of the land is now part of Red Gables Farm.

An invasion of foreigners!

It is of major significance to the life of our village in the last century that in this period around the sixties, the population of Bozeat all but doubled in size. The three new private housing estates brought new and young families, many from the London overspill and thereabouts to rejuvenate village life – school, Working Men's Club, pubs, football team, churches, etc. Inevitably at first there was a feeling of "us and them" but the old Bozeat village spirit prevailed and, 30 years on, the new families are as proud of being Bozeat as those which have been here for centuries.

Jim and Marjorie Gregory bought the last bungalow to be built in Hillside Close (No. 6) in 1970. Jim was born in Tunbridge Wells, Kent in 1907 and apprenticed to be a plumber in Bedford. His father had had a fish shop in Tunbridge and then moved to Bedford as a manager of Sell & Willshaw, the famous fishmongers. Jim did not go to war in 1939 as he was on WARAG work – providing water supplies to farms in North Bedfordshire. They lived at Clapham just outside Bedford where their only son, Derek was born in 1936. Derek followed Dad into the plumbing trade and bought one of the new houses in Fullwell Road (No. 48). His Dad followed him here on retirement at 63. Derek's son Martin, like father and grandfather before him, entered the plumbing business and married Denise, the daughter of two Londoners, Kit and Peg Pratt, who came to live in the village and whose story we will take up later. They now live at Irchester. The Gregorys are one brick in the growing personality of the village in the second half of the 20th century.

Jim Gregory died on 26th March 1996 at the good age of 89. As Marjorie chatted about their lives together and the past, she disclosed that she was a Yardley Hastings girl and that they were married there in April 1931. "Alfie Underwood built this bungalow in 1971 for £3,000. We were at school together in Yardley. There were three Underwood boys, Harry, Bill and Alfie – all Yardley boys. Bill (now Church organist at Yardley) and Alfie are totally different. Bill is all up here," said Marjorie holding hand horizontally at the height of her forehead! "Alfie was quiet and retiring. He started work doing odd jobs, chimneys and that sort of thing. Then he built a house for himself at Wollaston, started a building business and has never looked back. He now lives at Wollaston House. He's built estates everywhere – Rushden, Irthlingborough as well as Wollaston and Bozeat. He's 84 this year (1996), the same age as me and doesn't do building any more. His two sons are not interested but the business is still there. When he called in for a chat he said to me, 'I've got lots of land but it's not worth building houses. I've not sold all the houses I have built. Of course the recession hit the business hard.'" For after the boom of the sixties and seventies, the property business reached a crisis point in 1988/89 when prices shot up and then slumped catching people (especially young first time buyers) in a negative equity trap and crippling the building trade. It was only in 1996, with mortgage interest rates dropping to about 5% (they were nearer 13% in the late eighties), and house prices bottoming at last, that the housing market and building business began to gain confidence again, to return house values under a more controlled inflation to much the same values in 2000. Alfie was at the right place with the right skills at the right time and did well – and as folk still say in Bozeat, "If you've got an Alfie Underwood house it will be well built!"

Dennis and Audrey Allen came to Bozeat in 1954 from the South-East of England largely in the pursuit of work. Previously Dennis had worked in Sussex at a stud looking after race horses. They found accommodation in the tithed cottage at Grange Farm and have since remained good friends with the Howkins family there. Dennis was offered the job of Peterborough representative for Spillers Seeds with the task of visiting local farms seeking to sell to their requirements. He remembered how Mr Tompkins, a local man, advised him on visits to farms to take with him free notebooks and pencils, to be friendly and to give the farmers one, business or no business! Slowly he got to know the farmers and they him and eventually purchases were made.

Having no money to afford a home they applied for a council house and were given one of the new ones (No. 13) at the top of Queen Street. They were one of the first trickle of real outsiders to enter the village before the flood of 'immigrants' in the sixties and were inevitably regarded with some suspicion – and in consequence found the village initially rather unfriendly. Indeed when the news got round that 'outsiders' had been given a new council house a reporter from the local newspaper appeared on their doorstep to get the story! Bozeat School was much smaller then and more insular so that when their two boys joined the school with their 'foreign' accents and unfamiliar surnames and outlooks they did not easily accommodate to the school ethos under the leadership of Miss Bettles.

But slowly friends were made and Audrey was soon involved helping at school and as a member of St Mary's Church and the W.I. Dennis soon became a familiar figure visiting local farms and it was not long before they felt at home and part of the village. For example, they soon made friends with the Botterills whose children went to school with their two boys. Dennis remembers how old Mr Botterill said to him one day in 1954, "My brother's house at 8 Easton Lane – a lovely stone house – is empty. You can have it for £1,900 if you like." "I only had £200 at the time so couldn't, though I would have dearly loved it. As it was, Mr Terry, headteacher at the time, bought it." Eventually, when Fullwell Road was built in 1972, they bought their present house (No. 22) for £2,100. Christopher went to Cambridge and is in 1999 a vicar in Leicester and William had done a variety of jobs and at the ripe old age of 40 in 1996 is an ardent globetrotter when he can afford to be!

"Then the village was an industrial village," remembers Dennis reflecting on these early years. "Almost everyone worked at the shoe factories, men and women. And if, like us, you didn't, it was not so easy to get to know folk. The factories were geared to women working there. They were given one and a half hours break at mid-day to give them time to get their husbands' lunch and they finished early to be home for the children after school."

Kit and Peg Pratt are Londoners from Plumstead. They bought 3 Fir Tree Grove in February 1973, new from the builder Alfie Underwood, the price of which then was around £4,300. Kit or Herbert Kitchener (someone bet his mother a shilling she wouldn't name him after the great man but she did!) was born in 1915, the youngest of 12, at 13 Albatross Street, Plumstead Common, London. He started work aged 11 helping the coal man and the milkman on their rounds. His mum got him a job in the building trade. "I was apprenticed to a hard man. Sometimes I had to work so hard with the bricks that by the end of the day my hands were bleeding. I showed him once. 'I'll make your heart bleed before I've finished with you!' was his only reply." Kit joined the Royal Navy in 1942 and was posted on *HMS Phoebe* to the Malta convoys. Despite catching pneumonia he continued to work on the guns till they got to Freetown when he collapsed and had to be invalided home and out of the Navy. Eventually he got back to the building trade.

Kit and Peg were 60 and 56 years of age respectively by the time they came to the village to start a new life, having been Londoners all their lives. They knew about Bozeat because their cousin was an evacuee here in the war and married a Bozeat boy and they came to visit her at weekends. (She is now Norah Drage and lives at 7 Hewlett's Close.) Six months after them their daughter and her husband, Jacky and Ray Edmunds, bought the new house backing onto theirs on the same estate, at 28 St Mary's Road. Kit was a skilled bricklayer so, with plenty of building around, found work even at 60 years of age. He did bricklaying for the builder Arnold Dobbs from whom he learnt to work in the local stone. ("I worked on Arnold's cottages opposite the Paper Shop.")

The double garage at Chequers and that at the Gilliam's at 46 Allens Hill and the fine stone wall of the Coles at 90 London Road are some examples of his work and he proudly remembers how he taught Malcolm Threadgold, the landscape gardener, to work in stone so that he could build his own garage! His son-in-law, Ray, was a butcher and for the first 15 years in Bozeat, Ray drove down the M1 to London every day to the butcher's shop in Charlton. Sometimes Kit went with him and helped deliver the meat around London to hospitals, etc. Eventually Ray was made redundant and became a travelling butcher selling at different markets around about while his wife worked at the Hinwick Home for the Handicapped. At 83 and 79 in 1996 Kit and Peg were still living at 3 Fir Tree Grove. Being an old soldier of the last war he enjoyed the comradeship of other men with similar experiences which they

From the left: Ralph Tompkins, Anne Tompkins, Donald Brooke, Trevor Tompkins (baby), Mrs Laura Higham (née Tompkins), Jim Tompkins, Percy Roberts, David Higham. (D. Roberts)

shared in the Working Men's Club and through the Bozeat branch of the British Legion. Kit died at home on Sunday 24th March 1996.

George and Pat Summers bought the plot of land in 1970 on which now stands their house at 27 Mill Road and into which they moved in 1971. Pat remembers the culture shock moving to live in Bozeat after life in Dunstable. "It was like going back in time. I hated it at first. People were so suspicious of us newcomers, especially Londoners. They didn't trust us – not surprising I suppose when you hear of all that goes on in London. But I hated it! It took two years before we really began to settle down. Then the whole of village life revolved around the shoe factories. There were five of them I think. It was all so different. Take the doctors. You would sit in the hall or on the stairs at 1 Allens Hill with the family who lived there going in and out with their lunch or whatever, waiting your turn; and after you were seen in their front room used by Dr Swan as a surgery, Mavis would count out your pills on an ordinary table…. We went to a posh new medical centre in Dunstable! And it was the same for their daughter Shirley at school. The old school in Camden Square was so basic and old-fashioned compared to the modern school in Dunstable. She wouldn't use the school toilets as they were so 'primitive' compared to the ones she was used to.

"And people were so inward looking. After all they only knew the life of the village and had little interest in anything outside it then. I went to work at the BBC as we called it – the Bozeat Boot Company up Easton Lane. Some of the ladies there looked to be in their eighties. They had spent their whole lives there. And shifts were arranged so that wives could clock off at noon till 1.00 pm. They would talk about what they were going to cook for the men – stew, dumplings, steam pudding … and then they would clock off earlier in the afternoon to meet the children from school and see to their domestic duties … it was devastating when the boot factories closed (the last, Gola, in 1981). It affected the whole of the village – pubs, the Club, shops closed ... people's lives were totally centred in the village. It had to change. Mind you, if the village had not expanded in the sixties with the coming of the outsiders it would probably have died in consequence." – or been taken over by prosperous commuters or wealthy retired folk and turned into a pretty dormitory village.

Pat's honesty about feelings and reflections of those early days makes one realise what could have happened – the demise of a village preserved for centuries. Thirty years later we can see how those outsiders were accepted and integrated into a community, that its continuity with the past has not been lost but strengthened. George with son Steven has played his part in the survival of the Club and Pat working for the Social Services cares for many of the older folk in the village ("If we have another winter like this it will be my last" she says with a wry smile) and is secretary (now churchwarden 1999) to the PCC at St Mary's. Daughter Shirley is a nurse, married to a chef from Scotland and lives in Portsmouth.

Pam Freely agreed with many of Pat's sentiments as we talked together. She came from Nottingham with her husband Pete in the 1950s. They felt total outsiders in the early days, save for their friendship with Roy and Marian Brown, a village family who persuaded them to settle here. Pam is now (1996) a supervisor in one of the Griggs factories in Wellingborough making Dr. Martens shoes for children. On 30th January 1958, she opened the 'Pamela Freely School of Dancing' in the Methodist Church. "It really was quite a novelty for the village folk," she recollects in her still strong but warm and friendly Nottingham accent. She is amazed with the way that Griggs have taken over virtually the whole shoe industry in the area. "Griggs have bought up everything. They must have about 26 or 28 factories. It's amazing that N.P.S. in Wollaston held out against them. Now even the Pope wears Dr. Martens – white of course! There's no stopping 'em. Why they've not a factory in Bozeat beats me. There must be some reason for it...."

The new road
The Rural District Council bought the land east of Sunbury or Sunberry Lane and to the South of Harrold Road, known to older residents as New Road. But the Enclosure Act of 1799 speaks of a public carriageway and drift road to be called Harrold Road (*Marlow*, p.75). Then it was only a stone-covered track and Bill Silsby remembers seeing the roadmen working on it breaking up the larger stones to make it smoother. This land stretched up to where the road dips down to Dodson's Close. All this area was rented out as allotments and Ted Drage remembers the schoolmaster Mr Lack in 1920s measuring out the land into acre strips for people to rent. It became known as 'The Allotments'. In fact what you had here was really smallholdings. As you passed up Harrold Road you would see pigsties, chicken runs, people growing wheat as well as vegetables and even small orchards of fruit trees.

Dolly's grandfather, father and Uncle Sid joined forces and combined their strips of land to make quite a sizeable little farm or farmlet! which together with their allotment in Bull Close would provide their families with most of their food the year round. The Council combined a larger section of land to hire out for more substantial farming and it is now known as Three Fields Farm, farmed by Keith and Anne Baddrick. Walter Drage had a smallholding where their farm is now situated. There is a photo of Walter with his tractor working the land. He and his brother Fred ran the first bus service to Wellingborough in 1920s. He also had a lorry in which he would transport cattle to and from market. Walter had five daughters. One of them, Glenda, still lives in the family home at 2 Hope Street.

When County Councils were encouraging villages to improve their recreational amenities, the village bought from them a large part of this land in about 1969 to create what is now Bozeat Playing Fields. Eric Brook, managing director of Marriotts, living at the Old Rectory, Easton Maudit, at the time was one of its main fund-raisers (along with a string of villagers) and became the first chairman of the Playing Fields Committee. As Church Warden of Easton Maudit Church, Eric also helped to raise many thousand of pounds for the restoration of that church.

Gola sports equipment made here

These were heady days for the village when Gola Sports was at its height and there was plenty of work and salaries were good. At the end of the '70s the Gola trade name was bought by an electrical company and boot and shoe making virtually came to an end in the village. It brought to a close one of the most important and longest periods in Bozeat history stretching back to at least the 17th century. It is therefore appropriate to finish this chapter of memories with two of Dick Botterill's from those good years of the '50s to the '70s.

The Botterills made up, for their American distributor, "a special pair of shoes for a well known American athlete who had been born with no feet. He decided to demonstrate his ability by running all the way across the US from Boston on the East Coast to Seattle on the West. Glad to say that he succeeded and the shoes – with some spare socks to be attached on route stood up to the job."

"In the early days of television publicity for sports shoe brands, Gola, which had close links with a number of top clubs, set out to make friends with the team trainers. It became a fairly noted bit of advertising – when a player was injured the trainer would run onto the field with his Gola bag, pause, look round to see where the cameras were sighted, turn the bag to face the cameras and then attend to the player. It became much more sophisticated and expensive as time went by."

The end of an era

The 1980s opened with the closure of the boot and shoe factories and the laying off of their staff and the ending of the era of boot and shoe making in Bozeat on any significant scale.

An anonymous poem in *About Bozeat* for December 1982 captures this change of mood well:

FAREWELL

On a cold, snowy morn in '63
I joined the local BBC,
A rich new life it was to be –
And, oh! how those ladies welcomed me!
We worked so hard from morn to night,
To get those Bozeat boots just right!
But also laughed and sang with all our might,
Shared joys and sorrows, in this light.
For many a year we shared this boom,

*And then more ladies entered our room.
No longer was it Botterills, Stripeys, and BBC,
But Gola Sports, combined the three.*

*For a few more years we laughed so free –
Then came a new word – 'Redundancy'!
So sad, some ladies left our sight,
And soon, more followed in their flight.
Some say its progress and well they might,
For only a few were left to fight.
"You others to London Road must go,
To carry on the firm", was said, and so -
Once more we worked from morn to night,
To get those Bozeat boots just right!*

*Then again came that word – "Redundancy'!
And a neat typed note was thrust to me.
"No longer will boots be Bozeat made,
To Raunds and Italy has gone our trade"!
So, to all my friends, so tried and true,
I know I shall always remember you -
For the good times spent, – and bad times too,
For all we said and had to do.
No need to sign my name for all to see.
For these memories will belong to YOU and ME!*

Rachel Mallows, a teenager at the time, remembers the sense of bewilderment and loss that prevailed in 1981 at the closure of Easton Lane Factory. Men drifted around the village as in a dream stunned by their sudden loss of livelihood. No more was time measured by the life of the factory – men streaming out when the hooter sounded, on foot or on bike, filling the streets and shops and pubs or off home – dictating the pattern of life in the village, its pulse, its rhythm. All this suddenly vanished and a boot and shoe industrial village with it. Suddenly the streets were empty and there was an eerie silence everywhere.

This is the lasting impression it left on one young person but as Graham Clarke pointed out, "Most people knew it was coming and many had already left to other jobs."

There are comparisons here with the closure of the coal mines in the valleys of South Wales in the 1970s, a strong sense of community, solidarity and purpose locked into village life isolated by it from the outside world suddenly deprived of purpose and meaning.

Fred Dilley who has lived in the village all his life and who now lives at the top of Hope Street was 38 when he was made redundant by Gola in the 1981 closure. Using his experience of sports footwear production and sales from Gola he formed Ram Sportswear Ltd in Irchester selling a full range of sports wear (e.g. adult jogging suits at £11.99) in partnership with Bob Lymn who had a company making shoe components. Fred has had to turn his hand to other things since then (including a spell as video photographer for weddings, etc.) whilst others remained in the industry working for Griggs or N.P.S. at Wollaston, for example. Fred's wife Irene works part time in the village Post Office for Keith Cullip the Postmaster. Bob Lymn has established Ram Sportswear as a retail shop in Gloucester Place, Wellingborough.

Austin Furniss at 1 Hillside Close was also made redundant from Gola in 1981 and took this as an opportunity to do what he always wanted to do – gardening. "But the money was too good when Gola was there not to take it," reflected his wife Janet as we chatted at their home in July 1996. There was not much money in gardening, so Janet got a job at a residential nursing home in Olney to get some extra money, working nights which meant she was able to be home for her children during the day. (My mother, Marian Bligh, died there in August 1996, at the age of 88, having lived her last four years in Bozeat at 26 Wollaston Road.) "I do that so I can be at home for Kay (their then 14-year-old daughter at Wollaston School). I haven't any nursing qualifications but I've got plenty of T.L.C.!" she said, smiling. "Actually I'm not from Bozeat, nor is Austin. Austin's father Richard Furniss came from Grimscote near Towcester where he worked laying cables for the electricity, and this is why he came to Bozeat in 1922 when the electricity arrived here. Through his work he met and married Sara Bayes." (The daughter of Johnny (Bundlehead) Bayes, who we shall meet again in the chapter on Spencelayh.) "They lived in Bozeat and had six children, Austin being the fourth child born in 1942 when Richard was working at Mr Austin's farm at Strixton doing some electrical work. Someone from Bozeat came running up to Strixton to tell Mr Furniss that his wife had just given birth to a baby boy and his first words were 'Well as I am working on Mr Austin's farm, I shall call my son Austin!'"

"I was born and bred in Weston Underwood (famous for Cowper's Oak and the Arbour in which Cowper wrote much of his poetry overlooking the River Ouse). Of course only well-to-do people can afford to live there now but in the 50s and 60s, when we were children, there were many there who were quite poor and we ran around in our bare feet. I shall never forget how, in 1960 when I was 14, on my leaving day my mother met me out of school and took me down to the Lodge Plug Factory in Olney to get my first job. I dared not say a word! It was only two miles away and I would bike there leaving home at 7.10 am and getting back home at 5.50 pm." (Incidentally this red brick building in Olney is typical of the boot and shoe factories in this area built in the early part of the 20th century. Later it was bought by Robert Maxwell for his publishing business but after his mysterious death the factory stood empty.) "The redundancy at Lodge Plugs made me hear of the good money at Gola so I went to work there at the Gola factory in Bozeat which was no problem as there was a minibus that picked us up at Olney and took us back in the evening. This was free of charge thanks to the boss of the Gola factory. This is where I met Austin at the age of 16 and we married in 1968. We have had a lovely, happy 27 years in Bozeat with our children Stephen and Kay."

For several years after its closure, Gola Employees had an Annual Reunion Dinner, an opportunity to keep alive old friendships and past memories.

CHAPTER 6

Bozeat Today 1980-1999

The poor man in his straw-roofed cottage
The rich man in his lordly hall,
The old man's voice, the child's first whisper,
He listens, and He answers all.
　　　　　　　Mrs Cecil Frances (Fanny) Alexander (1818-95)

Written in the middle of the 19th century, these lines of 'All things bright and beautiful' remind us so well of the world from which we see Bozeat emerging over the period of history we have been remembering here. A century and a half later we reflect on some of the striking contrasts of Bozeat then and now as we have passed another millennium.

Understandably, it is easier to reflect on Bozeat Past than Bozeat Present but it is, nevertheless, worthwhile to consider life as we now enjoy it and ask what village life means to us today.

When is a village not a village?

First we should remember that during the last ten years in England the rural population has increased by about 8%. At the same time we have seen the continuing decimation of village community life. This may be partly because the upwardly-mobile commuting business person at the higher end of the income scale is moving into the village for the environmental benefits to themselves and their young families. For many of them 'the village' is a pleasant environment away from the demanding pressures of city life rather than a community of which they wish to be a part.

We must remind ourselves too that one third of our nation is in the retirement bracket and a vast reservoir of the nation's wealth is tucked safely in their pockets. The village and the seaside town have become what has been rather cruelly called 'God's Waiting Room'! But retirement is of course, nowadays, a very active part of human life which can make an important financial and human contribution to village life. But the danger is that wealthy retired folk put all their capital into this final investment and develop modest village accommodation into superb dwellings, driving out the young families and others of modest means with their crucial contribution to village life.

The lifeless and 'pretty' picture postcard village can be a frightening reality. As folk say of Bozeat, "During the day the village is so empty." When I first came to the village and asked what was the high point of the week in Bozeat, I was told, "Thursday – Pension Day! The village comes alive then!" A recent (1996) survey of villages in Cambridgeshire, a county not untypical of many, showed that 40% of the villages had no village shop, 50% had no school, 70% had no bus service and 90% had no day care for the elderly. Now Bozeat is fortunate for it has all these things. The developers have not yet targeted us for 'destruction' but there is a feeling in the air that that day is not far away.

There is another factor which is perhaps far more worrying and far more influential. It is in the nature of modern life as we pass the millennium. Rising affluence and over fifty years of peace have brought with them a materialism and a self-interest which is undermining community life. The uniformed organisations are going because there is not the parental support for those who run these youth groups. "We are just being used," said one leader. "Parents come and dump their kids on us and collect them at the end of the session and that is their sole interest in what we do." An article in the *Church Times* of 20th October 1995 helps to explain this local leader's frustration. Working women are too busy and too tired to take on the role of Brown Owl and Guide Leader, reflected in a 10% drop in membership of the Girl Guides from 814,000 in 1983 to 750,000 in 1995. "The vicar's wife with time on her hands is no longer around," said one Guide Leader and County Commissioner. "So many ladies today go out to work, so their evenings are devoted to their families and in doing chores they can't do during the day."

This greater pressure on families is seen as we watch children driven to school, driven to Minimusic, driven to dancing, driven to keep fit and all the other social activities in a frantic round by which young parents, usually both working often long hours and pursuing careers, have so little time or inclination to create any other kind of life for their children. So although we do have an excellent drama group in the Bozeat Players, a fine youth club once a week, a lively village choir, a first class pub and a working men's club, keep-fit classes galore, a primary school of some 140 pupils and three churches which all offer a rich and varied programme, a historical and archaeological society and women's fellowship and institute, an over 60s club and a weekly lunch club for senior citizens, village community life is in one sense a shadow of its former self. There is not the same taste for community involvement and interdependency that there was. Private pursuits and mass entertainment are of greater interest than commitment of an evening to involvement in co-operative living – beyond the nuclear family.

And human expectations and opportunities have changed out of all recognition over the last century. Marjory Drage and Don and Dolly Roberts in their contentment to find all their expectations fulfilled within the life of village and countryside are no more. The achievements of the 20th century have outstripped all those of past history in terms of human science, medicine and technology, making aspirations once available only to kings and princes now realisable to the most ordinary of persons as our planet has truly become the global village.

The 20th century has seen a revolution in the home and the role of women. The rise of the modern middle class (compare with the 'middling sort' of 17th century Bunyan) at the beginning of the 20th century found about one-third of the nation's women in service to them. The labour-intensive domestic chores of cooking, washing and cleaning in a dirty environment of coal-burning stoves and fires, grimy streets of mud and stones and horse-drawn vehicles meant a continual process of washing and cleaning. My mother, born in 1908 remembered how, in her parents' home in Finchley, North London, net curtains had to be washed every week! In the tall narrow town houses where servants slept in the attic and toiled 80 hours a week in the kitchen and workroom basement with only a cold water tap and coal stove to heat it, the perpetual process of carrying hot water and chamber pots and food and clothing up and down interminable flights of stairs was the miserable lot of those in service to the rising middle classes. The increasing availability of gas at the end of the 19th century was providing cleaner lighting and heating.

The establishment of the National Grid in 1926 was to herald the arrival of the electric clean home in the 1930s. Its arrival with all its labour-saving domestic appliances was 'accelerated' by the increasing shortage of 'domestics' between the wars as more and more girls were finding better paid employment in factory and office, a process hurried on by the First World War and even more so by the Second World War in which some would claim 'woman power' won the war at home and in many ways showed itself to be equal to that of men. So great was the shortage of girls to go into service between the wars that village girls were coming from the countryside into the towns to fill such posts. The new age domestics are the washing machine, the floor cleaner, kettle, fridge, electric fire, freezer, etc., serving the new clean two-storey middle-class house of the comfortable city suburb, now the universal style of village and town. So we see the middle class woman of the '50s and '60s with time on her hands but traditionally required to stay at home to raise the nation's children. Many in consequence found social occupation in running uniformed organisations, charities, church, institute and guild, 'full of good works'.

From the '70s onwards significant and increasing numbers of them realised that they could now develop a successful career outside the home and this has been the most striking development in the last decades of the 20th century as the career woman has handed her home and her children over to the cleaning agencies, the professional child carer, playgroups and nurseries, previously the privilege of the upper classes. This pursuit of profession and personal interest means that the home is no longer the centre of these activities and interests, but rather the base to which parents return from the health and sports centre, choir and drama group, and evening classes which have increased in popularity as a way to relax after the demands of a working day – a creative and self-fulfilling way of recharging their batteries.

The women of our village as a working-class community remained immune to these influences. For centuries women worked in their cottage industries at pillow lace and the loom as well as gleaning and harvesting, cooking and cleaning and darning and sewing, providing a home for men and children, as a centre of human activity. With the coming of the boot and shoe factory at the beginning of the 20th century, they worked alongside the men as well as running most of the retail in the village. The village shop was so often, if not always physically then metaphorically, an extension of the front room of the family home.

So we see the women of the village from the first half of the 19th century in home, factory and shop, helping the men on the small family allotment and providing the backbone to the church and social life. And for most of this time there were few labour-saving devices and amenities (sewage, etc.) and services which those in towns and cities were able to enjoy. But nevertheless there was to be had a quality of life that was not in all respects inferior to that of people with these modern advantages, as the memories of the previous pages have hopefully made readily apparent.

A typical day for Don and Dolly

In 1996 at the age of 84, Don Roberts, on a typical day, would get up at 7.15 am and, weather permitting, spend the morning gardening – growing vegetables and flowers, cutting hedges and trees. As Dolly remarked, "It was thought a sin if you could not provide your family with vegetables." So Don, more for pleasure than to avoid sin, continued to grow his vegetables, thankfully still being physically able to do so, and thankfully still growing enough to have fresh vegetables for lunch and to freeze some for the winter. Lunch is their main meal of the day, our ageing digestive systems preferring not to eat too much at night, with plenty of fresh vegetables and a varied

Don and Dolly Roberts in the conservatory of 55 London Road, c.1993. (*D. Roberts*)

diet of fish or chicken or sausages followed by a substantial pudding. Dolly is a good cook "who likes experimenting" so there is always a gastronomic challenge to add to the pleasure of a plain wholesome meal! After lunch they have a rest followed, if possible, by a good walk to Easton Maudit or up Harrold Road with the scenic pleasures and ever-changing seasonal interests of the farming way of life.

Don has always taken a newspaper. Now it is the local daily *Evening Telegraph* and the weekly *Methodist Recorder* (they both find a tantalising pleasure in doing the *Recorder* crossword!) and these form the main content of Don's reading. In younger days he had photography but "that's become too expensive". For the first time in their lives (1995) they have a colour television after having had a black and white set (probably the last in the village!) for many years. "In earlier days, every evening was occupied with chapel, choir practice on Mondays, Class Meetings on Tuesdays, Preaching Service on Wednesdays, Wesley Guild on Thursdays and committees on Fridays, not forgetting three times to chapel on Sundays!" – the whole of their social recreational and cultural life was centred on the Methodist chapel/church and its faith.

Dolly, gets up earlier than Don, between 5 and 6 am, and reads. She loves cooking and playing the piano, and organ music. "Everyone passes on music to me. Vicar Marlow gave me all his organ music when he left (in 1944). I love classical music and Gilbert and Sullivan and of course religious music." Dolly still plays the organ for chapel services. In earlier days she sang in many choirs such as the Raunds Ladies Choir which was once broadcast on the BBC. They retire to bed well contented at 10.00 to 10.30 pm.

Indeed they still find, as they have always done, their entire contentment and satisfaction within the village in which they have spent all their lives. Looking out of their front room window onto the London Road, Dolly reflects on life as it was and now is: "We do miss the crowded busy streets," as men poured out of the factories for the hour lunch break, the main meal of the day, into the homes and shops and pubs, and women worked hard in keeping and running their homes. Life was labour-intensive then and there was no end of jobs to be done in factory and on farm, in home and shop and on the allotment. "But everyone knew each other and helped each other and there was always time to talk and give a hand, real neighbourliness there was.

But now the streets are so empty and so quiet. We don't even know our neighbours. We miss too not having a resident doctor and a village policeman. Dr Christmas was the last resident doctor. He lived at 29 Allens Hill and he and his wife were wonderful. They joined in and supported all the local activities. Mrs Christmas was on the school management and the hospital committee, etc. and Dr Christmas was president of the cricket club and the football club and so on. And of course we had the Co-op and the manager lived in the village. Divvy Day was a great social occasion when you went to get your divvy. Mr Hayes, two doors away from the Co-op, in his drapery would always be sure his Sale coincided with Divvy Day in the hope that people would come and spend their divvy money there!

Sadly all that has gone. But the village would have died completely without the London overspill people. Now nearly everything in the village is run by the newcomers – the shops, the Parish Council, the Playing Field…. I don't know what many of us older folk would do without our village magazine, *About Bozeat*, edited by Penny Brannon since 1980. It's always full of news and tells us what's going on."

The coming of the bypass

"And the coming of the bypass made such a difference to our lives. (It opened in 1989.) It pushed up the value of our property! The sudden peace and quiet! The house used to shake as the lorries passed. Dennis Evans across the road said plaster fell off the walls with all the shaking. Three alternative routes were proposed. The conservationists made strong objections to the proposals – and the Matchams at York Cottage who would be closest to the bypass. There was such a meeting in the Church Hall. The hall was packed and feelings ran high. The Traffic Commissioners were there and VIPs from London and the school children too with their notebooks to record everything. Some objected that the bypass would cut across their walks with the dog, and Bish (alias Colin Curtis of Bull Close), a staunch conservationist, shouted angrily that all they were worried about was not the loss of the trees but of somewhere for their dogs to wee! But suddenly, by the next meeting, the opposition all seemed to fade away and the proposals were passed without a murmur."

Mr Matcham bought Slype Farm across the way and his son and family moved into his previous home, York Cottage. Mr Matcham's restoration of the farm produced an impressive mansion and courtyard, a modern miniature of the Yelverton Manor and Park which stood just up the road centuries before. Sadly for him he is now having to cope with another contentious issue affecting the village at present, the proposal by the Marquis of Northampton to start an extensive sand and gravel excavation just below Slype farm and down the valley towards the River Nene, with all the environmental issues that raises.

Two families a century apart

Karen Ryan came to Bozeat in 1985 when she and her husband Rob were looking for a three-bedroomed house within 30 minutes travelling distance of Bedford that they could afford for themselves and their two young boys, Christopher aged four and Joshua one. They had come from Leighton Buzzard where houses were just too expensive. They bought 5 Allens Hill, the council house into which Dolly Roberts had moved at the age of three with her two sisters, Joyce the oldest and Margaret the youngest (the fourth sister, Mabel was born some 11 years later!), when it was first built in 1926. Originally it had three bedrooms, but no bathroom of course. After Dolly's mother died in 1952, Dolly stayed on to look after Dad. In the 1960s, council houses became available for purchase and Dad bought the house for £900. In 1969 he had an extension built on the side, a garage with a bedroom above. Today it still has three bedrooms as one has become a bathroom. In 1985 it was on the market, and Rob and Karen bought it!

At first Karen hated the village. The people around seemed unfriendly, almost snobbish. She had never lived in such a small community. But she slowly got involved, going to Carers and Tots, then chairman of the playgroup, and joining the Bozeat Players of which she has been a member for eight years and now (1996), "I couldn't imagine wanting to live anywhere else!"

Her youngest, Rosie aged eight, born in the village, wants to be an animal nurse. Joshua aged eleven loves the countryside, roaming the fields and ditches and hedges with his friends, and wants to be a cartoonist. Christopher aged 14 has just started the first of his two GCSE years at Wollaston School, is in the top set in science and wants to be a designer like his father or work with computers. Such are the youthful ambitions of three village children today. How do they compare with the three Tompkins girls who began their lives in the same house in 1926, all those years ago? Dolly remembers she wanted to be an opera singer and Margaret a housewife and a mum. Sadly Joyce, the eldest (born 1921) died in 1986. Her ambition was to be a farmer which was fulfilled when she became a land army girl in World War II. Mabel, the later addition to the family, who now lives at 99 London Road and has just celebrated (1996) 40 years of marriage (to Richard Pettit), still enjoys singing as a member of the Windmill Singers and has a remarkable gift for icing cakes for special occasions. Dolly remembers them all as little girls in those far-off days putting on their plays for all to see, doing acrobatics, and Joyce aged three standing on the table reciting poems!

A typical week and the people I meet

In order to leave you with a snapshot of the village today (1998) I shall record the immediate memories of this week in the life of the village and its vicar, the activities that usually take place here only one and a half years before the millennium comes to an end. There will be much naming of names as we encounter real people who, after all, are the village we live in here.

Sunday, 5th July 1998: All three churches are in action today and our Catholic friends like Tricia Roche and her daughter and two girls, Bernadette Woodford with Clare and Catherine (both at Bozeat School) go to the Catholic Church in Olney.

The service at St Mary's is at 9.30am heralded by our bell ringers: Rex Line, Tim and Anne Hickling, Helen and Tony Manktelow, Christine Downey and Bob Wright

The three Tompkins sisters, Joyce, Dorothy and Margaret in 1934 in the St Mary Guides, when the captain was Mary Smart. *(D. Roberts)*

Joyce Tompkins, Dolly's sister, worked at Spring Farm for Will (Duckie) Drage, and married Dennis Fisher. *(D. Roberts)*

It is the first Sunday of the month so there is a crèche and Sunday Club in the vicarage led by Audrey Bligh, Joyce Wesley (née Dilley) Elizabeth Shepheard and Anne Fletcher (the last two being retired head teachers!). Our servers/eucharistic assistants are Phil Drage and Tim Hickling aided by Christopher Howkins (aged 13). David Flint has been our organist on the first two Sundays in the month for the past 15 years using traditional Rite B but not today so the vicar has to play it! On the third Sunday Penny Brannon our Lay Reader leads non-Eucharistic Family Worship when Jackie Garrett plays the piano, and then on the fourth and fifth Sundays we have the modern service of Rite A when Stan Silsby or his son-in-law Philip Ansell plays the organ.

At the Independent Wesleyan Chapel, Sue Partridge-Underwood is the organist whilst husband Tom takes the main leadership role along with Gloria Wallis, and sisters Lyndis Payne and Ellie Minney are active members along with those like Marjory Stanford and Mary Wallis. They are looking forward to a retired Wesleyan minister moving to the village and becoming their minister next year.

At the Methodist Church, Dolly Roberts is still their organist whilst their senior steward is Mavis Holman and their lay reader in training is Sue Woods. History will be made this autumn when they have their first lady minister ever, Enid Ransom. Then there will be two Methodist ministers in the Wellingborough Circuit (she will join Superintendent Gordon Chisnell) serving the two Methodist Churches in Wellingborough along with those at Earls Barton, Irchester, Wollaston and Bozeat.

In the afternoon we have Village Cricket on the playing fields (20 overs each way, max. score 25, two overs bowling each, i.e. it has to be a real team effort!), Bozeat versus Abington Church where the vicar was Curate from 1988-90. They won 75 runs to 55 (making us two games to one in the series!) The unique feature of the match (including a magnificent tea) was an over by one of their team which consisted of 12 balls (i.e. six no-balls) in which he took three wickets! Afterwards, Abington organist, choir and new rector Stephan Adams led us in choral evensong in the Church. And this was to be a week dominated by the final rounds of the soccer World Cup in France and the stand-off of the Orangemen at Drumcree Church threatening the peace process in Northern Ireland.

Monday, 6th July: It is 'Carers and Tots' coffee morning and playtime in the Church Hall. There are anything up to thirty tots and the same number of mums or carers, such is the influx and number of young families in the village. The playgroup which meets in the playing fields pavilion led by Barbara Deviny is full until September. Anne Hickling is in charge of the 'Carers and Tots' with the help of Joyce Wesley as well as Josie Crofts and Mac Holt.

After a weekly one-mile lunchtime swim in Rushden Leisure Pool there is the junior confirmation class of five teenagers, Hollie Coles, Nathan Jones, Stephen and Lucy Howkins and Edmund Downey. Tower Captain Rex Lines, who has rung these bells since a boy and winds the clock daily, took them up to see the bells and the clock – quite an experience.

Before the class Audrey and I went to the last shoe factory in the village, twelve ladies working on special orders in the room behind the Nelson pub in the High Street supervised by Sharon Dorrington who took over from her father, Ralph Tompkins, when he died in 1993. We wanted a picture for the artist who is designing our millennium window for the church, Christopher Fiddes, but unfortunately the girls were not working today as there was no work to be done, possibly because of a running down in orders as factory closure week approaches at the end of July for the summer holiday break.

Churchwarden Tim Hickling, taxi-driver by trade, came round with George Sharratt in the evening to plan a half day for the Parish Church Council (PCC) to look at the report of the new Bishop of Peterborough (Ian Cundy) on 'Our Common Task'. In addition to them our PCC members are: Kath Silsby (Churchwarden). Alison Botterill (Treasurer), Pat Summers (Secretary), Rex Line (Vice Chairman), Penny Brannon (Lay Reader), Gordon Brannon (Electoral Roll and Archivist), Jackie Howkins, Margaret James (Deanery Rep.), Cyril Morgan, John Smith, Pat Smith (Pastoral Assistant and Deanery Rep.) and Derek Taylor.

Monday evening (first and third in month) is when Bozeat Parish Council meets in the Independent Wesleyan Chapel. The Council includes: Andrew Underwood (Chair), Marjory Stanford, Gloria Wallace, Lyndis Payne (Clerk), John Smith, Colin Curtis, Fred Dilley, and Tom Partridge-Underwood (Borough Councillor).

Today Emily Walsh of 1A Council Street died aged 100. She came from London to Wollaston with her four children as evacuees in 1939, Maureen, Nora, Eddie and Eileen. Maureen married Eric Kilsby a member of St Mary's, Wollaston and Nora married John Drage in Bozeat and still lives in Hewlett's Close. Friday this week Eric was helping Eddie move from his house in Brookside next to the clinic to the bungalow at 5 Church Walk. Emily was not the oldest person in the village. This distinction goes to Mrs Blanche of 77 Queens Street who is 104 and comes from Guernsey!

Tuesday, 7th July: Coffee Morning at Grange Farm farmed by the two brothers Peter Howkins (with his wife Jackie and children Christopher, Lucy and Andrew) and Gordon (with wife Judy and children Caroline, Steven and Richard). They are the third generation of Howkins to farm here. Jackie's large kitchen in the main house is where it all happens around its Rayburn cooker and large solid kitchen table. The house is the first of three fine houses (or villas) build by the Berrills in the same style. Built in 1862 it is on the most grandiose scale with tall ceilings and spacious rooms. The tiles in the hall are the same as those in the church! The other two houses are both in London Road, one known as Rock Villa, now Greenwood and the Hedges' farmhouse almost opposite the Chequers which has now been sold for private ownership this year. So incidentally has Wykes Farm (sold by Len Holt) bringing to an end this year their roles as working farms as they turn into private residences. Many at the coffee morning were those with rich village memories and tales to tell, as well as raising £55 towards Church funds.

At noon I went to Bozeat Cemetery for the burial of Salvatori Bovenzi who, as I have related earlier, had come as an Italian Prisoner of War in 1939 and worked on Garrett's Farm at Dungee Corner. Last Monday he collapsed in the garden of his house at the top of Hope Street aged 78. He had married Sheila Drage of Arch Villa and they had eight children. He was a jovial and friendly man who was much liked in the village.

In the afternoon it is the Bozeat School Sports held on the playing fields. This is a spacious area large enough for both cricket and football, having an excellent children's playground and tennis court (with money from the Lottery) as well as a pavilion where the playgroup meets. The Committee are: Ron Burnside (husband of Christine our community nurse), Terry Gibbins (chair and treasurer and one of the longest serving members), Brian Gibbins, Mavis Higginbotham, Anne Fletcher (secretary), Annette Hunt (our post lady), Bridget Jones, Nicola Wood, Paula Cutts and Philip Higginbotham.

Our village primary school this year has 143 pupils and a possible bumper intake in the autumn of 23 new children. The sports consisted of obstacle and straight races finishing with a toddlers' and parents' race with coloured ribbons for the first three to finish. The rain just kept off and there were a good number of parents and friends to cheer. The staff of the school are Richard Wilkins (head), Jim Stopps (deputy), Maureen Sowden, Julie Williams, Carolyn Jacobs and Doreen Dryburgh and Kath Green (secretary) with chair of Governors Margaret James, a farmer's wife with four daughters and one son who have all attended the school and she has been its chair for 20 years. Anne Hickling is the school caretaker and lives on site with Tim her husband and three basset hounds, two cats and a parrot!

After hymn singing in the vicarage (a weekly event for seven years!) for an hour several of us depart to the Independent Wesleyan Chapel for singing practice as members of the village choir, the Windmill Singers. Since it began in 1993 it has been led by Marian Brown of Manor Farm whose sheer vivacity and joy of singing have infected us all and enabled the choir to bring pleasure in singing to others, as it has to themselves, with a wide repertoire from the Beatles to Verdi. Some of the present members are: tenors – Gerald Corby, Matthew Woodford, Brian Skittrall, John

Bozeat Lunch Club 1998. (*Lunch Club*)

Back row: Pat Rathrell, Shirley ?, Doug Browning, Ted Alston, Lena Payne, ? , Gordon Mines, Jim Gibbins, Arnold Howarth.
Third row: Gloria Wallace, Eadie Ingram, Nona Darnell, Arthur Clapham, Margaret Alston, Joan Underwood, Peggy McCrae, Rene Nutt, Evelyn Bayes.
Second row: Max Elliott, Philip Drage, Cyril Morgan, George Brotherston, Hilda Brotherston, Mary Wallace, Jean Price, Stan Wheeler, Alan Underwood.
Front Row: John Price, Gladys Green, Gerty King, Eileen Clapham, Mary Barnes, Win Threlfall (organiser), Nancy Pettitt, Marion Bligh, Floss Drage, Carol Jefferson.

Parrott with help from Lynne Collier: bass – Peter Cartwright, Harold Smith, Gordon Mines, Philip Bligh, Bill Shepheard, Barry Fletcher: sopranos – Julie Mines, Jackie Ford, Linda Tomkins, Sue Evans, Gwyneth Wiggins, Mary Clarke, Tara Potter, Betty Watson: contraltos – Carol Razzell, Helen Manktelow, Janet Furniss, Eleanor Minney, Lyndis Payne, Mabel Pettit, Jean Knightley, and Sue Partridge-Underwood our pianist.

Two other activities occur on Tuesday nights. There is the Bozeat Historical and Archaeological Society which meets in the room above the Working Men's Club. Among its long-standing members are David and Elizabeth Mallows, Peter Drage, Arnold Dobbs, Ian and Carol Fearnley, David Stafferton, Mavis Holman and David Green (chair). And across the road in the Methodist Church the Bozeat Scouts meet. Those who lead our Cubs and Scouts are Hazel Green, Alan and Jackie Missenden and Graham Tompsett.

Wednesday, 8th July: This is the day in the week when some 36 of our senior citizens come to the Lunch Club in the Church Hall and enjoy some two hours of sociality in terms of bingo, raffles and entertainment etc, and an excellent lunch cooked by Jim Griffin (whose wife Joan is a nurse at our clinic) all for the cost of £2.40! It started five years ago with the help of Age Concern. It would not happen but for the fine band of volunteers who provide transport, wash up and serve the meal etc, all under the lively leadership of irrepressible Win Threlfall now in her 80s. (She was once the Avon lady for the village.) Other helpers include Doug Browning, Gordon Mines, Ted and Margaret Alston, Barbara Drage, Lena Payne, Carol Jefferson, Audrey Bligh, Richard Holman and Anne Fletcher. Some of the regular customers are: Nona Darnell, Nancy Pettitt, Floss Drage, Hilda and George Brotherston, Eadie Ingram, Arthur and Eileen Clapham, Gwen Carter, Cyril Morgan, Stan Wheeler, Phil Drage, Betty Partridge, Jean Price, Ken and Pat St John, Alan and Cathrine Underwood, Phoebe Murphy and Margaret Mann.

In church in the afternoon 'Carers and Tots' meet in the church for a story, some songs and a prayer and a cup of tea, etc., again under the able leadership of Anne Hickling (Pastoral Assistant) and Joyce Wesley, with help from the vicar and his wife! Some of the mums who come with their tots and babies are; Kirstie Betts, Helen Betts, Marion Green, Sharon McGeechen, Christine Burnside, Tara Potter, Kim Needham, Paula Jackson, Wendy Linnell, Caroline Dickens, Paula MacGreggor, and Tara Willey.

At the same time as 'Carers and Tots' meet in the Anglican church, the United Women's Fellowship meet alternate weeks in either the Independent Wesleyan Chapel or the Methodist Church, including ladies from all three churches under the leadership of Gloria Wallace and almost entirely composed of ladies in the retirement bracket. Driving round on my motorbike (the best form of travel in the village!) this afternoon it was sad to see a 'For Sale' board fixed to the front of the factory at the bottom of Hope Street – as Knapp Toolmakers are selling up the factory because they need larger premises. I popped in to see Agnes Jones in her fine if unpretentious brick house at 6 Bull Close with its beautifully kept cottage garden with a quaintness and modesty all of its own. "I am the oldest inhabitant of the road now," she remarked. "My father built several of the houses in the road." The next oldest is Colin Curtis near its entrance into Allens Hill – his little house facing the double fronted house on the other corner and facing onto Allens Hill whose garden backs on to that of Agnes. Mary Clarke lives there now but it was once occupied by Dr Christmas. Working in the boot and shoe business all his life, Colin regards himself as one of the few remaining characters ("There's not many of us left, Vicar") in the village with a rich knowledge of village and country life. For the other details and inhabitants of Bull Close, see Chapter 16.

In the evening it is The Women's Institute where a few younger women appear as well. The committee of the Institute consists of: Agnes Jones (secretary for 24 years), Marjory Stanford (president for 26 years), Win Threlfall, Margaret Holt, Sally Hewitt, Eileen Humphreys, Barbara Keogh, Margaret Mann, Iris Noble, Pat Smith, and Gloria Wallace. Margaret Elliott remains as the only founding member having joined at its inception in Bozeat in 1949, so next year will be the 50th anniversary. Margaret Elliott also is responsible for the over 60s which meet on Thursday afternoon in the Independent Wesleyan chapel on the weeks the fellowship does not meet.

On *Fridays* it is to Oakfield Home in Easton Maudit for an hour with the guitar and an hour of singing with the residents, mentally disadvantaged adults. And in Bozeat in the evening the Working Men's Club (proprietors John Saving and Lynne Smith since 1996 when they bought it for a pound but took on its debts running into tens of thousands!) as it does most nights provides a social centre along with the Red Lion (proprietor Glen Ward since 1995 – with help from his wife, a college lecturer) and ably supported by 'Yum Yums' the take-away in the High Street. And it is on Friday evenings that the Bozeat Players rehearse in the Church Hall for one of their three performances in the year, the pantomime being the most popular. Leading lights in the Bozeat Players are John and Sue Burgess, Mike Simms, Garry Mines, Stan Silsby (the dame!), Bill and Pat Conroy, and Bill and Belinda Ogilvie. The Carpet Bowls Club meet in the afternoon as well as on Mondays. Regular members of Carpet Bowls are Phil Drage, Dorothy Cave, Gordon Mines (treasurer) Harry Bayes, Mick Corby, Lil Perkins, the two Dorothy Dunkleys, Iris Noble (secretary) and Fred Noble, Margaret Drage, Bernard Line, Joyce and Ernie Muirhead, and David Higham (chairman). Two founding members were the late Geoff Partridge and Dennis Perkins.

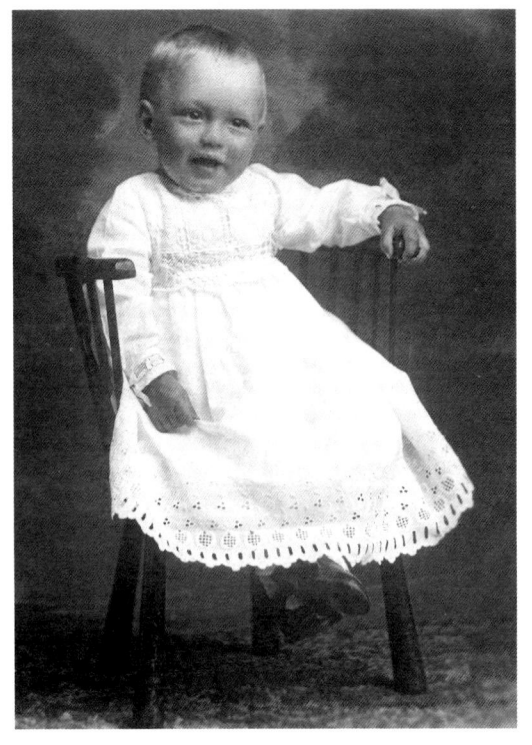

Harry Bayes, of Council Street, whose grandson Andrew Buckton runs the Paper Shop.
(D. Roberts)

Then on *Saturday, 11th July* we have Cream Teas on the vicarage lawns for one pound to the music of Rushden Mission Band together with a raffle, half of the proceeds of which go toward the cost of the millennial village sign and half to the church restoration fund. Richard Holman organised the band's visit for us. At lunch club, Hilda Brotherston (née Underwood) reminded us that when she was in her teens (she is 80 this year so that would be in the 1930s) the Rushden Mission Band came and played on Armistice Day each year and then stayed on and played in the Methodist Church in the evening, so we are keeping alive a long-standing tradition. And so was the weather as we had to retreat into the church for the second half of the concert as rain began to fall on this the wettest of summers for many a year!

Groups active in Bozeat 1980-2000
Information from *About Bozeat*. Names given are the contacts at the time.

Carnival	Diane West (1980-), Sue Ward (1980-)
Christian Aid	Cyril Morgan (1980-86), Kate Bowe (1986-88), Kate Morton (1988-)
Sandwell Lodge	Richard Zang (1983), Arnold Howarth (1983-)
Over Sixties (was Darby and Joan)	Margaret Elliott (1983-)
British Legion	Vic Green (1980-87), Len Holt (1987-)
United Women's Fellowship	Phyllis Silsby (1980-), Gloria Wallis (1990-)

Arthritis and Rheumatism	Snip Reeves (1980-), Tom Partridge-Underwood (1990-)
Conservatives	Snip Reeves (1980-), Mary Steel (1980-), Bernadette Woodford (1988), Charlotte Tipping (1989), Diane West (1990-)
Camera Club	Steve Higham (1980-), Stan Silsby (1980-)
Brownies	Sue Evans (1983-), Caroline Mooney 2nd Gp. (1980-), Annette Hunt 1st Gp. (1980-)
Playgroup	Ann Turnbull (1980-), Elizabeth Drake (1987-), Karen Ryan (1990-)
Youth Club	Michael Bartlett (1983-86), Dave Brooks (1983-), Joan Bayes (1987), Arthur Minney (1988-95)
Playing Fields	Richard Holman (1980-), Ian Houghton (1980-), Terry Gibbins (1988-90)
Bozeat Players	Penny Brannon (1986), John Burgess (1986), Jill Mapp (1987) Marian Brown (1988, 1990), Anne Simms (1989)
Cubs	Sandra Drage (1980-)
Scouts	Pat Taylor (1988-90)
Historical and Archaeological Socy	David Stafferton (1981-)
Teapot Club	Penny Brannon/Sue Emberton (1978-), Sue Villiers (1986), S. Dorrington (1987), Sue Coady, Jane Lewis
Community Watch	Irene Edmunds (1986-89), Belinda Ogilvie (1989-)
Guides	Pamela Cutts (1987), Annette Hunt (1989), Carol Gardner (1990), Lynn Skelton (1990)
Bowling Club	Iris Noble (1990-)
Methodist	Sandra Drage (1980-90), Sue Woods (1990-)
Independent Wesleyan	Ivy Line (1980-91), Marjorie Stamford (1991-)
Anglican	Kath Silsby (1980-), Pat Summers (1997-)
Action Research	Brenda Bould (1987), Belinda Ogilvie (1988), Jill Mapp (1990-)
Football	Matthew Woodford (1980-), Nikki Sharman (Juniors 1986-87), Ian Houghton (1988-)
Tiny Tots	Karen Johnston (1988), Jill Mapp (1988), Ruth Webb (1989), Gwyneth Wiggins (1989), Jill Mapp (1990)
Children in Need	Paula Drage (1988-)
Girls Club	Glenda Drage (1989)
Adult Education	Anne Dunkley (1980-), D. Billett (1990)
Jack in the Box	Gwynneth Wiggins (1987-88), Elaine Salmons (1989)
Aids Support	Mary Steel (1988), Sue Villiers (1989)
Muscular Dystrophy Lift Up Appeal	Jill Mapp (1990-)

The congregation assembled following Philip Bligh's last service as Vicar of Bozeat. Philip is to be found front row, fourth from left.

Boot and Shoe

HONEST JOHN FOOTWEAR
Reg. No. 387176.

This is an actual photograph of the boot

Smart but Serviceable

No. 317
Price **30/-**
POST FREE

AN excellent Glace is the leather of this boot, which is made on the whole golosh principle. For a delightfully comfortable, fairly light boot, it is remarkably serviceable—and moderate in price, too! The all-leather soles, $\frac{5}{16}$ in. thick, are sewn and stitched, and substance is added to the boot by a nice leather lining. You will find this model a real bargain in every way.

Also a cheaper line of the above.

No. 318 PRICE **25/-** POST FREE

Sizes 5 to 11 in medium and broad fittings.

Machining the uppers together

Whether you walk for business or pleasure, you will find a pair of "Honest Johns" the best foot-covering.

Page 15

A page from Honest John's catalogue.

CHAPTER 7

Northamptonshire and the Rise of the Shoe Trade

Historical Review based on an article in Tony Ireson's
Northamptonshire.

Why boot and shoe?
Why did the shoe trade survive commercially to the present day whereas other traditional trades have disappeared except as crafts?

Lace making was probably the most extensive of Northamptonshire industries that preceded boot and shoe making. Lace making was also the principle manufacture of neighbouring Bedford in the 17th century (population about 200 in 1640) where it was introduced by the Huguenot refugees in the reign of Elizabeth I. In about 1800, 10,000 people, mainly women and children, were working on their lace pillows in and around Wellingborough and in the south and south-west of the county earning from two to eighteen pence a day. Until about 1850, thanks to the Napoleonic Wars, French lace not available, so salaries rose with demand and men left the land and joined the trade, earning more here than following the plough. But hand lace making could not compete with Nottingham machinery which by 1853 could produce a piece of lace for seven shillings which in 1809 had by hand cost £17.

Spinning of cotton was pioneered in Northampton in the 18th century, thirty years before Arkwright perfected his machine, after which it died out here and Lancashire towns like Bolton became the centres of the industry.

Weaving also did well for a time. Silk weaving started in Desborough as an offshoot of the Coventry industry in about 1820 and spread to Rothwell and Kettering, but French competition killed the silk trade. Desborough also excelled in linen weaving, embroidering net for ladies dresses and working designs for fancy waistcoats, but it was not destined to survive. Burton Latimer wove carpeting and in 1849 had a mill employing 400 people that could work 16,000 yards a week, but it could not compete with the northern towns and their cheaper water power for the cotton industry.

As these various trades declined, the boot, shoe and leather industries emerged as those on which the future industrial prosperity of Northamptonshire would depend. The story of their rapid growth is largely the story of the 19th century industrial expansion in the County.

How did it happen – and why Northamptonshire?
The rise of the shoe trade as a staple industry began in Northamptonshire which has a reputation for hard-wearing leather from early times. The County's famous pastures grazed cattle to provide the hides and Rockingham Forest oak for tanning. Northampton leather was taken in large quantities to the famous three-week Stourbridge Fair from which merchants all over England bought their supplies. By the mid-17th century an industry capable of supplying much more than local demand began to develop so that Fuller could write: "The town of Northampton may be said to stand chiefly on other men's legs, where (if not the best) the most and cheapest boots and stockings are bought in England."

When in 1642 trouble broke out in Ireland and hurried preparations were made to send an army, thirteen Northampton shoemakers rapidly supplied 4,000 shoes and 600 boots for the troops. The boots and shoes reached London under armed escort (and costing £1,000!) but Charles I still had not paid for them by the time the Civil War broke out. The unfortunate manufacturers could not persuade the Commonwealth under Cromwell to pay for them either! Eventually all but £200 of the bill was paid out of the Estate of a recalcitrant family at Walgrave.

It was Northampton that, in 1648, sent 1,500 pairs of boots to Leicester for the Parliamentary infantry who were literally marching "without shoes or stockings". By one account, in 1689 Northampton dispatched 400 pairs for the ill-equipped troops of William III in Ireland.

During the American War of Independence in the middle of the 18th century, very large demands by the government for army boots and shoes attracted more workers into the industry in Wellingborough, Kettering, Raunds, Daventry, Long Buckby, Thornby and Cold Ashby. The volume of work increased enormously right up to the end of the Napoleonic Wars. The lower rates asked for by shoemakers in Northampton over those in London meant that they captured the market, so that by 1806 the town became the principal shoemaking centre for the whole country. Already we can see a pattern that was to continue into the next century. War made high demands for boots and shoes and in such times the industry flourished and expanded, particularly while the foot soldiers and infantrymen remained the backbone of the army. But also, in the wake of war, boom could so easily be followed by bust! For example, after the defeat of Napoleon, there was such a glut of unused shoes due to overproduction that thousands of pairs were sent back from the war zone. These were thrown onto the home market thereby flooding it with cheap products so causing a serious depression in the shoe trade until it picked up again in the 1820s. There would also be a sudden drop in the demand for shoes with the cessation of war aggravated by the return of men from the front looking for work which was often not there. This was exactly the situation in the shoe trade after the Great War in the early 1920s a century later.

Life before the machine

It was the arrival of the machine in the late 19th century that was to turn a home industry into a factory operation. Until then, shoemaking like lace making was a craft that ran in families, father, mother, sons and daughters all co-operating in the work which was done at home, in the little workshops or 'barns' at the back of the house. Many are still there in the memories and buildings of Bozeat today. "At the beginning of each week one or two of the children, who helped by fetching, carrying and waxing thread, called at the warehouse of the firm for which the family worked, and collected a bulging sack of leather. The contents, ready prepared, were soft, pliable pieces for stitching together into uppers and tough ready-cut soles for attachment afterwards. Work, we understand, did not begin until Tuesday morning because these happy-go-lucky shoemaking men would patronise the local taverns so well at weekends that they were not up to starting work again until Tuesday – hence Monday became known as 'Saint Monday' in such towns! The family would then unpack their leather in the little workshop attached to the house or across the yard, to isolate the noise of continual hammering. Sewing together the uppers, or 'closing' as it is still called, was the job of mothers and daughters, while fathers and sons attached the soles and heels, and gave the footwear its final finish. Shoemakers would often work frantically into the night to finish by Friday in order that they could sell their finished products and enjoy the weekend!" (*Ireson*)

The advent of mechanisation

The arrival of the machine was to do away with this carefree style of life. But because of the difficulty of making a machine to match the individuality of skills, shoemaking held out until 1857 as "the trade to which machinery has never been applied." When, however, machines were made that enabled workers to sew uppers faster than by hand (i.e. closing machines), the shock was so painful that it brought a violent reaction from fierce protagonists of this ancient trade. As several firms started to use machines, workers in Sheffield, for one, objected on the grounds that machinery would deprive them of their livelihood. In Northampton a mass meeting of workers in the Market Square decided to oppose use of machines although several were already installed. Extremists threatened employers operating closing machines and some went to prison. But, there was no turning back from the new age of mechanisation and after nine weeks on strike, workers reluctantly returned to the factories after a loss of 20 months' worth of orders due to disruption and closure.

Business blossoms

Exports began to boom. By the middle of the 19th century, Northampton supplied "the army, the colonies and the principal markets of England, Ireland, and Scotland." Australia, with money to burn after the Gold Rush of 1851, made big demands on Northampton shoes, an export link that happily continued until recent times. Apparently, Australians "prefer English footwear – it makes them feel just that little better than the next fellow."

The new work ethic

After the labour troubles in the 1850s, use of machines rapidly increased to such an extent that in 1894 the Operative Union requested that, except for closing and hand sewing work, all work at home should cease and all workers should be employed in factories. So the old freedoms slowly went and, with the coming of the railways which opened up central Northamptonshire to the world, so the appearance and character of her boot and shoe towns changed. Now there appeared the rows of dull red brick houses built close to the square ugly factories, soon to become typical of this part of the county along with the factory and its bells and sirens disgorging their hoards of workers on bicycle and foot after a long, monotonous day on the factory floor. But there was security and salaries and better working conditions and better pay and a life beyond the factory when the whistle blew at 6.15 pm. – that is after a 9¾-hour day (plus Saturday mornings) and a 52½ hour week with a weekly pay of between 25 and 29 shillings, to pay the bills and make the most of the weekend, albeit shorter than in the good old days!

But there was still hardship and poverty in the new work ethic. Life was often hard in villages such as Bozeat as we shall see. But workers in villages often fared better than those in towns, for families still had their own smallholdings or 'allotments' to grow their own food. For, although in the middle of the 19th century the village changed within a generation from being agricultural to industrial, there was still a close affiliation with farming and the land. So we find in the depression following the

Boer War that workers were hard hit, and in towns like Kettering workers were stripping their homes in the winter to feed their children. Two free meal centres were opened to serve food to the poverty-stricken there, with some 18,500 meals given away, while the Salvation Army was providing free breakfasts.

Note: Quotations and some paraphrasing are from the article by Tony Ireson.

The Drage Shoe Company staff, 1891. (*Bozeat School Scrapbook*)

Mr H. Partridge's closing factory staff, 1890. The building in Bull Close is now the Brierley-Linnell's house. Note the familiar Berrill herringbone patterning on the wall. (*Bozeat School Scrapbook*)

CHAPTER 8

Shoemaking in Bozeat

Norman Palmer (with supplementary material by Philip Bligh)

The 17th century – the working man comes of age
Who the first shoemaker was in Bozeat we shall never know, but as most communities had a shoemaker purely for local needs it is probable that Bozeat had at least one for many hundreds of years.

If only there were some personal records especially from the turbulent times of the 17th century when ordinary men were gaining literacy and political voice and muscle. "Before the 16th century an educated man was almost necessarily a priest or a gentleman; only the Reformation emphasis on Bible-reading made possible, and economic circumstances demanded, a spread of literacy." (Christopher Hill, *Bunyan and His Church*, p.139). The uprising of such ordinary men under Cromwell against the Crown, the Church and the Landed Gentry was in many ways the birthplace of Parliament as a governing body over against the Crown, the establishment of the House of Common Men (Commons). Archbishop Bancroft's contemptuous remarks in the 1640s about places "where half a dozen artisans, shoemakers and tinkers … do rule the whole parish" reflects both the fear of the ruling classes of the rising influence of those of lowly origins and those categorised as such – shoemakers, tinkers like John Bunyan born nearby at Elstow, and the like. "'Those venerable and reverent Fathers, Master Cobbler, Tinker and Button-maker, rising from the very dunghill, beating the pulpits.' Cobblers, tinkers, peddlars, weavers, sowgelders and chimney sweeps.' An indignant royalist in the south-west during the Civil War denounced Parliament implausibly, as 'a company of tinkers and pedlars.' On the other side Richard Overton declared that 'bellow menders, broom-men, cobblers, tinkers or chimney sweepers … are equally freeborn with the loftiest.'" (Hill, *ibid* p136ff).

Believing our village church probably housed Cromwell's men and horses, who will have relieved their boredom by damaging our statues and ornamentation, etc., one wonders how willingly the village accepted the lay intruder Paynell Hargrave sent by Cromwell to occupy our vicarage. What were the political interests and activities in our village in these times? – and the names of the shoe workers who presumably shod Cromwell's men? We say 'presumably' because by 1671 when a Religious Census was taken of the Province of Canterbury, there were in Bozeat 380 Conformists (i.e. Church people), no papists and only five nonconformist families (*Marlow* from a MS at Stafford) which not only gives us an idea of the size of our village (i.e. some 400 souls) but also suggests an overall loyalty to the crown.

It is in 1685 that we find an earliest reference of a shoemaker in Bozeat "Neil described as a shoemaker/cordwainer". (*David Hall.*)

The evangelical revivals of the 18th century and the powerful unions of the 19th continued to enable the common man, tinker, tailor, shoemaker, to gain his birthright.

Our earliest records – the 18th century
One of the first references in Bozeat records to a shoemaker is in the marriage transcripts for the year 1709, when Samuel Styles, shoemaker, married Hannah

Lawton, lacemaker. By 1781 when a list of men who could serve in the militia (Home Guard of the time) that is between the ages of 18 and 45 was compiled, we know of two names – Richard Smart, Cordwainer and James Wright, Cordwainer. There would have been others out of this age range.

A note on terminology: a Cobbler was a shoemender, a Cordwainer made shoes from new leather and a Shoemaker made shoes from old leather. We may infer that the cordwainer was the highest on the socio-economic scale and the cobbler the lowest of the three. In the early 1670s, Nehemiah Cox, a cordwainer in Bunyan's congregation at Bedford was able to plead before the magistrates in Greek and Hebrew! (Hill, *ibid* p.140)

We know of other shoe workers in Bozeat of this period because the names of those who made shoes for paupers or were paid for by the parish appear in Parish Accounts. Note that spelling was not of great importance to those who wrote these accounts! In 1779, "Daniel Stiles (probably the son or grandson of Samuel Styles) making and mending shoues workhouse 10s-10d." We know that Daniel Styles lived at 1 Pudding Bag Lane. The village workhouse is now Lavender Cottage adjacent to the churchyard in what is now called Mallows Yard. The inmates had to be fed, clothed and shod by the parish. In 1786: "Humphrey Bettell for mending shoes for workhouse children 9d." There were seven shoe workers in Bozeat at the latter end of the 18th century, which suggests that they were not meeting the demand for shoes from the village alone, but were making them for men serving in the Napoleonic War. It seems probable also that shoemaking was taking over from the traditional craft of lace making amongst men. Humphrey Bettell continued to make shoes for parish paupers, often for orphans for, in April 1817: "Paid Humphrey Bettell for John Corby's New Shoes 8s-0d" And in March 1825: "Hump Bettell for making Sarah Talbot Children Shoes 7s-0d." We know he was making shoes as late as 1829. John Roberts was another making and mending shoes. In Sept. 1812 we read: "Pd John Roberts sho bill for Pore of parish £2-10s-1d." Robin or Robert Wooding is also mentioned in 1795: "Paid Robard Wooding for Shoo Mending 1s-0d." In the Line family, who later had shoemakers, there is mention of one James Line in the Bedford Methodist Circuit membership list for Bozeat in 1792, an early mention of Methodist converts in the village.

As the 18th century closes, there is an appreciation of the industry from the pen of William Pitt who toured Northamptonshire at the time. "In Northampton and some of the neighbouring towns, upward of a thousand hands are employed in making shoes for the Army and Navy and for the shops of London and also for export to the world. About seven or eight thousand pairs are manufactured weekly in time of peace, but at present (July 1794) in consequence of the war, ten to twelve thousand may be manufactured in the same period. The price runs from 3/6d to 5/- and upward a pair. The medium price may be reckoned at 4/2d of which about 1/6d is paid for labour. The leather is purchased in this and neighbouring counties, but chiefly from the London market. A journeyman earns from 7/- to 14/- a week and from 9/- to 10/- may be considered average."

The ups and downs of the first half of the 19th century

As we have already seen, the prosperity brought to the local shoe industry by the Napoleonic Wars followed the pattern shown by the two wars of the next century, not to speak of the Boer War. Slump followed boom. We saw how masses of unused shoes were dumped on the domestic market at half price after the Napoleonic Wars ended in 1815. The damage to the shoe industry and its later recovery on a local scale is probably reflected in Bozeat's baptismal records for 1813-20 which gives five fathers stated to be shoemakers and this increases in 1821-30 to ten.

We gain some idea of what the trade meant to the village in the first half of the 19th century from various other sources. In April 1809 there is an item: "William Partridge for instructing John Partridge for makeing of shoes 18s-0d." This was probably the first part of a premium of a pauper apprenticeship. In October 1811: "John Partridge for shoemaking Tools 1s-0d". What would their value be today? In December of that year it was probable that the last part of the apprenticeship premium was paid by the parish: £1-4s-0d. It is probable that William the master shoemaker was practising his trade as early as 1798 when he was married. In some parish minutes (as it is from parish records like this that all this information comes), for September 1827 we read: "Frances Partridge making application for the parish to assist him in apprenticing his son Thomas Partridge, agreed to allow him 3 pounds at the time of binding and 3 pounds more in two years time." Thomas Partridge was 12 years old at the time, bound to Richard Riseley of whom more will be said later.

Life was not easy for the shoemaker as we can see from the case of John Mallows. Born in 1799 he was son of the first John Mallows who himself may have been a shoemaker, which we infer from the fact that the name of John and the trade of Cordwainer were together carried down the family. The second John Mallows married Ann Partridge in 1820 and between 1821 and 1839 had 10 children baptised. When the old workhouse was sold in 1837 and lalter bought by Charles Green of Northampton, John Mallows and his family became one of the tenants. John had fallen on hard times, as did many other craftsmen, for in 1832 the parish had to assist him: "Relieved John Mallows 2s-6d." In 1840 the churchwardens recorded: "1½ days to John Mallows Sweeping the Church 4s-6d." He appears to be very literate for in 1842 they were paying, "John Mallows for Riting Register 3s-0d" (In view of his spelling it is probably fortunate the churchwarden did not write them!).

John continues to write these for many years up to 1858. In 1848 they were paying, "John Mallows pulling Nettles in the church Yard 5s-0d" and in 1854, "Pd John Mallows for crying the church Rents 6d." i.e. he was acting as town crier, and others of his family would continue to do this. Because there was no unemployment pay, a shoemaker, as we shall see later, often did other kinds of work besides his own craft. By 1851 his sons Harry aged 22, John aged 21, Christopher aged 16 and Frances aged 13 were living at home in what we now call Mallows Yard helping their father in his trade as a cordwainer. As we have already seen, whole families from youngest to oldest helped the craftsman in his trade. Also we find in 1851 that Thomas Mallows (cordwainer) aged 25 and his family lived in Pudding Bag Lane whilst William Mallows (shoemaker) aged 30 lived with his family in Meeting Yard later called Line-Prop Yard off Easton Lane where the factory is now situated.

Metamorphosis – from agricultural to industrial village?
By the middle of the 19th century we begin to see a slow growth in the shoe trade. In 1851, there were 15 Cordwainers and 22 Shoemakers in Bozeat, two of who were as young as eleven! In addition there were two men who were utilising the work of cordwainers before the coming of the factory era. One was John Osborn who lived in Sanders Yard (now demolished), described as a "Boot and Shoemaker" and

appeared to have had some capital, for the family employed a nurse.

The other was Richard Riseley, aged 60 in 1851 and described as "Boot and Shoe Manufacturer". His wife obviously helped him for she was classed as "Boot and Shoe Binder". We know more about Richard Riseley from other sources. He lived where the Gillihams now live at 46 Allens Hill, which was known as 'The Picle'. In 1851 they were three cottages which in later years had the nickname 'Riseley Garden'. The landlord was Charles Tabot of Olney. Richard Riseley was paid for making shoes for the parish poor as early as 1825 and was training apprentices in their craft. According to the *History of the Methodist Church* he was also the first Methodist local preacher resident in Bozeat. He was also described as a 'Bespoke Boot Maker', that is one who cut his own patterns, cut the uppers, closed and finished complete. In other words he made the complete shoe from start to finish.

Here we see the first signs of industry in the making. It was still of course a home or cottage industry with whole families making the shoes in their own workshops or barns which, when a new house was built, would automatically be built at the back as 'necessary services'. And there were those like the publican of the Chequer's Inn who made shoes during the day and served at the bar at night! The same was true of Thomas Corby, landlord of the Nelson who in the 1876 Business Directory is described as a "Shoe Agent and Beer Retailer" (the Nelson never had a licence to sell spirits) and in the same directory William Pettit was a "News Agent and Boot and Shoe Maker" and there were others who likewise combined two trades. It is remarkable that in 1998 there is still a workshop attached to the Lord Nelson (now closed as a pub) where twelve or so ladies are still making shoes – run by Sharon, daughter of the previous owner Ralph Tompkins who sadly died in 1993.

From the 1851 Census, it is apparent that Bozeat is still primarily an agricultural village. The Census shows that there were only 39 men (and families) connected with the shoemaking industry out of a total of 207 families (total population 921). Twenty years later, in one generation, the picture had entirely changed. Men whose fathers had worked on the land now opted to work in their shoe workshops at home or with increasing frequency in the small but growing factories which were fast appearing in the village.

Take as an example the Drage family which was to become a famous name in the shoe industry in Bozeat as well as being one of the most common names in the village. From the marriage registers we learn the following:

James Drage, Shoemaker, married	1870 – father	Joseph Drage, labourer.
James Drage, " "	1872 – "	Thomas Drage, "
George Drage, " "	1872 – "	John Drage, "
William Drage, " "	1874 – "	James Drage, "
James Drage, " "	1874	John Drage, "
Charles Drage, " "	1875 – "	Thomas Drage, "
Alonzo Drage, " "	1878 – "	John Drage, gamekeeper.

Even from this short list you can understand why each Drage was to have a nickname in order to identify them! (But where did all these Drages come from? There was only a handful of them at the beginning of the century. Did some migrate here? There were Drages at Yardley Hastings and some came from there, and were more 'produced here' than in earlier times?)

By the late 19th century, agricultural labourers were few in number compared to shoemakers.

The factory arrives

We have already seen how the factories with their machinery came to the towns of this part of Northamptonshire, helped on by the arrival of the railway which opened up the trade to a wider market here and abroad. Towns like Northampton and Rushden found that labour was cheaper in the countryside and relatively abundant as they could pay workers more than farmers could. There are examples of factories handing out work to be done in the home workshops around the end of the 19th century but at the same time entrepreneurs like John Osborn and Richard Riseley became manufacturers in their own right and small factories began to appear in the village itself, for it was obviously more economical to have factories where the workers lived if possible.

We can see this in the case of Benjamin Belsher whose family ran the shoemaking craft. He is mentioned as a shoemaker as early as 1826, and in 1851, the year of the Census, was living in Skevington's Yard and classed as a cordwainer. By 1861 he had risen to the status of Shoe Agent. We then read that in 1876 Thomas Belsher, presumably his son, was also a Shoe Agent. Some Bozeat School notes, compiled over 40 years ago say that, "Thomas Belsher was the first man in living memory who let work out from a factory in 1870" – located on the other side of the present Paper Shop in the High Street. We have already noted how these early shoemakers were men of many parts and Thomas was no exception. From the Trade Directory of 1877 he had the first sub-Post Office: "Thomas Belsher receiver …. Letters arrive from Wellingborough about 8.15 am, dispatched at 4 pm. Sundays 10.10 am". A year later in a trade directory he is named as "Boot and Shoe Manufacturer".

The boot business gets technical

The different classifications in the shoe trade are revealed in the baptismal and marriage registers. Before 1880, all workers in the trade are classed as 'Shoemakers'. It is highly probable that the different classifications existed long before they appear in the registers. In the following list we have the first date when they do appear:

Shoe-Riveter (1882): with the shoe-finisher, one of the most common of trades.
Shoe-Finisher (1881): one who trims, scours, smoothes, colours and burnishes.
Shoe-Clicker (1897): very few compared with the two previous trades and must have been more highly skilled. Cut out sections of leather to form upper part of shoe. Name comes from the sound the knife makes as it is turned while cutting.
Leather-dresser (1897): one who tidies the finished shoe, cutting off cottons etc.
Press-man (1896): perhaps one who pressed the leather together in the making of heels.
Shoe-Machinist (1883): see below. Always a woman, perhaps in the closing room.
Fitter (1885): another women. "Their job was to fit together the sections of the uppers in readiness for the machinists." (from *Life in Old Northampton*, 1975)
Shoe-Closer (1897): stitching together the 'uppers'.
Rough Stuff Man (1898): one who worked on the rougher, stouter, leather sections of the shoe, i.e. the soles (only one registration of this trade).

Shoe-hand: probably just a general term to cover the shoe trade.
Knife-filer (1894): this may have been an associated trade to the 'Clickers'.

Here come the machines!

The introduction of machinery can be seen in the marriage registers, where from 1883 some brides appear to have been employed as 'Shoe Machinists'. In 1852 the Howe sewing machine, adapted for sewing leather was introduced and several were used in Northampton factories and worked by female labour – for lower wages! It is probable that hand machinery was introduced in Bozeat at some date after 1870. Whilst the marriage registers of the parish church only show some of the weddings performed in the village at that time, between 1883, when the first mention of a woman shoe worker is shown, until 1889, the number of the female shoe workers getting married was between one and three a year. But after that there is a jump in numbers, five in 1890 and six in 1891. This would suggest that from 1890 onwards, women were turning from the traditional employments of housewife, lacemaker and 'in service' to work in the factories.

The Drage family and shoe manufacturing

The establishment of the factory system in Bozeat will always be associated with the name of John Drage and his brothers.

John was born in 1833, the eldest son of William Hooton Drage. There were altogether seven sons and two daughters in the family, although one son (Jess) died in infancy and another possibly died young. The father, William Hooton, was sometimes classed in the baptismal registers as shepherd and at other times as agricultural labourer. Whilst William could not sign his name on his wedding day in 1830, his wife Sarah Allebone could, and the fact that most of his family seemed to be literate suggests that it was not a pauper family as many labourers were at that time. There is also the interesting fact that this branch of the Drage family had many connections with the Allebone family.

There is a tradition in the family that John, the eldest, showed initiative at a very early age by running away from home with the intention of seeking employment in Northampton, with all his worldly goods wrapped up in a large red handkerchief which he was carrying on the end of a stick over his shoulder – a budding Dick Whittington! – but the family caught up with him at Easton Maudit! Somewhere about the age of 18 it is said that John was apprenticed to a baker in Northampton. He probably married his first wife in Northampton, but she died and he came back to Bozeat with their only daughter and was remarried to Emma Chambers, aged 25, when he was a widower at the age of 22. He was classified as a shoemaker at the time of the wedding in 1855. Perhaps he changed his trade in Northampton? It is probable that he returned to the family home in Dag Lane, where his brothers George and Henry were already making shoes (in the 1851 Census).

About 1870, it is said, he built Arch Villa (now the Paper Shop) and encouraged men to leave the land and learn the trade of shoemaking for which instruction they were charged £1. When the Old School at the bottom of Mile Street was closed in 1873 and the children were moved to the new Board School in Camden Square, John Drage took it over as an extension of his business and his premises. Towards the end of the century he was making heavy boots, lighter men's boots, school boots, football boots and tennis shoes. He was assisted at the time by his sons, W. C. Drage

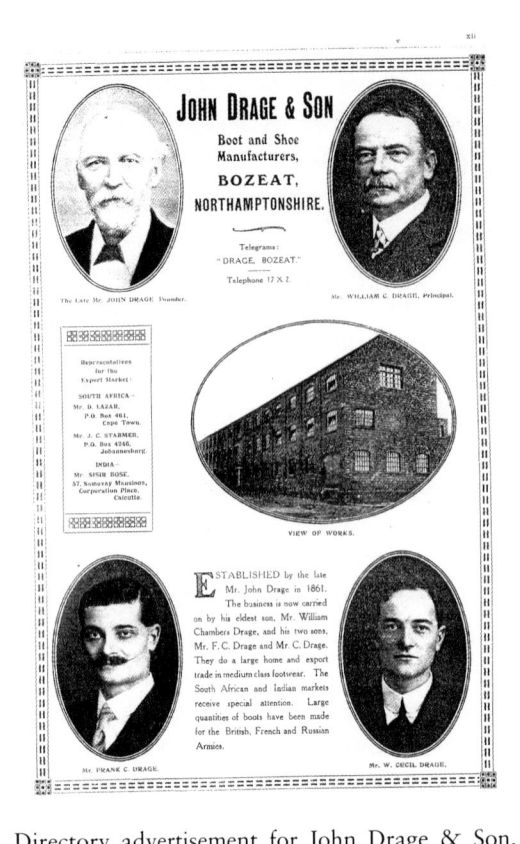

Directory advertisement for John Drage & Son, Boot and Shoe Manufacturers established 1861.
(R. Mallows)

and J. E. Drage. According to a published report he had a good export business to the colonies which were then demanding Northamptonshire footwear in great quantities (see previous chapter).

John Drage's five brothers (Thomas had disappeared from the records – probably died) were well known in the village and district and all were connected with the Boot and Shoe Trade. John and his brother William took an active part in the public life of Bozeat all their lives. William Drage (baptised 1838) started his business in some small cottages on the left hand side of the road going from Bozeat to Olney. He lived at Rock Villa now known as 'Greenwood', and was fond of hunting with the Olney Hunt. George Allebone Drage (born 1835) had an agency at Olney making up boots with materials supplied by Joseph Boswell (see later on the Boswells of Olney) until he began manufacturing on his own. Henry Drage which seems to have been the name for Harry Drage (baptised 1840) also lived at Rock Villa. He was more of a boot manufacturer and also took an interest in farming. Joseph Drage (baptised 1843), the youngest of the brothers, married the daughter of the Olney boot manufacturer and was manager of the Boswell business as long as it lasted.

Both John and Joseph owned a number of houses in the village. All the brothers were fine singers and formed themselves into a 'Glee Party' and were in great demand, even at Castle Ashby House when the Marquis of Northampton was entertaining guests. They travelled all over the district either by horse and trap or on foot to give concerts, carrying with them a small organ.

David and Elizabeth Mallows, who own Arch Villa and the associated factory buildings, have in their possession a shoe catalogue issued by John Drage probably towards the end of the 19th century, showing the 'old school factory' and the Arch Villa Building. From it we can appreciated the wide variety of shoes they made:

Bluchers – open tab form and laced with metal eyelets. This was an early form of ankle boot once used in the army. Catalogue prices from 3/6d to 7/6d.

Derby – with curved side seams. This was a later form of ankle boot. Catalogue price from 4/6d to 12/6d.

Oxonian Shoe – (with front lacing) which came in the earlier years of Victoria's reign. Catalogue price from 3/9d to 7/-.

Buttoned Boot – was a fashion which came in around the 1850s. Catalogue price from 5/6d to 11/-.

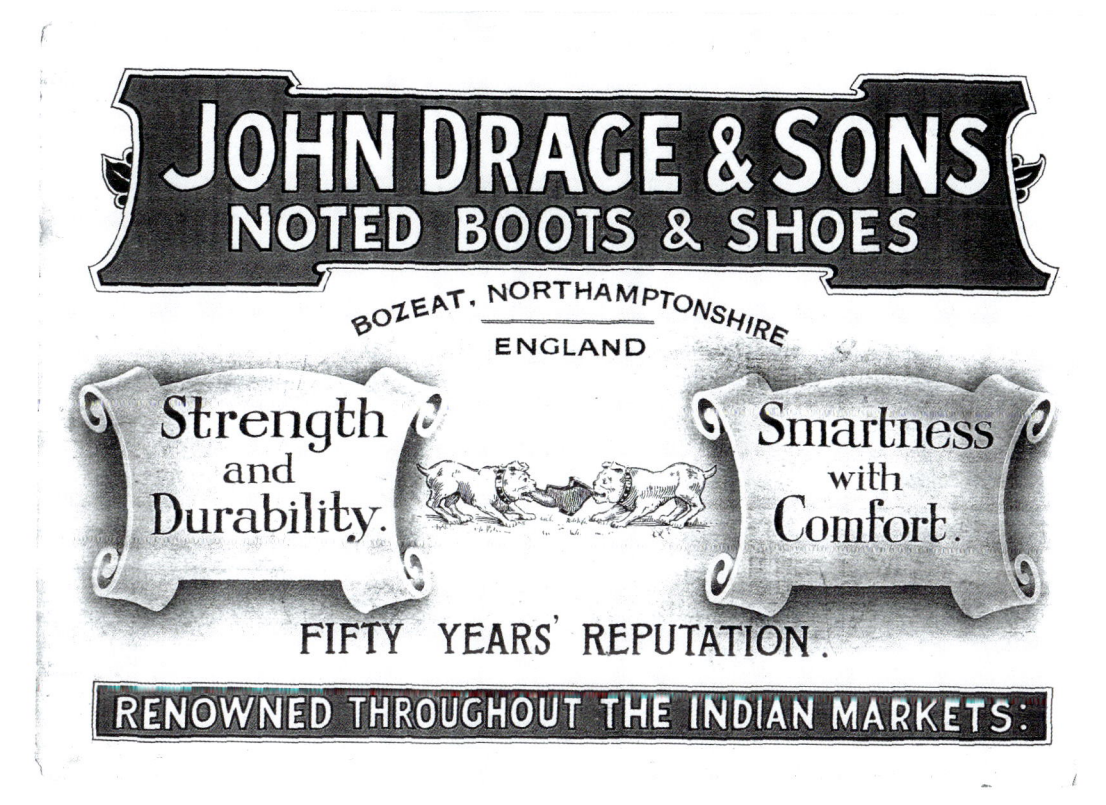

JOHN DRAGE & SONS
NOTED BOOTS & SHOES
BOZEAT, NORTHAMPTONSHIRE
ENGLAND

Strength and Durability.

Smartness with Comfort.

FIFTY YEARS' REPUTATION.

RENOWNED THROUGHOUT THE INDIAN MARKETS.

Directory advertisement for John Drage & Son 'Renowned throughout the Indian Markets'.

Chelsea or Military Boot – Catalogue price from 4/1d to 7/6d.
Men's Canvas Shoes – Catalogue price from 2/6d to 4/6d.
Waterproof Boots – the entry reads: "These Boots have stood the test of twenty-four hours standing in water, and can be fully recommended to Farmers, Sportsmen, Butchers, Game Keepers, Policeman and others. 13/6d. No more bad colds through damp feet. A trial solicited."

Other shoes being made were 'Elastic Sided', which came into fashion about 1837, Balmoral shoes, School Boots, Football Boots and Tennis Shoes. As you can see, this one small factory was able to produce a great variety of footwear. Apparently hand-sewn shoes were a speciality.

There were others besides the Drages

About 1890, F. Goodman & Sons, Boot Manufacturers from Northampton built a factory at the bottom of Hope Street which was much smaller than the present building. We have already seen that it was not uncommon for Northampton-based manufacturers to build factories in the countryside where the rates of pay were lower and there was no lack of labour. Such labour also lacked the protection of labour organisations, so forcing the workers to accept lower wages. Little seems to be known about this first building. It is believed that William Bradshaw was manager and in

1892 they were classified as 'Boot Manufacturers' and later as 'Boot and Shoe Manufacturers'. However, it is said that the firm went bankrupt which seems to have been the common fate of other factories. William Drage, son of John Drage, took over the factory which acquired the nickname 'The Shanty'.

Later his son Frank and his brother Cecil came into the firm and the company ran until 1929 when Caswells of Kettering took over the business and put Frank and Herbert Boswell in charge. Under the Drages the first enlargement of the factory took place in 1914 at the outbreak of the Great War (a period of expansion as we have seen). The trademark of the business 'Honest John' is said to have originated in the fact that John (grandfather) paid his creditors 20/- in the pound following his bankruptcy. Within living memory the factory was making shoes for light wear, as well as heavy footwear, such as boots.

After the boom years of the war, the 1920s and Drages saw a sharp decline in their business as pre-war markets to India, South Africa and West Indies were lost. Their problems were further exacerbated by what in retrospect was a poor business decision. As Dick Botterill remembers hearing of the story: "Frank and Will Drage at some time in the 20s decided to sell shoes direct to the public and placed a full page advert in a National Daily, I think it was the *Telegraph* which was then the *Morning Post*, offering their boots under the Honest John brand direct by post. Their regular customers reacted by ceasing to order and that was the end of the Drages!"

Frank Drage not only owned 1 Allens Hill (the history of which is picked up elsewhere) but he also bought Red Gables Farm from Mr Welch in 1921, who consequently moved to 'The Gold' in Mile Street (where David Mallows' house now stands). Cyril Drage came and farmed the land for him and Cyril's two sons Malcolm and Graham farmed it after him until Malcolm died in 1998. Their sister Alison married Dick Botterill the boot manufacturer (wheels within wheels!). Frank himself went to run a cinema in St Ives, Cornwall.

Many factories were so small as to employ only a handful of men. Such a so-called factory has been described by Clarry Drage. Born in the village in 1894, Clarry lived his whole life here except for a short spell in London between the ages of about eight and fourteen. He remembers working as a lad in the long shed which is now in his garden, for he was now living in his former employer's house at 3 Peartree Close. The small factory made heels and so the employees were described in footwear terminology as 'Lift Makers'.

Clarry's employer, Mr J. Barnes, made cheap heels as did other small 'lift makers' from odd pieces of leather from the cast-offs of boot and shoe manufactures. They were stuck together using paste and water and then nailed. These were then used on cheap workers' boots. A piece which had not been gripped by a nail during the process of manufacture was often forced out during wear and had to be trimmed by the wearer with a knife. Six women worked there in Clarry's time and he, as a lad, earned eight shillings a week. He was offered work by William Taylor, a friend of the family, who by then had a factory in Easton Lane, at ten shillings a week. Other young men in that factory were getting twelve shillings a week.

Thomas Corby was another 'lift maker' and appears in an 1898 trade directory. In 1909 he built a factory up the London Road and a bungalow was built for his occupation in front of the factory in 1910. The bungalow was next to what was Herbert Cave and Son (Thomas), Funeral Directors and Carpenters at 81 London Road. The factory was very modern for the times having a glass roof and electrical fittings. After passing it on to his son, it was sold to William Nutt of Wollaston and burnt down in 1935. Heels had been made in this factory by punching out small pieces of leather which were then stuck together by women. The leather used was a tough leather from the belly of a cow and could not be used for the 'uppers'.

Another type of factory, common in Northamptonshire, was the co-operative. In these ventures a few men would combine to engage in shoemaking, pooling their savings, electing a manager and then going into production. Such a group of men were said to have started up a co-operative in Easton Lane, perhaps in Meeting Yard or Line-Prop Yard, but there is no information on this at present. What is known is that at the end of the 19th century they occupied a house in London Road, now demolished, which was on a patch of ground, now grass, on the right as you go to Olney just down from the alleyway through to Mill Road. In an 1885 trade directory, William Bradshaw is manager and the business is called the 'Boot & Shoe Co-operative Industrial Society Ltd.' In September 1901 the shoe co-op closed and many in the village, we are told, lost their savings. The building later became a garage where a coal lorry was parked.

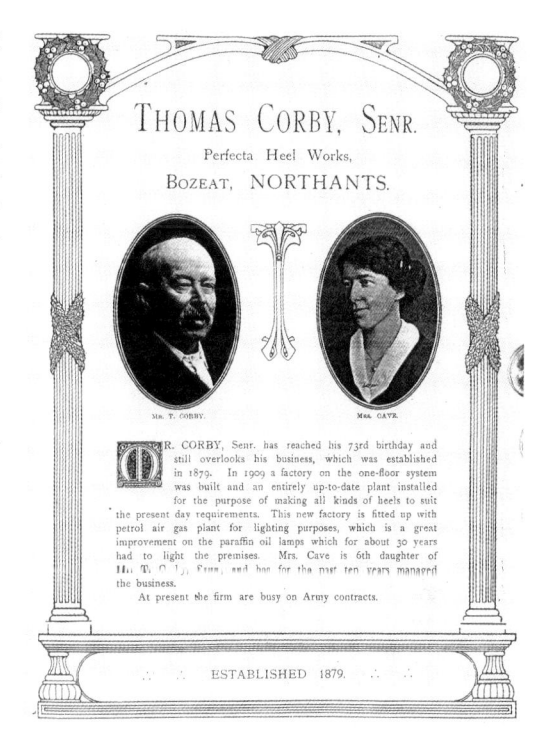

Directory advertisement for Thomas Corby, Perfecta Heel Works, established 1879. Mrs Cave was married to carpenter Mr Cave.

Trade directories tell a tale

The development of the Boot and Shoe business in Bozeat from is beginnings in the 19th century to the opening two decades of the twentieth, can be appreciated by listing the inclusions of the trade in these directories (D). Other sources for the date information show just the year:

John Mallows, shoemaker 1849 (D).
Richard Risely, shoemaker 1849, 1861 (D).
Benjamin Belcher, shoe agent 1861, 1874, 1877 (D).
John Drage (Honest John), shoemaker 1869, 1897, shoe mfr and grindery, etc., boot and shoemaker 1876, 1877, 1885, 1891, 1903 (D), wholesale boot mfrs, High St 1904, 1911 (D).
William Drage, shoemaker 1896 (D), 1874 shoe mfr, 1876 boot and shoemaker, 1877 (William Hooten Drage) boot and shoe mfr, 1885, 1891 (D), 1893 (London Rd).
Thomas Belcher, shoe agent 1876 (D), 1872 (D). Thomas Belcher boot and shoe mfr, Post Office and shopkeeper.
Thomas Corby, shoe agent and beer retailer 1874, 1876 (D), 1898 lift maker, 1904 lift mfr, London Rd 1911 (D).

Samuel Monk, boot and shoemaker 1876 (D).
William Pettit, news agent and boot and shoemaker 1874, 1876 (D), shoe mfr 1874 (D), Shopkeeper and Boot and shoe mfr 1877, 1885 (D).
George Coles, boot-upper closer 1877 (D).
Henry Drage, boot-upper mfr 1874 (D), boot and shoe mfr, Rock Villa 1877, 1885 (D), 1893 (D).
Boot & Shoe Co-operative Industrial Society Ltd, William Bradshaw manager 1885 (D), William Bettles manager 1891 (D), 1893(D).
F. Goodman & Son, boot mfrs 1891, 1903, 1904 boot and shoe mfrs, Hope St.
William Goodman, boot closer 1891, 1893, 1903 (D), boot and shoe closer 1920 (D).
Henry Partridge, boot closer 1891 (D).
Frank Smith, boot dealer 1891 (D), 1893 (D) boot and shoe dealer, 1904 boot and shoe dealer and sectional heel maker, 1911 (D).
John Walker, shoe agent and grocer 1874 (D).
William Botterill, boot and shoe mfr 1903, 1904, 1911 (D), 1920 (*Kelly Leather Trades*).
J. Barnes, lift maker 1904 (D).
H. Corby, boot and shoe closer, London Rd 1904 (D).
W. Craxton, boot dealer, 9 Wollaston Rd 1904 (D).
T. Freeman, boot and shoe closer, London Rd 1904 (D).
J. Laughton, boot lift mfr, High St 1911 (D).
T. Robinson, grocer, shoe grindery dealer 1911 (D).
Tom Corby Jun, boot and shoe leather heel maker 1920 (D) (*Kelly Leather Trades*).
Hooton & Barnes, as above and boot and shoe mfr 1920D (*Kelly Leather Trades*).
Fred Curtis, boot and shoe mfr 1920 (D).
John Drage & Sons Ltd mfrs of reg. brand 'Honest John' medium footwear, 1920 (D).
Taylor & Drage, boot and shoe mfrs 1920 (D).
George Pettit, Church Lane, boot and shoe maker, warehouse and dealer 1920 (D).

The story of William Taylor
William Taylor, left his job as manager of William Goodman's factory to go into business on his own. He set up in an old butcher's shop on the lower corner of Church Lane with Pudding Bag Lane which he rented at 2/6d per week. Eventually he needed larger premises and when Elwin Drage, son of John Drage, built a factory in Easton Lane, William went into partnership in a business described as 'Taylor & Drage'. William employed some good craftsmen who made a good class of shoe. The building occupied by William Taylor in Easton Lane was previously a grocer's shop owned by Mr Sellick. 'Clarry' Drage remembers it as a one-storey building but at some date, probably after William Taylor vacated the premises, it became a two-storey building with a gas-engine room downstairs and a closing room upstairs. It was related by a woman who worked at the Easton Lane factory about 1928 that York Bros owned the factory at that time. York Bros had a large factory in Wellingborough and the Easton Lane factory was a closing room for their operations. But in 1928, the Wellingborough Shoe Operatives went on strike and so the Easton Lane factory was closed by the Company.

But to return to William Taylor, when he outgrew the building that he then occupied in Easton Lane, prior to the Great War, he moved again, this time up the London Road just below and adjacent to Spencelayh's house, No. 105, (see Chapter

27) and behind what was Mrs Pettit's house. As with the rest of the trade, the end of the war brought a slump and fewer craftsmen were needed. Those who were left, and 'Clarry' Drage was one, can remember the feeling of insecur-ity over how long their jobs would last.

A fire broke out in 1928 which destroyed the factory and William Taylor eventually moved to Northampton where he opened a billiard hall. He took an active part in village life and for some time was Church Warden. In his prosper-ous days he took over the cottages in the Pightle, one of which had been occupied by Richard Riseley, demolished them and rebuilt one single house out of stone.

Dick Botterill remembers how in those days there was a 'set' in the village com-prising those who belonged to the managerial side of the boot business and those of similar status who played tennis together and formed the more 'genteel' side of Bozeat society. Dick remembers Richard Riseley as quite a refined man, "Too good for the shoe trade," he added with a smile!

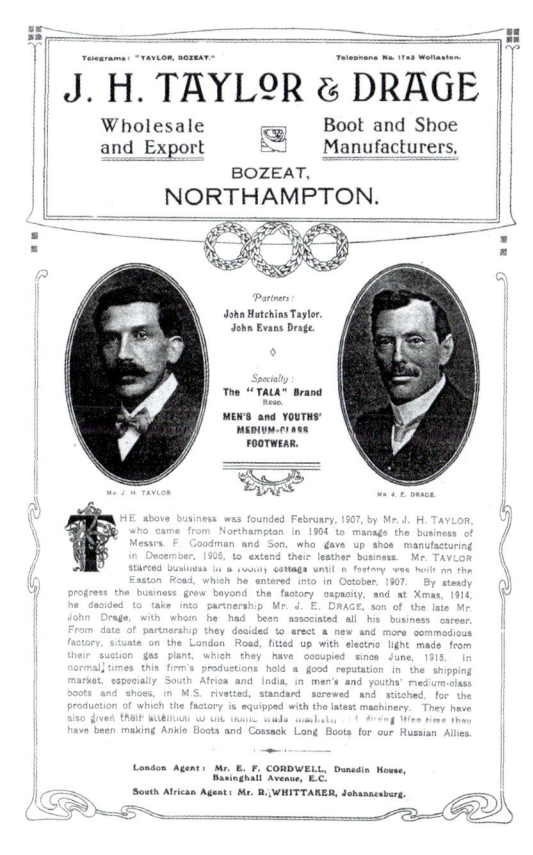

Directory advertisement for J. H. Taylor and Drage Co. 1907. *(R. Mallows)*

W. Botterill & Son from Wollaston

"The Company was founded by William Botterill in 1895 to manufacture Boots and Shoes as a Cottage Industry." (*Pictorial History of Bozeat*, 1992). In about 1903 William moved from Wollaston to a house towards the top of London Road and a factory grew round the house until the site was full in 1974. The family went to live in a house further down London Road – first to what was to become Spencelayh's house and then to No. 91, the attractive stone house where Peter and Rose Drage live. The bay window of the original house still remained part of the original office until recent years. Originally there were two 'clickers' and two women 'closers', the work being mostly sent out to home workshops. Gradually machinery was introduced and army boots were made during the Great War.

"William was joined by his sons Alfred and George who took over the management after the First World War and expanded the company to make all types of boots and shoes and football and rugby boots.

After the Second World War, Alfred's sons John and Dick, later joined by brother-in-law Herbert Nicholet, took control of the Company. Sales were concentrated on Gola Sports shoes and the business grew to employ over 200 people making over 20,000 pairs of Gola Shoes each week in factories in Bozeat, Lavendon and Earls Barton. Gola shoes and sports equipment were sold worldwide.

In 1974, Botterills, along with The Bozeat Boot Company, were bought by

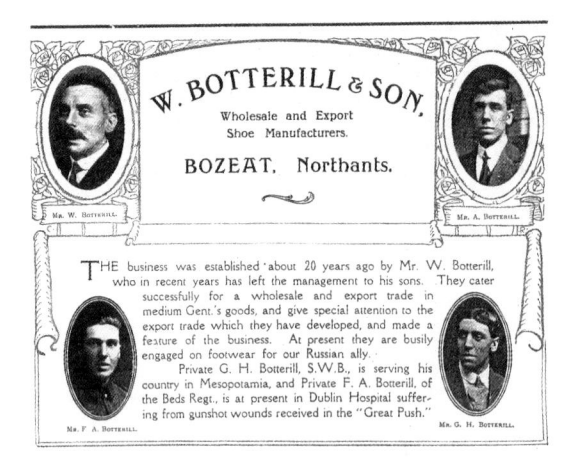

Directory advertisement for W. Botterill & Sons, Shoe Manufacturers. *(W. Botterill)*

Electronic Rentals Ltd and formed a new company, Gola Sports Limited. The last member of the Botterill family left the Company in 1979." (*Pictorial History of Bozeat*). The full story of the Botterill family and its affair with shoemaking is told in another chapter of this history.

The rise and fall of the Bozeat Boot Company

After the Second World War, in the late 1940s, Spencer Clarke of Northampton became the owner of the Drage shoe business with a Mr James as manager. At that period the main work was army and football boots. They also had a 'clicking room' in Arch Villa, the old home of 'Honest John' Drage which is now the Paper Shop. Just before this, also in the late 1940s, Spencer Clarke had acquired the Bozeat Boot Company which at that time was situated in a small building in Hope Street. Mr Clarke had advanced Bozeat Boot monies for the manufacture of footwear from his retail shops but unfortunately the owners found themselves in financial difficulties and unable to complete the contract. In consequence, the business was passed to Spencer Clarke in settlement. It was after this that, with the acquisition of the Easton Lane factory, the whole business moved up there. During the war, the factory had been used as a school for London evacuees. After Mr James, it was managed for a short time by a Malcolm Clarke (no relative) who retired due to illness. Up to this time the factory had manufactured, in the main, the Bo-Shu sandal.

"Ron Coles joined the company after demob from the RAF in 1950, taking charge of the accounting side, having been previously involved briefly in the tanning industry, prior to service in the RAF.

The company had been and was still struggling, losing money each year. The owners had been attempting to make various kinds of shoe constructions to sell in the shops which they owned, irrespective of competitiveness.

In 1952 Ron Coles was appointed Manager and that year the company for the first time and to the pleasure of the owners did not lose money. The manufacturing policies were changed and the company began to specialise in these products only: sandals for the summer season, balanced by work boots, shoes, and football boots for the winter season. With product specialisation the company began to prosper and expand, opening units in Kettering, Wellingborough and Olney, and profits increased.

The company discontinued making sandals with the introduction of the training shoe. They were the first company in the country to manufacture trainers and one of the first to produce football boots with moulded multi studs. Mr Coles was made a director in 1960 and then Managing Director. He met and signed Bobby Charlton, then aged 19, who helped to design the Bobby Charlton football boot. Bobby Moore was also signed and the products carrying his name were sold through the G.U.S. catalogues.

Looking north from south end of London Road, Botterill's Shoe Factory (after the house has been absorbed into the factory). The Bozeat Women's Institute planted the avenue of trees.

In 1970 the company decided to introduce a new brand and the Managing Director approached Jimmy Hill, who at the time was setting up a consultancy. The brand name that was evolved was 'Lightning', with a lightning flash being designed for the products.

The success of the company began to attract offers from other companies, the shareholders being tempted to sell in 1973. "It owed its success to many long-serving and loyal local employees." (*Pictorial History of Bozeat*, 1992)

As we have already seen, in 1974 the company along with Botterills was bought by a major public company and traded under the name of Gola Sports Limited. Sadly in 1981, the Gola Shoe Factory (as it was then known) in Easton Lane closed and all its workers were made redundant.

With the Hope Street Factory closing down as a shoe factory in 1978, in 1981, after a century as a thriving village of the Boot and Shoe industry, this branch of Bozeat's history as such came to the end, one of the most important chapters in its history which, as we have seen, had its roots in the 17th century if not earlier.

The impact of these events on the lives and memories of the village is told elsewhere (see Chapter 5).

So what happened to the factories?

What happened to the three factories after their working life for shoemaking had ended? Knapp Toolmaking moved into the Hope Street Factory in 1982. They are making precision tools particularly for the motor and electronic industry. They undertake jig boring, spark erosion, wire erosion and pressing. Mike Knapp, the owner, had 10 years experience in the tool making trade before moving to Bozeat from Olney and was pleased with the easy access to the factory, particularly after the new bypass was opened. To enable them to install the machines needed for their work, Mike had to gut and rebuild the ground floor.

Originally the upper floors were to be let but were eventually retained for their own use. The firm brought their nine existing staff with them, all living near Bozeat in Earls Barton, Rushden, Olney and Wellingborough, but by 1995 the staff had increased to over 50. In 1982 Mike lived with his wife Susan and their two children, Michael aged seven and Mary aged nine, in Stoke Goldington (see *About Bozeat*). The work has continued to expand so much that in 1998 they sold up and moved to Wellingborough as they needed larger premises. The factory was bought to store documents and archival material.

The Easton Lane factory has provided accommodation for a small company – Electrosite (UK) Ltd.

The factory up London Road, originally established and developed by the Botterill family, then the property of Gola sports was bought in October 1984 by Mr Neville Spiers director of Stonnig Products. He moved his firm from North London to the 25,000 square feet of the Gola factory to assemble furniture from kit form which involves gluing the components together and then finishing with a hard wearing polish. Mr Spiers had been associated with the furniture trade for some 60 years supplying timber to the trade. He recruited Mick Corby of 124 London Road (see Chapter 27), formerly with Botterills for 18 years and appointed him head of the firm's warehouse and security and Mick helped them recruit a labour force from the village.

One of their main customers was Olney Galleries who originally put Mr Spiers on to the Bozeat factory and for whom they continued to assemble furniture. This, together with taking over Surecraft, a contract polishers at Milton Keynes, represented a total investment of £250,000. "I am showing my confidence by selling my home in London and moving my family here. I am a Londoner, and it is quite a wrench," he told the *Evening Telegraph*. Sadly, the furniture side of the business ceased operation in 1994 and Mr Spiers has since then rented out the premises to small firms for office use. In 1996 it traded under the catching sign BBC – Bozeat Business Centre!

Terms used in shoemaking

Traditionally, 'boot and shoemaking' was divided between six departments:

Clicking, where the leather was cut out for 'uppers' of shoes.

Closing, where the leather upper pieces were stitched together.

Ruff Stuff Room, the department where thick hides were matched and cut for soles and heels.

In the *Making and Lasting* room, the upper and the sole were joined, and the heel attached.

The *Finishers* trimmed and smoothed, and then coloured and polished the heels and edges.

Finally, the *Shoe Room* gave a final polish to the shoes and prepared them for packing.

CHAPTER 9

The Botterills – the History of W. Botterill and Sons

Dick Botterill

Beginnings

William Botterill and his family moved from Flore to Wollaston in the early 1880s, and in 1895 he set up in business as a boot manufacturer. His was a cottage-based business, as was common at that time.

In the late 1890s William moved to Bozeat with his family. There is a story that he was offered a plot of land in London Road if he would come to Bozeat and develop a manufacturing business to offer employment. He moved into the house at the top of London Road, which it is thought that he had built. The original house can still be recognised by the bay window and the front door to its right.

Here William started making working type boots and shoes at Bozeat. Over the years he was joined by his sons Alfred, Frank and George, and the first part of the factory was built on to the house. Some workers were in the factory, while others worked from their homes.

During the First World War boot making continued, including boots for British and Empire soldiers and probably for the Russian army. Frank and George both joined the British Army. Sadly, Frank was killed in France in 1917 (Chapter 4).

Between the wars – 1919 to 1939

During this period the business developed, managed by William, Alfred and George. Heavy Boots were made, and Football Boots and Rugby Boots became a speciality. Remember that in 1919 there was no electricity in Bozeat. As the years passed the business grew. Extensions were made to the factory, an engine was installed to drive the machines by a maze of pulleys, shafts and belts and a generator produced DC current to provide lighting. As production became more mechanised, workers moved into the factory and home working stopped. As the years passed, William, who had moved from the Factory House in London Road to the stone house further down the road now owned by Peter Drage, retired. His son George and his wife moved into the Factory house where their children Alan and Lena were born.

During the middle 1920s the public electric supply and the telephone came to Bozeat. As the years passed into the 1930s W. Botterill and Sons grew and workers came in from outside the village. Two hired buses brought workers in daily from Olney and Lavendon and others came from Grendon and Wollaston. In 1936 Botterill's became a Limited Liability Company, and in the same year the decision was made to have a company brand for football and rugby boots. The name chosen was 'GOLA', an anagram of GOAL, and the first slogan, which appeared on the sides of buses was, 'Gola means Goals'.

Can you remember what football boots were like in those days? The uppers were all from russety coloured leather in three quality grades, split leather for the cheapest, side leather for medium and russet kip butts for the most expensive. All had high legs, about the height of a modern work boot upper, a reinforcement strap across the toe area, and a hard tan coloured toe cap, with lots of clearance for the toes. The soles of leather were machine attached with rivets and reinforced with machine-applied screwed wire. Each shoe had six pre-built leather studs attached with three or four nails. Screw-in studs were unknown and a small number of boots had rubber studs nailed on. Boots were made in sizes from 7 child's up to size 13 men's. The ex-factory prices for men's sizes started from less than 3/- per pair (15 pence today).

By the late 1930s the company was producing around 5,000 pairs per week for home and a few for export. George Botterill and his family had moved to his new house at the top of Allens Hill, where his daughter Lena and husband David Payne now live. The factory that grew around the house in London Road and had grown to about half its present size was supplemented by the large black wooden building known as the Cinema that had been bought in the mid-thirties to store finished stock.

The Second World War
September 1939 brought rapid changes as Britain went to war. The Ministry of Supply immediately took control of production, which was reduced to essential levels. For Botterill's this meant that sports boot production practically ceased. About a third of the factory was taken over by the Ministry for storage and the remaining part of the factory made heavy work boots and boots for the armed forces under government contract. Young men and women went away to join the services, work on the land and into munitions factories. A much reduced workforce carried on at Botterill's until the war ended in 1945.

The years from 1946 to 1974
With the return to peace, there was no immediate return to freedom from control. People will remember food rationing, points for clothes and utility standards for furniture and household goods. The Government controlled the production of industry, and boot and shoe manufacturers' production was controlled in the quantity, design and quality they could make. Botterill's quota in the early post-war years was 2,000 pairs per week, and they had to make boots to Government Specification BMC/3 (Boots Men's Common Grade 3), HMC/3 (Boots Heavy Common Grade) and SM/3 (Shoes Men's Grade 3). Exports were encouraged and rewarded by exemption from quota controls, but an export licence, difficult to obtain, was required.

The Company suffered an early post-war blow with the sad and unexpected death of George Botterill. This left William's oldest son Alfred as the major shareholder in W. Botterill and Sons Ltd. Alfred was joined by his sons John and Dick when they were demobilised from the RAF and the Army in 1947 and after a period they joined their father as directors of the company. Alfred retired at the end of the 1940s, and control moved to the third generation.

Gradually restrictions were eased and production was built up. Closing Rooms were opened in rented premises in Lavendon and Olney. Ladies were less willing to travel to work and it became common for branch factories to take more work to the workers. Also in the late '40s the first post-war extension was built at Bozeat. Underwoods of Wollaston was the builder but all later extensions at Bozeat, Lavendon and Earls Barton were by Elliot & Dobbs of Bozeat.

Production through to the mid-'50s was still heavy boots and shoes, and football and rugby boots, still mainly in pre-war styles and made by long-established machine methods.

The latter years of the 1950s saw major changes. Botterills heavy boot and shoe production was changed to directly moulded-on rubber soles. These were sold under the brand name of OTTER, derived from bOTTERill to compete with the highly successful TUF brand. These boots for the first time in the shoe industry offered a written wear guarantee for one year. Demand was good and shift working started in the moulding departments.

At last football boots started to change. Uppers were cut lower to little more than shoe height, russet leathers diminished and disappeared to be replaced by black, brown and even white leathers. The soles were still leather riveted on with leather studs. Screw-in studs of rubber, metal, and plastic started to appear.

Production grew, exports started to grow, mainly to the USA, Scandinavia, South Africa and Australia, and the first training shoes were made. Almost all the early production went for export; the home market was not ready for trainers.

During these last years of the '50s the important decision was made to develop the GOLA brand as the company's main product, and to widen the sports range to cover athletics, cricket, sports accessories and the emerging market for training shoes. The critical decision was made to appoint a sole distributor for the United Kingdom and to seek and appoint Gola distributors in overseas markets.

During this period a third director had been appointed, Herbert Nicolet who had married Alfred's youngest daughter Janet. Herb specialised in material buying.

So, in the late 1950s the development of the Gola brand went into its stride. Training shoes with leather uppers and a variety of rubber sole materials became very successful and further space was needed. Already the main floor at London Road had been extended forwards to the front of the site, and now a new Closing Factory was built at Lavendon and the small Olney premises closed. A factory was rented at Earls Barton for making training shoes. The rubber moulding was doubled and moulds were installed to make directly attached soles for football boots incorporating multiple rubber studs as part of the sole. Production continued to rise, the old pre-war level of 5,000 pairs per week had long been surpassed, and 10,000 pairs per week was in sight.

In the 1960s the strength of Gola grew, allowing the company to concentrate almost entirely on sports and to sell almost all of its production through its sole UK Gola distributor and its overseas Gola distributors. More building was carried out with a new factory at Earls Barton to replace the rented premises.

By the end of the 1960s the link between the company and its UK distributor became so close that the distributor asked that it be cemented by the purchase of a 30% interest in W. Botterill and Sons Ltd. This was agreed in the early 1970s, and Electronic Rentals Group Ltd, a major and wealthy public company and the owners of the distributors, became 30% owners of W. Botterill and Sons Ltd.

The 1970s opened well with growing Gola sales in UK and widening sales abroad. Export sales had reached around 50% of production, going to a wide range of countries, from Finland to Canada to New Zealand and to Japan. Weekly production went through the 15,000 mark, the Moulding Plant had been replaced by a new, more efficient faster injection moulding line and direct moulded training shoes went into production. The decision was made to double the size of the Lavendon and Earls Barton factories, and soon after, to put a second storey on the office block at London Road and to build up the rest of the site.

Production moved on to 20,000 pairs per week, supplemented by more shoes bought in from manufacturers in the UK and sports bags and clothing sourced mainly in the Far East. To provide a warehouse for future growth the old Drage Shoe Factory in Hope Street was purchased.

In 1974 it appeared that Gola had established a strong place in the world market for sports and leisure equipment, and encouraged by a leading merchant bank survey, Electronic Rentals Group decided that they wanted to invest and aim to compete with the world market leaders and that Gola was to be the vehicle. This led to the proposal that ERG should take over Botterill's totally and take over other companies to increase volume, range and market penetration. After a great deal of heart-searching the Botterill family agreed that this was the best course for the business to expand.

So in 1974 W. Botterill and Sons Ltd passed out of the ownership of the Botterill family.

As part of the deal to sell Botterill's, the new owners agreed to purchase the Bozeat Boot Company Ltd and to merge the two companies with the distribution company that had its sales and administration at Dorking, Surrey, and its warehouse operation at Liverpool. The merger of the three companies formed the new company Gola Sports Ltd.

Gola Sports Ltd – 1974 to 1983

The new Company started to operate in September 1974 with its head office at London Road, Bozeat, with manufacturing on the same site and further manufacturing at Easton Lane Bozeat, Earls Barton, Lavendon, and small closing units at Olney and Kettering. There were storage sites at the old Drage Factory in Hope Street, Bozeat and the old Cinema in London Road, Bozeat. All the employees of Botterill and Bozeat Boot Company transferred to Gola and were joined by a number of the former employees of the distribution company from Liverpool, altogether approaching 450 people. The new company inherited a production capacity of around 30,000 pairs per week.

A new Managing Director was appointed by the new owners, and the former directors of Botterill, Bozeat Boot and two from Dorking were appointed to the Board.

During the Christmas holidays of 1974, a major reorganisation of the company's manufacturing facilities was carried out, with the object of raising efficiency and of moving people doing similar jobs together so that they would think of themselves as working for Gola, not one of their former employers.

Gola's expansion plans proceeded, a large warehouse was opened at Sywell fed by large trailers that transferred finished shoes from Bozeat and Earls Barton daily. A new advanced polyurethane moulding plant was installed at Earls Barton to make lightweight training shoes. Gola continued the practice established by Botterill's of showing at all the major international Sports Fairs and intensified overseas sales visits.

By 1977 it was becoming clear that sales were not growing as fast as planned, and that competition from other international brands was intense. The other problem was the arrival on the international market of well-made training shoes from the Far East at prices that European manufacturers could not meet.

Disagreement built up on the proper course for Gola to remedy its problems. This resulted in the resignation of a senior and highly experienced director, quickly followed by the owners' decision to replace the Managing Director.

A new Managing Director arrived with the problems of the company continuing:

strong competition, more Far East imports and now deteriorating relations with established customers. By 1979 four more of the company directors had gone.

The run-down of the company began and Managing Director No. 2 departed. The owners appointed Managing Director No. 3 and further contraction followed until manufacturing finally ceased in 1982 and all the premises were vacated in 1983.

The Gola brand was sold to a North of England company.

Botterill Sports

In 1979 John Botterill's son Michael, who had worked for some years for W. Botterill and Sons Ltd, and became Export Sales Manager for Gola Sports Ltd, decided to set up a company to make and market sports shoes. A small building was purchased in Irchester, and, with help from his father, Michael started manufacturing a range of football, rugby, cricket, track and training shoes. The shoes were branded BORTA, and national distribution was quickly established for the United Kingdom.

The company started well in a difficult market, and in the early 1980s, having outgrown its Irchester premises, the old Bozeat Boot Factory in Easton Lane was purchased from Gola Sports Ltd.

Although the business operated satisfactorily for several years, the pressure of cheap imports from low labour cost countries made it obvious that prospects were poor. The decision was made to cease production before losses developed.

The Easton Lane factory was sold and divided between the new owners, Electrosite and Glenco.

The Red Lion advertising 'Good accommodation for cyclists', with local flat-capped youths posing for the camera.

CHAPTER 10

Boot and Shoe – From a Personal Point of View

Philip Boswell

The Boswells
Herbert Boswell came to Bozeat to work for the Vol-Crepe Shoe Company in 1928. Their factory was situated on the north side of Hope Street once used by the Drage Shoe Company as a store for their factory across the road. After Vol-Crep moved to Glossop the building was taken over by Dunmore & Edmunds and eventually pulled down and houses built in its place.

Herbert was an expert in shoemaking. It was said that he could take a whole factory apart and put it together again. He knew the workings of shoemaking machinery inside out and personally made special sandals for the Royal Princesses, Margaret and Elizabeth when they were only three or four years old.

The Boswells came from Olney – a name still linked with the shoe trade there. When Herbert was born, his father moved to Rushden which was then, along with Northampton and Kettering a great centre of the shoe trade. Philip remembers that his grandfather became steward of the Athletic Club at Rushden. Like his son after him, Herbert joined the shoe trade as a boy and worked his way up from the factory floor. Philip remembers stories his father told him of the Boswells of Olney. One Boswell was legendary for his strength – it was said he was the strongest man in England and once wheeled a fully loaded wheelbarrow from Olney Market to Emberton (some three miles away) without setting it down! Another was a Carrier. He was so strong that he never had to back his horse and cart – he just lifted up the rear wheels and walked them round!

The Boswells come to Bozeat
Herbert and Jessie Boswell moved into 1 Allens Hill, 'Bona Vista', which was owned by Mr Frank Drage. Initially they rented the house until they were able to buy it. It was known as The Doctor's Surgery, and still is, and even after they had moved in, Dr Baxter, the village Doctor at the time, continued to use their front room on the left as his surgery and the hall was the waiting room for his patients! The Surgery did not move from there till the time of Dr Swan and his wife when the new clinic was built in Brookside in 1978.

The Drage Shoe Company, since its inception in the late 1890s under Honest John and his brothers at Arch Villa in the High Street, had had a rather chequered history having been shut down twice because of bankruptcy. The then owner Frank Drage wanted to start the business up again and asked Herbert to go into partnership with him. He agreed but before they could get started Messrs Allen & Caswell from Kettering made a better offer for the business and were willing to make Herbert the Works Manager and Frank the General Manager. So, in 1929, under the ownership of Murray Caswell, the Drage Shoe Company came to life again for a third time. It was on Feast Day c.1932 that Jack Walker, the local painter and decorator, painted the huge boot on the road-side of the factory wall inside of which he painted the outline of a man with a stick, Union Jack and waistcoat, and a British bulldog i.e. John Bull. The painting became a landmark for the village before it was painted over by a later owner of the factory. It was still visible in outline through the masking black paint, but, for the year 2000, it has been repainted by Mr Steve Linnell. Incidentally, Betty, Jack Walker's daughter, was to marry Philip, Herbert's son, some years later.

The company continued to operate in the factory in Hope Street until 1972 when Mr Caswell moved it to Kettering where it still trades under the name of The Drage Shoe Company! So after a century, a business which started so modestly in Bozeat lives on.

Herbert and Jessie took an active part in village life. There is a photograph of them both in the Parish Church together with the vicar, Rev. Powell, the organist Mr Hol Smith, members of the boys' and men's choir and members of the PCC from c.1949. Jessie was secretary to the PCC and Herbert was Churchwarden along with Mr Wyman. Herbert continued as works manager until ill health got the better of him and he handed more and more of his responsibilities over to his son Philip.

Philip was their only child and was nine years old when they moved to Bozeat in 1928. He, with Albert Drage and Freddie Furr were among the first batch of boys to start at Wellingborough Grammar School when it was first opened in 1930. He started work at Drage's at the beginning of 1935 when he was 16. He was apprenticed to learn the trade right through and soon felt that he was part of the family business. With his father and Frank Drage managing it that is not surprising. When he was eighteen, a man from Southern Rhodesia (Zimbabwe) came to ask Herbert to buy the machinery to start a factory, take it to Rhodesia and stay with it until staff had been trained to use it and it was working satisfactorily. Philip was included in the deal. Herbert bought most of the machinery from Fred Hawkes of Rushden, but the doctor would not allow him to go since the combination of a weak heart and a factory at 5,000 feet above sea level could have killed him! So Philip went with two shoe men from Rushden. However, after twelve months he returned home as he saw the venture was not getting off the ground successfully.

Wollaston and Dr. Martens

In 1970 Philip left Drage's and went to work for N.P.S. at Wollaston. Murray Caswell had sent his eldest son to a shoemaking college, and it soon became clear that he was destined to become the future managing director. Herbert, his father, suffered increasingly from ill health and Philip took over more of his duties and became in effect the works manager. Eventually his father died but Philip carried on until he saw the advert for staff at N.P.S. at Wollaston. He wrote asking for an interview, was asked to meet the committee, met them and within an hour had been appointed manager. It was a wise move. In 1972 Murray Caswell had moved his Drage Shoe Company to Kettering, as we have already seen.

N.P.S. (Northampton Productive Society) was a workers' co-operative governed by a committee elected every year. Philip found the firm to be in a very poor financial state, making too many types of footwear with very little profit. A short time previously Mr Bill Griggs and the previous manager of N.P.S., Mr Sargent, had gone to Germany and Mr Griggs had bought the patent to make Dr. Martens-type footwear. Naturally N.P.S. was offered first chance to participate in this and in fact the first samples were made at N.P.S. because they were the only firm in Wollaston that had the machinery to make welted footwear, with the heat welding machine as the crux of the process. They persisted with the new process and Philip gradually eliminated the loss-making footwear and DMs became the main method of manufacture used.

It was highly successful, not least because the method was simpler and more reliable. There was no need for repeated gluing and stitching of the top to the bottom as in the traditional method practised for centuries, where earlier nailing rather than stitching was used. In this process the sole and the heel are one piece of soft, flexible man-made plastic-like material with a recessed interior to make it lightweight and this was initially heat-welded to the welt rather than stitched and glued as in the traditional manner. The traditional method is more labour intensive and is still used at N.P.S. for some specialist boots. These boots are more expensive, heavier and have to be 'worn in'. The new method provides you with a lightweight, soft and flexible shoe from the start!

At first DMs were sold as a heavy working boot but now they are of the latest fashions particularly amongst young people, as popular with the girls as with the boys. And I myself have never had such comfortable, spacious, light and flexible shoes! When taking assemblies in the gymnasium at Wollaston School (1995) the young people have to take their shoes off and so I am typically confronted with 200 children and tidy rows of 200 pairs of shoes, nearly all Dr. Martens costing around £60 a pair, making a total of some £12,000-worth lined up at the door awaiting their owners!

Philip and Betty lived in retirement in Betty's parent's house (35 Easton Lane) until 1997 – built for Jack in 1939 by Alfie Underwood – with evidence of Jack's painting and decorating business in the workshop round the back! And what of 1 Allens Hill? Happily it is now the home of their daughter Sue with her husband Barry Wagstaff and their two children, Philip, born 1982, and Tara born two years after. We shall pick up their story a little later.

The Wagstaffs and Griggs
Richard Zang decided in 1977, at the ripe old age of 31, to work for himself as an electrician, having had only one boss since he left Wollaston School, who taught him his trade. Today (1995) he is a respected and skilled electrician well known in the district around Bozeat. He started out in 1977 with a small piece of paper with three jobs on it to be done in three weeks. One was to rewire Barry and Sue Wagstaff's house at 1 Allens Hill which he did, "And they don't seem to have had any problems since," added Richard with a smile as we chatted while rewiring power circuits in our Thornton Heath house in London in November 1995. Richard was kept busy in all the factories over this period. "I literally owed them a living," he remembers, as there was a continual need to upgrade and update their electrical systems with increasing demand and advancing technology.

Barry Wagstaff, from a large Northampton family, came to Bozeat looking for work with few qualifications to help him. For a time he worked on the roads as a labourer, straightening the A509 near Olney in 1972, and at this time struck up a friendship with Philip Boswell's daughter, Sue, who had just left Wellingborough High School and was looking for work. "I didn't want her working in my factory," said Philip, "that would be unfair. So I asked Mr Griggs if he could find her a job in his office. 'Of course I can,' he said, 'Send her along on Monday morning.' So I took Sue along on Monday, pushed her into the office at Griggs and said, 'Now it's up to you!'" At the time Barry was living with them and out of work, so Sue found him a job at Griggs. Barry worked all hours learning all the different stages of the trade, the operation of the various machines involved in their production, until he could make a shoe from start to finish. It was soon realised he had a real gift for working with machinery as well as managing shoe production and he began to climb the promotional ladder until he became part of the management team responsible for the development of machinery and mechanisation and establishing new shoe factories as far away as South Africa.

Nowadays, in 1998, Griggs Shoe Company in Wollaston makes all the Dr. Martens shoes having terminated the licence to N.P.S. and has virtually monopolised shoemaking in this area. Co-operatives of all kinds such as N.P.S. and Scott Bader's at Wollaston have done well to survive in the fierce trading markets of today, pioneered over a century ago by such men as Robert Owen and the great social reformers of the Victorian era. (We think of the short life of the Bozeat Co-operative at the turn of that century.) It is an interesting twist to the story that Philip Boswell's son-in-law, Barry Wagstaff, is now working for his rival company Griggs and is currently (1995) helping establish a factory in South Africa making Dr. Martens shoes. Interestingly enough, N.P.S. continues to make Dr. Martens-type shoes identical to the ones they have always made but can no longer do so under this trade name. They sell their product under the brand name *Solovair*. Their output of course is very small compared to Griggs which with its world market makes one pair every 26 seconds and is a multimillion-pound company. Max Griggs is currently investing much of his considerable fortune in realising a dream of making Rushden football club a member of the Premier Division. He has already invested £10 million in upgrading the stadium and there is another £17 million for a new grandstand. But will the business follow the trade's record in the past of boom and bust? After 50 years of virtual peace they have survived and moved into the world market of designer shoes – shoes as a fashion product – not just the brown and black boots and shoes of Philip Boswell's day.

Postscript
On a current poster (1998) we are reminded that Dr. Martens (*Air Wair*) boots were first made on 1st April 1960 – therefore called 1460 boots. Now a million pairs are made each month, 60% are exported and Griggs employ 2,800 people.

Taken from the church tower, this photograph from 1952 shows, left foreground, 'The Mount' in Mile Street, with Pudding Bag Lane behind, and the old school beyond.

Livelihoods

NORTHAMPTONSHIRE,
ON THE BORDERS OF BEDFORDSHIRE AND BUCKINGHAMSHIRE.

Particulars, Plans, & Conditions of Sale
OF
THE BOZEAT ESTATE

In the Parishes of Bozeat, Grendon, and Wollaston, about 10 Miles from the important Town of Northampton, 6 from Wellingborough, 13 from Bedford, 5 from Olney, and 3 from Castle Ashby Station.

A VALUABLE & COMPACT FREEHOLD PROPERTY
WITH THE MANOR OR REPUTED MANOR OF BOZEAT,
Including nearly the whole of the Parish of Bozeat, and comprising about

1972 ACRES
Intersected by good roads, and divided into

7 PRINCIPAL FARMS
OF VARIOUS SIZES, AND
10 ACRES OF WOOD, COMMODIOUS FARM HOUSES, AND CONVENIENTLY ARRANGED HOMESTEADS,

Accommodation, Pasture, Garden, and Building Land,

TWO FULL-LICENSED INNS & PUBLIC HOUSE,
VILLA RESIDENCES,
Shoe Factories, & Grocers, Drapers, & Butchers' Shops, & Premises,

70 CAPITAL COTTAGES, &c.;
OF THE ESTIMATED
Value of £3000 Per Annum.

MESSRS.
STAFFORD AND ROGERS

Have been favoured with instructions from T. REVIS, Esq. to offer this important and valuable Freehold Estate for Sale by Auction,

On WEDNESDAY, JULY 7th, 1886,
AT
THE HIND HOTEL, WELLINGBOROUGH,
AT TWO FOR THREE O'CLOCK IN THE AFTERNOON PRECISELY,
(SUBJECT TO CONDITIONS OF SALE HEREIN)
In Lots as described in the annexed Particulars, or in such other Lots as may be decided upon at the time of Sale.

Particulars with Plans may be obtained of Messrs. J. Garrard & Allen, Solicitors, Olney, Bucks.; E. J. Rickards, Esq., 2, Crown Court, Old Broad Street, London, E.C.; and as to the Land at Wollaston, of Messrs. Jeffery & Haviland, Solicitors, Northampton; or of the Auctioneers, Bedford.

First sale notification of the sale of the Bozeat Estate, to take place 7th July 1886. *(T. Drage)*

CHAPTER 11

Farms and Farmers

Anglo-Saxon origins
"Taking the Celtic Islands as a whole, agriculture was not the preoccupation it became in Saxon and medieval times." (Trevelyan, *History of England*)

In the Iron Age under the Celts we have a picture of herds of wild boar roaming virgin forests. It was the Anglo-Saxons who established the open field system of communal village agriculture (which was to last in our village until the Enclosure Act in 1799) and the large centred townships when they occupied the corn-growing districts of the Celts. The Celts tended to be scattered over the countryside in small family groups, continually subdividing, each group with its 'trev' or 'Hamlet' consisting of light structures of timber or wattle or mud, easily and frequently destroyed in tribal wars. The 'trev' stood in the middle of its enclosed land with the 'waste' beyond. The majority of land high and low was under forest and scrub with river valleys waterlogged and not drained.

Middle Ages
In the reign of Henry II (1154-1189) – see Appendix, Village Diary – the serf or villein was almost the slave of the medieval manor (ours stood just east of our present cemetery). This was before the days of freeholders or yeoman, which came only with the breakdown of both the old manorial system and the feudal economy. The slave who comprised 9% of the population recorded in the Domesday Book had risen to the villein class and he and his Lord shared the Manor and its produce. His cottage was still a hovel, without chimney or glass and sometimes without any separate rooms, just a door, built either of split logs erected side by side in old Saxon fashion (and as the first settlers in Australia!) with mud filling in the oaken framework. The art of baking bricks died with the Romans. The roof was turf or thatch. A small orchard or yard surrounded the cottage.

In the best agricultural districts (East and Middle England) there were large villages of between 2,000 and 3,000 souls grouped around a parish church and manor-house in the middle of an open or 'common' field cut up into a chessboard by hedges but further divided into hundreds of little strips each of an acre or half an acre and separated by 'balks' of grass or footpaths. They must have looked somewhat like our present-day allotments but on a larger scale and all under corn. These strips are still visible in the field by Red Gables Farm and in the fields on the west side of the cemetery, remembering that to the east of the cemetery stood our medieval manor.

Each peasant (freeman or villein) 'owned' several strips (typically 30) scattered throughout the fields within the Lord's domain. In fact there were three separate fields in the Three Field System, and in each of them every man had a share. Each year one of these three huge fields stood fallow, used for grazing cattle, one grew wheat or rye, and one oats or barley. Each field was generally enclosed by hurdles and the practice rotated each year. This system lasted from the Norman Conquest until the great age of the Agricultural Change in the 18th century.

We have a memory of the Three Field System in Bozeat in the oldest actual documents known to exist belonging to Bozeat, two inventories of land left by various people in their wills for the maintenance of the Vicarage dated 1633 and

1636, thanks to an instruction by William Laud on being made Archbishop of Canterbury in 1633. The first, written in ink on a kind of pigskin, reads: "Bozeat this 5th November 1633. Thomas Hull and Thomas Manninge Churchwardens A Terrier ofe all the land and grasse and houses appteyneth and belongeth to the Vicaridge of Bozeat aforesayd." (*Marlow*, p.40) We will give only an excerpt showing how strips belonging to the vicarage are identified as they are adjacent to others and are found scattered in all three fields:

Ditch ffeeld – Item 8 lands lyinge together in Ditches on the North side containinge one Aker and 3 Roods. Mr Wiseman lying on the Est and William Taylor West. Item, one land lying next Dungey leyes on lands the Earl of Kent on both sides.

Woodfield – Item 3 lands lying next the park greene containing 3 Roods William Bettell on the West. ... Item one land with a headland end, butting into Bullwell Slade containing a Rood, Thomas Dobbs west Thos. Bettle east.

Sandwell ffield – Item one half aker lying in the homermost overthrow William Bettell east and Richard ffeary, west. Item, one land lying near the windmill next two ways except one, containing a Rood Mr Childe east Thomas Dobbs west. ... Item one little headland lying near ffulwell, containing half a rood the Earl of Kent, south the ffurlongs North.

It seems that at this time three families were the principal owners of Bozeat: "The Wisemans possessed the Manors", with responsibilities for the Church, "and appointment of the Vicar, also five farms. The Earl of Sussex owned two farms and the Duke of Kent one farm." (*Marlow*, Sheet 5, p.9)

Many village officials were required to run the open system. In 1580 Sir Thomas Cecil was "ordered to repair the commount Pound of Bozeat before the Feast of Pentecost under penalty of 10/s." The Pound was an enclosure where all waif and stray animals were put. The last Pound known to exist was opposite Mr Garrett's, the butcher on the corner of Church Lane and Harrold Road. It is remembered by Tom Partridge-Underwood as a very wide verge on Church Lane, with a large stone in the middle, known as the Pound Stone. This vanished when the new houses were built. The 'Official' in charge of the Pound was called 'The Hayward' whose job it was to guard the crops in the open field from damage by trespassing animals and to impound them, a title which was to become a common surname. Each man did not plough his own land, but it was ploughed by the village plough (which was kept in the church) and divided into strips again afterwards. Village accounts from this period signed by John Wiseman, Lord of the Manor, include: 1688 "paid Wm Dodson for mending the town plow, 6d." and "1696 3/10d for mending the plow and 4d for sharpening the points." (*Marlow*, p.60) "The plough ceremonies (i.e. Plough Monday), held on the first working day after Christmas, were fertility rites, when young men of the village harnessed themselves to a plough which they dragged round the parish, ploughing up the ground before the door of any household which refused to pay a token." (*Duffey*, p.13), an ancient custom still practised in Bozeat within living memory. With the Enclosure the post of "The Hayward" became redundant.

Apart from the fields lay the meadow, possibly down by the brook. It was a common hayfield and common pasture subject to the elaborate rules laid down by the Manor Court, in which freeman and possibly villeins acted as judges and assessors. Astride the brook or millstream stood the watermill (e.g. Hardwater Mill at Great Doddington astride the Nene – 'Harold's Mill' in Domesday) usually owned by the Lord who could charge exorbitant prices to grind the peasants' corn. Windmills were uncommon in medieval times. They are said to have come from the East after the Crusades of Richard I. Our most recent windmill which stood in the gardens of the south side of Roberts Street was a Post Mill bought second-hand and moved there in about 1840 (there is a date cut into the post inside: R.H. 1761, presumably the date it was made). It was a working mill up to 1921 and stood there until it blew down in the storm of 1949. The Lumley Deeds of 1343 refer to 'The Windmill' in Bozeat and there is a 'Millway' in the 18th century so there was also another windmill in Windmill fields at the other end of the village and Marlow writes that, at one time, both were in action. "A reason given by a village humorist for the other one being taken down is that 'there was not enough wind for both of them!'" (*Marlow*, p.83)

Beyond the fields lay the Waste – marshes, heath and forest that once covered the whole island and still covered half of it in the Middle Ages. Horne Wood is a last vestige of our medieval forest. As generation followed generation, as new hamlets and farms sprang up and village fields enlarged and multiplied, heath, fen and woodland shrank and shrank until in Hanoverian times the 'waste' dividing townships had shrunk to a couple of village commons, until, with the 'enclosures', they disappeared altogether (but see Appendix, 'The Bogs').

Enclosures
From Tudor times onwards and earlier, quarrels and litigation compelled more able farmers into compact farms and hedged fields but much of the best land in the Midlands remained 'open fields' until the 18th or 19th centuries (*Trevelyan*), and this was the case at Bozeat. Also enclosure increased production and ultimately population (see population figures in Chapter 16 for Bozeat where its population rises from the 400 at which it had been static for centuries in concurrence with Enclosure at the beginning of the 19th century) after wholesale enclosure in the reign of George III. Such enclosure enabled capital to be poured into agriculture, imposing scientific methods and machinery and stock breeding of special strains of animals, use of certified grasses and root crops putting nourishment back into the soil (e.g. 'Turnip' Townsend) and proper methods of growing grain. By 1820s onwards what is significant is the number of farms and smart new brick and stone houses reflecting the rising status of the 'farmer'. Nevertheless the Census of 1831 showed that one in six was still the old fashioned husbandman working for himself and as late as 1851 two-thirds of farms in Great Britain were under 100 acres in size.

Enclosure may have produced the more prosperous farmer/landed gentry but it also created the landless labourer who once at least in times past had his own strips of land with the rights allotted to him. The alehouse became the only compensation for being a waged worker. Until the new Poor Law of 1834 it made the rural labourer a pauper and discouraged in him thrift and self respect. In the Reform Bill of 1884 the agricultural labourer (and miner) were at last franchised – given rights and political privileges as the establishment of elections and local self-rule in country (rural) districts replaced the patriarchal rule of Justices of the Peace (JPs).

Our Enclosure Act was in 1799. The Map showing the Awards of the New Allotments in 1799 is kept in St Mary's, Bozeat. Each owner received the same amount of land but in blocks instead of strips (see Terrier of 1633 above). Compare the allocation of the various strips to the vicarage and how these have been reallocated and consolidated into one farm, Glebe Farm up Harrold Road. Mavis Holman (née Line) remembers as a girl taking the rent to the vicarage each month when her uncle rented Glebe Farm. (Vicarage tithes were commuted for land in 1798.)

The title given to the Map is: *Describing some of the old Enclosures and Allotments as set out by the Commissioners on the Enclosure of the said Parish.* So now we find some 26+6+21+1=54 acres to comprise Glebe Farm and adjacent to it but nearer the village is some 30 acres which becomes an allotment awarded to Edward Skevington. By far the greatest amount of land is contained in the new Allotments to Earl Spencer: Allotments in Mill Fields 300 acres (where the Post Mill stood), Dungey Leys 200 acres, Dyches field 330 acres, Road Common for tithes 361 acres and Bozeat Wood 121 acres (a wood up towards Grange Farm) which alone gave the Earl some 1,000 acres. Where the new school now stands, and Manor Farm i.e. the area between Dychurch and Harrold, was Earl Spencer's Manorial Estate, hence the name of the farm now owned by the Brown family, dairy farmers from Cheshire. There are some six villagers who own land and were awarded new allotments. Apart from Edward Skevington already mentioned, William Church had two cottages, one house, one garden and an allotment in Mill Field, and Archibald Ruddick an allotment of some 121 acres in Wood Field and John Dexter 21 acres. Richard Orlebar Esq. of Hinwick had a modest three acres.

The Enclosure Act Award describes in paragraph 7: "One public footpath and drift 20 ft. leading out of South end of Dag Lane to allotment awarded to Baroness Lucas for use of their agents, tenants, servants and workfolk" And in paragraph 8: "One public footpath 4 ft. wide leading out of Stone Stile Lane in Southerly direction over allotments to John Dexter, Baroness Lucas, Archibald Roddick, Earl Sussex and Earl Spencer until it enters the parish of Lavendon". Stocken Hollow was the Allotment to Baroness Lucas. One of her descendants, Patie, sister of John Lucas of the giant electronics company lived there with her partner Gerald Lanyon whom she met in St Andrews Hospital, Northampton where both were receiving treatment. Gerald was a real character and a keen beekeeper, and when he died on 7th April 1995 the Lucas family claimed back the land and sold it by auction. At his funeral, our resident village poet, Tony Roche, read one of his poems written in memory of Gerald.

There is a small holding close to Bozeat
and you can bet your bottom dollar
you will find Gerald Lanyon there
The Hermit of Stocken-Hollow.

The place – it's most untidy
one or two things lying around!
The house dark and gloomy
No light and little sound.

Gerald lives there all alone.
looks ill – often in pain
Hobbles around very slowly
on two sticks – and a frame.

*Despite all his misfortunes
one thing is very plain
I've never heard him moan or groan
or ever once complain.*

*He manages to get to and fro
with a helping hand from people.
His sense of humour – and hearty laugh
Can be heard from Bozeat Steeple.*

*So if you think you've got problems
You will do worse than to follow
the example of Gerald Lanyon
The Hermit of Stocken Hollow.*

(At the end Gerald lived there in total chaos with cardboard boxes stacked to the ceiling and no electricity as the rats had chewed through the cables – a lonely man, good-hearted, who craved the company of his fellows.)

Bozeat Estate

In May 1736 Sarah, Duchess of Marlborough, bought the Manor of Bozeat of 1070 acres from Elizabeth Wiseman (whose family had owned it since about 1600) for £13,631. Her second daughter, Lady Anne Churchill, married The Hon John Spencer and the Estate was left to her by the Duchess on her death in 1744. Thus it came into the hands of the Spencer family. "In August 1831 George John, 2nd Earl Spencer sold the Estate for £27,000 part-payment to the Most Reverend Lawrence, Lord Archbishop of Cashel, in Ireland." This was merely a financial investment and as he was a Roman Archbishop, the Church property could not belong to him. The advowson, or right of presentation to the Vicarage of Bozeat, was still retained by Earl Spencer, until it was handed over to the Bishop of Peterborough in 1922. The Estate was passed on from the Archbishop of Cashel to others, until it came to Archdeacon Cotton, who sold it in June 1857 to Mr Thomas Revis. It appears as though Mr Revis bought it largely by mortgage …. "The Royal Exchange Assurance Company bought in most of the mortgage in 1880 and thus owned the larger part of the Estate." (*Marlow*, Sheet 35, p.8)

Sale of the Century

By order of Mr Revis an attempt was made on Wednesday, 7th July 1886 to sell by Auction in Lots the Bozeat Estate at The Hind Hotel, Wellingborough. – 1,972 acres divided into seven principal farms of various sizes and 10 acres of woods, two full licensed Inns and one public house, 70 cottages, Villa residences, shoe factories, Grocers, Drapers, Butchers' shops and premises, estimated value, £3,000 per annum. A Summary of the Sale is as follows:

LOT		
1. The Grange Farm	396	acres
2. Cottage and Land	9	acres
3. The Church Farm	500	acres

4. The Manor Farm	420	acres
5. The East Farm	129	acres
6. The Spring Farm	163	acres
7. The Town Farm	81	acres
8. Wykes' Farm	80	acres
10. Spring Villa, etc.	13	acres
18. White Wall	7	acres
19. Roses Pan	6	acres
20. Claylands.	10	acres
21. 22. and 23. Stoney Piece	15	acres
9. 11. to 17. and 24. to 48.	10	acres
51. Pulleys Barn	1	acre

Some descriptions are interesting:

Rock Villa in the London Road (Olney End) was rented at the time by Henry Drage and Spring Villa, also on the London Road (Wellingborough end), rented by Mr Davidson.

Lot 34 reads: "Four Well-Built & Commodious Cottages, pleasantly situated in the High Street, each having 4 Rooms and Wood Barn, BAKEHOUSE, SHOP, & STOREROOMS, GARDEN GROUND, SMALL YARD, 3 PIGSTIES, containing 8,984 square feet (more or less), Let to Messrs. W. H. Brown, Arthur Harrison, Henry Pettit, and Mrs Timson (excepting two of the pigsties), at a Rental of £21 per annum."

In Lot 3 there is an 'attractive' description of Windmill Hill Field: "There is an excellent Site for a Mansion on the Windmill Hill Field, having a nice elevation, from which there are charming views over Castle Ashby and the surrounding Neighbourhood, and in the centre of a considerable tract of Grass Land, forming almost a natural Park." This is the area over which there is much present contention regarding P14 and gravel extraction.

In Lot 1 'The Grange Farm', the house is described as an "excellent Residence" and the description bears this out and explains why Mr Revis himself resided here: "Substantially built of Stone, with Brick Quoins, and slated: containing Entrance Hall paved with Tesselated Tiles, 3 Reception Rooms, 6 Bedrooms, w.c., 2 Kitchens, Dairy, Cellars and Pantry; occupying a very pleasing position at a convenient distance from the Road and approached by carriage drive under a nice avenue of elms, and surrounded by 50 Acres of Grass Land of park-like appearance, with Flower and Kitchen Gardens and productive Orchard." The style and grandeur of the situation is well above anything else in the Estate, the closest we get to a manor house of the gentry. Jackie Howkins, who with her husband Peter and three children live there and farm the land with Peter's brother Gordon and his family, pointed out the impressiveness of the entry hall with its stained glass and its tessellated tiles that are the same as found in the church.

In the event, only a few lots were sold, e.g. 'Stoney Piece' to Mr Jos. Drage, and most of the Lots were withdrawn as they did not reach the reserve price. "On August 18th, 1909, the rest of the Estate was again put up for sale, 1,710 acres divided into 8 farms. There were certain obligations, and tithes paid in the past by the Lord of the Manor which had to be apportioned out between the several lots and the sale price of those lots was lowered accordingly. This time the whole of the lots were sold for what they would fetch. Mr Hucklesby, of Stamford Hill, London, bought most of the big farms and re-let them. Mr John Fawdry, of Birmingham, bought the Grange Farm. ... Since 1909 there has been no Lord of the Manor, but many owners of different parts of the Parish." (*Marlow*, Sheet 35, pp.8, 9). So after its continual ownership from Countess Matilda to the Latimers then the Wisemans then the Spencers and finally Mr Thomas Revis, who rid himself of it in 1909, 800 years of continuous Manorial Lordship came to an end.

Farmers of the recent past
We have seen how the farms of today evolved through Enclosure and developing technology and knowledge and wealth particularly through the 19th century, but what of the farmers who farmed them? We shall simply list the names of the principal farmers remembering that many villagers had smallholdings and allotments, for example the smallholdings along the south side of Harrold Road which were large enough to make the families like the Tompkins (see Chapter 1) virtually self-sufficient in food with little orchards, corn, pigs, chickens, vegetables, etc.

FARMERS/GRAZIERS IN 1849
(From *Whellan's Directory*)
1. Edward Boddington
2. William Faucett
3. William Faulkner
4. Henry, Mary and John Hensman
5. James Charles Robinson
6. Mary Saunders
7. Richard Skevington

IN 1874
(*Mr Hutchinson of Peterborough*)
1. George Ashwell   Spring Farm
2. Richard Deverall
3. Thos Fancott   Corn Merchant
4. Hy Hutchinson   Church Farm
5. Edward Maxwell,
6. Walter Maxwell   The Grange
7. Joseph Pollard
8. William Sanders

FARMERS 1904
(From *Bennett's Directory, Northamptonshire*)
1. Abbott, H. J.   Manor Farm
2. Bosworth, J.   Ashpole Farm
3. Drage, J.   East Farm
4. Knight, C.   Church Farm
5. Partridge, J.

FARMERS 1911
1. Drage, J.   East Farm
2. Felce, J.   Spring Farm
3. Knight, C.   Church Farm
4. Wallis, O.   London Road

Farmers between the wars (based on the recollections of Dolly Roberts)
Start at the Wrights at Dungee – the most easterly edge of Bozeat. Dungee means 'danger' – possibly as it was a favourite haunt for highwayman (*Marlow*, p.78). I worked for Mr Wright when he was manager of Bozeat Co-op. They had a large orchard and some two acres of land mostly for hay and rented out. Malcolm Drage at Red Gables was always a friend of theirs and grazed his sheep there, especially on their meadow of orchids, to provide nutrient without damaging their delicate structures.

Next towards Bozeat we come to Newlands Farm. It was then called New Barn, just as we called Harrold Road 'New Road'. Before the Second War Longdons farmed it and then in 1947 it was Gordon James' father from Wales.

Next we come to Glebe Farm. It was then farmed by Mr Coles and subsequently by Sid Line, Mavis Holman's uncle. This was owned by the church and rent was paid to the vicar. These are all on the north side of New Road. The other side belonged to the County Council, but this was made into Three Fields Farm, farmed by Keith and Anne Badrick, and the Playing Fields. In the dip in New Road east of Badricks, where a stream used to cross the road, Walter Drage (Glenda's dad) farmed and grew mangelwurzels. From Walter's and right along the south side of New Road to Bozeat it was all allotments. These were really smallholdings, usually half an acre in size, rented from the County Council I suppose. Dad, Uncle (Tompkins) and Bamp had allotments just opposite Glebe Farm and joined them together to give them over an acre. They grew wheat, had 60 hens, kept pigs and grew vegetables and had fruit trees. We were almost self-sufficient in food as a family. Mr Welch and George Pratt also had allotments there and a railway carriage! At the Dychurch end, Will Abbott grew flowers and had fruit trees. Will was the postman and was a wonderful gardener.

Next going down Dychurch we come to East Farm where Cyril and Gwyneth Brown now live. Next to it is Spring Farm, probably so named because the spring on this land provided the flow or jet of water which flowed off its high ground into Town Well just opposite the entrance to Manor Farm where John (Cyril's son) and Marian Brown now live. Before them it was the

John Perkins, lamplighter, taken on the Wollaston Road bridge in 1925.

(*Bozeat School Scrapbook*)

London Road looking south with the thatched cottage at no. 67 in foreground, and beyond that is Mr Cave's undertakers.

Hodgkins. Between the wars Will ("Duckey') Drage lived at Spring Farm. He was our boss and a 'Big Chapel' man. We sang hymns to him for years. He was our Rural Councillor as was Don's father, Percy Roberts. Hedley Brown now lives in Spring Hill Farm. The Browns are dairy farmers from Cheshire and now run all these three farms – East, Spring Hill and Manor Farms together.

Then coming to the middle of Bozeat, opposite the schoolgirls' gate to the old school in Camden Square was Townsend Farm farmed by Mr Drage (Ted Drage's father).

Then next to the Methodist Church (Big Chapel) Mr Howard farmed the land. The steep lane to his farm is still there alongside the Church and leads now to the Bradleys' house at the back. He delivered milk and sold cream and fresh butter.

Between the wars the thatched house where Barry and Anne Fletcher now live at 67 London Road was a farmhouse where Mr Howe lived. Then it was owned by Will Warner who married a Howe (Betty Warner's grandfather-in-law). At the end of the nineteenth century the only house beyond the farmhouse was Cave's the undertakers before the shoe factories arrived.

At the southern end of the parish is Grange Farm where 'Old Revis' lived – as Dolly's dad used to call him. This was Mr Revis the last Lord of the Manor who sold Bozeat Estate in 1909. Then it was farmed by Mr Fawdry who used to drive a carriage and pair, and then the Howkins farmed it for three generations.

Then up Easton Lane we come to Slype [then spelled Slipe] Farm then owned by Mr Simco who brought the milk round in a churn with a two-cans measure which was silver-coloured with a brass handle. The Matchams bought the farm and

The Flat, London Road looking north from the bottom of Hensmans Lane towards the Chequers with Spring Vale Farm on left. Note the oil street lamps. The lamplighter appointed by the Parish Council until the arrival of electricity in 1925 was Mr. John Perkins (see page 133). He would spend the morning polishing the glasses and filling and trimming the lamps, carrying a small ladder. Lighting them at dusk could be a difficult job in windy weather. He was latterly paid 16/- a week.

demolished it and built the large new building which is there now. They strongly opposed the new bypass as it would affect them most.

Coming back along Easton Lane to the London Road we have Church Farm, next to the church and farmed then by Mr Knight. Pat Silsby worked for the Knights, a wonderful character, as did his two sons Harry and Bill Silsby, who until 1999 lived side-by-side in the two bungalows at 2A and 2B Council Street, sharing their marvellous village tales which only they could tell in the broad Bozeat accent of yesteryear. Mr Roberts then had the farm and after him his son Raymond who sold the house to David Harrison in 1995 but he still runs a successful animal feed business situated in Windmill Field which has won a Queen's Award for Industry. Mr Everest had hens and apples where now the Downeys live at 6 Church Walk. His daughter Miri Everest played the organ at Little Chapel after Warren Drage (Don's Uncle).

Northward along the London Road almost opposite Pear Tree we come to Spring Villa and Spring Vale Farm. This was farmed by Mr Nottingham between the wars and before him Mr Babs and after the Nottinghams we had Nick and Christine Hedges who eventually sold it into private hands in 1997 to two doctors I believe.

Finally at the northern end of the estate we have Red Gables Farm farmed by the Drages – where I spent every evening from 1933-40 with my friend Winsome. I remember her sister Alison being born there. Dolly nostalgically considers it her second home.

I say "finally" but we should not forget Wykes Farm at the top of Allens Hill. It was then farmed by Arthur Smart, a big chapel man and a relative of Haydn Smart, recently rural dean of Wellingborough, and then it was farmed by the Holts until it was sold into private hands in 1997.

Farming Today

Farmers of the 1990s

Two headlines in the *Farmer's Weekly* this summer (1998) read: "Dire Harvest and prices at rock bottom," and "Just when you thought it couldn't get any worse." True we have not had the best of summers with it being cold and wet through to the end of June. But then we shouldn't forget (how could we!) that a succession of cold and wet summers in the late 1830s provoked the Bishop of Hereford to ask the Prime Minister in 1838 to issue a national form of harvest thanksgiving, presumably to persuade Providence to produce better weather, but Melbourne refused!

But it isn't only our weather that is against our farmers. Along with the above headlines there is an editorial in the same weekly which reads: "The last thing British farming needs is more food scares. The industry, reeling from the effects of BSE, is having to weather a catalogue of horrors, all stemming mainly from the strength of sterling. And the weather has been unkind to grass and grain harvests in many places. Never in living memory have so many things conspired against British farmers.... News that rats reacted badly to a diet of genetically engineered potato, and that the Crohn's disease might be linked to drinking milk were not what the farmers wanted to hear."

Business is bad. There is a crisis in the pig sector, where prices to the farmer have slumped to about half the cost of production and, in August, Scotland's biggest pig farmer filed for bankruptcy. Reports indicate that something like 2,500 dairy farmers are going out of business each year. The recent Hampshire Farming Study showed that 46% of farmers will retire in the next 10 years and half are without a family successor. The bleak truth is that on these farms, sons and daughters have decided there is no future in farming.

More depressing still is the evidence of the Rural Stress Information Unit that levels of suicide are high and rising within the farming community and the evidence of the Royal Agricultural Benevolent Institution of countless cases of poverty and destitution, particularly on small upland farms among our 71,000 hill farmers, paints an alarming picture of the future of farming which has for centuries lain at the heart and been such a proud feature of our national way of life.

At the end of the millennium who are our farmers and how are they managing, those who play such an important part still in our village way of life? Those still farming in the 1990s are as follows:

Badrick, Keith and Anne *Three Fields Farm.*
Brown, Cyril and Gwyneth, Hedley and Dorothy, John and Marian *Manor Farm* incorporating *East Farm and Spring Hill Farm.*
Drage, Graham and Malcolm *Red Gables Farm.*
Green, George and Joyce *White House Farm.*
Hedges, Nick and Christine *Spring Vale Farm* (sold 1997, now private residence).
Holt, Len and Margaret *Wykes Farm* (sold 1997, now private residence).

FARMS AND FARMERS

Howkins, Gordon and Judy, Peter and Jackie Howkins *Grange Farm*.
James, Gordon and Margaret *Newlands Farm*.
Matcham, Ronald and Brenda *Slype Farm* (now in 1998 a private residence).

Let us visit four farms and hear what life is like for the farmers of this generation:

THREE FIELDS FARM

Keith Badrick is a pig farmer from Radlett, Watford. He then moved to farm at Hertford. Northampton County Council who owned much of the land to the south of Harrold Road as we have seen, combined three fields here to make a farm in 1974 of just under 100 acres and Keith showed an interest in renting it. They could have built farm buildings and a 'kit-bungalow' but Keith was having none of it: "I'm not going to live in a shed!" Eventually they built him a proper bungalow. Before the building was complete he had to travel 60 miles each day from Hertford and remembers having to make silage that first autumn. He remembers too that the Tompkins worked the fields before him as smallholdings. (i.e. Dolly Roberts' dad and uncle). "There were apple trees then I remember." Keith's is the newest farm in Bozeat and one of the three farms left still milking (1996). He has some sheep, fattens cattle and sows a variety of crops, diversification being the safety net these days, but no pigs! His land stretches along to the Playing Fields (also once owned by the County Council) and behind them. He works the farm with his wife Anne and their three daughters Hazel, Jennifer and Catherine.

NEWLANDS FARM

"My father John James came from Shropshire in 1946 with two horses, borrowed a tractor and started to farm this land," said Gordon James with half a smile as we stood in one of his fields on a September morning in 1998. His father came from generations of dairy farmers from Monmouthshire in mid-Wales. "And dairy farmers we still are."

The farm John bought in 1946 was 108 acres. When Bozeat Estate was sold by Mr Revis in 1909, Mr Hucklesbury of Stanford Hill, London bought most of the big farms including this land. In 1910 he established the "Freehold Farm Situate and known as New Barn Farm" and built the Farm House in that

Newlands Farm. (*Bozeat School Scrapbook*)

same year where the James' now live. But, as Gordon showed me, the barns are much older, part stone and part brick, placing both buildings in the time of the Enclosure in 1799 where we have similar stone barns to brickwork from the early part of the 1900s and the end of the 19th century. (Is this barn[s] new enough and significant enough to give the new freehold its name of Newlands Farm?) It seems likely that cattle have been grazed on this land for some time and there is a memory of old giant shire horses being put out to graze here in the past.

Gordon's wife Margaret, a nurse but much involved in the farm, especially with regard to lambing, as well as bringing up a family of four daughters and one son, showed me the history of the Freehold from that date:

1.	1910	Abstract of Title
2.	29th October 1910	Conveyance F. J. Hucklesby to H. J. Abbott
3.	3rd November 1910	Mortgage H. J. Abbott to A. Rumball and G. H. Edwards
4.	23rd May 1912	Reconveyance A. Rumball and H. Edwards to H. J. Abbott
5.	29th September 1917	Conveyance H. J. Abbott to Mrs E. L. Kilsby
6.	22nd December 1937	Conveyance Mrs E. L. Kilsby and others to F. Heginbothan
7.	15th March 1938	Conveyance F. Heginbothan to R. Crowther
8.	14th February 1944	Conveyance R. Crowther to G. H. Purser
9.	1st March 1946	Conveyance G. H. Purser to J. James
10.	1946	Supplemental Abstract of Title
11.	18th March 1946	Mortgage to Midland Bank Ltd with receipt endorsed 31.3.65

As we stood in the seven acre field above, north of the house, Gordon pointed out the ridge-and-furrow system. "See how the ridges are made to drain the land, roughly east/west down to the brook. Without drainage this field would be waterlogged for much of the year and unusable. When we ploughed it we found an old tile drainage system – medieval? Roman? Who knows? These ridges may well be medieval. You know of course that a new ridge-and-furrow system was dug during the 20 years of the Napoleonic Wars at the beginning of the 19th century (I didn't!). When the French blockaded our ports then we had to grow all our own food, so every field had to be used. So you have to distinguish between Napoleonic ridge-and-furrow and medieval. This I think is medieval as is that at Red Gables I believe. The system followed the lie of the land or runs north/south (to dry out the furrows quickest). Same with the blockades in 1939 and the Second World War when we were producing only 20% of the food we needed at home!"

"After the first refrigerated ship in the later 1800s there was a slump in farming as cheap produce, meat and so on, flooded in from abroad. No wonder they could not sell the Bozeat Estate in 1886, when the asking price for the farms etc could not be reached!"

Pointing out the ridges and furrows Gordon started to explain how an acre is a day's work ploughing and equals one furlong (furrow long) times one chain. "These ridges are about half or a third of a chain wide." (Two bullocks or horses pulling the plough?) "That's how we still measure things in the farming world working on the land, with your body or simple implements such as rods and chains or a day's work. My forearm is 18 inches and the width of my hand 4 inches – we still measure in hands and I still pace out my fields to measure the amount of spray I need to use – one pace equals one yard – and my foot is one foot or near it! Can you remember your measures vicar? 4 rods = 1 chain, 10 chains = 1 furlong, 8 furlongs = 1 mile and 640 acres = one (square) mile. We still think in acres!"

"Of course the Enclosure changed farming. We used the old Norfolk Four Field System – one field of wheat, one of barley, one of root crops, turnips etc – they're easy to farm, and one of seeds – that's grasses and clover to put something back into the soil. That would be impossible on the Open Field System."

"The farm is 108 acres but we farm 250 acres by renting land. 40 acres from the Wrights at Dungee for example. We did rent 100 acres of Northamptonshire County Council land on the other side of Harrold Road but we lost the tenancy when they made a farm out of the three fields, Three Fields Farm which Keith Badrick now farms, 93 acres for him and 7 for the Bozeat Playing Fields."

In 1969 John James died and Gordon inherited the farm. "It's all mechanised today. We have 90 cows (for milking) and about 220 lambs a year (starting at Christmas), with 60 acres of maize (sweetcorn) or wheat mainly for cattle feed, much of it put down for silage." Gordon had just finished concreting over an area for a new silo to store cattle feed, with hay and silage everywhere in and around his barns and a machine for collecting waste and squirting it back onto the land, and a new machine that takes feed from the silo or silage and delivers the correct amount to each animal.

Gordon runs the whole enterprise almost single handed with the help of his son Haydn, recently graduated from Agricultural College, and his wife Margaret and in earlier years his daughters, Catherine, Elizabeth, Eleanor and Sarah now in their twenties and mostly away from home.

"You must see our litter of six puppies before you go – border collies, that's all we use on the farm. And we don't have piped water either. Once there were two wells but now we get all our water from a borehole 100 foot deep. That's why your cup of tea tasted so good!"

MANOR FARM

Cyril and Gwyneth Brown were sitting either side in their low-beamed fireplace, now occupied by an imitation wood electric fire! As usual Gwyneth warned me to watch my head on the heavy beams of the low ceilings as she welcomed me into East Farm House one late September afternoon as already the dark evenings were beginning to draw in.

"This house is the oldest – from the 1660s – and David Hall says the far (south) end is probably a hundred years older, from counting the rings in a trunk of wood," says Gwyneth as we sit down.

So why did the Browns come here? Thomas Hodgkinson, Cyril's mother's brother, his uncle, (their graves are in the cemetery just to the right as you go in the only vault there) owned Manor Farm – he bought it when Bozeat Estate was put up for sale in 1909. He wanted his brother-in-law, Cyril's father, John Brown to come south and help him farm it. John was a farm manager at Aspry in Cheshire, a dairy farmer. He was from a large family. Cyril has 32 first cousins on his father's side! John decided to come but his two sons, Cyril aged 16 and brother Hedley hated moving and leaving all their friends, as Cyril (now aged 81) remembers the experience. That was in 1933. "Then you could buy land for £10 an acre. The cottage across from us in Dychurch sold for £65 in 1909." Thinking back to those early days, Cyril continued, "I remember farmers were up early to get their animals to the Town Well before the rest. Then it had a low wall around it, like a cattle trough, and the water came from the spring from the high ground behind it. The well had a sort of cover over it I remember." "And the well never dried up," added Gwyneth, "until they brought electricity and then the spring never flowed again!" We presume that this is how Spring Hill Farm on the high ground behind the well got its name. Earlier, this waterlogged ground may have been the site of Marshes Manor referred to in 1556

(*Marlow*, p.9). There are many references to the Town Well for its repair and lettings over the centuries. (*ibid* pp.60,70)

In 1940 John Brown bought East Farm and then in 1954 he bought Spring Farm from William Drage. This gave them a total of 550 acres. In 1997 they bought two fields in Wollaston from their owner Miss Watts from whom they had rented them since 1942. In their heyday in the 50s they had a herd of 413 Friesian milking cows and young. In fact in 1949 the Browns carried away most of the prizes for their herd in the Northampton Show and in 1947 their Friesians were Second in all England and Wales. Today they have all gone and there is no more milking. Instead they have a herd of 120 pedigree Angus and grow wheat, rape and beans, the latter to feed the cattle, and Whitworths the flour people in Wellingborough still take the wheat. They have even stopped lambing as there was so much harassment of the animals from domestic dogs.

This year (1998) they have planning permission to build a small estate of houses in front of the Manor Farm House where Cyril's Son John and his wife Marian and daughter Emma now live. The new estate incorporates the old barn, one of whose stones has the date 1805. We remember that on the Enclosure Map of 1799 this area is designated the Manorial Estate. Presumably from here Earl Spencer, who lived at Althorp some 20 miles away, planned to manage his Estate. There is still a small two-storey building to the south of the farm house which appears to date from this period and was used as a farm/estates office. Perhaps the large barn was erected at this time to provide storage centrally for farm implements, produce and animals. During the Second World War the office housed Italian prisoners of war sent to help work the land and produce food, one of whom was Salvatori Bovenzi. After the war there was a Ukrainian refugee and his wife who came to live there and work on the farm, at a time when the Browns employed about seven farm hands, several living in the cottages behind East Farm in Dychurch. Cyril recalls how the Ukrainians' baby died in a tragic accident while they were living there when it rolled off the table into a bath of scalding hot water on the floor below. "I was one of the first called there after it happened. I remember the wife because she had gold fillings in her teeth which glistened in the sun. One day the two of them went shopping to Wellingborough. She was wearing a fur coat. The story goes that when they got to Woolworths she handed her fur coat to her husband, went into Woolworths and was never seen again."

Manor Farm House is also a mystery. It dates from the late 1700s and is long and narrow with its floors on different levels, particularly upstairs which is like a rabbit warren in places. If our theory is correct and because it is next to the Estates Office, one wonders if it was not used as accommodation for those working on the estate and not living in the village, with a large communal kitchen and washing/domestic area at the north end which is still used as such today.

Cyril's wife, Gwyneth Austin as was, came from a family with a long association with Bozeat. Her grandfather Luther Austin had White House Farm on the Olney Road until 1933 when it went to his son Luther Stanley Austin. Eventually he sold it to Mr Deakin. Her great-grandfather Levi Austin had an outhouse for making shoes in Wollaston and the business grew until the family built the big shoe factory in Eastfield, now Eastfield Road, which is now owned by Griggs. Her father also farmed at Greenfield Farm at Strixton and then Gwyneth's brother farmed it. Gwyneth and Cyril met when she came as a land girl to work on the Browns' farm in the Second World War in the desperate drive to feed the nation.

RED GABLES FARM (through the life of Malcolm Neil Eyles Drage, 1927-1998)
Malcolm was born on The Ides of March, 15th March 1927, at Red Gables Farm, the same day as his twin sister Kathleen. The story goes that when his second presumed 'child' was due to be born, his father Cyril, having no telephone of course, arranged with his sister and parents living in Hope Street to signal the arrival by standing outside the front of the farmhouse (his sister living at the top of Hope Street) and waving his arm, the left for a boy and the right for a girl. We can imagine his sister's consternation when she saw him frantically waving both arms!

In one sense Malcolm was never to leave Red Gables. He was born there, he lived and worked there as man and boy and died there peacefully in his bed just 11 days short of his 71st birthday. In this restless age with its demands for change and progress, we must ask ourselves what advantages we have over this good man in terms of life fulfilment?

What was the history of the farm before Malcolm's arrival? Bill Thompson was born at Red Gables soon after the house was built, just after the turn of that century. At his request, his ashes were scattered on its land when he died. His grandfather Mr Welch was a tenant farmer there when it was owned by one of the Oxford Colleges, All Souls, just as neighbouring lands at Strixton were owned until recently by the Duchy of Lancaster (i.e. the Crown).

In 1918, the farm was bought by Frank Drage who also owned the Drage Shoe Factory at the bottom of Hope Street. In 1921 Cyril Drage, who was previously a baker working for Mr Smith whose bakery was where the Spar shop now is in Camden Square (note the brick bakehouse at the back), became the tenant farmer at Red Gables. Cyril had served in the Sixth Northamptonshire Regiment in the First World War and was awarded the Military Medal for his bravery at Westhock Ridge. Cyril's brother Neil lived at Arch Villa (now the Paper Shop and where the Drage Shoe Company had its origins) and started a taxi business there. Neil had a son Barry who currently (1998) has a television repair shop in Wollaston and a daughter Sheila who married Salvatori Bovenzi, the Italian prisoner of war who worked for the Browns, and she still lives at the top of Hope Street.

Cyril's cousin was Walter Drage who lived at 2 Hope Street who with his brother Ernest started the first bus service to Wellingborough in the 1930s. Walter is also famous for having had five daughters, Glenda, Mary, Gladys, Jean and Ruth, and Glenda still lives at the family home, married to Robert Welch. Beyond this, the complex web of Drage relationships in Bozeat becomes almost impossible to disentangle!

Farming in the years between the First and Second World Wars was very different from today. Most farms produced mixed crops with small dairy herds, pigs and hens. Milk was delivered from the farms direct or by a local roundsman and served directly out of the churn into the customer's jug. Ploughs were horse drawn or later by small low power tractors. Harvesting usually started with the farm worker cutting round the edge of the field with a scythe which made space for the binder to get to work. The binders, which were pulled by horse or by tractor, shot out bundled-up sheaves of straw and ripe corn which were stacked by hand into shocks then carted away to be built up into stacks in the rickyard. In the autumn a contractor went round the farms with his steam engine and threshing tackle to thresh out the corn to complete the harvest. Much changed during the Second World War when it became essential to raise farm production to the absolute maximum to avoid national starvation. There was no electricity until the late twenties and all water had to be drawn from the wells until quite recently.

Cyril married Phyllis Scouse in 1921 and they had six children. The eldest was Winsome who married a young American airman, Eddie, stationed at Podington during the war who now lives in America. Then there were twins Kath and Malcolm born in 1927 and, after a gap of seven years, remarkably twins again with the birth of Alison (who married Dick Botterill, the shoe manufacturer's son) and Ian and then finally Graham.

Malcolm was twelve when the Second World War broke out and he went straight to work on the farm after leaving Bozeat School at the age of 14 or 15 at a time when feeding the nation was a desperate responsibility for those working on the land. And Malcolm would have been only 17 when 22-year-old Lt. John Ahern from Baltimore, Maryland, crashed his crippled Flying Fortress, still loaded with bombs, in the field behind their farmhouse, the explosion creating a large crater which became a venue for admirers and souvenir hunters for years to come. For his bravery and for avoiding the village, Lt Ahern was posthumously awarded the Purple Heart.

As a young man Malcolm played football for the village team and joined the AYPA, the Anglican Young People's Association, started by Vicar Powell, which used to meet in the barn behind the old vicarage (and which still stands today). And it was Vicar Powell who persuaded him to come on to the Parish Church Council at the tender age of 19 in 1946 and he had been on it ever since, a period of faithful service to St Mary's spanning half a century.

In the very demanding seven-day-week profession of a farmer, particularly one with a dairy herd to milk and visits to Northampton Market to sell calves etc, a welcome interlude from the daily routine was to yarn with the fraternity and keep up with the farming gossip. And such human intercourse was the lifeblood of such a sociable and warm-hearted person as Malcolm. Small wonder he also enjoyed the regular dances in the old Church Hall which, I understand, were lively social occasions. And he was best man to Gordon James at Newlands Farm and has ever been a close friend, if not part of, the James family. Few of us could resist his warm smile and friendly welcome and you always felt better for his wave and a chat. Sister Alison remarked that he seemed to know more about the village than anyone for he always had time to catch up with the news, with Graham holding the fort back at the farm! And of course his egg deliveries became a village event we all miss. "Another dry summer," we agreed as Malcolm delivered our eggs on Wednesday, 11th July in 1996, as he had done every Wednesday for six years, making every Wednesday better for his visit. "Still the hay is not bad and there seem to be no restrictions from Anglian Water. We are on mains water now of course, ever since the bypass was built (1989). Before that we got all our water from the farm well but that dried up when they built the bypass. We complained but we would have had to take it through the courts and then most probably it would have made no difference. These people have all the answers but the fact remains that building the bypass dried up our well! – and now we have to use mains water!" concluded Malcolm with that wry smile of his. Such incidental conversations were repeated a thousand times over, and always with that philosophical and reflective mood that made them so congenial. I remember once how he and Graham were chatting outside their farmhouse while their inquisitive cows licked my motor scooter clean, how they looked over to the bypass and said. "A petrol company wanted to build a petrol station on our land over there and would have given us a lot of money but that would have spoilt the view and the countryside wouldn't it!" So much for the values of our materialistic world.

I don't think Malcolm ever had a holiday and there is no memory that he ever went to the doctors. There is little time to be ill if you are a farmer even at 70! I gather he did take a trip to America some 20 years ago one Christmas to see Winsome and her family and I understand, such was the affection generated that they are still asking, "When is Malcolm coming back?" No social occasion, no tombola stall at the vicarage garden party will be quite the same again without him. His warm sense of humour and winning smile will always be sorely missed.

Postscript

Since Malcolm died his 500 chickens have had to be sold and milking has come to an end as Graham bravely keeps the farm going with help from the rest of the family. It was proposed that the £2,500 given in his memory should go towards the millennium window in St Mary's depicting the life and faith of the village of which he was so much a part. This window was finally installed on 2nd August 2000 and dedicated by the Bishop of Brixworth on 3rd September.

GLEBE FARM

Glebe Farm is the first farm on the left you come to as you leave the village up Harrold Road. Arthur Coles rented the farm until he retired in the 1930s. Thereafter from 1936/7 Sid and Bernard Lines rented it from the Church until 1956, the year before their sister Loreen married Ted Drage the village carpenter whose father rented and farmed Town Farm.

Glebe Farm was farmed by Mr Holbrook, and was then bought by Dr Ronald Carpenter whose practice was in Wellingborough. It is one of those curious twists of history that his wife Mollie was the sister of my wife's guardian (whom she knew as Auntie Jessie) with whom she lived as a little girl while her parents were missionaries in China. Auntie Jessie was a well rounded, bubbly, vivacious lady as I remember her from our courting days when she lived at Westcliff-on-Sea where she had looked after old Dr Oliver Bartlett, founder of the Bible Church Missionary Society (B.C.M.S.) and my wife Audrey stayed with her as a child in the 1940s. Later (1960s) Auntie Jessie moved to Sidmouth and lived with Dr Carpenter's sister Mary as two spinster companions. Auntie Mary was more placid and quieter in character.

The Carpenters had three children, Sally who became a Sister at Exeter Hospital, and David who was the farmer, and Christine. Ted Drage remembers how he and David enjoyed a practical joke and how his father would mix his medicine with his farming! "Here comes Dr Carpenter for some drugs for his sheep!" – they would say at Wellingborough Cottage Hospital.

Ronald had been a missionary in India. The Carpenters lived at Farndish in the 1960s before coming to Glebe Farm. Ted remembers helping do up the house for them there when he was working for Tom Cave. "They had to have nothing but the best. I remember that everything had to be Formica then. Arnold Dobbs reconstructed the house and they had a swimming pool from the Frosts at the Garden Centre. His father was a vicar." Audrey Brook from Easton Maudit remembers dining with the Carpenters at Farndish with her husband Eric, how it was Dr Carpenter who did the cooking and how Eric would comment that the food was very rich, "Too much cream!"

Dr Carpenter sold Glebe Farm to Mr Reeves a farmer from Hinwick. Judith Line and her husband managed the farm for him in the 1970s and she remembers that Dr Carpenter did much renovation work there. She loved the farming life and mixed it with her professional work as a teacher, getting up at five for lambing and milking before going off to school! Today (1996) Mr Reeves' daughter Heather uses the farm and stables, etc. as a Riding School with much of the land rented out to other farmers including Gordon James at Newlands Farm next up the Harrold Road. It is currently (1998) a thriving equestrian centre offering riding instruction and experience as well as stabling for horses.

Taken from the Red Lion Hill, looking at the Cross Keys Inn, with a smart group of schoolchildren and an interesting motorbike.

CHAPTER 12

Inns, Innkeepers and Beer

Inns and Innkeepers
Written by Norman Palmer (edited and updated by Philip Bligh)

How did they originate?
Inns were always associated with roads and those who travel. Strictly an Inn is a house where travellers are provided with anything necessary for their journey – refreshment and overnight accommodation. They are required to have a licence once taxable liquor is sold.

An innkeeper was obliged to accommodate anyone entering his house provided that person had the money and was of good character. Inns seem to have originated in the hostelries provided by monasteries for travellers and pilgrims on the road. Presumably the modern equivalent is the hotel with a bar.

There is another type of establishment called the tavern, victualling house and later beer house. It differs from the inn in not providing overnight accommodation and so its main purpose was to provide drinking on the spot, the pub being the modern equivalent. Taverns probably had their origin in the Church House. This was often a brew house for the brewing of ale for the various feasts of the Church, of which there were many. At one time, these, along with many other kinds of village events, took place in the people's part of the church, the nave, the chancel being reserved for the priest and his activities, i.e. the Mass. A poem of 1671 entitled "Ex-ale-tation" goes:

> *The Churches much owe, as we all knowe,*
> *For when they be drooping and ready of fail,*
> *By a Whitsun or Church-Ale up again they go,*
> *And owe their repairing to a pot of good ale.*

Church ales not only raised money for church repairs, etc. but also for charity. The Church House often housed paupers and the elderly, before there were workhouses (our workhouse is built into the east wall of the church yard, Lavender Cottage, 4 Mallows Yard). There is evidence we had a Church House, the 1605 All Souls College Map of their lands in Bozeat shows land for the upkeep of the 'Towne House', which could not have been a workhouse as these had their origin a century later. Church Houses often became taverns and in some cases inns.

Inns and taverns had to be licensed in the reign of Henry VIII (1509-1547) to sell ale which was brewed on the premises. Many people brewed their own ale but a licence was required when it was sold to the public, i.e. in the 'public house'. In the Middle Ages brewers were under the control of the Lord of the Manor and could be required to pay a rent for selling ale. Inns and taverns showed their function to an illiterate people by a pole, or a bush on the end of a pole. Then came the inn signs which proclaimed their special purpose and buildings built for that purpose began to appear in the 1600s.

Joseph Macknis – Innkeeper and Churchwarden
Before the formation of Parish Councils in 1887, the village was governed by an

elected body called the Vestry. On this body amongst others (see later) were two constables and thankfully we still have their accounts for the latter part of the 17th century to give us a glimpse of life in our village in those days. Sadly we do not have them for the period of the Commonwealth under Oliver Cromwell, 1648-60.

Accounts for the year 1685 include the item: "Pd Jo Mackanesse ffor lodging two women and two children ffrom Sat'day night to Monday morning 1s 4d". And for the same year: "Pd Joseph Mackandes ffor Lodging foure Seaman, 6d" Whilst in 1673/4: "Spent on a merchant man att Joseph Makines 8d."

Clearly, Joseph Makeness (or Makness or Macknis), whose family was known in Finedon in the 15th century, was an innkeeper in our village. Joseph was a Christian name of the family used in Finedon, there being another Joseph there about the same date in 1693. Not only was he an innkeeper, but he was a Churchwarden, the earliest known, for his name is carved on our old Church Chest as 'J Macknis CW 1686'. We still have three pieces of a remarkably well preserved headstone to a grave which tells us that a Joseph Macknis buried a son, also Joseph, in 1709 aged 27. He himself was buried as a widower on 15th November 1719, age unknown. Being illiterate, as so many were at that time he had an interesting way of putting his mark – 'I M'. He clearly had a contemporary who was another innkeeper, and also sometime churchwarden, for we read in the accounts for 1687/8: "Paid Tho Tombs and Jo Mackanesse ffor bread and beere when the towne plow went out. 9s 1d." What this actually means can be seen from an inclusion in the accounts for a hundred years later where for January 1787 we read: "Joseph Partrig for going with Town Plow 2s-6d." As the date is January this probably refers to Plough Monday, the Monday following the end of the 12th night (6th January) and the beginning of the year's festivities. It was the custom of farmers' boys to dress up with bright ribbons over their clean smocks and dance in procession round the village, singing, joking and shaking collecting boxes. Most people contributed money or drinks but if the owner of any substantial house failed to pay up, then the lads would plough up the ground outside his front door! (see Chapter 11). The village plough must have been heavy and there were memories (via Mr Kirby, school teacher) that it was kept in the Parish Church when not in use. [*Duffy*, p.13, says that such plough ceremonies were fertility rites carried out by young men in the village, early pagan observances absorbed into the Christian calendar.]

Besides Thomas Tombs and Joseph Maknis there was another innkeeper referred to in the Constables' Accounts, Thomas Hull, at various times between 1670 and 1694 e.g. 1672/3: "spente upn A man and his wife 9 children and one horse At Tho hulles 1s 10d." and again 1694/5: "It (item) paid to Tho Hull for 5 travellers with a pass from Saturday night to Munday morning 2s.6d." It is possible that another innkeeper, Thomas Davey, may have followed Thomas Hull, for there is no reference to the latter after 1694, whereas Thomas Davey appears as one in the Constable Accounts from 1694 to 1699. So it appears that there were at least three inns in Bozeat in the last decades of the 17th century, all actively involved in providing accommodation for travellers of all sorts (including soldiers, etc.).

THE RED LION
How long a building has been on this site is unknown but from what has been said there may have been one for hundreds of years, from the 1660s or back even to the Middle Ages. The Red Lion was used as a badge of John of Gaunt, the powerful son of Edward III (1327-77), but any link between the two seems tenuous.

INNS, INNKEEPERS AND BEER

Early view of High Street with Red Lion on right and Cross Keys on left, showing the Berrill-style cross hatch herringbone stone on the Cross Keys. The thatched building just visible down High Street is the old Co-op. (J. Darker)

The earliest mention of a brewer in Bozeat is in 1670: "spent at Will Glover on a man and his wife 1s-6d." (Constable Accounts). In the 1970s Peter Haggar found in Easton Maudit one of his trade tokens – locally minted small change to be used at his hostelry, with 'William Glover' on one side and on the other side 'of Bozeat, His halfpenny 1686'. So William Glover was an innkeeper in Bozeat in 1686. He appears as such in the Constable Accounts from 1670-85 and a man of this name is on the jury lists for Bozeat in 1657. Other examples from the Accounts are:

1671/2: "ffor lodging a woman and her daughter att Will Glouver. 1s.0d."
1672/3: "Spent upon a man and his wife 2 children 2 nights at William Gluver 1s.6d."

N.B. People who came in need to the Village Constable were passed on to the innkeeper and paid for out of parish rates. *Paupers* could not claim right of settlement except in the parish of birth. For such reasons there were always *travellers* and *passengers* passing through our village. So we read: "for straw to lodge passengers." (Accounts 1678/9) – probably provided in an outbuilding.

Palmer makes a 'calculated guess' that William Glover was the innkeeper of the Red Lion. He is last mentioned in the Constable Accounts in 1685 and Thomas Tombs appears in them first in 1687 as innkeeper i.e. possibly taking over the Red Lion from Glover. This Thomas Tombs may be the widower buried in 1725. It must have been his son, also Thomas, who took over the inn and who married Jane Addis in 1753. Thomas Tombs (the second) was buried in 1763 and described in the Burial

Trade tokens of William Glover, an innkeeper in Bozeat, dated 1668 – found at Easton Maudit. (*N. Palmer*)

Registers as 'Publican'. The Church Warden Accounts describe his widow as continuing: "Jan(e) Tom hor Bill 4s-8d." Mrs Toms' bills occur from 1770-79. Then on Sept. 29th 1780 Jane Toms, widow, married Joseph Douglas of Easton Maudit. The Douglas family were farmers and butchers at Easton Maudit. Mr Douglas is mentioned in the Bozeat Churchwardens Accounts, the Vestry, (forerunner of the Parish Council) having a "town meeting at Mr Duglas".

Every village was governed by its Vestry – the parochial parliament consisting of officers elected by those who paid the rates. The poor had no voice until the coming of Local Government in 1895. They would elect their legal officers: two Churchwardens, concerned with the fabric of the church, two Overseers of the Poor, for under Elizabethan Law each parish was responsible for its paupers, and two Constables who were concerned not only with law and order but also for carrying out the decrees of central government. Two Overseers of the Highways were elected to be responsible for the state of the roads. They met monthly in one of the inns, in our village alternately in the Chequers and the Red Lion. Needless to say the innkeepers were very often on the Vestry!

Mr Douglas then disappears. Jane Douglas was buried at Bozeat on 7th October 1794, whilst 'Mr' (that word is only used in a burial register for a leading parish personality) Joseph Douglas was buried at Easton Maudit just over 3 weeks later on 30th October 1794. We do not know their ages. However Ann, the daughter of Thomas Tombs and Jane, married John Gough (born 1761) in 1785 and he was buried in 1799 aged 42. It seems likely that John Gough took over his stepfather's inn from 1787, for from that date onwards he shares with Mr Brown of the Chequers the duty to act as host for the Vestry meetings. By Ann his first wife he had children baptised 1786-97, the eldest of whom was Jane. As a widower he married Sarah Barker in 1804 by whom he had several more children baptised 1805-19 when he is named Victualler i.e. licensee of a public house. (N.B. a victualler is an innkeeper licensed to sell spirits.) John Gough was buried in 1837 aged 76, but before then his eldest daughter Jane had married Charles Woolley of Castle Ashby in 1816, the year after the Battle of Waterloo. He in his turn is shown as having 'town meetings' in his inn in 1830. He too is described as a victualler.

Charles Woolley was buried in 1838 aged 57 as he must have taken over the inn before his father-in-law died. Thereafter Mrs Jane Woolley managed the Red Lion Inn even at the age of 64 in the 1851 Census. She had with her at the time a daughter, Jocosa Woolley, aged 26 (born at Grendon), and Sarah Bettel, a servant aged 45, and Henry Oliver, a customer, aged 23, a clerk obviously sleeping the night. Jane Woolley was buried in 1854 aged 68.

The Red Lion was owned by the Earl of Sussex at the time of the Enclosure in 1799 and when he, being the last of the family line, died the whole of his estate at Easton

Maudit, including the magnificent Manor House to the north of the Church which boasted one of the finest libraries in England (his ancestor was Christopher Yelverton, Speaker in the Parliament of Elizabeth I) and parts of Bozeat including the Red Lion, were purchased in 1801 by the then Marquis of Northampton. To bring friends and relations from the London Coach which stopped at the Red Lion to Castle Ashby House, conveyances would meet them. In those days the Marquis had a road which ran in a straight line across the fields at Easton Maudit crossing the village street at the bottom of the village and then straight on to the House. Part of this road is still clearly visible today. Horses were kept at the inn for that purpose. It was no coincidence that the innkeepers had some 26 acres of land during Jane Woolley's time, which was classed as a homestead at the time of Enclosure. It was of course land which belonged to the Marquis and later went by the name of 'Woolley's Land'.

The Red Lion was probably a 'staging inn', where teams of horses could be changed for the long distance rides. The service required a change of horses every ten miles. Also it may have been a 'post inn', which had nothing to do with mail, but horses could be hired out to draw a private carriage to the next posting inn or, alternatively, where the customer did not have his own carriage, hire out a 'post chaise' as well as a team of horses, each team being accompanied by a 'post boy' (much as we would hire a taxi today!). A number of horses could then be stabled at such a building as well as some out in pasture. The changeover of horses and their care required an ostler, and there is one mentioned in the 1851 census in the village. As we have already observed, these early decades of the 19th century were the great age of the horse and of the road before the car replaced the first and the railways the second.

Red Lion on the right with a row of buildings beyond (now demolished) including the Cross Keys and sweet and grocery shops advertising Cadburys Cocoa and Cadburys Chocolate.

At the same date after the death of Mrs Jane Woolley, William Frederick Hill took over the Red Lion being described in the 1869 Directory of Trades as having the Red Lion and being a farmer. He appears to have left the Red Lion in 1876 and is described only as a farmer after that date, dying in 1884 aged 72.

In 1874 the Red Lion was conveyed by the Marquis to Thomas Revis of Clifton Reynes who owned the Bozeat Estate. He erected a new building which is now the present one. It occupied roughly the space of the courtyard of the older building, so we must imagine the previous building as being on the site of the spaces round the present one. The courtyard in the earlier building would have been for the entry of coaches and carts and at the rear were stables which could accommodate a large number of horse-drawn vehicles. There was a house on the right hand side of the present Red Lion, pulled down some years ago (previously occupied by Mr and Mrs Bird), which was part of the original inn. In it were three large rooms upstairs and cellars underneath. There was a paddock at the rear. Recently, in one of the outbuildings at the rear of the present Red Lion a date of 1734 was found on the beam which had been painted over. One wonders whether the building on that site, prior to that date, had been burnt down in the village fire of 1729. Looking across from the Fish and Chip Shop in the High Street one can see more than one aperture plainly blocked up with stone. One aperture stands at a height from the road and one can only guess that there may have been a 'mounting block' at that point for the customers to mount their horses.

Thomas Revis erected the new Red Lion and the adjacent four cottages in London Road in the early 1880s. He died on the 9th July 1886 after which the property was conveyed to Messrs A. W. Hipwell and others, then later in 1921 to P. Phipps & Co., the last owners being Watney Mann.

Richard Cave, grandfather of Tom Cave (Tom's wife Dorothy lives, 1999, at 17 Fullwell Road) appears to have taken over the Red Lion by 1876 and in the 1903 Trade Directory it was managed by his wife Nancy Emily Cave.

The forecourt would have been the centre of village activities. There are memories of three rings fixed to the wall where owners tied their horses when going in for refreshment. Men from home, workshop or factory would meet here for a cheese sandwich and a pint. Pedlars would come to Red Lion Hill. Clarry Drage remembers as a child, women outside the Red Lion weeping into their aprons (which they all wore then) on hearing the news of the death of Queen Victoria (1901). Travelling showmen, usually Hungarian with dancing bears, organ grinders with their monkey in its red jacket travelling from village pub to village pub are remembered here.

The pig supper for clients' entertainment was another custom in days when many families had a pig up the garden, a custom which sadly died out at the start of the Great War.

And the Coroner's Court would be held here in times past, held to enquire into accidental or suspicious deaths. The Red Lion seems by tradition to have been such a place as far back as the time of Thomas Tombs for in the parish accounts for 1699 we read: "Pads (paid) Henry Church for goeing for the coroner. Spent on the Juy (jury) at Tho Tombs." Mary Smart of Bozeat in the time of the 'Commonwealth' of Oliver Cromwell (January 1656) appeared before the Justices to answer by whom she had had a bastard child! Through the next two centuries inquests were held there. In 1891 we have what must have been a common cause for inquest before maternity care became common: "An inquest was held at the Red Lion Inn, on Thursday week

INNS, INNKEEPERS AND BEER 151

1917 photograph showing The Flat, London Road and the Chequers with the Hope Street factory in the distance. The window in the low building on the right is Benny Squire's bakers shop (note the 'Lyons' sign).

on the body of Louisa Tompkins.... Sarah Drage, midwife of Bozeat gave evidence of attending the deceased in her confinement on the previous night, and stated that the deceased died about an hour from the time of birth."

THE CHEQUERS INN

At one time this was the last building on the road leading out of the village to Wellingborough. There is more than one theory as to how such inns derived their name. One strong contender is that the 'chequer board' upon which merchants, clerks and accountants once made their calculations (hence the Exchequer) was also applied to the inns where they kept accounts. It is supposed, on this theory, that these inns served as meeting places where matters of local rent payments were made between the steward of the manor and his lord's tenants. In such cases the innkeeper may also have been a money-changer. The fact that the building was at the end of the village suggests that it may have been a meeting place for the collection of rents from the tenants of the surrounding countryside. That is pure speculation for the name may simply have been the name favoured by a landlord long ago. Still many Chequers are found in seaports where the pub was used to pay off sailors after a long voyage.

So far there is no evidence that prior to 1800 there was any other owner than the landlord himself. The 1799 Enclosure Map shows, as already stated, that it was in private hands whereas, had it been estate property, it would have been either under the control of the Spencer family or that of the Earl of Sussex. The fact that it is at the end of the village may only have been due to the foresight of some landlord who wanted it to be the first inn to be reached in the village with incidentally the only well (for drovers and others) after leaving Wellingborough.

There is a date on the building of 1751 AD but this does not necessarily mean the date of its construction, only of a reconstruction. In living memory, stables were part

A recent photograph of the Chequers spring in London Road, the first stop for horses from Wellingborough. Gladys Line remembers circus animals drinking from the spring while passing through the village.

of the outbuildings, and further up the yard was a shed in which traps and carts of travellers would be accommodated.

The first known innkeeper was John Brown, who appears in the first of the Overseer of the Poor Accounts providing refreshments 1778-1793 for the parish meeting. John and Mary Brown had a child baptised in 1779, but as there is no record of a marriage one must assume they came from away. John Brown was of course on the Parish Vestry but then he was buried in January 1793 and for the next year it was "Mrs Brown Hur Bill" in the Churchwardens' accounts.

In September 1794 James Carvel of Odell married Mary Brown. If we go by the ages on burial, James Carvel would have been 29 at the time of his marriage when his bride was aged 44. She appears to have kept the land – perhaps there was a marriage contract, for a woman's property in those days normally came to her husband, for in the 1799 Enclosure, James Carvel is described as being a 'Yeoman' having four acres "in right of Mary his wife". He appears to have kept the inn until round about 1807. If it was property he married for, it could not have lasted, for John Danes the next owner appears on the Vestry in 1809 and by the rent accounts of Earl Spencer, James Carvel is found renting what must have been an estate house. In 1825 the parish were paying him a sum as a pauper. "James Carvel ill 6s-0d." and he was buried that same year aged 60. Mrs Carvel lingered on with sundry payments by the parish to those who nursed her, e.g. in 1827: "Mrs Clayton applying for Widow Carvel, She being ill to have per week 2s.0d.," and later that year: "Ann Smart made application on behalf of widow Carvel she being ill. To be left to the discretion of the Overseer (of the poor)." She was buried in 1832 aged 82.

John Danes took over as innkeeper of the Chequers, as mentioned previously, somewhere about 1807 or after, for James Carvel was named in the 1806 poll list. He too was on the Vestry and was once the chairman. One gets the impression that he was more wealthy than his predecessor. The inn was in his hands for at least 30 years, although he does not appear to have been resident there towards the end. In the 1831 poll he is named as 'Publican' and his name appears on the poll list of 1837. But somewhere between 1840-1850 he retired to Weston Favell, leaving the inn in the hands of others.

The land to the rear of the Chequers extended in a triangle to the bottom of what is now Allens Hill. There was in it a large pond. It is possible that this was a pasture land for horses needed by the inn. John Danes and some of his predecessors seem to have rented other land as well, such as the Wellingborough Feoffes and Church and Town Well land, possibly for the growing of hay or barley. The land adjacent to the inn was in living memory often used for village activities on such occasions as the Feast Weekend.

By 1845 George Allin was the landlord who probably gave his name to Allens Hill, the road at the rear of the property. In the 1851 census the name is spelt 'Allen' and he was described as a 'Victualler' aged 52 born at Hanslope in Buckinghamshire with wife Mary two years younger. They appear to have managed the inn between them with no servants.

At some date in the latter half of the 19th century, Campbell Praeds took over as Landlords. Thomas Swingler, who was once a constable (in 1892) in the County Constabulary at Bozeat, by 1897 was a 'clicker' and in 1900 became a licensed victualler of the Chequers, probably continuing his shoe trade at the back of the house during the day, and keeping his clients in order at night!

In 1960 The Chequers ceased to be a public house when it was bought from the brewery by a Mr Mitchell. At the same time the land was bought by a builder Arnold Dobbs and he built two houses and two bungalows along the London Road in the 1960s (numbers 3, 5, 7 and 9) and then two more houses were built on the Triangle at the very end in 1998 when Arnold sold this land to a builder, one of these being bought by Robert and Pat Driver who ran the Paper Shop for many years.

In 1969 Mark and Pat Allebone bought the Chequers. "There were only two rooms you could live in then," remembers Mark, since when they have carried out extensive alterations inside but preserved the traditional appearance.

THE BEER HOUSE IN MILE STREET

John Dexter, the last of his line in the village, was born in 1778, the son of Thomas and Martha Dexter. He married Catherine Lawton in 1799. He had two children inside of marriage and a greater number outside. John Dexter seems to have been

Mile Street with the beer house at top on right. In front of that is the yard known as 'The Gold'. Church Farm on the far left. The allotment ground on the left was to be used by the electricity board to store telegraph poles and treat them with creosote when electricity came to the village. On the right is a shoe lift manufacturing shop.

fond of wine, women and song, although we cannot be sure if they came in that order. He had served in the Northamptonshire Yeomanry during the Napoleonic Wars – possibly a dashing young officer. When the village was enclosed in 1799 (the year he was married) he was in military service and being a minor and absent, his land was being farmed by his uncle John Lewis of Town Farm.

It seems that through the years after the war his land decreased, until by the time he died in 1839 aged 61, he owned only the Bull Inn. His wife Catherine carried on with the 'Bull Inn' (1847 Directory) being described as a 'Beer Retailer' in the 1849 Directory. She appears to have given this up about this date for in the 1851 census she is described only as a 'visitor', that is one visiting but living away. She died in 1855 aged 78.

Here one must resort to a calculated guess. Thomas Houghton was a butcher who lived at the 'Mount' further up Mile Street. We know from the Rate Book that he had a Beer House in 1851. It was probably the same building as 'The Bull'. And it would have been fitting perhaps for a butcher to call his beer house 'The Shoulder of Mutton' which was the name given to the building prior to it being called 'The Royal Engineer'. Mention will be made later of the Corby family who also appeared to rent or own beer houses and pubs. It seems that blacksmiths, being thirsty men, had an appropriate second line!

In 1773 (Churchwardens Accounts) William Corby was a blacksmith who had an ale house. When Robert Stanion was glazing the Church windows, there is an entry: "Wm Corby for ale for Robert Stanion." Also in the same year was another entry: 'Pd two Men Goen with the man that Brok his Leg at Corbeys 3s-0d". Was there a 'rough house' or did he miss his step as he left?! William Corby died in Olney in 1821 aged 74 but was brought home for burial. John Corby a grandson of William was a pauper boy apprenticed by the parish to John Monk the blacksmith in 1822. By 1869 he appears to be a Beer Retailer as well as a blacksmith but we cannot be sure that this was the then 'Royal Engineer'. William as son of John and Sarah, born 1834, had been working with his father but tradition has it that he was also apprenticed in London to an engineer and returned to Bozeat. Certainly he calls himself an 'Engineer' at his daughter's wedding, probably an agricultural engineer. However, he had a blacksmith shop on one side of Mile Street, (later occupied by Mrs Harriet Partridge until 1994), and took over the Beer House named 'Shoulder of Mutton' changing it to the 'Royal Engineer'. When William was buried in 1889 his wife Mary carried on the trade. At the beginning of this century, Harry Corby, son of Thomas (who once had the Cross Keys) took over the Royal Engineer, leaving his sister to run this when he became the first steward of the Working Men's Club in 1897. There were to be other landlords of the 'Royal Engineer' and the last was Ben Tompkins when the licence was withdrawn in 1932. Village memories said that the Beer House was a scene of much leg pulling and joking and was also a meeting place for poachers which were once plentiful in the village. This is now a private house – No. 40 Mile Street.

THE LORD NELSON
Over the front of the building is a triangle in the stone with 'D TS 1743' carved in it. The date may be that of the reconstruction of the building and the initials possibly those of previous owner Thomas Skevington or a Spencer? The porch is a late addition for it appears as one of the earliest bits of 'Planning Permission' by the newly

The Lord Nelson selling 'Dulley's Ales and Stout', which were brewed in Sheep Street, Wellingborough.

appointed Parish Council (elected in 1895) after the Liberal Government established Parish Councils (to replace the 'Vestry') in 1894, which in 1897 saw no objection to a step projection from the house into the High Street so long as it was no more than 4 feet 6 inches from the outside wall and a proper protection provided. (It must have been quite a step down before then!) From some 200 years ago we see Inn Signs commemorating famous individuals, and most probably soon after the Battle of Waterloo in 1818 the Beer House displayed the name of Britain's Premier Admiral. It must be about this time that Low Farm in Easton Maudit, (now owned by a Yorkshireman Ken Bowe (1996) and previously by Mr Ingram) was named Waterloo Farm. It is not known whether the Nelson was an inn in the 18th century or just a large house or who occupied it. The walls are in places some 30 inches thick. Traces of a former thatched roof can still be seen from the exterior before a slate roof was laid and oak beams could be seen in the interior. In the living room an oak beam supports the ceiling.

The first known landlord of the inn was Samual Skevington born 1793 and buried in 1848 aged 55. He was the son of a butcher, Thomas (and Anne) Skevington. For a time it seems that Samuel was also a butcher, but he did not prosper in that trade, probably because, in the early 19th century, meat was too expensive for the average labourer. Samuel married in 1812, but seems to have fallen on hard times as a year later he was given pauper's pay by the parish. The five children he had were baptised between 1815 and 1825 when he is documented as a butcher. His wife Catherine died in 1839 and by 1840 he had married Nancy, a widow from Pitsford with two children. On an 1843 Rate Book he has the 'Lord Nelson' and may have had it for some time previously, but was only the occupier. His brother, Thomas Dexter Skevington, a baker, was actually the landlord, owning many other properties in Bozeat. This brother was married to Martha, with family including (another) Thomas and William. Samuel also appears to have some 10 acres of land. After his death in 1848 his widow Nancy carried on the trade being described as a 'Beer House Keeper' in the 1851 census. She was buried in 1866 aged 62.

Three years after Nancy had died, Thomas Dexter Skevington is named as Beer Retailer in the 1869 Trade Directory, named as having a 'Beerhouse' in 1874 and being a 'Beer Retailer' and 'Butcher' in 1876 and 1877. As Samuel had no son named Thomas it may be assumed that this brother Thomas Dexter Skevington, who was the landlord, put in his own son Thomas as the landlord. This Thomas Skevington probably died in 1879 aged 41. (His brother William died in 1904 aged 59.) Samuel's only son John became a gamekeeper at Denton probably safeguarding the Marquis's Estates. (None of these landlords seems to have lived to a ripe old age!)

Murder!

The *Northamptonshire Herald* for Saturday, 13th August 1887, records an Inquest at Bozeat on Tuesday afternoon (9th) "touching the death of a young man of the village named George Partridge", before William Tomalin, the deputy coroner. The jury, members of the Vestry, etc., seem to include all the 'Notables' of the village; Mr J. Drage (foreman, presumably John Drage the shoe manufacturer who was to give a good word for the accused at the Assizes), Mr T. Wallis (shopkeeper and blacksmith who owned many houses in Bozeat), Mr H. Drage (probably John's brother Henry, another shoe manufacturer), Mr J. W. Kirby (the first Board School headmaster and churchwarden), Mr William Packwood (draper and tailor), Mr W. Drage (presumably William Hooton brother of John and Henry, boot and shoe maker, Mr J. (John) Smith (shoe finisher) and Mr R. (Richard) Cave (landlord of the Red Lion), where the inquest took place.

From the evidence given, there was a long-standing three-year grievance between this young man and another villager Arthur Harrison. Harrison challenged Partridge to a fight whilst they were in the Nelson on the previous Saturday night (6th). He refused, but after leaving the pub at closing time Harrison knocked Partridge down. Subsequently Partridge was found severely injured lying in Dychurch Lane where lived Police Constable Blackburn (presumably Partridge was on the way to report the attack). He was taken to his home and visited on the Sunday by Dr Orr of Wollaston and subsequently died at 1.45 am on Monday morning. The inquest reported several kicks and blows to the body and the jury, after hearing the evidence, returned a verdict of 'Wilful murder'. "It would seem that the majority were for a 'hanging verdict'." (*Palmer*). But the jury at the Three Counties Assizes at Bedford on 26th October 1887 threw out the charge and returned one of 'Manslaughter'. John Drage, the shoemaker, said at the trial that he had known the prisoner since he was a boy and he was honest, hard working, upright and courteous. He had never seen him drunk and the prisoner had a wife and four children, one of whom was blind. The Judge in his summing up said there was no evidence to show that the prisoner did no more to the deceased than give him a black eye. As the defence pleaded that the prisoner had already been in prison for three months he was sentenced to one month's hard labour.

Peter Horn was mentioned as the landlord of the Nelson at the time, continuing at least up to 1892. Harry Spakes seems to have followed him at the turn of the century and was still there in the 1911 Trade Directory. In his day there was an event which could be remembered by Mrs 'Mim' Warner which occurred a few days before the

Feast Weekend, when village housewives turned out en-bloc. The Village Crier would walk around the village with his bell announcing the coming of the crock auction. Marriott's of Wellingborough would bring crockery (probably seconds or discarded lines) and sell them outside the 'Lord Nelson'. Straw would be put down and crowds of housewives would gather round to obtain some cheap crockery in the days before unbreakable plastic plates – and if the rubbish tips were anything to go by there must have been quite a massacre of crockery! The auctioneer would run the plates up his arm in his professional way as he asked for bids. Meanwhile children mingling with the housewives, all of who wore the traditional apron (or 'pinny'), would pin these together creating unexpected ties between the women! After the auction the landlord would bring out a four-handled chamber pot for the auctioneer to quench his thirst. It remained an unforgettable sight. (See a similar memory of this event in Chapter 3). The yard at the back of the Nelson contained six houses which remained into the 20th century. Considering how small they were, they must have been very crowded when in the 1851 census, one had two families living in one of them – seven persons in all – and the others having five or more persons in them. By 1892 (rate lists) there were there ten family 'heads' paying rates. They were owned by the landlord of the Nelson.

The Anglia Television *Village* programme, filmed in 1992, interviewed the then owner of the Nelson, Ralph Tompkins who, in the room at the rear had a closing workshop called the 'Kinston Closers', the last remaining 'shoe factory' in Bozeat! Ralph bought the old pub in 1960 as a private house, the pub having lost its licence to sell beer in 1955 – it never had a 'spirits' licence. As a shoemaker himself he was encouraged to start a small closing room there which he did. In the doorway at the back there is still the old clocking on and off machine for the workers! In 1992 there were still some dozen ladies working there, one being Viv Smith whose husband John works for Dr. Martens at Wollaston. "We just do small runs, 12 pairs of shoes say. Larger factories cannot deal with these small numbers," said Ralph on the programme. Sadly Ralph died in 1993 but his daughter Sharon kept the business going. "It's a bit 'iffy' these days," said Viv in 1998, who lives just round the corner from the Nelson in Camden Square. "We make everything from ballet shoes to motorbike boots mainly for N.P.S. at Wollaston or George Cox at Wellingborough but there's not much work at the moment. John (her husband) says I should get a better job but I don't want a full time job, and it's so convenient." Sadly in January 1999 it had to close as Sharon, who toured the factories around looking for work, could no longer find enough to keep it going and the surviving ladies (including Viv) had to be laid off.

As I write in July 1999, Mark and Lynda Rudd move into the Nelson to take over its ownership from just across the road for they have been living at Miller's Corner for the past five years carrying out several improvements there but maintaining its traditional feel and quality. Mark has also purchased a small wood towards Harrold and is busy learning tree craft, so has a real investment in the traditional values of these parts.

THE CROSS KEYS

This was a 'beer house' but the date of building is unknown. It is known that Thomas Corby held this in 1876. He was already a 'Shoe Agent'. It appears that about 1877 the Cross Keys which was part of the Bozeat Estate under Thomas Revis was given

The Cross Keys, c.1920. In the doorway are Fred and Mary Perkins, with daughter Dorothy aged 10.
(G. Mines)

to another landlord. Thomas Corby had his own shoe works in 1879, building a very modern building further up London Road in 1901. The 1886 Sale after the death of Thomas Revis tells us that it had an annual rent of £47 and let on lease then to Messrs Allfrey and Lovell and contained a Parlour, Tap Room, five Bedrooms, Underground Cellars and a Brew House. By the 1909 Sale it was held on a yearly tenancy by Newport Pagnell Brewery Co. although after the death of Thomas Revis the Royal Exchange Insurance were the landlords of this and the rest of the Bozeat Estate.

About 1887 James Drage, who may have been in the shoe trade previously, became landlord. By some strange coincidence (or was it?) his two daughters married men in the shoe trade whose fathers were also 'Licensed Victuallers' The fathers were Thomas Swingler (Chequers) and Thomas Corby, deceased (Royal Engineer). If blood is thicker than water so was ale! One of his daughters recalled as a little girl holding the horse of the outrider (the old term for a commercial traveller) who called from the Newport Brewery for the order. The agent for the Royal Exchange collected rents on quarter days, she remembered, and a farmer's dinner was usually held afterwards. In 1901 Horace Brown became landlord. He must have been quite a character. He was noted for his teeth pulling. When a difficult customer arrived for an 'extraction' he is said to have sent for Thomas (Derry) Dobbs, the thatcher, a strongly built man who held the patient's head whilst Mr Brown did the necessary for sixpence! Another version says that he called in the brother of the spinster lady next door, Miss Rice (shopkeeper), who would hold the patient's ears whilst the proprietor did the necessary. Sometimes he got the wrong tooth but the charge was still the same – sixpence! The patient would be given a bowl of hot water to wash out his mouth. Of course there was a 'proper' dentist at Olney, if you cared to walk that far and pay more. Horace Brown was also noted for his musical ability and he had a small string orchestra, which is remembered by 'Clarry' Drage. As Horace Brown played the violin his nickname (a Bozeat habit) was 'Catgut'! Neil Silsby played the piccolo, William Robinson, who played the organ at Castle Ashby Church, was the pianist, Charles Craxton (nicknamed 'Wag') played the clarinet, Ernest Drage the flute and George Dobbs who in years gone by when the parish church had no organ had played it in the Musicians' Gallery (fixed to the church tower wall), played the cello. Sadly we have no record of the music they played. It appears that they only played for the benefit of clients. But as Clarry tells us the children would stand outside and would sing whilst "'Catgut' played the fiddle. Horace his son played the drums. Misses plays the old banjo and the kids sing 'tiddle, tiddle dum'."

Garry Mines has a photograph of his grandparents Frederick and Mary Perkins standing at the door of the Cross Keys and with them his aunt Dorothy aged about ten, showing that Fred was landlord there in about 1920. On the board above them fixed to the wall we read "The Cross Keys. Noyes Ales and Stout Drawn from the Wood, Newport Pagnell Brewery Co." And then on the board above the door: "Frederick Perkins. Licensed Retailer of Beer. Consumed on and off the premises, Dealer in Tobacco".

When the licence was withdrawn from the Cross Keys in 1931, Charles Wells of Bedford were the last brewers to own the building, which is now demolished, along with neighbouring buildings. The last landlord, Mr R. Byrne, continued to live in the building, working as a saddler, until the 1950s, until it was condemned by the government health inspectorate as unfit for human habitation as were the neighbouring buildings, and the site is now a village green, for children to play on and for maypole dancing.

Reading Room and Library

"A Reading Room and Library was started in October 1872. In 1874 *Whellan's Directory* says there were 50 members who paid 5/- each per annum. It is said to have been started at the instigation of Mr Henry Hutchinson, of the Church Farm, and kept by Mr Joe Laughton in the double fronted house in Mile Street, now occupied by Mr Stokes, nearly opposite the gate of the Church Farm. The Reading Room extended over both the downstairs rooms. A Good Templars Lodge was formed there, and downstairs a refreshment room for hot teas or coffee, etc. In the Directory of 1877 John William Kirby [schoolmaster] was the Secretary of the Bozeat Reading and News Room. Charles Partridge and later Mr William Surridge occupied the house and took charge." (*Marlow*, p.86)

Working Men's Club and Institute

"In 1894 a Working Men's Club was founded in a house in High Street, now occupied by Mr William Hewlett. The Secretary was Mr Thomas J. Robinson. ... In 1897 the present Men's Club Buildings in High Street were built on land previously called Riseley Gardens. Ten residents made themselves responsible for £10 each. These were Rev. Sargeaunt, Messrs Joe Laughton, Tom Corby, T. J. Robinson, G. E. Craxton, Charles B. Drage, Arch. Dobbs, Arthur Harrison, Ben Pratt, William Bettles. The cost of the building was about £400. Messrs Joe Laughton and George Dobbs made a good part of the furniture." (*Marlow*, pp.86,87)

Fred Elliott who lives (1999) at 38 High Street is 85 (born 1914) and was steward for over a quarter of century, for 27 years, from 7th October 1949 until 5th November 1976. "They built it with a passage down the middle so it could be two

This is the building in High Street where the Working Men's Club started in 1894. In the 1950s it was a café run by Mr Owen, and now is a private house 'Short Stagger Cottage'.
(*Bozeat School Scrapbook*)

houses if it didn't work as a club," Fred remembers. There were only originally three rooms downstairs but there have been two or three extensions since and many alterations. In 1952 two of the three rooms were knocked together to make a bar and the third into a games room with a screened-off area for a television set. Membership then was 270. Then in 1973 they built a room onto the back, all this in Fred's time. Fred remembers particularly the big flood in 1952: "It was May 19th I remember as it was my wife's father's birthday – the seats of the chairs were under water!" "After the war, Dick Strange the butcher was the steward but he packed up because of ill health, so I took over. There were several stewards between the wars – two of them I remember were Sam Bayes and Sam Humphreys."

The last Stewards were Mr and Mrs Leach. The Club had got into heavy debt partly because clubs were becoming less popular than pubs with young people who didn't like the idea of membership. Also the image of a 'men's only club', even though families used it, did not help. So in 1994 it was taken back by the brewery to which it was in debt to the tune of £90,000. In that year John Saving and Lynne Smith took on the Loan and reopened the Working Men's Club under the new image of 'Bozeat Club'. It still operates on the basis of membership but is very much for all the family and, with live music, etc., it aims to draw young people back and restore its important function as a social centre for the village.

High Street with the Working Men's Club on the left, and the school in the distance.

Brewing of beer
Alcohol

"For most of the past 10 millennia, alcoholic beverages may have been the most popular and common daily drink, indispensable source of fluids and calories. In a world of contaminated and dangerous water supplies, alcohol truly earned the title granted it in the Middle Ages: aqua vitae, the 'water of life'." (Bert Vallee, *Scientific American*, June 1998). Indeed alcohol must be considered as one of the primary agents in the development of our entire culture – and that includes the daily life of Bozeat since its inception!

Possibly our Stone Age ancestors left a jar of wild honey too long and it fermented giving us our first alcoholic drink – Mead; likewise with fermenting wild fruits, dates or sap, etc. creating meads, ciders and wines.

Beer, which relies on large amounts of starchy grain, had to wait until the development of agriculture and the cereal-based civilisations around Egypt and Mesopotamia two millennia before Christ. Agriculture would give a boost to the production of wine and the developments of vineyards. A painting from the Khety's Tomb in Egypt, c.2100 BC, shows guests being carried away from a banquet, the worst for wear after too much wine.

Creation of agriculture led to food surpluses, leading to ever-larger groups of people living in close quarters in villages and cities. This resulted in problems of supplying enough water for their bodies' requirements, and the problem of water contamination through human and animal waste, making it dangerous to drink. Contaminated water carried the ancient killers – dysentery, cholera and typhoid. In such circumstances alcohol provided a potable (and storable) beverage. We see on the continent of Europe that beer and wine still play a large part in the liquid consumption of the inhabitants of all ages and at all meals, and this dates back to the comparatively recent past when the water was not safe to drink. Whilst those

High Street looking towards Camden Square with Smiths Buildings on the left and the Methodist Church on the right.

countries have now caught up with our standards and indeed surpassed them, this habit has remained as part of their culture, but not so in ours.

Thomas à Becket, Archbishop of Canterbury could stomach no alcoholic beverage like wine, ale or cider. On one occasion in 1171-2, while at Croydon Surrey, his servant scoured the district for some whey (the thin watery part of milk that separates out from the curds after clotting) for his master to drink. Hugh of Meymac recalled offering Thomas whey in a silver cup in 1156 or 1159. (Thomas had an attack of colitis in Northampton in 1164) (*Thomas Becket*, by Frank Barlow, Weidenfeld & Nicolson, 1985, p.25)

Throughout the Middle Ages, grain remained the basic food of peasants and beer their normal beverage, along with mead, cider and wines. In the Mediterranean climate enjoyed throughout Europe then, vineyards were widespread even in England and the church operated the biggest and best vineyards to considerable profit. Beer was the generic name for malt liquor including ale and porter – from malted barley flavoured with hops. Whereas beer was made by fermentation in which the yeast settles to the bottom, in ale the yeast ferments on the top of the liquid. David Hall points out that fines for brewing beer were regular in the 15th century. There are records of several cases in Bozeat of fines for brewing beer and not having it passed by the Ale Taster. One Bozeat man was fined in 1435 for selling beer at two different prices although the same brew! (*Marlow*, p.63) In Bozeat, church documents show that provision of ale was often given as a part payment for work done (e.g. three quarts of ale for workmen scouring the Bozeat clock in 1701). Payments were made to parishioners or church officers like the sexton or clerk for maintaining constant watch over the blessed sacrament from Good Friday till Easter Day and for "bread, ale and fyre" to see them through the chilly night hours and are common in pre-Reformation churchwardens' accounts. (*The Stripping of the Altars*, Eamon Duffey, Yale Univ. Press, 1993 p.30) One suspects that such items would have been found in accounts at Bozeat, with the rich medieval structures and functions of its church.

Distillation, developed about AD 700 by Arabic alchemists, was introduced into Europe circa AD 1100 in the distillation of wines to produce spirits which, with their high alcohol content, brought both relief and misery. The widespread drinking of spirits followed closely on the heels of the 14th century bouts of plague, notably the Black Death of 1347-51 which culled over half of Europe's population in a single generation, and helped to relieve the misery and destitution of the poor of Victorian England in the wake of the Industrial Revolution, reflected in apt sayings such as "Gin was mother's milk to her." And its medical use in dulling pain for operations and in disease is typified in Darwin's wife who ministered gin-and-opium concoctions to the sick of her village, Downe in Kent, in the mid-19th century. The Overseer (of the Poor) Accounts in Bozeat refer to Mr Lettice, Apothecary from Wellingborough, son of a former vicar of Bozeat, engaged to serve the poor of this parish: 1790 "Mr Lettice for wine for Riseleys 2s-5d." Thomas Surridge was ill in 1803 and in March, "Gin and wine 5s-5d.' and in 1833, "paid for brandy for Wm Craxton 1s-0d." – he died that same month aged 67. And presumably to dull the pain, March 1805: "Sarah Drage midwifery for Jane Jolly 2s-6d. 2 Quarts of Ale 1s-2d. Gin for Jane Jolly 2s-6d.," (*Palmer*) quite a hefty dose! The advice in the *Book of Proverbs* has stood the test of time: "Give strong drink unto him that is ready to perish, and wine unto them that be of heavy hearts. Let him drink and forget his poverty, and remember his misery no more." (c.500 BC)

The fact that our village of some 1,000 folk could sustain five pubs at the beginning of the 20th century shows the widespread importance of beer as a beverage and its role in social cohesion and village life in the culture of the earlier part of the century and in the previous, when agriculture and village industry was contained entirely within village life. Pubs like the Lord Nelson had no licence to sell spirits, reflecting a satisfaction with beer, cider (and wine) as the working man's regular beverage.

If the pub was the cultural centre for men, the Church provided a similar role for women though not exclusively so and there is still some gender polarisation here today. The rise of Methodism and its establishment in the village (first chapel opened in Mile Street in 1834) coincided with an increasing awareness of alcohol abuse and its associated diseases. As early as 1813, Thomas Trotter, a graduate of Edinburgh College of medicine, influenced probably by moralistic anti-alcohol Methodism, wrote an essay on how the habitual and prolonged consumption of hard liquor causes liver disease, accompanied by jaundice, wasting and mental dysfunction, evident even when the patient is sober – a realisation that was to lead to the American Prohibition (1919-1933). Dolly Roberts' grandfather (6 Burton Terrace) was a strict teetotaller and belonged to the Band of Hope (which met in the Methodist chapel) in the latter half of the 19th century and encouraged her to sign the pledge. The increased influence of Methodism in the 19th/20th century in this village is told in the appropriate chapter and offered an alternative social centre to men through the Methodist Wesley Guild with its emphasis on self improvement and abstinence. Even today no alcohol is allowed on our Methodist Church premises.

NORMAN PALMER

It is said that it was common in rural England at the turn of the 19th century for every cottage to brew its own beer, for the average consumption for a labourer's family was four pints a day in winter and about 10 pints a day in high summer. Home brewing was done in October after the barley had been harvested.

William Pitt in his *General View of Agriculture in Northamptonshire*, written in 1809, says that for the farmer, his family and farm workers who 'lived in', "that breakfast included beer and for supper ale was allowed on many occasions and small beer at command at all hours." He goes on to say: "A great proportion of the barley crops is made into malt and consumed in the county." Strong beer is that made with the first brew of the hops, the second brew produced a mild beer called 'small beer'. We know that barley was grown in the district, for in Earl Spencer's 1818 Rent Returns the Vicar was growing barley on his Glebe Land. However, the high cost of barley and hops during the Napoleonic War changed the habit of home brewing and so came the rise of the Beer House and the drinking of tea. J. Kirby, the headmaster, writing over 100 years ago, said that Bozeat people once brewed their own ale and brew houses could still be seen in his day.

Home brewing continued on the farms, for in the 1886 and 1909 Sales of the Bozeat Estate, Town Farm and Church Farm both included a brew house, and village memories can go back to the time when beer brewed at Church Farm could still be bought. It is interesting that in the catalogues for these Sales, the Red Lion and the Cross Keys both had their brew houses. Seeing that both places were supplied by outside brewers one assumes that these were not then used. Before the days of large commercial brewers, local farmers appear to be the prime source of beer and ale, the wines of course being imported. One such farmer, who was described as 'Maltster' in his will of 1808 was Edward Skevington, forebear of the Skevingtons. Born in 1736, he lived through the Enclosure of 1799, dying in 1814 aged 78. His latter years, ending a year before the Battle of Waterloo, was a prosperous period for the farmer, and especially for one who grew his own barley, as I think he must. He had three farms in Bozeat plus a farm elsewhere. One of these farms was probably that of Len Holt, Wykes Farm. Exactly where he did his malting is not known, but in his will he decrees: "I give all my stock of barley and malt and utensils of a Maltster", which enabled him to give to his heirs, "all my household utensils, wines, ale, spirits and other household stores."

There is another picture of a Maltster, John Allebone of Easton Maudit, which is mentioned in *A History of Methodism in Bozeat*, by John Warren Partridge, referring to a time about halfway through the 19th century. "… he put his best into everything he undertook. He kept an outdoor beer house at Easton Maudit brewing his own beer. It is said that he purchased his malt from the best maltster he knew and it was a saying of his, 'I will make them come a long distance to fetch it', his motto being, 'Give the best value you can for their money'." This was of course before the days of the Temperance Movement.

Village tales
The men of the Windmill Singers were standing in the kitchen of our Independent Wesleyan Chapel having a cup of tea after a Tuesday practice in December 1998 – and I jokingly said, "According to the BBC News our medical experts say we ought to be having a tot of whisky or a glass of red wine, not drinking tea, as they are good for the heart!"

"What, in the Chapel!" exclaimed Gerald Corby (born and bred in the village) in mock horror, "that would never have been allowed in my younger days. You had to be tee-total to come in here. The preachers then preached the evils of drink!"

"I remember Ted Wallis – a great Chapel-goer. Every Sunday morning he would walk home from chapel in his best Sunday suit and bowler hat. I remember one winter Sunday – it must have been in the 1940s – and we boys were in the High Street making snowballs as it had been snowing heavily. The snow was melting so, as we squeezed the snow into balls, it became balls of ice! We saw Ted Wallis (brother of Alfie Wallis the blacksmith) coming out of Chapel so we dared each other to knock his hat off with a snowball as he walked down the High Street. One ice ball hit him smack in the back of the head – just here – and knocked him clean out. They carried him into the Working Men's Club and as he came round gave him some whisky to revive him. 'Where am I?' he asked as he came to his senses. When they told him – and he realised what evil substance had just passed his lips – he cried in horror, 'Who brought me in here. Get me out. Get me out of this den of iniquity!' Whisky and Working Men's Club did not mix with Chapel-going in those days."

On recounting this story to Tom Partridge-Underwood, he told me the tale of a Chapel preacher he remembered from his youth who would stand in the middle of the High Street and proclaim in a loud voice, "If you go in *there* (pointing to the Chapel) you will get *Salvation* – If you go in *there* (pointing to the school then in Camden Square) you will get *Education* – And if you go in *there* (pointing to the Working Men's Club) you will get *Damnation*!"

CHAPTER 13

Business and Trade

Market Forces

Man has traded his goods from the dawn of civilisation, exchanging the surplus of the products of his business with the surplus of others to meet his own needs. The Market Place was where this happened and the larger communities became Market Towns (e.g. Market Harborough). King Alfred "was a notable pioneer in founding and refounding towns, and, in the 10th, 11th and 12th centuries, towns sprang up again all over Western Europe. They were communities whose centre and *raison d'être* lay in the market in their midst and in peaceful occupation, yet also the home of fierce independence, internal riots and external wars, so that the walls and gates which surrounded them were as characteristic as the markets, as were the innumerable churches which adorned them...." (Rosalind and Christopher Brook, *Popular Religion in the Middle Ages*, Thames & Hudson, 1984, p.48)

Northampton had its castle, and was a walled market town. Wellingborough's market charter was granted in 1201. The cattle markets of Wellingborough and Northampton need no explanation and men such as Newman Darnell's father were drovers with the specific task of driving cattle and sheep to market, before the mass transport by train and lorry or even by plane took over. In *Kelly's Directory* they are described as Carriers and Coal and Wood Dealers, being carriers to both Wellingborough and Northampton as were Thomas Drage and William Surridge, such was the demand.

Although Wellingborough was famous for its healing waters, attracting nobles and royalty such as Charles I and his Queen Henrietta Maria in 1627 and 1637, county historian Norden pointed to "the importance of the markets held there since the reign of King John," noting that it was "... often called Wellingborow Forum, because of the Market there...." The market grew in importance from the granting of the first Charter until it swamped and eclipsed that of the ancient Borough of Higham Ferrers and with its attendant privileges, brought growing prosperity." (Joyce Pearson).

Guilds (or gilds), crafts and trade

The Medieval Guilds were probably urban in origin. Many were craft organised with important social and economic functions over and above their religious activities but the overwhelming majority, "were religious in character designed to regulate not trade or manufacture but the devotional lives of their members. By the end of the Middle Ages they were as much a rural as an urban phenomenon and most villages had a guild ..." (Eamon Duffey, *The Stripping of the Altars*, Yale 1992, p.142)

The golden age of the craft guilds was the 14th and 15th centuries. They were associations of the members of a particular craft or trade in a particular town. Their primary purpose was the social and economic regulation of the craft or trade, but almost all of them had a religious dimension. Some guilds emphasised secrecy on guild matters, had their own livery and had subscriptions but in general it is not correct to see the guild and the parish as different types of religious/social allegiance, as guilds often gave generous and loyal support to the parish church and community. A 20th century version could be exampled in Arnold Howarth as the last active member of the Brotherhood of the Royal Antediluvian Order of Buffaloes which

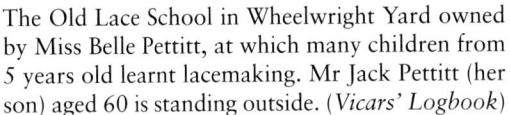

The Old Lace School in Wheelwright Yard owned by Miss Belle Pettitt, at which many children from 5 years old learnt lacemaking. Mr Jack Pettitt (her son) aged 60 is standing outside. (*Vicars' Logbook*)

"Mr and Mrs James Bayes aged 74 and 73 outside their cottage next to the Chequers. Mrs Bayes has made lace from an early age and still (1924) makes and sells privately." (*Vicars' Logbook*)

opened their Sandwell Lodge No. 7276 in the village of Bozeat on 17th March 1937 – a quasi-religious body which continued to have their Harvest Festival in the lounge of the Red Lion into the 1980s with Stan Silsby at the piano, the sermon by Vicar Palmer and support from Eric Brook, Churchwarden of Easton Maudit, auctioning their produce and giving the proceeds to local charities, £153 worth in 1981. Arnold, an amiable, lithe lanky, droll character, who drove for Gola and actively supported the chapels and was typically seen in a smart dark blue blazer plus badge, sadly died in his little bungalow by the church on the morning of Saturday 28th September 1996, just as he was packed ready to go for a week's holiday to Cromer with his friend Mary Wallis, Gloria's mother.

A central feature was the annual 'day' of the guild, usually the feast day of the saint to whom it was dedicated. Many guilds made provision for members in need, whether in sickness or poverty, and a few had their own hospitals. They took part in civic and religious processions, and the craft guilds were normally responsible for the mystery plays. After the scourge of the Black Death in 1348/9 (which reduced the population of England from four to two million) the Churches were beautified by the rich Trade Guilds, the Merchants and private citizens.

Weaving

"During the 14th and 15th Centuries the Weaving Industry flourished in our part of the country and many cottages would have their hand looms made of wood.... One of the earliest Trade Guilds was the Weavers' Guild, and in the Parish Church they had their Guild Chapel. Their patron saint was S. Catherine, because she was

BUSINESS AND TRADE

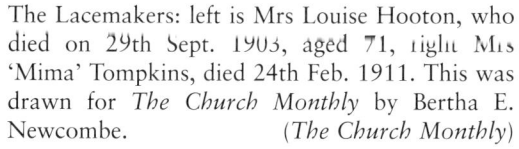

The Lacemakers: left is Mrs Louise Hooton, who died on 29th Sept. 1903, aged 71, right Mrs 'Mima' Tompkins, died 24th Feb. 1911. This was drawn for *The Church Monthly* by Bertha E. Newcombe. (*The Church Monthly*)

Mrs Lydia Rice of Bozeat, who died on 9th July 1916 aged 85, teaching her granddaughter Ethel Johnson lace. Drawn by Bertha Newcombe in 1908 for *The Church Monthly*. In later years Ethel lived with Jacqueline Cave in Easton Lane.
(*The Church Monthly*)

martyred on a wheel, and her Festival, 25th November, was the Weavers' holiday." (*Marlow*, p.15) Our Guild Chapel would have been in the east end of the south aisle. There would have been an altar, as is shown in the inventory of gifts for 1512: "The altar of St Catherine, a linen cloth, Joan Bluet," and on one of the two corbels above, which are still there, there would have been a statue of St Catherine with her wheel. Vicar Palmer describes the ornamentation on one of the stone corbels as "stalks of foliage running into one another, a symbol of continuous life often used in connection with St Catherine. The piscina is still there and of very beautiful design." Virgin Saints such as K(C)atherine were popular in the Middle Ages as virginity and chastity were believed to have sacred power (see *Duffy*).

Marlow suggests that the row of cottages once found in what is called 'The Gold' in Mile Street was originally 'The Guild', i.e. that part of the village where the weavers lived.

Lacemaking
Lacemaking, pillow lace in Northamptonshire, was very active in the past. In 1702 Paul Collinson was apprenticed to Edward Hooton of Bozeat, Lacemaker, for fourteen years. In 1726 Elizabeth Laughton was apprenticed to Robert Brice of Clifford, Bucks, Yeoman to the same trade and, in 1807, Charles Corby aged twelve was apprenticed to John Corby of London, etc. Many of those living in Bozeat in the 1930s remember attending the lace school kept by Miss Belle Pettitt, up Wheelwright

Yard. Boys and girls in the last century would leave school as young as five or six to attend lace school and would pay 1½ pence a week to learn. There were many lace schools or workshops in Bozeat. James Nichols who was buried in 1884 aged 77 kept one at the corner of Easton Lane and sold some of his lace to Mrs Sartoris of Rushden Hall. In Bozeat the noonday bell was rung on St Andrew's Day, 30th November and Tandrew toffee was still made on that day until the 1930s. It seems to have been a village holiday with St Andrew, as well as for St Katherine, the patron saint of lace makers, possibly because he was a fisherman and was therefore a netmaker.

Boot and Shoe trade

The Boot and Shoe trade has been the hallmark of this part of Northamptonshire for centuries, probably making boots for Cromwell's soldiers in the Civil War in the mid-17th century, for English soldiers in both the American War of Independence in the 18th century and the Napoleonic Wars around the start of the 19th century, and for British troops in the Great War of 1914-18. (In each case war provided a handsome boost to the trade.) Again they would have their Guild and in Bozeat there are everywhere little sheds called 'barns' in back yards or attached to the houses where the home industry of shoemaking thrived for centuries. The Patron Saints of shoemakers and leatherworkers are St Crispin and St Crispinian. There is not only a pub called 'The Boot' in Wollaston, our next door village where Dr. Martens shoes are made and business continues, but there is also 'The Crispen Arms'. There is a leather banner and pole in St Mary's presented by the Boot and Shoe Industry of Bozeat (designed by Alison Botterill) to their patron saints, making a link between the Church and the daily work of the village. The Legend says that Crispin and Crispinian were brothers who settled in Soissons in the third century with the intention of bringing the Christian Gospel to the people of Gaul. To avoid attracting attention they worked as cobblers but the excellence of their work and their charity – they shod the poor free – attracted many customers and thereby many were converted to the faith. For this they were arrested and beheaded on 25th October in AD 285. There is a sixth-century church in Soissons dedicated to their memory and their emblem in art is a shoe and a last. The history of Boot and Shoe in Bozeat is dealt with elsewhere.

With the mass migration from the countryside to the town and the consequent urbanization of England in the late 18th and 19th centuries as a consequence of the Industrial Revolution, the guilds were reincarnated as the Trade Unions, a secular corporate organisation of workers which continued to play a major role through the 20th century. With the coming of boot and shoe factories to Bozeat in the late 19th century we could say that the Industrial Revolution had belatedly arrived in our small corner of England and the village became more than less an industrial village. The establishment of union membership in the village and the formation of the Bozeat Co-operative at the end of the 19th century were a reflection of the growing solidarity and confidence of village working class.

Money

The use of money in Bozeat can be traced back to Anglo-Saxon times as a few coins have been found (*Bridges History*, 1791) and there is evidence of a Saxon hamlet from excavations in Hewlett's Close area. An Iron Age coin of Tasciovanus, who was a Trinovantian chieftain, was found near the Church. It was known as a gold slater and was minted around 20-15 BC probably at St Albans. The obverse is three crossed wreaths of corn and the reverse a Celtic warrior on horse.

Money and poverty

Churchwardens' accounts of 1670 and onwards, not kept in the vicarage so not destroyed in the fire of 1729, showed unemployment was as bad then as it ever was. "The third, fourth and fifth decades of the 17th century witnessed extreme hardship in England, and were probably amongst the most terrible years through which the country has ever passed ... many experienced extreme poverty living desperately from one meagre harvest to the next." (Peter Bowden – quoted by Christopher Hill in his *John Bunyan and His Church*, O.U.P., 1988 p.16.) The two generations, before John Bunyan was born in November 1628 not far from our village at Elstow near Bedford, "had been a paradoxical period in which England as a whole was getting richer but the poor were getting poorer." The combined effect of plunder of the church at the Reformation and the growth of population, of world trade and piracy, produced what Bowden called 'the great divide' – 'a massive redistribution of income in favour of the landed class ... as much at the expense of the agricultural wage-earner and consumer as of the tenant farmer.' Real wages halved in the sixteenth century, and the continued drop in the first three decades of the 17th century. As a document of 1591 put it, economic changes "made of yeomen and artificers gentlemen, and of gentlemen knights, and so forth upward; and of the poorest sort of stark beggars." (Hill *ibid*). Our Parish Church accounts reflect these turbulent and difficult times:

"Given to a man and his wife and four children 4d...."
"Given to twelve passengers, 6d."
"Given to a seaman, 6d."
"Given to a young gentlewoman, 2d."
"Spent upon a poor man and his wife, three nights and two days, being lone and weather very weate, 1/s."
"Given to two women which did make that husbands was killed in warre, 6d."
"Given to 8 Jewish people, 8d."
"Spent upon a man and his wife which came out of holand, 1/s."

(Examples from Accounts of Constables between 1670 and 1690. *Marlow*, pp.57,58.)

Trade tokens

These documents indicated that many passengers or wayfarers were lodged by one Wm. Glover. He was evidently a tavern keeper. (*Marlow*, p.57) The smallest coin in those days was the silver penny. As smaller coins of exchange were found necessary in the villages, tradespeople, tavern keepers and others were allowed by the government to use halfpennies and farthing 'tokens' in brass, copper, tin, pewter, lead and even leather. When copper coinage became sufficiently abundant, these private 'tokens' were forbidden. As we have already seen, a Trade Token was found in a field at Easton Maudit by Peter Haggar. It is of the earliest known innkeeper of Bozeat, for on one side of it we read, WILLIAM GLOVER . W G. On the other side we have written OF BOZEAT HIS HALF PENNY 1668. He may well have had the 'Red

Lion'. "Government orders no more minting of trade tokens." This was the message of the Proclamation of 16th August 1672 and on the 22nd of that month, the London Gazette announced that Royal farthings would be issued at an appointed office in Mincing Lane. And in 1673, Royal copper halfpennies were issued, but this did not stop the practice of traders issuing tokens – a practice which continued into the next century. The number of Northamptonshire trades found on 17th century tokens gives us a vivid record of the range of trades practised in those times. They are:

Grocers	Fruiters
Publicans	Glovers
Mercers	Tobacconist
Chandlers	Dyers
Candlemakers	Butchers
Coat of Arms	Ironmongers
Drapers	Millers
Haberdashers	Cordwainers
Bakers	Goldsmith
Carriers (Packmen)	Blacksmith
Weavers	Fruiterers
Officials (Mayor/Overseer/Bailiff)	Booksellers

(Details from Northampton Numismatic Society and Northampton Museum.)

Trades in 1849
(*Whellan's Directory* for this year)

COMMERCIAL

BATTLE, James	Butcher
BIRRELL, William	Stonemason (a Berrill?)
CORBY, John	Blacksmith
HAUGHTON, Thomas	Butcher
HOOTON, Thomas	Carpenter
MALLOWS, John	Shoemaker
MONK, John	Baker
PARTRIDGE, Frs.	Parish Clerk
PEARSON, Robert	Schoolmaster
PETTIT, John	Cattle Dealer
RISELY, Richard	Shoemaker
SANDERS, Thomas	
SKEVINGTON Dexter, Thomas	Shopkeeper and Baker
SKEVINGTON, William	Baker
SQUIRES, Thomas	Tailor
WALKER, John	Tailor
WALLIS, Thomas	Grocer, Draper, Blacksmith
WARNER, Thomas	Baker
WYKES, Thomas junr.	

Carriers: to Northampton, John Nichols, Sat.; Luke Smart, Tues. and Sat.; to Wellingborough, both on Wed.

PUBLIC HOUSES
ALLIN, George	Vict. *Chequers*
DEXTER, Cath.	Beer Retailer
SKEVINGTON, Nancy	Beer Retailer
WOOLEY, Jane	Vict. *Red Lion*

FARMERS AND GRAZIERS
BODDINGTON, Edward
FAUCOTT, William
FAULKNER, William
HENSMAN, Henry
HENSMAN, Mary
HENSMAN, John
ROBINSON, James Charles
SANDERS, Mary
SKEVINGTON, Richard

Trades in 1874 – just as the Bozeat Boot Factories were beginning. (Information provided by Mr Hucknell in Peterborough to *About Bozeat*, September 1994)

COMMERCIAL
BELCHER, Benjamin	Shoe Agent
BROWN, Mrs Ann	Baker and Shopkeeper
CHAPMAN, Stephen	Cottager
DRAGE, Hy	Boot Upper Mfr
DRAGE, John	Shoe Mfr and Grinder
DRAGE, William	Shoe Mfr
GREEN, Miss Susan Annie	Mistress (Infants School)
HARRISON, William	Grocer
HOUGHTON, Thomas	Butcher
KIRBY, J. Wm	Schoolmaster
MONK, John	Baker
PETTIT, Jas	Manager Co-op Stores
PETTITT, William	Shoe Mfr
SKEVINGTON, Mrs Martha	Shopkeeper and Baker
SKEVINGTON, Mrs Mary	Shopkeeper and Baker
SKEVINGTON, Thomas	Butcher
SMART, William	Higgler
TIMPSON, Joseph	Carpenter
WALKER, Dexter Jno	Painter
WALKER, Jno.	Shoe Agent and Grocer
WALKER, John	Miller
WALLIS, Thomas	Blacksmith, Grocer, Draper, Assistant Overseer

PUBLIC HOUSES
BERRY, John	Vict. *Chequers*
CORBY, John	Smith and Beer House

CORBY, Thomas   Shoe Agent and Beer House
HILL, Wm. Fred   Vict. *Red Lion*
SKEVINGTON, Thomas   Beerhouse

FARMERS AND GRAZIERS
ASHWELL, George   Spring Farm
DEVERELL, Richard
FANCOTT, Thos   and Corn Merchant
HOWE, Henry
HUTCHINSON, Hy   Church Farm
MAXWELL, Edward
MAXWELL, Walter   The Grange
POLLARD, Joseph
SANDERS, William

CARRIERS
Frank and Jacob Shrives   To Wellingborough Monday, Wednesday and
                                      Friday and to Northampton Tuesday and
                                      Saturday

Trades in 1904
(*Bennett's Business Directory – Northamptonshire*)
Population 1,478. Early closing: Wednesday at 2 pm. Nearest Railway Station: Castle Ashby, 4 miles distant.

BARNES, J.   Lift Maker, Pear Tree Close
BATTAMS, F. C.   Baker, Grocer and Flour Dealer, Church Lane
BOZEAT Industrial & Provident Society High Street, T. Robinson (manager)
BOTTERILL, W.   Wholesale and Export Boot and Shoe Mfr,
                                          London Road
CORBY, F.   Horses, Traps and Wagonettes for hire, Mile St
CORBY, H.   Boot and Shoe Closer, London Road
CORBY, MRS E.   Grocer, Confectioner and General Grindery
                                          Dealer, Mile Street
CORBY, J.   Fishmonger, High Street
CORBY, T.   Lift Mfr, London Road
CRAXTON, W.   Boot Dealer, 9 Wollaston Road
DRAGE, C.   Builder, London Road
DRAGE, J.   Wholesale Boot Mfr, High Street
EVEREST, G.   Wheelwright, London Road
FREEMAN, T.   Boot and Shoe Closer, London Road
GOODMAN & Son   Boot and Shoe Mfr, Hope Street
GRAY, H.   Grocer and Provision Dealer and Shoe
                                          Grindery, High Street
HARRISON, W.   Grocer, Coal and Wood Merchant, High St
HAYES, W. J.   Tailor, Draper, Milliner and General
                                          Outfitter, London Road
JAMES, W.   Butcher, Church Street

BUSINESS AND TRADE 173

MONK, J.	Miller, London Road
NICHOLS, F.	Pork Butcher, Ham and Bacon Curer, Agent for Yarde & Co. Seeds, High Street
PARTRIDGE, J.	Carrier (W'boro. and Wollaston daily, N'ton Tues and Sat) Church Street
PARTRIDGE, J. W.	Postmaster, Post Officer, London Road
RICE, MISS M.	Grocer, Draper, Haberdasher and Smallwear Dealer, London Road
SKEVINGTON, T.	Family Butcher, Church Street
SMITH, C.	Baker, Pastry Cook and Confectioner, High St
SMITH, F.	Dealer in Boots and Shoes and Sectional Heel Maker, High Street
SMITH, H.	Grocer, Confectioner and General Dealer, Hope St
SMART, W.	Timber Merchant, Church Street
SQUIRES, B. T.	Baker, Grocer, Flour and Offal Dealer, Mile St
SUMMERLIN, A.	Carrier (W'boro Wed., Fri. and Sat; N'ton Tues, Wed. and Sat), Mile Street
SWIFT, F.	Lift maker, High Street
TURNER, F.	Grocer, Tea, Coffee and Provision Dealer, Crockery and General Merchant, Agent for W. & A. Gilbey's wines, London Rd
WALKER, MRS S.	New and Second-hand Furniture Dealer, High Street
WALLIS, W.	Grocer, Ironmonger and General Furnishing Stores, Church Street
WALLIS, W.	Shoeing Smith, High Street

PUBLIC HOUSES, ETC.

Chequers Inn, London Road,	Proprietor, T. Swingler
Cross Keys Inn, High Street	
Red Lion Inn, London Inn	Proprietor, Mrs N. F. Cave
Royal Engineer Inn, Mile Street	Proprietor, H. Corby
Bozeat Working Men's Club and Institute	Sec. J. T. Robinson

Trades in 1911 – Two years after village is sold, three years before the First World War (*Bennett's Business Directory, Northamptonshire*)
Population 1,478. Early closing: Wednesday at 2 pm. Nearest Railway Station, Castle Ashby, 4 miles distant.

BAILEY, R.	Fancy Draper, Hosier and Milliner, High Street
BARKER, T.	Grocer, etc.
BOTTERILL, W.	Wholesale and Export Boot and Shoe Mfr, London Road
CAVE, W. H.	Carpenter, Joiner and Undertaker, London Road
CORBY, F.	Horses, Traps and Wagonettes, London Road
CORBY, J.	Fishmonger, High Street
CORBY, MRS E.	Grocer, Mile Street

CORBY, T.	Lift mfr, London Road
CRAXTON, G. E.	Grocer, Mile Street
DRAGE, J.	Baker, Grocer & Flour Dealer, Church Lane
DRAGE, J.	Wholesale Boot mfr, High Street
EVEREST, G.	Wheelwright, Carpenter and Undertaker, High Street
HAYES, W. J.	Tailor, etc., London Road
HEWLETT, W.	Confectioner, Tobacconist & General Dealer, High Street
JAMES, W.	Butcher, Church Street
JAMES, W. A.	Hardware Dealer
LAUGHTON, J.	Boot Lift Mfr., High Street
PARTRIDGE, J.	Carrier, Church Street
PARTRIDGE, J. W.	Postmaster, Post Office, London Road
RICE, MISS M.	Grocer, Draper, Haberdasher and Smallwear Dealer, London Road.
ROBINSON, T.	Grocer and Provision Dealer, Shoe Grindery, The Square
SELLICK, H. G.	Grocery and General Merchant, Easton Lane
SKEVINGTON, J.	Carpenter, Joiner and Undertaker, Mile Street
SKEVINGTON, T.	Butcher, Church Street.
SMITH, H.	Grocer, Hope Street
SMITH, C.	Baker, Pastry Cook, Confectioner, etc., High Street
SMITH, F.	Dealer in Boots and Shoes and Sectional Heel Maker, High Street
SQUIRES, H. T.	Baker, Mile Street
SUMMERLIN, A.	Carrier, Mile Street
WALLIS, W.	Shoeing Smith, High Street
WALLIS, W.	Grocer, Church Street

PUBLIC HOUSES, ETC.

Cross Keys Inn, High Street	
Lord Nelson Inn, High Street,	Proprietor, H. Sparkes
Red Lion Inn, London Road	Proprietor, B. Bounds
Royal Engineer Inn, Mile Street	Proprietor, H. Corby
Working Men's Club, High Street	

Butchers and bakers
By Norman Palmer

Butchers and bakers are very old trades and appear to have been in existence for at least 200 years and perhaps much longer. The Militia List of 1777 gives us much information as to trades. Robert Cercuit is named as a Baker, but we know nothing else about him or where his bakehouse was.

The Wykes family seemed to have prospered fairly well in both butchering and baking. Thomes Wikes or Wykes appears as butcher in the 1777 Militia List, who may have been the same Thomas buried in 1775. James Wykes was named as Baker

Craftsmenship in Wood

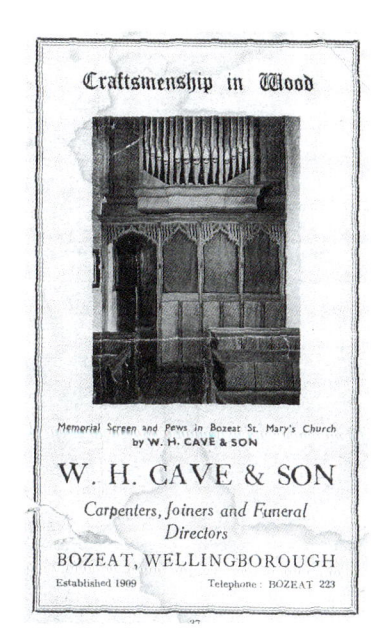

Memorial Screen and Pews in Bozeat St. Mary's Church by W. H. CAVE & SON

W. H. CAVE & SON
Carpenters, Joiners and Funeral Directors
BOZEAT, WELLINGBOROUGH
Established 1909   Telephone: BOZEAT 223

W. H. Cave and Son, publicity poster showing St Mary's Church and Yates organ
(*Vicars' scrapbook*)

in the 1781 Militia List, although what the relationship between the two was is obscure. This son of William and Susannah Wykes was baptised in 1759 and buried on Sept.6th 1846 aged 88. It is probable he had kept the same trade for most of his lifetime, spanning the latter half of the 18th century and well into the 19th. In the Rate Books for 1838-40 he had a house and bakehouse in Dag Lane owned by John Dexter. Like other bakers during the poor period of 1800-1812 when harvests were bad and a war in progress, we find him supplying the parish poor with bread funded by the rates. Bakers were needed by the parish at pauper funerals when bread was given with the liquid refreshments. Such is the meaning of the Overseer's Accounts for Sept. 1812: "James Wykes Bill for Bread for Burials 11s-10d." It is possible that John Monk took over the bakehouse.

In the 1781 Militia list we find Graveley Lawton named as Baker. He was Overseer of the Poor a number of times beginning in 1778, so it is not surprising that like other bakers he too supplies bread to the parish poor. In 1791 for instance he is paid 2s-2d for bread, and continues to do so in the bad years ahead.

The Skevington family appears to have produced both butchers and bakers. Edward Skevington, born 1736 and buried 1814 aged 78, was a Maltster in his will, but apparently had a hand in more than one trade, for he bequeaths his Butcher's shop to his son Thomas, who is classed as Butcher in the 1789 Militia List. This Thomas was baptised in 1767, but we are uncertain of when he died, it may have been in 1835. Samuel, son of Thomas (1793-1848) was also for a time a butcher, but eventually became the landlord of the Lord Nelson, so trade could not have been too good. William Skevington (1795-1868) was another son of Thomas and two years younger than Samuel. He appears with his wife Mary as a lace-buyer in 1833, but times were bad for lace, for with the competition of machine lace there was little profit. It seems that they ran a lace school for a while, but about 1840 the premises where they lived were converted. By 1842 he is described in a Baptismal entry as a Baker and in an 1854 directory as Baker and Grocer. The yard in the 1851 Census was known as Skevington's Yard. It seems probable from what the writer has heard that William took over as butcher, whilst his wife was the baker. After his death his widow is described as 'Baker and Shopkeeper'.

To go back to an earlier period, the Dexter family was another with a tradition of baking. They held the right parish offices, Overseers and Churchwardens, to profit by the connection. With the other bakers they also supplied the poor during the critical period after 1800. Thomas Dexter (1741-1830) as baker appeared to have considerable property and some land. Like the other bakers he supplied bread for pauper funerals e.g. Sept.1812: "Pd Mr Dexter for Bread John Johnsons Child Burial 2s-0d." He probably had a house at the rear of Mile Street.

Samuel Boddington, the family from which Susannah Church came, was another butcher in the 1798 Militia List and was still carrying on his trade when his child was baptised in 1813. At the same period (1813-1818) Daniel Hooton, as a father in baptism is described as a poulterer.

Thomas Houghton (1816-1894) was a long-time resident in Bozeat, in the house known as 'The Mount' in Mile Street. He apparently came to the village from away and continued his trade as a butcher. He also had some land for keeping his stock. 'The Mount' continued as a butcher's shop into living memory, and before renovation a cold storage unit could be seen in the cellars with slaughtering house at the rear complete with drain-away. There is some specialisation in the trade when, in the 1904 Directory, P. Nichols was a pork butcher and curer of ham in the High Street, and to diversify his trade was an agent for a seed firm.

It is when we come to the 20th century that the details can be 'filled out'. The bakehouse, which once stood in Pudding Bag was sold to Joseph Drage, the oven being heated by faggots, three or four bundles being used daily. It was his son John who converted this oven to coal in 1894. The daily batch of loaves then was about 200, chiefly 'cottages' a 2lb loaf at 2d per loaf and 'penny batches' – 1lb loaves. Flour was about 17/- per sack. Pastries and cakes were also made and after the bread was done, customers' dinners were cooked in the still warm oven – the charges for these were ½d for 2 large tarts, ½d per fruit pie, 1d for a family cake, 1d per Yorkshire pudding or large tin of potatoes. When John Drage retired in 1922 his son William Sydney Drage took over until 1948.

Mention has been made of Thomas Skevington and two of his sons William and Samuel. Another son, the eldest, named after his mother's maiden name, Dexter Thomas Skevington probably worked with his brother William for a time, but by the time of the 1851 Census was living in Mile Street. He lived from 1791-1871 classed in the Trade Directories as a 'Shopkeeper and Baker'. His wife, like her sister-in-law, carried on the business after her husband's death – one supposes that they had to before the era of old-age pensions. If these premises continued as a bakehouse, and this is possible as ovens would not be easily constructed and it would be simpler to take over an existing bakery, then the bakehouse may well have continued down to John Robinson, after which it was taken over by Benjamin Squires.

Benjamin Squires came to Bozeat before the turn of the century at the age of 11, working at John Monk's bakery in Camden Square for seven years. When he became independent, he took over the bakehouse in Mile Street in 1900. There he had a wood oven using four faggots a day. At first he delivered bread in a wheelbarrow, later a horse and cart. Flour was at this time 18/- for a 20 stone sack. The Trade Directory of 1904 says about Mr Squires that he was "baker, grocer, flour and offal dealer, Mile Street. Families called upon daily, wholemeal and brown bread to order." Bakers were remembered as pushing their carts up to Grange Farm and over to Harrold Wood Farm in order to deliver their goods and retain custom. Before the Great War, Mr Squires bought premises in London Road from Mr Warren, the butcher, and in 1913 built the brick bakehouse with a coal oven adjacent, which held 300 loaves in one batch, baked by hand 6 times a week and used to cook Sunday dinners for customers until electric cookers became available. He is remembered as being something of a 'character' and being very good to the poor.

Mention has been made of the bakehouse in Dag Lane. This was held by John Monk, Miller and Baker from 1845 onwards, diversifying his trade by adding 'Grocer' to the list. As miller he had the windmill, but used both wind and steam to grind his flour. Village memories are not very kind sometimes, but they do give some semblance of truth when as Overseer of the Poor he was not thought to be generous to those in need. However, he brought an orphan named Charles Smith from Northampton as an apprentice baker. In time Charles Smith was to marry the daughter of the local shoe manufacturer, John Drage, and thereby, through family connections to increase trade and to buy the bakery from John Monk. There were enough bakers around to increase the competition and one elderly resident could remember a fist fight over custom with another baker. Three years after opening as a baker Mr and Mrs Smith built a dwelling on to the property (in Dag Lane) and the old bakehouse was pulled down and rebuilt. He is advertised in the 1904 Directory as "Baker, pastrymaker and confectioner, etc. Wedding, birthday, school, and all kinds of cakes made to order". His late daughter told the writer that they were baking seven days a week. The fires were started with faggots, and then the coal was put on. Housewives would arrive on a Sunday with their joints of meat in one can and their puddings in another. When the bakehouse was rebuilt the first baking was on Good Friday making a batch of hot cross buns. The flour house was above the bakehouse. This later, so the writer is told, was used as a storeroom for the Home Guard. The oven was capable of baking over 200 loaves, and above the oven was a boiler. Mr C. Smith had a large round taking in the villages of Podington, Hinwick, Easton Maudit and Grendon, using a horse and cart. Older residents of Bozeat could remember the bakehouse baking the Sunday dinners having as many as 40 pans of different sizes, each with a name, having to be taken away by 12 o'clock. There would be trouble of course if the dinners for various owners got mixed after cooking and delivery – but it did happen!

Trade in Bozeat: 1980s – just after Bozeat boot factories close
(based on information advertisements in *About Bozeat* – first edition March 1980)

TV Repairs/Sales	Barry Drage (1980-), Rushden and Wollaston
Post Office and Spar Stores	Keith and Carol Cullip (1980-) Camden Square
D. B. J. Builders (1980-)	Bob Ingram, Hope Street
Carpenter, etc: (198?-)	Paul Ingram, Wyman Close
Landscapes: (1980-)	Malcolm Threadgold, Goffs Yard
Takeaways (1982-)	J. M. Batty (1982-), Pat and Roger Alderman (1985-), Arthur and Linda Walsh (1985-), Yum Yums, High Street
Professional Services (1987-)	Rachel Mallows, High Street
The Paper Shop (1980-)	Barry and Sandra Carvel (1982-85), Robert and Pat Driver (1985-98), Barry and Steph Strain (1998-)
Joinery and Carpentry (1980-1994)	Steve Laughton, High Street
Skip Hire (198?-)	Doug Brown, Knights Close
Videos (199?-)	Fred Dilloy, Hope Street
Insurance (198?-)	Geoff Betts, Fullwell Road
Hairdressers	Studio/Salon One (198?-), High Street
Greengrocers, etc.	Toni's (1988-), Martin and Ken Gibbs (1991-)
Red Lion (1980-)	Jim and Jan Baker (1988-), London Road
Garage/Service Station (1980-94)	M. and D. Young (1980-89), Mike (1990-94), London Road

Carpenter and Joiner, etc. (1980-)	W. H. Cave and Son, London Road
Co-op (1980-91)	London Road
Provisions and Groceries (1956-)	Vera Askew, London Road
Glass Specialists (1980-)	Beckfords, London Road
Electrical Contractor (1980-)	Richard Zang, Fullwell Road
D.I.Y., Builder, Carpenter (1981-)	John Spriggs, Camden Sq./London Rd
Builders and Contractors (1980-)	Elliott and Dobbs, Peartree Close
Wellingborough Building Co. (1982-)	Peter and Tony Spencer, Bull Close
Butchers (1980-)	Tottman and Gell (mobile to Bozeat), Harrold
Butchers (1890-1990)	Garretts, Mile Street
Health Foods, etc. (1983-)	The Little Shop, High Street
Electrical Retail/Trade (1983-85)	Sparkies, London Road
Grendon Roofing (1983-)	Eric Green, Wyman Close
Driving School – Three Shires (1985-)	Gordon Bayes, Harrold Road
Taxi (198?-)	Tim Hickling, Harrold Road
Taxi (1988-)	Paul and Jean Summerfield, High Street
Sinclair Fabrics (1989-)	London Road
Working Men's Club	Collin Neunzer (1988-), London Road
Riselky Rustics (Garden Structures) (1990-)	John Cox, Fullwell Road
M&M Stores (1991-1995)	Mohan Singh and Mohinder, London Road
Greengrocer and Flowers (1991-92)	Martin and Ken Gibbs Little Hut, High Street

Conclusions

The trade lists above, spanning a century and a half, tell their own story. Those for 1849 and 1874, though not a complete picture of village trade, do reflect the transformation of Bozeat over this period from a basically agricultural to a rural industrial village as shoemaking moves from a cottage based industry to a factory-driven one. We see an increasing sophistication in trades (shoe agents, lift manufacturers, wholesale and export, etc.) paralleled by that in farming as small farmers and graziers are superseded by bigger and more specialised farms as each must become more competitive to survive, e.g. milk farmers like the Browns from Cheshire with their pedigree Friesian herd.

In the boot and shoe trade, mergers were required to make the technical innovations to meet the market needs, until we have a giant company Gola with an international market growing ever more rapidly, until in about 1980 the bubble bursts and the long history of the shoe trade in the village suddenly comes to an end. Farming has followed a similar growth over the two centuries peaking somewhere in the mid-20th century, but then a less spectacular decline and at the turn of the millennium we see our farmers hard pressed to remain competitive within the wider European market. And alongside these major breadwinners there are what we may call the supporting service industries of the village, aiming to meet every human need and making it almost self-sufficient in itself. These peaked in the thriving and relative prosperity of the early decades of the 20th century, ensuring the rich self-promoting village culture of these years (see 'Memory Lane'). But these were to suffer a similar decline and fall.

Through these lists we see them in their heyday in the booming retail trade with its 30 or so shops in the village selling everything (Chapter 14) and the Co-op (Chapter 15) which survived for a century as a village institution with its proud boast of selling "everything you need" – together with the carriers, tailors, confectioner, grocer, baker, blacksmith, miller, Post Office, carpenters and three undertakers!, etc. – see the lists for 1905 and 1911 when the sale of the village must have brought new forces of free enterprise and innovation.

Population size also reflects this growth in prosperity. It remained static at about 400 for centuries but began to rise with increasing momentum at the beginning of the 19th century after Enclosure reaching 1,000 by the beginning of the 20th and then suddenly doubling in size to nearly 2,000 in the 1980s following the influx of outsiders from the London overspill, etc. into the new estates built on the small holdings and allotments of the old farming community signifying the burial of this aspect of the past.

And we must not forget the dramatic rise in Nonconformity in the village with the building of the chapels representing the increased dignity and self awareness of the 'working man' – alongside the flourishing pubs and the creating of the Working Men's Club as a reflection of the modest but real rising prosperity and rich diversity of village life. But again all these institutions and activities have experienced their own decline since the Second World War as the village as a closed community lost its invisible but invincible barriers to the outside world, and now its residents live and work and play beyond its borders and our self-sufficient village is no more. We see this in the decimation of retail life and the trades listed from this latter half of the 20th century which are supplementary to the larger businesses and trades and supermarkets and DIY of the wider world now on our doorstep (our village undertakers are no more!) and survive by their convenience, filling the gaps in our modern multiplicity of needs and wants and interests in the new millennium.

Postscript on the Bozeat Windmill
We have already noted how windmills possibly came from the East after the Crusades of Richard I. The Lumley Deeds of 1343 refer to "The Windmill" in Bozeat as does a Terrier of 1633 and there is reference to a Millway in the 18th century.

"Our latest mill is a Post Mill and has initials 'R.H. 1761' on its main 2 foot 8 inches square oak Post – possibly those of the Miller at that time," writes Marlow and continues: "There were two mills at one time, the other being in Windmill Field." (*Marlow*, p.83). A field to the north of the village is still known as Windmill Field and in the 1886 Sale of the Bozeat Estate in Lot 3 'Church Farm' there is reference to "an excellent Site for a Mansion in the Windmill Hill Field, having a nice elevation...." Mr Hensman, who owned Church Farm before Mr Knight, planted an avenue of elms and Lombardy poplars in preparation for building a mansion there but never did (see Dolly Roberts' description of them in Chapter 1). The trees have since disappeared, possibly through being diseased.

In his book *Windmills of Northamptonshire* (W. D. Wharton, Wellingborough, 1991 p.33f), Trevor Stainwright questions Marlow's conclusion above. In the first Ordnance Survey Map of the area circa 1833 (Old Series 1 inch) a post mill is depicted to the north of the village – and no windmills are shown in Bozeat in the Eyre and Jeffrey's map of Northamptonshire in 1779. This is curious with the regard to the initials R.H. and their date 1761. The windmill had presumably disappeared by 1846 for in that year another is offered for sale with the inducement, "there is no other windmill within 6 miles." From this information, Stainwright believes that there was only one windmill, a post mill, originally built to the north of the village

Looking from the site of the windmill to the north of village, looking down Cow Lane towards village with remainder of the avenue of trees.

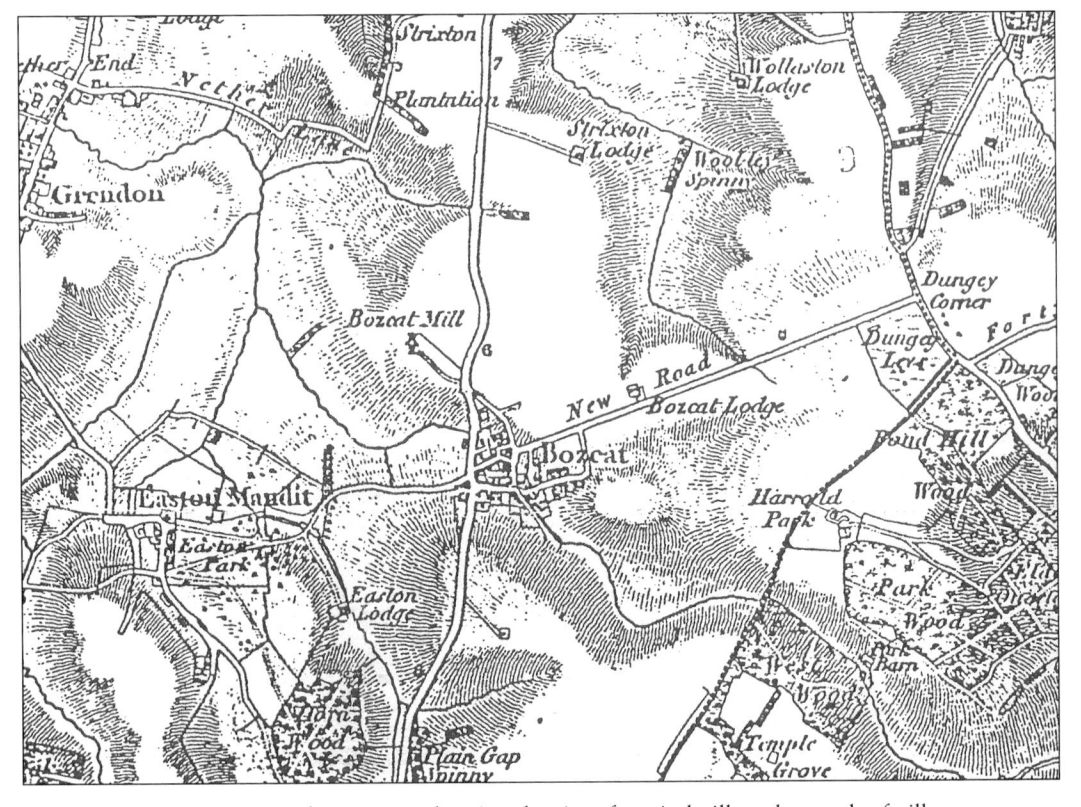

Map of the region from 1835, showing the site of a windmill to the north of village.

and there by 1833 which was then dismantled and re-erected on the southern edge of the village. Lack of information from residents suggests that he is right, although there undoubtedly have been other windmills around Bozeat in earlier times.

But on the Enclosure Map in St Mary's Church for the Bozeat Estate of 1799 there is at the centre a large Allotment (No. 16) designated for the Town Well Acre (presumably for its upkeep) which is situated to the north of the village and west of the London Road a drawing which is remarkably like a post mill. (N.B. Mill fields as they are called on this map where we now find Windmill Field.) So a mill was there in 1799 if not in 1779. As it was made/first used in 1761 do we conclude that Bozeat acquired it second-hand? (Village tradition is that it was bought second-hand and came from Peterborough way in the mid-1700s.)

Further information cames from a map based on the survey by William Mudge and Thomas Colby between 1808 and 1817, extensively revised in 1834 with the railway from Northampton to Peterborough along the Nene Valley added in 1854. On this, "Bozeat Mill" is clearly marked to the north of the village in the vicinity of Windmill Field with a road to it from the Wollaston Road which is almost a continuation of Allens Hill and about the same length (¼ mile). As it is on the 1854 version of this map do we conclude that the mill was still there in 1854 and had not disappeared by 1846 as Stainwright suggests? Whatever conclusion we draw there is no sign of another mill to the south of the village in this map.

The author and publisher, with Bernard Line, visited the earlier northern site by courtesy of Raymond Roberts and, where the 1870 map showed the mill to be, found what might well be a part of an old grinding stone under bushes. The site is at the highest point offering a panoramic view of the surrounding country facing towards Northampton which on a clear day can be seen on the horizon. Facing the prevailing westerlies above open flat land it would seem the most sensible place to position a windmill.

The post mill was the most famous and the last of its kind in Northamptonshire. It had four cross beams 20 yards long rotating in a clockwise direction and was three stories high. At the end of the long tail pole was a wheel and winch which could be hand cranked so as to turn the mill on its post till the sails faced into the wind. The trestle and buck were made of oak but the stocks of Norwegian pine. Its mighty grinding stones were geared directly to the four great sails and in a steady wind it would grind six bushels an hour – and nine bushels in a strong one.

In 1846 Thomas Saxby held the mill but soon replaced by William Spencer. In 1851 Denton Gilbert of Pudding Bag Lane had it with a single employee, Will Skevington the 21-year-old son of the village baker.

By 1871 John Walker aged 41 a miller from Bedfordshire had taken it over. He had formerly worked the watermill at Milton Ernest, post mills at Riseley and Yeldon and possibly also the watermill at Billing. He was assisted by his eldest son Jon aged 23 and George Hooton aged 20. Violent storms damaged the mill in his time. Between 1877 and 1890 it was sold to John Little and he and the last of his daughters Mabel Little (born 1888) were the last Millers of Bozeat and worked the mill until 1921 when it ceased commercial production. It was worked alongside a steam mill and was mostly used in winter months.

On the night of Monday 28th February 1949 the old windmill fell down (the money necessary for its preservation – some £200 to £300 could not be raised) after standing idle for 28 years. Mabel said it was a night of steady but light rain but the papers reported it stormy. On the morning of the 20th all that remained was a heap of broken woodwork and twisted metal exposing the massive giant millstones in the centre.

Mabel died in her 97th year on the 10th February 1985. A post mill is engraved on her tombstone in the village cemetery. The badge on the pullovers of the children of the village school shows a windmill, and the old millstones lie in their playground to remind them of the village past. And its foundations can still be seen in the back yard of 5 Roberts Street looking out on to Mill field.

The windmill in full sail, with perhaps the miller's wife and two children standing in the buck of the post mill at the top of the steps, c.1905.

The windmill working with two millers posing on the steps. The steam mill with its chimney can been seen, with the granary between.

The old Bozeat Windmill c.1930, in derelict condition and tilting.

(*John Darker*)

CHAPTER 14

Shops and Shopkeepers

The British are a nation of shopkeepers.
Napoleon

Shopkeepers of the eighteenth to the 20th century
Norman Palmer, with additions by Philip Bligh

The first evidence of a shopkeeper in Bozeat is found in the Churchwarden Accounts for 1729: "Paid for Nailes 5 pound to Nath Jakes 1s-10¾d". Nathaniel Jakes is known in the Poll Books as early as 1702. When he made his will in 1746 he described himself as Grocer. There is no mention of a shop or goods in his will but apparently he had a dwelling and an orchard. It would seem he had no family, only nephews and nieces. He was buried in 1752 aged 79, named as the husband of Mary Jakes. We do not know whether he had lived here all his life, but if so it would seem possible that there was a shop here in the late 17th century.

Most villages depended upon the local market town, until the beginning of the Industrial Revolution and the Enclosures. A very great deal of food was grown locally and the necessary goods manufactured in cottage industries. The Enclosures (in our case in 1799) meant the land for local food supplies was in other hands, and the factories provided competition which decimated the cottage industries. With the coming of the Turnpike Roads there were better roads for carrying goods – ours was turnpiked in 1754). The second incentive for shopkeeping was the coming of the railways, and the carrier services increased from the railway station, bringing more goods into the range of the village shopkeeper.

Susannah Church and her family
But, just before this era, there emerges 'out of the shadows' Susannah Church, who must have been a remarkable woman. William Church was a shepherd, with some land and property. As a widower he married Susannah Boddington in 1762. When the registers were signed he could not write, but she could, which was very unusual in those days as it was usually the reverse. It would seem that she came from a family with some money so she had some education, which was put to good use. William Church was obviously very possessive of his educated wife, for in his will in 1770 he says, "I give unto my beloved wife Susannah Church the house that I live in & the Commons of Pasture lying & being in Bozate fields hereunto belonging for Her Natural life. Provided she keeps her self a Widow of William Church. And also all my personal Estate of what kind so ever, but if she maryes again Then Nothing. Then I Give and Devoise (devise) unto my Son William Church the house that I live in for Him and for His Heirs for ever." But far from marrying anyone else she was to be buried in 1797, whilst he was not buried until a year later. The house of which he speaks is known now as Glebe Cottage in Church Lane. In the Methodist Bedford Circuit Membership List for 1792 Susannah heads the list, perhaps as Class Leader, with the trade of Shopkeeper, whilst her husband came second on the list. It would seem probable that this lady founded Methodism in Bozeat. [and she was a contemporary of the founder of Methodism John Wesley (1703-91). *phb*] The house

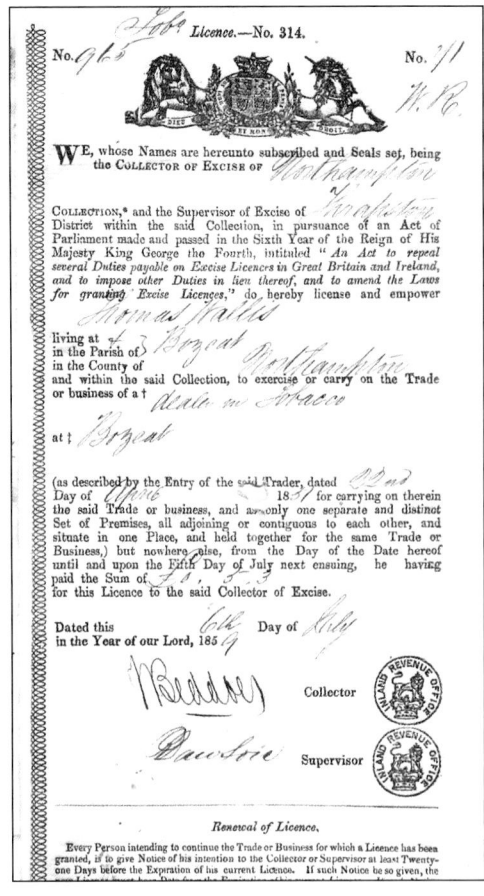

Thomas Wallis, Glebe Cottage. Licence to sell tobacco dated 1859. (D. West)

was to remain as a shop within the family for some years. So we have the impression of an educated personality able to take a lead in village life.

It was Susannah Church who supplied many of the goods bought by Overseers of the Poor for the village paupers. Here is a selection from the accounts:

> 1798 "Mrs Church 6 Ells Cloth 14s-0d", and in the same year, "Mrs Church for a shirt Henry Drage 4s-0d.", 1792 "Mrs Church for a shift 3s-4½d."

Meanwhile, and probably from the same premises, the shepherd's son, another William, was a lace-dealer, paying for the lace worked in the homes and supplying the thread, bobbins, and lace-pillows, both before and after his step-mother's death. Besides the lace, he was able to supply from distant markets further supplies of a very wide range of goods.

This was the era of the Napoleonic Wars when the local Militia (men called upon to do military duty in this country) and the village had to supply powder and shot. In an interesting bill for 17th October 1793 we find such items as:

"2lb Shott 7d. ½lb powder 12d." and in with the bill, items for paupers, "2½ yards buff karsey 2s-6d.", "Buttons 7d pockits 5½d thread 1d – 1s-1½d."

The above was for John Grange (a pauper) supplied on 9th November 1793 and in the following January:

"pare stockings for John Grange 1s-10d" "2½ Ells Cloth for Sue Hawkings 17½d - 3s 3½d."

It would seem that for a time the house was used for worship by the early Methodists, before building their first Chapel down in Mile Street. William Church (Jnr.) continued purchasing and selling to the parish into the 19th century:

Jan/Feb 1810 "Mr Church for 1½ yards of flanell for James Maycocks wife 1s-10d." June 1817 "Bought of Mr Church 2 Pair of Stockings for John Corby 4s-10d." Sept/Oct 1817 "Pd Mr Church for SM (Smock) Frock for J Corby 6s-0d." (a common item worn by all the labourers).

William's daughter Margaret married an Edward Stocker in 1833 and they took over the family shop, having three children, the father being described (in the baptism register) as 'Grocer'. In the Churchwarden's Accounts for 1844 there is just one item that was purchased there, obviously for the Church stove: "Mr Stocker Brushes and Black Lead 1s-2d." It does not appear that the shop continued in the same hands for many years, for at some date before the middle of the 19th century the property came into the possession of Mr Thomas Wallis, blacksmith, from Finedon, who had the old smithy whilst his family kept the shop well into the 20th century.

Thomas Wallis has an entry in the 1847 Trade Directory and in every directory onwards in that century, classed as blacksmith, grocer, draper and ironmonger (see Chapter 13). One has to remember that, like the village craftsman, shopkeepers did not, and could not, restrict themselves to 'one line'. Some of Thomas Wallis' sales appear in the Easton Maudit's Churchwardens Accounts:

May 27th 1870 "Brush 2/-, Hand Brush 8d, Mop 1/1d, Soap 4d, Soda 1d, Flannel 5½d, Scrubbing Brush 8d. Total 5s-2½d."

By 1904 the business appeared to have been taken over by Thomas' nephew William Wallis. Thomas Wallis died in 1901 aged 83, having at his funeral a choir of school children as a mark of respect to a school manager (see Chapter 17).

But to return to an earlier period. Another shopkeeper of the period when the shop at the top of Church Lane was in the hands of the Church family, was William Abraham, who possibly came from Olney and settled here marrying Susannah Pettit in 1791. It appears he could not write – yet he must have been able to do his sums, otherwise he could not have survived. In the 1798 Militia list he is described as 'Grocer', the ubiquitous term which meant he sold just about anything that was

Looking down Church Lane to Dag Lane, the cottages in the distance having since been demolished to make way for St Mary's Road. The School Houses are on the left.

John Drage had a greengrocers shop on the corner of Church Lane and High Street (Millers Corner) from 1925, and sold from his cart until 1946. Here he is pictured on his rounds, with two large money pockets, one for copper and one for silver. *(Bozeat School Scrapbook)*

needed for a village community. He certainly survived as far as the earliest Trade Directory, that of 1847 still as 'Grocer'. According to the 1799 Enclosure Map his shop was somewhere near the site of the later Baptist Chapel not far down Church Lane from the shop owned by the Church family. In the 1798 Overseer Accounts there is evidence of his trading for the parish; "William Abraham bill 6s-6d." On 6th July 1812 there is another entry: "Pd Wm. Abraham for Bread and Cheese at John Joley (Jolley) burrel (burial) 5s-2½d." he must have had a horse and cart for he was hired by the parish to take a sick person to Northampton Hospital. Nearly all the shopkeepers of this period seem to have been successful because they all did a little property speculation – in fact Thomas Wallis and the Skevington family were said to have owned the village between them (see Chapter 16). By 1851 William Abraham owned three cottages and appears to have retired to Dychurch to live with his daughter and son-in-law William Robinson, an agricultural labourer.

After the middle of the 19th century the number of shops and range of shopkeeping increased with a greater population and more wealth from the Boot and Shoe Trade, but, as mentioned previously, they were all prepared to sell more than 'one line'. William Skevington was a grocer and baker. John Walker was a tailor and grocer, and Miss Rice a grocer and draper.

Some notes in the Record Office record memories of earlier village shops. Many older residents will maybe remember Mrs Susannah Harrison keeping a sweet shop at what is called 'Miller's Corner', the corner of Church Lane and High Street. She had a printed notice in the window which read: 'Don't poke your nose where it isn't wanted. Come and buy!' She was obviously in the best position for the village school opposite. She is remembered as selling penny 'lucky p turnovers' – some having a threepenny piece inside – if the customer was lucky. Not all customers were lucky for it is recorded in the School Logbook of a pupil dying from a poisoned sweet, we don't know from whom, but it was a tragedy not unknown in those days where manufacturing standards were not so high. Mrs Harrison's son William had a waggonette and ran a coal business as well as being a general carrier, listed in the trade directories for the time as "Fly-proprietor, grocer, coal and wood merchant."

Another resident of the same shop nearer to our own time was John Drage, a general dealer and fruiterer. When he left school he went as an assistant to A. Knighton, grocer and wine and spirit merchant who had a shop on the site of the London Road Co-op around the 1900s. John Drage went round the villages with a horse and open van. He could remember selling sugar in those days at 1¼d a lb. After a period of shoemaking and army service in World War I, he started as a greengrocer operating from Wollaston Road. He was to come to 'Miller's Corner' in 1925.

Again about the turn of the century Mrs (Betsy Shep) Drage had a small shop at the top of Mile Street and is remembered for the notice extolling her ginger beer:

> *If you want pop, one momentary stop.*
> *At my door just rattle, 1½d for a bottle.*
> *The string untie the cork will fly,*
> *The pop begins to hiss.*
> *Then you will say, as well you may,*
> *I've never had pop like this.*

In the 1911 Directory, Thomas Robinson was a grocer and provision dealer, where the Post Office is now. In about 1920 he gave up his shop. He is well remembered by the children for taking a large box of sweets over to the school playground and throwing them out to the children to catch and scramble for – his parting gift!

Mention has to be made of the very long hours that shopkeepers and their assistants kept in those days. Up to 1912 there was no regulating the hours that a shop could stay open or how long an assistant had to stay on his or her feet. But in that year the Shops Act was passed which stated that in every week shop assistants must receive one day's half-holiday. When the Parish Council received notice of this it was resolved in April 1912 that shops in Bozeat be closed on Wednesday at 1 o'clock, and so it has remained ever since. At the same time they applied to local banks to open an office in Bozeat but it would seem at that time there was not enough custom to make it viable – what a pity!

But a look at the Trade Directories at the turn of the century reminds one what a diversity there was in the village. There was a John Drage hairdresser, J. Corby fishmonger, Mrs Sophia Walker new and second-hand furniture dealer, George Everest wheelwright, carpenter and undertaker (there were in fact three undertakers in competition around this time! – see chapter on Trades). And Mr William J. Hayes tailor, draper and milliner and general outfitter who had suits to measure from 32/6d, trousers 10/6d and the newest things in hats, ties, braces, fronts, collars, shirts, etc. Those were the days! What about the memories of some of our oldest residents? We shall test them out next.

Bozeat shops in the last century

BEFORE THE GREAT WAR
Starting from the Wollaston end we have along the London Road (as remembered by Harry Silsby):
Dennis Squires – Baker.
Hayes the Drapers.
John Partridge – Post Office.

Camden Square. (*John Darker*)

High Street, starting from London Road end:
Miss Rice – Sweets.
Cross Keys – Public house.
William Hewlett – Grocers.
Co-op.
Millers Barbers shop – opposite Methodist.
Mrs Harrison (Millers corner of Church Lane with High Street) Camden Square – Sweets.
Mr Walker – Grocer (opposite).
Dick Strange – Butcher (on corner).
Mr Robinson – Groceries and sweets (see above).
William Wallace – Grocer, Ironmonger, Blacksmith and all (shop on Square and also up Church Lane at Glebe Cottage) – a bit of everything.

Then up Church Lane:
Cephas Drage – Baker and Grocer.
Garretts – Butchers (started 1895).

DURING THE GREAT WAR
All those mentioned above except for Miller's, and Harry adds:
Ernie 'Laddie' Drage – Greengrocer.
Benny Squires – Baker (started up Mile Street/ now London Road). (But how does this relate to Dennis Squires?)

BETWEEN THE WARS
In this period the 'little shop' was booming. The following list as remembered by Don and Dolly Roberts and Harry Silsby and others shows that then there were over 30

small shops whereas today (1995) there are only four – a Materials shop in London Road, the Paper Shop and Takeaway at Arch Villa (also a ladies hairdressers) and the Spar Shop and Post Office at Camden Square.

London Road (starting the Wollaston end):
Feegan Drage – Sweets/groceries.
Sam Bayes (next door) – Sweets, etc.
Chequers Public House.
Squires – Bakery.
Don Roberts – Greengrocer in old school, sweets, etc.
Mr Hayes – Post Office (took over from Mr Partridge), drapery, material rolls, wool.
Co-op (next door and opp. Red Lion) – Groceries, drapery, spices, snuff, tobacco, medicinals.
Red Lion Public House.
Bill Warner's – (up from Red Lion) Threshing tackle and coal business later. Turned it into a garage – took it over from Sarringtons.
Deverills – (opp. Greenwood) Sweets.
Ted Partridge – Garage, petrol/repairs 105 London Rd.
Bayes – Newsagent (top of London Rd.)

High Street (starting at London Road end):
Miss Rice (opp. Cross Keys) Sweets, fruit.
Allebone – (next to Miss Rice) Comics, *Wellingborough News*.
Cross Keys.
Mrs Mabbutts – Tailors, stockings, etc.
William Hewlett (Baycock) – Grocers, sweets, drapery, fancy goods, shoe repairs.
Skevingtons (crippled lady opp. paper shop) – Sweets.
Spenny Drage – Arch Villa (from William Drage) Property business.
Coady Craxton – Cycle shop. His father Ernie had a bakery in front of it.
John Farey – (took over Ernie Craxton's shop) – Barber.
Mr and Mrs Corby – Fresh fish shop behind John Farey in Fish Alley.
Sarringtons – (in Warner's Yard) Bakery (cakes).
Working Men's Club.
Lord Nelson (no licence for spirits).

Camden Square:
Mrs Cave and Mrs Johnson – (now Spar Shop and P.O.) Groceries, sweets, took over P.O. from Hayes.
Dick Strange – Butcher.
William Wallace – Blacksmith, grocer, ironmonger (son Alfred took it over).
Yorks of Wollaston – Fried fish and take away (in Walker's old shop).

Church Lane (going up):
Powell – Fish shop (on Miller's corner).
Laddie Drage – Groceries, sweets (William's Corner).
Cephas Drage – Bakehouse in Burton Terrace/Pudding Bag Lane, also sweets, groceries.
Ada Wallace – (top of Church Lane) Sweets, drapery.

Camden Square. The tree on the right was planted to commemorate the Diamond Jubilee of Queen Victoria in 1897. In the centre is the Independent Wesleyan Chapel.

Garretts – Butchers (top of Mile Street).

Mile Street:
Lizzy Corby – Sweets, groceries, sausages.
Mabel Parker – Sweets, groceries.
The Engineer (Corby).

Dychurch:
George Drage – sold a few sweets up Dychurch.

NOTES:
(i) Spenny Drage – took over Arch Villa from William Drage, shoemaker and started a shop running a property business. Sold shop (and adjacent factory) to David Mallows after World War II (1960s) who took over all newsagent businesses in village. Shop now rented from David Mallows and part of factory used by daughter Rachel for 'Services to Business', part as Take Away and part as Hairdresser (1996).

(ii) Coady Craxton – bicycles. His father Ernie Craxton had the bakery in front of his cycle shop. John Farey took over Ernie's shop as his hairdressers. It is now (1995) the village charity shop BOZAID run by Eric Green whose grandfather was Ted Drage.

(iii) Walker's greengrocers stood empty for years – so did Mrs Harrisons. William Wallace died and son Alfred kept on as blacksmith while his daughters, Annie and Millie kept the shop.

(iv) Thomas Barker went to Olney and the Co-op took over – and Anne Skevington ran the shop for a year or two.

(v) When John Partridge died, the Post Office went to Hayes the Drapers then to Mrs Cave. Alf Mabbott went into the Drapery.

(vi) Fish Shops: Yorks from Wollaston took over Walkers old shop and then Spenny Drage rented it for a bit. Mr and Mrs Corby had a fish shop behind present BOZAID shop. Used to go around with a horse and trolley to neighbouring villages two or three times a week selling fish. "That's where fish started. The house were called Fish Row and the alley below Fish Alley. They were there when I was a youngster and old Mrs Corby was still alive when we was married." (Harry Silsby – born 1914)

Arch Villa in 1953. Spenny Drage operated a taxi business with four cars from the garage on the right.
(Bozeat School Scrapbook)

SECOND WORLD WAR AND JUST AFTER (1940-47)
Mavis Holman (née Line) remembers the shops from her childhood:

Co-op complex – Butchers, food, general stores selling virtually everything from clothes to paraffin (opposite Red Lion).
Post Office (Mrs Hayes) – next door to Co-op towards Wollaston.
Drapery (Mrs Mabbott) – next door to Post Office towards Wollaston.
Ethel Johnson – where village green now is to the left of the Cross Keys, selling haberdashery.
Laddie Drage – opp. old school (in Camden Square) at corner of Church Lane and High Street – Groceries and sweets.
General Store including groceries – top of Church Lane (Glebe Cottage where Diane West now lives) run by Ada Wallis. Jean Wellman and Eileen Jarvis were the Candy daughters. Their parents bought the shop off two spinster ladies (Wallis) for somewhere to live but carried on the business until 1958.
Garretts the Butchers – top of Allens Hill on corner of Mile Street.
Yorks on Camden Square (where council houses now built) – Fish and Chips.
Miss Cave – on Camden Square (where P. O. now is) – Groceries.
John Farey – Hairdressers on High Street.
Taxi Service – Spenny 'Nimp' Drage at Arch Villa (father of Barry Drage)
Newsagents, sweets and tobacco – Bayes, No. 3 Allens Hill

Glebe Cottage, Church Lane – a summary history
In the possession of John and Diane West, the present owners of Glebe Cottage, is a document which is the Indenture (i.e. a contract or written agreement or a deed under seal) concerning Joseph Duglas written on waxed parchment in which all the land "to be hereby granted … unto the … Joseph Duglas …" which as we shall see was once owned (the parchment is difficult to read) by THOMAS DAVEY and continues, "to be paid onto the said Joseph Duglas his executors administrators or assignes the full and … english money in manner following (that is to say) fourty shillings … at or on the one and twentieth day of June next … the day hereof and the … of at or on the

one and twentieth day of December next following which shall bee in the year of our Lord one thousand six hundred and ninety and eight ..." – suggesting that money is to be paid to Duglas in 1698. This is some 27 years after Glebe Cottage was built, for the readable part of the document opens: "... bearing the date of the eighteenth day of July Anno. Dom. 1671 being now in the occupation of the said Thomas Davey and also the Appurtnances situate and being in Bozeat aforesaid being since erected and newly built upon parts of the ground of the said first mentioned or late in the tennee occupatoid of one William Hawkins the younger as it is now divided and sett out from the parts of the yard and ... and ground of the said Thomas Davey ...", i.e. Glebe Cottage was built probably in 1671 on the grounds of Thomas Davey and occupied by William Hawkins as his tenant. His land is some 5 acres with the "comon streets" to the south (i.e. now the High Street, etc.) with "several houses and building, bankes, slades, watering wayes, slades parteing grasse, etc." but we read "purchased in his lifetime to him and his heirs forever of one T Davey ... bearing the date the fourteenth day of May, Anno Dom 1677 as in and by the said several indentures relatoid being ... now or ... the recited ... or occupatoid of the said Thomas Davey ..." So there may have been several sales of the cottage since it was built and now Duglas who owns it in 1698 is selling it again.

In the Will of William Church dated 1770 we read: "I give to my beloved wife Susannah Church this house that I have lived in ...", i.e. Glebe Cottage.

The Methodist Bedford Circuit Membership List of 1792 gives the name of Susannah Church at the head of a list suggesting she was a Class Leader with her husband second in the list. This suggests she held the first Methodist (Class) Meetings in Bozeat in the parlour at Glebe Cottage whilst the founder John Wesley was still alive. The Membership List also gives her trade as 'shopkeeper'.

Susannah died in 1797. William Church (Jnr) traded as a lace-dealer from the house, paying for lace made in the house and supplying bobbins, thread and pillows before and after his stepmother's death. He continued providing for the parish poor stockings, flannel, etc as his step mother had done.

Williams's daughter Margaret married Edward Stock in 1833 and in 1844 is described in the baptism register as Grocer.

Before 1850 Thomas Wallis, blacksmith from Finedon, bought Glebe Cottage and his family continued to use it as a shop well into the last century. He also bought the old smithy in Camden Square. He is described in the 1842 Trade Directory as Blacksmith, Grocer, Draper and Ironmonger. The shop was to remain in the family for the next hundred years. There are some interesting receipts, etc. from the period 1846-1869 in the possession of the present owner which gives some idea what the shop sold in those days:

(i) In August 1846 Mr Wallis bought from Richard Ward, Wholesale Grocer and Tea Dealer in Northampton – nutmegs, sugar, candy peal, raisins, plaster, lozenges, barley sugar, wellingtons, bulls eyes, ginger balls, etc.

(ii) In 1849 he bought a considerable amount of mutton and some pork from Mr Wykes. This could be a regular order as we have a similar order for 1852.

(iv) June 1867 an invoice from William Saddington, Newsagent, Stationery and Booksellers at Earls Barton for 24 Telegraphs for the period May to June at 1½d each, total 3/-.

(v) In October 1868 Mr Wallis bought sundry items from W. A. Hope, Wholesale Agricultural and Family Chemist of Silver Street, Wellingborough (also selling soda water manufactured by steam power!) including, tartaric acids, red lead in oil, poppies (opium?), strong mints.

(vi) Also in October 1868 an invoice from Shrive, Carriage and Harness maker, from which Mr Wallis had bought what appears to be a covering (for) carriage wing.

By 1904 the business was being run by Thomas' nephew William Wallis (whose son Alfred took over the business in Camden Square before the Great War). In the 1920s/1930s William's daughters Annie and Minnie kept the shop at Glebe Cottage selling sweets and drapery. Folk remember Ada Wallace running the shop. In 1942 Mabel Constance Candy bought the business – a grocery and hardware shop run by the two Wallis spinster ladies – from its owner a Mr Leat of London. The Wallis ladies retired to the two gabled house at 11 Bull Close where Fred Tivey (sometime manager of the Co-op) and his wife Floss once lived.

Mabel Candy had a mind for business. Her husband Percy was a farmer and they had a son Roy and two daughters, Jean and Eileen. Jean was born in Hayes, Middlesex where he was farming and she was twenty when they came to Bozeat. Roy was a farm manager in Northamptonshire and the family lived with him for a time (when Percy gave up farming after the War Agricultural Committee took over farming and dictated to farmers what they should grow and where) before Mabel saw this business advertised in Bozeat. Their son Roy joined the aircrew of an all Canadian Squadron based in Lincolnshire, flying Lancaster bombers and was shot down and killed on a raid on Munich in 1945. His name is on the War Memorial in St Mary's. Mabel never really got over his death which led to a breakdown. Her daughter Jean returned home and gave up her job in Market Harborough to look after her. The business declined and early in 1958 Mabel sold Glebe Cottage and she and Percy went to live at 16 Allens Hill next door to where her daughter Eileen now lives (1998) married to Jim Jarvis.

Len Welman met Jean when she was 15. His brother had a small holding opposite the Candy's farm in Hampshire. He came from a large family of five boys and five girls. Len joined the 5th Battalion Somerset Light Infantry when he was 24 and came out in 1946 aged 31. He and Jean were married one year later at St Mary's Bozeat on 7th June 1947 and Len resumed the trade of painting and decorating. "It was terribly hard to get somewhere to live in those days and for ten years we lived in two rooms at Glebe Cottage. It was a large rambling place with two staircases, four bedrooms, a sitting room, a big dining room and a kitchen at the back with the shop at the top end – and a cellar. The cellar was always cool and the milk and such-like were kept there. "The steps down were often wet with condensation," Jean remembers, "and once coming up with some milk I slipped and my arm landed on a broken milk bottle and I cut it badly. My mother rushed me into the yard and put my arm under the water from the pump to stem the flow of blood. I remember that there was a 'traveller' in the shop at the time and he took me to the surgery in Wollaston where I had five stitches." In those days Glebe Cottage was surrounded by tiny thatched cottages – "one up and one down" as Len called them – usually with a cellar. They must have been small for there were two such cottages in what is now the present parking space adjacent to the cottage. It was Vicar Knight who persuaded the Church to sell Len and Jean the piece of land in the corner of the glebe and the bungalow was built in 1956. Both of them had to work hard to pay for their home – Jean was the village post lady for 46 years until April 1968.

Such was the shortage of housing that Eileen and Jim also lived at Glebe Cottage for a time after they were married in 1955. Derek Taylor remembers the shop being in operation in the early to mid '50s when Olive Garrett sent him round the corner from the butchers to buy a bar of soap there to scrub out the wooden sides in the butchers: "You can't even use a knife with a wooden handle in a butchers these days at Tescos. Then each Monday we scrubbed all the wooden sides with soap!" remembered Derek in 1998.

We think that in the late '50s the cottage was bought by the Torrances from Rickmansworth – relatives of Waterfields the butchers in Wellingborough.

Then in 1970 it was bought by David and Joan Willis who ran it as an Antiques Shop and also sold shoes. The cellar was also blocked up in their time. They were in the business of buying property, restoring it and moving on. In 1972 they sold the property to John and Diane West and they moved on to Brixworth. The Wests still own the property in 1998 which they use as a private house.

Mr Summerlin's cottage on the right, and the gable end of the Royal Engineer is just visible at the top of Mile Street. (*John Darker*)

CHAPTER 15

The History of the Co-op in Bozeat

How it all began

In the summer of 1864 it appears that the Bozeat Co-operators started trading – only 20 years after the famous Rochdale Pioneers had first met. We do not know where these first Co-operators had their stores – although Norman Palmer heard it said it started in what is now the car park of the Working Men's Club.

"In *Whellan's Trade Directory* for 1874 it says: 'Co-op Stores, Jas Pettit manager'. In Churchwardens' Accounts for February 1879 it mentions a bill: 'The Co-operative Society 1-7s-4d. Do 2s-0d.' A later entry reads: 'Mr James Pettit's Bill 19s-9d.' These were probably bills for oil to supply the lamps in the Parish Church and a later bill indicates this: 'Oil Bill (Co-operative Stores) 1-5s-8d' and later 'The Stores for Oil 17s-4d'." (Norman Palmer)

In 1878 the management of the Bozeat Society bought new premises which "swallowed up" all their working capital. These premises, now a private house, were opposite the present Paper Shop. "Extra capital was badly needed and this was obtained on the security of the deeds of a field belonging to the Sick Benefit Club which field is still (1964) used as an allotment ground. This action, however, caused some members to withdraw their support from the Society at a time when the Society needed more co-operation rather than less and from then onwards it seems to have been a struggle to keep going."

Hope comes from Wollaston

"In 1890 two delegates from Wollaston Society attended a conference at Bozeat and four years later the two Societies agreed to slaughter a beast between them, one week at Bozeat and the next at Wollaston."

By the next year (1895) half yearly sales exceeded £2,000, but shortage of capital continued to plague the society. They appealed to the local District Association for financial assistance but were told they would only be given help if Bozeat members themselves increased their investments.

In 1899, when Thomas Robinson (later to manage the shop) was secretary and William Jolley chairman, mortgage on the premises and overdrafts were four times as great as members' own investments. The dividend was only 9d. (old pence) which prompted some Bozeat co-operators to become members of the Wollaston Society with a dividend of 2s 6d in the pound – over three times better! By 1903 the dividend had risen to 1s 6d but dropped again to 1 shilling in 1905.

This building in High Street housed the Bozeat Co-operative shop from 1878. It is now a private house.   (*History of Co-op in Bozeat*)

At this time the premises were all together. As in any typical village shop at this time a wide variety of goods were sold. Miss Burrows and Miss Annie Skevington were lady assistants at this time and drapery lines and groceries were sold. Behind the shops was a bakery at which many Bozeat meals would also be cooked, managed in latter years by Mr Fern. Beyond it was a butchery managed in the early days by Jim Pettit and then by Mr William Garrett who married Miss Skevington and started his own butcher's business in 1895 at the top of Mile Street. His business continued in the family until it closed in the summer of 1990 with the death of first his son Sam Garrett in 1978 and then his sister Olive in 1989 aged 93. (Another well known butcher at this time was Charlie Smith.) On a piece of land at the back of the premises were chickens giving a handy supply of fresh eggs. A limited postal service was also provided under the supervision of Miss Maria Hardwick who was to become the first Bozeat Postmistress in a house next to the present shop. She was followed by Jean Wellman and Stella Smart, Tricia Roach, Stella Nye and Annette Hunt were still post ladies in 1999.

In 1905 the shop closed at 7.00 pm with late opening until 8.30 pm on Fridays and Saturdays. The membership was 84, falling to 79 in 1907 when there were only 4 employees. These were times of depression and when the Bozeat Co-operative Boot Society ceased to exist at this time it was feared that the retail society would suffer the same fate. In 1908 such fears were realised and it was decided to wind up the society. The monies were divided between members and the books, deeds and documents were taken to Northampton by the youngest and newest member, born in 1869, Harry Edmunds who was a healthy 95-year-old when the booklet *A Century of Co-operation in Bozeat* was published in 1964, from which much of this information comes and quotations are taken. (Harry was also one of the last boys to attend the school at the bottom of Mile Street as mentioned in Chapter 1.)

Wollaston takes over
But Co-operation in Bozeat did not die. Bozeat members were able to join the Wollaston Society and have their goods delivered from Wollaston. "Membership in Bozeat must have increased since, in 1914, in response to many requests, premises in the High Street were rented by the Wollaston Society to open a Branch Shop. A Mr Russell, from Stoney Stratford, was appointed the first branch manager and the sales of his first complete half year amounted to £305. Space must have been inadequate for increasing trade since, within a year, a room in an adjoining house was rented. Co-operation in Bozeat had taken on a new lease of life. Mr Russell was later enlisted to serve his country and, for a brief period, the shop was managed by a Mrs Rivett, who resigned because of ill health. The position was then offered to Miss Esther Dobbs, who managed this shop through the difficulties of World War I until 1919.

From High Street to London Road
In 1919, when trade had reached £84 per week, the Society bought the block of buildings of Mr Knighton in London Road facing the top of the High Street for £450. Because of the high cost of building materials it was not possible to make improvements to the premises until 1923 when the sales had reached £100 per week. The president, Mr Catlin, opening the newly refurbished shops, in that year asked for a trade of £100 per week. He did not live long enough to see this target realised thirteen years later in 1936.

THE HISTORY OF THE CO-OP IN BOZEAT

Wollaston Co-operative Society's Bozeat branch shop in London Road, Bozeat in 1919.
(*History of Co-op in Bozeat*)

The management of the new shop was given to Mr Wright who was previously manager of the Wollaston grocery shop. He lived at Dungee Corner at the far end of the Harrold Road out of Bozeat. His three unmarried daughters, now in their 80s (1996) still live in the fine house he had built there maintaining a genteel quality of life, unbeatable at croquet laid out in their garden and managing the unique meadow of orchids adjacent to the house.

Miss Dobbs, after a short period at Wollaston returned to Bozeat where, in addition to grocery duties, she was responsible for the drapery section and achieved 39 years of loyal service to the Wollaston Society serving the Bozeat Co-operators. Her length of service has only been bettered by Glenda Drage who will have worked 40 years for the Co-op by December 1996 without ever having had a day off sick!

Mr Wright continued to serve Bozeat throughout World War II with its shortages and rationing and when he retired the weekly trade averaged £313. The butchery shop seen in the 1923 photo continued through his 25 years of service but with modest sales. He was succeeded in 1948 by Fred Tivey who was manager of Grendon Branch and whose father had been manager of the Wollaston Branch. This was the period of emergence from wartime controls and by 1953 Bozeat sales were well past the £500 a week mark. "Whereas in 1923 sales had been only 38% of Wollaston Grocery, 30 years later they had risen to 62%" But by 1958 there was a sudden slowing down of sales in the Bozeat Branch although these were still averaging nearly £580 per week. "Supermarkets and now multiple shops were emerging in the surrounding towns and their cut-price policies were beginning to attract trade from our Bozeat members. It was appreciated that something must be done to stimulate trade and, arising from revision of the Society's rounds in general, an improved delivery service was commenced in September 1960. Sales commenced to improve but only to a limited extent and it seemed that what Bozeat members needed was a block of modern shops comparable to those at Wollaston."

The Co-operative in London Road, Bozeat Branch 1923, after refurbishment.
(*History of Co-op in Bozeat*)

New shops for a new age
On 4th July 1961, the Committee visited Bozeat to inspect the existing premises which had not been altered for 38 years, and a week later, after discussion of provisional plans, it was decided to consult Pollards of London, a leading firm of shop builders. Plans were produced and a quotation for a new block of shops was obtained by February 1962. It was decided to open the new grocery shop as 'self-service' after visiting similar shops belonging to the Northampton Society. Current sales were about £600 per week and it was appreciated that a considerable increase in trade would be necessary to pay for these new developments.

The rebuilding programme began with the demolition of the old butchery shop and adjoining cottage and the excavation of the rising land behind these. The butchery department temporarily went into premises rented from Spencer 'Spenny' Drage in the High Street. "Then the new Dry Goods shop was built on the cleared site and was temporarily occupied by the Grocery Department using new fixtures purchased for eventual use in the new warehouse. The Drapery Department was also accommodated in one corner of this shop and the other shops demolished, being replaced by the Grocery shop and warehouse and the new Butchery shop. During this time, while plans and prices of fixtures and refrigeration were considered and decided upon, sales at Bozeat were, regrettably, decreasing."

"Eventually the new grocery and butchery shops were completed and fitted out and on 15th October 1963 the new self-service shop opened its doors after a very hectic weekend transferring goods into the new fittings and re-assembling the temporary fixtures in the grocery warehouse. To mark the occasion parcels of C.W.S. groceries were given to all customers spending £1 and over in the first week of trading. After the initial strangeness of self-service the system has operated successfully and has been well appreciated by our loyal Bozeat customers.... In the week following, the

THE HISTORY OF THE CO-OP IN BOZEAT

The new self-service Co-operative shop opened in 1964, taking £660 a week.
(*History of Co-op in Bozeat*)

new Butchery Shop was opened and 1lb of sausages was given free with every purchase of 10 shillings and over."

"During these two weeks the Dry Goods Shop was fully completed and on October 27th the President, Mr C. W. Perkins, formally opened the premises witnessed by several Bozeat members and delegates from other Societies, all of whom were greatly impressed with the new shops. Dry Goods purchased immediately after the opening and during the following week qualified for double dividend and amounted to £695."

"For that half year the combined Grocery and Dry Goods sales averaged £666 weekly and in the following half year, which was the summer period without the high opening figures, averaged £616. Last half year the average weekly sales were £660 or, including the Butchery sales, £727." The 1964 Report continues optimistically: "These three shops are capable of handling £1,000 trade per week with ease and Bozeat co-operators are capable of providing this amount of trade. An extra 10s. per week per member would achieve this figure and increase the dividend into the bargain."

The Report concludes: "For many years Wollaston Society has provided Bozeat members with as good services for the delivery of milk, bread and coal as are provided for the Wollaston members and now they have provided even more modern and well-built shops than those at Wollaston. These are probably the best branch shops of a village Society in the country, of which our Bozeat members can be justly proud."

The end of Co-operation in Bozeat

When Joyce Wesley was made redundant from Gola in 1982, she worked for a time in the old Sainsbury's in the Wellingborough Arndale Centre until it closed down in 1989. It was then that she went to work for the Co-op in Bozeat in London Road.

The manager was Glenda Drage who had worked there since she left school at 15 in 1956 and her deputy was Kim Nye. "They were the only full timers but several of us worked part time – Christine Line, Mary Andrews (Glenda's sister), Joyce Corby, Teresa Robinson from Allens Hill – oh yes and Margaret Jones – Joyce's sister. I remember Glenda phoning me up one day and saying, 'Joyce, the rumours are true. The Co-op – they're selling it!' The Co-op closing affected Keith and Carol at the Spar badly as well. The Co-op kept folk in the village doing their shopping. Now they went down to Tescos or Sainsbury's and did it all there." So in 1991, 127 years of Co-operation in Bozeat came to an end, and Glenda, its last manager, went to work at their shop in Olney.

Happy Shopper
The Co-op was sold and bought by the Singhs from Bedford. They bought their goods from the wholesaler 'Happy Shopper' and so they traded under that name. "It was such a struggle," Joyce Wesley remembers. "They had to go back to work and leave the children in charge. I worked part time for them and they were very good to me. Their two older children, Ravi and Pups, did it together but they were young and wanted to enjoy themselves. If there had been somewhere for the family to live it would have been much better. Sharon, their youngest, went to Bozeat School and made many friends and spoke English well. But the older village folk, who mainly used the shop for convenience shopping, found it difficult to understand the parents and older children and this might have put them off a bit. Another difficulty was that, although at the end the Co-op was taking £5,000 to £6,000 a week, this was mainly in milk checks and solid fuel. When they closed, the milk checks went to Keith who with the paper shop also sold fuel, leaving the Singhs with a much smaller income." Sadly, the consequence of these difficulties for the Singhs was that they had to give up and so the Happy Shopper closed down in 1996. For two years the premises stood empty but in 1999 they became a carpet warehouse.

Garretts the Butchers
William Charles Garrett started a butchery business in 1896 having previously had a butchery shop (working for Tom Skevington) as part of the old Bozeat Co-operative, then in the High Street, which he took over from Jim Pettit. William married Tom's daughter Martha Skevington who worked at the Co-op.

When he started on his own in 1896 he worked up the business from virtually nothing from the thatched cottage which he owned at the top of Mile Street which was dated 1731 and therefore built two years after the Great Fire of Bozeat of 1729, and it was here that his daughter Olive Franklin was born in 1897. His son Sam was born three years later in 1900 and he went into the business helping his father at a very early age.

In 1955/6 Sam bought the whole of the yard known as Burton Terrace for a modest sum – £850 – from a man going abroad and desperate to sell. This was a few years after Derek Taylor had started working for them as the butcher's boy at the age of 15 straight from school. "My father wanted me to learn a trade. That's why he sent me to Sam. 'You've got to learn a trade, boy', he said, 'and I worked for them for forty year!'" said Derek giving his infectious cackling laugh as he reflected on a lifetime of service to the Garrett family. "Burton Terrace was very run down when Sam bought it." Derek remembers. There were five little cottages, now pulled down, ours at No. 6

Mr Sam Garrett's butchers shop at the top of Mile Street in 1953. He had 3,000 registered customers, and visited 16 villages. (*Bozeat School Scrapbook*)

and next door which was once a butcher's shop. ("It's always been damp in there due to all the salt butchers used," added Pat, Derek's wife.) Also there was the grocer's shop where George Line now lives and next to it a bakery and two other cottages I think. The Council condemned most of the cottages and a firm charged £50 to take them down. I remember Sam saying to me, 'Now George has offered £400 for those cottages. I'd have had to pay £200 to take them down so that's £200 clear profit!' It's all money you know," said Derek laughing as he told me. George Line still lives in the end cottage – what he now calls 'the bakery' having pulled the other cottages down and created one of the most interesting village gardens you could imagine. Derek and Pat came to live at No. 6 38 years ago when they were married. Sam had it done up for them as it was then occupied by his cowman, Stan Johnson, who moved into a council house.

Work at the butchers was hard with long working hours. Sam himself would arrive at the shop at 6.00 am and Pat and Derek not much later. Olive would always be at the till in the shop taking the money. "Typically we would start work about 7.00 in the morning and often we would still be working at 10 at night. We would often start our last round at 7.00 in the evening." Dorothy Cave remembers Derek arriving with the meat late on a cold evening and Derek remembers how she often gave him a glass of sherry to warm him up. "He looked so cold," remembers Dorothy, the undertakers wife. "I had known Derek since he was a boy. This year (1998) I would have been 50 years in the village since I married Tom."

"At our busiest – in the 1960s that would be," continued Derek, "we could be killing every week, 4 bullocks, 14 lambs, 6 pigs and we had to prepare all the meat ourselves. We also made all our own sausages as well as potted beef, haslet (pork with sage, etc) and we made faggots which we took on big baking trays down to Berty Squires, the baker in London Road to bake them in his oven and then we would sell them hot in the shop as well as cold. We had three vans going then. Sam bought his vans new from Bob Reeves at £405 each. And three of us did the all the deliveries – Pat, me and Willie Line as well as Sam – and we covered a lot of villages – Bozeat, Easton Maudit, Grendon, Wollaston, Hinwick, Podington, Wymington and even some as far as Emberton. And we had to visit our customers three times a week – at the beginning, in the middle and at the end of the week." Willie Line (Bernard's brother) joined the business as an errand boy at the age of eight and worked at Garretts until October 1978 when he was too ill to carry on.

William handed his business over to Sam and Olive and went into farming up Hinwick way. He was able to buy farm land cheaply at that time. He bought the farm at Dungee and gave it to Olive, and her husband (Mr Franklin) farmed the land for a time. Eventually Sam and Olive went to live in William's fine thatched house at Hinwick. Due to their frugal lifestyle, despite the great wealth they inherited and the healthy butchery business, the house fell into dilapidation through neglect. "When we arrived in 1990 the roof had caved in and was covered by a large green canvas." Derek remembers visiting Sam lying in bed dying of cancer and him saying pitifully, "Derek would you move that bucket of sand over there to catch the water (dripping through the roof), the noise upsets me."

Sam died in 1978. That same year Olive's sheep dog knocked her over and several bones were broken but, then in her eighties, she worked on with Derek running the shop and dealing with all the van deliveries in the surrounding villages. He worked long hours under harsh conditions and with no holidays, ably supported by his good wife Pat. Commenting on his present job at Tescos with those 40 years with the Garretts he laughed and said, "It's a doddle!"

Olive worked until three years from her death just before Christmas 1989 aged 92. In those three years, Derek and Pat did almost everything for her, getting her up and getting her meals and to putting her to bed at night, as well as running the business. She never had the luxuries of hot water or central heating and Derek had to make the fires. Apparently she had never registered with a doctor. And her home at Hinwick (a listed building like her thatched house in Bozeat) was broken into many times and valuables including furniture taken. There were rats everywhere although Olive would not believe it. When she notice a loaf partly eaten by them she said, "Derek, take that loaf back to the shop and get our money back and tell them they've got rats!" Apparently she read a chapter from the Bible each evening and always gave an ox tongue to the Church fayre each year as well as supplying the harvest loaf for the Harvest Festival, bringing it out of the freezer year after year.

After she died, the shop closed in 1990. Relatives appeared from various parts of the world to claim their part of the inheritance, Olive and Sam having had no children, for they were worth millions so it was believed, in a business that had lasted for 94 years. Their thatched house, the slaughter house next to it and a single-storey shop at the top of Allens Hill were bought and developed into three attractive residences, two cottages and a bungalow, with little indications of the previous life as a butchery business.

To the end Olive refused to change to the new decimal coinage and customers had to do business in her shop in the old currency of pounds shillings and pence! Derek has many tales to tell of the eccentricities of Sam and Olive and their frugal lifestyle. "Olive made eight wills," said Derek, "but never signed any of them. I remember going to the Solicitors office with her when she went to make one of them and the Solicitor came out to see me in the waiting room, took me aside and said to me, 'Now you stick close to her and you'll be a very rich man.' But I never got nothing for she never signed them! And they are still sorting out the will. One cousin has died of a heart attack already and it dragged on so long I expect the solicitors got more out of the Estate than anyone!" said Derek with his mischievous laugh with not a hint of bitterness in it. Fortunately Pat and Derek now live in and own 6 Burton Terrace (where Dolly Roberts' grandparents once lived) on account of their having lived there for 30 years working for the Garretts and entitled to claim ownership through residence.

CHAPTER 16

Buildings and Builders of Bozeat

Introduction

In Chapter 11 we reflected on how our Celtic Islands in the Iron Age and painted a picture of herds of wild boar roaming virgin forests with our forebears scattered over the countryside in small family groups constantly subdividing – each group with its Trev or Hamlet consisting of light structures of timber or wattle (mud, straw and wood, etc.) and roofs of turf, etc. to keep out the miserable weather. Survival was mainly by hunting and grazing and living between the vast forests and waterlogged and undrained river valleys. Wood, wattle, mud and turf and stones would be the natural building materials available to them then.

The Anglo-Saxons who followed them were farming communities using an open field system reflecting a communal village agriculture. They built modest cottages of split logs erected side by side with mud infilling the oaken framework and a roof of thatch or turf – there were not always separate rooms or proper windows as there was no glass to keep out the bitter weather. The Roman legions brought with them the sophisticated building methods of the East and Christianity and we may well imagine that the Saxons had their wooden Saxon church here just as the Romans had their villas like the one recently excavated on Low Farm, resplendent with its elegant floor of coloured tiles and presumably stone walls and brick and tiled roof – a striking contrast to the Saxon hovels of wood and wattle. They appear to have taken their advanced building skills and materials such as tiles and cement and stone back with them when they could no longer stand our miserable weather! and the Romans left our shores in about AD 410. Was there a Saxon hamlet and Roman settlement at Bozeat? "Intensive fieldwork and air photography have led to the discovery of a notable number of Iron Age and Roman settlements, mainly on the boulder clay areas on which the greater part of the parish is to be found." (*Palmer.*) David Hall was involved in much of the excavation work in this area and with others has published much of the results of their work with several articles in the *Bedfordshire Archaeological Journal*. Norman Palmer has made a helpful summary (unpublished) of all the work done in this area. An early name for the village was Bosgate "points to a Saxon origin as Earl Bosa's land was near, so it might be bosa-gate." (*Marlow*, p.1)

With the Norman invasion of Anglo-Saxon England, two kinds of stone buildings suddenly appear studding the English countryside changing its appearance in a striking way, the Manor and the Norman stone church, the latter being a constant reminder of the profound change in our culture and the skills of the early builders. Our medieval manor was situated on the rising ground to the east of the present cemetery, and our church on an area which was still known as Bury Yard in the early 18th century (Bury – a fortified hill). Remains discovered there are probably those of the main manor of Bozeat, usually known as 'Latimers' who were Lords of the Manor from 1311 until 1577, i.e. 250 years. The lord's house (originally occupied by a knight) may have been barely distinguishable from other village dwellings, unless it was fortified or moated, and it seems ours was on a fortified hill. From the 15th century onwards the house in which the lord or squire resided was rebuilt and often re-sited.

The church dedicated to St Mary, built about 1130 on the highest ground opposite it on the other side of the brook, was to form a landmark for centuries to come.

St Mary's Church in the 1880s. (*A Dobbs*)

Details of the building are given in Chapter 22 but it is worth reminding ourselves that our village church stands as a living history of the evolution of building techniques throughout the Middle Ages as detailed in that chapter. Originally it was simply a dark empty box built of huge blocks of cut sandstone three to four feet square and consisting of the present nave with four corner pillars (still to be seen) and a steep thatch roof and tower with its curved Norman Arch and a small chancel. Shafts of light came through slits in the walls piercing the gloom, relieved otherwise by light from smoking rush lights and later wax candles. It was a comparatively giant but clumsy building with its huge stones placed one upon the other with no mortar and no foundations as it floated on its bed of clay (but see note at end of Chapter 22 for details of a stone wedge shaped structure that formed the simple foundations of the tower). It was two centuries later that the whole structure was enlarged using more advanced building techniques. The nave wall was pierced and its lower part replaced by four stone pillars supporting the old wall which was extended upwards to form a clerestory (clear storey) and the thatch was replaced by a wooden roof insulated from the weather with malleable sheets of lead. Two aisles were added and the chancel extended and a heavy stone spire built on the tower in the fashion of the day. All too often these proved too heavy for their Norman towers and over 90% collapsed under their weight in the ensuing centuries – ours doing so in 1877!

Two striking innovations were to be seen at this period. The first was the introduction of windows with the advent of glass, flooding the building with light. Our fine windows reflect the early English Perpendicular style, the most sophisticated of these being the Ogee window in the tower dating from around 1420. The second innovation is the introduction of wooden furnishings, with our original oaken pews still there as well as our rood screen with its simple but modest ornamental carving and fine medieval paintings on its panels. Part of the wooden roof in the north aisle is from this 15th century development while the present fine oak roof to the nave has the date 1680 on one of its beams, but others suggest an earlier date. And we should not forget the stone carvings of the masons as the hilarious faces around the top of the tower and later the more dignified of saints etc that brought to life the solid slabs of stone – as well as the beautiful stone ornamentation such as around our southern door.

It must have been a magnificent building compared to the primitive hovels of wood, wattle and stone clustered around it with their roofs of turf and smoking thatch. It was the public hall of the village. Its porch with its two stone benches served as a school and a place for medieval plays and pageants as well as a manorial court and its nave was the only public meeting place big enough to assemble the whole community. Marlow (p.13) quotes the judgement regarding the 13th and 14th centuries that, "Architecture in England reached heights of refinement to which it has never attained since," and we are fortunate to have an example of this at the centre of our village. It is Marlow also who points out that the window in the east end in the north aisle is of exactly the same design as one in the north aisle of Barnwell Church, suggesting it to be the work of the same itinerant craftsmen of the same masons guild. And the pews in the church at Yielden, a village just outside Rushden, are of the same period and have the same structure and ornamentation as our own reflecting again possibly the same itinerant craftsmen in wood. But the ornamentation is more universal, as it is to be found at Stoke Bruerne and in the parish church of Mere, Dorset, amongst others.

The long reign of Elizabeth (1558-1603) brought stability and prosperity reflected in a housing revolution and major rebuilding and development of medieval England, and we would hope to find evidence of this in Bozeat as it occurred also among yeoman class and successful members of the agricultural community. Last traces of building in wood were replaced by building in stone. At the bottom of the social scale the one-roomed cottage began to give way to the house with two rooms, hall and parlour, often with a chimney stack between them. "The cruck house and the aisled

Artist's impression of the medieval hall which once stood where now is the car park of Bozeat Club (from an article in notes of Northamptonshire Historical Society c.1980).

hall were still living elements in the local vernacular." (M. W. Barley, *The English Farm House and Cottage*) (A cruck house is a crude building, a pair of curved wooden timbers supporting the building's roof.) There was a Mediaeval Hall with cruck truss in Bozeat High Street (behind the club) which survived in part to the 20th century but was demolished (see drawing). Not only did more chimneys appear with Elizabethan prosperity but glazing of windows became common as did comforts in the home – feather-bed and the pillow replacing the straw pallet, even in the humbler homes. Beef, bacon and rye bread hung from the roof. Chests in the parlour were full of homespun cloth and, once winter evenings came, the housewife fetched down the spinning wheel from the chamber above and "the husband sitteth by the fire and hath nothing to do, then may he make his forks and rakes ready...." (*A. Fitzherbert*)

The pace of new building seems to slacken in the 30 years prior to the Civil War which began in 1642, and does not seem to have begun apace once again until after the Restoration of the Monarchy in 1660, for which we see evidence in the building life of our village (see below). Serious outbreaks of plague in the East Midlands (like the plague in London in 1625 which killed 35,000 people i.e. around 10% of its population) reduced populations as burials outnumbered baptisms and the 'stinting of the commons' caused commoners to loose their grazing rights and livelihood, while some 'enclosure' of land meant larger farms, and farmhouses were appearing and developing with capital to put into the land, increasing hay production, etc. with the draining of meadows.

In the Midland Revolt in 1607, which was part of the widespread revolts against enclosures leading up to the Civil War, it was reported that the rebels were craftsman, as well as husbandmen and labourers. In this period the habit of making wills was even more widespread than before and had spread down the social scale with inventories of the possessions of labourers to be found, allowing historians to see into their homes with such terms as 'firehouse' and 'solar' appearing. Subsistence farming of the Middle Ages was giving way at the level of the small husbandman to farming for profit with the small holding consisting of barn plus hovel for the cattle plus a three or four room house – a parlour for the dairy (milk, butter, cheese), a chamber above for storing corn, wool and hemp, one for living and one for sleeping. So by the 1630s the two roomed house was often no more the largest category of home in this part of the world. And with London and market towns growing apace and the need to search for work, the rural populations with families staying in the same village for centuries was becoming the exception rather than the rule as people became more mobile. Like Dick Whittington they were looking for prosperity elsewhere. The population in London was then (c.1300) 15,000 and swelled to three times this size in the century, becoming 220,000 by 1600. It then doubled to 450,000 by 1650 (the year after when Charles I lost his head), mainly due to the influx of Englishmen from the provinces (plus many Scots during the reign of James I).

We have a possible example of a late medieval/Elizabethan stone farmhouse in East Farm House in Dychurch, which, from its wooden beams, David Hall dates from the 1660s but is possibly 100 years older in parts. It is believed that parts of Church Farm may well be from the same period. We have too the title deeds of Glebe Cottage at the top of Church Lane giving its date of building as 1671 (see Chapter 14), after the restoration of the Monarchy. This is quite a substantial stone building and we can expect that similar such buildings, many smaller and more modest and packed together in the old village would be built over this period of growth and stability in

Dychurch Lane from Camden Square with Jack Bayes' thatched cottage on the right and the Town Well just beyond it.

the nation, rather like the three that occupied the garage space of 6 Church Walk. And the fine thatched cottage round the corner owned by the Garretts reflected the quality of building of this period. Its date given as 1731, so it might be a rebuild after the great fire of 1729. The modest cottage called 'Little Thatch' adjacent to the Town Well thought to have been occupied by Johnny 'Bundlehead' Bayes who brought round the night cart, was bought by Chris Saunders in early 1999 and beautifully restored and rethatched. On stripping off the old thatch (one thatch upon an older one in fact), it was found to be supported by thin saplings of willow over which appeared to be laid branches, etc before thatch was laid on top – possibly of straw, the poorest sort – dating again most probably from the 17th century. Many of the cottages built at this period at the end of the 17th and beginning of the 18th century would have been built with stone from the quarry field in which Len Holts cottage now stands, with higher quality stone for cutting brought from further afield. Mortar and cement would come from the Limekilns such as that near Bull Close at the back of the adjacent allotment and in 1886 we know there was a lime kiln and valuable bed of stone up Dychurch on the right in the grounds of the cottage there. The poorest had the poorest stone and thatch, and some would live in little more than hovels. The hearth was the centre of the building, its life providing heat for cooking and warmth and hot water with the bath tub in front of the fire on bath night. In 1664 Charles II introduced a Hearth Tax as a measure of wealth. The Wisemans at the Manor had eleven hearths!

The Great Fire of 1729 which started in Widow Keech's house at the top of Mile Street near the churchyard on 9th September and destroyed 41 dwellings and four farms probably destroyed a third of the village, sweeping through its closely packed thatched buildings. The site of her cottage is now the appropriately named Burnt

Close. Part of No. 6 Church Walk was damaged and Wykes Farm or Skevington's Farm behind it was damaged at its southern end, being thatched at the time. This too must be one of the oldest houses in the village and has a grade II listing. There is a date stone 1730 giving the date of the repair and initials M Svc which may be those of the stone mason – possibly Mercer Skevington mentioned in the deeds. The house may therefore have been built at least 50 years previously, possibly when we have our first mention of a Berrill as a village stone-mason in 1687.

From Chapter 12 it is clear that there were some kinds of hostelries well back into the 1600s as we have records of travellers, tinkers and travelling salesman, (reflecting as we have seen the increased mobility in this century), as well as folk on the move for various other reasons being given accommodation in such places, sometimes at the parish's expense. But as mobility and travel became more of a feature of normal life and business and letters and goods were increasingly transported as with the coming of the stage coaches and improved – turnpiked – roads, so inns and/or coaching houses became a regular feature of villages and towns in the 1700s. "The gay and rapid life of the English road reached perfection only during the Napoleonic wars" – with "the glory of its hard 'Macadamised' road (the work of capitalist companies recouped at the toll-bars) with its Tally-ho coaches and post-chaise speeding along at 12 miles an hour ..." (*Trevelyan*) – but 20 years later the railways were already foreshadowing its end. The Lord Nelson (it must have been named as such during these wars) was rebuilt as a coaching house in 1742 and round the back was substantial accommodation for horses, coaches and travellers, the horses being led the modest 80 yards to the Town Well (in reality built as a small pond or watering trough, fed with fresh water from the spring above it. It closed as a public house in the spring of 1955 but is a fine stone building of this period. Bozeat was fortunate to lie on the London Road and the Red Lion must have been built possibly in the latter part of the 18th century and served as one of the stages for the London coach where travellers to Castle Ashby could alight and horses be changed. (There were stables behind in living memory.) The old inn was pulled down in 1874 and a new one erected in its place by Thomas Revis who owned Bozeat Estate. It occupies the courtyard of the older building where coaches and carts entered and the stables were at the rear which could also accommodate a large number of horse drawn vehicles. There is evidence to show that the inn existed in the 17th century and possibly dates back to mediaeval times. To the right of the present building was a house with cellars and three large rooms upstairs which was part of the previous inn.

The long reign of George III (1770-1820) – with the magnificent Coat of Arms in our Church of George III dated 1770 – not only saw the most rapid improvement in transport since the Roman era and the Industrial Revolution but also a doubling of the population from 7.5 to 14 million and the wholesale

The Royal Arms of George III dated 1770, restored by Clifford Ellison in 1997.

Looking up the London Road southwards with in the foreground on the left No. 91, the house of Charles Drage, who dug and lined many wells in the village, and Rock Villa on the right. (*John Darker*)

enclosure of land. The last of these helped produce a generation of prosperous farmers towards the end of the reign with their smart new stone/brick houses, who drove a gig to market, had wine on their tables and a piano in the parlour – although the old-fashioned small 'husbandman' had by no means disappeared. So the coming of the Enclosure Act in 1799 to Bozeat opened the way for remarkable developments in village life – and the change in its social fabric is reflected in the nature of its buildings dating from this time. Methodism grew rapidly in these parts and by 1877 there was built the fine stone church/chapel in the High Street. The vicar in his splendid double-gabled 18th century vicarage was to be joined in the 19th century by the doctor who now lived in the village, as well as prospering farmers and the managers of the new Boot and Shoe factories each wanting fine stone and brick houses/villas built for themselves. And we see in the second half of the century a transformation in building style and practice with this increasing use of brick. In 1862 the Lord of the Manor, Mr Revis, often to be seen out with his coach and pair, had The Grange built in splendid style at the top of the hill on the southern edge of the Estate, on London Road, its fine stone house with the windows embossed in brick, and brick work interlaced with stone in the walls giving a noble appearance – a style which was becoming increasingly popular. The well-built outhouses and barns were also on a grand scale, roofed with bright orange-red tiles matching the brickwork. Some walls are built with a hatchwork or 'herringbone' pattern of flat stones and mortar, presumably to strengthen the wall structure. This is a feature of building peculiar to Bozeat and practised we believe by the Berrill family. The house is described in the sale of 1886 as "brick quoin and slated containing an entrance hall

Looking northwards down London Road towards the Red Lion sign. W. Cave's carpentry shop is central.
(*John Darker*)

with tessellated tiles, three reception rooms, six bedrooms, WC, two kitchens, dairy, cellars and a pantry."

There are in the village three similar buildings but built on a more modest scale (i.e. Georgian in character, square with squat-slated roof) and again one wall with the same hatchwork construction which suggest the work of the same builders.

(i) Spring Villa – (almost opposite the Chequers) – entrance hall, two receptions, four bedrooms, drawing room, kitchen, scullery, dairy and pantry built as a farm house.

(ii) Arch Villa in the High Street (now the Paper Shop) built as the home of the Drage family, who were shoe manufacturers.

(iii) Rock Villa (or Greenwood) up the London Road – again the home of the Drage Shoe Managers but also Dr Selby lived there at the beginning of the 20th century.

The coming of compulsory education in 1870 meant the construction of the first purpose-built school in Bozeat at the bottom of Mile Street and alongside it a house for the full time teacher, and next to it a house for the village doctor – all in stone. Note again the same hatchwork style on the end wall. The evolving social hierarchy and structure of the village is reflected in its buildings. And this goes too for the Working Men's Club in the High Street which was built all in brick at the end of the century (1889) almost opposite the Methodist Church. And then there are the three shoe factories all built in brick with the one at the bottom of Hope Street in the classic style of shoe factories seen all around this part of Northamptonshire, as are the terraced brick houses for shoe workers up the Olney end of the London Road and similar ones in Hope Street and round the corner along the London Road at the other end of the village. They all date from the end of the 19th and beginning of the 20th century and are associated with the developing shoe industry.

So we see how, as the 19th century progresses, more and more brick is being used. We know that in 1881 in part of the Church Farm there was a brickyard and a kiln 19 feet by 10½ feet. In the 20th century the village, its population and the quality and number of its dwellings and other buildings continued to grow, but before we enter the 20th century we must take a another look back at the people who have built our village so far.

THE FAMILY THAT BUILT BOZEAT
Norman Palmer

Introduction
When in 1980 the village experienced the most serious flooding for years, the culvert near the bottom of Hensmans Lane was damaged. The conduit under the lane was inspected to see whether it would be in danger of collapse. Surprisingly enough it turned out to be a stone tunnel made with stone slabs with no mortar in between, yet it was a piece of craftsmanship which had stood up to the worst the flood water could do for probably two hundred years. Possibly it had been constructed somewhere about the beginning of the 19th century and had been built by men with an eye for the shaping of stone and for placing them in exactly the right position, with none of the mechanical aids that are now available.

Without doubt the men who were responsible for this piece of craftsmanship were of the Berrill family, a family who had been resident in Bozeat for well over two hundred years, plying their craft as masons.

A walk round the village will show how the older buildings were all made of stone, quarried for the most part locally. Not only had the mason to choose a block of stone with a practised eye, but he had to know how it could be shaped and then laid to form a perfect fit with others in the building of walls, houses, barns and also the church fabric.

It is not always easy to distinguish an old house at first sight because it may have had a plaster rendering on the outside with the windows and door later having a brick edging. But they are there in the village, and even some of the more modern brick buildings built in the 19th or 20th centuries very often have a stone base, which reveals that there once stood a stone building on the site.

What's in a name?
But what of this family who built Bozeat? From many sources we know that the Berrills – sometimes spelt Beril, or Beriel – were practising their trade from the late 17th century onwards. The family surname was not only known in Bozeat, but also in Olney, where too they practised their trade of masons, and they either came from that town to here or vice-versa. Much of Olney was also built by them.

We have to remember that skilled crafts were handed down from one generation to another, over many hundreds of years, with all the inherited experience that lay behind it. Of course there were a few in every skilled family who departed from the tradition, such as Levi Berill who in the mid 1800s was a shoemaker. But not only

The Town Well in Dychurch.
(Marlow's History 1936)

were crafts inherited, so were the family Christian names, and each family appeared to have its chosen names. They may jump a generation or two, but they still stayed 'within the family'. Somehow one can imagine the feelings of a young wife being told by the older members of the family that the child they had borne simply had to be given the family name. The wife did of course insisted on a bit of individuality in later times by giving a middle name which was her maiden name – so rose the habit of the middle name! Thomas and John appeared to be the family names given to the children, very often the first child, with an occasional William. But when William Berrill married Jane Wykes in 1818, then the first son was named Thomas Wykes Berrill, an early example of a middle name. Thomas, John and William were the family names until the family died out in Bozeat about the beginning of the 20th century. It must have been confusing at times – for instance in 1851 there was a Thomas and a John Berrill living in 'Spangle Row', another John Berrill, stone mason, lived in Mile Street, and yet another Thomas Berrill lived in 'Nelson Yard'. Hence the rise of nicknames to distinguish individual members of the same family name.

The Town Well

The two Berrills we have record of – they were of course Thomas and John – are found in entries in 1680 onwards. The village wells were vital to the life of the village so in 1680/1; "The towen welles Coost mending ... Thomas Bearill for ... Boayes well. 6s 6d. Thos Berrill ffor Works there ... 6d." This was long before the era of piped water supplies, and it seemed that many wells were given a name, probably of their owners. In 1685 "pd for Carrying a loade of Clay to mend the Well ... 1s " "pd Thos Berrill & Willm Serridge for mending the Well." 1688/9: "Pd ffor three Quartn of Lyme ffor Blackwell 12s. 0d. ffor ffetching the Lyme frrom Olney 2s. 0d. ffor 9 Loade of Stones. 9s. 0d. pd ffor ye Chariage of Nine Loade of stone & thre Load of sand. 4s. 0d. pd Thos Berrill ffor 17 ds (days) worke at ye sd well. 17s. 0d. pd Jo (John) Berrill ye Like. 17s. 0d."

Because these wells were in constant use it was necessary to keep the stone walls in good repair to prevent them being fouled.

John Berrill appears to have practised his trade up to 1726, and then had the rare distinction of being named by trade in the Burial Register: "John Berrel, Mason, buried 1730."

The Town Well, and presumably the other public wells were being constantly repaired down the next two centuries. Thomas Berrill, a descendent of probably the original John or Thomas, in 1860 had an entry: "The Berrill Bill £8-2-6d. Do for repairing Town Well 5s-0d." This is 200 years after the first entry, and bills were presented until 1880 by the same Thomas. Of course it was thirsty work and it was customary in days gone by to give ale as well as wages to men at work, for in 1790 for the men working on the Town Well it was recorded: "6 pints ale the men Town Well at Mr Browns 1s-0d." (Mr Brown was the Chequer's Innkeeper), and in February 1792: "5 quarts of beer the masons 1s-8d."

The Town Well area has been restored as part of the Bozeat 2000 Millennium Celebrations.

Quarries

Nearly every village had a quarry, provided suitable stone was available. It seems most likely that the stone for most of the village houses was quarried from the site on which Mr Len Holt has now his bungalow and which stretched down as far as, and including the allotment field in Allens Hill. It must have been a quarry used for many hundreds of years, for by the Enclosure in 1799 it was already let out for grazing and so was then disused and grassed over. Mr Holt tells us that the turf is only a few inches thick and underneath is hard rock. If one looks at his field, with its bumps and mounds, and looks also at the original earth level by the council houses, one can see how many tons of rock must have been extracted. There is a tradition, and it is only a tradition with no written proof, that the Church itself was built from this rock. This is sensible, for those who had to drag the rock would bring it from the nearest available source. The rock slabs when cut would have been placed on sledges and horse-drawn to the site. This is probably what is meant when in 1716 there is an entry: "paid to Jon Berrill for three Load of Ston 2s. 0d." – three loads being drawn by sledge. The entry says further: "Paid to Jon Berrill for 3 days at ye brig 3s. 6d." This seems to refer to some bridge which must have spanned the brook possibly on the road to Wollaston. Wood was also used on this bridge for: "Paid Jon Tomkins for 6 days and a half about ye Brig & Plank 7s.7d. Paid to Jon Tomkins for 13 foot and half of timber. 13s 6d. Paid Jon Tomkins for a post & roof and boud (board) for ye Bridg 5s 8d." So John Berrill must have built the supports to the bridge and John Tomkins the wooden bridge itself.

After the Allens Hill quarry was worked out, we know from the Parish Accounts that other quarries were being worked. One was opened up Dychurch about the beginning of the 19th century, and though there is a modern house now built upon it, it can still be identified. The other quarry known as the Dag Lane Quarry was, I am told, not far from the present surgery in Brookside. A lot of material was used on the roads, but there must have been a great deal of stone used for building extracted. The size of some of these blocks was seen when one was revealed when the Vicar's present garden had to be fenced. It was at least three feet wide and possibly as deep. Such a block, used for the base of the old vicarage (in about 1730), must have been a heavy object to move, even on a sledge. We must remember that quarrying such rock was a skilled task, especially splitting it to size.

The Church Cottages

The mason's work was a very important part in the building of every house in the village, except of course the wooden houses for the poor (more like shacks to us). We have a fairly detailed account of the building (or rebuilding) of the Church Cottages, which were condemned before the last war but not demolished until after the war. They were condemned in 1935 but Vicar Marlow protested to the Minister of Health, London and the demolition was delayed until war broke out, when all demolition was stopped. The original bequest was eight acres of land and one church house for

Church Cottages situated where the garage of 6 Church Walk now stands. (*Vicars' Logbook*)

the upkeep of the Churchyard Cross – which no longer existed in 1791 when Bridges' *History of the County of Northampton* was written. The cottage was rebuilt after the great fire of 1729 for £30! In 1858 it was divided into three cottages and it was in one of these that the family of Paul Geeves lived when they came as evacuees during the Second War. The back wall of the double garage of 6 Church Wall is the only remaining stone wall of the cottages left – see photograph. Most of this information is from a hand-written note of Marlow's with photographs.

In 1721-2 a complete account of materials and builders employed are shown. The masons are not named but without doubt the masons mentioned were Thomas and John. To quote the materials first: "Paid to Robert Bodinton 44 Load of Ston & Morter fetching 14s-8d. Paid for 4 bushills of Lime and Carrig 2s-8d. Paid to ye Masons for work don at ye hous £2-0s-10d. Paid for Watling for ye Butrey 6d." (A buttery was where the provisions for the house were kept. (Watling is the application of wattle, a rendering of clay and other material, usually twigs or straw.)

Over the years further repairs were done to the house (for, as we have seen, it was really a building divided into three). 130 years after the first account the house needed complete renovation, which included taking up the old stone floors and replacing with brick, walls pointed and various other alterations. The contract was drawn up in 1858 and after the work was completed an entry says: "Tho Berrill Bill £3-6-0d" which was a considerable amount for those days. And the expense included, "Carpenters & Masons at Church Hoses for ale 7½d."

What's in a wall?

The stone houses that the Berrills built in Bozeat two or three hundred years ago had a considerable amount of stone within them. Each exterior wall would in fact be of two wall thicknesses, one on the outside and one on the interior. Between the two walls would be a rubble filling of smaller stones and fragments of large stones left over after shaping to size. Opposite the Independent Wesleyan Chapel, the old smithy which had been used by Thomas Wallis was converted into a house in the 1980s. One part of the old stone wall had collapsed and the rubble filling had come out like flour from a burst bag. When work was done on the Church porch in recent years the rubble filling could be seen from the top when the roof of the porch was removed. The rubble filling would act as insulation, provided the exterior walls were in good

Workhouse in Mallows Yard.
(Marlow's History 1936)

repair and that the thatch above did not allow water and frost to penetrate. It has been said by an inhabitant of a stone house that it was warm in winter and cool in summer. However, the thatch always provided a problem as can be seen from the various parish accounts. Norfolk reed would not have been transported far, so the thatch came from the straw of local farmers. And thatching was done very much on a Do-It-Yourself basis, sometimes by labourers who were only too glad to earn a little extra. The fact that the parish was probably parsimonious in its expenditure probably didn't help. In any event the old workhouse needed patching to the thatch every two or three years, which indicated that the craft was not as it is today. When after a few years the moisture had crept into the rubble filling and the frost had pushed out the exterior wall, the time had come to call in one of the Berrill family to completely rebuild.

William Berrill repaired the workhouse (now the building in Mallows Yard, adjoining the Churchyard) and presented the bill to the parish in 1828 which read: "William Berrills Masonry Bill for Workhouse £6-2-0d." (William died in 1851 aged 62.) And there were many other repairs to the Workhouse and Church Cottages by the same family over two hundred years. [When Horace and Ethel Andrews moved into the house soon after they were married in 1934 it was in a terrible state. It was owned then by a Mr Stevens of Wellingborough. Horace and Elsie lived in the top half and Horace often had to climb out and replace the tiles on the roof. "Next time you can get a young monkey to climb out and do this for me!" Horace once complained to the owner. The sanitary Inspector then came along and condemned the building and it remained derelict for a long time. Eventually it was restored and is now in good condition and lived in by John and Irene Collins and their three daughters and called 'Lavender Cottage' – a far cry from the days when it was the village workhouse.]

The Church walls being built of the same stone in the same fashion also needed constant repair over the centuries, an example in 1804: "John Beriel for pinten (pointing) Church Leds (leads) 6s-8d. " [I wondered who cemented in the leads in the chancel window making them impossible to remove for restoration!] But a few years before that, in 1800, another bill was recorded, "John Beriel his Bil for Wite Washen Church £7-1-8d." [making it even more difficult to restore any mediaeval pictures painted on them!] These old craftsmen were fairly adaptable in what they undertook. The earliest mention of masons in connection with the Church goes back to 1704 when: "Paid to John Berril for mending ye Church yard wales 5d." It was here that the mason really came into his own, for his work could be clearly seen, and his reputation as well! Now the interesting thing is that when in the early accounts of repairs to the Churchyard walls are mentioned there is no mention of lime, or sand or mortar. In other words it is highly likely that the Church walls, and others in the village, were examples of 'dry-stone walling'. This is a technique that we normally associate with walls in remote moorlands. But, it was possibly fairly common in all districts two hundred years ago. It is said that a skilled man can lay about six yards of double wall in a working day. So we can work out from the following entry in a parish account book of 1832 how long and how much was paid on this occasion: "Pd Joseph Berrill for 44 yards of Whalling at 7d Yd £1-5-8d." It took Joseph probably just over seven working days. We have no idea where all this building or rebuilding of walls took place, but certainly about that time a considerable amount was being put up, as another entry for 1829 shows: "John Berrill towards the wall building 12s-6d." This looks like a pre-payment in hard times for the next month. "The Balance of John Berrill Bill for building 50½ yards of walling at 8d per yard, £1-1-2d" Which makes a total of £1-13-8d for over eight days work. The walls if over four feet high would (somewhat like the two walls of a building) have two walls with solid pieces of filling between. At intervals along the wall would be a solid piece acting as a tie across the full width of the wall. As the different courses were laid, the larger stones at the bottom gave way to smaller ones so that the wall slopes in towards the top. Although all the stones would have been irregular, the capping stones at the top would be fairly uniform. The dry stone walls of estates or farms were usually of double thickness whereas the dividing walls within a boundary wall were usually of single thickness. Again, as with buildings the stone had to be carted from a quarry as we find in 1798: "Wm Berril for carien 4 louds [loads] of ston to Churchwals 2s-0d."

Bozeat at the end of the 18th century
We are given an insight into the buildings and people of Bozeat at this time from (a) the Inoculation List of 1788; (b) The Militia List of 1798; and (c) Enclosure Arrangements of 1799.

The Enclosure gives us most of the details. The Village is clustered around the High Street and the Church with most of the buildings found in the High Street stretching on up Dychurch westwards. Then into the London Road up towards Olney for about 100 yards up from the Red Lion and likewise a hundred yards or so up Easton Lane towards Easton Maudit. Then going south off Camden Square we have dwellings up Church Lane/Pudding Bag and likewise into and down Mile Street, and continuing south along what is now Allens Hill as far as Pear Tree Close. Then northwards off Camden Square we have dwellings up Dag Lane for about 200 yards. The majority of these would consist of modest stone, thatched cottages with one hearth and smoking chimney. The actual details are as follows:

(i)   19 Homesteads (often described with orchard) – the most substantial buildings e.g. Red Lion, farms, vicarage, etc.

(ii) 15 Houses often described with yard and/or garden) – still good substantial stone buildings, e.g. 46 Mile Street where the Fenns now live.

(iii) 64 Cottages (usually with garden and sometimes orchard) – ranging from extremely modest to those of some quality (many of the less substantial were demolished in the 20th century – see later.)

This gives a total of 98 dwellings/homes. In addition we have in the village: Bury Yard (the site of the original Manor to the right of Easton Lane), Burnt Yard, the site origin of the Great Fire of 1729, a few fields, 21 Closes (a Close was a small enclosure for containing animals e.g. Bull Close, or property, or a cluster of buildings, etc), five woods/spinneys, an Inn (Red Lion – owned by the Earl of Sussex), and 49 Allotments. The Allotments were like smallholdings of land which were rented or owned by villagers on which they made their livelihood, the replacement of the old open field system (e.g. many of the allotments were the result of dividing up Mill Field). The main land owners were Earl Spencer with the majority of land and buildings but also among the gentry the Earl of Sussex (at Easton Maudit) and Baroness Lucas and the Church (Rev. Corbet Wilson). But there were some villagers with substantial property and land such as Edward Skevington (three homesteads, fields, allotments, etc.) and Thomas Dexter (a house and cottage, Burnt Yard and allotments in Mill Field and the Leys), John Dexter (two cottages and gardens, a house, a homestead and an allotment), William Bettell (a house and garden and an allotment), George Hooton (a house and garden and allotment) and Will Church (a house, two cottages and gardens and allotment in Mill Field). These were the major property owners but there are also 24 villagers named as owners usually of one cottage. Familiar names appear: Hooton three times, and once Drage/ Smart/ Cracstone(Craxton)/ Partridge/ Laughton. Also All Souls College, Oxford owned a homestead, a cottage and an allotment.

Jim and Anne Bayes outside the Old Cottage (now demolished) in London Road, next to the Chequers.

Comparison with the Inoculation List of 1788 (in the possession of William Bettell and Thomas Dexter) of 10 years earlier – those inoculated by John Lettice were 361 persons coming from 97 homes, which compares with 98 homes above so it seems that virtually all the village was inoculated, perhaps fearing an epidemic. These numbers give an occupancy on the average of 3.7 people per home with a range from 1 to 9, which is perhaps similar to today. There were also 53 different family names then with Drage only appearing five times (which compares with the early 20th century) – and we also have Bates/Church/Line/Taylor/Hooton/Pettit/Bettel/Tyler/ Meacock/Insfield/Eastall/Smart/Smith/Wykes/Lewis/Jolley/Negus/Riseley/Ross/ Walker/Tomkins/Smart/Berril/Surridge/Partridge/Bayes/Gibson/Craxstone/Lawton to mention some names still in currency today.

The Militia Lists were raised by the Lord Lieutenant and deputies of Northamptonshire for the defence of the realm when there was a threat of war, e.g. Declaration of Independence of American colonies on 4th July 1776 and declaration of war with France first in 1778 and then in 1793: our list seems to have been drawn up because of the last of these. Presumably it contains all the able bodied young men who would be able to fight if necessary, and there are 91 of them in all – compare the list of 210 young men who volunteered to go to war in 1914 from Bozeat – again virtually all the young of the village seem to have volunteered. What is interesting is that we find 50 different family names (compare 53 on the inoculation list) and these names are familiar from the lists above. There are eight Drages, three Pettits and four Hootons among these young men, but in addition there is a Warner/ Skevington/ Osbourne/ Boddington/ Bradshaw among others. What is interesting is the range of occupations which are as follows:

Cordwainers 7	Shepherds 1
Carpenters 2	Masons 1
Grocer 1	Taylors 2
Labourers 65	Millers 1
Farmers 7	Blacksmiths 1
Butchers 2	Cottagers 1

The Enclosure means business
In 1817-1818 the agent of Lord Spencer (who owned the greater part of Bozeat land and farms) was building walls and farm buildings, which was probably a gradual process after the 1799 Enclosure when the land was re-distributed. John Berrill in 1818 was employed on building boundaries. James Drage dug the stone for £5-13-7d, whilst John was paid £12-13-10d. Also for farm buildings James Drage dug stone for £6-10-0d, whilst John Berrill was paid £35-5-4d. They must have been golden years for the masons who could find employment on the new buildings. But harder years were ahead.

Hard times follow
Following the end of the Napoleonic Wars in 1815, a deep recession came which was only to improve towards the middle of the 1800s. All classes were to feel the 'pinch', and the tradesmen were no exception. In the same year of 1818 John Berrill (maybe the same or another of the family) was paid by the parish: "1 day to seek work 1s-0d." Then 12 years later the same or another John was given by the parish: "John

Berrell for Masons Tools 5s-0d." One wonders what would have been their comparative worth today.

Pebble paths and pitching

We find in the Churchwarden's Accounts another side to the Mason's trade. To quote the 1738 entry in full: "paid for gathering poables for the Church Yard 4s-9d. Paid for Caridge for pebley and sand and stone 10s-0d. Paid to thom Beriell for Pichon and Wallen 15s-9d." Now whilst the stone was for the walls, the 'pichon' and 'poables' were for the paths. Large cobbles were gathered from the fields by women and boys, and then laid for paving. The work of laying the cobbles was termed 'Pitching', and the area laid called 'the pitch'. Not only Church paths, but many old yards and paths in Bozeat, now overlaid with tar, must have been 'pitched'. These pebbles were laid with the aid of a 'Pitching Hammer'. This was a long piece of wood with a handle on the side and the base of the wood had a metal plate to stop it from splitting. With one hand on the side handle and the other holding the top of the piece of wood the pebbles were driven into the ground until they were even. They no doubt prevented the walking public from being immersed in the mud, but what a problem those churchyard pebbles were to be. For weeds would grow in between and an annual entry in the Churchwardens' Accounts for the next hundred years was payment to paupers and old men for weeding the pebbles. A typical entry for May 1843 is: "J. Smart and 5 Old men weeding pebles 3s-6d.". This seemed to be half a day's work for they were paid about 1s-0d a day. This continued until 1874 when the local landowner had the pebbles removed, "By sale of pebbles to Thos Revis Esq £1-0-0d."

Here come the bricks and tiles

During the last half of the 19th century the building of houses in stone became obsolete. Stone was heavy and awkward in carriage, and the building of a house with what was in reality two walls was time-consuming when the age of brick arrived. Brick began to be used in Bozeat early in the 19th century but not on any great scale until the great expansion of the village which coincided with the Boot and Shoe Industry after 1860. There were new people – 'outsiders' – and all had large families. New houses had to be built and brick was the new mode. Brick made for ease of construction, as well as cheapness, even in such an area as our own with building stone not far away. From now on the local stone would be used as 'chippings' put by the local roadman on the village highways and byways. Brick was for cheaper building – and sometimes slum buildings. Somewhere about 1860 Thomas Bignall was making bricks in his brickyard over the fields, where there resulted a large hole, out of which the clay was dug. This came to be filled in with old tins, bottles, etc. from the village and came to be known as "Tin Pits". Local brick can be seen in various places round the village being often of differing hues, and showing marks of burning, instead of being the uniform hue of the mass-produced brick. Supplies of tiles and bricks came from this brickyard and kiln, but not within living memory (1980s), so possibly it came to an end before the turn of the century, to become a rubbish pit when the parish council were looking round to see where they could dispose of their rubbish. I am told that many of the houses at the top of London Road were built of these bricks. So the Berrills if they were to survive had to change with the times. In the 1876 Trade Directory Thomas Berrill is named as Bricklayer, and Thomas and Charles Berrill were builders and contractors in 1892. Thomas lived in

Peartree in a brick house, no doubt of his own construction. It was an end of an era, and it was also the end of the family. From Thomas Berrill in 1680 to another Thomas in 1892 is a long time, but it was this family who must have built most of the older houses of the village, the farmer his barns, the walls to keep in his stock. The Church fabric received their constant attention, and under the surface of the paths, we tread the pebbles which they laboriously laid.

[The transition from stone to brick is clearly seen in the house once belonging to Eli Berrill who owned a brick kiln and where Ruth Webb now lives at 6 Mile Street – just above where Derek Summerlin once had his stone cottages and carrier business and where now stands a house built in the 1990s. Ruth's house has a fine brick front with a date 1908 on it but her deeds which include wills from the 19th century show that it was probably built before the Enclosure in 1799. When she had it treated for subsidence, digging down several feet revealed the original 100+ year old stone walls on which the new brick walls had been built in the early part of the 20th century. Another example of this building brick on stone is to be clearly seen on the side wall of 25 Mile Street which is also a classic example of how a front room was converted into a shop in the boom days of the little village shops in the early years of the 20th century. Similarly the barn of the Carvels of 58 Allens Hill but facing onto the top of Mile Street is brick upon stone]

Square brackets [ ] indicate additions to Palmer's text.

Postscript – Paul Geeves and the Church Cottages

On seeing me by the churchyard gate (spring 1997), Paul stopped the car he was repairing, got out and took me over to stand with him in the double garage of the fine old stone house at 6 Church Walk (Burnt Close). "We are standing exactly where our cottage was. I can remember it as though it was yesterday! Up there was a hole in the ceiling to the up stairs, but no stairs, just a ladder through the hole."

This was once the middle of the three Church Cottages described earlier and all that is now left of them was their end wall which now forms the back wall of the garage. From the photograph you can see that they were in a line almost at right angles to the road with Wykes farmhouse behind.

Paul was born in West Ham, London in 1939, the youngest of four boys. His father worked in the docks. As soon as the war started, the docks were the target it seemed for every enemy bomb, so the family were evacuated to Somerset to a vicarage in the Mendip Hills. They were not particularly happy there but they did have a distant relative living in Bozeat so Paul's mother brought her four boys to come and live here, and the middle of the three church cottages was their first home. Paul recalled his life as a lad in those war years. "There were no toilets – just a bucket in the barn which was emptied by the man with the night cart. I remember how it slopped around on its iron wheels and how the driver sat on it to eat his sandwiches! And there was no water – we had to go through the garden of 5 Church Walk to get our water from the well. The milk came in churns from the farm at the centre of the village and it was ladled out into jugs. We got our meat from the Garretts, the butchers round the corner – they were an education! (I have modified this London lad's blunt words!) – and the baker brought the bread. One of the cottages was full of papers. It was lucky there was no fire or we would all have gone up in flames!"

"School was strict. I remember as soon as you got home from school you went out again or you'd be given jobs to do. You only complained, 'I'm bored' once! We went

Looking from the top of Hope Street, 1920s, with Honest John's shoe factory at the bottom.

out anywhere – or we'd be cleaning the house or digging the allotment."

"Then we lived for a time at what was 'The Engineer' (a beer house at 40 Mile Street). It was owned by Mr Elliott (Joyce Corby's father) – looked at us foreigners as though we'd come from another planet (again recalling a boyhood memory). I've been here 56 years and I'm still not really Bozeat! (Paul smiles) My mother is 91 and still lives at the bungalow at 1 Queen's Street but she was just a girl when she came then."

"My brothers remember the war better than I do but I remember going up to the old airport at Podington and the huge lorries that thundered along the road. It was at Dungee Corner that one of them nearly blew my mum and the pram into the ditch! We were always finding bits of planes and equipment in the woods around there."

Paul first went to work at Unilever in Sharnbrook and then in 1972 bought Harrold Green Garage and built up a business there over the years – the amiable Paul who keeps our cars going today! His wife Julia runs the hairdressers next door to his garage in Harrold. They live at 41 Fullwell Road.

Building in the 20th century

1. *Before the Great War*

There is an extant receipted invoice from T. & C. Berrill, Builders and Contractors at Irchester to Mr (Henry John) Edmunds, dated Michaelmas 1902 "for building House at Bozeat As per Contract" – currently 14 Hope Street – for the cost of £212. It is a fine double fronted house in rich red brick with some stonework and for a "Stone Bottom and Tar paving" there was an additional cost of 1 pound 4 shillings with a further 12 shillings for "12 Sets Blind Rollers & Furniture" There is a row of red bricks faced with sea shells along the top of the front wall just below the gables. It is a fine building from the early 1900s standing nobly half way up the street on the right. Many of the terraced brick houses are typical of the houses of this time built for shoeworkers in such places as Rushden and Wellingborough, etc., together with the typical brick shoe factories such as the three in our village – the most classic being the one at the bottom of Hope

14 Hope Street. (*D. Edmunds*)

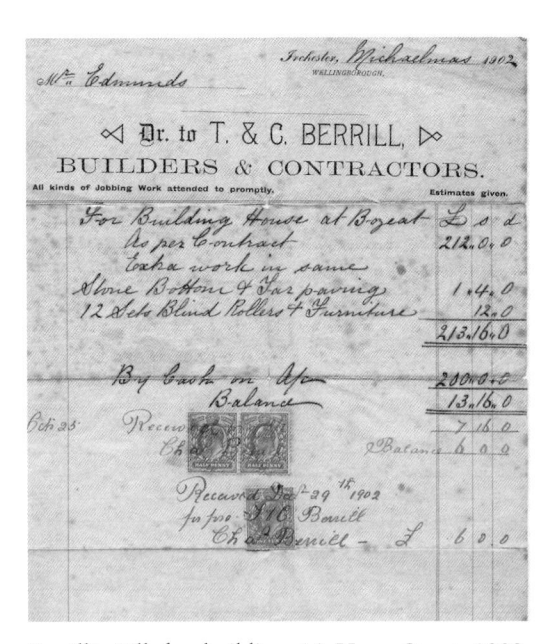

Berrill's Bill for building 14 Hope Street 1902. This was paid in gold sovereigns in two lots of £100. Derek Edmunds was born there in 1936 and built his own bungalow across the road. His grandfather Harry is named as a tenor horn player in the Bozeat Band in the time of Queen Victoria's Jubilee in 1887 (Marlow's History p.89). There is a Charles Berrill in Bozeat Cemetery, born in 1863, died 18th Jan 1931. (D. Edmunds)

Street. There are 17 such houses in Hope Street on the south side and 12 along Wollaston Road as well as 26 semi-detached and terraced brick houses at the top of London Road towards Olney (evens 116-164, odds 142-154) – some 55 terraced brick houses in all. William Botterill moved into a brick house in 1903 and around it grew a shoe factory until the site became full in 1973. We should also mention White House Farm towards Olney built in the early 1900s by Owen and Edmund Wallis, now a whitewashed square stone building with flat roof and mock battlements – quite different from anything else in the village. It was probably built, as was the red brick farmhouse at Newlands farm, in 1910, after the sale of the Bozeat Estate in 1909 and the consequent reorganisation of the land. Benjamin Squires built his brick bakery adjacent to his stone house at 21 London Road with its coal oven baking 300 loaves at one time in 1913. And there are three brick houses in Peartree which appear to be of this period, one in Bull Close and three up Allens Hill so there may well have been some 65 dwellings added to the village in the first decade of the century before the outbreak of war.

2. Building after the Great War

In the building boom that followed the war and with a Labour government, the first council houses were built in Bozeat – the very first is 5 Allens Hill and occupied by the Tompkins family from Shepherds Lodge – leading to an estate of 12 council houses in Allens Hill. Then in 1930, 12 council houses were built behind them in Bennes field which became Council Street. (The four council bungalows at the bottom of Council Street were built later in 1978.)

Towards the end of the 1930s after the completion of Council Street it was decided to build an estate of similar mainly terraced council houses in Harrold Road – 16 in all – giving us a building boom of some 40 houses.

And there were odd bits of 'infilling' taking place over this time with private houses added here and there. In the London Road what is called Spencelayh's house (No. 105) was built in the 1920s by Albert Partridge and when the old cinema burned down a bungalow was built on the site (No. 87). And up Easton Lane the Boswell's house (No. 35) was built in classic 30s style in 1939 with curved bays and light metal window frames with horizontal divides, as was the house next to it and further up number No. 55, overall a modest 14 houses (including Nos. 1, 3 and 49 Allens Hill, two houses in Bull Close and three in Peartree) or so were added to the village

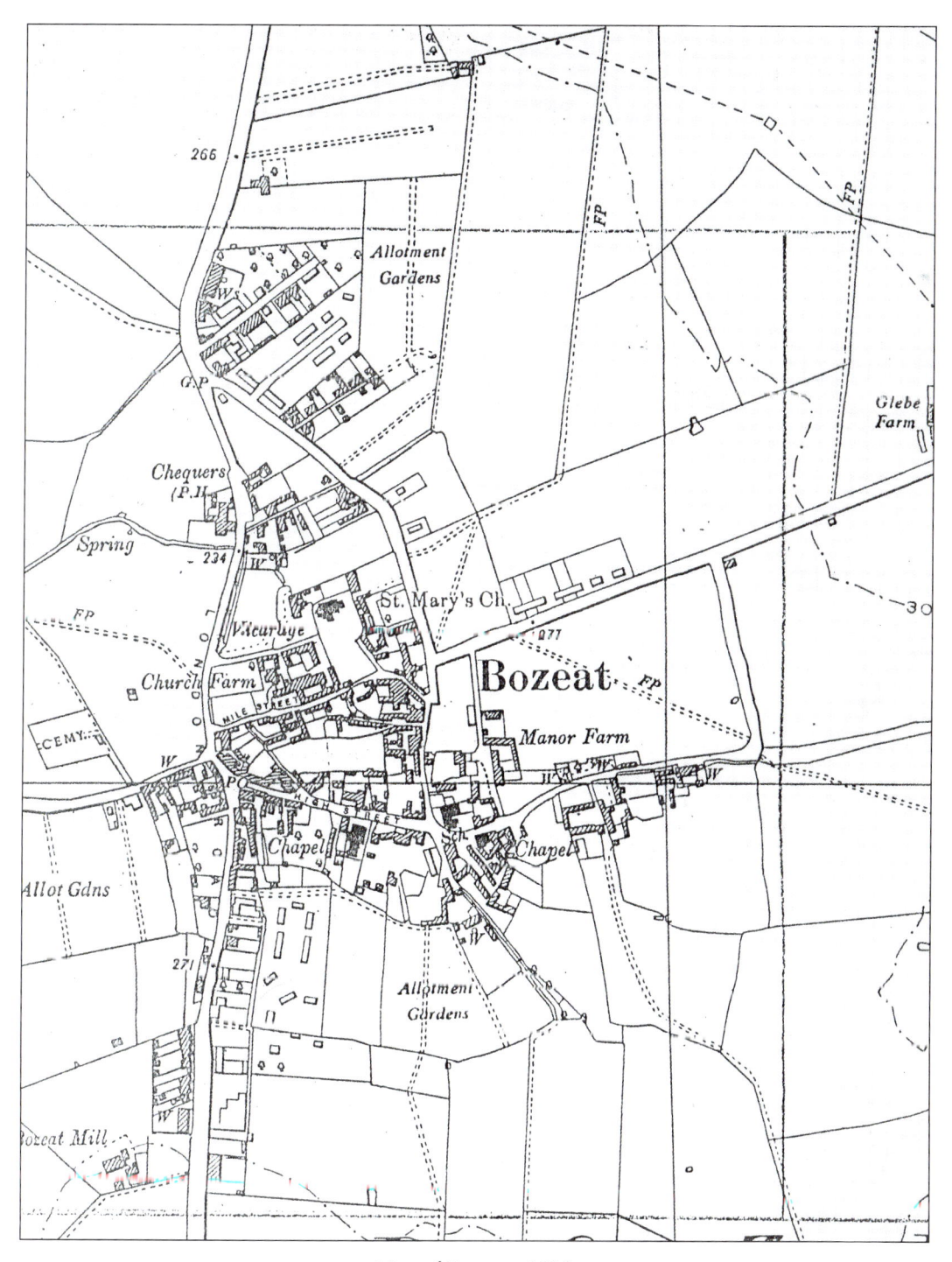

Map of Bozeat c.1920.

privately between the wars giving a total of some 54 dwellings from c.1900 to 1939.

3. Building after the Second World War
Here again we see another building boom of council homes with another Labour government.

Gerald Corby moved into his new council house at 11 Queen Street in 1956 as part of a fourteen house development at the top of this road, presumably named to commemorate the Queen's Coronation in 1956. Behind these in a cul-de-sac called Roberts Street (in memory of Percy Roberts a well known public figure, councillor and Methodist in the village) the council added a further eleven houses, on land where the mill once stood which was sold to them by the miller's three daughters – the Misses Little. On this land they added five more at the top of the road which was named after the celebrated mill, including one splendid detached house for the Little ladies, which is now 7 Mill Road). On the other side at the top of Mill Road they built ten dwellings more giving a Council Estate of 37 houses at the top of the village to the west of the London Road.

To the east of London Road lay Warrens Garden Field where the Empire Day Sports took place each year and the Council bought this by compulsory purchase to build a further estate also in the 1950s: 14 houses in Hewlett's Close (named after another village public figure, Frank Hewlett, a JP and parish councillor), and eight at the top of what is now St Mary's Road (named after the village church) giving a further council estate of 26 houses. So the Council's post-war home building programme in Bozeat provided a total of a further 59 homes, including the four in Camden Square.

Some modest private infilling was also going on at this time. One builder put up four dwellings at the Wellingborough end of the London Road (Nos. 3, 5, 7, 9), two bungalows and two houses and lived in No. 9 himself, and Vicar Knight enabled the Wellmans to build a bungalow on the Glebe land (No. 25 London Road), the piece of land sold for £100 in 1955. And on the edge of the Glebe facing Allens Hill, permission was given to build three bungalows (36, 38, 40) (land sold for £500 in 1956 – in 1907 it was a proposed site for a generating station for a tram company!) built by the village partnership of Elliott & Dobbs. Ted Drage the village carpenter bought number 40 in the 1950s and did the woodwork himself as it was his trade. "They offered me to extend my garden across the glebe field to the London Road for £70 but I could not afford that – I could hardly afford the mortgage!" remembers Ted (1999) as we sat in the back room looking over the glebe past the little garden shed where he still makes his beautiful wooden furniture at the age of 82. If these three bungalows had extended their gardens there would be only half the glebe there is today and only the old vicarage orchard between Ted and the churchyard. No. 50 was built at this time giving us around ten new private homes, a total of some 70 homes in this post-war period up to 1960.

4. Immigration and the private house building boom of the 1960s and '70s
London overspill programmes and the creation of New Towns such as Milton Keynes resulted in businesses moving out of London with a consequent migration of people looking for new homes near their new places of work. Suddenly we find Bozeat doubling its size with people who have no historic association with the village or the area.

Mrs Botterill sold Stoneypiece, previously allotments, for building in 1964/5. Abbey Homesteads built the first phase of houses constructing 34 bungalows (mainly detached) in the lower half of Queen Street (the top part being the council estate). Just below this estate they built 15 houses and also created a cul-de-sac, Clayland Close, of a further 15 houses – 30 in all. Another cul-de-sac off Queen's Street further down had 17 semi-detached bungalows built, and retained the name of Stoneypiece in memory of the whole area and the nature of the ground.

Then out from the bottom end of Queen Street they created the lower end of Mill Road and built the first two bungalows, number 47 for Cliff and Eileen Fenn and next door to them one for Jo and Betty Watson. In all 41 bungalows were built in the bottom half of Mill Road and then between them and council property at the top they built 17 semi-detached houses and a cul-de-sac off which is appropriately called Abbey Close (after the builders) with a footpath through to Clayland Close of 17 more houses giving 34 there. George and Pat Summers bought a plot of land in 1970 on which was built 27 Mill Road and they moved into it in 1971.

So in the mid-'60s there suddenly appeared on the other side of the London Road from the village a new private estate of 92 bungalows and 64 houses – 156 dwellings in all. At the top of Mill Road the Council built a further 16 bungalows which with the 1950s estate on the higher ground and the new private one provided a total 210 post-war housing development to the west of the village.

Mr Oddfellows owned Backside which stretched from the brook alongside Dag Lane to Wyman Close. It was bought by the Wollaston builder Alfie Underwood who built a private estate on the land in the '60s and early '70s consisting of: Brookside (19 houses); Firtree (14 houses plus three bungalows – Kit and Peg Pratt, Londoners, bought No. 3 in 1973); Wyman Close (13 houses plus three bungalows, named after Mr Fred Wyman, a parish councillor, school governor and Methodist, whose daughter Winnie at 80 years of age lives (1999) at 1 St Mary's Road); Knights Close (11 houses – named after Vicar Knight); St Mary's Road (13 houses plus two bungalows); Hillside (four houses plus four bungalows – the last bungalow to be built was that of Jim and Marjorie Gregory in 1971.) All this gives us a total of 88 new houses.

Finally Alfie Underwood bought land which was originally part of Church Farm but also garden fields/allotments, at the top what was known as Dock Hill and owned by Walter (Tompy) Drage including part of Red Gables Farm, an area which on the old maps was called Fullwell – so that the resulting road of new houses, 80 in all (including about eight bungalows), became Fullwell Road. Bill and Margaret Maycock bought the bungalow at No. 11 and were the first in. Stan and Pat Silsby were married in 1964 and went straight into the new two-storey house opposite at No. 14. The first houses were built at the bottom and worked upwards. Dennis and Audrey Allen bought No. 22 when the builders got that far in 1972. These three private estates, two to the south and one to the north of the village give us an increase of 318 dwellings in all. Also in this period we note some infilling in Hope Street (eight), bungalows at the top of Allens Hill/Harrold Road (five) and further down Allens (four) High Street (three) and Bull Close (one) raising the total to 339. Some modest council building occurred at this time (six bungalows in Church Walk/Mile Street plus eight bungalows at the top of Mill Road) making the total for this period of around 350 – some 542 new homes in the century, with the biggest (private) building boom in the last 30 years.

5. The 1980s, 1990s filling in the gaps and flowing onto farm land
As farming becomes harder and the desire to live in the country becomes greater, infilling and the sale of farmland for domestic dwellings continues. So in the old farmyard of Church Farm we now see seven fine stone-faced detached houses in Church Farm Close. And on land belonging to Manor Farm which on the old maps is marked as an orchard we have four similar houses called 'The Orchard Church Lane.' Another farmyard turning into a domestic dwelling at this time (1999) is that of Wykes farm which with the house and Yard both sold in 1998 as private dwellings, as was Spring Villa bought by two doctors and sold by the Hedges who once farmed the land. And the old butcher's shop with the slaughter house next door was turned into two more domestic dwellings at the corner of Church Lane with Mile Street. Infilling went on slowly in the 1980s with two houses at the bottom of Fullwell, and two in Bull Close, two in Peartree, one at the top of St Mary's Road, three in Hope Street and six in London Road (two village men built two of these – the one at the very top of London Road by Mike Coady and Paul Willey, one for himself just above the old shoe factory in 1998) and one in Camden Square and two bungalows in Brookside, slowly increasing the total to 34. Then on the hill to the south of the High Street belonging to the Warner family there have appeared six (eventually eight) executive houses, creating Warner's Close, giving us some 41 houses so far.

Finally in 1999 we see two major developments in the middle and to the south of the village:

(i) Starting December 1998, Dean Homes of St Ives are building four- and five-bedroom and three-bedroom properties on Manor Farm field as well as converting the historic barn to give some 20 homesteads.

(ii) Also starting in December 1998 Bellway Homes of Bedworth are creating the 'Summerfields' Estate behind the Shoe Factory up the London Road of about 35 dwellings – six of which will belong to a Housing Trust bought in collaboration with Wellingborough Council for local young people.

This gives us a total of some 96 dwellings in the last two decades of the millennium so that overall some 638 homes have been added to the village in the 20th century.

The numbers game
We know from the Electoral Register there were 739 houses in 1998 as compared to 148 houses in 1821. We also know that some 120 families lived in the village (*Bridges*) around 1720 so then there would have been no more that 120 homes. A simple calculation gives 739-583 (638 minus 55) = 156 homes in 1900 suggesting only about 8 homes were built between 1820 and 1900 and some 28 between 1700 and 1820.

A story in stone
The value of 8 above is clearly incorrect – for at least two reasons: (i) A significant number of buildings from the last century were pulled down and we have not accounted for this; (ii) Two or more stone buildings from the 19th century have frequently been combined into one home whereas previously they were two or more. How can we correct for these two factors? Here we have a remarkably useful fact to help us. Virtually all the buildings in the village before 1900 were built in stone and

virtually all those since then (apart from stone-facing in Church Farm Close and the Orchard in 1980s) were built in brick. If this is so then all we have to do to determine how many homes there were in the village in 1900 is to count the number of stone buildings there are, evaluate how many homes that is equivalent to and add to this an estimate of the number of stone homes demolished this century.

Before we do this we note two other interesting features of building in the second half of the 19th century:

(i) Brickwork is increasingly added to the stonework both as ornamentation, but increasingly as part of the essential structure, e.g. around windows, as brick is much easier to work with than stone. Also one or two buildings, such as 6 Church Lane and 6 Mile Street, look like fine brick houses dated from the first decade of the 20th century when seen from the front, but they are in fact stone houses, one or more of whose walls have been rebuilt in brick (see later).

(ii) During this period the Berrills used a characteristic way of building at least one of the stone walls in a building – making the wall up as a hatchwork of stone and mortar with the stones at some 45 degrees to the horizontal, presumably to add strength to the wall, giving a herringbone appearance – a similar wedge style was used as a foundation to the church tower by builders some 750 years before them! (see note at end of Chapter 22). They added this feature into the fine detached villas – Spring Vale and Greenwood in London Road, Stanley House at the top of Bull Close and The Grange. In addition it is found elsewhere in detached and semi-detached homes in Bull Close (six), Dychurch (two), Peartree (two) and No. 6 Church Lane (one) and London Road (five) including the old school and the Teacher's and Doctor's houses adjacent. If we include the extension to the Methodist Church then we have a total of some 20 in all built by the Berrills in the last half of the 19th century which is a style they developed at this time almost unique to themselves and to Bozeat.

COUNT OF STONE DWELLINGS:

Public houses (Nelson/ Red Lion/ Chequers)		3
Farms (Spring/SpringVale/East/Manor/Wykes/Homestead/Town/Grange)		8
Private dwellings:		
London Road	14	
Easton Lane	6	
Mile St/Church Walk	46	
High Street	26	
Allens Hill	12	
Dag Lane	6	
Bull Close	9	
Burleigh Terrace	4	
Dychurch	19	
Pudding Bag Lane	11	
Wheelwright/etc.	7	
Peartree	5	*165
Total		176

*165 is a calculated estimate of the original number of homes the present buildings represent (i.e. one family to a building).

Estimate of number of stone houses demolished mainly just before and after the Second World War (including the old vicarage in 1964!):

>Mile Street/Church Walk (including Church Cottages) 11
>High Street 3
>Pudding Bag 8
>Village Green (i.e. Cross Keys, etc.) 9
>Vicarage 1
>London Road (i.e. Chequers Cottages) 2

Total 34

Adding together these two totals, this gives us an estimated number of dwellings in 1900 of approximately 210.

Compared with our previous figure of 156 which ignored these two factors we now have an estimate of 210-148 = 62 houses built between 1820 and 1900 which is more realistic than eight.

These are only rough approximations but do give striking information about the changing nature of village life over these last three centuries. To put these figures in perspective we must finally look at the changing population over this period.

Population trends in Bozeat

When the Domesday Records were compiled, the population of England was perhaps 1¼ to 1½ million. By the middle of the 14th century it had risen to some four million but the Plague (Black Death) of 1349 culled the population by a half to some 2 million – and similar but less severe outbreaks, infant mortality, poor hygiene, housing, diet, etc kept the population in check for the centuries to follow – England being remarkably free from devastating wars until the 20th century. By the end of the long and increasingly prosperous reign of Elizabeth I the population rose to some 5 million (1605) and despite the Civil War of the 17th century continued to rise to about 6 million by the beginning of the 18th compared to 20 million in France and 1 million in Scotland. The 18th century was to see revolutionary changes in agriculture and medical knowledge and practice as we have seen so that by the coronation of George III in 1770 the population had risen to 7.5 million and by the end of his long reign in 1820 had doubled to 14 million. Then during the 19th century the exponential explosion in population gathered pace so that by 1935 the UK population had reached 45 million – nearly quadrupling in a hundred years. The present figure of some 70 million at the end of the 20th century measures the slowing down of this exponential stampede as family sizes have reduced to the frequently quoted 2.4 children – closer to the average in our village of earlier centuries of around 2 that kept our population at 400 for so long.

Information on the population of Bozeat comes from various sources:

1377: 210 paid Poll Tax in Bozeat (*David Hall*). If this 'head' or poll tax was for adults we can estimate a total population of some 400.

1381: There are 82 taxable people in Bozeat, i.e. adults giving a population of about 380.

1671: The Religious Census of this year (see *Marlow*, p.48) gives 380 Conformists (C of E) living in Bozeat, no Papists (Roman Catholic) and five nonconformist families (i.e. Cromwell's war seems to have had little impact on our conservative village!) – suggesting a population of some 400 again.

John Bridges (1666-1724) began in 1719 to collect information on the history of the county and says of Bozeat: "The town consisting of about one hundred and twenty families." This again would give us a population of some 480 people approximately. (*Palmer – Marlow*, Sheet 25, seems to be in error here).

1789: Inoculation of the village that year was carried out on 361 persons, which if you assume some 10% needed no inoculation gives a population again around 400.
1801: First Government Census gives population 680, i.e. this is the first significant increase in the village population which had remained constant at around 400 since the 14th century for some 450 years – depicting a village of families averaging two children assuming insignificant migration in and out. Hereafter there is an exponential climb through the 19th century.

1811	754
1821	754
1831	812
1841	845
1851	921
1861	955
1871	1,086
1881	1,189
1891	1,273
1901	1,478
1911	1,192
1921	1,145
1931	1,157

Note how the population peaked about 1901 – and almost doubled during the 19th century.

1998: c.1800 (electors 1467). The population has nearly doubled again from after the Great War to the end of the century, mainly due to migration into the village.

Compare this increase with the known housing figures:

1720   120 homes.
1799   98 homes as determined from details of the Enclosure Settlement (average 3.7 persons per home).
1821   148 homes (ave 5.1 persons per home).
1900   156 homes (+33 demolished + mergers gives us about 210, i.e. 54 more) (average 6.9 persons per home – just about the peak of house population density at the end of the Victorian era).
1914   224 homes + 54 = 279 (average 4.2 persons per home).

1939   278 homes + 54 = 322 (average 3.6 persons per home, i.e. back to the 1799 occupancy).
1960   348 homes.
1980   698 i.e. the village (number of homes) doubled in size in 20 years!
1998   739 homes (average of about 2.4 persons per home – the lowest on record in a village with 7.8 times more homes than it had 200 years earlier in 1799!)

Conclusion: The number of people living in a dwelling was 3.7 in 1799, 5.1 in 1821, 6.9 in 1900, 4.0 in the 1930s and only 2.4 in 1998 – a steady increase in house occupancy density during the 19th century peaking around 1900 and then declining for a century to the lowest value in the largest and most luxurious accommodation at the end of the millennium.

By way of comparison and historical reflection, I remember Bill Silsby, born in 1918 living in a small cottage in Spangle Row, a family of 13 in all (two families from his parents' previous marriages and seven together) saying to me: "There were a lot of us. Some were already grown up so we never really knew them. But still there were a lot for a small cottage. Harry and I shared the same bed."

Bull Close [*Agnes Jones has kindly collected much of this information*]
I presume we must suppose that Bull Close got its name as that enclosed area where the village bull was kept – a Close being, in the context of a village, a small enclosed field or more generally an enclosed space. There were many Closes in Bozeat mentioned in the sale of 1886 – Dobson's Close, Orchard Close (several), Pond Hill Close, Windmill Close, Home Close (several), Little Close, Great Close, Barn Close (site of Newlands Farm), etc.

On the 1799 Enclosure Map the Bull Close area is designated, 'Allotment for Stone Pitts' which was allocated to 'Surveyors of Highways' presumably for the acquisition of stones for the repair and making of roads in the village.

On 9th October 1901 Arthur Smart borrowed £150 from the Working Men's Club to build a brick house, 6 Bull Close. He was a farmer at Wykes Farm, the first of six children plus one who died soon after birth. He was born on 24th September 1855. His sister Lucy Smart was related to Mavis Holman (née Line) and Arthur was the grandfather of Frederick and Peter Jones. He was a strong Methodist man. Arthur died in 1936 aged 80.

Several of Arthur's brothers built themselves houses before the Great War (i.e. in period 1900-1914) on the same area of ground which on the sale map of 1886 was on the edge of Glebe Land adjacent to that of Wykes farm and the Smart family:

(i)   One brother built the fine double fronted stone house on the south corner of Bull Close and Allens Hill – where the Clarkes lived (29 Allens Hill), which was then a farmyard.

(ii) Another brother built in brick – 15 Bull Close where Anthony Coles now lives with Hollie and Ashley.

(iii) Another brother built No. 11 in brick – where The Grays now live.

(iv) Yet another brother built a fine brick house opposite 29 Allens Hill on the corner of Peartree (i.e. 22 Peartree). Joe Smart (descendant) died in 1979. In the 1970s, one bungalow and two houses were built in the garden of this house.

On the north side of the opening into Allens Hill stand two attached stone 'Wolesley Cottages' which were built in 1882 (1 and 3 Bull Close), and carved on the stone front wall is the name and date and a Star of David. Telford and Melissa Walker lived at No. 3. Telford was a painter and decorator. They had children Jack and Cicely. Jack's daughter, Betty, married Philip Boswell the manager of the Hope Street shoe factory and they lived in 1 Allens Hill, afterwards the house and surgery of doctors Donald and Sheila Swan. Cicely married Stan Curtis from Earls Barton and they had three children, Colin, Francis and Mavis. Francis was the subject of a fine painting by Spencelayh while still a student at Wollaston School in 1955, depicted as a young student seated at a table pondering on a picture of Sir David Wilkie's 'The Blind Fiddler' on the wall in front of him. Colin Curtis still lives at No. 3.

Arthur Smart from Earls Barton (no direct connection with the previous Smarts) had No. 8 built just before World War II in 1939. His wife Louis (née Robinson) died in 1988. Rod and Caroline Bolton are now living here. It was built by Alfred Underwood of Wollaston for £238.

No. 12 was built in the 1990s and is presently owned by Nicholas and Kaye Loizou. This plot was owned by Ernest Drage and Fred Smart in the 1950s.

No. 18 is a long stone house from the 19th century and was once lived in by Harold and Clarice Drage with their parents when part of it was used as a Closing Factory. Derek and Pat Cox lived there from 1969-86 and Derek remembers that, as you entered the front door, the Closing Room was on your left and the living quarters to the right. Steve Linnell is there at present with his wife Wendy (of the Brealey family) and their two young sons Joshua and Luke.

No. 21 is a fine stone Villa built by the Berrills in the second half of the 19th century identified by the herringbone pattern of bricks and mortar on one of the walls. The Berrills built a cluster of houses up this end of Bull Close as Nos. 18, 19 and 17 also have walls with this same trade mark, which appears in about 20 houses in Bozeat as discussed previously in this chapter. One of these, the schoolmaster's

Looking down Allens Hill with children gathered at end of Bull Close. On the right was the doctor's house. *(John Darker)*

house, built in 1857, was once called 'Stanley House' and the present owners Andrew and Paula Lees tell us there is evidence that it was once used as a shoe factory.

No. 19 is a semi-detached stone house from the 19th century built by the Berrills. In 1962 Richard and Mavis Holman came to live there and it is now occupied by Tony and Helen Manktelow and their two young sons, Michael and Christopher.

No. 17 is the other half of No. 19. Peter and Julie Cartwright came to live here in 1977 with children Jonathan and Elizabeth.

No. 7 is a new house built in 1991/2 by Mick and Kim French and presently owned and occupied by Ian and Tara Potter and their young sons Elliot and Henry. This plot was originally owned by farmer Arthur Smart.

No. 5 is a fine double-fronted brick villa from the first decades of the 19th century. Previous to 1955, Edmund, Millie and Alf Wallis lived there and he owned the shop at the top of Church Lane, called Glebe Cottage. Then in 1955 Fred and Floss Tivey came to live there, Fred being appointed the manager of Bozeat Co-operative in London Road. Fred had a beautiful singing voice and was active in the Church while Floss was a lively lady and actively involved in the Women's Institute and Methodist Chapel. Fred died in 1991 and Floss left in 1994 to live with her daughter in Northampton. Stephen and Susan Bryden came to live here in 1995 and since then have had a son Ethan.

29 Allens Hill

Grahame Clarke gave me a view of the deeds of the house which contained the following information:

(i) 16th April 1879 Messrs James Pettit, Thomas, Tho' Robinson, H. Partridge and William Jolley and their mortgagees to Mr William Smart. [So this appears to be the date when it was built]. Indicated on the plan is a proposed road (Bull Close) 15 feet wide plus 4 Lots.
(ii) 20th January 1915 Messrs W. C. Drage, A. A. Drage to Mr Wm Cecil Drage [marking a transfer of ownership]
(iii) 27th April 1925 Mr W. C. Drage to Mrs E. W. Corby [another sale]
(iv) 18th April 1928. Personal Rep. of Mrs E. W. Corby to Dr R. W. Christmas. [Dr Christmas was the village doctor from 1928 to 1936. The extension at the back was once a stable and seems to have been converted as a surgery by the doctor]
(v) 6th April 1938 Mortgage. Dr Christmas to Messrs Pratt, Drage and Robinson. 8th April 1938 Conveyance by referee for Dr Christmas (deceased).
(vi) 22nd November 1946 [another sale].
(vii) 1966 Graham and Mary Clarke buy the property.

A Memory: The Frosts rented the house before Graham and Mary Clarke. "Mr Frost was a sort of engineer," Jim Jarvis recollected. "He used to sharpen scissors, I remember. When he died Mrs Frost and her sister lived together but they didn't get on too well. It was a cold house then and each stayed in their own room with a coal fire. Mrs Frost would tap on the window and call me over when they wanted a job done. I'm sure Tom Cave's father lived there sometime. His wife was a very fashionable woman – always fashionably dressed. Tom Cave married Dorothy Corby."

Infrastructure

Misses Esther and Edith Dobbs in 1914. Esther Dobbs went on to work for the Co-op.
(*Bozeat School Scrapbook*)

Mrs M. A. Dobbs, aged 82 in 1928.
(*Bozeat School Scrapbook*)

Old School in Camden Square c.1905. (*John Darker*)

CHAPTER 17

Education

Education in England

King Alfred (849-899) founded the first 'public school' teaching letters to sons of noblemen, the first evidence of the gift of learning being given to some of the higher laity, previously the monopoly of monastery and cleric.

"In the Middle Ages education had been sought by poor scholars destined to be clergy while the lay classes had despised learning." (*Trevelyan*)

The coming of the French speaking Normans in 1066 caused John of Trevisa, a humble schoolmaster writing in 1385, to say: "Children in scole, against the usage and manere of alle other nacions, beeth compelled for to leve thire own langage, and for to construe thir lessouns and these thynges in Frensche, and so they haveth seth (since) the Normans first came into Engelond."

Yet these centuries after the Conquest were the formative period of the English language – what Trevelyan calls "the chrysalis stage between Saxon caterpillar and Chaucerian butterfly." (Chaucer died in 1400.) The end of the Middle Ages was a great period in the founding of schools – besides William of Wykeham's Winchester and Henry VI's Eton and with Guilds and private persons endowing Chantries and attaching schools to them, other schools were founded on an independent basis sometimes by lay headmasters, apart from the collegiate, cathedral and parish schools of an earlier foundation. So reading and writing ceased to be the monopoly of the clergy. The 15th century saw new schools for the Middle Classes, the new printing press of Caxton and new endowments to establish the Elizabethan grammar schools remodelled on the new Protestant teaching based on the new modern English language of Chaucer who enriched it with many French words – and Wycliffe who did likewise with words from the Latin Vulgate – only to reach its full flowering in Shakespeare and Milton in the centuries to follow.

Largely under the Puritan influence founding of schools went on more rapidly in the first half of the 17th century than in the previous hundred years. The founding of Charity Schools for the Poor began in Queen Anne's Reign (1702-1714) followed by the Sunday School Movement in about 1780. The Society for the Promotion of Christian Knowledge (established 8th March 1695) played a significant part in the founding of such schools in its concern to establish a wider basis of Christian and moral teaching. "The schools founded by this Society increased so much that in 1818 a branch association was formed called 'The National Society for the Education of the Poor', which made grants for founding schools under the supervision of the Parish Church. They were known as 'Parochial Schools' and that is why so many village schools are still Church Schools." (*Marlow*, p.85). And we must not forget the old Apprentice system of Tudor and Stuart times which still played an important role in education right through to the present time where the teaching of technical skills has now been integrated into the national system at all levels.

It was not until the Education Act of 1870 that Primary Education was established on a national basis. When no other school existed one was set up subject to an Elected School Board (under Gladstone and the Liberals) and the only religious teaching permitted was to be nondenominational. Church Schools were allowed to continue in villages, much to the disappointment of dissenters who had to send their children there when there was no alternative. (The Schooling Act of 1714 suppressed excellent nonconformist schools and Hanoverian England excluded all dissenters from university education.) But at last, thanks to 1870, we had a nation that would now be able to read and write.

It was the Balfour Act of 1902 that handed over both Primary and Higher Education to County Councils and County Boroughs and put Secondary Education on a proper financial footing.

1930 saw the establishment of the new Grammar Schools with the opening of one in Wellingborough for those children from Bozeat who passed the Eleven Plus, and a Secondary Modern at Wollaston if you did not. It was the 1944 Education Act that laid the ground for the modern educational system we now enjoy and the Comprehensive System that was to follow.

Beginnings in Bozeat
(The following history up to the end of the 19th century is based, verbatim, on the work of Norman Palmer.)

For the majority of our parents in our village in the past, education would have been an unaffordable luxury as well as depriving the family of an income through the labour of their children. When and where the first school was erected in Bozeat we have no idea. There is an entry in one of the Church Registers which says that a large school was kept at Strixton by a Vicar resident there towards the end of the 1600s and the beginning of the 1700s and, because this fact was written down in the one book that was likely to survive, this must have been considered important and it is reasonable to suppose that many scholars from the village went there. ["From 1688 – 1707 George. Harding was Rector of Strixton and we have a note that he kept a large school there and was buried with his wife in the chancel rails of Strixton Church." (*Marlow*, p.43)]

Our first school?
The very first information we have of a school in Bozeat is in the Rent Returns made out by the agent of Earl Spencer, who owned a great deal of Bozeat, in the year 1818, three years after the Battle of Waterloo. There are two entries. The first is "John Riseley's Salary two half years to October 1818, 10-0-0d" and on the next line, "Subscription to the school one year payable 1st January 1818 5-0-0d." Now whether this was a proper school as we know it today we don't know, because the Riseleys had been a lace-making family and it is just possible that it was a lace school. [An article in *About Bozeat* for June 1980 says that in 1811 there was a school in Bozeat run by the National Society for Education of the Poor, i.e. Church Sponsored] Nor do we know the location. Richard Riseley, possibly a son, was classed as a Boot and Shoe Manufacturer and lived in one of the four cottages in the Picle (various local spellings – also pightle, pyghtle) in the 1851 census, now one of the houses at the rear (i.e. east) of the Church. But again we do not know whether the house had been inherited and whether it had been used as a school as well as a house. But it seems obvious from the agent's entry that Earl Spencer paid the teacher's salary and gave a subscription to the already existing school to which others must have given fees or subscriptions.

Bozeat has a Parochial School

The next item of information about a school is to be found in one of the first Trade Directories which mentions Bozeat 30 years later. In *Whellan's Directory* of 1849 we read: "Bozeat has a Parochial School supported by the inhabitants, Robert Pearson, Schoolmaster." We get more information about this school two years later, when the 1851 census was published. Robert Pearson then was aged 48 and his wife Sophia was 10 years older. He came from Huntingdon and she from Olney. They lived in what was called Church Street (now known as Church Lane) but exactly where we do not know.

It is possible that the school met in their house as this was often the case. *Marlow* (p.85) says the school was held for a time in a house in the top yard of Easton Lane. There were 74 scholars in 1851 but we must not be misled into thinking that the same conditions applied then as now. Schooling had to be paid for and it was not compulsory, which meant that such a school was under a handicap because poor parents needed the little money their children could bring in and local farmers needed the cheap labour.

So the numbers attending school in those early days depended upon the purse of their parents and the agricultural season. If it were hay-time or harvest there would be an absence of the older boys. Nor must it be thought that all the scholars in the village attended the parochial school, as it was then called. The sons of more wealthy farmers would probably board at Wellingborough School. Then we must remember the many who did not attend school. Some of these were already engaged either in farming (the boys) or in lacemaking (the girls). There were 19 boys in 1851 under twelve years of age who were classed as agricultural labourers, some as young as nine years of age. There were 36 girls under twelve years of age who were lacemakers, two of whom were as young as seven. Then there was a young shoemaker aged eleven.

Of the 74 scholars who attended this school in 1851, their age range was from two to eleven years. There were three older girls of 12, 13 and 16, but they were probably assistants or monitors. The majority of the children went to school about the age of four and then left in their ninth year. So it was usual for children to be at work by the age of ten in 1851. So whilst some of your children of that age would be in primary school, 150 years ago a plough boy of ten would be leading one of those great shire horses, often being cuffed over the ears by the ploughman when he made a mistake.

It was only after the 1875 Act that the minimum age for a boy working on the land was ten years and then he must have completed 150 school attendances – or 30 weeks, which is less than one year's schooling today. Of the average of five years spent at Parochial School for the majority of scholars, that is far less than the required attendance today. And the fact that half as many boys attended school as girls suggests that boys were required more to enhance family income than read or write or do arithmetic.

A new school

In 1857 the school which stands at the bottom of Mile Street as you look up it was built with a little bell over the top of the front. It appears to have been a Church School then, for in the Trade Directory of 1869 it is called the National School (i.e. the Church of England National Society) and the Mistress then was Miss Keziah Jones with Vicar Pizey and his wife going in to teach. Teachers in the School were Miss Kate Horn, Miss Polly Deverill, Miss Hopley, Mr Vicars and Miss Green (from

May Day in the school playground c.1923. The teacher right of the piano is Mrs Eagles. The girl second from right is Joan Roberts, Don Roberts' sister. *(D. Roberts)*

Marlow) and a Mary Bate who, according to Norman Palmer, married a Railway Guard from Dover. According to *Marlow* (1936, p.85), the Rev. Pizey and Mr Revis (who owned Bozeat Estate) were possible responsible for building the school. It was built with a house for a teacher and doctor next to it, all in the style of the Berrills. After its closure in 1871 it seems to have been bought by the Drage Shoe Company. In Marlow's time (1930s) it was a warehouse and in Palmer's (1970s) in was Don Roberts' gardening and produce shop. In 1988, 131 years after opening as a school, it was converted into two domestic dwellings. But its educational value was not entirely lost, for in the 1990s Ruth Allen living next door used it for her Minimusic School – so it has had an interesting and varied history.

Bozeat gets its Board School

The great education act of 1870 made education compulsory and therefore possible for the masses, but this took time to implement. Attendance Enquiry Officers were appointed to bring pressure on parents to send their children to school which was now a legal requirement. In the Trade Directory for 1885 we find that one had been appointed to Bozeat. To enforce the law a bigger building was necessary but not until 1873 did Bozeat get its larger Board School. Bozeat actually formed their School Board in 1871. It consisted of five elected members, Thomas Drage (boot and shoe manufacturer), Walter Maxwell (steward for the Royal Assurance Company which then owned the whole estate) and Thomas Wallis (blacksmith, ironmonger and draper), being three of them. The school building erected in Camden Square in 1873 cost £2,250 inclusive of site purchase (£300) and money borrowed to do so to accommodate 230 children, but the average attendance was only 150 (*Whellan's Directory*). Compulsory education came in 1880, and by 1885 the average attendance had risen to 250.

Laura Bettles, Infant School teacher, who, as a leading campaigner for the bypass, cut the ceremonial first turf. *(D. Roberts)*

The school log from this time shows that children started school at barely three years of age and were expected to work at reading and writing from the beginning. School Log: 3rd April 1874: "I admitted three children on Tuesday, M. Bayes, A. Minney and N. Corby. I found after I had entered the last name that she is not three years old until next month, so I have not marked her attendance." Not surprisingly considerable mention is made of these young entrants creating a disturbance, e.g. "the babies were very fractious." In 1877 the 'babies' class consisted of 40 children between the ages of three and four who were "very tiresome and disorderly." And children seem to have left school at the age of twelve or thirteen. In 1898 the Factory Inspector sent three girls and a boy back to school who had turned thirteen but had not passed Standard 5 (*School Log*).

Frederick Manning was the dreaded 'Attendance and Enquiry Officer', followed later by Henry Drage. With compulsion on the parents, the school had to be enlarged in 1892 at a cost of £600 to hold 330 children. By the turn of the century the average attendance had risen to 280 – nearly double that of when it was first built. The School Board was in debt over the building for at least 30 years for in 1906 £1,500 was still owing. The school was built of local stone with Bath stone dressings (*Marlow*).

Mr Kirby, appointed to the old school in 1871/2, was made Headmaster of the new school when it opened in 1873 and Miss Christina MacLean was the Infant Mistress. Infant Mistresses following were Miss Kircop, Miss Noinette, Mrs Bennell, 1893 to 1921, who became well known in the village after her retirement, and Mrs Eagles, appointed in 1922. Mr Kirby retired in 1909, having served for 37 years to be followed as Headmaster by Mr Lack (*Marlow* p.86).

Norman Palmer continues: I am told that Mr Kirby was rather a crude character. He had a thick stick of which he would chew the end and spit it in the face of a pupil. He was a strict disciplinarian and made his scholars learn. It was he who, I believe, in the days when there were supposedly 400 Drages in the village, gave them each a nickname to differentiate them. But we must remember that teachers in those days had to be tough for they had to enforce a system not accepted by all. Payment of fees was still continued although it was abolished later. The teachers were paid at first by a bad system of payment by results, the results being assessed by how well children performed in the examinations, so it was hard luck if a teacher had a dim class.

A newspaper report of 1883 says, "The teachers handed in the school fees for the first four weeks (pupils' payments). The Clerk read a letter from Miss Thomas, the infant mistress, applying for an increase of £10 per annum. The Board thought the application premature as Miss Thomas had only been in Bozeat seven months – the report of the recent examinations had not been received." Payment by results? We

Old school in Camden Square with school children behind the railings c.1907.

should note that in 1875 the weekly school fees went up from a penny to tuppence. *School Log*: "Very few children attended Monday Morning. This was owing to the advancement in the School Fees from 1d to 2d per week." Mrs Dunmore told Vicar Palmer that when she went to school (about 1890 onwards) the labourer paid 1d and the shoemaker 2d and this was paid on Monday for the week.

What difference did these schools make?
What effect did these three schools have on the children of our village? One way to tell the progress of education is to study the signatures in the Marriage Registers for they show the progress in literacy. Those who could not write or read, and for hundreds of years this meant the great majority, simply put a cross in the Marriage Register and a note was made by the Parson or Clerk to say that this was his or her mark. From 1800 to 1867, and this means those who had been educated in the old Parochial School before 1857, just over 20% of those being wed could sign their names, which must reflect the same average for the whole population. Of the 20% who could write, roughly 58% were male, which shows that education was not given to women in general, in fact only 7% of all females being wed could sign their names. For the first half of the century the majority of farm labourers could not write their names (only 13% could). But over half the tradesmen being wed could and most of them had tradesmen fathers, which shows that the average tradesman was going to be sure that his son got the minimum of education and was prepared to pay for it.
Then the signatures in the Marriage Registers show that the level of literacy began to rise from about 1875 onwards, which if one goes back 20 years reveals that the 1857 school was having a limited influence in the village. It was about 1880 before half the newly-weds could sign their name. This level of literacy rises until, by 1893, that is 20 years after the Board School had been built, very few illiterates show up in the

Mr Lack and staff at the school.
Left to right: ? , Mrs Lack, Mrs Eagles, Mr Lack, Percy Roberts (Don Roberts' father), ? , Miss Bettles.

Registers. The great majority by the end of the century could read and write. So Mr Kirby and his assistants made great progress during the last 30 years of the century.

In 1969 Harry Edmunds aged 100, the last surviving pupil of the old Parochial School of 1857, died.

The reign of Mr Lack (1909-1946)

Mr Lack was headmaster during the two World Wars and the intervening years – a notable achievement. He came at a difficult time for we read in the School Log for 1908: "Classes are smaller than they have ever been before on account of the depopulation of the village because of bad trade." He taught the Seniors with Mrs Lack and Miss Smith, and Head of Infants was Mrs Bennell (who lived in Bull Close). On 15th January 1915 a young assistant teacher named Miss Laura Bettles joined the staff of the primary school. Her association with Bozeat was to span the century, remaining a spinster and one of the great characters of the village, living in the attractive double-fronted brick house at 4 Wollaston Road. In 1988 as the oldest inhabitant of Bozeat she cut the first turf of grass to herald the start of the construction of the long awaited village bypass.

Mrs Bennell retired in 1920, marked by her being pulled round the village by children with ropes attached to one of the few cars around in those days.

"Before 1883 the boys did sewing as well as the girls, but equality didn't extend to teachers' salaries. In the early 1920s a pupil teacher – male – earned £35 per annum but the woman only earned £26. In 1881 a school monitor was paid two shillings per

Schoolchildren in 1925 – Class II. (*T. Drage*)
From back row left to right: Jack Drage, Fred Elliott, Max Smith, ?, ?, ?, Jack Bayes
?, Rex Shipton, May Luck, Margaret Blundel, May Frost, Dol Corby, Emily Squires, ?, May Lovell
Gordon Bayes, ?, ?, Gladys Coleman, ?, ?, Dora Partridge, Marion Drage, Phyllis Gooding, ?
?, ?, Dick Warner, Harold Drage, Jack Corby, Harry Drage (Ted), Jack Goodman.

week which rose to 3/6d in 1893. The health picture is frightening – cushioned today by all the wonders of medical science, we can forget just how recently measles, whooping cough, scarlet fever and diphtheria were killers. Measles epidemics in 1877 and 1890 caused many deaths among the schoolchildren and the school was closed several times because of it – especially in 1911." (*About Bozeat*, June 1980)

Bill Silsby went to school in 1921 aged about four and he remembers his primary school teacher, Miss Bettles for her voice. "You could hear her at the Club!" he recalls. "I was always playing truant. I don't know why. As soon as I got home they sent me straight back to school again! I remember Miss Bettles chasing me round the square as I tried to run away. 'I'll catch you young Willie I will,' she cried. 'No you won't,' I shouted back! Mr Lack was a disciplinarian. He had to be. He really made the school – gave it a good standard. He carried a stick up his sleeve. I remember when he took us up Harrold Road to see the airship come over and some of us boys misbehaved and disappeared in the hedgerows. When we got back to school he lined 30 of us up in the playground and we all tried to get to the end of the line; 'It will make no difference where you are,' said Mr Lack, 'I've got enough energy to cane you all.' And he did. Three each. I remember too how Miss Bettles made us stand on the chair when we misbehaved so Mr Lack could see us through the glass panels from his office – and we knew what that meant!"

Children in the playground of the old school in Camden Square dancing round the maypole in 1940/41. The teachers are Mary Brown and Miss Bettles. The boy in dark clothes on the left is Derek Edmunds. Second child from right is Olive Johnson's daughter Norma. Third child from right, on the maypole, is Eileen Line. The older girls at the back were at the same school. (*D. Edmunds*)

In 1922 the Infants and the 'mixed' sections were combined into one, under one head. Previously there had been a Mistress for the Infants and a Master for the Mixed. In 1928 electric light was fitted. In 1929 the school closed on 21st November for the opening of the new Church Hall by Earl Spencer of Althorp House (the Patron of the Church) accompanied by Lady Anne aged eight and also Lady Cynthia.

Wartime

As recollected in 'Memories', the war brought with it the evacuee children who swelled the ranks of the School, some 120 of them. The School Log for 11th September 1939 reads: "Opened School – War with Germany – Children evacuated from London 121 at Bozeat. Working shifts." Mr Cooper, a Methodist Lay Preacher from Cuffley, Herts came as their headmaster with others to help him and they shared at first the same buildings as the village school, led by Mr Lack, each doing half a day. Later the Evacuees used the factory building in Easton Lane as their school. In 1944 there was a tragic accident when a 10-year-old girl, Florence Drage of 18 Council Street, died from an accidental shock from an electric iron during the absence of her mother. At her funeral were "Headmaster Mr A. H. Lack and Mr W. T. Cooper, Miss L. Bettles, Mrs B. Bellamy and Mrs James of the teaching staff of Bozeat Council Schools." (*Newspaper Report*)

Post-war until yesterday

In 1946 Mr Lack retired after 37 years to be followed by Mr Gulliford. He was succeeded by John Terry in 1949. Mr Terry was a well-known radio and television ventriloquist during and after the war. He served as a physical training instructor with the RAF but ill health forced him to leave. Before the war he was a secondary school teacher in County Durham and after 1944 he was headmaster at Nassington, near Oundle for some six years before coming to Bozeat. Both he and his wife (who started the Bozeat Women's Institute) were active in the community, John being a freemason, interested in local history and active in the NUT and friend of Vicar Knight. Tragically he died in Northampton Hospital in 1963 at the age of 57 leaving a widow and three children – David an architect in Plymouth, Nigel a student at Wellingborough Technical College and Heather at Northampton High School for Girls.

Let us look briefly at three children of those days who since then have played their own special part in the life of the village right up to today (1998):

1. Rex Line, Captain of the St Mary's Belfry and bell-ringer since a boy, left school in 1945. "I remember that I took the Eleven Plus in 1942 and could have gone to Grammar School if my parents had been able to contribute. With seven children in the family, this was out of the question, so I left school at 14 and got a job. I started work two days before V.J. Day and because we had no wireless, I was surprised by the V.J. celebrations and the fact that there was no bus to take me to Wellingborough – everyone was out celebrating." Eventually he worked for the Ministry of Defence and was recognised for his achievements by receiving the British Empire Medal just before his retirement in 1994.

2. Mavis Holman (née Line) born in 1936 and grew up in Homestead Farm just across the road from the school in Camden Square until her parents, Frank and Dolly Line moved to the top of Peartree when Mavis was 12 years old. She went to Bozeat School when Miss Bettles and Mrs James were teaching there and Mr Lack was still head, as he had been since 1909 On his retirement in 1946 she remembers Mr Gulliford becoming head to be followed by Mr Terry three years later. "Mr Terry had a beautiful blonde wife, rather heavily made up and he was a bit of a singer," were Mavis's childhood memories. It was Mr Gulliford who announced in assembly one morning in 1947 that Mavis had passed the Eleven Plus which qualified her to go to the Girls' County High School in Wellingborough. By a curious coincidence Graham Clarke, then living in Higham Ferrers, destined to become a neighbour of Mavis, entered the Boys' Grammar School in that same year.

At 17 Mavis went to Technical College for a year and then went to work at Bozeat Boot Company in 1955 and continued there until her first daughter Suzie was born in 1961. In 1967 she decided to start work again when her second daughter Christine was three years old. Joy Farey (daughter of the village barber) was in charge of the reception class at the time and made a last-minute decision to go for teacher training, leaving the post vacant. Mavis solved the problem this created by offering to take over the reception class, where she stayed for 12 months. After this in 1968 a new teacher was appointed, Maureen Sowden, whose father was school caretaker for some years and Maureen was to begin a long career in the school where she is still teaching 30 years later in 1998. Eventually Mavis went to work at the Bozeat Clinic where she worked for 26 years until retirement in 1996, as we shall see.

3. Joyce Wesley (née Dilley) was a younger contemporary of Mavis but didn't pass the Eleven Plus exam, so went to the Secondary Modern School in Wollaston. Joyce

Bozeat County School Senior Children 1951. (*Bozeat School Scrapbook*)
Martin Drage, David Mallows, Bill Brightwell, Peter Elderton, Colin Curtis, Alan Clements, Peter Sharman.
Jacqueline Barker, Jennifer Furniss, Janet Line, Mary Forth, Carol Coleman, Mavis Curtis, Yvonne Wyant, Julie Brown, Zena Darnell.
Barry Gibson, Martin Line, Ann Coles, Mr John Terry (Headmaster), Janet Ingram, Graham Drage, Paul Geeves, Peter Saving.
Fred Dilley, Peter Strange, James Beard, Russell Line.

was born in 1941 at 10 Hope Street at the home of her auntie Nellie and uncle Laurie Roberts (Laurie was Don Roberts' brother). She left Bozeat School when she was 14 and went to Wollaston School for her final year (1955) which was then in the present Wollaston Primary School building. The headmaster there was Hollingsworth Smith, who lived in Peartree, Bozeat and was organist and choirmaster at St Mary's. "I did not know him in the village," said Joyce. "He was very strict I remember that – wore his glasses on the end of his nose! But I got on marvellously with him. He got me out in front of school assembly and said, 'I wish you were all as good at mental arithmetic as Joyce.' He got me my first job – at Drage's Shoe Company, Hope Street. Instead of just writing a reference he went to see them. I was 15 then. I was receptionist but did all the office work. Mr Holmes from Wellingborough was in charge of the office then (1956) and Phil Boswell in charge of the factory." Obviously Joyce's mental arithmetic was put to good use!

Following the death of John Terry, Barry James was appointed headmaster in 1963 along with his wife Sheila as Deputy – the Authority advertised for a married couple to fill the posts. When they took over there were 75 pupils and 3 classes. By the time they retired in November 1984 there were 200 children and 7 classes (there were 130 in 1969/70). Barry and Sheila met in Bolton in Lancashire where he taught at a secondary school and moved to Northamptonshire in 1964. They lived in Raunds. Barry's family background was Norfolk and before the War he was a trainee surveyor. After war years spent with the RAF in Lancasters, he spent some time working for Metropolitan Vickers before going to Didsbury College for teacher training.

A new school
On 1st May 1973, exactly one hundred years since the old school had been built, after a short assembly in the old school, the children filed out into the spring sunshine and walked with their teachers along the farm track of Manor Farm to their new school in Harrold Road. The youngest pupil, Anthony Westray locked the door of the old school and handed the key to the chairman of the School Managers, Mrs 'Snip' Reeves (later to become chairman of Wollaston School Governors) and she presented the key to the door of the new school to the oldest pupil, Darren Elliott, for him to open it as they arrived. The building was designed by a team of architects (Downes and Edmunds) from Northants County Architects Department. It was the first school in the county to be built with the co-operation of the school staff. There were 193 pupils on the roll.

In October the Old School was up for sale for £40,000. There was considerable local pressure for the authorities to buy it for a Community Centre or Village Hall but it was sold privately and developed into three domestic dwellings.

In 1980 the staff were: Mrs Maureen Sowden (Reception), Mrs Patricia Finke (Middle Infants), Mrs Sheila James (Third Year Infants), Mrs Rosemary Bates (First Year Juniors), Mrs Jessie Dalton (Second Year Infants), Mrs Madeleine Newton (Third Year Juniors), Jim Stopps (Fourth Year Juniors).
Pupil Numbers: 96 Infants and 115 Juniors.
School Managers: Four Parish Councillors: Dennis Evans, David Higham, Mavis Holman and Ted Spicer, four members recommended by Northants County Council: Margaret James (chairman), Fred Dilley (parent representative), District Councillor Geoff Smith and County Councillor John Grose, Mary Clarke (co-opted village representative), Maureen Sowden (teacher representative) and Barry James (headteacher).

Today
In 1984 Richard Wilkins, who was then head of Denton Primary School, was appointed head of Bozeat School. Jim Stopps is currently his deputy. Teachers are: Doreen Dryburg, Carolyn Jacobs, Maureen Sowden, Julie Williams. Secretary: Kathy Green. Caretaker: Anne Hickling (1998). In 1984: 200 pupils and 7 classes. In 1996: 140 pupils and 6 classes.

Richard Wilkins lives in Olney with his wife Mary, a teacher at the First School in Olney and daughters Claire aged 10 and Louise aged 9 in 1985. He comes from Windsor and did his training for his Teachers Certificate at Avery Hill College, London, followed by an Open University Degree. Since qualifying he has taught in the Bahamas, London, Cambridge and in Berkshire both at Primary and Junior levels and before coming to Bozeat School he taught for seven years at Denton. Richard has a particular interest in teaching the 'basics' of maths and his personal hobbies are stamp collecting and work for Olney's Floral Fiesta. (Information from *About Bozeat*, March 1985)

The story of Catherine Ross (born 1843) – a child of 18th-century Bozeat
Norman Palmer

Catherine was the third daughter of Anne Ross, a widow and pauper living in Dag Lane. In the 1851 Census, Catherine is described as a lacemaker, as were her older sisters Caroline aged 13 and Elizabeth aged 18. She had probably been working 'at the pillow' (as it used to be called in Bozeat) since she was seven, crowded with her sisters into a stuffy room with what natural light they gained from the windows, or the light of a single candle shining through a glass globe filled with water. Like so many other young lacemakers, she would probably suffer from poor eyesight all her life. Or, if she worked in a lace-school, it could be a 10- or 12-hour day, taking home a solitary 6d a week for the first year and something between a shilling and two shillings a week after that.

There was nothing unusual about Catherine starting work so young, for in 1851 there were 35 other girls in the village between the ages of seven and twelve making lace. Her elder brother Thomas, aged eleven, was classed as a 'shoemaker'. Again there was nothing unusual in that boys would be starting out in other trades, especially that of agricultural labourer, as early as nine years of age. In 1851 there were 64 children between the ages of four and twelve working at some trade in the village. Because of the poverty of the agricultural labourer, and then Bozeat was mainly agricultural, only 77 children attended the village school (aged between 2 and 11 years), possibly about a third of the village children.

Catherine would then be amongst the great majority who could neither read nor write. Over half of those who came to be married would have "X his (or more likely her) mark" in the space for their signature. We can only imagine what life was like when it would have been impossible to understand the weekly newspapers. Not that this family could have afforded the luxury of *The Northampton Mercury* or the *Northampton Herald* – separate papers then and brought by carrier. And books would have been completely outside their known world. What limited information Catherine received would come by word of mouth, and gazing out of the window was a favourite spare-time occupation of the illiterate – not that they had much time to spare! The four growing Ross children, for that is what these young workers really were in today's terms, had to keep themselves in food and clothing, and their pauper mother as well. If widow Ann was given some parish relief by the Overseers of the Poor, it would certainly have been reduced at haytime and harvest when she would be forced to go and work in the fields. But then paupers in this parish had been doing this since time immemorial.

However, changes were to come in that home. Catherine's sister Caroline married in 1858 and, whilst she could not sign her name, her husband could which was most unusual for an agricultural labourer. Her mother Ann remarried in 1861 and neither she nor her husband Joseph Parnell, the local chimney sweep, nor the two witnesses, could sign. Catherine herself married in 1864 at the age of 21 and neither she, her husband nor the witnesses were able to sign. From 1813 to 1867 the wedding registers show that under half of those being wed could sign their names. But the headmasters won in the end, for by the end of the century, as we have seen, at least 90% of the brides and bridegrooms in Bozeat could sign their names. And with a new age of literacy came new horizons.

Triennial election to School Board – Parish of Bozeat (1886 and 1898)
The 19th century "was the age of the Trade Unions, Co-operatives and Benefit Societies, leagues, boards, commissions, committees for every conceivable purpose of philanthropy and culture." "The extension of the political franchise to all compelled the nation to elaborate a system of national education out of the fragmentary efforts of private and denominational enterprise." (Trevelyan's *History of England* p.730) – and so came the Education Act of 1870 of William Edward Forster which established primary education on a compulsory national basis replacing the voluntary system that preceded it and producing for the first time in its history by the end of the century a nation who could read and write.

The Times in that year wrote that what diverted the public from anxieties over the Franco-Prussian War "was the creation of a London School Board" (not surprisingly with women voting for the first time in British history). With half the nation's children running loose, the Education Act enabled the setting up of education authorities (school boards) to sweep the street urchins into a countrywide system of schools. Radical London gave every ratepayer the vote in its school board election. One can read between the lines and imagine some of the same competition between nonconformist and church, radical and up-and-coming in the working classes competing for the prestigious places on the new boards even in Bozeat!

We have copies of the public notice displaying the results of these particular elections and they are interesting for the names and professions of the candidates and their degree of success in election:

1886 Election took place on the 5th day of July

Names of Candidates	Description of Candidates	No. of Votes
1. Secker Augustus William	Clerk in Holy Orders	144*
2. Bradshaw, William	Boot and Shoe Company's Manager	135*
3. Drage, John	Shoe Manufacturer	113*
4. Drage, William Hooton	Shoe Manufacturer	78*
5. Wallis, Thomas	Grocer and Draper	70*
6. Pollard, Saunders William	Shoe Riveter	61
7. Maxwell, Walter	Land Steward	34
8. Corby, Thomas	Shoe Riveter	28
9. Davison, John Wykes	Farmer	3
Total:		666

* those elected to the Board

The population in the village was 1189 in 1881 and 1273 in 1891 and 1478 in 1901 after which it declined. This election was in the 13th year after the school opened i.e. 7th school board. We can see from this that some 55% of the total population of the village voted. We have a copy of the actual tally written in one hand presumably from

School Group c.1914. (*D. Roberts*)
Staff: Lucy Nichols, Harold Roberts, Norma Hayes, Mabel Hayes, Bill Partridge, Percy Roberts.
Pupils: May Luck, May Lovell, Margaret Drage, Margaret Blundell, Gladys Coleman, Emily Squires, Mabel Pollard, Cecilia Partridge.
Jack Drage, Ted Drage, Bert Drage, Bill Drage, Ena Johnson, Betty Mooring, Margaret Drage, Rose Dunmore, Dora Partridge, Kathy Bradshaw, Marion Drage.
Walter Driver, Dorothy Bayes, Fred Dunmore, Florence Ross, Gordon Smith, Loreen Line, Ena Line.

a meeting in Bozeat School on this day and it appears that it was by a public show of hands, which may have coloured the voting pattern! But nevertheless it does reflect the candidates' position and significance in the eyes of the villagers (most of whom were there) with the Vicar at the top and boot and shoe managers, including two of the five famous Drage Brothers, just below, with employees and the one farmer well below and a well-known family of shopkeepers receiving enough support to get Mr Wallis on the Board – the top five candidates being elected.

Compare this result with that 12 years later:

1898 Election took place on 5th day of July.

Names of Candidate	Description of Candidates	No. of Votes
1. Sargeaunt, William Drake	Clerk in Holy Orders	190*
2. Wallis, Thomas	Draper	179*
3. Monk, John	Miller and Baker	106*
4. Robinson, Thomas James	Pressman	106*
5. Drage, John	Shoe Manufacturer	104*
6. Maxwell, Walter	Land Steward	104
7. Corby, Thomas	Lift Maker	58
Total		847

* The top five were elected to the Board

Comparisons with twelve years previously show a more even spread in the votes with an increase in the number voting (some 80%) with the population up by about 20%. With two fewer candidates and only one shoe manager interested there may be less kudos and less interest in being a school manager – particularly as four of the candidates are the same as 12 years previously, and two of these fail yet again to get on the Board! Once more the Vicar tops the votes, but some notable tradesmen (the miller and the draper) are above the shoe manufacturer and now dominate the Board.

Board of Governors – Bozeat Primary County School 1998
The 1944 Education Act did for Secondary Education and the 20th century what the 1870 Education Act did for Primary Education in the previous. No longer was primary education the only compulsory education for all but the same now applied to secondary and a minimum school leaving age of 15 – and this inevitably influenced the primary system all of which now came under Local Authority Control. In the 1990s under the Conservative government of Margaret Thatcher we see power being taken from the local (council) authorities and transferred back to parents and the local community as well as central government. So our village school has seen many changes in its government from an optional charitable establishment with the church having a notable influence to a Board School and then to the post-war establishments we have today.

The content of the governing body of the village school exactly a century after that of the last Board given above makes an interesting comparison and reflects some of these changes:

Parent Governors
Richard Allen (teacher by profession – his wife Ruth teaches music in the school and runs Minimusic in the village)
Gwynneth Wiggins (housewife)
Jill Nellis (housewife)

Education Authority Representative
(Two represent the political party in power – Labour)
Margaret James (farmer's wife) – chairperson
Penny Smith (parent and housewife)
Elizabeth Ayres (parent)

Parish Council Representative
Marjory Stanford (retired)

Co-opted Members
Audrey Browning (retired – classroom assistant)
Tom Partridge-Underwood (Wellingborough Borough Councillor for Bozeat)
Susan Wagstaff (clerk – also school secretary at a primary school in Wellingborough)

Staff Representatives
Richard Wilkins (headteacher)
Maureen Sowden

There are some striking contrasts with 100 years ago:

(i) Nine out of the 12 governors are women compared with the all-male board in 1898.

(ii) The board had only five members compared with 12 governors now.

(iii) The representation is totally different now with the education authority and parents and staff having a constitutional proportional representation, as well as co-opted members. Whereas before members of the board were elected by the village at a public meeting, now individuals volunteer or are approached to make up the necessary number.

(iv) Under the old regime the church in the person of the Vicar had major influence and control which is no longer the case.

Margaret James has been a governor for 27 years and remembers how when she began the governing body was much smaller and much more like the old school board with most of the members from the Parish Council and village. ("I remember Mrs Knight whose husband once farmed Church Farm was a governor.") Then of course the responsibility of the governors was more to do with law and order in the school, and bricks and mortar, and receiving one-way information from the headmaster. Nowadays it is totally different in that the entire management of the school is now the responsibility of the governing body – its educational policies and practice as well as its budget and the appointment and performance of its staff.

This new control was the result of the Conservative policy in the previous government reducing the power of the Local Education Authorities who effectively ran the schools before this, controlling the governing bodies with staff and the headteacher in their employment and under their control. Schools can opt out totally of Local Authority control and be funded directly by central government.

Introduction of parental choice allows parents to choose which primary school they wish their children to go to. So if they choose to send their children to another village school because they offer special subjects, etc. or feed into a secondary school they prefer, they can control the size and future of their village school by doing so. All this puts pressure on the school to compete with neighbouring schools to provide what parents want. "Schools are now subject to regular government inspection and league tables which compare school performance and results of Standard Assessment Tests are published. They handle their own budget and compete with their neighbours to attract pupils, each one of whom brings more money into the school. These are pressures which were unthought of a hundred years ago." (*Judith Line*)

CHAPTER 18

Health

Universal 'cure' for all pains
Norman Palmer gives us glimpses into the past through the eyes of the Accounts which we still have of the Overseers/Constables of the Poor.

The provision of ale or beer did not occur only when the pauper died but also when he or she was in the process of dying. It is likely from the Accounts that such items were given when a terminal stage was reached and there were no pain-killing drugs available. In 1790 Mr Lettice … was prescribing, "Mr Lettice for wine for Riseleys 2s-5d." Thomas Surridge in 1803 was ill and in February was given by the parish a bottle of wine costing 2s-3d, in March Gin and wine 5s-5d. In 1829 "Thomas Berrill Ale when ill 1s-3d." and in June/July of that year, "Relieved John Tites wife ill 8s-0d (pauper payment). Wine for John Tites wife 2s-2d." In Aug/Sept 1833 "Bot (bottle) Wine for Sarah Line ill 3s-6d" and a month later "Bottle of Port Wine Sarah Lyne 3s-6d." In the same year 1833, "Paid for Brandy for Wm Craxton 1s-0d." He died that same month aged 67.

The insane were not forgotten either and perhaps the beer increased their already fuddled wits to make them harmless. In 1806 the parish paid James Bradshaw, the local tailor to make for John Bettle a "Stret Wascoot" (straightjacket). There are in these Accounts numerous entries for payments made whilst he was watched and fed, which suggests he was violent, and in that year of 1806 John Gough of the Red Lion is paid for "Beer and Cheese" for John Bettle.

The parish also paid for pauper mothers when their children were delivered by the local midwife, for they too had their alcohol presumably to deaden the pain. We know from writers of the time that a bottle of gin or brandy was kept in the household for the deliveries which averaged out about once every two years. In April 1798 we have the entry: "Robt Church's wife Bot (Bottle) of wine 3s-4d. Midwife for Robt Church's wife 2s-6d." In March 1805, the local midwife and 'wise woman' "Sarah Drage midwifery for Jane Jolly 2s-6d. 2 Quarts Ale and Gin for Jane Jolly 2s-6d." Even after delivery the alcohol supply was continued and one must assume medical complications. In July 1806 Mary Line was delivered of a child and the next month the Innkeeper of the Chequers, "James Carvel for Beer for Mary Harrison 3s-1d." One wonders who would have been the more inebriated at the time, the mother or the midwife, for the latter had a reputation for the 'bottle'!

Medicine on a firmer footing. Bozeat gets its first doctor – Richard Lettice
Rev. J. H. Marlow published in his *Church Magazine* in the 1930s invaluable information from records of the village and these have recently been collected together and republished in a book by Bozeat Historical and Archaeological Society.

On Sheet 24 (and p.46 of *The History of Bozeat Village*, 1936) we read:

> 25th March 1788. "An agreement between the Minister and the Parish Officers of Bozeat and Mr Lettice, Surgeon and Apothecary of Wellingborough. Mr Lettice engages to furnish the Parish Poor resident in Bozeat with Attendance and Medicines (the Small Pox excepted), Surgery and Midwifery, for £5. 5s. to

Easter next ensuing 1789."
John Lewis and Joseph Manning, Overseers. Rd. Lettice.
Ed. Shevington and Thos. Dexter, Churchwardens.
(This is 'Dicky' Lettice, son of a former Vicar who caught sparrows.)

Smallpox in the 18th century was the cause of one tenth of the deaths in the country. Evidently there was a special epidemic of it in 1789, for we have two receipts: "July 10th, 1789, £22.10s and Oct. 8th, 1789, £22.12.6d, making the sum total forty-five pounds two and sixpence for Inoculatin the Parish Poor for the Small Pox, by me, Rd Lettice. Received of Thos. Dexter, Baker, Overseer of the Poor." One of our Parishioners has "Mr Thos. Dexter's and Mr William Bettel's List of People inoculated." It is the earliest list we have of the inhabitants of Bozeat and Marlow quotes it in full. It shows that a total of 361 persons were inoculated at 2/6d each giving a total of £45.2s.6d. No wonder his contract fee states "the Small Pox excepted"! These numbers also give us an idea of the size of our village, some 400 souls, the same as it was in the earliest record we have in the religious census of 1671, again around 400. (*Marlow*, Sheet 10, p.46)

Richard Lettice was a contemporary of Edward Jenner (1749-1823), the pioneer of vaccination. Inoculation for smallpox as practised by Lettice on the good people of Bozeat meant using the lymph from someone already affected mildly from the disease (or 'matter' i.e. puss from a skin eruption) and giving some to a healthy person in the hope they would likewise suffer only mildly from the disease and have immunity from it in the future. (A risky business!) Jenner noticed that girls who milked cows and got cowpox never got smallpox. He found a young dairymaid with fresh cowpox lesions (a disease harmless to humans) and using 'matter' from these inoculated a boy who developed slight fever and low grade lesions. The story goes that he likewise inoculated three condemned men and had them put to bed with a bad case of smallpox. None of the three caught smallpox and so also escaped hanging (see *Marlow* p.73). Marlow also refers to a note on 9th November 1791 that: "William Dodson, a Bozeat boy, did some seven years since serve apprentice for a year to Rd. Lettice, Apothecary."

Health in the 19th century
Norman Palmer writes from his own researches:

"Had you been born in the first half of the 19th century, I would estimate that at least a quarter of you would not have reached your 21st birthday. And should there have been an epidemic during those years of childhood and early adulthood then the figure would probably have risen to a third. One thing we find it very hard to realise is that people had to live and die with the fact of high child mortality. The significant thing about those deaths of children is that many died before even reaching their first birthday.... We do not know the numbers of children still-born or who died at birth and therefore unbaptised, because their burial is never recorded, but it is safe to imagine that they too would have been considerable. We get some idea of the dangers of the early years of life from the fact that in the 10 year period, 1860-70, nearly half (actually 49%) of those buried were under 10 years of age, the greater part being under 1 year of age: whilst only about 20% of those buried were over 60 years of age. It is only after the turn of the century that we find the critical period of life

Priscilla (Grandma) Tompkins, Bert Tompkins, Sidney Tompkins, Hilda Tompkins, Frederick ("Bamp") Tompkins, in 1918. (D. Roberts)

coming at the end and not at the beginning." Lack of hygiene and medical knowledge (at least before 1840) were two causes of high infant mortality. Sanitary Inspectors came to perform their duties at the end of the century (the first one was named Bayes) and constantly the association of drains and disease finds its way into the Council Minutes from the Inspector's reports. But there were other causes too, one being malnutrition. The food value of milk was not widely realised and meat was expensive, so men would go to work on a breakfast of cold potatoes and this plus bread and cheese was a labourer's staple diet. To make matters worse, a parasitic fungus, native of Peru, succeeded in establishing itself in Europe's increasing potato fields, destroying crops and creating the 'hungry forties' and potato famines of 1845-49 all over Europe, followed by typhus, etc which resulted in millions dying. Bozeat had an epidemic at this time causing an increase in burials from 12 in 1847 to 38 in 1848 when the epidemic seemed to be at its peak in the winter months. (Two children died of measles at the time.) In 1849 it dropped back to 21 burials, then to 13 in 1850. "There was a typhus victim in Bozeat in 1858 and probably others. Scarlet Fever was another killer and we know there was an epidemic of this in 1885. A person wrote at the time: 'During the year 1885 the Scarlet Fever raged in Bozeat. Even grown up people did not escape. Out of a population of 1189 there were 39 deaths of which 17 were the result of Scarlet Fever. During the early months of the year the bell (Church bell) seemed to be tolling every day.' Of the 17 who died of Scarlet Fever, 14 are shown in the Burial Register as being under 11 years of age." Then there was Whooping Cough. In the Easton Maudit School Logbook for 9th

January 1872, there is the entry: "Low Attendance the children suffering from whooping cough," and a similar entry three days later, and at the end of the month, and at the beginning of February.

We should remember too that it was not until 1902 that the Midwives Act was passed, creating a central register for midwives and laying down rules of conduct. Before then it was left to 'wise-women of the village' such as Sarah Drage who was in practice from 1779 to 1805. One item in the Overseer of the Poor Accounts reads: "Sarah Drage for attending Sarah Line and Sarrah Joley (Sarah Jolly) 5s-6d."

Olive Johnson was 94 in 1998, born on 20th November 1904. She was the village laundrywoman noted for the way she could iron shirts, and has lived a hard working life. She was born in a little cottage up Dychurch Lane. On that November day they asked her mother what she wanted for supper: "Blackberry and apple pudding," she replied. So they went out and picked some blackberries as there were still some on the bushes that year. "But she never got her pudding," said Olive with a smile, "I arrived instead and the rest of the family ate the pudding." Olive was making blackberry vinegar when I popped in to see her on 3rd September 1996. "If you've got a sore throat, you take an eggcup-full of this with some hot water. If you can't get to sleep it will send you off. My grandmother taught me this recipe. You take a pint of vinegar and add enough blackberries so they are just covered and leave for eight days. Then you add a pound of sugar and boil for 20 minutes – but you must watch all the time or it will boil over as milk does. Then I pour it into a pillowcase in a bowl and squeeze through the juice and bottle it. I've done four bottles and it's all gone. You taste some." I dipped my finger in the thick creamy juice – sweet and tangy and heavy with blackberry – delicious!

"I remember the diphtheria epidemic. So many little children dead. I wasn't married then so it must be about 1920. We had to wear blue dresses with white gloves and we girls carried the little coffins into church on poles covered with a white cloth and laid them on a table in church. Then we had to carry them up to the cemetery for burial. When we got back to the village we heard that another baby had died."

Olive gives us a glimpse into the medicine and tragic maladies of a village past. Now (1998) she lives in one of the little bungalows just outside the gateway into the churchyard – and her kitchen is as clean as a new pin. And she still makes blackberry vinegar!

The doctors of Bozeat
At the end of Sheet 54 of Marlow's *Church Magazines* from the 1930s we read: "There are no other traces of other doctors until 1877 when the directory of that date says Dr Blyth was resident in Bozeat." So we have:

1. Richard Lettice, surgeon and apothecary from Wellingborough (1788)
2. Dr Blythe was resident in Bozeat (Directory of 1877)
3. Dr Warnford
4. Dr Forsythe
5. Dr Bennett (during his time Dr Baxter came to Wollaston)
6. Dr Selby – came before the Great War and lived at Rock Villa, London Road
7. Dr Underwood
8. Dr Gluckstein (for one year – 1927)

Mavis Holman, who worked for the Swans for 20 years until their retirement to Spain in 1989 continues the list:

9. Dr R. W. S. Christmas (1928) lived and held his clinic at 'Hillcrest', 29 Allens Hill where Graham and Mary Clarke now live (1995).
10. Dr Carter-Locke came to live in Bozeat as an assistant in January 1936 when Dr Christmas was ill. Dr M. McLeod was a lady doctor who came as a locum during Dr Christmas' illness. His life came to an end at the age of 78 when he was found dead in tragic circumstances, face down in the stream alongside his beloved cricket field, dressed in his pyjamas, on 30th January 1936. He seemed to have left his bedroom about 2 am and climbed through the bathroom window which was only 5 feet from the ground and found open. P.C. Willey was informed and organised a search but it was not until about dawn that the doctor was found. In his pyjamas he had walked in the darkness from his house down the hill and crossed over the London Road to his beloved cricket pitch where he was fond of strolling. The path to the pavilion runs beside the brook with steep unfenced banks and it appears that the doctor fell into it and was drowned. He was found by Jack Drage. The newspaper report continues: "Dr Christmas took a leading part in the life of Bozeat and was president of the Cricket Club, Football Club and the local British Legion. He was a Major in the R.A.M.C. during the War, and before coming to Bozeat was in practice in Essex. For the past 12 months his health had not been good. Mrs Christmas, who is his second wife, was prostrated with grief when the facts were broken to her. She also is an active public worker in the village and is vice-president of the Hospital Week Committee and president of the Girl Guides attached to the Parish Church. The inquest is to take place at 'Hill Crest' tomorrow at 11.15 pm."
11. Dr Baxter of Wollaston bought Dr Christmas's Practice but died suddenly while on holiday in Eastbourne later that same year on 6th August 1936 (buried at Wollaston 11th August).

The Practice was held at 1 Allens Hill when the house was owned by Frank Drage and it was the home of Herbert and Jennie Boswell, until the new clinic opened in 1978.

12. Dr P. Hebden Flockton (1936)
13. Dr Eric Shaw (1943)
14. Margaret and Cyril Carter (1943)
15. David and Sheila Swan (1964). The new clinic was opened in Brookside in 1978.
16. Sudhir and Sulabha Marathe (1990), from Stoke-on-Trent.

The Bozeat Ambulance Brigade

Amos Roberts, 10 Wollaston Road was Methodist chapel official ambulance man for the village c.1920, and a photograph of his house has the notice "Stretcher Depot". After Amos died Percy Roberts dealt with the ambulance dressings etc. from the Club House. Jack (Tricky) Drage was ambulanceman after Percy for many years and the service was always free to everyone. Bill Silsby remembers when the old Independent (Baptist) Chapel in Church Lane became the Ambulance Room. Before he came to Bozeat Fred Tivey was official ambulanceman in Grendon (N.B. Most people knew all the herbal remedies and used them to save the doctor's bills. Free National Health did not come until 1946.)

Memories of the St John's Ambulance are recalled by Phyllis Celia Windhaber (née Partridge) – taken directly from *The Pictorial History of Bozeat*:

"Writing from memory, I recall that in years 1936-37, Mr 'Jack' Drage had reformed the St John Ambulance Brigade Men's Section in the village, and it was suggested that a Nursing Branch be formed for the ladies. After discussion and enquiries from interested parties, a section was formed under the guidance of Mrs M. Campbell of the Victoria Nursing Brigade Section, Wellingborough. Miss Laura Bettles was appointed leader, after training at Wellingborough, and under her leadership the following ladies were recruited: Mrs Mabel Craxton, Miss Maud Elliott, Miss Margaret Pratt, Miss Dora March, Miss Edna and Miss Hilda Underwood, Miss Amy Fleming, Miss Celia and Miss Joyce Partridge.

A suitable room for meeting was provided by Mr 'Spen' Drage in the old factory warehouse. This was thoroughly cleaned, chairs were provided and a small electric fire fitted. Meetings were commenced.

Miss 'Cis' Britton from Easton Maudit, who was a member of the Victoria Brigade, came to instruct us in bandaging and First Aid techniques, Dr P. Hebden Flockton, the village doctor, came to give instruction and lectures on First Aid. This examination having been passed by all members, Home Nursing lectures and instructions were given. This examination was passed in 1938. Members became proficient in giving injections and treating minor injuries when called upon to do so by villagers, keeping a record for inspection at any time.

Uniform dresses were made for us by Mrs Mabel (Cody) Craxton, and coats, hats (coal scuttle-style), aprons, caps, cuffs and belts were purchased from the St John Ambulance outfitters department. Cuffs and belts were beautifully laundered by Mrs Dunmore of London Road. Drill instruction was given by Mr Drage and we attended all the Hospital and Remembrance Day Parades in the village and elsewhere.

By 1939 the war was becoming a reality. The Red Cross and Brigade came under the control of the Civil Defence, and the Civil Nursing Reserve was formed. We were detailed to attend Northampton General Hospital to gain experience and insight into hospital training and nursing on the assumption that we would be called for duty at any time in an emergency. As we were all 'working girls', we gave up our Saturdays for this training, travelling on York's bus at our own expense, taking our own food, but having drinks provided. All duly completed this course, some with very mixed feelings about general nursing!

The early 1940s claimed some of our youngest members for the Forces. Margaret Pratt decided to take her Nursing Training and in 1942 I myself became a Nursing Auxiliary before commencing Nurse Training in 1943.

I do not know what finally happened to members of the Brigade, or how it disbanded, but I do recall my friend Mabs (Mrs Craxton) telling me that both she and Miss Bettles were called to London to help in the air raid shelters, and during that time Mrs Winston Churchill visited the shelter and spoke to them. It was a very happy and interesting period in my life, and we all enjoyed the experience."

Mavis Holman (née Line) and the Swans.
Ted Drage (born 1914 and uncle of Mavis) remembers how "Dr Selby had his surgery

at Greenwood and Dr Christmas at Hillcrest. Both were very nice men. Dr Christmas was mad on cricket.... After him there was a man from Wollaston – I don't think he was so popular in the village."(possibly because he did not live here!)

Joy Farey remembers 'Dr Margaret' (Carter) and 'Dr Cyril' (Swan) as they were known and how in those days the doctor was an authority whose judgement was not to be questioned! "I liked Dr Swan. Once when I went to the Wollaston Clinic with terrible stomach pains. I sat on his chair and it collapsed under me! He gave me an injection for the pain and I was all right then. He always smoked one of his cigars at the surgery – you could not do that now," remembered Derek Edmunds with affection.

It was in the time of Dr Baxter that the Practice moved to 1 Allens Hill, when the house was owned by Frank Drage, and Herbert and Jennie Boswell lived there. The doctors held surgery in the front room on the left and patients waited in the hallway. It continued as the venue for the doctor's practice in the village for 38 years until the new Clinic was opened in Brookside in 1978.

Mavis Holman's mother Dolly Lines (born 1904) lived at the top of Peartree Close until 1998, the granddaughter of one of the famous five Drage Brothers, William Hooton Drage (1830-1920), shoe manufacturer and on the School Board in 1886. (Her mother died in 1964 aged 96.) Mavis was born in 1936 and in 1947 aged eleven, as we have seen, was the only child from Bozeat School that year to pass the Eleven Plus Examination and go to the Girl's High School in Wellingborough. We followed her involvement in village school and factory and how when her second daughter went to school she was able to look for a full time job. In those days you could pick and choose, and three jobs were offered her – secretarial work at Scott Baders, Botterills Shoe Company or with the village doctors, David and Sheila Swan. They had taken on the practice four years earlier in 1964. Mavis chose the last of these. "It offered the best salary!" and so began her long career with the medical practice in the village. She began in November 1969 and retired 26 years later in January 1996 on her 60th birthday. (In fact Mavis worked for the Swans for 20 years, her predecessor being Sandra Carvel who later ran the Paper Shop.)

In those early days, with no special training for the work, Mavis had to turn her hand to dispensing, accounting and overall running of the Practice. There were few stand-in doctors in those days and so she was as much 'on call' (in the sense of 'holding the fort') as were the Swans. Looking back over her quarter of a century of work in general medical practice she has noticed three major changes that have occurred:

(i) drugs and medicines – their huge increase in variety and relative cost.

(ii) public expectation – there was in earlier days an acceptance that the doctor knew best and a more unquestioning respect for his or her decisions. Nowadays people are more ready to criticise the treatment they are given.

(iii) increasing bureaucracy – as much to safeguard the doctors as the patients and to deal with the increasing complexity of modern medicine.

In 1989 the Swans retired after 24 years as our village doctors and went to live in Spain. At the very end of 1996 Mavis had a phone call from Sheila Swan to tell her that, on the Monday before Christmas, David had had a heart attack. They had come over to London to do Christmas shopping and amidst the crowds of shoppers he had collapsed and died. He was 66. "It was terrible," said Sheila, "crowds of people around and nobody stopped to help." David had organised his funeral – just a quiet family affair but he wanted Mavis to be present, a touching tribute to their long partnership. The Swans have three children, two boys, one of whom is a doctor and the other a vet, and a daughter who is in professional photography. Ethyl Andrews (1912-97) of 3 Hewlett's Close had helped look after them when they were little. David's older brother, Jeremy, is a leading heart specialist working in Hollywood, but his younger brother Gordon sadly, having qualified as a dentist, is now (1995) with dementia as a resident of Hemmingwell Lodge Old People's Home (along with Harriette Partridge who died in 1997) – but still with a courteous charm about him. "The best part of Dr Swan was when someone was seriously ill," remembers Mavis. "I remember when Graham Clarke was diagnosed as having cancer, David Swan said to him, 'You won't be in pain, I'll see to that.'" Graham, who lived where Dr Christmas once lived in Allens Hill across the road from Mavis, lived with his cancer for 10 years, showing great courage and determination, an inspiration to us all, until he died, as did his doctor David Swan, in December 1996, aged 60.

Doctors Sudhir Marathe and Sulabha Marathe (1990)
Having experienced work in a largely rural area like Whitehaven (in the General Hospital), in a town like Middlesbough and in a city like Stoke-on-Trent, they definitely prefer general practice in a rural area, so took the opportunity of the Practice in Wollaston and Bozeat. They also prefer general practice to hospital work, having experience of both.

A husband and wife team, they both were born and brought up in India in a town called Nagpur. They graduated in India in 1972 and worked there for seven years before coming to England in 1979 where they have undertaken postgraduate work and training to increase their speciality experience. Dr Sudhir achieved membership of the Royal College of General Practitioners (M.R.C.G.P.) as well as his MD specialising in the care of the elderly but with particular interest and some research into asthma and diabetes and has started clinics in both these illnesses.

Dr Sulabha can put M.B.B.S, D.G.O. and D.C.H. after her name which indicates her interest in general medicine but with gynaecology/obstetrics and child health/paediatrics as areas of speciality. She is also interested in the elderly having been responsible for the medical care in two old people's homes whilst working in Stoke-on-Trent.

They came with two sons, Mandar aged 15 at Wellingborough School and Manoj aged 6, and officially started surgery on Monday 2nd July 1990.

CHAPTER 19

Roads and Travellers

Introduction
"At its height the Roman Empire could boast more than 50,000 miles of major roads and the journey from Rome to London could be made in a fortnight, a standard not to be improved until the second half of the 19th century ... no one made any more roads in this island until the turnpike movement of the 18th century. Thanks to the Roman legacy, Britain had better natural highways under the Saxons. If the bridges soon fell in from neglect, the paved fords remained.... Gradually the stones subsided and men were too careless and ignorant to replace them. Next, the road was used as a quarry, when the medieval Englishman, having somewhat exhausted his timber, began to build for himself dwelling places of stone. From driving roads they declined into pack-horse tracks, finally disappearing for the most part into moor and ploughland." (*Trevelyan*, pp.56, 57)

In the latter half of the 18th century "the heavy coaches (still) lumbered along in the ruts in a very different style from that in which their light timbered successors in the years following Waterloo (1815) scoured the roads remade by Macadam....The gay and rapid life of the English road reached perfection only during the Napoleonic wars, and twenty years later the railways already clearly foreshadowed the end. Brief, but characteristically English while it lasted, was the age of the all-worshipped horse, with Horncastle Fair for its Mecca, with fox-hunters, stage-coachmen and jockeys as ministers to the national enthusiasm for the noblest of animals," (*Trevelyan*, pp.156, 714) – of which our local poet, William Cowper, just down the road from Bozeat at Olney, wrote in his saga of John Gilpin.

ROADS AND TRAVELLERS
Norman Palmer (edited and updated)

Bozeat to London by Coach early 1800s
"Wellingborough, Olney and Woburn Post Coach," the advertisement reads, and goes on to say, "The Public are respectfully informed that the above Coach leaves the White Hart Inn, Wellingborough, every Tuesday, Thursday, and Saturday Mornings, at a Quarter before Seven o'clock, through Dunstable, St Alban's and Barnet, to the Windmill and Cross Keys Inns, St John's Street, and the George and Blue Boar, Holborn, London. The down Coach leaves the George and Blue Boar, Holborn, the same Morning precisely at eight o'clock, and goes by the same route to the White Hart Inn, Wellingborough. B. W. Horne, Wm. Page, Proprietors, Wellingborough, 24th May 1834."

A traveller had to be up early to be sure to catch the coach. When he took his seat, it could be with 11 other passengers inside, which would leave very little room. If he were too poor to pay for an inside seat then he could perch on the roof, finding there the worst of all weathers. Fares were not cheap for the fast coaches charged their inside passengers 4d or 5d a mile, whilst those on the outside paid 2d or 3d per mile. For instance a journey from Northampton to London, inside the coach, would cost about £1 each way, which, considering the value of money in those days of the early 19th century, makes it a very expensive form of transport compared with today.

It is possible that the coach stopped at the 'Red Lion', Bozeat, on the journey, for the Red Lion in those days had an open space where the present building stands (erected in the early 1880s), and buildings where there are now open spaces, i.e. there was a central courtyard for coaches. Certainly there were travellers from Bozeat, for in 1811 there is an entry about a Jonathan Hooton who went insane and had to be taken to St Luke's Hospital, London (now the hospital for clergy!). Sept. 1811: "Expenses taking Jonathan Hooton to St Luke's Hospital London.... coach fare for Ditto £3-8-0d" (for two it must be presumed), and again in October of the same year: "paid Mr Church (a lace-merchant) Expenses for fetching Jonathan Hooton from London.... coach fare from Ditto 3-0-0d" It is possible that they were 'outside' passengers – the patient died the next month! The average speed of the coaches could be as much as 9 to 10 miles per hour including stops, travelling at 20 or 30 miles per hour to keep to their schedules. R. L. Greenall writes in his *History of Northamptonshire* of these days: "The principal road-towns of Northampton were then (in the 1830s) alive with the bustle of numerous coaches regularly passing through, the fastest of which were performing the 72 miles or so to and from London in the remarkable time of 7¾ hours." (p.94)

Turnpikes and toll-gates
The road over which coaches travelled through Bozeat had been taken over by a private company and the surface improved. At certain stretches along the road were set up toll houses with toll gates to receive payments, with which to keep the road in good repair, and in theory, to make a profit. The main road from Kettering to Newport Pagnell (now the A509) had been turnpiked by Act of Parliament in 1753. Of the three turnpikes on the road, one was built on the county boundary at Northey Farm. The rates which were at first levied were 3d for a horse drawing a cart or carriage, 1d for animals not drawing vehicles, cattle herds at 10d per score, and hog and sheep flocks at 5d per score. These rates were later increased. By 1806 a new toll house was built at the site of the present cross-roads with the Bedford to Northampton road, and the old buildings became known as the 'Old Toll House' and were pulled down in the 20th century.

There are a number of references to toll gates in the parish records. In 1804 the Churchwardens had to travel to be sworn into office and their account reads: "The turnpike and corn and hay for the horse 9d." And in the same year William Bettles, who was a pauper living outside the parish, had to have his wife buried, for which the entry reads: "For carrier Willm' Bettles wife and Gate (toll gate) 5s-0d." In 1825 Mary Harrison was taken to Northampton Hospital: "Paid Danl Hooton Horse Cart 6s-0d Paid Expenses and Tolls 2s-2d." William Pitt writing in 1809 about Northamptonshire said: "The great roads leading through the county are all turnpiked and are supported by the money collected at the different toll-bars and partly by the statute labour imposed by Act of Parliament. Each tenant who occupies a farm of 50 pounds of rent being required to perform three days labour of a cart with three horses and two men, yearly, on the turn-pike roads within the parish and the same on the private and parochial roads." We can see how this worked out in some documents deposited in the County Records Office. In a list covering one year, 1815/16, Thomas Hensman, a farmer, paid a rental to his landlord, Earl Spencer, of £281, which meant that he had to provide 5x3 days labour from his farm = 15 days per year or else this could be commuted for money payment. John Pell, another

The Flat, London Road with the thatched cottage in the background, now demolished. In the foreground is the roadman's wheelbarrow, and Fred Corby is driving the wagonette with passengers. This is pre-1913 as Benjamin Squires built the brick bakehouse on the right of the house in the centre of the picture in that year.

farmer, paid £228 rent which was 4x3 days labour = 12 days per year for 2 men and 3 horses.

Repairing the roads
William Pitt goes on further to say: "The private parish roads are in many places in ruinous situation and in general so narrow as to admit of only one track. The stone of the countryside is apt to grind into powder. It is placed on the roads as it was raised out of the quarries and, instead of being broken with hammers, that operation is performed, in course of time, by cart wheels. The numerous droves of cattle in wet weather are nearly as injurious to the roads as any kind of carriage. In some parishes statute duty is done whilst in others little or nothing is done. This is frequently the case in grazing parishes, where if a horse or an ox can get along, the rest are satisfied having little occasion for carriage roads." Somewhere about a hundred years later the Bozeat schoolmaster, obviously drawing on the memories of older folk could say about the Bozeat roads, probably the side roads: "The state of the roads is terrible. In summer they resemble a desert, in winter the mud is knee-deep. Very little travelling was done."

Roads were made good in a very haphazard fashion. Those in whose care they were who held office for one year only were the 'Overseers of Highways', local men with little experience. And those who actually did the work were either paupers or later the aged. Road-making seemed to be the last resort for a man unemployed.

Minutes of a meeting held on 23rd October 1827 read: "Richard Pettit making application for employment he not having a place of service to go on the Road to have per week 2s-6d" (which works out at 5d per day for the 6 day week – he was probably a single man). The minutes of a meeting held the next year read: "Thomas Abraham made application for the advance of wages on the Road he now receiving 4s-0d per week. To continue as usual." (This is 8d per day and he was probably married.) There was a great deal of unemployment at the beginning of the 19th century, and as each parish was responsible for its poor, many parishes, including Bozeat, put their unemployed 'on the road' or in the stone-pits to save on the poor rate. At first there were 20 to 30 men so employed, but after 1830 something like 60 or more. It must have been during these early years that Harrold Road was laid down, Easton Lane, the width of which was to cause trouble in later years, and Church End Road, later to be called Allens Hill, probably after George Allin, the Innkeeper of the 'Chequers', whose land at the rear formed its boundary.

There were obviously some slackers on the road, for from 23rd October 1827 they were ordered "to come to Church when the bell rang and not to go home again until the Bell rang at 12 o'clock." They had to return when the bell rang one o'clock and the man five minutes late was to lose half a day's pay. The next year it was ordered they should bring their tools with them – obviously some made the excuse to slip back home. The bell-ringer (probably the Parish Clerk) received 3d a week ringing the bell four times a day for six days.

With greater prosperity about the middle of the 19th century, there was no need to use the unemployed 'on the roads' but older men, no longer fit for work on the farm, were given the task. It must be remembered that there was no Old Age Pension then, for many only the prospect of the workhouse at the end of their days. One can imagine that road making was a fairly easy-going occupation and the payment had improved from 20 years before. William Denton was 53 in 1851 and earned from 1/1d to 1/3d per day. Thomas Nicholls at 51 was getting about the same. Henry Nicholls aged 57, William Whittington aged 66, Thomas Harris aged 60, and James Taylor aged 55, earned between 9d and 1/1d per day. John Maycock earned from 1/- to 1/1d a day, being paid at the end of the week on 5th January 1850 and was buried the next month aged 75. Their names disappear during hay time and harvest, when it appears road work was suspended, and they had one day off in the year – Christmas Day.

Materials
Pebbles were collected from the fields and stone was quarried (mostly during the winter months) from the pit up Dychurch Lane (now built upon), and from the Dag Lane pit, which used to be near the doctor's surgery. (On the Enclosure Map of 1799 there is an 'Allotment for Stone Pitts' allocated to Surveyors of Highways which was in the region of Bull Close and the present adjacent allotment.) Gunpowder was used to break up the stone after the top soil had been removed, with entries such as in 1830: "Paid for one Pound of Gun Powder for Stone Pit 1s-10d."

Under new management
Continual losses and competition from the railways finally led to the winding up of the Turnpike Trusts, and to the disappearance of the stagecoach. The Kettering to Newport Turnpike was taken over by the Local Government Board in 1878. (In the

1886 sale of Bozeat Estate the field between Northey Farm and The Grange which straddled the parish and county boundaries was still known as 'Old Toll House Field'.) An Act of Parliament in that same year abolished parochial responsibility for its own roads. The newly formed County Council administered all road maintenance after 1894, and a Local Government Act of the following year provided help from central funds for County expenditure. The new County Councils were responsible for maintaining all 'main' roads in their area, and it was left to them to decide how much, if at all, they would subsidise the repair of secondary roads left in the hands of the rural districts or parishes. There came a gradual improvement in road maintenance.

The carrier
One common sight in this and every other village in the 19th century was the carrier, with a waggonette capable of holding six people, or the brake which could hold more. Local farmers and tradesmen seemed to have performed the service earlier, with such entries as in 1813: "Expenses for James Lines Daughter 2s-11d Pd into the Infirmary for Lines Daughter £1-0-0d. W. Church (Lace merchant) for horse and cart 5s-0d." and in 1827: "Paid William Abrahams (local shopkeeper) for carriage of Tho Berrill to Northampton" (to the Infirmary). Gradually a regular carrier service was built up between Bozeat, Northampton and Wellingborough. It started off on a journey twice a week (later in the century nearly every day) or in the case of Easton Maudit once a week. They were always on market days and in this way local people could take their produce to market, and in turn bring some home. Town tradesmen used it to send supplies to Bozeat. The passengers would sit on the parcels with their feet in the straw. It was a slow journey for it could entail a good many stops. The journey to Wellingborough could take 1½ hours depending upon the stops. When it came to hills like the Red Hill, Wollaston or Cogenhoe Hill, the passengers must get out and walk for the horse had only strength for the cart. I am told that the carriers often bought their horses after they had seen better days, and it was not unknown for them to drop dead between the shafts overworked with heavy loads. A 'hoe' or 'drag' was placed under the wheels when descending to retard the motion. One very notorious hill was Cogenhoe which, before the road was improved, led straight to the bottom where the farmhouse now is, before turning to continue to Grendon. 'Clarry' Drage tells the story of a relation of his, a carrier, who as a favour for a friend was bringing back a donkey to Bozeat and had him harnessed between the shafts. When they reached the top of Cogenhoe Hill and were about to descend, the donkey refused, and sat down. But he really had no choice with the weight of the cart behind him and he was pushed down on his backside and a very sore one it must have been by the time he reached the bottom!

The earliest carriers we know of are to be found in *Whellan's 1849 Directory of Northamptonshire*: "Carriers (to Bozeat) Nichols, Horse Shoe" (The Public House in Wellingborough from where he started the return journey). "Wednesday, and Smart, from Bee's Wing Wednesday." John Nichols was a carrier and lived in Mile Street. Various entries tell us what he and others carried: (1855) "John Nichols for carridge of Coal 7s-9d." In 1856: "paid Jn Nicoll cartage of coal 3s-6d." In 1861: "John Nichols for use of Van to the Confirmation Wellingboro 6s-0d." In 1869: "John Nichols conveyance to Confirmation 6s-0d." One can only hope that John Nichols washed his cart of the coal dust before he took the female confirmation candidates in their white dresses!

Summerlin's cottage in Mile Street just above Fish Alley c.1928 shows Nancy Bayes (now Pettitt) holding step-brother Derek Summerlin (died at about 12 months old) with Cecil Bayes. Note the bicycle tyre on the roof! (N. Pettitt)

The Smarts were a family of carriers living at 'Millers Corner' (corner of Church Lane and High Street). Luke the father in 1844: "L Smart 2 B (bags) Coke and carriage 1s-4d." But after his death in 1851 the sons carried on for in 1859 "John Smart for carting and attending Wellingboro County Court 6s-9d." (for the 'ejectment' of a non-paying tenant, who the landlord probably asked John to convey.) And in 1873 another son, "W. (William) Smart for Wood 2s-0d."

William Surridge about 1890 went to Wellingborough four days in the week, and Northampton on Saturdays, picking up at Easton Maudit. He was remembered as having a horse with sore eyes and a dog which performed tricks. His favourite performance was for him to say, "Spin, Charlie, spin," whereupon the dog spun round like a dancer on its hind legs. Frank and Jacob Shrives were carriers who also did some farming. They worked from Church Lane, eventually selling their business to Mr Charlie Summerlin, who lived in the thatched house next to Garrett's the Butchers. His wife ran a shoe closing room inside the house, which helped to bring him trade.

We notice an increase of carriers at this time due to the expansion of the Boot and Shoe industry, as parts of shoes would be brought into the village from the main suppliers in Wollaston or Rushden by the carrier, and, after closing and finishing, would be returned in the same way. Charlie Summerlin's brother continued the business from a house now demolished at the bottom of Mile Street with their vehicles, two horse vans. This was Derek Summerlin. He married Sarah Bayes after the death of her husband Charles Bayes, a labourer who had fought in the Great War, bringing with her three children, Nancy (now Pettitt living in Hope Street 1999) born in 1916, Gladys (now Green living in Roberts Street) and Cecil Bayes. The total of five children in all lived in these two cottages in Mile Street (just below the present No. 6) rented off Mr Leate from London.

Mr Jos Partridge of Church Street was another carrier to Wellingborough and Northampton. The last carrier in Bozeat was Arthur Elliott, who lived in a now demolished cottage behind the (now) Bozeat Club in the High Street. It was well remembered that on the return journey the carrier would often 'nod off', and it was left to the horse to bring the carrier, parcels and passengers safely home. Mr Elliott's wife, Nancy, was the village layer-outer who prepared bodies for burial.

A horse bus also used to run through Bozeat. A hunting horn was blown as the bus came down Harrold Road and passengers were picked up in the High Street once a week between 10 and 11am, and returned about 6 pm. This continued until 1906.

Then there were those who hired out their vehicles, and also their own services. William Harrison, who in the Trade Directories is called the 'Fly Proprietor' was remembered as having a wagonette for hire. He was also grocer, coal and wood merchant. There was great competition between Frank Smith and Fred Corby for customers for their horse brakes, Fred Corby advertising as "horse, traps, waggonettes for hire on reasonable terms" lived up London Road. These men really came into their own for Sunday School Outings, and visits by large families to relatives for the 'Feast' weekends of local villages.

The bicycle becomes popular

Gradually the popularity of the bicycle grew. "Penny-farthings' were once quite common, we are told, in the period prior to the turn of the century. Owners very often held races, which had its hazards on roads with a loose stone surface. One owner stated that he could ride from Bedford to Bozeat (about 13 miles) in under an hour. But there were accidents, and one of the last owners of such a machine fell off and broke his arm. The amusing story is told by 'Clarry' Drage of the rider of a penny-farthing who started to ride down Cogenhoe Hill. It must be appreciated that the penny-farthing was braked by the rider with his pedals, but in this case the rider lost control and careering down the hill towards the wall of the barn, hit a stone and was catapulted on to the roof with very little harm except to the penny-farthing.

Mr Ben Pratt, who used to live in Mr Dilley's house in Pudding Bag, used to own a tricycle and carried children in a specially adapted basket. He is said to have used an umbrella to assist him on a windy day.

By 1888 the bicycle was moving up the social scale. The advent of the 'Safety Bicycle' in 1887 and the pneumatic tyre in the following year made the new transportation fit for women, and there came about the bicycle craze of the 1890s. Margaret Dunmore has said that her brother, Mr Fred 'Poddy' Dobbs (who was a professional cricketer for Yorkshire) owned the first bicycle in Bozeat with pneumatic tyres. (He was later killed in the Great War.) Kate Corby and Mary Hudson had the first normal two-wheelers as we see them today. There was a bicycle repairer up Dychurch Lane, Mrs Johnson's father assisted by his daughter. She tells how she would have to mend as many as 40 punctures a week, for her father was a member of a team of bell-ringers, who brought their bicycles for repair and they would cycle out to ring the bells in neighbouring parishes. They always kept a large amount of carbide in stock for the old type of bicycle lamps.

Here comes steam propulsion

The first mechanically propelled vehicles on the road were steam driven traction engines, used for agriculture and heavy goods. The traction engines were kept in the village, behind what is now (1996) the garage. John Johnson who was the driver of one of these was so tall that he is remembered as resembling another chimney at the rear! These engines were used for ploughing and threshing. But this was in the days before the repeal of the notorious 'Red Flag Act' of 1865, which imposed a speed limit of 4 mph in open country and 2 mph in towns. The Act required that all 'road locomotives' be attended by at least three persons, one of whom was to walk 60 yards ahead of the engine carrying a red flag by day and a red lantern by night. Margaret Dunmore, once our oldest inhabitant, remembered these being carried in front of the traction engines when they went out to the farms. The Act was repealed in 1896.

There were various other restrictions on these engines, one of which governed the use of water drawn for the boiler from a public well. The well outside the Chequers Inn was the first one to be met by any drovers bringing their cattle or sheep from Wellingborough. Messrs Whitworths of Wellingborough had some of these early wagons with horizontal boilers. Evidently by the time the engine reached Bozeat it was time to 'top up' the boiler. But the local inhabitants also needed the water from the well, otherwise they had to carry water from a distance. In 1903 the Bozeat Parish Council made a complaint that the drinking water from the Chequers well was being taken for the use of the motor wagons and asked Messrs Whitworth to desist, to which they replied saying they had warned the motor man. But two years later the minutes say that the well had been frequently used by motor wagons and great inconvenience had been caused to the inhabitants. Messrs Whitworths undertook not to use the well again. The Rural District Council was asked to affix a notice to the well warning persons against improper use. In 1909 the Parish Council Clerk wrote to Miss E. Shrives and Mr Warren requesting them not to wash down their vehicles on the side of the well.

Why no railway?
There was a proliferation of small railways at the end of the 19th century. It seemed that no community was too remote for a pair of lines to reach it. Remembering the increased population of the Nene Valley with the growing Boot and Shoe Industry it is not surprising that enterprising business men saw a way of linking the busy shoemaking communities and making a profit. The first attempt was a company formed under the name of 'Wellingborough and District Tramway Company'. It was intended to convey passengers, goods and mail 'by steam power and other mechanical means' and to link Wellingborough with Little Irchester, Knuston, Rushden, Higham Ferrers, Strixton, Lavendon, Olney and Bozeat. They obviously contacted all the parishes concerned to gain their support. The predecessor of the Parish Council, 'The Vestry', gave its consent to the formation of the company in 1889, agreeing to give it further powers in 1890. The country people, especially the shoe-workers, were going to benefit from this, especially those without any means of transport. But conditions imposed upon the company caused the Bill to be dropped. A few years later another attempt was made, only this time it was to be powered by electricity. This was a quite revolutionary step at that time. In one large city after another the tramways were electrified at the end of the 19th century. The British Electric Traction Company was an organisation which promoted the development of tramways and, later, buses in various parts of the country. Their greatest opponents were the unprogressive municipal authorities and the company became the target for much political abuse. In 1904 the Parish Council was examining a map showing the position of the tramway suggested by the company. The company secretary said in a letter that they were making application to Parliament and asked the various parish councils for their support. This again never 'got off the ground' probably because of the various restrictions imposed. One is left with the feeling that a good opportunity was missed.

The first motorcycles in Bozeat

One is not quite sure who had the distinction of owning the first motorcycle in Bozeat. Some would say it was Frank 'Wassy' Tompkins, who used to mend bicycles. Certainly the first powered tricycle was owned by Dr Bennett somewhere about 1904. The first motor bicycle had belts instead of chains, the disadvantage being that the belts would sometimes slip. 'Clarry' Drage had the first chain-driven motorcycle in the village. Clarry worked with Mr Craxton who had the first garage. He started his business across the road from the school, next to the 'Lord Nelson' where there were some thatched cottages. Later the garage moved into one of the three cottages standing on the site of the car park of the Working Men's Club. The main employment for the garage at first was with bicycles, then motorcycles, followed by cars.

Dick Edmunds (right) on his Triumph in Bozeat High Street, 1930s. (*D. Edmunds*)

There is a story of one owner of a motorcycle with a bad temper and a loud voice, living in the High Street. He had an early side-car of woven rush work. His wife's name being Louise, he would shout as they turned a corner "Lunge Loo!" (to balance the combination). In typical Bozeat fashion she was given that nickname. One day when coming down the London Road the order was given but Loo lunged the wrong way with the consequence that they parted company, so husband and wife landed up on opposite sides of the road!

The state of the roads

Elderly citizens of Bozeat can remember the bad state of the roads at the beginning of the 20th century. Pieces of large stone were laid on the road to be covered by gravel and compacted by a steamroller. It was not a safe surface for either a bicycle or motor-bicycle. Clarry Drage tells us that he would choose to go to Bedford on his motorcycle for shopping, for the roads over the border in Bedfordshire were better and safer. The roads were also of concern to the Parish Council who, in 1903, drew the attention of the County Council "to the shocking state of the 'Flat' (area of London Road between Mile Street and Allens Hill) owing to its sides having been made higher than the middle," thus the water was unable to escape. They also pointed out that the stones on the main road from Bozeat to Wollaston had been rolled but were lying loose. Such surfaces would cause many a cyclist, when cycles were popular, to have a skid and to have punctures. Old photographs show the rough surface of the roads and a horsebrush was used to sweep the village streets. The Parish Council drew the attention of the County Surveyor to the fact that the horse brush was used in the village Friday and Saturday mornings, and that the mud was left lying by the side of the pavement during the whole of the Saturday night and Sunday "much to the inconvenience of pedestrians". The surveyor said he would ensure that the mud by the pavements adjoining the houses would be removed the same day. We are told that pattens (overshoes with a wooden sole raised by an iron ring) were used to keep the wearer's feet out of the mud.

The mud in winter turned to dust in the summer and the hedges by the side of the road were covered by it. In 1908 the Parish Council were again drawing the attention of the surveyor to the bad state of the road from Bozeat to Wollaston. At the same meeting, the Council requested that the carter living in Bozeat, and who carted stone for the roads, should have preference to outsiders. In 1914 the Parish Council drew the attention of the surveyor to Wollaston stating that carts and other vehicles were wearing away the banking and that there was nothing to prevent the water flowing off the road on to the footpath and into the houses and suggested some form of kerb be put down to prevent the traffic encroaching on to the bank.

To show the leisurely pace of those days (1920s), George Knight, who farmed 'Church Farm' up Hensmans Lane was in trouble because he allowed his cows to wander through the streets unattended and he was asked not to allow them out without someone in attendance. They obviously knew their way home, but they did appreciate what was grown in the gardens when the gates were left open. Two years later he was again in trouble when it was reported to the Parish Council that the "footpath from Church Corner to Rear Street" was in a "very unsatisfactory state" owing to Mr Knight's cows. He was asked to instruct the person in charge (he must have had one by then) to keep the cows off the footpath. Due to the Great War and the shortage of manpower the Council minutes after that war are full of complaints about the condition of the roads. In 1922 it was stated that the main road was in a bad condition and so was Red Lion Hill which was said to be dangerous owing to the Bus Traffic (first mention), and the Brewer's Wagons – a letter was sent to the Brewers.

The internal combustion engine

This is the place to mention the coming of the internal combustion engine. The Red Flag was done away with in 1896, and the Act of 1903 allowed motorists to have a maximum speed of 20 mph. But the car was very much an object of suspicion and hostility. For many, the car created dust (not the fault of the car), would backfire and cause horses to bolt, frightened the old ladies, and left a nasty smell behind. In turn it brought the wrath of the local JP (no doubt a 'hunt'n and shoot'n' man) down from the bench having obtained evidence from the police constable, who had been crouching behind a hedge observing the approaching dust cloud with a large pocket watch in his hand. This attitude was to pass with the Great War. But, where the car did do damage was to the local road surface, for the sucking action of the tyres destroyed a badly bonded top surface, which was not the case with horse drawn vehicles or even traction engines. We can understand then the attitude of mind of the Parish Council, who in 1906 made application to have warning posts placed at the corner of Easton Lane and London Road. But the County Council did not agree then or three years later, so the Parish Council directed the Chairman "to see the Police Constable and request him to report any cases of furious driving."

Signposts

Signposts had been in the village at least since 1827, when there is an entry, "Paid for painting and writing a Hand Post 7s-0d."

The Daimler Motor Company (formed 1896) was one of the early pioneers of the car and it was resolved by the Parish Council in 1909 to write to the Daimler Car Company of Coventry telling them about the dangerous corner of Easton Lane and asking it if it could see its way "to erect a caution or danger signal to warn motorists and others." The company said they were willing but could it also have an advertisement on it? In 1913 the Council approached the Motor Union for further signs "warning drivers of motor cars and other vehicles of the dangerous corners." Unfortunately when the signs were received they had misspelt the name of the village for it appeared as 'Bojeat' (perhaps they had only heard it pronounced!). In 1918 a signpost was erected at the bottom of Harrold Road. In 1923 permission was asked of Mr Leete (who owned property in Bozeat, and this must refer to what was known as 'Lime – or Line – Prop Yard' where the factory now is) to place a danger sign on the house owned by him opposite the cemetery. With his permission the sign was painted on the wall of the house. The first car owned in the village was one purchased by Mr George Knight, the farmer mentioned, before the Great War. He bought it second-hand in Bedford.

Here come the buses

After the Great War came the era of the bus, motorised now. A company known as the Buffalo Bus Company ran from Olney to Wellingborough, but did not long survive, as was the fate of others. The Coleman brothers bought a First World War army lorry and, in the space at the back, chairs were placed, and this was run to Wellingborough to the cinema on Saturday evening, which in those days was considered a great night out. The mail van, which was a vehicle on private contract, used to carry passengers whom it is remembered were locked in for the journey.

Dick Edmunds (left) and Eddie Drage with their Rio 20-seater outside the Red Lion in the 1930s. In the bus is Mr Pettitt who kept the Red Lion. Note the Wellingborough sign in the bus front window.

(D. Edmunds)

United Counties bus in Bozeat High Street in the 1930s. (*D. Edmunds*)

In 1920 Grose Bros of Northampton ran a bus from Red Lion Hill to Northampton, via Lavendon. It was an open-topped bus with solid rubber tyres and slatted seats. In January 1921 the Drage Bros ran a regular 20 minute service to Wellingborough and two journeys to Harrold on Sundays, one in the afternoon, and the other in the evening. They started with a 14-seater Model 'T' Ford. Seats were up the side with a door in the centre at the rear – but 14 people had to sit very close to be accommodated. It was called 'Red Emma' by the village. Later came a 20-seater Thorneycroft, followed by an additional one. Walter Drage drove one and his brother Ernest drove the other. The colours were red and cream. The fares were 5d single and 9d return to Wellingborough.

At the same time Dick Edmunds and Eddie Drage had a Model 'T' Ford, later an American "Rio" 20-seater, which was a type commonly used by small coach companies. This service specialised in workmen's buses, in fact one driver himself worked in a Rushden Shoe Factory. There was a great deal of competition between the small companies. It is said that when the bus of one company waited in the 'Square', another waiting by the Red Lion belonging to another company would be watching their departure in order to depart at the same time and get ahead to pick up passengers before the rival coach. Maurice and Joyce Palmer in their *History of Wellingborough* tell us that these small operators would also compete with the Wellingborough Omnibus Company, who could only run at a regulation speed of 12 mph, by overtaking them to pick up waiting passengers at the bus stops, leaving the more nervous to be picked up by the Omnibus Company. But one by one the small bus companies had to sell out to the United Counties Omnibus Company. Mr Walter Drage later went in for transporting cattle.

In 1920 the Bozeat Parish Clerk was writing to the Wellingborough Bus Company protesting against the high fares being charged by the Company. It resolved to ask the

Northampton Omnibus Company to run a service to Wellingborough via Bozeat and Wollaston. As the bus stop against the Red Lion was causing inconvenience, the United Omnibus Company and Road Transport Ltd were asked by the Parish Council in 1923 to make the Square near the school a stopping place, "because of the narrowness of the road and the dangerous corner at the bottom of Easton Lane." The reason for that was because at that period there were houses opposite the Red Lion which made it a narrow road. But later it seems the practice of stopping in the Square was also found to be dangerous for in 1925 the Parish Clerk wrote to the Superintendent of Police to ask, "If a constable could visit the spot on Wednesdays and Saturdays when the traffic was busiest."

It would be interesting to know how busy the traffic really was in comparison with today. The Superintendent of Police replied by saying he had written to the owners, "to discontinue the practice" – whatever it was. Later it was reported to the Council that "considerable danger was caused through the stoppage of bus users at the bottom of Olney Road" and "could there be a different arrangement". But buses still continued to stop in "the narrow way near the Co-operative Society premises" and the parish clerk was asked to write to "Messrs Drage & Son and Mr Davies of Lavendon to request them to discontinue this practice." With more than one company operating, the narrow road was causing blockages.

It is interesting to note how old some of the problems were. In 1914 the Parish Council said that the road through Wollaston to Bozeat was very unsuitable for heavy and motor traffic by reason of it being so hilly and the detrimental effect this had upon the trade and business of the parish and suggesting that a new road should be made from a point at the bottom of Red Hill to the bridge at the bottom of Strixton Hill. David Hall in his *History of Wollaston* mentions that "the subject of a bypass had been brought up at Wollaston in 1922 and then almost every year since. If the Wollaston bypass is finished by 1984 then it will be 70 years since it was first mentioned."

As early as 1919 the Council were receiving complaints about the condition of Hope Street. After a survey it was resolved that nothing be done. In fact nothing was done for 57 years. As early as 1904 there was talk of improvement to the dangerous corner of Easton Lane, and after various alterations, a new road was completed in 1979.

When in the post war years the first of the motorways was being planned (M1) it was first suggested that it should be to the East of Northampton on the A509, Newport Pagnell to Kettering. Had it done so there would undoubtedly have been a bypass round Bozeat. But the motorway was eventually routed towards the West of Northampton. It is interesting speculation to wonder if Bozeat will one day be bypassed.

So writes Norman Palmer in 1980/1 giving us the story so far. We shall now take it up and see what came happened next.

Bozeat gets its bypass
The *Evening Telegraph* of Thursday, 4th April 1974 featured an article on Bozeat entitled 'Crash Village' where angry residents demand speed restrictions (speed ramps and signs) following a spate of serious pile ups in the village, particularly where Easton Lane used to enter the High Street opposite Don and Dolly Roberts' House at 55 London Road, on a blind bend, which they claim until recently averaged one a

month. "We live in perpetual terror," said Mr John Steele of 16 Wollaston Road. In the same paper on November 21, John Ellis, landlord of the Red Lion, warned that someone one would soon be killed at this junction if nothing was done. "My daughter was knocked down near the junction and had to be taken to hospital to have several stitches in her head." On complaining to the County Council the Chief Executive replied that "the flow of traffic through the village did not warrant further improvements." "This is ridiculous. It is the main trunk road link of Wellingborough with the M1.

Public meeting for the bypass in May 1984, including Harold Morton, Michael Garratt, Kate Morton, Brenda Bold, Danny Bold, Maxine Simpson, Mavis Bates, Ian Houghton and Michael Foster. (*Evening Telegraph*)

Also, they have recently widened the road either side of the village," replied Mr Ellis.

The work to re-site the entry of Easton Lane into the London Road towards Wellingborough away from the blind corner (but also away from Don Roberts' shop threatening some of his trade!) was carried out in 1979 leaving a triangle of land between the old end of Easton Lane (now turned into a cul-de-sac) and the new. Harold and Kate Morton have a letter from the County Council dated July 1980 with permission for them to rent the triangle to keep their horses there. After the entry was complete, a huge mound of top soil was placed in the middle and local youths used the ground as a speedway track, racing round the mound in the middle on their two-stroke motorbikes – and they can be noisy machines! Harold levelled the ground, put fences round and peace returned. He still (1999) rents the triangle from the County Council.

In 1982 a letter to the new village magazine *About Bozeat* from the county surveyor promised a bypass "within the next 10 years." The A509 was now signed as part of the M1 South Route carrying increasing traffic, especially lorries, through the village.

On March 1984 a Public Meeting on the Bypass was held and questionnaires were distributed to all adults in the village offering a choice of different bypass schemes. The returns showed that 45.7% were for the finally approved scheme, 14.7% the same but with a roundabout at the junction with the road to Easton Maudit instead of a bridge, 6.3% were happy just improving the present A509 through the village, and 16.2% questionnaires were not returned. On 21st/22nd July of this year the County Council set up an exhibition of proposals in the Church Hall.

Then in 1985 Peter Fry, the Member of Parliament, met the Action Group and Parish Council on 3rd May regarding the bypass proposal.

Two years later on 20th June a formal Enquiry into the Bypass Scheme was held in the Church Hall and conducted by Major General Sawers. Finally on 25th February

1988 bulldozers began to carve out the path of the new bypass, a scheme that was to cost the County Council £3.2 million. The oldest inhabitant, former schoolteacher Laura Bettles aged 92, cut the first turf aided by Parish Council chairman Mavis Holman and vice-chairman Tom Partridge-Underwood.

On the eve of its opening on 31st January 1989 the contractors gave permission for a torchlight procession along the complete bypass – 3.3km long and 7.3m wide single carriageway road with 1m hard strips, equivalent to 11.5 hectares of land, requiring the removal of 100,000 cubic metres of surplus excavated material onto fields adjacent to the bypass or to landscape or provide noise bunds.

■ STANDING ROOM ONLY . . . a huge crowd turned out to see their bypass end years of traffic misery

Newspaper picture of the opening of the bypass.
(*Evening Telegraph*)

Then in the presence of the Mayor and Mayoress of Wellingborough, Councillor and Mrs John Jessop, Alan Northen, leader of Wellingborough Council, and other dignitaries, Councillor W. D. Morton CBE leader of Northamptonshire County Council, at 2 pm on 1st February 1989 cut the tape and officially opened the Bozeat Bypass.

Postscript

Alan Brealey (1933-99) died suddenly from a heart attack on the evening of Tuesday, 2nd February sitting at home at 22 Brookside watching the sports results on TV. He was a passionate man, uncompromising and controversial on the Parish Council and the Action Group opposing the Sand and Gravel excavations behind Slype Farm and always fighting for causes to preserve the countryside and the way of life he loved. He took early retirement from Scott Baders to give time to these causes, and was typically seen with his dogs and his gun out in the fields and woods – born and bred in Easton Maudit, never failing to be at the harvest auction there and bidding for groceries he never wanted! His last public service was to write a fierce and powerful letter to the County Council about the appalling number of accidents, some fatal, occurring on the A509 in the region of the Bozeat Bypass. With the lobbying from farming brothers Peter and Gordon Howkins at The Grange this at last triggered a response with the promise of signs, speed cameras and possibly a slip road into the village.

Alan's concern for the bypass, road safety and his specialist knowledge of highways may well have been driven by the fact that his mother was killed on the A509 in the village before the bypass was opened. It must have been triggered too by the tragic and untimely death of Sue Coady, who lived in the High Street with her husband and three teenage sons, killed in a head-on collision just below the Grange on an icy Sunday morning in December 1998 on her way to work in Northampton, an occurrence that shook our village. After the increasing number of accidents on this dangerous highway, increasingly overloaded with lorries and M1 traffic, improvements have been made with further warning signs and the construction of a roundabout at the Bozeat junction.

CHAPTER 20

Fire!

Norman Palmer

Our forefathers' fear of fire
One cannot help being aware, in looking at old documents, of the threat of fire to our forefathers. This is hardly surprising when so many lived in the wattle and daub dwellings with so much wood in their construction. Even the stone-built houses would have had thatched roofs. Fire-fighting equipment was virtually non-existent and the only way to bring water to a fire from river or well was by a continual chain of buckets.

Most communities of any size appear to have had a fire of devastating proportions at some time or other besides the single outbreaks which appear to have been contained. Travelling through Bozeat were those who sought out the parish constables for shelter and food and these were sometimes those who had been made homeless by fire.

Constable Accounts 1679/80:
"Given to 1 man his wife & Children having great losses by fier … 1.0d
1680/81: "gave two women & three Chelld burnt by fire … 3d gave a poore woman & nine Chelld burnt out (by) fire … 2d.
1681/2: "to a Man yt had losse by fire … 3d"
1682/3: "to 2 Men and One Woman had los by fire … 4d. … to A Man & his Wife who had losse by fire … 2d" and so for nearly every subsequent year.

Occasionally in the village accounts there is a passing reference to a fire when someone had to be paid to watch the ashes, that a spark may not cause a fresh outbreak. Constable Accounts for 1761/2: "paid for beer for Watching the fire of John Eastol's house. 2s:0d." John Estell was a lacemaker.

The great community fire of Bozeat – 1729
Bozeat suffered its 'community fire' in 1729 and Easton Maudit in 1737. Both were the result of carelessness. The information comes from the Register Books of both parishes. Bozeat's fire is recorded by Thomas Drake in front of our earliest Register Book of Births, Marriages and Burials. The previous registers were burnt in the fire.

"Be it known to succeeding ages that on Tuesday, the Ninth Day of September, Anno 1729, a Sudain and Violent Fire broke out in the Parish of Bozeate about Two of the Clock after Noon at one Widow Keech's; who was baking upon the hearth in a poor house amongst the Church Yard houses. Which in the space of Three or Four hours (with a strong Wind) consumed Fourty One Dwelling houses besides all out Buildings (not Five Shillingsworth of useful timber saved). Four farms were burnt with full crops of Harvest, and great Quantitys of Household Goods: The Bell Frames were Twice on Fire. The whole Loss Amounting to Near Four Thousand Pounds. Blessed be God there were no Lives Lost, nor anybody hurt amidst so great Danger. And Whereas the Vicarage House was Burnyt with the Register Books, I, Thomas Drake (above Twenty One Years Vicar of this Parish) Having quitted this for another Living To my successor Mr Humphry Bradford: But having not removed my Family and Goods, became a Considerable Sufferer in this Dismal Fire…."

John Bridges (1666-1724) began in 1719 to collect information on the history of the county. He says about Bozeat: "The town, consisting of about one hundred and twenty families." It is possible that there were in some cases more than one family per house, and this would have been especially true of the farms. Then, ten years before the fire, there would have been between a hundred and twenty houses in the village which would not have changed very much by the time of the fire. Therefore something like a third of the houses were burnt down.

There is a puzzle about the Bell Frames being twice on fire. It seems to the writer to need a great number of sparks from an adjacent building to cause a combustion in the belfry, especially when the points of entry are not very big. Thomas Drake writes of the cause of the fire – Widow Keech, as having a "poor house amongst the Church Yard houses." Was there literally some kind of dwelling (probably shacks) in the Churchyard then, nearly adjacent to the Belfry? This would explain a puzzling entry in the Churchwarden's Accounts shortly after the event which mentions filling in some part of the Churchyard, which was not to do with graves, but could have been filling in the area where houses once stood. All conjecture of course.

Easton Maudit also catches fire – 1737
The fire at Easton Maudit occurred eight years after that at Bozeat, and the account is carefully preserved in the old register.

"Anno 1737. Whereas it pleased ye divine Almty Justice to visit this town with a Fire which began on Tuesday March the 7th 1737 between one & two O Clock in ye afternoon by ye CARELESSNESS at least of one Thomas Fisher a discontented Labr living in one of my Lord's Farm Houses & suffering his Boy to carry out hot ashes & lay them down on some straw near ye said house as is alledged: By means whereof ye Sd house barnes & Stacks of corn as also ye Barns Stables Hovels outhouses Stacks of corn & implements of Husbandry occupyd by & belonging to John Smith Farmer together with other small houses inhabited by John Pierson Thatcher & Wid Harris a poor woman & ye Shop & Stable of Tho Douglas Butchr were entirely Burnt & Concumed ye Dammage thereby sustained exclusive of ye Buildings which all belongd to ye Rt Honbl ye Earl of Sussex being on a moderate Valluation as follows:

John Smith farmer	£158 - 0 - 2
John Pierson thatcher	£15 -10 - 6
Tho Douglas Butcher	£4 - 1 - 6
Wid Harris	£2 - 2 - 6
Thos Fisher Labourer	£3 - 7 - 6
Total	£183 - 2 - 2

And whereas Certificates hereof have been signd by ye Minr & Churchwardn of this parish at ye desire of ye sayd poor Sufferers attesting the truth of the premis & ye Sum lost by them & amounts in ye whole to the sum of 183 as aforesaid up which Certifict ye County having been collected the SUMES FOLLONG have been received for ye use & relief of ye poor sufferers to be divided among them in ye proportions aforesd according to their respective losses."

(There follows a list of 55 donations received from parishes and landed gentry in Northamptonshire and Bedfordshire of which Bozeat gave £6-0-0. The total coming to £122-2-4½) "out of which takeing ffive pounds nineteen shillings & two pence expended in collecting the same there remains 116 pounds 3 shillings & twopence half penny the said sume as before in the following proportion amounting to twelve shillings and Eight pence in the pound for our respective Losses and no more.

John Smith have received	£100 – 0 – 4
John Pierson have received	£9 – 6 – 4
Thomas Douglas have received	£2 –11 – 6
Widow Harris	£1 – 6 –11
Thomas Fisher	£2 – 2 – 9
Total	£115 –18 –10
Overplus	£0 – 4 – 4½
SUME	£116 – 3 – 2½

For which we return thanks to God and the several persons who have comiserated our suffering. Witness our hand this 18th day of April 1738." (There follows the signatures of the five who lost by fire – Mary Harris, the widow, could only sign with a mark).

Now the turn of Wellingborough

It was the turn of Wellingborough to suffer from fire the year following Easton Maudit's conflagration, for we find this note in the Easton Maudit register: "This 13th day of Aug 1738 Being Sunday after Evening Service I collected the Summ of 3.18s.2d for ye Relief of the Sufferers by Wellinboro' Fire as Follows" (there follow 34 names.) The Vicar who heads the list gave 10s-0d. The two richer farmers of the parish, which included John Smith who suffered from the fire the previous year, £1.1.0d each. A Guinea would seem to be the acceptable donation for those in the higher income bracket. Then comes the donation of lesser men, such as Thomas Douglas Butcher who gave 2s-6d each or less, to those who had the lowest income – and this included Thomas Fisher the 'discontented labourer', who gave 6d each, the poorest 2d or 1d.

Fires nearer our own time and hopes of a fire brigade

There appear to be problems nearer to our own time with coal-fired central heating, as it was reported by Mr Kirby, the first headmaster of the old school in Camden Square, in his *School Logbook* for 22nd Dec 1897: "We had a narrow escape this morning of being burnt down. The Caretaker came at 7am and found the school full of smoke. She came for me at once and we found the wainscoting and floor at the back of the furnace on fire. We pulled up some of the woodwork and found the joists burning, not in a flame but burnt quite through. A few buckets of water quenched it; but if it had happened a few hours earlier, we must have been burnt out."

The predecessor of the Parish Council (begun 1895) was the Village Vestry Meeting. At the Easter Vestry of March 1884 there was a suggestion to make a reservoir at the Town Well to provide water in case of fire and a committee was formed to consider this. But nothing seemed to come of this suggestion. How, one would ask, would the water be transported to the other end of the village in such an emergency?

The theme of firefighting recurs in later Council Minutes. In 1905 a letter was received by the Bozeat Council asking if they would contribute towards the upkeep of a fire engine and appliances proposed to be purchased by the Wellingborough Urban District Council. It was decided that the Parish Council could not do anything. Consideration was given to the provision of chemical fire extinguishing appliances. Although this was discussed at length nothing came of it.

It appears that a fire brigade was formed in 1906 after the Parish Council declined an invitation to contribute to the cost of a new steam-pulled fire engine purchased by the Wellingborough Council. In 1919 Earls Barton offered their fire engine for sale but the offer was declined.

In July 1920 the Bozeat Parish Council received an offer of help from Earls Barton Parish Council informing them that it could have the use of the fire engine but Bozeat would have to provide the horses. Bozeat Council resolved that in case of necessity Mr T. Drage (grandfather of Eric Green) be asked to supply horses, ride to Earls Barton and collect the fire engine. One can only presume that Bozeat was still providing the firemen.

In 1924 the Northampton Town Clerk asked whether the Council would like to enter into an agreement with the Northampton Corporation for the use of the Borough Fire Brigade in case of fire in this parish, but there was a negative reply. The next month Northampton Town Clerk wrote again enquiring if the Council wished to purchase a steam fire engine, but the offer was declined.

THREE FIRES THIS CENTURY
Philip Bligh

A factory fire
Just to the south of 105 London Road, where Spencelayh once lived (1941-1952) there was a narrow alley and then a shoe factory stretching some 50 yards down London Road to where John Farey's bungalow now stands at number 95. Before the

The Taylor & Drage factory fire in London Road. (*Bozeat School Scrapbook*)

Great War, William Taylor (sometime churchwarden) started a shoe business in a grocer's shop in Easton Lane but business grew during the war and just afterwards he built this new factory. It was in 1928 that a fire broke out in the factory one night. Max Laughton, then a young boy, remembers it vividly. "They had to spray the wall of Ted Partridge's house (No. 105) continually to prevent it being burnt down." Dick Botterill, a very young boy then, remembers the night because someone ran to their house in Easton Lane and had to throw gravel at their bedroom window to wake them to tell them Taylor's factory was on fire – of concern to the family as his grandmother, Frances, lived next door and her house could catch fire. If it had, you never know, Spencelayh, the great painter, may never have come to Bozeat and immortalised Bozeat folk and village life in his marvellous paintings. As it was, the factory was completely destroyed and William Taylor moved to Northampton where he opened a Billiard Hall. In its place the council built a new house for the village policeman, PC Forth, his predecessor, PC Willey having lived up Hope Street. The last village Policeman, PC Peter Fry, lived there till 1974 (died 1998) after which the council put it up for sale, when Peter and Pam Freely bought it.

Two farm fires

Three hundred tons of hay and straw were badly damaged by fire when they caught alight in the 200 foot barn at Church Farm one night in 1962. The barn was situated where now stands a cul-de-sac of seven elegant stone houses built in 1987 and known as Church Farm Close which opens into Mile Street. Up from this opening are still to be found the row of old cottages which backed onto the farm yard where the barn and cowsheds, etc once stood. The magnificent old farmhouse dating from the 18th century and some parts even earlier still stands looking down on the Flat (i.e. London Road). The Hensman family who farmed the land in the 19th century gave their name to the lane alongside. One of them had eleven children and, as a churchwarden, made a pull-out extension to his churchwarden's pew in the Parish Church (at the top of his lane) to accommodate his family!

The *Evening Telegraph* report was that:

"Firemen from Wellingborough and Rushden worked all night and farm workers loaded trailers with burning hay and straw bales and carted them to a nearby paddock. Two cows with calves – one born only yesterday – were rescued from the yard in front of the L-shaped barn as flames leapt through the 200 ft by 40 ft building.

About 30 ft from the barn was a two-year old pedigree bull locked in his pen. It was decided that he was out of danger. Mr J. A. Roberts, the farmer, who has lived Bozeat for about ten years – he formerly farmed at Hinwick – was concerned about the bull, Newboze Brutus. 'You can never tell with those fellows,' said Mr Roberts, 'He's sort of reconciled himself now. When the sparks stopped flying and the tiles stopped falling he settled down. If he'd got loose I don't know what would have happened but a lot of people would have been hurt.'

Mr Roberts said that the thick walls of the 30 ft high barn had helped to contain the blaze. 'I spent £200 having the roof repaired.' he said. "The barn was absolutely packed.' It was his son Raymond Roberts, who gave the alarm soon after 9.00 pm. He was watching television in the farmhouse when he heard a loud crackling noise outside. He went out and saw the smoke rising from the barn about 100 ft away. All over the village people heard the sound of tiles cracking.

'It was like fireworks night.' said one man who was in the Chequers public house when the outbreak started. Others left the Working Men's Club to help salvage hay and straw. A trailer brought out of the burning building was found to be damaged.

The vicar, the Rev. W. C. Knight, was in the Vicarage nearby when he heard the crackling sound. 'I looked out and saw the barn on fire and dialled 999, but the alarm had already been given.' he said. Among the volunteers who helped fireman were youths who stripped to the waist in the heat of the flames.

The barn is one of the oldest buildings in Bozeat, and is said to have Roman origins.

'Youngsters are always going in there, although we've got a 'Keep Out' sign up.' said Mr Roberts.

Two appliances from Wellingborough and one from Rushden were at the fire.

Soon after the fire started there were rumours that someone may have been trapped in the barn, but these were dispelled by police."

Richard Roberts still owns some of the farmland adjacent to the new bypass at the lower end of the village – a meadow known as Windmill Field. He now runs a successful business on it producing animal feed which in 1987 won a Queen's Award to Industry. Richard still lives in the village.

A similar farm fire was started in the Dutch barn owned by farmers Cecil and Hedley Brown in 1973, when the building of the new primary school was nearing completion in the adjacent field. (The £100,000 contract had been won by Robert Marriotts the Rushden builders whose managing director, Eric Brook, lived in the Old Rectory at Easton Maudit and was churchwarden there.) The fire was first spotted at 4.30 pm in the barn nearest the new school and which contained 70 tons of hay and 35 tons of nitrogen fertiliser worth thousands of pounds. Three fire tenders, two from Wellingborough and one from Rushden, went to the fire but the firemen could only join the dozens of children and older people watching the blaze fanned by a strong breeze as it destroyed the barn and its contents. While the fire burnt itself out, police and fireman examined a small rubbish fire on the building site where the new primary school was being completed some 30 yards from the barn and thought the blaze could have been started by a spark from this fire.

John Brown was in his mid-20s at the time and remembers (1999) the occasion well. "I was drilling up towards Dungey when they came and told me about the fire. It must have been spring as I was drilling and fertiliser bags were still in the barn waiting to be used. The hay went up just like that – it was so hot it destroyed the asbestos roof but left the metal frame still usable but buckled by the heat. The firemen sprayed the fertiliser bags but the fire damaged every one of them. I remember having to break up the fertiliser and then throw it onto the fields."

A house fire

Joyce Wesley was working in Ron Coles' factory (i.e. Bozeat Boot Company) on the morning of 6th January 1975 – built where Line Prop Yard used to be and next door to Joyce's thatched cottage down the hill at 11 Easton Lane when someone shouted out to her, "Joyce, your chimney's on fire!" "Rubbish," Joyce called back, "we don't have a fire with thatch." But the thatch was alight – a spark had been blown from a cottage up the hill. It was only a red patch when they looked but it was soon ablaze and the whole of the top floor was gutted – even the timbers in the kitchen burnt before the firemen from Wellingborough could put it out. "They were as much concerned with spraying water on the thatch of the Morton's cottage next door as ours!" remembers Joyce, "They didn't want another to go up in flames. We had to have a completely new upstairs. When Dunkley the thatcher came to persuade us to have a new thatch I told him, 'Unless you can guarantee me 99% it won't catch alight I'm not having thatch.'" He couldn't so we got tiles! But people were so kind at that time. Folk couldn't have done more to help us."

Apparently it was a van driver drawing up at the factory who noticed it first. Factory workers and neighbours helped to remove personal belongings. Mr Wesley, a commercial traveller, could not be contacted and the children, Richard(13), Nicholas(12) and Clare(10) were at school. One fireman Mr R. Nash was taken to hospital unconscious after part of the burning thatch roof collapsed and another fireman was slightly burned pulling him from the blaze. "Apparently part of the roof collapsed on me as I went up the stairs. Then I don't remember a thing." (*Evening Telegraph*) Most of the furniture was sound but everything upstairs was burned.

Camden Square c.1910. On the left is the blacksmith's (now a house called The Forge), with the narrow Striker's Cottage next to it, and Thomas Robinson, grocer. (*John Darker*)

In 1953, members of the 1st Bozeat Scout Troop won two prestigious cups. The Patrol which won the Gilbey Cup comprised Patrol Leader J. Bryant, Seconder R. Pettit, and Scouts P. Elderton, B. Roberts, David Terry, David Mallows and Frederick Dilley. The Silverwood Cup for camping and general Scout standards was won by Patrol Leader David Terry, Second David Mallows and Scouts Colin Curtis, Ray Langford, Frederick Dilley and Martin Line. In the lower picture, the Group Scoutmaster, Rev. Knight, is at the back in the centre. The Scoutmaster was John Fleming, the A.S.M. Jim Tompkins, and they had a celebratory dinner at the Bozeat Café.

Religion

Methodist Chapel anniversary tea 21st May 1952. (*D. Roberts*)

CHAPTER 21

Methodism and Nonconformity in Bozeat

"My chains fell off."
"The serious concern of the English Puritans for salvation was one of the living forces in religion in the 17th century." (Stephen Neil, *Anglicanism*.) Another influential movement in society of that age was pietism. These two forces came together and had a powerful influence on John Wesley (1703-91) the founder of Methodism.

Both John and his brother Charles, the hymn writer, were sons of an Anglican vicarage and were greatly influenced by the devout faith of their mother, Susanna Wesley and by the piety of the German Moravians. It was at one of their meetings at Aldersgate Street in London on 24th May 1738 that John had his conversion experience at the age of 35. He spoke of his heart being "strangely warmed" in a deeply emotional and personal experience of Jesus in his heart which convinced him that God accepts us not on the basis of our good works but on his unconditional love for us.

So began the evangelical revival in England under the Wesley brothers. The puritanical emphasis on discipline and the conviction that genuine spiritual experience must find its outward experience in practical holiness, earned their followers the nickname, 'Methodists' and their quest was to promote spiritual holiness throughout the land.

The impact on the poor of this land, in mine, field and factory, to whom the Wesley's message made such a powerful appeal, brought about a great revival amongst the ignorant and uneducated giving them a new heart and dignity. Education in 18th century England was deplorably low and it was Wesley's conviction that a serious Christian must learn to read and be suitably provided with edifying reading material. Wesley also followed the practice of other pietistic groups of his time in forming Societies provided with teachers and leaders suitably qualified to nurture their spiritual growth, which was to be realised in the weekly class meeting which became the local power house of early Methodism. Each class would have a leader and to ensure they had adequate teaching they were linked and fed by an itinerant and trained group of local preachers travelling between and preaching to the 'societies' in their local circuit.

Susannah Church – the first Methodist of Bozeat?
Norman Palmer
Towards the end of the 18th century before the full impact of the industrial revolution there emerges from 'out of the shadows' Susannah Church, who must have been a remarkable woman. William Church was a shepherd with some land and property. As a widower he married Susannah Boddington in 1762. Further details are given in Chapter 14 where we noted they lived in the house known as 'Glebe Cottage' in Church Lane. In the Methodist Bedford Circuit membership list for 1792, Susannah heads the list, perhaps as Class Leader, with the trade of Shopkeeper, whilst her husband came second on the list. It would seem probable that this lady founded Methodism in Bozeat. The house was to remain as a grocer's shop within the family for some years. So we have the impression of an educated personality able to take the lead in village life.

Did her Methodism give her education or at least promote it and develop her natural gifts of leadership by giving her that evangelical faith and consequent upward mobility as it did for many of her and following generations? She would have been almost an exact contemporary of John Wesley, possibly like him born in the first decades of the century, so probably a first generation Methodist and convert (she married William 24 years after Wesley's conversion experience when Revival was in full bloom). Wesley first preached at Bedford on 16th October 1753 "on St Peter's Green at seven in the morning and five in the evening," when Susannah may have been in her impressionable teens/twenties and she may well have been there in the crowds. Three years before her marriage, Wesley was again in Bedford and in his diary for Friday, 23rd November 1759 he writes: "The roads were so extremely slippery, it was with much difficulty we reached Bedford. We had a pretty large congregation; but the stench from the swine under the room was scarce supportable. Was ever a preaching-place over a hog-sty before? Surely they love the gospel, who come to hear it in such a place." Well it seems Susannah for one fell in love with the gospel that fell from Wesley's eloquent lips!

If not the first Methodist in Bozeat, Susannah was almost certainly, therefore, the leader of that first little group of believers whose class meeting would undoubtedly have been in their leader's house – Glebe Cottage, Church Lane. Is it more than a touching coincidence that Susannah should have the same Christian name as the influential mother of the founder of her Methodist faith?

Bozeat Methodism in the 19th century
(Based on the history by John Warren Partridge written in 1924)
John Partridge writes that the origins of Methodism in Bozeat go back as far as 1804. Then the first Methodist preacher we know of visited Bozeat and preached in a cottage occupied by a man named John Weeds at the bottom of Pudding Bag Lane. "It was pulled down some years ago – nothing but the ground remaining where it once stood. How many met there we do not know. It would almost certainly have been a small low-roofed thatched cottage with one or two rooms, small leaded windows which did not allow much light to enter the room, with shutters either on the inside or outside of the windows and a broad window board which would answer for seating accommodation for two or three of the congregation. The floor might consist of stone slabs or earth sprinkled with clean sand as was customary in days long past. The humbleness of the cottage reflects the folk who met here for worship – agricultural labourers in the main and possibly one or two small tradesmen."

The second preaching place of Bozeat's early Methodists
This was the parlour of a house in Church Lane now known as Glebe Cottage. This had been purchased by William Church and his wife Susannah, and they ran a grocer's shop from it. They were living there in 1770, and we have read earlier in this chapter, Susannah probably held the first Methodist Class Meeting there. We know (c.1810) another William Church traded in lace from the cottage. Partridge tells us that a John Church also occupied or owned it, and thereafter it was known as Mr Church's Parlour. (In c.1840, it was bought by Thomas Wallis, blacksmith from Finedon, and in 1924 it was still in the Wallis family and still a grocer's shop, occupied by the family of the late Mr William Wallis, retaining the name of Glebe Cottage).

The third preaching place

Precisely how long these Methodist folk worshipped at Mr Church's Parlour we are not sure, but possibly c.1815 they moved to the house of Mr Dobson in Church Lane. We know nothing more of Mr Dobson, but these were times of bitterness and persecution where such places of worship where spoken of as 'Cysim (i.e. schism) Shops', (where they 'sold' their religion) and in some places, where the Squire and the Clergyman held power, a Methodist who was bold enough to open his house for preaching had to leave his cottage under the Squire or close it against Methodist preachers – as did Sam Tompkins at Mears Ashby for example.

Mr Dobson's house had a change of religious direction as it was to be demolished and the Baptists built a chapel known as 'The Meeting Place' on its site in 1844. The pulpit was at the end up the hill, and the entrance was from the bottom end, and one of the most prominent members was William Garrett, the butcher. Latterly it was used as a hall to be hired out, and was also used as the St. John Ambulance Room. In its turn it too was demolished and on its site we now (1999) find two cottages, Nos. 30 and 32 Church Lane, called Tanyard Cottages.

The fourth preaching place

This was the house of Mr Richard Risely – "who belonged to the early Methodists and opened his house for preaching. His house was situated down what was known then as the Pykle Garden and was the bottom part of a house now (1924) in the possession of Mr Taylor, shoe manufacturer and known by the name of Stoneleigh (now 46 Allens Hill). The loan of this house was only for a few weeks however as they began to think about a place exclusively for the worship of God.

A fifth and 'set apart' place of worship

"The Methodists then rented a barn from Mr E. Skivington and it was converted by them for use as a chapel. Now (1924) it is pulled down and a house occupied by Mr Sarrington (carrier) built upon the site" – in Mile Street just above Fish Alley. Nancy Pettitt (née Bayes) born 1916, who still lives (1999) at 35 Hope Street was his step-daughter and showed me an old photo from about 1928 of the two cottages where she grew up. "How long the Methodists used this place for holding their services we know not, but we do know that the five places mentioned represented thirty years of Methodism."

A chapel at last

After these 30 years of Methodism at last a chapel was built, a new one and the first one for the Methodist people of Bozeat. "It was built on a piece of land in Mile Street, given by a member of the Methodists named Henry Nichols, grandfather of Mr Thomas Nichols one of the first trustees of the present new Wesleyan Chapel and father of the late (1924) Mrs Arthur Smart and Thomas Nichols who lived at the top of Peartree Close. (It is now 16 Mile Street and the house is called appropriately 'The Old Chapel'.)

This first chapel was opened on 13th November 1834 by a minister from London, Rev. George Cubitt (died 1850). This was in the old coaching days and this gentleman was unfortunate enough to miss the coach and was fetched by a Mr Inkly, a Bozeat Miller, in his own trap – and arrived half an hour late at 2.30 pm instead of 2.00 pm. We can imagine some of the anxiety and excitement of the officials and congregation on this important and long awaited event. The text for the occasion was from the First Letter of Timothy Chapter 1 Verse 15. Methodism in Bozeat was further encouraged by the coming of Rev. William Taylor in 1833/4 (his daughter married the Reverend Joseph Payne, minister 1835-1855) for the membership doubled and the debt on the building cleared."

The Wellingborough circuit

"Until this time the Wellingborough Circuit had only one minister but as things improved the circuit took on a second minister. It was wider then including both Grendon and Lavendon with half again as many places of worship. We must also remember the difficulty of getting to the different places in this wide circuit; conveyance was scarce and the minister's stipend small and no horse hire fund and no cycles. The local preacher of necessity had to reach his appointment on foot. Long journeys and roads were not as good as they are today and travelling not as safe. A description of a Methodist travelling preacher in the coaching days of 1820/21 is recorded of the Reverend James Burley. On his first coming to the circuit, he walked into Wollaston Chapel in top boots with a great coat on his arm and a thick stick in his hand. Whether he tried to affect the character corresponding to his name, he looked sufficiently fierce in himself to overawe an ordinary congregation. It is also told of another preacher, being tired with his journey, astonished his host by taking off his wig and presenting himself in a new aspect while he laid it on the fender to dry and wiped his heated brow."

A Sunday School is first started in July 1835

"They tell us the chief difficulty arose from the lack of teachers. However, brother Talbot did his best with the assistance of James Sargeant, a farmer from Wollaston Farm, known in 1924 as Poplar Lodge. The scholars could sing only two hymns both to the same tune and both by Bishop Kenn, 'Awake my soul' and 'Glory to my God this night'."

The Society class meeting

"The weekly class meeting was, in early days, the test of membership and amongst the most helpful and beneficial of all its meetings. Probably the first class leader (see *Palmer* on Susannah Church) in Bozeat was James Nichols. He was a tall dark thin man and wore large round spectacles. This gentleman kept a lace making school so we are told. We are also told his wife was a member of the Baptist Church which was fairly strong in those days. It is said of James Nichols, when on his death bed, that he said, 'I stand in my Iron Shoes' indicating that he stood firm in the truth and safe in Christ."

The Sunday morning class

Mr Richard Riseley also had charge of Sunday Morning Class. In the 1851 census he is stated to be the Senior Steward. The census also gives us an indication of the number of Methodist worshippers in Bozeat in their two chapels, the Wesleyan Methodist (erected 1834), and the Union Chapel, Denomination Baptist and Independents, Church Lane (erected 1844) with Robert Pearson, Manager.

Taking the total from the most well attended Services i.e. the evening, the total in church or chapel on the evening of 30th March 1851 was 377 – which out of a total village population of 921 was 40.9%. Of these 18.5% were in the Wesleyan Methodist Chapel, 8.7% in the Union Chapel and 13.8% in the Anglican Church, i.e. the majority of worshippers in the village were Nonconformists, 27.2% compared to 13.8% Anglicans, i.e. about twice as many. Bozeat was definitely a Nonconformist village but far from completely so.

Spiritual giants
So we conclude that the majority of worshippers in Bozeat at this time were Methodists. John Partridge writes that "to the Sunday Morning Class belonged some distinguished men: Thomas Nichols, Joseph Warner, William Shrive, William Pettit who served the school as teacher and Superintendent for a remarkable period of 40 years and were respected and beloved by all. These four brethren were all converted together in the month of February 1848."

Partridge remembers these renowned men and some of the hymns they were accustomed to give out. For example, at the Sunday 11 o'clock prayer meeting Brother Thomas Nichols very frequently gave out number 43 in the old hymn book "not in the present book":

And am I born to die,
To lay this body down,
And must my trembling spirits fly,
Into a world unknown,
A land of deepest shade
Unpierced by human thought
The dreary regions of the dead,
Where all things are forgot.

This second was his favourite verse:

Soon as from earth I go,
What will become of me,
Eternal happiness or woe,
Must then my portion be
Waked by the trumpet's sound,
I from my grave shall rise,
And see the judge with glory crowned
And see the flaming skies.

Brother Joseph Warner's favourite was No. 44 in the old book, third verse being as follows:

No room for mirth or trifling here,
For worldly hope or worldly fear,
If life so soon is gone,
If now the judge is at the door,
And all mankind must stand before,
The inexorable throne.

We savour here something of the stern Victorian spirituality and the seriousness of

Joe Bosworth with a Methodist Sunday school class. (*D. Roberts*)
Back row: ? , Elsie Deverill, Lizzie Ross, Nellie Corby, Mrs Partridge, ? .
Middle row: Maud Church, Elsie Church, Nancy Drage, ? , ? .
Front row: ? , ? , ? , Mrs Perkins.

these early Methodists. Life was hard and uncertain for such working class men subject to their own mortality and with little prospect in this present life so their hope was chiefly in the life to come. As Partridge writes: "these men ... were in deadly earnest about spiritual things, so it was no wonder that they were noted men. There were other members of this class, namely Thomas Pettit, James Drage, James Hudson father of the noted William Hudson ... also Daniel Surridge, John Allebone and John Labutt – the last two from Easton Maudit." "Later on during a revival under the Reverend Joseph Payne (1835-55) others joined the church and society, namely John Chambers, John Drage and William Surridge. The two former names soon appeared on the preachers' plan and proved very useful and welcome preachers to the end of their earthly life."

John Allebone
"John Allebone Senior used to put in a pretty good Sabbath Day's work. He would walk from Easton Maudit to attend 7.00 am Prayer Meeting and 8.00 am Class Meeting then home for breakfast. At 11.00 am he would again be present and return home for dinner. He would appear at 2.00 pm for the preaching, back home for tea and then attend the service at 6.00 pm, stay for either Sacrament or Prayer Meeting, after Preaching Service.... This gives us an insight into the character of a man who put his best into anything he undertook. He kept an outdoor beer house at Easton

Maudit, brewing his own beer. It is said that he purchased his malt from the best maltster ... his motto being 'Give the best value you possibly can for their money.' Remember that the Temperance Cause and Teetotalism were both practically unknown (then)."

Indeed in these days before the Temperance Movement, in the middle of the 19th century, there was a saying in Methodism here (according to John Partridge), "Drink and Dancing play the Bear with our People!" "Even Mr Riseley himself being weakly, used to bring a flat bottle of wine together with some baked pudding to strengthen himself for the services, the fact that he also sat on a velvet cushion is scarcely in accordance with the ideal picture which we conjure up of the self sacrificing of the old Methodists."

"Mrs Riseley took charge of the collections made in the Chapel and carefully kept each in a separate cup or basin. She also collected money in penny a week subscriptions to help people to buy bibles. The first Local Preacher resident in Bozeat was Mr Thomas Riseley, a small farmer and brother of Richard Riseley who afterwards moved down to Surrey where (as he quaintly put it) a different style of preaching from his own was required by the congregations."

Music

At this time the "musical part of the service was of a makeshift type there being no choir at all and when Mr Samuel Brown came to preach at the service to celebrate the Centenary of Methodism in 1839, he first asked the congregation if they could sing hymn 75 ('See how great a flame aspires') before venturing to give it out. At one time the singing was led by three women named Ruth Drage, Elizabeth Hudson and Mary

Methodist Chapel anniversary tea in the 1950s. (*D. Roberts*)
Front: Edna Drage, Mabel Tompkins, Dolly Tompkins, Don Roberts.
Others from the left: Enid Tompkins, Reg Beard, Flos Tivey, ?, ?, Marjorie Drage, Laura Bettles, Dolly Smith, Mary Silsby, Mrs Horden, Heather Partridge, Win Beard, Mrs Tom Bayes, ?, ?, ?, Miss Eadie Johnson, Miss Jacqueline Cave.

Heaton who was blind, but soon afterwards John Allebone, uncle to the Mr John Allebone who did so much for the present Chapel, led the congregation with a clarinet, while Joe Drage helped with a flute. The aforesaid Joseph Drage was brother to Mr John Drage, Boot Manufacturer, who was also a good helper to the present Chapel (See Memories of Ted Drage, nephew of John Drage and now 82 in 1996). The same Joe Drage is living at Doddington at the time of writing August 1924."

"The orchestra was sometimes further strengthened with a violin played by Thomas Robinson, father of the present (1924) Mr Thomas Robinson also Mrs Thomas Dobbs of Pear Tree Close who is also a member of the present congregation and Chapel (her son Arnold Dobbs the builder still [1999] lives in the same fine brick house overlooking the glebe) also with a brass viol by William Harris, sometimes they broke down altogether. Later on Mr Sam Monk played the brass viol, George Drage the flute and J. P. Osborne the concertina."

"One of our members who was favoured with a seat in the singers' pew when a boy has a lively recollection of the first practice he attended. The late Thomas Mallows then led the orchestra with a clarinet, the bass or cello was the above Sam Monk, brother to William Monk who put forth such energy in rendering the bass runs in the Creation that the boy could not help laughing. He was however summarily checked by a stroke on the back of the head from the bow of the musician. In the days of the old Mile Street Chapel, discipline was sometimes roughly administered so the above was not an isolated case, a wand of twined deal measuring about six feet in length being used to keep the boys in order. On one occasion during prayers conducted by Mr Riseley, a teacher broke it over the head of one of the scholars, where upon the good man stopped and said, 'Don't you ever do that again.'"

A Love Feast at Wellingborough

"The oldest surviving member of Methodism in Bozeat in 1894 was Mrs Drage who lived with her daughter Mrs Monk at the Mill and at the advanced age of 82 years was then blessed with the enjoyment of all her faculties." She was born in 1812.

"She was one of the party who accompanied Mrs Richard Riseley when she drove her donkey waggon to attend a Love Feast at Wellingborough in the year 1830 (when aged only 18). There were 20 or 30 young people in all, members of Mrs Riseley's class. Most of the party walked both ways though some were allowed occasionally to take a rest in the waggon. On the old Wellingborough Bridge the Reverend Robert Melson, father of Dr Melrose of Birmingham, met the party as he was walking out to an appointment and by the leader requesting wrote out for her a ticket as follows: 'Admit the Bearer June 6th 1830 Robert Melson'.

This Mrs Drage possessed this ticket together with her tickets of membership for 64 years. At the above Love Feast the excitement was so intense that two or three rose at the same time to speak. Mrs Drage was then a young girl in the service with Mrs Wykes of Greenfield (the fine stone house up London Road later to be occupied by the Boot and Shoe Drages and then Dr Silby).

In the same year 1830 she heard a sermon from Mr Chater from Wollaston, then a young man, on the text 'Let both grow until the harvest' which struck home to her conscience. Previously she had often slept during the sermon, and been annoyed by the pokes given from behind by Mr Riseley. But Mr Chater's dramatic picturing of members of the same family separated at the Judgement made her realise her lost condition. Mrs Wykes warned her not to let her convictions die and helped her constantly by writing little pieces of counsel and Scripture on paper and putting them in the kitchen where she had to sit.

She tells us that she was at first very dark and did not understand the nature of Saving Faith, till Mrs Wykes explained it to her and even then she did not find peace for weeks. One day when her Mistress had gone to Chapel she took up a long piece of paper she had left for her to read with these lines at the bottom, 'Believe, Believe in Jesus' name, And you shall be forgiven.'

While reading this verse her chains fell off. She felt full of Happiness and as free as the air she breathed. Now she rested alone in the atoning death of Christ for her Salvation."

"Mrs Wykes who was for a long time lame with rheumatism and gout, and used to be wheeled in the invalid chair (which was also wound upstairs bodily by means of a winch through a trap door on the landing floor) died at Strixton on 14th February 1880 aged 81 years."

Partridge comments: "The Methodists of that time seemed to have had wonderful fire, but they seemed to have depended a good deal upon sensationalism hymns about the Judgement Day as were much relied upon in the early Revivals, from Hymn 54 to 66 inclusive in Wesley's Old Book. They may be considered out of date by some and too terrifying...."

1860 and the purchase of the harmonium

The "purchase of a harmonium was considered a great advance on the former instruments (i.e. flute, concertina, fiddle and cello, etc.) and we must remember that it was the first instrument of that description in a Nonconformist Place of Worship in Bozeat." Remembering the modest income of ordinary working and small business people who were the majority of the congregation this was a purchase of some considerable expense in 1860. Partridge writes: "I was informed by one of the then young people that it was raised by sixpences, threepenny pieces and coppers chiefly and then only at the sacrifice of some personal luxury. Miss Wykes, now Mrs Bell was the first player and is still living at Easton Maudit (March 1925).

She was followed by Miss Lizzie Maxwell then living at the Villa then when they left Bozeat, Miss Maxwell was followed by Mr George Coles, who was followed by Miss Annie Maxwell of the Grange, Bozeat and after Miss Maxwell, Mr G. A. Drage.

The harmonium was to play its part in the opening of the new Chapel in 1875 when Mr W. Bradshaw was appointed Leader of the Choir and Instrumentalist, his principal helpers being Mr George Johnson, Miss Lizzie Drage, G. A. Drage and John Bradshaw ... and (it) provided the music for the Great Revival in the years from 1883 to 1885, the greatest known in the History of Bozeat Methodism. It also provided the music for the Choir when the Choir was in its most efficient state that it has ever been."

"Coming down to later days, Mr Toliday recalls that in 1866 Mr and Mrs Wykes Senior of Strixton, Miss Wykes, Mr T. Wykes of Greenfield, their son and also the Drages, Partridges and Craxtons were supporters of the Bozeat Methodist Church. At the time Miss Wykes was Foreign Missionary Collector and anticipated the Blake System of gathering a farthing per week from forty-eight subscribers.

Nine years later 1875, there were a number of farmers' families worshipping at the old Mile Street Chapel, among whom were those of Mr Harrison, Mr Coles of Easton

The present Methodist Church, viewed from High Street in 1889, showing a well set into the wall.
(D. Roberts)

Maudit, Mr Walter Maxwell of the Grange, Bozeat, Mr John Allebone, Mr E. Maxwell of Spring Villa, Bozeat and Mr Wykes of Greenfield."

Mr Harrison
"Mr Harrison was a big stout North Country man possessing the North Country Fire and Zeal, a very acceptable Local Preacher. I have heard it stated that one gentleman of the congregation said that he would give five shillings to anyone who could go to sleep during his preaching, and some time after this Mr Harrison's youngest son went home after one Sunday afternoon service and said to his father, 'Father what was wrong today as you did not shout so much as usual. I went to sleep during the Sermon.' The gentleman was as good as his word handing over to the lad the five shillings. This same Mr Harrison was preaching at Lavendon one Sunday afternoon in the summer and the Chapel windows were open, looking towards the established Church. Mr Harrison warmed to his subject so that the clergyman sent and requested the friends to close the windows as he could not proceed with his own service."

1877 and the building of the present Methodist Church in the High Street
"It was felt that the time had now come to build a better Chapel for the Worship of God. The present freehold site was accordingly secured by Mr Walter Maxwell, from Thomas Revis Esq and mortgages for £250 on 5th October 1875, and conveyed on 18th October 1875 to the following Trustees: John Allebone, Fred Maxwell, Walter Maxwell, John Drage, James Pettit, William Pettit, John Chambers, Thomas Robinson, George Coles, William Jolley and James Silby."

"The stone was laid on Whit Monday in the year 1877 by the Reverend John Clulow, Chairman of the District, who died in 1879. The day of the stone laying dawned wet and dreary, but the members assembled in the old Mile Street Chapel at 5.00am before they went to work to pray for a fine day. It seemed as if they all were inspired, so earnest were their pleadings and sure enough in the afternoon the sun burst out and splendid weather followed for the ceremony. I well remember the ceremony."

"It had been decided at a meeting of the Committee and Teachers held on 29th May 1876 that each teacher be provided with a book, and that 100 collecting cards be provided for the use of the scholars and that the amount collected may be laid on the foundation stone by each scholar or their teacher. So keen and enthusiastic were the scholars of the senior class that one member gave 3d spending money and also his three half-pence he had given him weekly for a glass of beer to his teacher James Pettit to enter in the book."

"The present Gothic, somewhat cut down however from the original design, was opened on 13th December of the same year 1877 by the same gentleman who laid the stone. The following Sundays the pulpit was occupied by the Reverend William Hurst, James Chapman and Alexandra Mo Aulay. Dr Puncham preacher the following Whit Monday."

"The Bozeat Chapel occupying as it does such a fine site and presenting such a perfect interior, will stand for a great many years as a solid and worthy monument in stone to the enterprise and zeal of Mr John Allebone Maxwell and John Drage and all the above Trustees and Subscribers who gave liberally in money, time and labour (all carting being done free of cost) also the many friends who loyally supported the work by giving according to their ability and whose praise is recorded above. Considerable difficulty had to be overcome in the course of construction. The front wall having fallen down when partly built and the foundation having to be renewed at a depth of ten feet below the present surface – but Faith and Perseverance WON."

"In 1893 the schools were further extended and three more class-rooms built, all being carried out on the same substantial scale. There remains a large plot of land occupied at the back which will be useful for further extensions and yet the total cost of all including site and construction, up to the present time has only been about £2,000. It must, however, be remembered that all the stone was quarried on the site itself during the ministry of Reverends Bailey and Haliday 1883 to 1885."

Revival in the 1880s
"A revival broke out at Bozeat during the time of Reverends Bailey and Haliday which continued during the stay of Reverends Davis and Bate. At that time a hundred persons might be seen at the 7 o'clock Prayer Meeting and the Class Meeting having as many as 27 present, would take two hours to meet. On a certain Sunday in March 1885 as a result of this Revival a novel service was held at Bozeat when 27 members were recognised publicly. This was referred to at the Quarterly Meeting and the further remarks made that such services tend to deepen the feelings of responsibility in the younger members of our Church and to encourage the older ones in showing that their labours are not in vain in the Lord."

The Sunday School grows
"The Sunday School work has marvellously grown in Bozeat since the days of Brother Talbot and a few others began it in 1835. There are now 235 Scholars in October 1894 and Bozeat ranked third in the Circuit as regards numbers, Earls Barton being first with 348, Irchester second with 285 and Wellingborough having 219. Wellingborough has however about a hundred young men and women in adult

Methodist Church Sunday School room, now used for the playgroup. (D. Roberts)

classes, not included in these figures. A tablet in the School Room tells of the death on 9th November 1888 aged 65 years of William Pettit who was teacher and Superintendent for 40 years, an unassuming worker all his life. Other Superintendents were William Shrive, Jonathan Drage, James Robinson, Mr Bradshaw, Mr Monk, Mr Walter Maxwell, J. T. Drage, W. J. Hayes, Harry Partridge, A. Dunmore, William Partridge, A. Deverill and Jonathan Burrage."

In conclusion
Apart from the final list of names just given, from this history particular families stand out in the leadership of Bozeat Methodism – the Riseleys in the first half and the Wykes and later the Maxwells in the latter part of the 19th century to be followed at the turn of the century by the family of John Drage the Shoe Manufacturer at Arch Villa in the High Street (now the Paper Shop) – not forgetting its initial establishment of Methodism with Susannah Church and Glebe Cottage.

Looking forward into the 20th century, the best of Methodism is typified in Thomas Percy Roberts born in Bozeat in 1880, a shoe operative working in Bozeat shoe factories all his life until he retired in 1947 aged 67 and who died at the age of 73 in 1953. He was one of Bozeat's most notable public figures in the first half of the 20th century – an ardent Methodist being a Lay Preacher for 35 years. He was also chairman of the School Managers and Parish Council being a member for 35 years, and in the last six years of his life represented Bozeat on the Rural Council, as well as a member of the St John's Ambulance Brigade for 50 years. He was also Sunday School Superintendent for 30 years as well as serving for a time as Society Steward and represented the church on various circuit committees. During the Second War he was secretary for the village parcel fund and helped raise £1,100 to send gifts to servicemen.

But we must not forget that great company of Methodists these represent, whose stirring faith and sense of social responsibility have contributed so much to the making of modern Bozeat over the past two centuries. The continuing story of Methodism is told through the Memories of Percy Roberts' son Don and his wife Dolly as well as of the niece and nephew of John Drage, Marjorie and Ted in Chapters 1 to 5 together with the diary of this village in the Appendix of this book.

ORIGINS OF NONCONFORMITY AND THE INDEPENDENT WESLEYAN CHAPEL

DISSENTERS IN BOZEAT

"The earliest record of nonconformity in Bozeat is given in a manuscript which exists at Stafford. It is a copy of a religious census taken in 1671 in the Province of Canterbury. 'In Bozeat there were 380 Conformists, no Papists and five families of nonconformists.' In 1731 a family named Ward took their two children, Mary and Martha, to Yardley to be baptised by Mr Drake, a dissenting Teacher. On 15th August 1746, a Dissenting Preacher, John Oram, was buried in Bozeat Churchyard. These most probably were all Baptists. It is not certain where the Baptists first met before the present Chapel in Church Lane was built in 1844." (*Marlow* p.48.)

This Baptist Chapel was constructed for a congregation of 50. It was known as 'The Meeting House', so Meeting Yard may have been the area to the side. The front (pulpit) end was up the hill, and the entrance was from the bottom end. The cottage next to it, down the hill before Homestead Farm, was a cottage in which lived a real village character known as Johnny 'Hard Hat' Pettit – because he always wore a bowler hat! In its last years, as numbers dwindled, the Baptist chapel ceased to be a place of worship, and it was used as a hall to be hired out, and as the St John Ambulance Room from 1943. It was pulled down in the 1960s, as Tom Partridge-Underwood remembers. Behind it (away from the road) was a row of cottages where leather workers lived and their yard behind them was their way out, via Pudding Bag. On the far side of their yard (which was always full of washing lines, as Tom remembers) were the barns or shops where they did their tanning, and Jack Tebbut, the rag-and-bone-man used to live in one of the cottages. The cottages were demolished at the same time as the Chapel, but the 'shops' are still standing, and the Council is now trying to get preservation orders on them. It is no wonder that, when they pulled down the Chapel, the two cottages they built in its place were named Tanyard Cottages. One of the most prominent members of the Baptist chapel was William Garrett, the butcher, whose family story we have followed.

Baptist Chapel in Church Lane, now demolished. The site is now in Tanyard Cottages' gardens.
(*Bozeat School Scrapbook*)

INDEPENDENT WESLEYAN CHAPEL

To quote from a newspaper cutting on the occasion of the funeral of Mr Thomas Wallis: 'In 1849, the year of the great Reform agitation in the Wesleyan Church, Mr Thomas Wallis, of Bozeat, was expelled from the Wesleyan Church for leading the class of another leader, who was suspected of sympathy with the reformers. This compelled him to throw in his lot with the movement. He became a local leader in the Reform Movement, taking an active part in the foundation of the Wellingborough Circuit.' He was for 50 years a local preacher and died in 1901, aged 83.

Mr Gilbert at the Mill was also associated with Mr Wallis in forming the Independent Branch in 1852. The chief financier was Mr Stevens, of Strixton, uncle of the late John Gibbard. Mr Stevens built the first Chapel (1861) on a plan that would enable it to be turned into two cottages if not successful as a Chapel. On 31st May 1862, the Wellingborough Circuit of Wesleyan Reformers united themselves to the Reform Union. Moved by James Parker of Wellingborough, seconded by Thomas Wallis of Bozeat, the Chairman of the meeting being Ezra Lack. By 1882 the Chapel building was paid for (over £180) and the Porch added, on which was placed the date 1882. Also the School-room was added at this time.

Thomas Wallis was the blacksmith from Finedon whom we have already met, and his family who owned Glebe Cottage up Church Lane and had the shop there. Was Mr Lack, Headmaster of Bozeat School during the Second War and who attended this chapel related to the Mr Lack in this story?

The chapel went through a total refurbishment in 1991 modernising it and giving it a contemporary and comfortable feel together with a kitchen, and the school-room has had a complete restoration in 1999. Also in 1999 the chapel looks forward to having its first (non-stipendiary) minister ever, the Revd Geoffrey Lee, from Milton Keynes, who is to be inducted on 25th September 1999, and was

The earliest known picture of the Independent Wesleyan Chapel, with the founder Thomas Wallis.

sometime a tutor at London Bible College. The leadership of the chapel today consists of Tom and Sue Partridge-Underwood, Gloria Wallis, sisters Lyndis Payne and Ellie Minney, and Marjorie Stamford. It is the venue for the Windmill Singers, the Over 60s Club, the Parish Council, the Women's Institute and the United Women's Fellowship (alternating with the Methodist Church). In 2002 it celebrated its 150th anniversary.

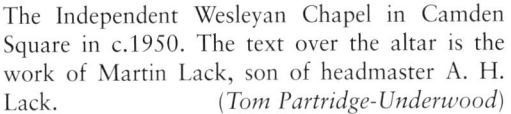

Thomas Wallis and his wife Elizabeth.

The Independent Wesleyan Chapel in Camden Square in c.1950. The text over the altar is the work of Martin Lack, son of headmaster A. H. Lack. *(Tom Partridge-Underwood)*

Independent Wesleyan Chapel, 'Little Bethel' in 1953. *(Bozeat School Scrapbook)*

Others seeking after religion

After the First World War, spiritualist meetings were popular as people sought to make contact with their dead soldier loved-ones. We have already seen how many young men in the village went to war and how many never came back. It was not surprising therefore to find in the 1920s and '30s two spiritualist meeting places, one at the top of Mile Street, and one up Dychurch. Another religious group that appeared after the Great War was 'The Brotherhood of the Royal Antediluvian Order of Buffaloes', a working-man's Masonic movement, with Arnold Howarth taking a leading role. This continued until 1990, although Arnold still wore his sash and emblem on Remembrance Days in the 1990s.

CHAPTER 22

The Church of St Mary, Bozeat

St Mary's Church in 1914.   (*John Darker*)

My Quiet Church

The Church is quiet
The church is old
I feel alone, with no-one there except God
While I'm sitting in the pew I then think of God
Peaceful and happy
I look around and see colour and beauty
I look around and see different shapes
I feel safe in this church
I feel small in this huge great hall
Sometimes I come to church, I feel relaxed
Sometimes I feel very cold
And I call this church, My quiet church

Daniel Bayes, Bozeat Primary School, aged 10 (1995)

A treasure in stone
The survival of enormous numbers of medieval churches in almost every part of Europe is a remarkable expression of the faith of that period for "in all sorts of ways their site and setting, their design and style and ornament, have much to tell us of the interests and devotion of their builders. They also disguise the hidden world of the

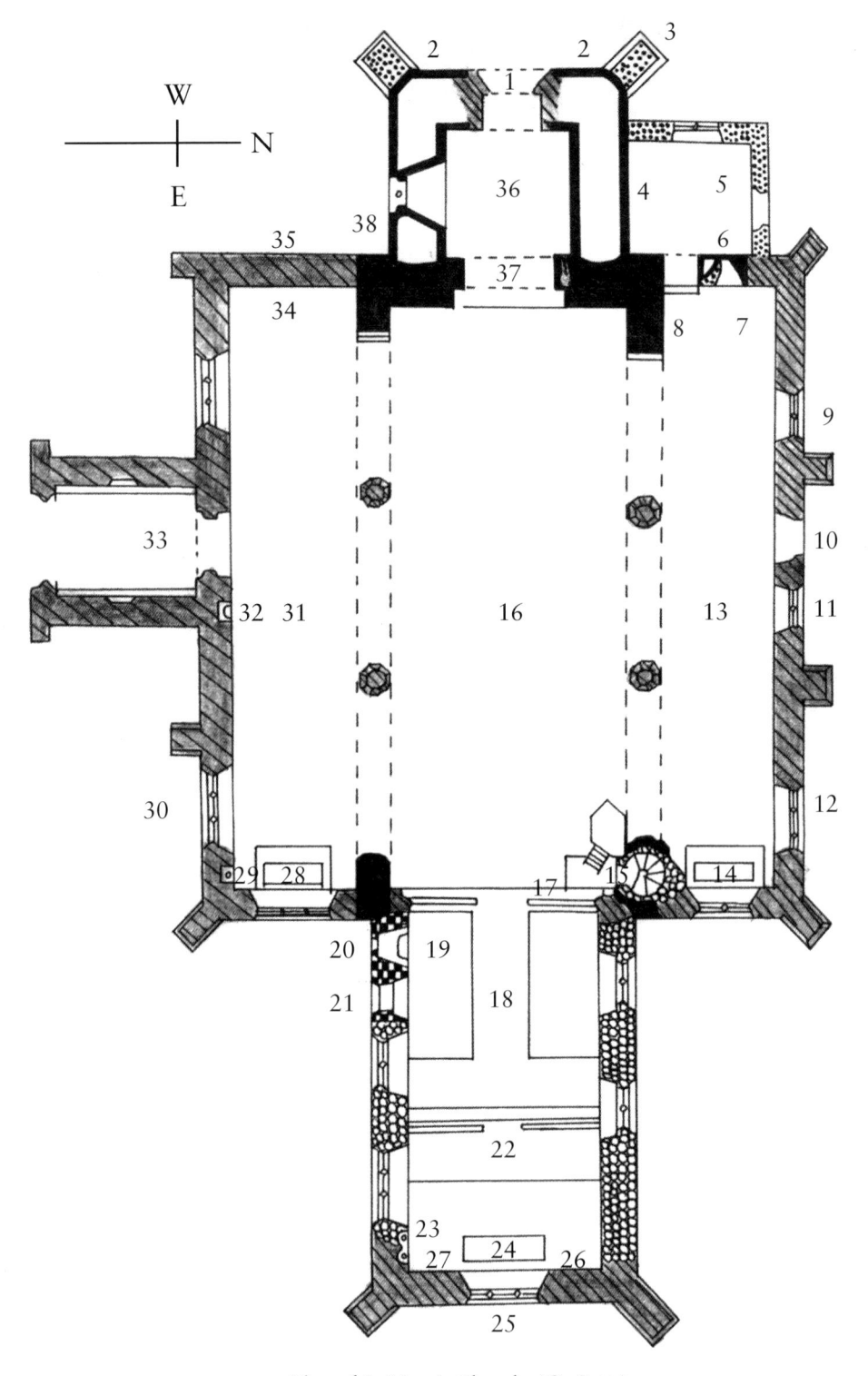

Plan of St Mary's Church. (*G. Betts*)

Key to numbered locations

1. West Door with Ogee window c.1420 above it.
2. Heads on west wall are possibly of Henry V and wife Catherine, or Lord and Lady Latimer. Both men were at Agincourt. (Marlow's History p. 19f)
3. Time capsule behind stone with crosses, 1883.
4. Toilet 1992.
5. Kitchen 1992, with toilet was previously the old vestry and boiler room.
6. Leper window.
7. Organ Loft with pipes of the Yates organ.
8. Names of the 210 men who fought in the First World War.
9. Window restored in 1994, donated by the Dilley family.
10. North Door (the Devil's door) in front of which is the Church Chest 1680.
11. Stained glass window by Geoffrey Webb 1921.
12. Window restored in 1995, donation by Botterill family.
13. North Aisle 14th century with original oak beam roof and elegant tracery around its east window.
14. Victorian altar given in memory of Vicar Seeker 1894.
15. Spiral staircase which once lead to Rood Loft (15th century).
16. Nave with 15th century oak pews and piece of old roof on which is carved "1680 WD WS CW RH" (William Dodson and William Surridge were Churchwardens CW).
17. Rood Screen with damaged medieval paintings.
18. Choir.
19. Consol of the Yates organ.
20. Blocked-in Priest's (early English?) window.
21. Blocked-in Priest's door (clearly visible from outside).
22. Sanctuary.
23. Medieval combined Piscina (bowl and drain) and Credence (table for bread and wine).
24. Mahogany Communion table in Jacobean style given by Mr and Mrs Taylor in 1948.
25. East window in memory of Thomas Revis 1869.
26, 27. Lord's Prayer and Ten Commandments on tin sheets.
28. St Catherine's Chapel with remains of wall carvings, now used as War Memorial including that to Lt. John Ahern.
29. Piscina for south aisle altar.
30. Millennium window 2000.
31. South Aisle with parts of original roof and with east and south west windows of the perpendicular period, 14th century with reticulated tracery.
32. Holy water stoup.
33. 14th cent Porch with beautiful tracery over its pointed arch.
34. Baptismal Font which fits the description in a Church Terrier of 1736: "1 stone font lind (i.e. lined) with lead & decent cover of wood."
35. Rose window, early 15th century, an exact replica of the original, carved in 1995.
36. Norman Tower (with new vestry and belfry floor 1995) and Spire.
37. Original 13th century Norman Arch on wall, above which is Coat of Arms George III 1770 where once was the Musicians Gallery.
38. Brick Cross on ground where skeleton of a priest was found, possibly that of Vicar Barlow, died 1794.

heretic, the blasphemer, the drop out, and the pagan." (Rosalind and Christopher Brooke, *Popular Religion in the Middle Ages*, Thames & Hudson, 1988, p.63) The formation of new parishes became fixed in many parts of Europe in the 12th century (when our church was built) when the uneven process of development became fossilised through the "strengthening of Episcopal authority, which made the informal establishment of parishes impossible, and of the Church's courts and Canon laws, which provided a legal framework much more difficult to break." (*ibid* p.82)

Who built our church?
It is unfortunate that we are not able to trace who built our Church but the date of its foundation is about 1100 to 1120. At the Norman Conquest (1066), William the Conqueror gave most of the land around here to his niece Judith. Judith's daughter, Matilda had two husbands. The first was Simon de Senlis, Earl of Huntingdon, a great Crusader who died in the Second Crusade. In 1113 she married David who became King of Scotland in 1124. In the Survey of Henry II completed in 1154 it says: "In Boseyate King David of Scotland holds 2 hides (120 acres). There was a rule even from Saxon times that an owner of substantial land must not only attend to the material wants of his tenants but also to their spiritual needs. So it is likely that Matilda and her husbands gave instruction and money for the building of the Church of St Mary at this time. And they would use local stone, as from the quarry field at the Harrold side of the village (now owned by Len Holt). Some of the foundation stones are massive – some 4 by 3 foot blocks – and so difficult to bring from a distance. Villagers would most likely have been involved in its building and the more artistic of them have carved the humorous characters that decorate the top of the tower.

The whole stone edifice would be built up on these huge stones without further foundations, so the building literally floats on its clay and gravel bed, and has stood like this for nearly 900 years – see note at the end of this section. Its dedication to St Mary tells us that the date it was consecrated by the Bishop of Lincoln was 26th August, the Festival on which, ever since, has been known as Bozeat Feast Day.

The vicarage is ordained
In 1220 Bishop Hugh of Lincoln (originally Hugh of Avalon) 'ordained' the Vicarage of Bozeat, along with about 300 others, out of concern that there was no one to take services in many of the village churches in his diocese. The man ordained to be the first Vicar at that time was Ralph who was here for 38 years. Since then Bozeat has always had its own Vicar, the present (1999) one being the 67th. This does not include the two 'Intruders' installed here by Cromwell from 1655 until possibly the Restoration of the Monarchy in 1660 and it is worth noting that Bozeat was able to support a curate from 1756 to 1766 and 1795 to 1825 in addition to the vicar.

The original structure
The original structure (little more than a dark, clumsy, stone box in Romanesque style) would have consisted of the Nave, a small Chancel stretching to just beyond the Priest's Door and Window (still clearly visible from the outside) and the square Norman Tower. The craze for building Spires came two centuries later, and over 90% of those built on Norman Towers collapsed, for these towers were never built to support such massive stone structures! Ours fell down in 1877 (its wall being only

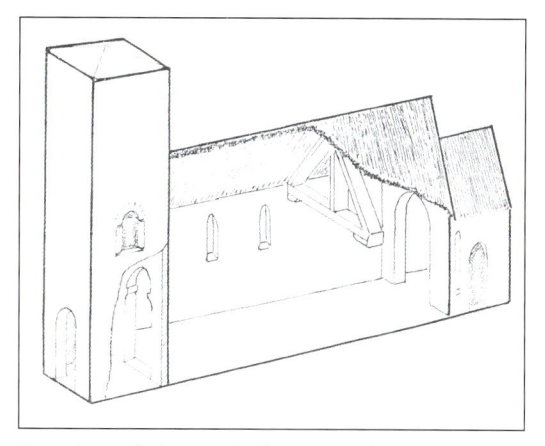

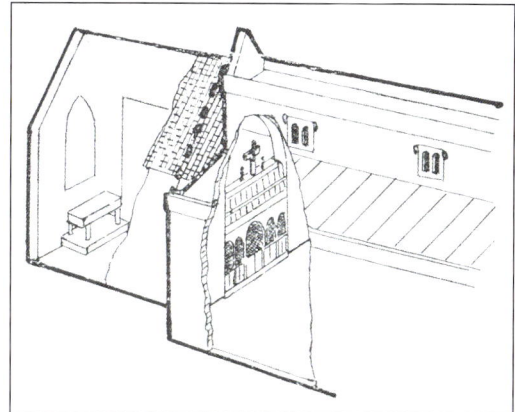

Drawing of the original St Mary's as it was in Norman times. (*N. Palmer*)

Drawing of the expanded St Mary's, post c.1400AD. (*N. Palmer*)

four feet thick) after repeated warnings, and was rebuilt in 1883, the oldest bell recast (presumably damaged in the fall), the whole peal re-hung and the old clock dating from the end of the 17th century (only a few decades after the Dutchman Huygen's invented the escapement which made such clocks possible) repaired at a total cost of £1,000 – taking 13 months to complete. The Tower contains a beautiful Ogee window dating from about 1420, the West Door to the Tower being from the same period, and the two carved heads on the mouldings round the window probably represent King Henry V and his French wife Catherine.

Expansion

The original roof to the Nave and Chancel would have been a steep sided thatch – the stone supports of which are still visible along the Nave walls. In the middle of the 14th century, mortified by the Black Death in 1348/9 which reduced the population of England from 4 million to 2 million, but also reflecting the increasing wealth and developing piety in the 12th and 13th centuries, churches were enlarged and beautified and ours was no exception. In addition to the Spire, a Clerestory was added to the Nave, giving greater height, ventilation and light and the Chancel extended eastwards to its present size. (The old Priest's Door and part of the long narrow window adjacent to it used for confessions have been blocked up but are still clearly visible from the outside.) The Nave walls were pierced leaving us the two rows of pillars and the creation of a North and South Aisle.

The stone seats running along the sides of the porch remind us that the Church Porch played an important part in the life of the community in the Middle Ages. Its date is 14th century. Excommunicants had to stay here for they would not be allowed to enter the church (or they would watch the celebration of Holy Communion from the slit-like window in the north-west corner, which may have been one of the purposes of this so called Leper's Window). Here were held burial services, the first part of the marriage service (the vows) and inquests. The first schools were often held in the church porch. Here also the parish elders met and business was transacted, a reminder of which are the Parish Council notices which may still be seen there. Miracle or mystery plays would possibly be staged here with the audience in the churchyard.

A fashion in furniture

The internal south porch doorway – a richly moulded pointed arch – is early 14th century and one of the most beautiful features of the church.

"A fashion came in with the 14th century in many parts of Europe for much more elaborate furniture of wood than had hitherto been used." (*ibid* p.83). So, as in many churches, our Chancel became separated from the Nave by a Late English Decorated Rood Screen on whose panels can still be seen medieval paintings, two showing Adam and Eve being driven from the Garden of Eden, two of the Angel Gabriel announcing to Mary the birth of her Son, two of the Adoration of the Magi and two of the Baptism of Jesus by John the Baptist. The spiral stone staircase to the left of the Screen was the way up to the Rood Loft – a platform on which would be a life sized Crucifix with life sized statues of Mary and St John standing on either side. The paintings show evidence of vandalism probably by the swords of Cromwell's soldiers who with their horses may well have barracked in our church. There is certainly damage to pedestals, all the statues have been destroyed, and there are signs of damage, possibly by the horses, to our ancient pews which are 15th century and the first to be installed – with holes for rushlights and all (one church inventory of gifts reads: "Torches given by Joan Bluet, 1512"). So did our church, as many did, have its fire due "to candles guttering in draughty churches", ornaments of wood and linen cloths stored under altars" (*ibid* p.90).

During 1896-8 the Nave Roof was extensively repaired for about £700 and one piece of the old roof was inserted in the middle beam and is carved: "1680 WD WS CW RH" – William Dodson and William Surridge possibly the Churchwardens

Rood screen in St Mary's showing medieval paintings. (*Vicars' Logbook*)

The Church chest dated 1686.

(CW). After RH there is: IF J.C(?) IHC on a metal plate, which may well be from an older beam. If so we have a record of three periods of the roof on that beam since the thatched roof was removed on building the Clerestory.

Our fine oak church chest dates from 1686 on which is carved: "H. Partridge. J. Macknis CW 1686". One of its three padlocks is one of the original handmade locks for which we still have the key. Our Communion Chalice and Platen date from earlier in this same century (1636) at a time when Archbishop Laud was seeking to raise the standards of church ornamentation and worship. If Vicar Drake had only kept the Parish Register in this chest rather than in his Vicarage it would not have been lost in the great fire of 1729 and with it much of the history of the village since possibly 1538 when Thomas Cromwell ordered that all Parishes keep such Registers.

It was fortunate too that Vicar Pizey removed the Organ from the Minstrels Gallery fixed to the East wall of the Tower and placed it in the Chancel when he restored the Chancel in 1875 largely at his own expense. "A small gallery is at the west end, on which was formerly the organ, which has recently been removed to the north side of the chancel. The chancel was restored in 1873-4 at the expense of the vicar, assisted by the lay proprietor, at a cost of £400, including an organ." (Whellan, *History of Northamptonshire*, 1874 p.909) Otherwise it would have been destroyed along with the Gallery when the Tower fell in 1877. The pipes from this old organ were used by the well-known organ builder Roger Yates (b.1905, apprenticed with Henry Willis III – see *Organist Review*, Nov. 1993) when he built our fine present organ in the NW corner of the church, completed in September 1939 at the outbreak of the Second World War and one of the first to have an electro-acoustic operation.

The Ten Commandments are fixed to the east wall of the church in the sanctuary, alongside the east window. They are thought to have been given by Mr Thomas Revis, the owner of the Estate, as church accounts show: Mr Revis, cheque on account of the 10 Commandments as per agreement, £6. 1872, 1 year's ditto, £3. 1872, ditto, £3. 1874, last instalment, £3. equals £15. They are beautifully painted on a long sheet of tin, in black and red paint in classical ornate Gothic style. The Lord's Prayer is on a similar sheet on the right side of the window. They both look to be from the same time and artist.

Let there be light
The 14th century flooded our church with light as windows pierced the gloomy walls of its dull Norman interior, matched only by the simultaneous increase in spaciousness and faith as its frame was pushed upwards and outwards by the elegance of early English architecture.

The North Aisle dates from that century and all its three windows have the flat heads and tracery typical of this period. At its east end there is a beautiful window of two lights with well designed tracery, almost identical to that found in Barnwell Church, Northants, suggesting the work is by the same itinerant craftsman.

The South Aisle at its south west end, and the chancel at its east end possess two windows alike in design, the tracery of reticule or 'net' pattern largely used in the 14th century and founded upon the equilateral triangle and the hexagon.

In the 15th century a further new style of architecture arose, called the Perpendicular style, and to this period belong all the windows along the sides of the chancel.

The window at the east end of the south aisle and the tower door and window above it are also from this Perpendicular period. This latter window was probably inserted to gain light and in the beautiful ogee style – ogee defined as "a wave-like moulding having an inner and outer curve; a pointed arch, each side of which is formed of a concave and convex curve." This window was put in about 1420 after the battle of Agincourt in AD 1415 and the two heads on the external mouldings of the window may represent Henry and his French wife Catherine. (after *Palmer*)

Stained glass
There are still traces of medieval stained glass in the Chancel typified by its garish hues. Our East Window tells the sad story of Thomas Revis, son of the Manor, who took his own life at the age of only 36 on 11th February 1869, when forbidden to marry the village girl with whom he had fallen in love. The modern (1921) stained glass in the North Aisle is one of the best examples of Geoffrey Webb's work (note his signature – the spider's web!). The windows on either side were in a dangerous state of disrepair and were renovated in 1994 and 1995 through the generosity of the Botterill and the Dilley families respectively, the work being carried out by Bryant & Sharman of Wellingborough (Dave Bryant who spent the early months of 1996 rebuilding windows on St George's Chapel, Windsor Castle after it was gutted by fire in 1993 said to me of these two windows: "You've got the same Polish glass in yours that I've been putting into St George's!"). So our church has examples of Medieval, Victorian and Modern stained glass.

Recent restoration – 1970s to 1990s
Considerable restoration work was carried out in the 1970s and '80s both to the exterior stonework and the old pews, during the time when Norman Palmer was Vicar. Earth excavations which he carried out to a depth of 15 inches revealed the base of the original walls lying between pillars at the middle and eastern ends on both sides of the nave. During the 1990s, restoration work on the South Wall and Parapet

was completed. Handfuls of ivy roots, which had once covered the south side of the church earlier in the 20th century and in the previous, were pulled out from behind the brickwork and were probably responsible for much of the damage to the stone, aggravated by the fact that the wall had been rendered in the past, sealing in the moisture. The more recent restoration work was carried out by Bowden & Ward, who in 1995 rebuilt part of the southern parapet, scoured the vicarage garden, etc. for stones to repair the south aisle wall and carved an exact replica of the disintegrating Rose Window dating from the early 15th century on the south-west wall under the direction of our Architect, Bruce Deacon.

Modernising the facilities

During the last decade of the Millennium much work has been done to improve the building for its use in worship and related activities.

In 1991/2 Faculties were obtained to convert the old vestry into a kitchen and toilet and to install a gas-fired/radiator central heating system to replace the oil-fired industrial hot air blower which was bought second-hand by the church in about 1976 and gave up in the autumn of 1992. In that year a large trench was dug to the vicarage to take water mains and a soil pipe, and gas, which came to the Village in 1991, was laid on to the Church. The old vestry was built in 1894 to hold the boiler for a hot air system of heating and contemporary records say how well the extension fitted in with the character of the church. This system was afterwards replaced by stoves and the old heating boiler chamber turned into a vestry on 27th September 1923. Also, from 1992 to 1995, extensive upgrading and improvements to the electrical system (under the supervision of Richard Zang) were made. The heating system went operational in March 1993 and was installed by Housdens of Bedford. Much of the work for all these schemes was carried out by men in the village (Gordon Brannon leads our men's working group) using professional skills in the village (e.g. Arnold Dobbs our builder), considerably reducing the overall cost. The heating system cost £14,000 and the kitchen/toilet around £7,000.

In 1992 the Borough of Wellingborough installed floodlighting at the Church. During our building work the old iron bar which held the Lych Gate Lantern was unearthed. Derek Cox with his son James, then blacksmith at Castle Ashby, made us a new lantern and now it is wired up to the floodlighting system to illuminate the main entrance into the Churchyard.

In 1993 an induction loop for those with hearing aids and sound enhancement system with radio microphone and sound recording and reproduction was installed by B & J Stevenson of Cambridge for £2,000, given in memory of Norman Bligh, the vicar's father, himself having been an electrical engineer.

Revival in the belfry

In 1994 a dream began to come true when a Faculty was granted to build a new Ringing Platform in the Tower creating a Vestry beneath and opening the way for the a sixth bell to be added to the Belfry. Donald Loe, Churchwarden of Abington Church, gave us of his professional services in the design of the platform and plate glass screen (supplied by Northampton Glass) and the work was carried out by Robert Hollowell of Cogenhoe and completed in September 1994 at an overall cost of around £5,000. The new treble bell was cast on Friday 24th March at 13.30 hours at the foundry of John Taylor of Loughborough and installed by Whites of Appleton,

West end interior of St Mary's showing new vestry with glass door with ringing platform above.

after considerable preparation and finishing work by Rex Line (Tower Captain) and his team of helpers, and was rung for the first time for worship on 26th November 1995. It hangs alongside the oldest (No. 3) bell dated c.1450 and recast by Taylors in 1885, No. 4 cast in 1605, No. 6 in 1633, No. 5 in 1635 and No. 2 purchased in 1723 for £37-10s-0d. Compare this with the cost of our new bell and fittings of around £4,000, a total of £10,000 including installation. The new bell was consecrated along with the dedication of the other bells and the Ringing Platform by the Bishop of Brixworth on 31st January 1996 in the presence of the Mayor and Mayoress of Wellingborough, Councillor and Mrs John Watts, and members of the Parish Council. (For more details see Chapter 23.)

Furniture for today
Finally a word should be said concerning church furniture. Much of the oakwork in the church from the last century was carried out by Undertakers and Carpenters Bert (W. H.) Cave and his son Tom. It was Bert who with his son made the aisle pews and choir stalls which were installed in 1938/9. ("Mr Cave deserves our praise for the excellency of his work. He can be justly proud." *Vicar Marlow*) More recently they made the bishop's chair and sanctuary chair. It was, however, Marriotts who made the War Memorial. It was in about 1938 that Bert met by accident in the street one day with a young man who was a carpenter from the village and out of work and said to him, "Don't be out of work. We've got plenty of work to do!" So he went to work for Cave's for most of his career doing much work in church and chapels as well in houses, particularly those built by Alfred Underwood of Wollaston who worked in collaboration with Caves. His name was Ted Drage. In particular in 1992 Ted made

the two oak chairs given by Cyril Morgan (Lay Reader) in memory of his wife Edna, and in 1994 the oak Vestry table and chair given by Lynne Houghton and her husband Ian in memory of her parents Harold and Mavis Bates.

And we should not forget the beautiful new carpet which the church has bought and had laid at a cost of £2,989 which was laid ready to welcome the vicar in January 1998 on his return with his wife Audrey after his nine-month exchange in Australia working as Rector of Holy Cross, Hacket, in Canberra; neither should we forget the completion of the new spot and floodlighting system for the chancel, choir and east end of the nave, installed and fitted by men of the church with the expert help of Richard Zang.

Still alive and well

In its 900 years our Church has seen the most remarkable changes in the social and religious life of England and our village, of which it stands as a permanent record and testimony. Gone are the days as in the 18th century when "the whole village met together with their best Faces, and in their cleanest Habits" at the Parish Church for Sunday Worship. But despite the continual decline in church attendance (as in most organisations) over recent years, St Mary's still plays an active part in the life of our Village. Presently (1999) its elected officers are: Tim Hickling and Kath Silsy (Churchwardens), Alison Botterill (Treasurer), Pat Summers (Secretary) with Penny Brannon as Licensed Lay Reader and our two Pastoral Assistants, Anne Hickling and Pat Smith.

NOTE: Foundations of the Church Tower
(From a newspaper article of the time, 1882/3)
"The church tower is now all down, the foundations are dug out, and all is in readiness for the foundations, which are to be of brick and concrete. The old foundations were remarkably curious. Their depth and thickness were about 5 ft. On the rock was a thick layer of clay; on this a row of ordinary stones was placed end ways, the sharp points bedded in the clay, and the whole closely packed together without mortar or cement of any kind. This bottom row leaned at an angle of 45 degrees from south to north. Then came a layer of road dirt about 4 in. thick; on this was placed another row of stones, the sharp points again bedded in the dirt, but leaning in the opposite direction to the bottom row. On this was placed another layer of road dirt, and another row of stones was set on this, leaning in the same direction as the bottom row. At the corners on the north-west and south-west, the middle row of stones, instead of being inclined from north to south, was inclined from east to west. No mortar of any kind was used between any of the stones in the three rows, but not a stone had given way, and all stood as they did when put in seven hundred years ago, thus showing that the architect was right when he said that the tower had been crushed between its heavy spire and rocky foundation. It is very probable that the first church and this tower was built by the villagers, under the direction of the priest, for there was no skilled work of any kind, the tower simply being four walls, each four feet thick, with a door leading into the church. The window and door which were inserted in the 15th century, and half of which were covered up by the huge buttress erected in 1753, were found to be perfect and will be put up again, and a beautiful little Norman window was found in the south side of the tower, under the many coats of plaster which have been used at various times to hide the cracks in the walls."

NOTE: The Mass and Medieval Piety

Eamon Duffey (*The Stripping of the Altars*, Yale Univ. Press, 1992) writing of medieval pity and the Mass in 15th/16th century England notes that "... for most people, most of the time the Host (sacramental bread) was something to be seen, not to be consumed. Since the end of the 12th century it had been customary for the consecrating priest to elevate the Host high above his head immediately after sacring (the repetition of the words of institution, *Hoc est enim Corpus Meum* which brought about the miracle of transubstantiation) for adoration by the people." (*ibid*) This was the heartland of medieval lay spirituality. To participate only once a year on Easter Day was no deprivation when you could say "This day I have seen My Maker" in the elevation of the Host everyday in the daily Mass, e.g. in the dawn or 'morrow' Mass for servants, labourers and travellers. This moment was the central embodiment for faith for our village folk centuries. And our Rood Screen was not so much a barrier or a blind but a beautiful and ornate framework to heighten the drama to be viewed through it (some such screens have peep holes deliberately drilled through them to ensure the faithful in the nave can see all that is happening). Our so-called Leper Window is a powerful reminder of this fact for it enabled those outside the building excluded for whatever reason (disease or disgrace?) to participate as it is exactly positioned to enable the Host held high above the celebrant's head to be seen as he stood in front of the stone altar facing east. So in medieval art it was the moment of elevation of the Host which is almost invariably depicted. (p.96) We find too that it is the provision of good wax lights, and especially of torches which burned from the Elevation to the Agnus Dei, that became one of the most common of all activities of the guilds.

It was also very common "for individual testators to specify that the torches burned around their corpses at their funerals should be given to the parish church, to be burned around the altar at the sacring time, forming a sort of proxy for the adoring presence of the donor close by the Sacrament at the moment of elevation." Similarly gifts of kerchiefs or bed linen to make altar cloths or corprases were "a gesture clearly designed to bring the domestic intimacies into direct contact with the Host." (ibid) These insights give us a glimpse into the world of the inventory of gift to Bozeat Church in the 16th century as listed for us by *Marlow* (1936, p.16) and enable us to appreciate their significance:

1516: To the image of Holy Mary of Pity (i.e. statue in the deep recess at east end of North Aisle), my best bridal veil, Isobella Kendale.

1512: To the Altar of S Catherine (below her statue on one of the remaining corbels at east end of South Aisle), a linen cloth, Joan Bluet.

1521: Agnes Everton to be buried before the image of the Blessed Trinity (on the damaged ledge just to the north of the present pulpit).

1528: Towards the buying of candlesticks for the Loft.... T Luatt.

1521: To the Sepulchre light, a schyppe (sheep), Richard Everton.
To the Sepulchre light, one bushel barley, Rofe Aberge.

1505: I leave to the Church of Bozeat one cloth equal to linen, and my best bridal veil to be made into a Corporal, Alice Plowright.
Torches given by Joan Bluet, 1512; J. Brygg, 1525."

CHAPTER 23

Bells and Bell-ringers

THE BELLS OF ST MARY'S
Rex Line

The art of bellmaking

Anyone who has seen church bells at close quarters must marvel at the skill displayed by bell founders in centuries past. The decorations and inscriptions on many early bells is pure artistry, and the problems associated with casting them, often on site, and then hanging them in towers up to 100 feet above ground must have been considerable.

Many of the early founders were itinerant, casting their bells in church or churchyard, preparing the frames and fittings whilst the bells cooled and then lifting the bells up the tower and hanging them in their allotted places in the frame – before moving on to the next town or village which had work for them. This way of working would have raised many problems. In particular the vitally important clay for the moulds would vary from place to place and failures would have been common. So eventually permanent foundries were built on sites where raw materials were either ready to hand or could be easily transported in. The Whitechapel Bell Foundry in London, which is only a short walk from Tower Bridge, has been casting bells for over 400 years.

Bells are cast by pouring molten metal (a mixture of brass and tin) into a clay mould, the inscriptions and decorations which are to appear on the bell having been pressed into the mould before the clay set. Metal hoops, known as canons, were cast into the crown of the bell to provide for its attachment to a wooden headstock or axle, but with the introduction of steel headstocks it became more convenient to dispense with these canons and in recent years many were removed when bells were re-hung. This was the case with our bells when they were re-hung in 1947. The note of the bell is determined by its size, shape and thickness, and it can be tuned in one direction only, by lowering the note. This is achieved by removing metal from the inside of the bell to make it thinner. In the past the bell founder would chip the metal away with mallet and chisel, tuning by ear to the other bells; a risky operation as a heavy-handed approach could result in the bell being cracked. Nowadays tuning is more precise with electronic equipment being used to measure the vibration frequency of the bell and hence its note, the metal being removed in a large vertical lathe at the bell foundry.

The art of bell-ringing

The ringing of the bells 'in peal', swinging them full-circle with rope and wheel, is a peculiar English art, and a very ancient one, which developed in the early 17th century and has now spread all over the English-speaking world. Requiring as it does a team of people willing to work together, with calmness, perseverance and a sense of order, it seems to appeal to, and spring from, some special qualities in the English character.

It is an art which calls for skill rather than physical strength, a keen ear, and loyalty like the Christian life. Its only standard is a perfection which is rarely attained but should always be striven for, and a good ringer is one who never stops learning or trying to do better – like a good Christian. It produces the most powerful and far-reaching music made by man, and the loudest sound that man makes for no other purpose than the glory of God. In a world full of noises which man makes for his own profit or glorification, this is no small testimony.

Bells hung for ringing vary in weight from less than 1 cwt (50kg) to over 4 tons (4,000kg), and chiming or clock bells can be much heavier. For example, Big Ben – which is, of course, a bell and not a clock, weighs 13½ tons. Although some bells are named, the majority of ringing bells are known only by their number, where the highest note (treble) is sounded first, followed by all the others in descending order and ending with the lowest note (tenor). Thus the six bells at Bozeat are known as treble, 2nd, 3rd, 4th, 5th and tenor. Most of the bells in our churches and cathedrals were cast between the 16th and 18th centuries although some earlier examples exist. In common with most other churches the bells of our own parish church were not installed as a set, but were added to in ones and twos over the years.

The Bells of St Mary's
No. 3
The bell was originally cast about 1450 at Bury St Edmunds and was ornately marked with flowered crests. Unfortunately it became cracked, possibly by falling masonry when part of the spire fell in 1877, and had to be recast at the Loughborough foundry of John Taylor in 1884. The crests were the trademark of the original founder so Taylors could only reproduce the inscription which now reads "*Sancta Maria Ora Nobis. Recast by John Taylor and Co. MDCCCLXXXIV*" The translation of the Latin is "Holy Mary Pray For Us". When recast it had a diameter of 34⅛ inches and weighed 7¼ cwt. This changed to 7cwt 2qrs 12lbs during the re-hanging and tuning, again by Taylors, in 1947. So this, our second newest bell, was cast from the metal of the oldest.

No. 4
This bell is now our oldest, being cast in 1605 and inscribed "*Newcombe of Leicester Made Me*" with a diameter of 38¼ inches, its weight was quoted as 9½ cwt, but after removal of canons and returning in 1947 it tipped the scales at 9 cwt 1 qr 5 lb. The discrepancy probably arises from the fact that years ago bell weights were often calculated from their dimensions and errors obviously occurred.

The Tenor (No. 6)
This was cast at Hugh Watts foundry at Leicester in 1633 with a diameter of 45¾ inches and carries the inscription *I.H.S. NAZARENUS REX JUDEORUM FILI DEI MISERERE MEI* (Jesus of Nazareth, King of the Jews, O Son of God have mercy upon me). During the 1947 overhaul its weight fell from over 17cwts to 16 cwts 2 qrs 6 lbs. This is the bell with the deepest note (E) and is the one on which the clock strikes.

No. 5
Dated 1635 with a diameter of 41⅝ inches, this bell is from the same foundry and bears the same inscription as the tenor. Originally shown as 12½ cwt, Taylors weighed it as 12 cwt 2 qr 7 lb in 1947, another instance of a bell apparently weighing much the same after the removal of fairly heavy canons.

No. 2

This bell was purchased in 1725 for £37-10s-0d, its replacement price in 1991 was estimated at around £3,000! Cast by Henry Penn of Peterborough with a diameter of 31¾ inches, it was billed at 6¼ cwt and was inscribed: *THO.DRAKE, VIC: WILL JAKES, THO.WRIGHT, CH.WARDENS: HENRY PENN, FOUNDER 1737*. The churchwardens accounts for 1723 carry an entry: "Spent with Mr Pen when he clipt ye bell 4/s." The founder evidently chiselled away about 14 lbs of metal during the tuning process, because its weight was given as 6 cwt 14 lbs by Taylors in 1884 when, together with the second, it went to the foundry for repairs. The present weight is 5 cwt 2 qrs 26 lbs.

The new tenor bell 1995 showing the names of the churchwardens and tower captain. (P. Bligh)

The Treble (No. 1)

This was cast on Friday, 24th March 1995 at 13.30 hours at the Loughborough bell foundry of John Taylor in the presence of a small party from Bozeat – [Rex and Judith Line, Tim and Anne Hickling, Tony and Helen Manktelow, Gordon Brannon, Derek Cox, Philip and Audrey Bligh and Alison Botterill. It was remarkable to watch the process of making the bell, which had not changed over the centuries. The mould which was made of dung and straw and mud, shaped with bare hands wetted with water, was then buried in sand after a similarly shaped cover was placed over it. Molten alloy poured into the gap between whilst we each had a go pushing the rod down into the space to make sure the alloy was well distributed around the mould.]

Arrival of the new bell 1995. Left to right: Pat Taylor, Audrey Bligh, Christina Downey, Edmund Downey, Cyril Morgan, Gloria Wallis, Gordon Brannon, Rex Line, Tony Manktelow. (P. Bligh)

The bell has a diameter of 29¾ inches and a weight of 5 cwt 2 qr 10 lb, sounding note C sharp, and bears the inscription: *"Thanks be to God" E II R 1995 T. Hickling K. Silsby – Church Wardens. R. Line – Captain.* The bell and its fittings cost around £4,000 and the installation was most ably carried out by Whites of Appleton, the total cost being just over £10,000. Six bells were first rung for worship on 26th November 1995 [and A Service of Thanksgiving to mark the Consecration of the new Treble Bell and Re-dedication of the Bells and new Ringing Gallery by the Bishop of Brixworth in the presence of the Mayor and Mayoress of Wellingborough, Councillor and Mrs John West, and the Parish Council, was held at 7.30 pm on Wednesday, 31st January 1996.]

As can be seen from the descriptions, church bells are heavy things and, when ready for ringing, each bell is delicately balanced upside down. It requires only a moderate pull on the rope to cause the bell to swing down and over at an alarming speed. Without skilled hands to control it, disaster can occur. Never ever pull on a bell rope until you have been taught to ring by a qualified ringer. People have been killed by bells and by becoming entangled with flying bell ropes. Even skilled ringers cannot tell just by looking at the ropes whether a bell is up and ready for ringing or down and safe. This does not mean that bell ringing is fraught with danger. Those of us who practice the art derive a great deal of satisfaction and pleasure, and even relaxation, from ringing – unlikely though it may sound!

These then are the bells of St Mary, Bozeat It is a sobering thought that when all six bells are ringing, more than 2½ tons of metal is swinging continuously over and back again 40 feet above the heads of the ringers, controlled only by six lengths of rope and the skill of the ringers. And, furthermore, each bell is swung with split-second precision in order to follow its intricate path in the interwoven patterns that produce change ringing as we know it, an art which is practised (with few exceptions) only in the British Isles.

Ringing the Changes
The simplest way of ringing bells is to ring them down the scale, with the highest note (treble) sounding first (leading), and the lowest note (tenor), sounding last (lying). This is known to ringers as ringing rounds, and is the way bells usually sound both before and after ringing changes. From ringing rounds a trainee will progress to call changes where the bells are sounded in different sequences as directed verbally by the conductor, who will usually be ringing a bell himself. It is more pleasing to the hearer to have variations in the sound rather than the monotony of continuous rounds, provided that a good rhythm is both achieved and maintained.

The next step for the aspiring ringer is to acquire the skill of guiding his or her bell through the path of a plain hunt, where the bells change place or position at each swing of the bell, this of course producing continuous changes. A plain hunt can be shown thus – the bells sounding from left to right:

```
1 2 3 4 5 6
2 1 4 3 6 5
2 4 1 6 3 5
4 2 6 1 5 3
4 6 2 5 1 3
6 4 5 2 3 1
```

```
6 5 4 3 2 1
5 6 3 4 1 2
5 3 6 1 4 2
3 5 1 6 2 4
3 1 5 2 6 4
1 3 2 5 4 6
1 2 3 4 5 6
```

The bells will have rung several rows of rounds before the order 'Go Plain Hunt' is given, when at the next handstroke blow the bells will all start to plain hunt. If we follow the sequence of bell No. 2 we see that it follows a zigzag line with flattened turning points and the other bells follow similar zigzag paths. [Rex Line has acquired the software and developed the hardware for ringers to practise one at a time if needs be by watching the screen and ringing their bell at the right moment, but the sound you hear for all the bells is made by the computer as the clappers on the actual bells being rung are clamped so as not to disturb the neighbours! The computer prints out the table above with your number highlighted so you can see how well you are doing. The system came into operation in May 1999.]

With six bells the maximum number of changes is 6x5x4x3x2x1=720 and this is known as 'the Extent on Six'. With 7 bells it is 5040. A peal is defined by the Central Council of Bell-ringers as a true Extent on Seven Bells, or a minimum of 5,000 changes on any other number of bells. This will take approximately three hours on Bozeat bells, and a list of all the peals on these bells is as follows.
[Additions by Philip Bligh.]

Peal record (as from record book)
1. The First Peal ever on the bells was rung on Saturday 23rd November 1912, in 3 hours 7 minutes with 5,040 changes. Composition: Grandsire. Ringers: Henry Gayton (Treble), Arthur Minney (2), Charles Fairey (3), Edwin Jones (4), Henry Fowler (Tenor). Conductor: Harry Fowler.
2. Saturday, 28th February 1931, in 3 hours 3 minutes with 5,040 changes. Composition: London Singles. Grandsire. Ringers: Walter Fern (Treble), Henry Gayton (2), Alfred Elliott (3), Joshua Partridge (4), Sidney Corby (Tenor). Conductor: Joshua Partridge.
3. Monday 16th May 1932, in 2 hours 54 minutes with 5,040 changes. Composition: Manchester, Canterbury, Old Doubles, April Day, Plain Bob, St Dunstan, Antelope, Grandsire, London Single. Ringers: Sydney Corby (Treble), Horace Tyler (2), Alfred Elliot (3), Albert Minney (4), Joshua Partridge (Tenor). Conductor Joshua Partridge.
4. Sunday 21st May 1939, in 3 hours 8 minutes with 5,040 changes. Composition: Grandsire. Plain Bob. Ringers: Reswin Bayes (Treble), Edward Smart (2), Max Laughton (3), Donald Cockings (4), Thomas Fleming (Tenor). Conductor: Donald Cockings.
5. Tuesday 26th December 1939, in 3 hours exactly with 5,040 changes. Composition: 4 Methods (Canterbury, April Day, Plain Bob, Grandsire). Ringers: Thomas Fleming (Treble), James Stuart (2), Max Laughton (3), Edward Smart (4), Donald Cockings (Tenor). Conductor: Donald Cockings
6. Saturday 12th June 1948, in 2 hours 45 minutes with 5,040 changes. Composition: 7 Methods (Canterbury, April Day, Old Doubles, Plain Bob, St Dunstan, London

Bell ringers in the belfry c.1948: Alan Partridge, Ted Smart, Josh Partridge, Rev Powell, Dick Edmunds, Russell Elliot, Max Elliot. (*D. Edmunds*)

Single, Grandsire). Ringers: Dick Edmunds (Treble), Max Elliot (2), Joshua Partridge (3), Alan Partridge (4), Edward Smart (Tenor). Conductor: Joshua Partridge.

7. Saturday 5th May 1951, in 2 hours 47 minutes with 5,040 changes. Composition: 9 Methods (Chase, St Simon, Canterbury, Old Doubles, Plain Bob, April Day, St Dunstan, London Singles, Grandsire). Ringers: Joshua Partridge (Treble), Jack Mallows (2), Edward Smart (3), Frederick Holly (4), Harry Wooding (Tenor). Conductor: (Joshua Partridge).

8. Friday 27th June 1952, in 2 hours 48 minutes with 5,040 changes. Composition: 6 Methods (April Day, Canterbury, Plain Bob, Old Doubles, Grandsire, London Single). Ringers Dick Edmunds (Treble), Joshua Partridge (2), Jack Mallows (3), Frederick Holly (4), Harry Wooding (Tenor). Footnote: Half-muffled in memoriam Mr W. Fern.

9. Saturday 1st October 1955, in 2 hours 57 minutes with 5,040 changes. Composition: 14 Methods (Plain Bob, Old Bob, Norfolk, April Day, Kennington, Reverse Canterbury Pleasure, Southrepps, Cliffords Pleasure, All Saints, Grandsire, London Single, Northrepps, Fortune, Reverse St Bartholomew). Ringers: Delia Miller (Treble), Ronald Daniels (2), Rex Line (3), Norman Line (4), George Roome (Tenor). Conductor: Rex Line.

10. Saturday 7th April 1956, in 2 hours 52 minutes with 5,040 changes. Composition: 21 Methods (St Simon, St Albans, St Martin, St Paul, Reverse Canterbury Pleasure, Southrepps, St Columb, Cliffords Pleasure, Northrepps, Fortune, Reverse St Bartholomew, All Saints, Little Aston, Seighford, Marchington, Austrey, Plain Bob, April Day, Norfolk, Lennington, Old Bob. Ringers: Jean Packwood (Treble), Rex Line (2), George Roome (3), Norman Line (4), Alan Cozens (Tenor), Conductor: Alan Cozens.

Bell ringers in belfry with Vicar Knight in the 1950s. Left to right, Vicar Knight, Richard Torrance, Norman Line, Nigel Terry, P. Dobbs, Sally Laughton, Francis Curtis, Rex Line, Peter Haggar.

(*D. Edmunds*)

11. Saturday 29th September 1956, in 2 hours 52 minutes with 5,040 changes. Composition: 7 Methods (St Martin, Winchendon Place, Antelope, Grandsire, Plain Bob, Reverse Canterbury Pleasure, All Saints. Ringers: Joshua Partridge (Treble), Edward Smart (2), Christine Coleman (3), Rex Line (4), Norman Line (Tenor), Conductor: Rex Line. Footnote: for the enthronement of Dr Robert Stopford as Bishop of Peterborough

12. Saturday 1st December 1962, in 2 hours 45 minutes with 5,040 changes. Composition: 11 Methods (Stedman, Grandsire, Reverse St Bartholomew, Reverse Canterbury Pleasure, All Saints, Plain Bob, St Simon, Winchendon Place, St John, Old Bob, April Day. Ringers: Graham Paul (Treble), Roger Smith (2), Richard Danby (3), Alan Paul (4), George Roome (Tenor), Conductor: George Roome. Footnote: 50th Anniversary of the first peal on the bells.

13. Saturday 28th June 1969, in 3 hours 1 minute with 5,040 changes. Composition: Grandsire, Plain Bob. Ringers: Paul Hagger (Treble), Rex Line (2), Norman Line (3), George Roome (4), Edward Buckby (Tenor). Conductor: George Roome. Footnote: Half-muffled in memoriam Rev'd W. C. Knight.

14. Saturday 24th January 1981, in 3 hours 1 minute with 5,040 changes. Composition: Stedman. Ringers: William He (Treble), Michael Fiander (2), Timothy Wooding (3), David Garton (4), Peter Fleckney (Tenor). Conductor: Peter Fleckney.

15. Saturday 1st August 1981, in 3 hours 3 minutes with 5,040 changes. Composition: 5 Methods (Winchendon Place, All Saints, Reverse Canterbury Pleasure, Plain Bob, Grandsire). Ringers: Helen Knightley (Treble), Christina Downey (2), Elizabeth Taylor (3), Rex Line (4), Andrew Williams (Tenor). Conductor: Rex Line. Footnote: For the wedding of HRH The Prince of Wales and Lady Diana Spencer – first attempt by all, except conductor.

16. Thursday 18th August 1983, in 2 hours 57 minutes with 5,040 changes. Composition 21 Methods (Shipway Place, Antelope, Grandsire, Plain Bob, Reverse Canterbury Pleasure, St Simons, St Osmund, St Nicholas, St Remigius, Westminster, St Hilary, New Bob, St Vedast, St Martin, Eynesbury, Winchendon Place, Huntley Place, Blackburn Place, Dragon Place, Huntspill, Blaisdon). Ringers: Jayne Spencer (Treble), Catherine Richardson (2), Philip Ellis (3), David Garton (4), Mike Pidd (Tenor), Conductor: Mike Pidd.

Rex Line
Philip Bligh
Rex was born on 19th June 1931 in Church Lane where brother Russell now lives in what was known then as Roberts Yard or Wallaces Yard after the Wallaces who had lived at Glebe Cottage for generations. The yard consisted of three cottages and opened into Church Lane. His mother Eleanor Drage (a Drage from Yardley Hastings who married John Thomas Line) bought all three cottages in the latter half of the 1940s. Two of these were pulled down to widen the entry of Mile Street into Church Lane and the piece of stone wall still there is all that is left of the old entrance. The family house where Russell still lives might have once been stables and the two-storey shed alongside was a workshop for shoemaking.

Rex was one of nine children – four girls and five boys – Russell, Eileen, Rex, George, Norman, Ivy, Jack (buried in Italy), Nora and Ena. There seem to have been three families of Lines:

1. That of Bernard and Ron Line living at 21 Harrold Road who followed their dad, Bert, into the shoe trade while brother William worked for Garretts the butchers.
2. Mavis Line (now Holman) whose family were farmers at Home Farm and Glebe Farm
3. The Lines of Wallace Yard. They followed a variety of careers. For example, George worked on Holts Farm and then on the War Agricultural Committee. Russell was always good with machines and after starting in ploughing, now works on large road making machines.

Rex was in the RAF from 1949 to 1954, first as part of his National Service, and then as a volunteer for five years as an Aircraft Instrument Mechanic. On leaving the RAF in 1954 he joined Brookland Aviation at Sywell (buying a motor cycle to get him there!) repairing aircraft for the RAF under contract. Then in 1960 he joined the Royal Aircraft Establishment at Thurleigh, based on the Second World War American airfield there. The MOD took it over, working on aircraft experiments, blind landings, naval aviation, helicopter research, etc.

In 1994 Rex was awarded the British Empire Medal for his services to aviation.

Rex took over the responsibility of the Belfry at Bozeat in 1960; previous leaders included Jim Stuart and Joshua Partridge. He started ringing shortly after the ban on the ringing of bells was lifted during the Second World War. Rex remembers ringing for the special service held in memory of Lt John Ahern, on 8th March 1945 – the 22-year-old American pilot who was killed steering his crippled bomber clear of the village.

The Diocesan Guild was formed on 5th January 1924. Rex remembers the bells being taken down for repair in 1947 and that he wound the clock occasionally as a boy in the 1940s but began winding it regularly in 1954, which means he has been winding the clock on a daily basis for the past 45 years.

Rex instigated the AGM for the Bozeat Belfry in 1989 putting their work on a more formal footing. As Tower Captain since 1970 he has trained numerous men and women as bell ringers keeping this ancient profession in good heart – and in the last year is currently training up teams from Wollaston, Easton Maudit, Grendon (and also helping ringers in the locality) ready to ring in the new Millennium at 12 noon on 1st January 2000.

Note:
In May 1915 the Ellacombe Chiming Apparatus was fitted to the Bells by John Taylor of Loughborough, cost £14.

This aerial picture of St Mary's also shows Church Farm buildings, gutted by fire in 1962.

CHAPTER 24

Vicars of Bozeat 1220-2000

	1220	Vicarage ordained
1.	(?)	Ralph
2.	1258	Geoffrey de Foxton
3.	1274	Robert de Brockhall
4.	1280	Geoffrey de Dunewye
5.	1281	Roger de Haregrave
6.	1281	Philip de Brampton
7.	1284	Roger de Rivers
8.	(?)	Walter de Buckingham
9.	1322	Robert de Dodington
10.	1349	Thos. Catelyn de Ringstede
11.	1350	Simon de Bosgate
12.	(?)	John Dene
13.	1374	Ralph Hayward
14.	1378	Thos. Everard
15.	1380	Robert Gray
16.	1383	Richard Welles
17.	1390	Elias Wythiford
18.	1392	John Aude
19.	1403	William Peers
20.	1417	John West
21.	(?)	John Aleyn
22.	1436	John Wright
23.	1449	Rich. Frankysh
24.	1455	John Lylly
25.	1463	Thos. Curteys
26.	1468	Wm. Haryet
27.	(?)	John Lely
28.	1480	John Hobson
29.	(?)	Ralph Elkington
30.	1497	John Campynett
31.	(?)	John Newman
32.	1511	Wm. Atmere
33.	1527	Hugh Lidington
34.	1554	Wm. Stringar (?)
35.	1561	Thos Carter
36.	1569	Thos. Hill
37.	(?)	Oliver Houghton
38.	1576	Humphrey Norbury
39.	1607	Joshua Cock
40.	1617-50	William Collinson
41.	1652	John Manning
42.	1655	Paynell Hargrave*
43.	(?)	Edmund Dickenson*
44.	1663	Samuel Hart
45.	1680	Nath. Bentford
46.	1686	John Lettice
47.	1702	Edmund Godwin
48.	1708	Thos. Drake
49.	1729	Humfry Bradford
50.	1740	John Lettice
51.	1753-94	Ralph Barlow
	1756	T. G. Bennet (curate)
	1757	Samuel Edwards (curate)
	1766	J. Liptrott (curate)
52.	1795-1825	Wm. Corbet Wilson
	1795	J. Rodick (curate)
	1809	James Gibbs (curate)
	1825	W. C. Wilson Jnr (curate)
53.	1825	W. C. Wilson Jnr
54.	1853	John Pizey
55.	1880	Arthur Kinch
56.	1883	Augustus Secker
57.	1892	Wm Drake Sargeaunt
58.	1901	Hy Reginald Moule
59.	1906	Mordant Laird Warren
60.	1912	C. B. Jennings
61.	1922	C. N. Daybell
62.	1927	W. H. Britton
63.	1929	J. H. Marlow
64.	1944	S. F. W. Powell
65.	1950	W. C. Knight
66.	1969	Norman E. Palmer
67.	1990	Philip H. Bligh
68.	1997	Allan Huggins
67.	1998	Philip H. Bligh

*Intruders under Cromwell

"We are indebted to Mr Dorman, of Northampton, and Rev. Isham Longdon, of Heyford, for an almost complete list of our Vicars since the Vicarage was ordained in 1220, possibly 80 years after the Church was built." (*Marlow*, 1936, p.38)

VICARS OF BOZEAT 1220-2000

As the Church at Bozeat was known to exist in 1130 when David was King of the Scots and also owner of the Estate of Bozeat he might well be the founder of the church. The right of patronage was later placed in the convent of Dryburgh in Northampton and in the records of Dryburgh Abbey (founded in 1150 by Hugh de Morville, King David's Constable, this document exists: "Richard de Morville, to all friends and honourable men – greetings. Be it known to those of the present time and equally to those of the future, that I have granted and confirmed by my charter, to God and to the Church of the Blessed Mary at Dryburgh, and to the Canons who serve God in that place, a donation from my mother of the Church of Bosyet and of the mill .... in perpetual alms gift, as freely and quietly as it is possible for alms gifts to be freely and quitely (bestowed). To be granted and helde for the welfare of my soul and of the souls of my predecessors and successors." His mother, referred to, was Beatrice de Beachamp, who married his father Hugh de Morville. (*Marlow*, pp.11,12). We may not know the actual year our Church opened for Divine Worship but we do know the day of the year because this day has been kept ever since as our Holy Day, or Feast Day, the Fe(a)stival of St Mary, to whom the church is dedicated which on the old calendar was 26th August or the first Sunday after this date.

"The Victorian History says: The Parish Churches of England were at first all Rectories possessing the tithes, glebes and offerings. Vicarages had their origin in appropriation, *i.e.* the giving of advowsons [the right of presentation of Incumbent] and subsequently the rectories to religious houses. The monasteries steadily refused to assign definite stipends or securities of tenure to their Vicars." (*Marlow*, p.41.) Marlow also quotes another writer who says: " 'As many a Vicar knows to his cost, the very name Vicarage often implies that the benefice was anciently robbed of its endowments.' In 1220 Hugh Bishop of Lincoln fought this scandal and ordained 300 Vicarages (of which Bozeat was one)."

"Notice that up to 1350 the Surnames (of the Vicars) were taken from their birthplace. Several of the Vicars were Northamptonshire born. 1350, Simon de Bosgate may have been a Bozeat man, as Bozeat was sometimes spelt Bosgate." (*Marlow* p.39) This may reflect the origin of the name – possibly Boza-gate as the lands of the Saxon, Earl Boza were near here. "After 1350 the Surnames were taken from their ancestors' trade or profession, e.g. Haywood (1374, official who protected crops from 'trespassing' animals) and Wright (1436, i.e. wheelwright) There are many records of where our vicars came from and went to e.g. Robert Gray, 1380 came from Duston and left us for Whiston and John Lylly, 1455, went from here to Lois Weedon and on to Harlestone.

When Oliver Cromwell came to power and King Charles I was beheaded in 1649, he issued his Edict against the use of the Prayer Book and many clergy were evicted from their vicarages for still using it. So at Bozeat John Manning was ordained at St Andrew's, London for Bozeat, but in 1655 Paynell Hargrave was sent in 1655 from Lambeth Palace (then in the hands of Cromwell) to be in charge of Bozeat. He would use the Dictionary of Public Worship and was not an ordained clergyman so was called an 'Intruder'. Hargrave was followed by another Intruder, Edmund Dickenson, but with the Restoration of the Monarchy in 1660 (Charles II crowned), Samuel Hart was ordained in Peterborough Cathedral in 1663 – a year after a conference met and revised the Prayer Book in 1662 – the one that is still used today.

Retracing our steps for a moment, William Collinson was made Vicar on 1st March 1617 and stayed until 1650. "He evidently was left alone when so many were turned out in 1645, and their places were taken by laymen. John Manning, Vicar, 1652 was presumably evicted in 1655 for continuing to use the Prayer Book and replaced by our first Intruder, Hargrave. Our Communion Chalice and Paten date from 1636, so during the time William Collinson was Vicar. Below the foot of the Chalice is the inscription: 'The Communion Cupp and Cover of the Parishe of Boziatt in Northampton weigheth 21 ounces 3d. weight.'" (*Marlow*, p.19) This was the time of the reforming zeal of William Laud, made Archbishop of Canterbury in 1633, sometimes called the founder of Anglo-Catholicism as he sought to restore high church practices in terms of the centrality of the Mass, the altar and sacraments and associated vestments, holy vessels, etc. (note four holes, two on either side of our altar where the tabernacle legs, which Laud would have insisted was reinstated over what would now be an Altar rather than the bare Reformation Holy Table). His reforms may explain why our beautiful solid silver chalice was purchased at this time.

During the 1990s we brought it back to Bozeat from the Central Museum in Northampton, where it was kept, for use on Easter Day. Thanks to Laud we also have the oldest actual documents belonging to Bozeat that are known to exist – two inventories of the land left by various people in their will for the maintenance of the Vicarage. On being made Archbishop in 1633, he sent out certain orders for uniformity, and gave notice that he would make a visitation throughout his Province of Canterbury. This took him three years to accomplish and evidently each parish had to prepare an inventory – our two, one dated 1633, on a kind of pigskin and signed William Collinson (Vicar) and Thos Hall and Thos Manninge (Guardians) and the other dated 1636 are kept at Peterborough.

"It was about 1707 that Strixton first became attached to Bozeat. From 1688-1707 Geo. Harding was Rector of Strixton and we have a note that he kept a large school there and was buried with his wife within the Chancel Rails of Strixton Church. He had no connection with Bozeat, but his successor was John Lettice, Vicar of Bozeat, who left Bozeat in 1702 and went to Rushden for five years. In 1707 he became rector of Strixton and died there in 1720, aged 59. This must have started the connection between the two Parishes, for we know that in 1729 Strixton Registers were burnt in Bozeat Vicarage in the big village fire. Then another John Lettice (his son) became Rector of Strixton in 1733, Vicar of Bozeat in 1740 and Vicar of Grendon in 1746 and held the three Livings until he died, aged 43.... From 1740 to 1929 Strixton was attached to Bozeat but on August 23rd, 1929, it became part of Wollaston Parish." (*Marlow*, p.43), i.e. a period of 189 years.

Three generations of the Lettice Family lived at Bozeat, and some members of the family reached exalted positions. The first, John Lettice, matriculated at Clare Hall, Cambridge, 1679, BA 1683, and was ordained Vicar of Bozeat on 1st December 1686. He was married at Farndish on 1st October 1702 to Elizabeth, third daughter of Thomas Scriven, Rector of Souldrop and Knotting, and they had two daughters Martha and Elizabeth and one son John. Martha was to have two famous sons, William who became subsequently Bishop of Chester, Bangor and St Asaph, and Euseby who became Archbishop of Dublin in 1809. Son John took his BA at Sydney College, Cambridge in 1729, took a curacy at Holcot and became rector of his father's old parish at Strixton in 1733 and Vicar of Bozeat in 1740. Mary his first wife had died on 6th January 1746 at Bozeat and he then married Ann Catlyn in 1750 who died two years before him on 4th April 1752. He is buried with his two wives in the same vault within the chancel rails at Bozeat church, but tiles put down about

1860 covered up all the gravestones. By his first wife Mary he had six daughters and two sons. The boys get a mention in the Churchwardens' Accounts: "1751, paid Jackey Lettice for 4 sparrows, 1d." and "1752, paid Dickey Lettice for 8 sparrows, 1d." The eldest John (the third) was born 27th December 1738, educated by his father at Bozeat vicarage, Oakham School for three years, then in 1756 to Sussex College, Cambridge, BA 1761, MA 1764 and in 1764 obtained the Seaton Prize for a poem on the 'Conversion of St. Paul.' In March 1765 he spent an evening with Dr Johnson at Cambridge, who was a friend of the vicar of Easton Maudit, Eustace Percy, who was a well known literary figure and who with Dr Johnson and Oliver Goldsmith was a member of the Garrick Club which used to meet at the vicarage at Easton Maudit. John was Chaplain and Secretary of the British Embassy at Copenhagen and in 1797 gained a Doctor of Divinity and in 1804 became Prebend of Seaford in Chichester Cathedral. "So Jackey Lettice who caught sparrows at Bozeat became a great Divine and Poet and died at the age of 93 and 10 months and is honoured in the biographies of England. Richard Lettice his younger brother became more well known locally as an Apothecary and Surgeon in Wellingborough. On 25th March 1788, he was made the first Parish Doctor to Bozeat." (*Marlow*, p.46.) Richard Lettice died aged 59 and was buried on 1st April 1800 according to the Register of All Hallows Church, Wellingborough, but no gravestone for him has been found in their graveyard. (See Chapter 18 for more details on Richard Lettice.)

"A Terrier of 1730 (now at Peterborough) says: The Vicarage house before it was burnt contained three bays of buildings and a little Buttery, a Stable and two barns, a garden on the South side of the house, a yard on the North side, a close on the East between the Churchyard and Lays Close." (*Marlow*, p.42.) We have not been able to

The old vicarage. (*Vicars' Logbook*)

locate the exact site of this vicarage. Humfrey Bradford was inducted into the living about a fortnight before the outbreak of the fire on 9th September (see Chapter 20) 1729 but the previous vicar, Thomas Drake, "Having quitted this for another living ... having not removed my Family and Goods, became a considerable Sufferer in this dismal fire ..." as did the Parish Registers of Bozeat and Strixton which he unfortunately kept in the vicarage so these precious records of our past were lost for ever. It was Humfry Bradford who rebuilt the vicarage with the generous help of patroness Elizabeth Wiseman to the tune of one hundred pounds and contributions from his friends. "T'would have been injurious to the memory of this worthy vicar to bury in silence what he hath caused thus to be done for the benefit of his successors," writes Thomas Drake in penitential mood over the loss to parish and family by the fire. So we have Humfry Bradford to thank for the fine vicarage which stood from about 1730 to 1963, over 230 years, to be replaced by the present building.

"... an old copy of *Bridges' History* in the possession of the Architectural Society of Northampton is interleaved, and gives additional information apparently written by a member of the Bridges family. This was a fortunate find as it is probably the only place where this information could have been found. It says: 'Within the Altar rails is a defaced slab to Rev. H. Bradford, Dec.10th, 1739-40. Also one to Rev. John Lettice, Rector of Strixton and Vicar of Bozeat, Easter Day, 1753, aged 43/4 and his two wives. Nave slabs: (1) Mary Ashton, 1740, (2) Thos. Drake, husband of Mary Drake,

Line drawing of the church in the 1870s by 9-year-old Ernest Hutchinson showing two iron bands clamped round the bulging tower. (*Vicars' Scrapbook*)

VICARS OF BOZEAT 1220-2000

The church after the collapse of tower and spire in 1877. (*Marlow's History*, 1936)

1751; Margaret Drake, 1719; John Drake, 1717, age 5, children of Rev. Dr Drake ... on the West side of the Churchyard is a tombstone: 'Sacred to the memory of Rev. Ralph Barlow, A.M., forty-two years Vicar of this Parish, who was interred near this spot at his own request. He died January 27th, 1795, aged 80 years." (*Marlow*, p.23.) This reminds us at least that Ralph Barlow was probably the longest serving Vicar of Bozeat ever, and of the practice of interring vicars in the chancel in the 18th century. Barlow's tombstone presently (1999) leans against the church wall adjacent to the vicarage garden. When the tower was rebuilt in 1882, a skeleton was found by the side of its foundations with feet to the west showing it to be that of a priest. The above information suggests it was that of vicar Barlow. The body was left there and its place marked by a cross of red bricks under the Church clock in the corner.

Spencelayh's dramatic 1951 drawing of the collapse of the spire in 1877. The original is in the Central Museum, Northampton.

Notice too that Ralph Barlow, 1753 and Wm Corbett Wilson, 1795, had Curates. "This means those Vicars held other Livings and came here later on when they were older." (*Marlow*, p.39.) Note too that one curate was Corbet Wilson's son and became vicar after him.

"The only memorial tablet to be seen in the Church is one to Rev. William Corbett Wilson, who died 25th May 1853, aged 58, Vicar of this Parish and Rector of Strixton for 28 years. 'O the depth of the riches both of the wisdom and the knowledge of God. How unsearchable are His judgements and His ways past finding out.' This text no doubt was chosen because of the manner of his death. He was thrown from his trap on the hill leading out of Wollaston towards Wellingborough. Apparently he lingered a few days after the accident. The memorial is also to an infant son, 1831, but there was another son born in 1833, and daughter, 1837." (*Marlow*, pp.23, 24.)

The Chancel of the Church has had many restorations. "The Lord of the Manor was responsible for the repairs of the Chancel. But the Estate was going through a bad time during Mr Revis' ownership and it is recorded that in 1873/4/5 the Reverend Pizey restored the Chancel chiefly at his own cost of about £400 including the gift of the Organ. It was fortunate that the Organ was moved at this time from the Gallery at the West End to the Chancel, because when the Tower fell in 1877 it broke the Gallery and it was never repaired, but taken down. The staircase to the Gallery is now used as a staircase in a house in Easton Lane." (*Marlow*, p.22.) John Frederick Pizey was instituted vicar in 1853. It was Vicar Pizey who stained the Rood Screen and Panel brown all over presumably because they looked patchy and untidy. (*Marlow*, sheet 39.) The collapse of the spire and tower was an event immortalised in the dramatic sketch made by Spencelayh in 1951 and now hanging in the Central Museum at Northampton. Despite buttresses built to support it and an iron band put round it to stop it bulging – see the line drawing of nine-year-old Ernest Hutchinson drawn in the 1870s – the tower caved in, never having been built to support the weight of its heavy stone spire. Arthur Kinch, inducted vicar in 1880, inherited a church without a spire and only stayed until 1882, so he never saw it restored. In a farewell letter to parishioners he said how he regretted never hearing the bells ring. During rebuilding, four bells stood in the churchyard and the treble was erected on a tripod near the south door to call people to church. Vicar Pizey died on 21st April 1884 at Kingswear, Devon aged 66, having been Vicar of Bozeat for 28 years.

The Reverend A. E. Kinch 1880-83.

Rev. Augustus Secker was instituted and inducted on the same day, 20th January 1883, as Vicar of Bozeat by Ven. R. P. Lightfoot, Archdeacon of Oakham. Rev. Secker was previously Curate of Harlestone, Northampton from May 1869 to January 1882 and of Rushden from Jan. 1882 to Jan. 1883. On 27th June 1883 Ven Lightfoot laid the corner stone of the restored Tower. A bottle was included containing coins of the realm and an inscription: The Church of St Mary the Virgin, Bozeat in the County of Northamptonshire 'Except the Lord build the House they labour in vain who build it.' The ceremony was held in pouring rain, so incessant that the tea on the vicarage lawn had to be moved to a neighbouring barn. The original tower had not been built to support a spire as well, so in the rebuild all of the tower had been taken down and the stones numbered. The walls were to be built as much as twice as thick.

The Reverend A. W. Secker 1883-92.

The completion of the work (undertaken by Margetts & Neale, monumental masons from Kettering) was celebrated on Tuesday 15th July 1884 with a service in church followed by tea attended by 400 on the lawn in front of the vicarage. The committee in charge of the whole occasion being Vicar Secker, Mr J. W. Kirby and Mr H. Howe, churchwardens, Mr W. F. Hill (ex-churchwarden), Mr F. Drage (organist), Mr R. Brown and Mr J. W. Davidson. Vicar Secker died on 1st February 1894 and was buried at Strixton. In April a new lectern, used for the first time on Easter Day, was presented by Vicar Secker's sister in his memory and of another sister. Also friends (and Miss Secker) in 1894 gave the new High Altar to the Church costing £19-15s, in his memory.

On 22nd April 1892 William Drake Sargeaunt was instituted Vicar of Bozeat and Rector of Strixton. He was born 1859, son of Lt. Col. W. T. Sargeaunt and was from Stanwick with BA (1883), New College Oxford, an ardent Liberal and great friend of the MP for E. Northants, Francis Channing. Whilst Vicar of Bozeat he published a collection of poems (privately, 1900), *The Banks of the Nene* and *Poems* (Dent, 1902). In one poem Sargeaunt says that his devout wish is to:

The Reverend W. D. Sargeaunt
1892-1901.

> *Help live again beauty shewn*
> *Of old in Gothic arch and spire*
> *And music's full harmonious tine*
> *Restore to the four voiced choir*
> *From Peter's stately western pile*
> *To lowly Bozeat's pillard aisle.*

In 1893 Vicar Sargeaunt was involved in founding the Working Men's Club and in 1907 the present club building was built on ground called Riseley's Gardens with ten residents making themselves responsible for £10 each, one being the vicar, toward the cost. (*Marlow*, Sheet 54.) In his time the North Aisle roof was restored for £85 with further repairs to the roof costing £600. There is a photo taken in 1901 of choir and churchwardens, the Vicar and his wife and their two young children William and Mary ages about 8 and 6 respectively. He saw the New Century in and his last Sunday here was Easter Day 1901 – when he went to be vicar of Stoke Abbott, near Beaminster, Dorset. On his death on 27th January 1940, aged 81, Vicar Marlow wrote of him in memoriam: "So many of you still remember Mr Sargeaunt and have spoken to me so frequently about what was done in his day, that I felt when I first went to stay a night with him that I already knew a lot about him. In spite of differences of outlook on some questions when he first came, Bozeat people soon learnt to love him and his family, and many are the pleasant memories still brought by a mention of their names. His musical abilities made an impression on the Choir of his day that has not been lost in 40 years, and I often hear of the Yattendon tunes

TO THE PARISHIONERS OF BOZEAT.

MY DEAR FRIENDS,

It seems only right that, before leaving, I should lay before you a statement as to the present position of the Fund we have been trying to raise for the Restoration of the Tower and Spire of the Church.

At Michaelmas, 1880, there was in hand on this account £22 19s. 3d.: £2 2s. 0d. of this a donation from the late W. B. Higgins, Esq.; £2 2s. 0d. collected by Mrs. G. F. Corby; and £18 15s. 3d. raised by Collections in Church. The List of Subscriptions amounts now to £651 18s. 7d. Of this sum, £406 14s. 7d. has been actually paid, and now lies at the Union Bank, Northampton, in the joint names of the Vicar and Churchwardens. At the end of this month there will be another £3 10s. to be added for the half-year's Interest.

This £651 18s. 7d. is within a hundred pounds of the sum required by the lowest estimate for the work of re-building Tower and Spire. There will be the expense of re-hanging the bells, and Architect's charges to be added to this. So that a good deal yet remains to be done: but I think we may hope that the main difficulties have been overcome.

I need hardly tell you that it would have been a very great happiness to me could I have witnessed the undertaking and completion of the work in my time here. But I trust that nothing may occur to delay the work, and that at no very distant date I may be allowed to visit Bozeat again and to look upon the Tower and Spire restored in all their beauty, and to hear for the first time the bells of Bozeat Church.

In bidding you "Good-bye," let me add the hope—which is also my earnest prayer—that the restoration of the fabric of the Church may be but the outward and visible sign of another and a better restoration—namely, a true and lasting revival of Christian life and Christian work in the parish.

Believe me to be
Always your faithful friend,
ARTHUR E. KINCH.

Advent, 1882.

Bozeat Church Restoration Fund.

FIRST LIST OF SUBSCRIPTIONS.

	£ s. d.
Earl Spencer, K.G.	150 0 0
Marquis of Northampton, K.G.	25 0 0
Lord Alwyne Compton (late Archdeacon of Oakham) towards Tower	10 0 0
„ Spire	10 0 0
	20 0 0
Thomas Revis, Esq.	50 0 0
Rev. A. E. Kinch	25 0 0
G. J. Sale, Esq., per Rev. A. E. Kinch	25 0 0
The Mr. Benn's	10 10 0
Mrs. Kinch	10 0 0
Wm. Kinch, Esq.	10 0 0
Mr. John Monk	5 0 0
Mr. John Drage	5 0 0
Rev. F. J. Ponsonby	5 0 0
T. H. Kirby, Esq.	5 0 0
Miss Richards	5 0 0
Mrs. Savage	5 0 0
Mr. Wm. Hensman	5 0 0
Miss Clarke	4 0 0
Miss C. M. Kinch	2 2 0
W. B. Higgins, Esq. (the late)	2 2 0
Mrs. Percy Brent	2 2 0
Rev. C. H. Burnham	2 2 0
Mr. Henry Howe	2 2 0
Mr. W. F. Hill	2 2 0
R. W. Arkwright, Esq.	2 0 0
Frederick Kinch, Esq.	1 1 0
Mr. Foster	1 1 0
Mr. George Scriven	1 0 0
	£382 4 0

	£ s. d.
Brought up	382 4 0
Miss Hunter	1 0 0
Mrs. Alibone	0 10 0
Mr. Dent	0 10 0

BY COLLECTING CARDS—

	£ s. d.
Mrs. G. F. Corby	2 2 0
Mr. John Monk	1 15 9
Per do. by Mr. Peach	5 0 0
Miss Clarke	1 0 0
Miss M. A. Howe	0 5 0
Mr. J. W. Kirby	2 15 6
Mrs. Coles	3 3 9
Mr. Brown	8 18 6
Mrs. Wm. Drage	2 14 0
Mrs. C. Bass	13 4 6
Miss Marquis	1 17 0
Miss Wykes (Brington)	5 12 6
Miss S. A. Robinson	0 14 0
Mrs. Alibone	1 0 0
	50 2 6

BY COLLECTING BOXES—

	£ s. d.
Church Almsbox	3 15 6
Mrs. Wm. Drage	2 2 0
Vicarage box	3 10 10
	9 8 4
By Collections in Church	48 16 10
„ Bazaar at Whitsuntide, 1882	136 14 11
„ Sale of Work, Dec. 2nd	21 0 0
„ Interest at Bank to June 30th	1 12 0
	£651 18 7

Restoration Fund Appeal Account 1882. (*Vicars' Scrapbook*)

and we still use parts of Adlam's communion setting which he taught the Choir. The little Plays in the garden and elsewhere caused a great deal of enjoyment and amusement, and some of you will remember 'Bluebeard', 'Chimney Corner', 'Box and Cox', etc. In the bedroom I am sleeping in just now there are still two hooks in the beam – a reminder of the swing in the nursery of the children. The Working Men's Club has a special reason for very grateful memory of Mr Sargeaunt. They owe their existence to him, and he worked hard for their present building.... Here are a few things done in his nine years Vicariate. A hut placed in White Wall, Easton Lane for a Girls' Club, as there already existed a Boys' Club in Mile Street. 1894 Village Nurse suggested (but not obtained that year). 1894, hot air system for heating the Church. The Boiler Chamber built at NW Corner of the Church. Afterwards (1923) converted into present Vestry. 1894, Louvres to Tower Bell Windows. 1894, New Altar in Church, cost £19 15s, made by Ratter and Kett of Cambridge, a handsome addition to the beauty of the Church often admired by visitors as well as continually appreciated by our own congregation. New brass lamps bought for the Church. 1893, Working Men's Club founded in High Street. This was a lot to do in one year. I have a newspaper cutting (which reads) 'Some years ago the Steeple was rebuilt, but now the Church wants attention. The altar is a poor one and altogether inadequate and the Church wants properly heating.' 1896, Easter Day, new Lectern (made by Ratter & Kett), presented by Miss Secker in memory of her brother (the Reverend A. W. Secker) and her sister. The design is after an old lectern in Romsey Church,

Hants., of the date c.1450. 1896, Font Ewer (paid for out of offerings at baptisms). 1896, Brass Candelabra (C17th) hung in Chancel. 1897, Working Men's Club House erected at cost of £1,000 in High Street. 1897 and 1898, Church Roof extensively repaired. The cost, I have heard, was c.£600. August, 1898, Boys' Brigade started as Junior Section of St John's Ambulance.... Most of what I have quoted above is noted in the 'Log Book' of the parish I have made since I have been here, from things told me. So the memory of what this worthy Vicar and his family did for Bozeat will not lack definite record for generations to come."

On 28th January 1901 The Reverend H. R. Moule was instituted at Peterborough as Vicar of Bozeat and Rector of Strixton and started his parish duties in July of that year. During his time the last burial in the churchyard took place on 4th December 1903.

The Reverend H. R. Moule 1901-1905.

On 22nd July 1905 Vicar Moule's bicycle and clothes were found on the bank of the River Ouse near Ely. An ardent cyclist, Mr Moule, having been for a holiday in Norfolk with his wife, decided to make the return journey on his bicycle alone. At Ely he posted a card to his wife saying he intended to have a dip in the river. When his things were found it was presumed he had met with an accident but several days of dragging operations failed to yield evidence. A few months after, a rumour was circulated that he had been seen in Paris and it was reported later that he had gone to Canada.

Early in 1906 a Notice was fixed to the Church door summoning Mr Moule to attend before the Bishop. No response. A Final Notice declared that if he did not take up his duty with in a given time he would be deprived of his Living.

In our records there is an article with splendid pen and ink drawings by Bertha Newcombe from *The Church Monthly* of 1905 on 'The Making of Lace' written by Rev. H. R. Moule, BA, Vicar of Bozeat. And there is an interesting sequel to the story of this vicar's disappearance. We have a letter from Solicitors, Burgess and Chesher of Bedford dated 29th October 1956 and addressed to the Vicar of Bozeat which reads: "Dear Sir, We are endeavouring to trace the date and place of the marriage of the late Reverend Henry Reginald Moule to Miss Charlotte Wilcox. The Church Information Board informs us that Mr Moule became Vicar of Bozeat in 1905 [incorrect, 1901!], although there is no mention of him after that date in Crockford [that is the year he disappeared]. Could you give us the particulars of his marriage or failing that some information which might enable us to trace particulars. We are enclosing a stamped addressed envelope. Yours faithfully," [brackets mine]. It seems that the mystery of Mr Moule was still there 50 years later and possibly rightful inheritors of his estate still to be established.

"The Rev. Mordant Laird Warren, Vicar of Priors Hardwick, Warwickshire, has accepted from Lord Spencer the gift of the living of Bozeat-cum-Strixton vacant by the disappearance of the Rev. H. R. Moule" – so reads a newspaper article of the time. On 28th February 1906, Revd M. L. Warren was instituted and on 6th May

The Reverend M. L. Warren 1906-12.

took up his duties. But it was not until two years later on 10th March 1908 that he was formally inducted Vicar. He trained at Bishop Wilson's Theological School, Isle of Man, ordained deacon 1891 and priest 1893. From 1891-1894 he was Curate of Kirk Bradden, Isle of Man, famous for its outdoor services in summer, in autumn in the churchyard. Then 1894-96 Curate of Firle Glynde, Sussex, 1896-98 Curate of Daventry, 1898/9 Curate of Packington with Snibston, Leicestershire, and 1899 Vicar of Priors Hardwick, Warwickshire.

It was in his time that the pine pews along the side walls of the aisles were removed (1909) and replaced by chairs. The pitch pine pews are believed to have been put there by Vicar Pizey in about 1860 when box pews were removed. It was about this time also that the North Door was opened up and the Belfry partitioned. The belfry was to stay like that for almost a century until the partition was replaced by the present glass doors when the new vestry and new ringing platform were built into the tower in August 1995.

On 14th April 1912 Rev. C. B. Jennings took his first service at Bozeat (Patron Earl Spencer), instituted on 31st May and inducted on 9th June by Archdeacon E. M. Moore. Within two weeks of his arrival he was involved in a United Memorial Service after the *Titanic* disaster from which £4 was sent to the Lord Mayor's Disaster Fund. Later in that year the first ever Peal was rung on the Bozeat bells, the first of 15 of the 20th century, on Saturday 23rd, 1912 – the most recent (at 1998) being on Thursday 18th August 1983. He was to see the village through the years of the Great War and to leave two important additions to our heritage:

(i) It was sometime during the War (1914-18) that a painted panel kept in the vicarage suggested to Vicar Jennings that panels in the Rood Screen might possibly contain similar early paintings. After examination by the Rural Dean (Rev. Fry), architect (Talbot Brown from Wellingborough) and Rev. Paulkey (for Archaeological Society) they were taken away to be cleaned. The result was the discovery of four painted panels in addition to the one in the vicarage dating from the 14th century. Details are given in Chapter 22. The last two, those of the baptism, were found to have been cut off and replaced upside down – probably by Vicar Pizey so that he could squeeze through the screen from his clergy desk on one side from where he took the service to play the organ on the other and back again!

The Reverend C. B. Jennings 1912-22.

(ii) The second lasting contribution by Vicar Jennings is the fine Roll of Honour of all those Bozeat men, 210 of them (virtually every young man of the village), who went to war. This Roll of Honour was painted by Miss Diggle, a friend of Mrs Jennings and was dedicated by Vicar Jennings at the Evening Service of 12th October 1919. It consists of all those who enlisted and the names of those who died are in Red Ink. The preacher was the nephew of the Vicar, Rev. J. K. Jennings.

During this time the war memorial in the cemetery was erected (in 1920) at a cost of £80 and in 1921 the stained glass window in the North Aisle by Sidney Webb given in memory of Thomas Fancott Saunders by Elizabeth Osborne Hancock.

Vicar Jennings took his last service on 8th January 1921 and on 8th April 1922 was the institution and induction of Rev. C. N. Daybell who took his first service on 21st May (i.e. the parish had an interregnum of over a year). He must have been keen on musical tradition for he introduced the First Sung Eucharist in the church on 30th July 1922, and on Christmas Day 1924 the men and boys of the choir appeared resplendent in new blue cassocks and surplices (which are still in the vicarage loft 1999!). During his time the old heating boiler chamber (built in 1894 and now a kitchen and toilet 1999) was converted into a vestry and dedicated as such by the Rural Dean, Rev. Fry on 27th September 1923. Rev. Daybell's last service was 16th January 1927 and this was followed by the Institution of W. H. Britton as vicar, 12 days later on 28th January. Rev. Britton stayed barely 20 months, his last service being on 30th October 1928.

The Reverend C. N. Daybell 1922-27.

The 11th April 1929 saw the institution and induction of Rev. J. H. Marlow by Dr Claude Blagden, Bishop of Peterborough, and Archdeacon Greaves, as Vicar of Bozeat and Rector of Strixton in Bozeat Church. He came after two and a half years as Curate in charge of St Barnabas, Peterborough where he was attached to St Mark's Church, and prior to this he was at Abington Church, Northampton where he had been for 4½ years, being ordained at that church in March 1922 (as was the present 1999 Vicar Philip Bligh). A number of friends from Abingdon Church were present (as they were for me 61 years later!). Also present was Rev. F. T. B. Westlake from Easton Maudit who wrote a history of that village as Marlow was soon to write one of Bozeat.

Joseph Horace Marlow is remembered for many things but perhaps most notably for his *The*

The Reverend W. H. Britton 1927-28.

History of Bozeat Village which was published in 1936. It was thoroughly researched from original documents and reflects his own careful and meticulous recording of facts and events as witness his Log Book (kept up to date and held by his successors) of all that happened in his time here and in previous years. His researches, which formed the basis of his book, were first published in his monthly *Church Newsletter* in the 1930s and these were published together in the 1990s by the Bozeat Historical and Archaeological Society.

It was on 21st November of 1929 that Lord Spencer accompanied by Lady Anne Spencer, aged eight, and Lady Cynthia opened the new Church Hall in Allens Hill. The structure cost £500 and furniture £130. The Hall Fund was started in 1903 and the debt was cleared by January 1930. Previously the old building at the back of the Vicarage, originally a fowl house (and which is still standing 1999), was used as a parish council chamber, neatly whitewashed and furnished with chairs and electric light before the new hall was built. An equally enterprising spirit was shown in dealing with the problem of accommodating the Sunday School in the local cinema (building demolished in the 1980s) up the London Road – held on alternative Sundays in Rev. Daybell's time. It was used also by the Anglicans Young People's Association (A.Y.P.A.) which Marlow seems to have started in the 1930s and was still meeting there in the 1950s.

The Reverend J. H. Marlow 1929-44.

The new hall was built by a local builder. W. H. Cave and the vicar acted as architect and foreman! "The result is an attractive little hall, which any village would be glad to possess, constructed principally of asbestos and equipped with a large stage and dressing rooms, a kitchen boasting an up-to-date electric boiler, and electrically heated and lit throughout." (*Northampton and County Independent*, 23rd November) Three previous vicars were also present at the opening: the Reverend C. B. Jennings, the Reverend C. N. Daybell and the Reverend W. H. Britten.

In 1931 a Bozeat Scout Group was formed in May with the Vicar as Scout Master and earlier in that year (28th February) the Second Peal ever was rung on the bells.

On 14th August 1938, eight new aisle pews were dedicated each in memory of a parishioner and likewise four more memorial pews on 19th March 1939.

It was just after the outbreak of war in that same year on 18th September that the Roger Yates Organ in St Mary's was completed and dedicated, together with new choir stalls dedicated to the memory of a previous vicar, Arthur Kinch (1880-82).

These were the significant achievements of Vicar Marlow who was to see the village through almost to the end of the war as its Vicar. His churchmanship was broad and low and he wore only surplice and cassock and not vestments, a rather strict and formal bachelor who had time to play chess with the boys in the choir and involve himself with the Scouts. The following notes are to be found in the Vicar's Logbook: (unknown author) 30th January 1943: "Vicar J. K. Marlow rushed into hospital for operation (Wonderful recovery. Parishioners prayers and kindnesses very

Rev. Marlow outside the old vicarage with choir and church wardens in early 1940s. (*Vicars' Notebook*)
Front row in surplices: Ken Mallows, Kenneth Childs, Alan Botterill, Ron Drage, Vicar Marlow, Frank Hewlett, Philip Smart, Terry Drage, Philip Drage.
Back row: Bert Cave, Rose Smart, Mary Frost, Thora Hewlett, Hol Smith, Wally Bryant, Em Hewlett, Nancy Howard, Vera Smart, Gladys Pettit, Ern Dunmore.

great) After 3 weeks in Hospital, 3½ weeks in bed at vicarage he went to Devon for 11 weeks convalescing." In June he is back on duty.

22nd March 1944: "Vicar again to hospital. This time told he must give up his work at Bozeat." "Spoke to his congregation at Chancel Steps on Easter Morning at 10am Eucharist and administered the Cup. Passed away the following Sunday 16th April at Ideford, Devon where he is buried."

Phil Drage's sister, Mollie, was there on that Easter morning and told me how ill Vicar Marlow looked. "St Mary's was my second home." Phil used to say. It was his auntie, Annie Bryant, the older sister of his mother, who took the two children to church from a very early age and instilled in Phil the habit of a lifetime. "In Marlow's time we had 8 o'clock and 10 o'clock Communion (third Sunday was 10 o'clock Matins) and 6 o'clock Evensong. There would be 20 or so at 8 o'clock and 60 at 10 o'clock and about 40 at Matins. Of course there was no television then and nothing much else to do. Marlow was strict – very strict. We sat as a family in the first pew on the right, mother and father then me then Auntie Annie and then sister Mollie to keep us apart. Once, when we were older, about 16, a whole row of us boys at the back met together at 10 o'clock Holy Communion and when we had taken Communion Vicar Marlow said, 'I want to see you all afterwards.' We daren't but stay. He addressed us very slowly and said: 'If you boys want to come to Holy Communion you come at 8 o'clock not 10 o'clock (old folks come then). Then you can be off for the day. 8 o'clock is the proper time for you.' I agree with him – I always have – that's the right time for young people to take Holy Communion. When I see young people today coming later I don't think it right."

On 26th April 1944 the Reverend S. F. W. Powell was instituted into the Bozeat Living by the Bishop of Peterborough (Dr Claude Blagden). He was a younger man destined for higher things having previously been instituted Vicar of St Columba,

Corby in 1941 after a curacy at All Saints' Church, Peterborough and also a missionary in Johannesburg. "He was too good for Bozeat. He could go up into the pulpit and just preach without notes or anything. He was very, very, high. Marlow was low church. I think he went on to be a Canon. I don't remember much about Vicar Knight. We had a rota then for serving but he was high as well." (Phil Drage)

It was during his time, on the 8th March 1945 that a Memorial Service was held in memory of 22-year-old Lt. John Ahern who crashed his crippled bomber a few days before Christmas after steering it clear of the village thus saving many lives. 400 people gathered in memoriam to Lt. Ahern and an address was given by American Airforce Chaplain Everett B. Lesher of St Paul's, Minnesota who also presented the plaque on behalf of the 379 Bomb Group, U.S.A.A.F. which is still in the church today (1999).

The Reverend S. F. W. Powell 1944-49.

On 7th January 1950 the Reverend W. C. Knight was instituted Vicar to the Benefice of Bozeat by the Bishop of Peterborough (Spencer Leeson) and inducted by the Archdeacon of Oakham, Ven. E. N. Millard. An extract from *All Hallows Magazine, Wellingborough* for 19th July after his death on 18th June 1969 aged 61 reads: "with the sudden death of Cecil Knight, the Peterborough Diocese has lost a faithful parish priest, and All Hallows an old and loyal friend. The Vicar found him still here as curate of All Hallows in 1949 and priest-in-charge of the mission church of Saint Andrews, where he had done pioneering work for some 13 years and laid the foundation on which all others have

Bells standing in churchyard with Vicar Powell and son c.1946.

built and which remains solid to this day. Soon he was moved to Bozeat where he became Vicar, looked after his aged parents until their death and wore himself out in the fulfilment of his duties. Always an uncompromising Catholic (i.e. High Church), he was yet tolerant towards those of other communions and a man of compassion to all in need. As Chapter Clerk to the Higham Rural Deanery, he gave loyal service to the clergy, supporting the work of the Wellingborough branch of the Diocesan Guild of Bell-ringers as their president. His health had been poor for the past few years, but he bore the pain and frustration with his usual philosophic calm …"

His notes in the Vicar's Logbook bear out this picture of him. He continued Vicar Marlow's work with the Scouts and became their Group Scout Master, supporting their first camp in August 1950 at Denford. A strong traditionalist, he revived the old custom of Mothering Sunday of 'Clipping Mother Church' when, led by the vicar, the whole congregation joined hands and encircled the church singing "We love this place of God wherein Thine honour dwells." Also on Rogation Sunday the choir servers and congregation of both Easton Maudit and Bozeat led by the cross bearer processed through the village to Stoneypiece allotment ground where the vicar asked for blessing on "farm, field, allotment and factories of our village." As the procession wended its way through the village, the church bells rang. Afterwards the vicar and choir had supper at a local cafe.

The Reverend W. C. Knight 1950-67.

It was on Trinity Sunday, 4th June 1950 that Mr S. Centin was licensed as parish Lay Reader – perhaps our first lay reader and a sign of lay ministry to come. (Our Methodist friends had lay preachers from the beginning!)

In July 1951 the Spire was examined and found needing repair, carried out at a cost of £392-18-0. It was 18th July, two years later in 1953, that it was struck by lighting at 2.15 pm, just before Annie Bryant's funeral, damaging the clock and destroying the lightning conductor system. (Mollie Drage (as was) remembers how Auntie Annie was kneeling at her prayers as she always did, when she collapsed and died while the meal was burning on the stove in the kitchen! There is a brass plaque to her memory in church: To the Glory of God and in loving memory of Annie Bryant. A faithful worshipper in this Church. Died 15th July 1953.)

It was in Vicar Knight's time too on the evening of Monday 19th May 1952 about 8.30 pm that "a terrific storm broke out around Bozeat. The lightning and thunder was of the fiercest and the rain very heavy. A cloudburst between Bozeat and Harrold caused the brook to overflow, and the water rose in the district of the High Street to well above the lower window sills." as Knight describes the event. And it was in 1953 that Vicar Knight became also the Vicar of Ss Peter and Paul, Easton Maudit as the two Parishes were combined into one Benefice in that year.

In was in 1955 that carpeting was laid down (possibly for the first time) in the church on 1st November and was to remain there for 42 years to be replaced by another red carpet in December 1997.

Inspection of the church in 1955 showed there to be a bad infestation of Death Watch Beetle and the work of treating the wood and replacing badly damaged timbers took place between 3rd June and 24th September 1961 at the cost of £5,000.

Then on 1st October 1963 Vicar Knight took up residence in the new vicarage built by Messrs Marriotts Ltd of Rushden. The old vicarage, which was built in 1729/30 to replace the vicarage which had been burnt down in the great fire of that year which destroyed a third of the village dwellings, was levelled to the ground in 1964, sadly in the opinion of most villagers. Only the old steps leading to the front door and the barn behind which served as a church hall still remain (1999). On Feast Sunday of this year, 30th August, at the Parish Communion the new vicarage "was solemnly blessed, (these words underlined in red), sprinkled with holy water, and incensed by Vicar. A good Congregation assembled: Thurifer: Nigel Terry (son of headmaster, John Terry, Freemason and friend of the vicar who died 11th December 1983) Boat: Christopher Allen (son of Audrey and Dennis Allen and presently (1999) a vicar in Leicester): Crucifer: Christopher Bird.

Servers: Philip Drage and Jack Wright (Philip remained a faithful Server until his death on 29th September 1998): Organ: Mr Roger Tivey, who also played a Bach Fugue on the Organ after Mass. Mr Eric Brook managing Director of Messrs. Marriotts with Audrey his wife. These also came in for sherry and lunch afterwards." These notes of Vicar Knight clearly reveal the Catholic nature of his faith and practice. "There was no Sunday School in Vicar Knight's time so our children had to go to the Methodist Sunday School. When Richard was eight, Vicar Knight said to him, 'You're old enough to join the choir now', so he left the Sunday School and joined the choir." (Pat Cox)

Vicar Knight's final notes in the Log read as follows:

"Sept 20 1967 Vicar's Father (1876-1967), Mr William Ingham Knight died after short illness aged 91¼ years. Funeral Service Saturday 23. Interment at Easton Maudit Churchyard with his dear wife and sweetheart who died on Feb 27 1963. Sadly missed by his son Vicar RIP.

"Vicar still under Doctor with kidney trouble. Doctor says very run down and to take things steadily for 6 months. Vicar was in Northampton hospital for treatment May 9-31st 1966. Trouble failure of some kidney tubules to do proper work. Believed to have come from serious jaundice Vicar had at Wellingborough in 1942 everybody kind and helpful."

Cecil Knight died aged 61on 18th June 1969 and his funeral took place on St John Baptist's Day 24th June taken by the Bishop of Peterborough, and afterwards was buried with his mother and father at Easton Maudit.

At 7.30 pm on Wednesday, 19th November 1969 at the Church of Ss Peter and Paul, Easton Maudit, Revd Norman Ernest Palmer BD, Dipl.Th. (aged 40) was Instituted to the United Benefice of Bozeat and Easton by the Bishop of Peterborough and the induction was by the Archdeacon of Oakham.

Norman was formerly a Methodist Minister and previously Curate at Chipping Norton for two years. Born at Fairlight, Hastings and educated at Hastings Grammar School, he trained to be an engineering draughtsman in London and then became an engineering draughtsman in the RAF. In 1953 he entered Richmond Methodist College to train for three years for the Methodist ministry, and afterwards spent

10 years in Yorkshire and Devon. Vicar Palmer decided to become an Anglican and spent eight months at Rochester Theological College in 1966. In May 1967 he was made a deacon to serve at Chipping Norton Church and was ordained priest later that year. He came to Bozeat with his wife Beryl who was a teacher at a special school in London and two children Martin (6) and Julie (3). So why did Norman become an Anglican? From correspondence and comments it sees that he believed the Sacrament as central to worship and spiritual life. As more High Church Anglican practice emphasises the centrality of the Sacrament, so one sees evidence of such Catholicity in his ministry with the instalment of a perpetual light, an Aubrey for the Reserved Sacrament placed in the north wall of the chancel and the use of vestments in his time. He also introduced the Rite B Holy Communion service of the Alternative Service Book on its publication in 1980 at Bozeat together with the new Lectionary which was not an easy thing to do whereas Easton Maudit continued to use the 1662 Prayer Book as they do today.

The Reverend N. E. Palmer 1969-89.

Norman set off in great style by visiting every home in his parishes. Then in 1970 he re-established the Bozeat Parish Church Sunday School. Also that year he initiated an extensive programme of restoration for St Mary's, Bozeat, including replacing woodworm infected timbers supporting the old pews and in the roof, overhauling the 1939 electric organ, repairs to the windows and to the inside and outside stone work of the building. The estimated cost of structural repairs was £5,000 and that of the organ was to cost £1,000. Efforts of the parishioners over the years had put £2,810 into the Restoration Fund so another £2,450 needed to be raised, and over the next 19 years of his ministry Norman has left us a careful record of how this was done. A concert to celebrate the restoration of the organ was held on 24th March 1972 by organist Roger Tivey born in neighbouring Wollaston (and cousin of our own Fred Tivey – see 'Memories'), an internationally reputed organ recitalist, distinguished music teacher and composer. Along with this he carried out extensive research into the history of the village, writing excellent articles on the subject, several of which are published in this book and extracts of many appeared in the *About Bozeat* village magazine launched by Penny Brannon and others in 1980.

Vicar Palmer resigned due to ill health in 1989 aged 59 after 20 years ministry and retired to Bexhill-on-Sea, not far from the place of his birth.

Philip Hamilton Bligh aged 52 was instituted Vicar of the Benefice of Easton Maudit and Bozeat by the Bishop of Brixworth (Paul Barber) at 7.30 pm on Wednesday, 14th November 1990 with the induction by Basil Marsh Archdeacon of Northampton (after 25 years the longest-serving archdeacon I believe in the Church of England). He was ordained into the Church of England at Peterborough 3rd July 1988 and after 2½ years as Curate at Abington Church, Northampton came to this benefice. His previous life was as a professional scientist, having studied physics at University College, London, then medical research at the Institute of Cancer Research and Royal Marsden Hospital, London. At this point he felt called to full time Ministry and went to Wycliffe Hall, Oxford and St Catherine's College studying for the Ministry and taking a BA in Theology in 1963. Disillusioned with the Church of England (this was the sixties and the height of the 'God is Dead' theology) he returned to academia and went as a Lecturer in Physics to the University of Malaysia for three years, after which he returned to England and joined the staff of one of the newly established Polytechnics, eventually to become Head of the School of Applied Physics before responding for the second time to the call to full time Ministry. He came with Audrey his wife having a family of five children, Stuart, Rachel, Judi, Sarah and Jon. Audrey was daughter of Wilfrid Stott who was a missionary in China for 25 years.

The Reverend P. H. Bligh and his wife Audrey 1990-99.

Coming from a more charismatic and evangelical persuasion and, having been a Methodist Local Preacher for much of his life, he inevitably brought some of this flavour into his ministry. Bozeat introduced the use of a new Hymn Book, *Mission Praise*, published in 1990, which contains almost 800 hymns, the more popular of the old and the new. The Rite A Communion Service – the modern service – was introduced at Bozeat. The third Sunday of the month was established as non-Eucharistic All Age Family worship – already being developed before his time and led by Lay Reader Penny Brannon.

The restoration programme begun so well by Norman Palmer was continued with work on the south walls and the rebuilding of its parapet. Windows in the north aisle and chancel were restored and the Rose Window rebuilt out of new stone exactly to the old model. During this period the churchyard walls have been almost entirely rebuilt thanks to the work of the Parish Council.

The vicar inherited two medieval churches in sound condition thanks to the tireless work of parishioners and his predecessors over the last century and a half, so this enabled him to facilitate a programme of modernisation at Bozeat to enable wider and more effective use of this ancient building. As detailed elsewhere this has included an induction loop and sound enhancement system, conversion of the old vestry into a kitchen and toilet and a new gas-driven heating system and a new vestry in the Tower. Such modernisation made the church more available for use for parents and tots, a crèche, craft exhibitions and concerts in the church.

In 1992 Wellingborough Council installed floodlighting for the church and in 1994 a new lych gate lantern was made by Derek Cox and joined up to this system. Then in 1998 a new lantern for the gate into Hensman's Lane given in memory of Graham Clarke by his family.

In terms of the life of the church, Penny Brannon directed a performance in the Church of *Jesus Christ Superstar* (by Andrew Lloyd Webber) in March 1993 just after the new heating system became operational – packed out by villagers for its two performances. In 1993 we began our first series of what became known as The Bozeat

Lent Talks on Friday evenings in Lent held in our Independent Wesleyan Chapel and organised by all the churches. In the same year the first Holiday Club for children of Primary School age in August was held in the Methodist Church, drawing leaders from all churches (including Catholic) based on Scripture Union Holiday Club material, and this, as with the Lent Talks, has become an annual event attracting half the children in the village. In 1994 we had the first annual Bozeat Men's Dinner when some 50 men sat down to a splendid meal in the Church Hall with broadcaster and writer Brenda Courtie as the after dinner speaker. (The first women's dinner is scheduled for October 1999!). 6th June 1993 (the day when giant hailstones fell damaging houses and cars, etc.) also saw the start of the Lunch Club in the Church Hall organised in collaboration with Age Concern, with sometimes 40 senior citizens meeting for lunch, entertainment and company each Wednesday, thanks to the able band of volunteer helpers providing transport and serving at tables, under the lively leadership of our Avon lady Win Threlfall (now 82 in 1999!). The Hall itself is now completely double-glazed, has new tables, two cookers and improved heating to cater for these functions, and what with its use for youth club, carpet bowls, Bozeat Players, carers and tots and special events, it is in use most days of the week – managed so ably by Derek and Pat Taylor.

Finally we should record that Penny Brannon was licensed as our Lay Reader in May 1995 and Pat Smith and Anne Hickling (leader of Mums and Tots) as our Pastoral Assistants in March 1996. In April 1997 the vicar and his wife went on an exchange programme to be Rector of Holy Cross, Hackett, Canberra while their Rector, Archdeacon Allan Huggins, with his wife Jan, became Vicar of Bozeat and Easton Maudit. There was a live link in that year between Bozeat and Canberra on Bozeat Feast Day Morning Worship – the day that Lady Diana Spencer was killed in Paris in the early hours. The vicar and his wife returned in January 1998 to find the new lighting in the Chancel and Choir completed and a fine new red carpet beautifying the church. Just before their trip to Australia the vicar and his wife led a Pilgrimage to the Holy Land in February 1997 and another one is planned for February 2000 when a party of some 30, mainly from our villages (and four from Holy Cross) will be going to celebrate the new millennium.

On a practical matter, when Vicar Bligh arrived in 1990 the Parish Share was under £4,000 – now in 1999 it is over £13,000, reflecting the increasingly heavy financial responsibility placed on parishes themselves. It is a measure of the commitment of the parish that it has paid it in full every year.

CHAPTER 25

Closure of the Parish Churchyard
(A study in Parish Council practice and politics from the Minutes)
Norman Palmer

One of the great problems concerning all authorities (Church and Civil) from the middle of the 19th century onwards was that of overcrowded churchyards. These had been serving the population of this country for centuries, but what was satisfactory for the population of Medieval England simply could not cope with the increased numbers of 19th-century England and consequent burials. London solved the problem with large cemeteries on the outskirts; Brookwood Cemetery at Woking in Surrey opened in 1854 for the burial of London's dead and probably buried half of East London. And to facilitate this Waterloo Station had a special casket-loading platform.

The problem for Bozeat came towards the end of the 19th century. When one realises that the census for 1801 gave the population as 680 and that for 1901 was 1,478 you can see that it had risen by over 100% in 100 years. Neighbouring Wollaston churchyard was already closed for burials in 1882. There was a note in the Vestry Records (the village governing body before the establishment of a Parish Council in 1895) for 9th April 1885: "The question of the conversion of Bradshaw's Close" (which originally had been given for the maintenance of parish roads) "into a Parish Cemetery was adjourned for a time that the Vicar might collect information as how to go to work." There was silence after that in the records but obviously concern was growing about burial space. Bradshaw Close was not chosen.

In their very first year (1895) the Parish Council requested a report on the state of the Churchyard. The information given is interesting. It says it was possible to bury 107 more. The number of interments during the last three years (1892-95) had been 42, an average of 14 a year (even with a large population there are far fewer now). Of the 14, 10 had been infants of one year or under, showing the high infant mortality rates of those days. The Council felt in 1895 that there was no need to proceed to find a new cemetery. But obviously not all were satisfied for in that same year two sites were looked at according to Council records, one being called 'The Pickle', which must mean the 'Pightle'. But it was considered that the sites were too expensive. It was then proposed to hold a public meeting to discuss the Burial Act of 1879 which conferred on all Sanitary Authorities and Local Government Boards power to compel the provision of cemeteries where necessary, the land to be obtained compulsorily if not otherwise obtainable. The Local Government Board had powers to order burials to cease in any existing burial ground. It is obvious 'reading between the lines' that pressure was coming from somewhere for closure of the Churchyard, The expense of providing a cemetery was to form a charge upon the Poor Rate. This became a matter of debate in the village. When the writer lived in the village, there was a hint by an elderly person, now dead, that there had been some 'rearrangement' of previous burials to make room.

However, at Council Meetings, sites for a new cemetery continued to be suggested. Whitewalls, where the present cemetery now is was one and another site was Limekiln. A Mr Mobbs of Kettering offered some land but was declined as the offer was not considered suitable. Stoneypiece with its three acres was offered at £100 an

Remembrance ceremony at the cemetery off Easton Lane. (*Bozeat School Scrapbook*)

acre. The Council went from one considered site to another, obviously with some desperation. The Vicar had his own ideas and suggested enlarging the churchyard, but it would seem from lack of any further comment in the minutes that this was not taken up or adjoining sites were considered too expensive.

Then in 1903, the Local Government Board presented the Parish Council with what was in effect an ultimatum: either get another cemetery or we refuse further burials in your parish. It was their intention at the expiration of 10 days to present to his Majesty in Council that, for the protection of public health, burial should be discontinued in the church and churchyard. The Parish Clerk in 1903, looking back in the Council Minutes, found that they had approved a new cemetery in principle but had done nothing about it! The Council told the Local Government Board that they would proceed as quickly as possible, but could they defer the question of the cemetery? The Board said NO! – they must act. Something like panic must have set in at this stage, for this was pretty powerful pressure: the beloved dead would be buried in the corner of some foreign field, Wollaston or Easton Maudit!

Meanwhile the owners of the Bozeat Estate, the Royal Exchange Company, came to their aid and were prepared to give an acre of ground on Easton Lane for a cemetery. The offer was of course accepted. However, a loan of £600 was applied for to lay out the site, and £446 was actually spent on fencing and laying it out. A Burial Committee was formed in 1903 and fees laid down. A caretaker was appointed at £5 per annum in addition to fees for digging the graves. Mr Benjamin Pratt, father of the late Mr Pratt of Wheelwrights Yard, was appointed.

Coffins were carried on a hand-bier at the time and this was brought up for consideration. A hand-bier from a firm at Olney had been sent on approval at a price of £18-10s-0d, but on examination it was found that the hand-bier differed from the original photograph. Now a bit of bargaining took place. The Parish Council offered

£15 for it. The firm at Olney said £17 and eventually this was accepted. The bier had to be repaired three years later and, because Easton Maudit and Strixton wished to borrow it, a charge of 1 shilling was made for each loan in 1907. But profit could be made in other ways. As it was stony earth that was extracted for a burial, this was sold to the Rural District Council which may have used it for road-mending. The grass which was cut was also being sold at varying amounts each year totalling from 7/6d to £1-5-0d. Initially burials were segregated with Anglicans together in one block, and Non-Conformists in another.

In 1919 a letter was read from the caretaker of the cemetery complaining of a boy misbehaving in the cemetery and it was resolved by the Council that a letter be sent to the father of the boy. Some things never change.

Allens Hill with the doctor's house at the top of the hill. (*John Darker*)

The Arts

The Windmill Singers, assembled outside Manor Farm for their 1999 performance at The Castle in Wellingborough of *Thank You for the Music*.

Betty Watson, Tara Potter, Sue Partridge-Underwood, Linda Tomkins, Julie Mines, Sharyn Stein, Marion Green, Sue Carter, Viv Risby, Sue Evans, Gwyneth Wiggins, Faith Jones, Barry Fletcher, Lynne Collier, Harold Smith, Brian Skittrall, Marian Brown, Bill Shepheard, John Parrott, Cecil Farrow, Peter Cartwright, Gerald Corby, Jean Knightley, Ann Fletcher, Pat Summers, Lyndis Payne, Nicola Houghton, Eleanor Minney, Julie Williams. (*Marian Brown*)

CHAPTER 26

Music

Village musicians and the Minstrels Gallery
There is no trace of the maker of the Organ given by the Reverend F. J. Pizey. It was originally, in 1861, put in the Minstrel's Gallery high up at the West End fixed to the Wall of the Tower. The entrance to it can still be seen in the NW Pillar and part of the stairs is presently used in the thatched cottage up Easton Lane (see *Marlow*, p.22).

These minstrels must have provided the music prior to its installation. We have evidence of this in bills for the repair of instruments, e.g. "1827, paid Sparks of Yardley for mending the base viol, 9/6. Strings for ditto, 4/6. 1839 Paid J. Chesterton, Wellingboro, for 2 Clarionet Reeds, 6d.: 1 Violincello String, 1/6. 1841, For repairing the Base Viol, 14/6. 1850, Paid J. Chesterton, 1 set Violincello Strings, 3/6; 2 Violin 1st and 3rd Strings, 1/4d; 4 Clarionet Reeds, 8d." (John Chesterton was a bookseller, stationer and printer in Silver Street, Wellingborough.)

Thomas Dobbs played the Violin, Samuel Skevington the Bassoon, Thomas Mallow the Clarionette, Samuel Monk the Violincello or Base Viol.' (*Marlow*, Sheet 33 and elsewhere) We do not know when our Gallery was fixed thus, and one would like to know where the Coat of Arms, which now hangs in its place on the east wall of the tower, was hung when it was first put in the church in 1770.

Presumably the gallery was erected when music became popular in church. Popular music flourished in the great age between the Armada and the Civil War. German travellers to Elizabethan England noted with admiration how they:

> "'heard beautiful music .... for in all England it is the custom that even in small villages the musicians wait on you for a small fee.' ... and whole troops of able composers flourished in that great age of the madrigal. The arena of Tudor and Stuart music was not the concert hall but the domestic hearth.... Music and song were the creation and inheritance of the whole people. The craftsman sang over his task, the peddler sang on the footpath way, and the milkmaid could be heard 'singing blithe' behind the hedgerow, or in the North Country crooning the tragic ballads that told of Border fight and foray. The common drama was poetic drama.... It was no mere accident that Shakespeare and Milton came when they did.... And in the life of John Milton, born five years after Elizabeth died, we read clearly how the three chief elements in the English culture of that day – music, the classics and the Bible – combined to inspire the 'God-gifted organ-voice of England'" (*Trevelyan*, p.433)

It was Religious Revival under the Wesley brothers in the midst of the 18th century that was 'successful' amongst ordinary folk as much for the outpouring of hymns from brother Charles in popular music style of the day as for the passionate and unconventional preaching of brother John. Revival is so often accompanied by an outpouring of passionate and powerfully emotional music, and we can only believe that our instrumentalists found a place in our church from Elizabethan times onwards and also at our hearths and in our inns. And did something of the enthusiasm amongst ordinary folk in Georgian England find its way into the music of our parish church? Surely yes, as it was just down the road that the ex-slaveship

Captain John Newton came as Curate to Olney in 1764, joined three years later there by friend and poet William Cowper, who between them wrote the famous Olney Hymns, full of great devotion and evangelical fervour, such as *Amazing Grace* and *How Sweet the Name of Jesus Sounds*.

The old organ and organists and choir

As we have seen in Chapter 2, Marlow wrote in the 1930s: "There is no trace of the maker of the organ given by Rev. F. J. Pizey" (in 1861). "When it was taken down, diligent search was made. Some gummed labels still adhered to the large wooden pipes addressed to 'Rev. Pizey, Olney Station,' and written in pencil along another part (later addition) was 'Mr Shaw, Organ Builder.'" There have been several Renovations, including new bellows (1906, by Mr Austen of Irchester, who afterwards set up an organ-building business in America). In 1875 the Organ was removed from the Gallery and placed just inside the Screen in the Chancel on the South Side (where the console now is), so that the Vicar could play it through a hole he cut in the Screen, so it is said. The Choir desks and seats were set up in the Chancel at this time. Previously the Chancel was clear of anything except the Altar, etc. The organ was moved again in 1877 on to a platform made by Levi Hardwick on the North side, where it remains now (1999) and the piece of the Screen was replaced (except the feet of the two panels, which had been placed in upside down). The organist at the time of the Opening (1861) was Mr William Hooton Drage who opened it with the *Hallelujah Chorus*. He was followed in 1879 by his son, Mr George Allebone Drage." (*Marlow*.)

George was one of the five Drage brothers all connected with the Boot Trade as we have seen, all staunch Methodists (but George must have enjoyed playing the organ at St Mary's) and very musical being members of the 'Bozeat Glee Party' which toured many surrounding villages and were at Christmastide often invited by the Marquis of Northampton to entertain his guests.

Marlow writes in his notes kept in a book and added to by vicars of Bozeat since:

"From 1888 George Johnson, John Henry Drage, Tom Edward Drage, – Fisher: 1894, William Robinson; 1899 John

The old organ given by Vicar Pizey 1861.
(*Vicars' Logbook*)

Brearley; until in 1904 Mr George Hewlett was appointed and very faithfully carried on until 1932, when Mr H. Hollingsworth Smith became Organist and Choir Master and still is so today.

"Blowers are a most important part of the Organ! I cannot go far back, but we all remember Peggy Drage who, when Mr Smith came, objected to his using so much wind; and as she told me afterwards, 'I says, he shan't have it, so I let it out and he had to stop.' She was followed by Fred Jones; and the last of his line, Walter Bryant, who retires with the honourable record that he always found enough wind for the Organist although the bellows got very wheezy! As the Organ was opened with the *Hallelujah Chorus*, it was fitting that the last thing played on it on Sunday night, 22nd August (Feast Day) 1939, should be the *Hallelujah Chorus*. Mr Smith got all out of it that was possible that night, and the blower remained game to the end, although that last time tried him to the uttermost. Now electricity does the blowing in the New Organ, opened 16th September [1939] at 5.30 pm, free of debt; the cost, £525, which it had only taken six years to get together. Well done, Bozeat Church workers. It would be too great a task to mention the various members of the Choir since the time it removed to the Chancel, but it would be well to note that the men and boys who first donned surplices on Christmas Day, 1924. The choir then was: Boys in blue Cassocks: Arthur Dunmore, Len Dobbs, Frank Hewlett, Joe Dobbs, Joe Squires, Tom Cave. Men: Cecil Drage, J. H. Coles, W. Fern, C. Belcher, G. Britten, B. Robinson." (*Marlow.*)

From the records, the choir at the opening of the new organ in 1939 in their same uniforms were: Boys: Phil Drage, Kenneth Mallows, Kenneth Child, Phil Smart, Alan Botterill, Terry Drage, Max Laughton. And Men: Ron Drage, Sid Blundell, W. Fern, Paul Drage, Sid Drage and J. Edwards.

The Roger Yates organ
The dedication of the New Organ, console and Choir Stalls was on Saturday 16th September 1939 and was "presented for dedication by its builder, Mr Roger Yates, of Bodmin, Cornwall, and the dedicatory sentences were immediately followed by the singing of the doxology accompanied by the organ which up to this point had been silent, (played) by Mr R. Richardson Jones, B Mus. F.R.C.O. (All Saints Church, Northampton)." (*Marlow*) This was followed on the next day with a recital by Mr J. A. Tatam, B Mus., A.R.C.M., F.R.C.O. Director of Music at Oundle School.

In his October Edition of *St Mary's Church Magazine*, Marlow writes: "It was very appropriate that Mr Roger Yates, of Bodmin, the maker of the Organ, should say the words presenting the Organ to be Dedicated. He had worked most laboriously to get it ready for the day, most of the week 1½ hours before breakfast until late into the night, but was greatly hampered by transport difficulties and other delays in delivery, so there was still much to do after the Dedication. Mr Richardson-Jones was not able to use parts of the Organ. Mr Yates worked on Saturday night from 8 o'clock until 1.30 Sunday morning, and made great improvements for the Recital; but there was still three day's work to do. Mr Tatam, of Oundle, was most enthusiastic in his praise of our splendid instrument and asked to be allowed to come again and make further acquaintance with it."

In the *Organists' Review* for November 1993 there is an article 'Roger Yates – Organbuilder', from which we learn that he was born in 1905 and educated at Tonbridge School before taking up an apprenticeship with the Willis Firm of organbuilders. There he worked on such important organs as that at Liverpool and Westminster Cathedrals. In 1927 he moved to Nottingham and took over the local firm of Lloyd and Co; his work can be seen in and about the city and it was in the early 1930s he established a reputation for himself building and rebuilding organs in the Midlands. Quoting from the article: "Perhaps showing how as later in his career Yates' smaller organs were perhaps more representative of his thoughts and ideas was the 1939 rebuild of the 1861 Tristam organ at Bozeat Parish church." The following specification shows Yates' ingenuity albeit still with electro-pneumatic action and detached console. Clever duplexing and distribution of stops gives great flexibility for solo and plenum registrational possibilities. The console is in the chancel and the pipework at the west end."

The Specifications are: A two manual instrument of 32 notes – there being 13 speaking stops, four couplers, one tremulo, making a total of 18 registers and a total of 747 pipes.

In 1972, Vicar Norman Palmer had the organ restored at a cost of £1,000, renewing the "electric action which joins the chancel console to the pipework in the north-west corner of the nave (which had) progressively deteriorated and the pipes cleaned, thus ensuring its survival "an act of faith in these days when the unpleasant timbre of electric organs are being increasingly heard in our churches." (*Palmer.*) To celebrate its restoration, a Celebrity Recital was given by Roger Tivey on 24th March 1972, an organist of international repute, music teacher and composer and Wollaston born, cousin we believe to our own Fred Tivey.

Roger Yates Organ in St Mary's installed 1939. (*Vicars' Logbook*)

As to organists after Hollingsworth Smith – John Darnell learned on this instrument as a boy. He played at Annie Bryant's funeral in 1953 when lightning struck the tower. He started playing regularly from the age of 16 while still a boy at Wellingborough School in 1948 and continued until 1955 when he left to do his National Service. He remembers that he was followed on the organ by Sydney Jeffs and then Mrs Boswell. John himself has, for the last 25 years, been 'temporary organist' at Easton Maudit playing for the services (and singing) with great passion and dexterity for the 1662 Prayer Book worship of Mattins and Evensong he loves so much. Stan Silsby started playing the instrument at St Mary's as a boy of 15 in 1956 and was presented with a fine clock when he officially retired in 1984, only to be brought out of retirement and continue playing until 2001 – a period of 45 years. He has been joined over the period from 1982 by David Flint, brother of Marion Brown of Manor Farm, who is a fine soprano and director of the village choir, the Windmill Singers. In recent years, Stan's son-in-law, Philip Ansell, more at home on the electric organ, has been playing regularly for Sunday Worship on the Yates instrument (and his modern instrument for Family Worship) which in 1999 is going as well as ever under the careful attention of local organ builder Robert Shaftoe from Pavenham.

The Windmill Singers

In 1991 the Vicar introduced a new Hymn Book, *Mission Praise*, at Bozeat containing nearly 800 hymns, a selection of the most well known of the old and the new, so many of which are popular on BBC Songs of Praise. A small group began that year to meet to learn new hymns and songs and choose together those for each Sunday and practise them with the help of Marian Brown at Manor Farm. Then in 1992 Marian started her own Choir which became the Windmill Singers, meeting for practice (after our hymn practice now in the vicarage) at the Wesleyan Independent Chapel. It has gone from strength to strength and was featured in the ITV Village Programme about Bozeat in 1993. The choir sings for Weddings and Feast Days and Carol Services in the Village together with its own annual concert at Christmas as well as in villages and residential homes in the area. Members of the choir include: Sopranos – Julie Mines, Sue Evans, Jackie Ford, Betty Watson, Marion Green, Gwyneth Wiggins, Mary Clarke, Margaret Sharratt, Tara Potter. Contraltos – Ellie Minney, Lyndis Payne, Pat Summers, Julie Williams, Carol Razzel, Mabel Pettit, Jean Knightley. Tenors – Gerald Corby, John Parrott, Brian Skittrall, Matthew Woodford, Lynne Collier. Bases – Peter Cartwright, Harold Smith, Cecil Farrow, Bill Shepheard, Philip Bligh, Gordon Mines, – with Sue Partridge-Underwood our accompanist on the piano.

A climax to its history was a grand concert *Thank You for the Music* at The Castle in Wellingborough on Wednesday, 2nd June 1999, held in aid of the Marie Curie Cancer Care Field of Hope for which over £2,000 was raised. It was a sell-out with over 500 enjoying an evening of entertainment with readings by Peter Croft, features by the Vivien Lowe School of Dancing from Wollaston and Louise Wiggins, a 13-year-old harpist from Allens Hill, scholar of The Purcell School – and Peter Cartwright our compère, as always, with Harold Smith there to add further humour to the choir's natural mix of songs from the shows, with lighter and more classical items.

Mention should be made of Ruth Allen who runs Minimusic in the village and teaches music at the village school developing remarkable musical skills in many of our children – such as Louise. The school choir under her direction has performed in music festivals such as at the Royal Festival Hall, London on several occasions.

Bozeat bands – *Marlow*

"About the year 1873, a Drum and Fife Band was formed in Bozeat. Mr George Coles was the Conductor, Edward Corley (Big Drum), George Drage (Kettle Drum for a time then Fife), Neil Silsby (Piccolo). Others in the Band were, James Silby, William C. Drage, Alfred Maxwell, Eddy Maxwell, George Allebone. There are several tales told of going to nearby villages and of playing at Easton Maudit, and of playing for Feast Day, but no date of the last time they played. Some remember occasions when the field at Prescott's farm was used for dancing, and when George Allebone, Tom (Scott) Dobbs and George Dobbs played the Fiddle for the Sir Roger de Coverley (or was it called 'A hunting we will go'). One occasion was Queen Victoria's Jubilee, 1887. About 1887 a Brass Band took the place of the Drum and Fife. [They played at a Fête and Jumble Sale on the Vicarage Grounds on Thursday, August 11th 1892 which also included dancing, theatricals and a museum of curiosities!] Mr Neal Silby started this and conducted, also playing the Cornet at times. Other Cornet players were William Elliott and Neil Drage. Repiano: William Robinson. 2nd and 3rd Cornets: Levi King, Ernest Hooton, John Drage. Tenor Horn: William King. Baritones: Edward Hooton, Thompson Drage, Harry Edmunds, Euphonium: Thomas Hooton. Trombones: George Fairey, George King, Fred Tompkins. Bass: William Line. Drummer: Joseph Laughton. Other men who played in the band during its existence were: James Pratt, William Nichols, Robert Elliott, Dexter Daly, Frank Partridge, Len Partridge, W. Thompkins, Jack Mabbutt, Charles Mabbutt, Ted Corby, Harry Elliott, John Silby. Two men who helped as Instructors were: Walter Corby, a soldier who came home at times; and Walter Reynolds, of Earls Barton. The Band carried on by getting up dances and socials and was later conducted by William Elliott who started in the Bozeat Band at the age of 10, leaving to play for Kettering Rifles at age 18 and was chosen to play for 'Besses of the Barn', coming back again as bandmaster of Bozeat Band. They went to four contests: Stanion, Stanwick, Finedon and Rushden, winning two 3rd prizes at Stanion, under the conductorship of Walter Reynolds, who later went to the Queen's Hall Orchestra. It was at first called 'Bozeat Victoria Brass Band', and later 'Bozeat Prize Band'. Other places at which the Band played were: Silverstone, Kislingbury, Yardley Hastings, Castle Ashby, Wolverton. At Wolverton a boy stood on a box to play a cornet solo, now he is [1930s] Organist at Castle Ashby and an F.R.C.O., and has memories of playing on the terrace of Castle Ashby with the Bozeat Band (William Robinson). The members gradually left until only eight players remained. The date when it finally broke up is uncertain. A newspaper of November 17th, 1908, tells a story of a member of the Band who signed his name on the visitors book of a hotel and added B.B.B.B.B.B. and when asked what degree he had, said, 'I'm the Best Bass Bugler in the Bozeat Brass Band!' An entry in the Burial Register for January 18th, 1890 says, George Fairey, aged 27, formerly a Ringer, a Singer, and a member of the Band. The Band played at his funeral." (*Marlow*, Sheet 51, pp.89-90.)

CHAPTER 27

Spencelayh

A human camera

Charles Spencelayh was the youngest of 11 children. He was born at Rochester in Kent on 27th October 1865 (his father Henry having died a few months earlier). He is quoted as saying, "I was born in the usual way, number eleven, and so at six months I was given pencil and paper to amuse myself." He progressed to working in oils when he was eight! His genius blossomed in the 1880s when he was selling copies of the old masters to dealers for 7/6d each! (See *Evening Telegraph*, 26th June 1958). At 23 he had his first painting accepted for the Royal Academy Summer Exhibition – the youngest exhibitor there – and regularly exhibited pictures at the Academy throughout his lifetime being their oldest exhibitor at over 90. He married Elizabeth Stowe in 1890 in London and had one son, Vernon, in 1891. His wife died in 1937 from pneumonia. His son was also to live to a ripe old age, and was a painter in a similar style to Charles.

In 1951 he was commissioned to paint a portrait of Queen Mary. She became a lifelong admirer of his work, having several of his paintings in her collection. She was first attracted to his work in 1950 on seeing *The Accident*. Spencelayh painted a miniature for her famous doll's house which is still a great attraction to visitors at Windsor Castle. It is a portrait of King George V and hangs as a picture on the wall of the doll's house, being only the size of a postage stamp.

His father was an engineer and iron and brass founder, the family firm being W. & H. Spencelayh of Rochester. On one occasion Spencelayh said to Don Roberts of his father; "You have seen those water tanks beside the railways for replenishing the engines haven't you. Well next time you are on a train and pass one look carefully and you will see the name 'Spencelayh' painted there!"

His father was also a friend of Charles Dickens. Is this why he called his son Charles? Whether or not this is so, this link with Dickens does seem to have given a deliberate Dickensian touch to some of his paintings such as *The Old Curiosity Shop*. And like Dickens in much of his writing, Spencelayh in many of his paintings is fascinated by the flotsam and jetsam of life and visually describes it in great detail. In so doing he has preserved for us a social document of great historical value of the ordinary and mundane in English culture and society. This is particularly true of his work whilst at Bozeat where he brings to life in his paintings the chaotic detail and jumble of

Self portrait of Charles Spencelayh. (*M. Drage*)

life in a Northamptonshire boot and shoe village. There, in the tiny homes and backyards and alleys was where boots were surely made for Cromwell's men (who seemed to have used our church as their barracks), and made ever since by methods that have scarcely changed in 300 years.

How did he do that?
What was special about his methods was his painstaking attitude to detail, planning and designing his pictures like a draftsman or engineer (like his father). The apparent disorder of his studio betrayed this extraordinary attention to detail. His great preference for painting old men seems to lie in the rich store of visual history in their well-worn features and clothing and their cluttered habitats as a record of their past.

His lifelong fascination with detail is shown by his interest in Miniatures. He was a founder member of the Royal Society of Miniature Painters. His son Vernon Spencelayh, who at 85 was almost blind from painting miniatures himself, writes of his father's working methods. He would consider a new subject for about three days and then rough out the composition on the back of an old envelope. He would then build a set in his studio, furnishing it very carefully with props from his own several rooms full of junk. He would then hire one or two locals as models (see later). After making a drawing the same size as the proposed painting with the aid of many measurements, he would transfer it directly to canvas and start painting about 10 days later, finishing each part as he went along. Bigger pictures could take as long as anything from six weeks to six months.

In the early days he would get £3 to £6 plus copyright. Today these pictures can sell for tens of thousands of pounds! When despised by modern painters for his meticulous and almost photographic style he would answer: "As long as I see an apple as an apple, I shall paint it as an apple." To one local reporter who visited him in Bozeat when he was in his eighties, he said mischievously: "I shall change to this modern stuff as soon as I am old enough!"

Why Bozeat?
He had married again in 1939 to Elizabeth Boxall. They did not come to Bozeat until 1941 when he was already 75-years-old, after he and his wife were bombed out of their house in Lee, now part of the Borough of Lewisham in south-east London (destroying the house along with some 400 of his draft sketches and paintings!), narrowly escaping with their lives. That same night they commandeered a London taxi and raced through the darkness to old friends Mr and Mrs Coney at Lavenham Hill Farm, Olney, who were to find them their new home at 105 London Road, Bozeat. Charles knew the area, having lived in Olney in the early 1920s. At first they rented the house from Dick Botterill's mother, Frances Partridge (whose mother owned it before her), who thus became the great man's landlady and had to collect his rent! Eventually he bought the house and they called it 'St Mildred's' after their previous home. Now it is called, understandably, Spencelayh House.

Elizabeth, who shared his life in Bozeat, was previously married to Charles Boxall, headmaster of St John's School, Clapham. As wife of a famous painter, she entertained extensively and was a lively and witty conversationalist and was well known in the village. She was godmother to John Farey's only child, Joy, and was an active member of the Mother's Union at St Mary's and the Bozeat Woman's Institute. In August 1955 she was taken into the Park Hospital, Wellingborough, and died.

After his wife's death, Spencelayh was looked after by Mary Corby across the road at number 124. He was always 'at home' to visitors, remembers Mary. There was an old cobbler's workshop at the bottom of his garden, and he converted this into his studio. "You would squeeze past a mass of bric-a-brac and find yourself transported back five reigns, for the hut is packed with the Victorian furniture that has figured in so many of Spencelayh's pictures – old wall clocks, birds in glass cases, prints, a stuffed baby crocodile, oil-lamps, bellows and fishing rods." – So author and journalist Tony Ireson describes a visit to the old man.

Mary's husband Mick, who lived across the road, did his garden, helped him make the crates for his pictures to be sent to exhibitions, etc. and organised the sets for his pictures, remembers that, in winter especially, he also used the front room to the right of the front door as a studio. "The old man would sit there in his chair with his cigarette in his mouth, directing me exactly where to put every object. When the set was just how he wanted he would signal to me and we would leave the room and he would lock the door so nothing could be touched saying, "Now we must wait for the dust to collect! (an essential ingredient in so many of his paintings!) "And how he painted dust I shall never know – but he did!" said Mick reflectively.

Spencelayh was always ready to entertain new friends and to accept criticism or compliments with that whimsical humour that characterised him. On his 90th birthday he told a friend: "Now I am 90 I'm trying for the two 0s. They tell me they're more expensive. I do hope I can afford it." For his self-portrait at 88 he had borrowed Marjorie Drage's lucky double-eight domino (she brought it to show me) which he included in the top right-hand corner of this perfect mirror image of himself. Charles Spencelayh died at St Andrew's Hospital, Northampton on Wednesday, 25th June 1958 in his 93rd year.

Farewell
His funeral service was at 10.30 am on Monday 30th June 1958 at St Mary's, at which the Reverend W. C. Knight officiated, to be followed by burial beside his first wife Elizabeth at Chislehurst, Kent. In place of flowers donations were to be sent to the Artists Benevolent Society. According to Mrs Smith of Lavenham farm, Spencelayh loved to sing 'Amazing Grace' and wanted it sung at his funeral but Rev. Knight, a high churchman, also his executor (with Gordon Boxall, his stepson) vetoed the idea on the grounds that the hymn was unsuitable for funerals! In his address Vicar Knight said of Spencelayh: "He was a happy, homely man, never happier than when he had someone to talk to. He has enriched the world with his painting. He was a wonderful benefactor of the church here at Bozeat. He often told me if he could paint nature as well as the almighty God made it, he would be a proud and contented painter."

Characters in oil
Marjorie Drage became a good friend of the Spencelayhs and a companion to Charles after his wife's death. She remembers how he was always very interested in the elderly people of the village, and many of them became models for his pictures. These included Chrissie Mallows, Bob Robinson, Mr 'Rocker' Drage, Miss Sarah Maycock, Mr Bayes, Francis Curtis, and he painted Mick and Mary's daughter Maureen once when she was six, soon after he arrived in Bozeat, and again in the last year there when his eyesight was too poor to finish the picture – indeed he wanted to call it, *The Unfinished Portrait*.

'Nothing like Leather' by Spencelayh featuring Bob Robinson. (*M. Drage*)

Sarah Maycock was about the same age as Spencelayh and was the first woman he had painted for 20 years. Asked why he seldom painted women, he replied with a twinkle in his eye, "You can order men about better!"

Bob Robinson's only child Florence Louise was born in 1900 and moved into the new council house at 17 Council Street when it was built in 1926. His granddaughter, Sandra Carvel (née Smart), who with her husband Barry, ran the Paper Shop from 1982-85, recalled her still vivid memories of her grandfather while we sat in their cottage at 55 Allens Hill. "He was a lovely man. He was a slipper worker – worked for the family firm of Coleman in Irchester but I remember him working on his allotment behind our house in Bull Close which Alfie Underwood build for my parents in 1939, when he also build Jack Walker's house in Easton Lane. I used to go and peep through the door into the barn when Spencelayh was painting Grandpap, and Mrs Spencelayh would come and take us into the house and give us a glass of orange juice. He made bamp (local name for grandpa) take off his shoes to show he was relaxing and bamp was so embarrassed because he had a hole in his sock. But Spencelayh said, 'You must not mend it. We will make that hole a focus for the picture' – so there it is! The painting is of a man about 80 relaxing with a cup of tea, his old boots thrown off, looking thoughtfully at a new boot on the table in front of him. Spencelayh called the picture, *Nothing like Leather* and it is dated 1953.

Tom C. Drage, nicknamed 'Rocker' – there were so many Drages in Bozeat so they all had to have nicknames! – sat for Spencelayh no less that 14 times. The last 12

'Home Treatment' by Spencelayh featuring Jack Bayes.
(M. Drage)

years of his life until he died in the early 60s at the age of 93 he lived all alone in his tiny cottage next to the Cross Keys pub where there is now the village green, surrounded by his treasured mementos of a lifetime. A shoe fitter all his life until he retired he also used to play for Bozeat Rugby Club and up to the time of his death was a member of the village Darby and Joan club. Until a month before he died he would walk up to the house of his only son, Roland, in London Road every day for his dinner. He was the perfect Spencelayh character! Spencelayh painted him asleep by a table on which lay a trumpet and called the picture, *Much noise. Little music.* In an exhibition of 161 of his paintings at the Art Gallery, Guildhall Road, Northampton in September 1944 the picture is priced at £84. In another picture, 'Rocker' is a street musician invited into a cottage by the kind looking lady of the house (Mrs Spencelayh), seated at the table with a cup of tea and his French horn on the empty chair by his side. He called the picture, *Generosity.*

Then there was Jack Bayes, who was rather a scruffy character and was known by the nickname 'Johnny Bundlehead'. "He was quite an embarrassment to his family," Marjorie remembers. Jack lived in his tiny cottage just to the right of the old Town Well called 'Little Thatch'. He had the unpleasant job of taking the night-soil cart round the village. Tom Partridge-Underwood's mum, Olive Underwood, along with Olive Johnson, used to 'lay out' the village dead. Tom, when a boy, remembers how when Mum came home, having just laid out Jack Bayes, she said to Dad, "Stan, I never seen an 'ernia like it!" And his grandson Austin Furniss told me the other day (16th August 1999), "I remember going into Little Thatch one day to see my grandfather and finding him dead."

But Jack was just the personality that Spencelayh wanted to paint. Mick Corby recounted to me (7th November 1995 – and confirmed by Jack's nephew Alec Bayes) how on the appointed day Mr Bayes arrived on the doorstep with his face and appearance washed and shaved and Mr Spencelayh sent him away until they were grubby again! In the picture, Jack is cleaning the giant face of a grandfather clock with an equally large pair of bellows and Spencelayh called the picture, *Home Treatment*! The Furniss' have a print of another of his pictures portraying their grandfather, hanging in their hall.

Chrissie Mallows he painted sitting behind a round table resting his clasped hands on the huge leather-bound family Bible in front of him. Spencelayh called this picture,

Not Alone and told Marjorie that this picture "gave him more satisfaction than any others of his later years." When exhibited at James Green's Bond Street Galleries in April 1957 it was priced at 20 guineas along with another Bozeat painting of another village character which he called *His Old Wedding Hat* and which was going for 30 guineas. On the back of Marjorie Drage's print of *Not Alone*, Spencelayh has written: 'Exhibited at the Royal Academy 1946 (on the line)' i.e. one of the most outstanding exhibits. Hanging on the wall behind Mr Mallows is a picture of Christ with the crown of thorns which he painted for his wife. The Mallows are an old village family going back to at least the 17th century and his more recent ancestors – and his son as well as he himself – spent their lives in the shoe industry. The family had fallen on hard times in the middle of the 19th century and spent some years in the old workhouse adjacent to the churchyard and situated in what is now called, appropriately, Mallows Yard. Somehow, Spencelayh could capture much of this personal history in the features of the old man – or is this my imagination?

'Not Alone' by Spencelayh featuring Chrissie Mallows. (*M. Drage*)

Spencelayh painted Francis Curtis while he was still a teenager at Wollaston School. His brother Colin, known to everyone as 'Bish' (possibly because their father was a Methodist lay preacher!) is one of the remaining village characters knowing more about the fields and animals and plants and village life and history than most. "There aren't many of us left," he is fond of saying. Spencelayh, appropriately, called the painting, *In those Days Nature Was the Guide to Art*. In it, the young student is seated at a table gazing reflectively at the picture of Sir David Wilkie's *The Blind Fiddler* hanging on the wall in front of him. Characteristically we notice a picture of Queen Victoria on the wall behind him. Signed and dated 1955, some commentators believe the picture sums up Spencelayh's artistic philosophy.

Marjorie remembers ...

Marjorie Drage was living in Wellingborough as a companion to Irene Page during these years – and was so for 35 years. She came back to Bozeat twice a week to visit her mother who lived close by the Spencelayhs and would frequently pop in with friends to see the paintings as they both enjoyed company. "Mr Spencelayh always had a lot of letters to post on Sunday afternoons, and knowing what time my bus was due in, would wait for me, and I would go in to see how the latest picture was progressing. Every wall in the house was covered with oil paintings, water colours,

Painting by Spencelayh entitled 'In those Days Nature was the Guide to Art' featuring Francis Curtis. (*M. Drage*)

copper etchings, miniatures, etc. (You could scarcely see the wall paper for pictures, remembers Dick Botterill.) Mr Spencelayh was very generous and when a new picture was finished, he would give away many reproductions of it to friends. Most of mine he signed for my album, saying with his droll sense of humour, "That will add ninepence to its value!" He was such a jolly old gentleman, and delighted in relating anecdotes about the pictures and their models, especially if they were against himself. As soon as a new picture was finished he was surrounded by reporters from all around the district to hear of his latest adventures. He was never at a loss for something humorous to say, or to express his views on modern art.

"One of my favourite anecdotes was concerning an old lady who kept a junk shop in London and would let Mr Spencelayh know if she had found anything suitable for one of his conglomeration pictures. This time it was a fowl in a glass case, for which he paid one shilling. It was placed in a sunny bedroom, and after a few days the case was full of flying moths. Mr Spencelayh called on the old lady to complain and, in his mischievous way, said be must have sixpence returned. The old lady very quickly replied, 'Oh no, you owe me sixpence, you only paid for the fowl and case!'

"In most of the paintings would be a collection of oddments, pieces of string, keys, postage stamps, letters, cigarettes, pictures hung crooked on the walls, an old aspidistra turned up many times, old boots, Toby jugs, etc. Mr Spencelayh would borrow knick-knacks from villagers and friends who would be delighted to see them included in his pictures. In one such conglomeration, for example, called *Grandmother's and Grandfather's Treasures* dated 1945, there in the foreground is the metal hearthstand on which would hang the kettle before the open fire which belonged to Miss Rice who kept a shop on what is now the village green.

'His Old Wedding Hat' by Spencelayh featuring Bob Robinson. (*M Drage*)

"A great honour came one day, in a letter from one of Queen Mary's ladies-in-waiting requesting a specially painted picture, and on the wall in that picture was to hang a portrait of Queen Mary, which would be sent for him to copy. The Queen already had two typical Spencelayh pictures; one included a portrait of Queen Victoria, and the other Queen Alexandra. When the sketch was finished and sent for Queen Mary's approval, the reply was, 'Yes, the Queen liked it but would prefer that her portrait on the wall was straightened.' However the artist ignored this." Mrs Spencelayh is the model included in the picture – together with a canary which decided to alight on Queen Mary's picture, so it was painted there!

Once Spencelayh had prepared the set for a picture it was never touched, not even dusted, and with only occasional sittings that corner of the studio would be roped off for several months. Once a loaf was part of the set, and each day during painting a mouse came and gradually ate all the bread. But the artist's brush was quicker than the mouse and the finished painting included both the loaf and the little thief!

Sadly, a few years before his wife died, Spencelayh's eyesight began to fail. It had been marvellous all his life and he scarcely wore glasses – "Just for show," he would say. In a personal letter to Marjorie dated 5th September 1957 in a clumsy hand with blotches of ink everywhere he adds a P.S. – "Excuse my eyes abundance of ink." "I was his model shortly before he had finally to give up painting, and with weekly sittings, it took a very long time. Often he would have to paint out some of the previous week's work, and begin again. When finished, it looked very much like Mrs Spencelayh!"

Marjorie told me how once Mr Spencelayh gave her a painting – a fine painting of a girl in a hen house with a basket on her arm and a hen hopping through a hole in the door. Marjorie sent it to Sotheby's "to advise me on a suitable reserve to be put on it. This was ignored, and the picture sold for £50." Today it would probably be selling for thousands.

All good things come to an end
Mary Corby and Mick, her husband, looked after Spencelayh in those last three years in Bozeat when his eyesight was fast fading and his mind was becoming ever more confused, until at the last he was moved to St Andrew's Hospital, Northampton where his life was to end but a few months later.

Mary, across the road at 124, went in every day, seven days a week to get him up, give him his breakfast, make sure he washed, get his lunch, and then his dinner, and put him to bed. "He was such a lovely man," said Mary. "We all loved him. He could've only paid me a few pounds a week for looking after him. It wasn't much for all I did but it doesn't matter. I was pleased to do it. And friends always visited." Mary remembers Vicar Knight and Nurse Stoddard as frequent visitors.

Mick continued to do his garden, make his crates and help him with his sets to the very end. He remembers how in those last days the dealers and money men were frequent visitors – out for all they could get. They also made enquiries as to where they could find other Spencelayhs round about. With his prodigious output his pictures could be found in local homes and halls and the story is that some of these just disappeared. "Spencelayh was a shrewd business man," said Mick, "but he wasn't money-grabbing like that."

Mary had to go into hospital for an operation at this time so she asked Mabel Line if she would take over looking after Mr Spencelayh. Mabel, now 80 (1995) and living in the second bungalow just outside the churchyard gate, was at the time housekeeper to Lt. Col. Harold Selby, son of the village doctor who lived just down the road from Spencelayh on the other side in a fine stone house called Greenwood. Harold Selby was awarded the Military Cross in Italy in 1943 and became the First Commanding Officer of the Queen's Dragoon Guard in 1959, the year after Spencelayh died. He was also an outstanding horseman and show-jumper. He was a familiar figure in the village in those days, so the village could boast of two famous men at this time. "He was a real gentleman. He would raise his hat to a gypsy," is how Mabel described him. Mabel had been with the family to Germany and when they were to go to Malaysia she would have gone with them but for the fact that her husband had recently died. As it was she moved into Greenwood to look after old Mrs Selby. It was about this time Mary asked Mabel to look after Mr Spencelayh which she did for his last months in the village. Mabel remembers the last painting he ever did, of a redundant cloth and a wedding ring lying on the table. Mabel was not allowed to touch or even dust them. "He never did finish it, Vicar. He just couldn't see well enough to do so," she remarked.

The house that Albert built
This chapter of our village history would not be complete without a final word about the house which Spencelayh made famous and now bears his name.

The house remained empty after his death in 1958 for about two years and then went on the market at an asking price of £1,500. Max and Eta Laughton were interested in it. Max and his family were well known in the village. His father, Frank was born here in 1888 and started life as a milkman but became increasingly interested in furniture and antiques, so he built a small wooden hut in his garden and started his own business in Bozeat. He did well and also purchased a shop in Wellingborough in 1931, trading from 3 Newcomen Road as 'House Furnisher'. "For the rest of his life he was only interested in shops. He ran a furniture and carpet club and he would collect from prospective customers each Saturday morning on his bike. He continued in this way until his sudden death (in 1959), and I took over the business," remembers Max. 'F. Laughton, New and Second-hand House Furnisher, High Street, Bozeat' has been a familiar sight in Bozeat since the late 1920s until Max's son, Steve, sold up the business in 1994 with the sad loss of more commerce to the village. But to return to 1960 – because the house had stood empty for two years, Max offered £1000 for it. His offer was accepted and they lived there with the family until about 1970. Thereafter it had several owners – Margerite Newell and her family lived there till 1987, and Roy and Elaine Salmons with their children Kirsten, Sian and Andrew till 1995.

The house was actually built in the 1920s for Albert Partridge, whose daughter, Frances, was to own it and collect the rent from the Spencelayhs in 1944 until they bought it from her. Albert's son, Ted, opened the first garage in Bozeat in about 1926. The large garage still attached to the south side of the house was where he did his work with a petrol pump just outside on the corner into St Mary's Road, selling Pratts Petrol for a shilling a gallon!

Just to the south of the house with a narrow alleyway between them was a shoe factory stretching some 50 yards down London Road to John Farey's bungalow at No. 95. Before the Great War, William Taylor (sometime churchwarden) started a shoe business in a grocer's shop in Easton Lane but business grew during the war and just after built this new factory. We have already seen (Chapter 20) how in 1932/3 a fire broke out in the adjacent shoe factory and how Max Laughton, then a young boy, remembered that they had to spray the wall of Ted Partridge's house continually to prevent it being burnt down. If it had, you never know, Spencelayh may never have come to Bozeat and Bozeat may never have had its famous painter! As it was, the factory was totally destroyed and the house gained a new neighbour, the Village Policeman! For the Council built a new house here for the policeman, PC Forth. The previous policeman, PC Willey, lived up Hope Street. As we have already seen when we lost our village policeman in 1974, the Council put the house up for sale two years later and it was bought by Peter and Pam Freely from Nottingham. They brightened up the house in many ways – not least by fixing a shiny rectangular brass plaque on the front wall to cover over the words 'Northamptonshire Constabulary' and on it engraved the new name of the house – COPPERFIELD!

Marguerite Newell wrote in *About Bozeat* for June 1986: "The 'Old Shed where Spencelayh worked' has sadly gone, and with it a small part of Bozeat's history…. It was in a poor state long before we bought 105 London Road, and, although we did some repair work to it, the cost to totally restore and repair would have been out of all proportion to its usage. It had also suffered bad damage in the March storms and parts of the roof were unsafe, therefore forcing us to make the decision to take it down…. It was originally built many years before Spencelayh by Mr Albert Partridge, who was a carpenter by trade, and helped to build the actual house…." When his son started the garage at the side, commercially in about 1926, "Mr Partridge built the shed to use as a carpenter's workshop." If the dates are correct, the shed had stood for 60 years!

So we see how the history of houses is the history of people is the history of a village! The story of a house is the story of those who have lived in it – not in isolation but in a neighbourhood full of neighbours who belong to a community with its own life and character and characters – in this case a village and a village with a name as all its occupants have names – the village of Bozeat.

FOOTNOTES

1. Frances Partridge married Dick Botterill's father Alfred – the shoe manufacturer whose factory was only some 100 yards up the London Road towards Olney from Spencelayh's house.

2. Frances had an older brother Jack who was killed in the Great War along with 35 other young men from the village. Her younger brother was Ted.

3. Albert Partridge married Lizzie Drage whose father was one of the five famous Drage brothers of which Honest John was best known in the Shoe Trade. Their wedding day was memorable in that, at the Reception at the Falcon, Castle Ashby, the hot water for the teas was inadvertently boiled in a copper not properly cleaned after previously containing soap – so the tea tasted horrible! Staff hurriedly asked villagers to boil kettles and so remedy the situation!

4. John Partridge who opened the first Post Office in Bozeat at 70 London Road (in a business directory for 1904) was Albert's brother.

Appendices

A ladies' football team was formed in 1937 and played for two or three seasons.
(*Bozeat School Scrapbook*)
Back row: Winnie Coe, Lillian Ball, Rose Dunmore, Nancy Howard, Olive Wyman, Ena Bayes.
Front row: Olive Coleman, Rene Gale, Gladys Drage, Edie Lovell, Connie Gooding.

Bozeat Home Guard – 200 Years Ago!

J. H. Marlow (published 1941)

The Marquess of Northampton has kindly allowed me to search through several packets of old papers dealing with the Local Defence Volunteers during the time of the threat of Invasion by Napoleon in 1803. On 19th July 1803 the Lord Lieutenant of Northampton held a meeting "on account of the defence of the country". The County was divided into eight districts and circulars were sent out asking the Vicars to encourage the forming of Local Volunteers in their Parishes.

The inhabitants of 50 parishes in the County offered at once to enrol themselves. There is no trace in our own books of the forming of a Local Defence Volunteer Corps in Bozeat but evidently they did get a small company together because I found a paper which says:

"Castle Ashby, 19th September 1804, to Mr Hensman, Bozeat.

Sir, As you introduced the Bozeat Volunteers to join the Castle Ashby Company, I think you the proper person to apply to for payment of the clothing, etc., as by account £28-6-0 which the sum I must beg to be immediately remembered. The Gentlemen who have joined have done themselves credit.

I am, Sir, Your Humble Servant, Thomas Scrivens Captain C.A.V.T.

This was soon paid, as an item in our Parish book says, "Received from John Gough for Volunteers Clothing £28-6-0. Another paper dated 1st July 1804, at Castle Ashby gives the names of the Company and the village to which they belonged. The Bozeat men were: John Gough, William Bradshaw, William Drage, John Dexter, William Osborne, John Riseley, Thomas Skevington, William Taylor.

The cost of Uniform was: Jacket £1-16-0, Pantaloons 9/-, Gaiters 3/-, Cap and feather 12/-, Accoutrements 18/6, Haversacks 2/3, Stock 1/-, Braces 1/-. Perhaps some of those who now live in the village know whether "The Barracks," later known as "The Bunch of Four" opposite Burton Terrace was the headquarters? On 17th April 1804 "it was unanimously agreed to make application for the Castle Volunteers to be placed on Permanent Duty and to march to Northampton when required."

One document in the Buckinghamshire County Council archives describing the kind of service required of the Local Defence Volunteers ends by saying, "The greatest danger to which an enemy is exposed who dares to invade these Kingdoms arises out of the native Valour, Energy and Patriotism which have at all times distinguished the British character." One Bozeat man (whose name I have purposely left out of the list) evidently got lax in his attendance after a year, as the following shows:

"Head Quarters, Castle Ashby, March 4th 1805.

Sir, Your repeated neglect amounting at least in appearance to contempt of the Articles that you voluntarily subscribed to when you joined the Company of

Volunteers which I have the honour to command, has at length forced me to a measure that I can no longer forbear consistently with my duty, and the respect due to other members whose conduct entitles them to my best regard. Therefore I hereby request that you deliver up to Sagt. Jos. Smith your Clothing and Accoutrements. Having served with you in the Cavalry and imbibed a good opinion of your private character, I cannot but regret that you should be the first to drive me to this unpleasant exercise of my Commission.

I am, Sir, Thomas Scrivens, Capt. Commnt. C.A.V.T."

The last parade seems to have been in 1806. In September, 1805 Napoleon had to withdraw his invasion army from the Channel ports to march against the Austrian and Russian armies. Also the victory of Trafalgar 21st October 1805 relieved all fear of the invasion of England.

Postscript

It does seem that, despite Vicar Marlow's final sentence in his interesting article, "all fear" had not departed at least from one young lady's mind. We have in our possession in Bozeat Vicarage a Sampler beautifully stitched and embroidered by Eliza Bygott aged eight years in the year 1808 – who was the great, great grandmother of the Vicar's wife Audrey née Stott on her father's side on which are embroidered the words:

> *Shine mighty God on Britain shine*
> *With beams of heavenly grace*
> *Reveal thy Power through all her coasts*
> *And shew thy smiling face*
> *Amidst our isle exalted high*
> *Do Thou our glory stand*
> *And like a wall of gardian fire*
> *Surround our fav'rite land*

and in the bottom corner the words: *Hope the balm of life soothe us under every misfortune.*

The Bogs

Colin Curtis (From *About Bozeat*, March 1993)

The Bogs were a piece of marshland at the north end of The Meadow before the Brickyard (Tin Pits). It consisted of about five acres of rush grass and rough grassland marsh. Some parts were very wet and quite boggy. There was a patch or 'standing' of cricket bat willows at the Tin Pit end, which was particularly boggy. I spent most of my childhood days and youth down the meadows which included the bogs, with my schoolboy pal Martin Drage.

Our favourite time of the year was springtime when the birds were nesting. Our favourite bird was the Snipe, to sit and watch its display. We knew they were nesting by their drumming. The drumming was achieved with the help of two small feathers, one each side of the tail, which vibrated when the bird dived in its display. Other nesting birds were Reed Bunting, Yellow Hammer, Moorhen, Mallard Duck and Grey Partridge. Skylarks mounted the sky with their beautiful song.

Summer visitors were heralded by the Chiffchaff closely followed by the Cuckoo, Blackcap, Whitethroat and Yellow Wagtail. There was a large Wych Elm at the end of the slope in which Tawny Owls and Stock Doves nested. The meadow at the topside of the bogs consisted of sand, there was a site of old workings, large rabbit warrens, fox earth and the occasional badger.

The flora consisted of cowslips, lady's smock, cuckoo flower, ragged robin, sedge, and thistle. Frogs spawned in the brickyard. Mr George Knight (of Church Farm) was the farmer until he died, then Compton Estates became the new owners. They sold the farm and part of the ground to Mr Roberts which included the bogs but not the brickyard. Mr Roberts had a go at draining the marsh but it silted up again.

The land was again sold. Mr Hutchinson became the new owner of the bogs and meadow and set about draining the bogs by digging deep dykes and laying drains and filling with gravel. This method worked and the bogs were turned into arable land. The future of this land is again in the balance because it is in the proposed sand and gravel extraction plan. So it might be turned full circle and we might again see the Snipe.

Village Diary

1066	Invasion by the Normans with William the Conqueror
1085-7	Domesday Book: "The same holds for the Countess (Judith) 2 hides less 1 virgate in Bosieta." (210 acres). Judith 1½ hides & William Percival ½ hide. 1 hide approx 12 peasant farms. (*David Hall*.)
c.1130	A Norman Church is built on its present site of St Mary's. Hugh de Morville is Constable of King David of Scotland's lands and in charge of Bozeat.
1154	In the Survey of Henry II: "In Boseyate King David of Scotland holds two hides" (240 acres).
c.1160	Document in records at Dryburgh Abbey (patronage of Bozeat): "Richard de Morville ... to the Church of the Blessed Mary of Dryburgh ... a donation from my mother of the Church of Bosyet and of the mill...." (*Marlow*, p.11.)
1179	29th December: Four knights taking literally some rash words of Henry II, murdered Thomas à Becket in his own cathedral at Canterbury, an the whole of Christendom shuddered at the sacrilege. He became one of the most popular English Saints until before the Reformation.
1189	Richard I (the Lionheart), the Crusader King crowned on death of Henry II.
1195	Robert Bloet had an estate in Bozeat who sold it to the Earl of Sussex who in the reign of King John (1199-1216) bestowed it on William de Stokes his grandson. (*Marlow*, p9.)
1220	Bishop Hugh of Lincoln 'ordains' a Vicarage at Bozeat (along with about 300 others) and first Vicar Ralph, since when Bozeat has had its own Vicar, the present one (1999) being the 67th. Bozeat has 23 peasant farms. (*David Hall*.)
1246	John de Stokes succeeds William de Stokes.
1255	John de Stokes gave "all his possessions in Bozeat to S. James' Abbey, Northampton, in exchange for a house in Hecham (Higham Ferrers). Part of these possessions was a wood named Stanewey with the 11 acres and a half of assarts (i.e., thickets or coverts) with the custody of hernewode (?Horn Wood) belonging to the Crown." (*Marlow*, p9.)
1272	Third year of reign of Henry II. Bozeat manor in hands of the Crown.
1285	Manor in possession of Robert de Twengh.
1298	Earl of Lancaster Estate published. Shows he owned half of Bozeat. William de Ferrars came over with the Conquest and was made Earl of Lancaster and Leicester. (*David Hall*.)
1315	Ninth year of Edward II. Wm. de Latimer and the Abbott of St James (near Northampton) were Lords of Bozeat.
1316	Abbot of St James Abbey tried to overtax people in Bozeat with high rents and keep them in a state of villeinage. They appealed to the King against changes and dues by the Abbot. The King ordered that no increases be made until further investigation as the Manor was in the hands of the King. The Abbot tore up the order, imprisoned the conveyor from Bozeat in the Abbey taking their goods in the hope they would proceed no further with their plea. They didn't but must have returned to their village eventually. (*David Hall*.)

1327	William Latimer succeeds his father (William) to the manor.
c.1350	Church enlarged (after Black Death in 1348/9). The Norman walls were pierced, present pillars and arches built and aisles created along with Clerestory and Chancel extended. The spire was added about this time. Some beams in the north aisle roof are still original 14th century – enlargement supposedly by Lord Latimer. In the 13th and 14th centuries, "Architecture in England reached heights of refinement to which it has never since attained," it is said. (Marlow's *History*.)
1377	First recorded Poll Tax: 210 in Bozeat paid the tax – probably males, giving a probable population of about 400. (*David Hall*.)
1381	June: The Peasants' Revolt primarily against the Poll Tax – the beginning of emancipation of villeins and the ending of serfdom – freedom in return for 4d an acre rent. The age of Wat Tyler and Robin Hood! In Bozeat 76 people paid 4d plus 6 above the odds i.e. 82 taxable people, equating to a population of about 320.
1420	Ogee Window and doorway of Perpendicular design inserted in the west end of the tower. The carved heads on mouldings round the window are probably those of Henry V and his French wife Catherine. Visible around Henry's head is, "The casque that did affright the air at Agincourt and twice saved his life," as was said. (Marlow's *History*.)
1430	There was a Chapman in Bozeat. (*David Hall*.)
1435	"One Bozeat man was fined for selling beer at two different prices although the same beer." (*Marlow*, 1936, p.63). Fines for brewing beer were regular in the 15th century. (*David Hall*.)
1450	No. 3 Bell cast at Bury St Edmunds, ornately marked with flowered crests and inscribed in Latin: *Holy Mary Pray For Us*. Recast by Taylor's of Loughborough in 1884 after it was damaged when the spire fell in 1877. Present, probably original, pews date from c.1450.
1471	First know record of name 'Garrett' in Bozeat (*David Hall*.)
1496	First known record of name 'Dobbs' as Freeholders in the village of Bozeat. (*David Hall*.)
1509	Henry VIII comes to the throne.
1512	From list of gifts to church: "The Altar of St Catherine (in south aisle), a linen cloth, Joan Bluet." "Torch given by Joan Bluet (also by J. Brigg in 1525): Agnes Everton to be buried before the image of the Blessed Trinity" (ledge to north of present pulpit): "To the reparacon (repairing) of the Rood Loft, 6/8d, Richard Everton and Agnes Everton: To the guilding of the Rood Loft, 6/8d, Rofe Aberge. To the Sepulchre light, a schyppe (sheep), Richard Everton. To the Sepulchre light, one bushel barley, Rofe Aberge."
1516	"To the image of Holy Mary of Pity, my best bridal veil, Isobella Kendale."
1528	"Towards the buying of candlesticks for the Loft … T.Luatt. To the Sepulchre, a yew (ewe) lamb, T.Luatt."
1534	Act of Supremacy is passed, establishing Henry VIII as head of the Church of England.
1538	Every church in England commanded to purchase a large Bible in English and to read from it every Sunday.
1539	Henry VIII completed confiscations of all the monasteries. Bozeat Manor then belonging to the Abbey of St James and was valued at 10 pounds.

1549	Act of Uniformity by which universal use of the Book of Common Prayer (largely the work of Cranmer) in English was required.
1552	New Act of Uniformity under Northumberland (Edward VI) led to widespread destruction of imagery etc in churches in promoting the Prayer Book and the Protestant cause. Prayer Book of 1549 revised.
1556	21st March: Archbishop Latimer burned at stake at St Giles, Oxford (some 300 others likewise killed, 60 being women during six year reign of Queen Mary).
	Baldwin Payne and John Dobbs, merchants of the Staple, Calais, have possessions in Bozeat. (*Marlow*, p9.)
1565	First known record of the name 'Line' in Bozeat. (*David Hall*.)
1570	Information from an old will: there was a suit against church wardens of Bozeat because "the church coude be in decaye and allso the leads." (the lead sheeting on the roof)
1571	John Lord Latimer dies, leaving the Manor Estate to his daughters, and it is subsequently sold to John Wiseman, Esq.
1588	Defeat of Spanish Armada.
1591	Real wages halved in 16th century and continued to drop until 1630s. Document dated 1591 said economic changes "made of yeomen gentlemen, of gentlemen knights, and so forth upwards, and of the poorest sort of stark beggars." (*Christopher Hill*.)
1599	25th April: Oliver Cromwell born at Huntingdon. Died 1658 aged 59.
1603	James I (previously King of Scotland for 36 years) succeeds to English throne on death of Elizabeth I.
1605	No. 4 Bell cast and inscribed: *Newcombe of Leicester Made Me.*
	Year of Gunpowder Plot.
	Publication of All Souls College, Oxford Map of Bozeat showing their land and two windmills – one to north of Glebe Farm and one on high ground behind Red House Farm.
1607	Uprising of peasants in Midlands ends in failure.
1628	30th November: birth of John Bunyan at Elstow, tinker, soldier in Cromwell's army at Newport Pagnell, pastor in Bedford where in prison he wrote *Pilgrim's Progress*. He died in 1688 aged 59.
1621	John Wiseman, owner of the Bozeat Estate, dies, to be succeeded by his son Richard, and it remains in the Wiseman family until 1737.
1633	No. 6 Bell with inscription in Latin: *Jesus of Nazareth, King of the Jews, O Son of God have mercy upon me*. This is the bell with the deepest note (E) on which the Church clock strikes.
1636	Communion Chalice (with paten) inscribed: *The Communion Cupp and Cover of the Parishe of BOZIATT in Northampton weigheth 21 ounces 3d. weight*, in the time of Vicar William Collinson (1617-50) and during a period of restoration of high church traditions under Archbishop Laud (enthroned 1633).
1642-5	Civil War, when possibly Cromwell's soldiers and horses, barracked in Bozeat church, destroyed statues, carvings, ornaments and damaged screen, pews, etc. – as we see today.
1645	Jan 10: Archbishop Laud was beheaded, aged 72.
	Jan: Episcopacy abolished and use of the Prayer Book forbidden. Estimated

that 2,425 priests (30% of total) had livings confiscated for not conforming. 14th June: Battle of Naseby. Cromwell's victory.

1649 King Charles I, the Martyr, beheaded.

1655 Cromwell Intruder Paynell Hargrave followed by Edmund Dickenson in Bozeat Vicarage.
24th November: Deprived ministers might not serve as schoolmasters or private chaplains. Intruders were generally a mixture of Presbyterians, Independents and Baptists.

1660 Restoration of the Monarchy. Foundation of Royal Society.

1663 Samual Hart ordained to Bozeat Vicarage.

1670s The long or 'second' pendulum introduced by English clockmaker, William Clement using an anchor escapement as in Bozeat church clock (following the application of a pendulum as time controller into clocks by Dutch astronomer and physicist Christian Huygens in 1656 resulting in a huge expansion in clock making). 72 family names in Bozeat in the 1670s, 32 of these still in the village in living memory. (*David Hall*, 1980s.)

1670-7 John Smith described as bone lace weaver, one of earliest mentions in the county, probably spreading from Olney. (*David Hall*.)

1671 Religious Census taken of the Province of Canterbury shows that there were in Bozeat 380 Conformists, no Papists and only five nonconformist families (*Marlow* from MSS at Stafford) i.e. population about 400.

1674 The Wisemans at the Manor House were described as having 13 hearths for the Hearth Tax of Charles II, instituted in 1664.

1685 Neil described as shoemaker/cordwainer, again one of the earliest references to the trade. (*David Hall*.)
Last execution of a witch in England.

1686 Date of old oak chest with carving "H. Partridge. J. Macknis CW, 1686" with three Padlocks (one probably original, handmade) for each Churchwarden and the Vicar.
John Lettice ordained to Vicarage with Strixton.

1687 Berrill described at 'stonemason'. (*David Hall*.)

1688 Year of Revolution: James II deposed and William of Orange lands at Torbay. Accounts signed by G. Wiseman, Lord of the Manor and others, read: "Spent at Jos Mackiness when ye soldiers came first time 2/4d spent at Northton on ye men and myself when we carried ye soldiers before ye Justices, 2/6d. Paid for three horses to go to Northton to ye Soldiers 6d. Paid Wm Fayle for going for ye bone setter, 6d. Paid ye bone setter for coming to ye soldiers, 5/-. Paid Jos. Mackeness for Washing, Lodgens and Dyett for ye soldiers, 10/-." (*Marlow,* Sheet 11.)

1689 Act of Toleration under William III giving nonconformists right of separate worship in chapels, meeting houses, etc.

1691 Smart described as 'shepherd'. (*David Hall*.)

1693 Earliest known mention of a Drage Bozeat – William Drage, Parish Constable.

1700 Item: "Oyle for the Clock, 6d.". This is an annual item i.e. our clock was probably installed in 1680/90s after Clement's invention in 1670.

1701 Item: "Paid Will Dodson for cleaning clock and work in the Steeple, 4/6d. Paid Thos. Tombs for three quarts of ale for some workman at the scouring of the Clock, 6d."

1703	17th June: Birth of John Wesley who was to live 88 years.
1709	Three pieces of earliest existent tombstone now (1996) standing in the church at the entrance to the tower which reads: "Here Lieth The Body of Joseph Macknis – Son of (Joseph) Macknis – he (depa)rted this Life ye 23 (of) July – 1709 in ye (23rd year of his life?)" His father was churchwarden and innkeeper (see 1686).
1723	No. 2 Bell inscribed: *Tho. Drake, Vic: Will Jakes. Tho. Wright, Ch Wardens: Henry Penn, Founder 1723*. Purchased for £37-10s.
1729	9th October: Great Fire of Bozeat, starting at the top of Mile Street, which destroyed 41 houses and four farms, including the Vicarage. All registers and records destroyed as they were kept in the Vicarage. Luckily two inventories of Vicarage and property dated 1633 and 1636 kept at Peterborough so we have some information including list of vicars from these troubled times.
1737	Churchwarden's accounts: £9-3s paid to one James Ridey for "mending the Stepell" and "Paid to Madam Wiseman's men to help James Ridey to fetch the ladder, and setting it up to paint (point) the Stepell, 1/-." 30th August: Sarah Duchess of Marlborough bought Manor of Bozeat from Elizabeth Wiseman, 1070 acres, for £13,631. Her second daughter Lady Anne Churchill married Hon. John Spencer to whom the Estate was left by the Duchess on her death in 1744, and remained in the Spencer family until about 1830. (*Marlow*, p.8)
1740	John (the Second) Lettice made Vicar of Bozeat with Strixton and Grendon. Buried with his two wives in a vault within the chancel rails at Bozeat. Eldest son (also John) gained a DD in 1792 at Cambridge. In March 1765 he spent an evening with Dr Johnson there. For younger brother Richard see 1789. Sister of John (the Second) had two sons, one became Archbishop of Dublin in 1809 and the other consecutively bishop of Chester, Bangor and St Asaph.
1742	Laughton described as 'carpenter'. (*David Hall*.)
1748	Corby described as 'blacksmith'. (*David Hall*.)
1752	Church Accounts: "Paid Jackey Lettice (vicar's son John) for eight sparrows 1p."
1753	Extensive cracks and bulgings on north side of Spire.
1764	25th July: "My wife, Miss Williams, Mr Johnson and I took an airing by Bozeate." (from diary of Rd Percy, Rector of Easton Maudit and friend of Dr Johnson).
1770	Item in accounts: "Paid for the Ale and Attendance putting up of King's Arms 13/-."
1789	A note in Parish books: "An agreement between the Parish Officer of Bozeat and Mr (Richard) Lettice, Surgeon and Apothecary of Wellingborough. Mr Lettice engages to furnish the Parish Poor resident in Bozeat with Attendance and Medicines (the Small Pox excepted), Surgery and Midwifery for 5 pounds 5s. to Easter next ensuing 1789". Record for those inoculated for smallpox this year was 361 persons which, with about 35 with the disease, gives a population total of about 400.
1791	*Bridges' History* states: "The Tower is surmounted by a lofty but heavy spire, a large window and arched entrance to the tower is half walled up. Very little attention is paid to comfort or neatness in the Church. The old pews remain and the floor is neglected. There is a small mean West Gallery."

From the Enclosure to the Victorian and Edwardian era (1798-1912)

1798 Enclosure Act for Bozeat. Map issued 1799. Yelverton Dynasty ends. Tithes to Bozeat Vicarage were commuted to land.

1805 Opening of Grand Union Canal between London and Birmingham, the first direct trade route via Blisworth and its three-mile tunnel from the East Midlands to London.

1812-13 Violent Luddite protests, part of general movement of radicals and 'industrious' classes.

1813 In front of the Baptismal Register, 1813 there is a document:
"An Act for the better regulation and preserving Parish and other Registers of Births, Baptisms, Marriages and Burials in England, 28th July, 1812 … All Register Books to be kept in Custody of the Officiating Minister in an iron Chest which is to be provided at the expense of the Parish." We still (1996) have ours, 20in by 13in by 14in and too heavy for one man to carry! Perhaps the worst winter for a century, poor harvests.

1815 Corn Laws and general trade depression (blocking cheap corn from abroad hits poor hardest).

1827 Scratched on pane of glass in one of the Clerestory windows: "John Laughton. Wollaston, Plumber, Glazier, Painter, 30th October 1827. He set me here and bid me stand 100 years. Long may we live. Happy may we be. Born with contentment and misfortune free."

1834 13th November: First Methodist Chapel built in Mile Street by Rev. George Cubitt, the 'Old Chapel in the Gold'. There had been a national six-fold increase in Nonconformist Churches between 1800-1850, mostly in agricultural villages. The site of this chapel is now occupied by Burleigh Terrace.

1835 Chapel Sunday School started in July.

1838 Opening of Railway parallel to Grand Union Canal ending its monopoly in trade and speeding up transport from 4 to 40 mph.

1839 On the Tax Return forms for this year (the collectors for the village being Thomas Dexter Skevington and Edward Skevington) there were taxes for six horses for riding, six for business and two exempted. There were five dogs taxed and one exempted. Carriers Thomas Nichols had one horse and Luke Smart had two. (*Marlow*, Sheet 14)

1844 Erection of Baptist Chapel in Church Lane (where Tanyard Cottages now are). We are in the 'Hungry Forties'.

1849 *Whellan's Directory* for this year says: "Bozeat has a parochial school supported by the inhabitants. Robert Pearson, Schoolmaster."

1851 30th March: Census gives those in main service of worship as percentage of the population: Anglican (13.8%), Methodist (25%), Union (Baptist/Independent) Church Lane (8.7%), total 47.5% of the population of 921.

1852 Independent Branch of the Reform Movement, the Independent Wesleyans was founded in Bozeat in which Mr Thomas Wallis and Mr Denton Gilbert of the Mill took an active part.

1853 John Fred Pizey instituted as Vicar of St Mary's.

1857 Bozeat Estate sold to Mr Thomas Revis in June. Building of Church School by Estates at the bottom of Mile Street. Houses for teacher and doctor were built on alongside.

	Construction of the Independent Wesleyan Chapel in Dychurch Lane, paid for by 1882 (£160).
1861	Independent Wesleyan Chapel constructed in Dychurch Lane, paid for by 1882 (£160).
1864	Opening of first Bozeat Co-operative Society shop.
1868	Founding of the Trades Union Congress.
1869	Stained glass east window by W. Holland of Warwick, in memory of Thomas Henry Revis, by his parents.
1870	Visit of Northants Architectural Society reporting tower and spire in bad state and in danger of falling. Report reads: "The tower is in a very dilapidated state, being kept from falling only by bands of iron and by a heavy western buttress, which cuts the west doorway and west window. The insertion of them probably endangered the tower, which had been before imperilled by the addition of a spire to a tower not intended at first to carry it. The tower should be carefully underpinned, if practicable. No restoration of the Church can be complete, unless a considerable outlay is made on the tower." An ink drawing of the church at this time by Ernest Hutchinson aged 9 years 7¾ months shows two metal bands fixed round top of Tower.
1872	October: Reading Room and Library established, *Whellan's Directory* 1874 says there were 50 members who paid 5/- each per annum. Said to have started at instigation of Henry Hutchinson of Church Farm and kept by Joe Laughton in the double fronted house in Mile Street nearly opposite the gate to Church Farm. A Good Templars Lodge was formed there. (*Marlow*, Sheet 54.) 30th November First Football International between England and Scotland, a draw. Item (1872 Churchwarden Accounts): "Mr Revis, cheque on account of the 10 Commandments as per agreement, £6 1872, 1 year's ditto, £3, 1872, ditto £3. 1874, last instalment, £3 equals £15." (*Marlow*, sheet 45)
1873	The new Government School opened in Camden Square, cost £2,000.
1873-5	Vicar Pizey restored Chancel, moved organ from West Gallery and rebuilt it in Chancel, all largely at his own expense (£400).
1875	School Log for week ending 13th October: "Very few children attended Monday Morning. This was owing to the advancement in the School Fee from 1d to 2d per week."
c.1876	Screen and panels in church were stained brown all over by Rev. Pizey presumably as they looked patchy and untidy. (*Marlow*, sheet 39)
1877	Foundation stone laid for Methodist Church in High Street on Whit Monday, building opened later that year. Spire of St Mary's collapses. 14 tons of masonry from spire fell on and through nave roof.
1880	Spire rebuilt, paid for with help from Earl Spencer, completed in 1883. Tower standing as far as the clock. Spire and tower taken down and stones numbered. During rebuilding, four bells stood in churchyard and the treble was erected on a tripod near the south door to call people to church (see Chapter 24). Arthur Edoe Kinch instituted as Vicar.

Mangle Ann's cottage in High Street between the Methodist Chapel and Camden Square. It latterly was occupied by Will Abbott until demolished in c.1960. The house on the left of it still stands. *(Bozeat School Scrapbook)*

1881	Bad harvest nationally. This was a decade of depression and social riots.
1882	Independent Wesleyan Chapel building payment completed (see 1861) and porch added on and dated that year. Schoolroom also added at this time. Rev. A. E. Kinch, Vicar of Bozeat (1880-1882) in farewell letter to parishioners said how he regretted never hearing the Bells ring.
1883	20th January: Augustus William Secker instituted as Vicar. Spire and Tower rebuilt, paid for in part by Earl Spencer. Cost £1,000. On Wednesday evening, 27th June, the Memorial Stone of the New Tower was laid by Archdeacon Lightfoot who, in pouring rain, placed a bottle with coins of the realm in a hole in the stone marked with four crosses. *Northants Herald* of 28th July reports a 'Serious Scaffold Accident' at Bozeat Church on Saturday morning by the falling of a scaffold about 25 feet from the ground, whereby two brothers James and Thomas Ball, masons of Burton, were thrown to the ground. James sustained a bad fracture to one ankle and other minor injuries and Thomas had his head fractured in several places and was otherwise injured. "The spire of the church is in the course of re-erection, and it appears the scaffolding was overweighted at the time of the accident. The occurrence caused quite a sensation in the village. Dr Orr was hastily sent for from Wollaston, and attended to the injuries of the sufferers and prohibited them being removed further than to their lodgings, where they are both now lying. James Ball is progressing favourably, but Thomas is, we regret to say, in a critical condition."

Great Revival of Methodism brought about by two local ministers Revs Bailey and Haliday.

1885 "During the year 1885 there occurred the Scarlet Fever tragedy in Bozeat. Even grown-up people did not escape. Out of a population of 1,189 there were 39 deaths of which 17 was the result of the fever. During the early months of the year the bell seemed to be tolling every day." (Handwritten note by Vicar Secker.)

1886 Mr Revis attempts to sell Bozeat Estate by lots on 7th July 1972 acres were divided into seven principal farms with 10 acres of woods, two fully licensed inns and 30 cottages, estimated value £3,000 per annum. There were only few lots sold, e.g. Stoneypiece to Mr Jos. Drage and the old school to Mr John Drage, to use as a shoe factory.

1887 13th April: An entry in the Burial Register: "Ann Drage buried, age 67." In the margin is noted, "Best known as Mangle Ann". The last such mangle in Bozeat was broken up in 1929. It consisted of a number of rollers round which the clothes were laid and covered with cloths. A large box, full of stones, was moved along by a handle above the rollers, and so pressed the clothes.

House of Commons, Monday, 6th June: The House assembled after the Whitsun recess. A Petition was presented by Mr F. A. Channing from the School Board of Bozeat in favour of Sunday Closing of Public Houses.

Tuesday, 21st June: National Celebrations of 50 years of Queen Victoria's reign – the Golden Jubilee. "Early Tuesday morning the Jubilee was greeted with a salute by Mr Neil Silsby on his cornet and a merry peal rang out from the Church tower. Very early the people were astir, bedecking the streets with flags and wreaths. At half-past 11 o'clock a service was held in the Church, which was fairly well attended. The form of prayer prepared for the occasion was intoned by the Reverend A. W. Secker In the afternoon, at 1.30, the children under 14 years of age, numbering about 400, formed a procession and paraded the village headed by the Bozeat Fife Band. They afterwards had a free tea in the Board School, and afterwards 90 old people over 60 years of age, with a number of widows and widowers, were provided with a capital tea in the Wesleyan School Room. Tea over, all adjourned to a field belonging to Mr Prescot, when a capital programme of Jubilee sports, arranged by the Committee both for old and young, caused much amusement and interest. Messrs. H. Drage and R. Prescot acted as judges, Mr Thomas Johnson as starter, and Messrs. J. Laughton and J. Barnes as handicappers. Many tried in vain to climb the greasy pole. The Bozeat Fife Band, under the leadership of Mr Neil Silsby, played a selection of music, and the sports were kept up until 9.30, everything passing off in a pleasant and enjoyable manner." (Newspaper cutting of the day.)

1890s A decade called the 'naughty nineties' with its secularism, socialism and rediscovery of sexuality after decades of belief that morality was fixed, women in knickerbockers on bikes and climbing the winding stairs of open-top buses. Germany had the best-equipped army in the world and there was a flood of imports marked 'Made in Germany' with the Great War only 20 years away.

1891 Friday, 24th April: Bozeat Rural Sanitary Authority. A meeting was held at

Mr John Drage's house to consider the question of culverting the brook. This ran through the High Street (once called Brook Street) from Dychurch and then into the bottom of Mile Street (where it now emerges), along the Flat, eventually to the Nene. Those present were Revd. Secker, Messrs W. Maxwell, G. Drage, W. Drage, W. Abbott, and Mr Bayes, surveyor. The proposal was put to the Parochial Meeting held at the Board School on Monday, 27th April who agreed that the culvert of the brook should be carried on as far as Mile Street in that year with three ventilators, with further work to be held over.

Newspaper report: Sad Suicide of a Labourer. The County Coroner, W. Terry, Esq., held an inquest at the Red Lion, Bozeat, on Tuesday touching the death of William Bettles, a 63-year-old labourer. His wife, Sarah Bettles, said they had been badly off during the winter, and he was much troubled about having to go to the House (i.e. Workhouse). He had been dispirited about his want of work, said he should be sold up for rent and have to go to the Workhouse, and hinted about destroying himself. He left the house at 5 o'clock on Monday, saying he was going for a walk. As he had not got back at 6 o'clock she told her neighbours, who searched, but could get no tidings of him. She applied for relief three weeks ago, and got it for two weeks, when an order was given for the Workhouse. Deceased said he would never go there. Thomas Line spoke to seeing deceased walking fast in the direction of the fields in which the well was in which he was found. It was a disused well with about 7 feet of stagnant water. It was usually covered with a lid with bushes on the top. On hearing the deceased was missing he went to the well, and, with the aid of a rake, Harry Hewlett and himself managed to get the body out. After hearing further evidence, the jury returned a verdict that deceased committed suicide by throwing himself into a well of water, being at the time in an unsound state of mind. This is the second case of suicide which has occurred at this well during the last five years, and the jury recommended that it should be nailed down or secured by a lock.

1892 1st February: Rev. A .W. Secker buried at Strixton.

22nd April: Rev. W. D. Sargeaunt Instituted Vicar of Bozeat and Rector of Strixton. Church wardens: Mr Brearley and Mr H. Smith. William Drake Sargeaunt (b1859) from Stanwick, BA (1883), New College, Oxford, was an ardent Liberal and great friend of MP for East Northants, Francis Channing, the son of Lt. Col. W. T. Sargeaunt. Whilst Vicar he published collections of poems *The Banks of the Nene* (privately, 1900) and *Poems* (Dent, 1902). In one poem Sargeaunt says his devout wish is to:

Help live again the beauty shewn/ Of old in gothic arch and spire And music's full harmonious tone/ Restore to the four voiced choir From Peter's stately western pile/To lowly Bozeat's pillard aisle.

1893 Working Men's Club founded by Vicar Sargeaunt and others. Affiliated in 1895.

1894 March: Hot air heating system installed in Church. Boiler room built at north-west corner of church. It was later (1923) adapted into a vestry and in 1993 a kitchen/toilet.

July: New Altar bought, cost £19/15/- in memory of Rev. Secker, dedicated 14th December.

Establishment of Urban and Rural District Councils and Parish Councils by Liberal Government.

School Log in November: "No school in afternoon. The water was knee deep all down street and round the school."

1895 Girl's Friendly Society branch started.
Formation of Parish Council replacing village 'Vestry' Meeting.

1896 William Charles Garrett starts his own butchery business having previously worked for Tom Skevington at the Co-op. William lived in a thatched cottage at the top of Mile Street, with 1729 on the stone lintel over the front door, from which the business continued until it closed down in 1990 on the death of his daughter Olive, aged 92, just before Christmas 1989.
April: New Lectern used for first time on Easter Day. Presented by Miss Secker in memory of her brother, Vicar Secker). Made by Rather Kell of Cambridge (who also had made the new Altar), after design of lectern in Romsey Church, Hants c.1450.
June: Font ewer – a large brass jug for filling the font – an old Rum Measure bought and paid for out of offerings at baptisms.
Brass candelabra (18th cent.) bought by Rev. Sargeaunt and hung in chancel.

1897 North aisle of church roof restored. Cost £85.
New Lectern used for first time, bought in memory of Vicar Secker.
North Aisle roof restored £85.

1898 Further repairs to Church roof at cost of £600.
Further repairs to Church roof, cost £400 or more. Several subscribers including Earl Spencer (£50), and Churchwardens Henry Smith and Hamilton Drage. Church land was mortgaged to pay for repairs.
21st January, School Log: "The Factory Inspector turned up the other day. He sent three girls and a boy back to school who had turned 13 but had not passed Standard V." i.e. some parents removed their children from school at 12 to go out to work.
August: Boy's Brigade started as junior section of St John's Ambulance. Drill in Day School.

1899 Working Men's Club House erected for £1000.

1900 John Drage Factory opened in Hope Street.
Sisters Sarah and Emma Cave and their cousin Nell Monk, whose father was the Miller, went to Bedford by pony & trap to celebrate the Relief of Mafeking. All were in their late teens and each made her own dress for the occasion.
B. T. Squires started Bakehouse and Shop in Mile Street.

1901 28th January: Rev. H. R. Moule instituted at Peterborough as Vicar of Bozeat and Rector of Strixton.
Population of Bozeat 1,478. Easter Day was Rev. Sargeaunt's last Sunday as vicar. He goes as vicar to Stoke Abbott, Dorset.
The 'Shoe Co-op' closed. Many Bozeat people lost savings.

1903 Parish Council met to apply to Local Government Board to approve new Cemetery. Village meeting in July approved site of new cemetery in field known as White Wall. Last burial in churchyard 4th December and closed by order of Council 31st December.
July: Half proceeds from Sale of Work (total £26/1/-) to start Fund for Church Room (opened 26 years later in 1929).

1901 photograph of choir and others outside old vicarage. (*Vicars' Logbook*)
Back row: Frank Hewlett, George Hewlett, John Brearley, Ben Pratt (Sexton).
Next Row: Miss M. Skevington, William Robinson, Henry Smith, Hamilton Drage, Miss Emily Hewlett, Miss Agnes Dobbs, Miss F. Tomkins, Miss N. Townsend.
Middle Row: Miss E. Tompkins (standing), Miss S. Hewlett, George Furn, Revd Sargeaunt, William Sargeaunt, Mrs Sargeaunt, Arthur Tompkins, Miss Minnie Corby.
Small Row Sitting: Miss Rice, Frank Slindler, Mary Sergeaunt.
Front row: Miss Elizabeth Thompson, Mary Underwood, Charles Hooton, William Luddington, H. Ernest Drage, Walter Tompkins, Charles Corby, Miss Patty Brearley, Miss Annie Hewlett.

1905	22nd July: Incident where Rev. H. R. Moule's bicycle and clothes were found on the bank of the River Ouse near Ely and he was not seen again. See Chapter 24, 'Vicars of Bozeat'.
1906	28th February: Rev. M. L. Warren instituted and took up duties in Bozeat. Inducted as vicar of Bozeat and Rector of Strixton on 10th March 1908.
1908	Bozeat Co-operative Society wound up.
1909	18th August: Remainder of Bozeat Estate, 1,700 acres divided into eight farms, put up for sale and sold. Mr Hucklesby of Stamford Hill London bought most of the big farms and re-let them, and John Fawdry of Birmingham bought Grange Farm. So ended The Bozeat Estate after 850 years. Its ownership can be traced back to Earl Waltheof in Saxon times. The pitched pine pews in church along the side walls of aisles, believed to have been put there by Rev. Puzey in c.1860 when box pews were removed, replaced by chairs. Belfry arch boarded up and North Door opened out.
1911	B. T. Squires builds new Bakehouse at bottom of Peartree Close and with the help of his wife, Lorie, baked the first batch of village dinners on Feast Day Sunday.
1912	14th April: Rev. C. B. Jennings' first service at Bozeat (Patron Earl Spencer).

Inducted by Archdeacon Moore on 9th June.

28th April, 1.45 pm: United Memorial service after Titanic disaster. £4 sent to Lord Mayor's Fund.

Saturday 23rd November: First ever peal rung on Bozeat Bells. 5040 changes in 3 hours 7 minutes, conductor Harry Fowler. The ringers were: Henry Gayton (treble), Arthur Minney (2), Charles Fairey (3), Edwin Jones (4), Harry Fowler (tenor 16 cwt). (Central Northants Assoc.)

1914 Wollaston Co-operative Society opens branch shop in High Street, Bozeat.

The Great War 1914-1918.

1914-15 Vicar Jennings found a painted panel in the vicarage with illustrations of the Magi, and suspected that other panels in the Rood Screen in the church might possibly have been overpainted and retained their pictures under the brown paint. See Chapters 22 and 24 for details.

Alterations and extension to Glebe Farm House and buildings. Money borrowed from Land Improvement – repayable in 20 years.

210 men went to war from a village of 1,190 (i.e. 18%, or a third of the men).

1915 15th January: Miss L. A. Bettles began her duties as Assistant Teacher at Bozeat School.

May: Ellacombe Chiming Apparatus fitted for the bells by John Taylor of Loughborough, Cost £14.

1916 1st July: Battle of the Somme begins. 20,000 British troops fell in the first day and nearly ½ million in first five months.

1916-22 Lloyd George Liberal Prime Minister.

1917 Extracts from *School Log*, 22nd June: "A holiday was given on Wednesday because children have invested £100 in the War Loan." 21st September: "School closed on Friday afternoon for children to gather blackberries for His Majesty's Forces."

Between the wars 1918-1939

1919 6th July: Sunday 6.30 pm "A United Service of Signing of Peace. The Wesleyans (both) closed their chapels to join us. Mr Lack read one lesson and the Minister of the Wesleyan Methodist Church read the other. It was their own wish to close the chapels which much pleased the Vicar."

12th October: Roll of Honour for the Great War, dedicated by Rev. Jennings, painted by Mrs Diggle, a friend of Mrs Jennings.

1920 War Memorial in Cemetery erected at cost of £80 in memory of the 39 men killed.

The Co-op, the Bozeat branch of the Wollaston Co-op, moves to London Road.

Formation of League of Nations (United States does not join).

Northampton Motor Omnibus Co. Ltd started open-top bus service from the Red Lion to Guildhall Road, Northampton.

1921 Bozeat Post Windmill ceased commercial operations. Standing on a central 2ft 8in square supported by four cross beams and three storeys high, rotated by side arm and wheel to face the wind, it was 192 years old (post bears initials and date R.H.1729). Its mighty grinding stones were geared directly to the four great sails 20 yards long. It was the last of its kind in Northants and John Little its last miller. In a steady wind it would grind six bushels an hour, and nine bushels in a strong one. Mabel Little (John's daughter died in her 97th year on 10th February 1985. Her tombstone in the cemetery has engraving of a postmill on it). Wykes Farm or Skevingtons at the top of Allens Hill was purchased by Len Holt's father. The house is one of oldest in the village, originally thatched but damaged by the Great Fire of Bozeat, 9th September 1729, and repaired in 1730 as date stone on front shows. Deeds mention Mercer Skevington, stone-mason whose initials M S may be those on stone.

Stephen Craxton in 1921.
(*Bozeat School Scrapbook*)

Home Field, or 'Pit Field' across the road was quarried for stone to build many of the barns and cottages in the village 200 years ago. In 1998 the farmyard, barn and out-buildings were turned into a luxury private house.

Walter 'Tompy' Drage bought three buses and started the first bus service to Wellingborough with his brother George Ernest Drage (who married Floss Drage living (1998) at 11 Council Street). Walter had five daughters, Glenda still (1999) living in the family home at 2 Hope Street. The two brothers drove for the United Counties Omnibus Company when it took their business over.

Stained Glass window in North Aisle by Sidney Webb given in memory of Thomas Fancott Saunders by Elizabeth Osborne Hancock.

1922 Advowson or Right of Presentation to Vicarage passes from Earl Spencer to the Bishop of Peterborough.

8th April: Institution and induction of Rev. C. N. Daybell as Vicar.

April: Mr Stephen Craxton died in his 100th year. He left four children (three eligible for old age pensions), five grandchildren and 12 great-grandchildren. He well remembered the coaching days. He worked at Greenfield Farm for 20 years and looked after his allotment regularly until he was 97. The funeral service was in the Wesleyan Chapel.

30th July: The first Sung Eucharist in Church.

1923 Building of Council Estate at bottom of Allens Hill.

27th September: Old Heating Boiler Chamber in St Mary's (built 1894) turned into the Vestry and Dedicated by Rural Dean, Rev. H. K. Fry. Also new Altar Ornaments (silver plated) dedicated by Rural Dean at 7.30 Celebration Service.

Mr Everest, carpenter and undertaker, who lived at Burnt Cottage at the entrance to the churchyard and owned the paddock opposite where bungalows now stand (he kept a cow there) arranged the funeral of William

1923: St Mary's Choir and others (*Vicars' Logbook*)
Back Row: Mr W. Smith, Mr H. H. Smith.
Next: Mr J. H. Taylor, Mr Harry Drage (Churchwardens with wands)
The Misses: Freda Corby, Doris Bradshaw, Laura Corby, Ena Corby.
Men: Mr Furn, J. H. Coles, G. Britton, Rev Daybell, C. Belcher, R. Robinson, Cecil Drage.
Boys: Frank Hewlett, Son Dobbs, Len Dobbs, Tom Cave, Son Dunmore, Joe Squires.

Line of Homestead Farm for a cost of 12s-6d.
Stanley Baldwin, the dominant figure in British politics, heads a Conservative-dominated coalition with Liberals, with Labour the majority party.

1924 First Labour Government.
5th January: Formation of the Peterborough Diocesan Guild of Church Bell-ringers.
Christmas Day: Church Choir dressed in blue Cassocks and white Surplices, Boys: Arthur Dunmore, Len Dobbs, Frank Hewlett, Joe Dobbs, Joe Squires, Tom Cave. Men: Cecil Drage, W. Fern, C. Belchee, G. Britten, B. Robinson. Churchwardens: J. H. Taylor and Cecil Drage.

1925 Electricity supply came to Bozeat.

1926 The General Strike (1 week) in support of miners' strike.
First council house built at 5 Allens Hill. Bert Tompkins moved in with his family from Shepherds Lodge.
Creation of National Grid for national electric power system.

1927 28th January: Rev. W. K. Britton inducted Vicar of Bozeat and Strixton by Bishop Bardsley of Peterborough.

1928 R101 Airship on maiden flight from Cardington, the other side of Bedford came over Bozeat. Max Laughton, then eight, remembers Mr Lack let the school children out to watch. R101 on its way to India crashed in France killing all VIPs on board. "I remember once that we were all brought out into the playground to view a gleaming silver object, suspended high in the clear blue sky. It was the R101 Airship. (Lucy Jones in *About Bozeat*, June 1982.)

1929   Pipe organ installed in Independent Wesleyan chapel.
11th April: Institution and induction of Rev. J. H. Marlow as Vicar of Bozeat and Rector of Strixton by Bishop Blagden in Bozeat Church. Many people came from Abington where he was Curate (as was the exact same situation with Vicar Bligh in 1990).
21st June: Garden Fête 'fated' by rain, was held in Drage's canteen, a wooden hut known as 'Hope Street Room'.
21st November: New Church Hall built on Allens Hill on Glebe land. Opened by Lord Spencer accompanied by Lady Anne Spencer aged eight and Lady Cynthia. Structure cost £500 and furniture £130. Fund started in 1903 and debt cleared by Jan. 1930. This replaced the old building at the Rectory previously used, which was originally a fowl house, which had been used as a parish meeting place! The new hall was built by a local builder, W. H. Cave. The Vicar acted as architect and foreman!

1929. The Hospital Fête held in the Vicarage grounds. Left to right: Mrs Stapleton, Miss Wyman, Mrs Tompkins. (*Vicars' Logbook*)

Hospital Fête. Outside the vicarage gates at bottom of Hensmans Lane with banner.
(*Vicars' Logbook*)

Violin School opened by Mr Walter Nichols of 9 Council Street. He was the father of Pauline and Jean, and a member of the Methodist Church and in the Chapel orchestra.

John Farey's first shop opened in the High Street, Wholesale and Retail Tobacconist, Hairdresser, Fancy Goods, etc.

Dorothy Hayes (b1897) becomes Postmistress at 70 London Rd. Founder member of Wesley Guild and Women's Institute, also on Parish Council and School Manager (born in Miss Rice's house).

Formation of the Wesley Guild.

1930 Opening of Wellingborough Grammar School.

12 new council houses built in Council Street.

Dominated by economic depression and resurgence of Germany under Hitler who grasped power in 1933.

Churchwardens are Mr J. H. Taylor and Mr W. H. Cave.

Eight Variegated Privet Bushes planted by side of path in churchyard.

1931 28th February: Second peal ever rung on bells. Joshua Partridge (conductor), Walter Fern, Henry Gayton, Alfred Elliot, Sidney Corby.

May: Bozeat Scouts started (registered 29th July 1931). Vicar as Scout Master and limited to one pack till more help was found. Bob Green joined six months later and took troop to 22 members.

1931-2 First car owned by Jesse Boswell, church organist and piano teacher. She was the mother of Philip Boswell (shoe factory) and grandmother of Sue Wagstaff. Tom remembers how she would rap her piano pupils on the knuckles if she heard a wrong note.

1932 Jan: Miss D. Matthews at request of the Vicar started Guides and after five months there were 18. Miss Darnell took over as Akela in June.

3rd April: Organ fund Started at St Mary's.

7th Apr: A Toc H Group officially acknowledged and Rushlight presented. Responsibility for Churchyard upkeep 'handed over' to Parish Council. Vicar to retain freehold rights. No memorials to be without his permission and no alterations to be made by Parish Council without his consent.

22nd May: Mr H. H. Smith started as Organist of Parish Church, George Hewlett having retired the previous Sunday. Known as Hol Smith, he was also Headmaster of Wollaston School.

1933 8th August: Brown family come to Manor Farm from Astbury, near Congleton, Cheshire. They were the first to have Friesian cattle in Bozeat. Runners-up in national Dairy Competition in England and Wales in 1946. They finished milking in 1983.

1934 5th April: Bob Grace, Scoutmaster, says goodbye to take up work at a Borstal Institution in London. After six months the Scouts were discontinued as there were no leaders.

1st June: The Town Well stopped running into the cattle trough, the first time in living memory. It was dry for two weeks and was cleaned out for one week. The tap was only running slightly. 1933 had been a very dry year, followed by a dry winter.

2nd September: dedication of Clergy Stall in St Mary's, presented by Herbert Dobbs in memory of his wife Annie (died 4th March 1933) who did much needlework for the Church and was a Church Councillor.

1935   Mabel Line (née Pettit) confirmed by Vicar Marlow. Member of AYPA (Anglican Young People's Association) which met in the old barn behind the old Vicarage.
Driving Tests introduced.

1936-8   Spanish Civil War.

1936   20th January, 11.55 pm: King George V died.
30th January: Body of pyjama-clad Dr Christmas found face downwards in shallow stream bordering the cricket field he loved he was president of the Cricket and Football Club and the British Legion and had been a Major in the R.A.M.C. in the war. His wife was president of the Girl Guides attached to the Parish Church and vice-president of the Hospital Week Committee, see Chapter 18.
4th/5th November: Members of Mother's Union go to 60th Anniversary Pageant at the Royal Albert Hall.
Edward VIII abdicates to marry Mrs Simpson.
Vicar Marlow publishes his *The History of Bozeat Village*.

Bozeat Beauty Queen 1938, Vera Smart, in front of the old vicarage (the steps are still there).   (*Vicars' Logbook*)

1938   12th May: Funeral of Mrs Annie Maria Bennell at St Mary's, buried in Bozeat Cemetery. She had been head of the Infants at the school for 28 years and was a member of the Mother's Union and lived in Bull Close. She was 81. (see Chapter 17.)
14th August: Dedication of eight new aisle pews in St Mary's in memory of loved ones. "Mr Cave deserves our praise for the excellence of his work." (Vicar Marlow.)
In the North Aisle:
(1) To Thomas Bernard Smart.
(2) To Emma Maud Corby, Church Councillor, given by daughters.
(3) Dr R. W. Christmas by gifts from grateful patients.
(4) J. Ward by E. A. Partridge his grandfather and organist for 50 years.
In the South Aisle:
(5) Robert Timpson, sexton, bell-ringer, sidesman by gifts from fellow church members.
(6) Given by Mr H. W. and Miss E. Monk who worshipped with their parents in the old square family pew on this spot.
(7) Dr J. S. Selby given by Mrs Selby.

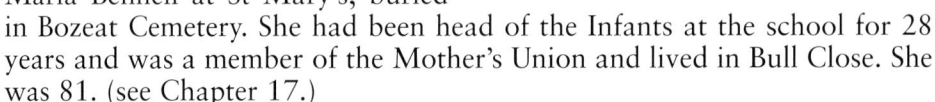

(8) Cecil Drage, past member of the choir and churchwarden.

16th June: Crowning of the Carnival Queen, Vera Smart, who (as Vera Askew) was to, in 1956, have a grocery and general shop at 129 London Road in the front room of their home. Her husband Stan persuaded her to start it.

29th August: Patronal Party in Church Hall. Proceeds to Organ Fund £14-1s-9d.

15th September: The Prime Minister (Neville Chamberlain) goes by aeroplane to meet Herr Hitler to arrange peace terms over question of Czechoslovakia.

Vicar sends Town Crier (Harold Tomkins) round village to call the people to Prayer at 2 pm. Although it was a workday, 80 people attended.

Chamberlain returns to an ecstatic reception in London from Munich with his 'Peace for our time' agreement.

In June 1938, the Carnival Queen is Vera Smart (Askew) of Mile Street. On the right are Elsie Brown (Spencer) and Hilda Underwood (Brotherston), on the left Olive Brown and Irene Gale. Walking the horse (below) is Mr Tebbutt, the rag and bone man. (*Bozeat School Scrapbook*)

Vicar Marlow sent substitute Crier Gee Hewlett to call people to church to thank God. 70 came.

1939 19th March: Four more memorial pews dedicated at 10 am Eucharist.
South Aisle:
Caroline Warner and Elizabeth Barnes (sisters).
Annie M. Bennell, schoolmistress (1893-1921) by Mrs Bridge (daughter) and brothers.
North Aisle:
Harry Furnell by his widow (née Drage).
Margaret Keep of Wollaston who attended Bozeat Church for five years.
29th April: New Organ installed at Methodist Church. Cost £250, housed in an oak chest with an electric blower with one manual build but built to accommodate another.

The 1939 Carnival Court, Gladys Pettit with Joyce Loveridge, Joyce Partridge, Cissie Elliott, and Hilda Underwood. The village forge is far left, next is Strikers Cottage which was a very small dwelling, then Mrs Cave's shop (now Spa). The cottages to the right are now demolished. (*Bozeat School Scrapbook*)

1939 Empire Day. Children in school playground (*Vicars' Logbook*)
Back row, left to right: Mr Paul Drage (Instructor), Geoffrey Coleman in front of Albert Brown in front of Keith Corby, Philip Smart in front of Eric Skinners, on his shoulders Malcolm Drage, Norman Line in front of Arnold Dobbs in front of George Line.
Front row: Richard Parker, Albert Furniss, Kenneth Tompkins in front of Harold Elliott, Walter Furn, Maurice Coles, Kenneth Mallows in front of Richard Drage, Newman Darnell, Philip Drage. Girls against wall: Joyce Craxton, Betty Bolton, Sheila Drage, Kathleen Drage.
Manor Farm is in the background.

Dedication of Organ and Choir Stalls on 16th September 1939. This was performed by the Vicar as, due to blackout restrictions, Bishop Blagdon could not come to officiate. (*Vicars' Logbook*)
Back row from left: Mr Walter Bryant (blower of old organ), Miss Gladys Pettitt, Mr Ronald Drage, Mr Ernest Dunmore (Vicar's Warden), Mr W. H. Cave (People's Warden), Mr Frank Hewlett (J.P.), Miss Mary Frost, Mrs Smart, Mr H. H. Smith (organist).
Front row: Phil Drage, Kenneth Mallows, Kenneth Child, Mrs J. H. Coles, Miss Nancy Howard, Vicar Marlow, Miss Thora Hewlett, Miss Vera Smart, Phil Smart Alan Botterill, Terry Drage.
Absent: Mr Sid Blundell, Mr W. Furn, Mr Paul Drage, Mrs H. Boswell, Mrs Smith, Drage, Mrs J. Edwards. Servers: Phil Boswell, Ted Smart, Max Laughton, Geoffrey Partridge, Jack Wright.

Battle for Britain 1939-1945

1939   24th August, Thursday: Situation in International Affairs over Poland so serious that at 12 noon Town Crier was sent out to call people to Prayer at 2.30 (Parliament was meeting at 2.45). 45 people came to the Parish Church.

3rd September: War is declared against Germany 11 am. Church services held at 5.30 and on 17th and 24th September, and 1st October. The Church is 'blacked out' for 8th October, so the service is put back to 6 pm. (from Vicar Marlow's diary)

11 September: "Opened school – War with Germany – Children evacuated from London – 120 at Bozeat. Working shifts." (*School Log*)

16th September: Dedication of new Roger Yates Organ at St Mary's, cost £525, and new choir stalls, given by Mrs C. M. Horniblow of Fleet in memory of her brother, the late Rev. Arthur Edoe Kinch, Vicar of Bozeat 1880-82, and made by Mr Cave.

1940   June: Ban on ringing Church Bells. One bell left ready to give warning of Invasion or landing of parachute troops in the district. Other bell ropes tied up.

Girls Life Brigade started with Lieutenants Winnie Wyman and Doreen Dimmock.

26th October: Scouts started again. Church (closed) Troop called 2nd St Mary's Bozeat Troop with Vicar as Group Scoutmaster, John Fleming as

Troop Leader, Phil Smart and Eric Shinner as Scout leaders. One Patrol of London boys joined on for the time being with George Messinger as Patrol Leader.

1941 Charles Spencelayh comes to live at 105, London Road.

27th January: Annual Parochial Church Meeting. Mr Cave retires as People's Church Warden and Mrs Cave as Treasurer. The Vicar very much regretted the retirements after a very happy period of work. Mr Wyman was appointed Churchwarden.

10th November: Mr Cecil Drage, well known in Bozeat for his tenor voice, and churchwarden for many years (appointed in 1924), and a member of the Church choir, having left Bozeat 17 years ago, was on this date elected Mayor of St Ives, Cornwall.

USA enters War after Pearl Harbour..

1942 Special characters who died during this year:

"George Everest aged 89, had been Undertaker and Carpenter … a good living man. Mary Anne Jolly aged 96. Her father died aged 99 (maiden name Craxton) and her uncle aged 90." (Marlow's diary.)

8th September: "Garden party at Vicarage for Waifs and Strays Homes. Got up by Boxholders. Turned out an unexpectedly brilliant sunny afternoon. Teas on gravel in front. Games on Lawn. 60 people for tea. Proceeds £5 7s 6d." (*Marlow.*)

15th November: "Ban of church bells lifted for a few hours … rung 9 am to 10.30 am to celebrate the Victory of our Forces in North Africa (Both the push from Egypt and the landing of American and British Forces in Morocco and Algiers). The Ringers were Messrs R. Hamilton, Hamilton Drage, J. Stuart (Wollaston), William Fern, Mrs Stuart (née Hewlett), Miss Vera Smart and Mrs F. Laughton taking different turns. R. Hamilton, a ringer of 20 years ago, took the lead. The Bells behaved themselves splendidly after this 2½ years rest, thanks to Donald Cockings' attention to them a year ago. Bell-ringers parted with a hope they would soon be called upon for another Victory! Heard (afterwards) that Donald Cockings was killed on a minesweeper on the very day we rang the Bells and thanked him." Donald aged 22 eldest son of Cyril Cockings joined the Royal Navy as able seaman in Sept. 1940 and had seen much active service. Previously employed by Chas. Pettit & Co. leather dressers, and was well known in district as bell-ringer. Lived at Harrold but trained junior team at St Mary's Bozeat where he sang in choir and "served at our Altar frequently with sincere Reverence." (*Marlow.*)

15th November: Also First Civil Defence Sunday. Civil Defence Corps parade in uniform. 23rd November: "Heard Fred Furr was Missing. He was in submarines. An old Scout (1934). Confirmed 7th March 1923. Came to Toc H when at home." (*Marlow*)

1943 30th January: "Vicar J. K. Marlow rushed into hospital for operation (Wonderful recovery. Parishioners Prayers and kindnesses very great) After three weeks in Hospital, 3½ weeks in bed at Vicarage he went to Devon for 11 weeks convalescing." 1st June back to duty.

22nd April: "Mr Henry Smith buried. Was Churchwarden for 38 years (about 1894 to 1923). Born in Bozeat. Sidesman at time of death. His son

H. H. Smith appointed Organist, 22nd May 1932. Did some duty at the Organ in 1904. Then went as organist to Easton Maudit." (*Marlow*)

6th June: "Hospital Sunday. Major Pyrah read one Lesson. Vicar preached. A large Parade. Home Guard, St John Ambulance Nurses, Scouts, Girls Life Brigade, etc." (*Marlow.*)

17th July: "Garden Fête in Vicarage backfield. Proceeds divided between three objects: Hospital, St Johns Ambulance (local fund), Servicemen's Fund. Speakers Major Pynch and Mr and Mrs Campbell. (Dr Eric Shaw Opener)." (*Marlow.*)

1944 22nd March: "Vicar again to Hospital. This time told he must give up his work at Bozeat." (*Marlow*)

"Spoke to his congregation at Chancel steps on Easter Morning at 10 am Eucharist and administered the Cup. Passed away the following Sunday 16th April at Ideford, Devon where he is buried." (unknown author in diary)

26th August: Institution of Rev. S. F. W. Powell to Bozeat Living by Bishop of Peterborough (Dr Claude Blagden). Previously Vicar of St Columba, Corby, Curate at Daventry, in Johannesburg as missionary.

27th August: Feast Sunday. First Sunday as new vicar. Afternoon of Feast, new vicar conducted first funeral, that of 32-year-old Bozeat RAF corporal, Albert Arthur Thomas Dunmore of 14 Council Street, killed when knocked from his motorbike. A much respected member of Toc. H and Scouts before joining Forces. Church full of parishioners for the funeral.

September: Farewell Service at Methodist Church to their Minister, Rev. B. L. Simpson after three years living in Bozeat (Senior Steward Mr T. P. Roberts presided).

Florence June Drage, the 10-year-old daughter of Mr and Mrs G. T. Drage, tragically electrocuted by electric iron. Buried at Bozeat. Teachers at funeral: Mr Lack, Mr Cooper Miss Bettles, Mrs Bellamy and Mrs James.

16th December: American Pilot Lt John Ahern, flying from Kimbolton, crashes behind Red House Farm (see Chapter 4).

1945 Atomic bombs dropped on Hiroshima and Nagasaki.

3rd August: Report in paper: "Mr A. J. Dobbs, the former Bozeat boy who became a member of Parliament last Thursday, was killed next day when returning to his home at Leeds after his victory for Labour at Smethwick." In Doncaster he swerved to avoid a child, collided with an army lorry and was killed outright. He was about 63. Worked as shoe laster at C.W.S., etc., Rushden, local leader of Boot Co-operatives Union, elected to Rushden Urban Council in 1905 till 1910, became leader of Labour group in Leeds and alderman, after First War officer of Leeds branch of Boot Operatives Union.

19th August: Victory in Japan, end of World War II.

After the War was Over 1945-1980

1945 BBC Country Magazine programme. Mr C. J. Walker, Farmer's plumber from Bozeat, pointed out that village has to rely on wells for water as there was no piped water and one well he went to repair on a farm was 150 foot deep.

26th October: "As the work and training of the Rest Centre has come to an end the leader, Mrs H. Boswell, arranged with the half of her staff a meat tea in the Church Hall to celebrate the closing down of a very happy and what might have been a very necessary piece of war work." The newspaper report continues: "The Parcel Fund which has recently made the final gift of 10s to all serving men and women is now closing.... The final work of the committee is to provide a memorial tablet in polished oak with the names engraved of those who have made the supreme sacrifice. A memorial and unveiling service will be held in the Parish Church."

1947 September: Dry spell means most wells dry up.
4th October: Rededication of Church Bells after repair and restoration.
20th November: Princess Elizabeth marries Philip Mountbatten.

1948 Spencer Clarke acquires Bozeat Boot Co. in Hope Street and moves into factory in Easton Lane.
5th July: Founding of National Health Service under Aneurin Bevan (Minister of Health). Labour swept to power under its promise.
Mahogany Table (Jacobean style) given by Mr and Mrs J. H. Taylor in memory of their son Frank Hutchings Taylor, who had died in the Second World War. His name is on the War Memorial in the Bozeat Cemetery. Mr J. H. Taylor had been a churchwarden.

1949 Monday, 29th February: Bozeat Windmill blows down in gale during the night. On the morning of 30th all that remained was a heap of broken woodwork and twisted metal exposing the massive giant millstones in the centre. It had stopped working in 1921.
Water supply piped to village.
Mrs Terry, wife of Headmaster of Bozeat Primary School is asked to form Women's Institute in Bozeat. First preliminary meeting 16th Nov. First General Committee Meeting, 6th Dec.1950, members joining fee 2/6d. Close friends Ethel Andrews (1913-97) and Harriet Partridge (1897-97) were founder members.

1950 7th January: Rev. William Cecil Knight instituted and inducted as Vicar by Bishop of Peterborough (the Right Reverend Spencer Leeson) and the Archdeacon, the Venerable E. N. Millard. In 1953, the benefice of Easton Maudit was added to his duties in the creation of the combined benefice.
Mothering Sunday: Vicar reintroduced old custom of 'Clipping Mother Church' where congregation joined hands and encircled the Church singing "We love the place of God ..."
March: Scout Group re-registered, with Vicar as Group Scout Master
4th June: Mr L. Centin licensed as Lay Reader at St Mary's.
Sewerage system established in village.

1951 January: Derek Taylor aged 15 from Podington came to work as Butcher's Boy for Sam and Olive Garrett, village butchers, and worked for them for 40 years till they closed in July 1990.
Festival of Britain.

1952 5th February: Death of King George VI.
Monday night 19th May: At 9 pm, torrential rail fell. 2½ inches in one hour fell on Bozeat (0.6 inches in Wellingborough and 0.02 inches in Kettering), submerging the centre of Bozeat to a depth of 6 feet in 15 minutes and

Don Robert's Shop in the first school in London Road with the doctor's house (No. 53) to the right. This was taken soon after the flood in May 1952. (*D. Roberts*)

producing a raging torrent tearing down walls and flooding 40 houses. Big Flood Scheme established.

Council Estate built including the top part of Queens St, Mill Rd, Roberts St, the top part of St Mary's Rd, and Hewlett's Close.

Ron Coles appointed manager of Bozeat Boot Co. Worked up from office boy, lived at 2 Hewlett's Close, next door to Ethel Andrews.

1953 2nd June: Coronation of Queen Elizabeth II.

18th July 2.15 pm: Lightning strikes Church Spire just as funeral of Annie Bryant (see brass plaque on organ console) is to begin and just as Alec Bayes looks out of his window in Mile Street for return of his brother's racing pigeons, so he saw it strike! Burnt the spire's lightning conductor to a frazzle and stopped the clock which was not started again till 4th November. John Darnell, still in his teens, was playing the organ at the time (he still does at Easton Maudit, 1998). "I was terrified," he remembers (1998).

1955 The Lord Nelson, built in 1742 as a Coaching House, closes as a Public House in the spring of this year.

October: Toc H Group in Bozeat closed

1956 September: Askew's shop – a miniature Co-op at top end of the village opens at 129 London Road in his front room. Extension to side built in June 1960.

1957 Fred Tivey becomes manager of Bozeat Co-op.

1958 30th January: Pam Freely's School of Dancing opens in the Methodist Church.

P.C. Fry appointed Village Policeman. He retired in 1976 (died Nov. 1998).

25th June: Death of the Bozeat artist Charles Spencelayh.

4th September: Wollaston Secondary School opens on its new site in

1963 aerial photo of church and old vicarage with London Road and Spring Vale Farm behind. Benny Squire's bakehouse to the right, Stoneleigh in the right foreground and old workhouse in the foreground.

Irchester Road to 357 children, with 14 staff and Alan Northen as Head until 1974, later to be Mayor of Wellingborough and Leader of Wellingborough Council.

1959 2nd March: Wollaston School officially opened by Dr Robert Stopford, Bishop of Peterborough.

1960 The Chequers public house closed.

1961 Repair and treatment of timbers in church damaged by Death Watch Beetle. Cost £2,000.

1963 Co-operative shop in London Road rebuilt as a self-service store.

1st October: Vicar officially takes up residence in new Vicarage built by Messrs Marriotts of Rushden.

Nov: The Old Vicarage dated 1729 was demolished and the site levelled. All that was left was the outhouse at the back which still stands (1999), and the stone steps to the front door, with the shoe scraper.

22nd November: President John Fitzgerald Kennedy assassinated.

11th December: John B. Terry, Headmaster of Bozeat School, dies in Northampton Hospital. He was Chairman of Bozeat P.C., a freemason and a friend of the Vicar.

1964 Harold Wilson and Labour win General Election with majority of 10.

30th August: Feast Sunday. At Parish Communion "new vicarage was solemnly blessed, sprinkled with holy water and incensed by the vicar. A

Good Congregation assembled." (Knight's diary) He adds "Thurifer: Nigel Terry, Boat: Christopher Allen, Crucifer: Christopher Bird, Servers: Philip Drage, Jack Wright, Organ: Roger Tivey ... Mr Eric Brook, managing director of Marriotts, came in for a sherry and lunch afterwards."

1965 Beatlemania!

1966 England win the World Cup.

Margaret Cross (nurse) married John Gordon James, only son of J. James of Newlands Farm.

Death of Frank Hewlett (aged 87) member of Church choir for almost 50 years, made Magistrate in 1937, member of parish council and cricket club for almost 76 years.

Jack Mabbutt, son of Mr R. V. Mabbutt, 2 High Street, appointed Professor of Geography at Sidney, Australia, previously head boy of Wellingborough Grammar School and captain of cricket.

First Bozeat Fête for 20 years in garden of Colonel and Mrs Selby in London Road, organised by villagers especially members of W.V.S. and Royal Antediluvian Order of Buffaloes, opened by Mr and Mrs Brook of Easton Maudit. Proceeds towards Christmas treat for elderly.

The model of the church made by Mr Herbert Edmunds, standing on the Church Chest, with the Enclosures map behind it.

1967 June: Funeral of Harold Elliot aged 41, building partner of Arnold Dobbs.

Bozeat F.C. Division II Champions of Rushden District League.

Bozeat Boot Co. (R. Cole, Director) wins contract to supply minimum of 25,000 pairs of heavy boots and shoes to Canada.

Mrs Florence Mabel Brown, Verger and Churchwarden at St Mary's for over 45 years retires. She lived at the top of Mile Street (No. 50).

Herbert Edmunds (85 yrs) had retired in 1947 as gamekeeper on Duke's Estates. He found he had a talent for making scale models out of miniature concrete blocks and made a model of the village church, still displayed in St Mary's, two medieval castles and a lighthouse since retirement. "You need a lot of patience and nimble fingers, And I'm lucky because I've never had to wear a pair of glasses in my life." (*Evening Telegraph*.)

Nursery set up in Methodist Church Rooms by two young mums, Mavis Holman and Mary Clarke, rooms which are already used as a welfare centre. This was the first playgroup in Bozeat, which Mary continued to lead for 11 years.

1968 Robert Welch (aged 21) completes his training at Royal Navy Supply School at Chatham. Signed on for nine years. He enjoys stamp collecting, football and church youth work. (Now married to Glenda Drage at 2 Hope Street – 1998.)

Adrian and Michael Jarvis aged six and eight of Allens Hill with friend Mark Line aged eight raised £2 from a toy and book sale towards village playing field and hall fund.

Three Drages – Thomas, Edward and Rowland rewarded for over 50 years as members of the Union of National Boot & Shoe Operatives (NUBSO). Rowland (67) started at Botterills on his thirteenth birthday in 1914. "I was one of the first people to join the union at Botterills. At that time wages were a pound a week and we worked over 50 hours a week regularly." Thomas began work at Taylors in London Rd. before it burned down 35 yrs ago and then went to the Bozeat Boot Co. (BBC). (*Evening Telegraph.*)

The Open University, brainchild of Harold Wilson, opens at Milton Keynes.

1969 18th June, 8.15 pm: Vicar Knight dies in Northampton hospital aged 61. He was Vicar of Bozeat from 1949, and Easton Maudit since 1953. Previously he was curate of All Hallows and Priest-in-Charge of St Andrews, Wellingborough. He is buried, with his parents, at Easton Maudit.

19th November 7.30 pm: Induction of Norman Ernest Palmer as Vicar of Bozeat and Easton Maudit, aged 40, previously Methodist Minister for 10 years in Yorkshire.

Neil Armstrong is the first man to step onto the Moon.

Henry John Edmunds of 14 Hope Street dies aged 100, one week before his 101st birthday. He was the oldest inhabitant of Bozeat. Born in the village of Gayhurst, he worked at the age of six with his father as a shepherd, moving wherever the next flock was when they bought it, so came to Bozeat in 1881 during the Boer War. He went into Boot and Shoe until he retired from Clarkes aged 80. Grandson Derek still lives (1999) at 15 Hope Street and great-granddaughter Caroline is a nurse with a taste for powerful motorbikes.

Joe Smart has lived at 22 Allens Hill since he was a toddler and still chooses to use the water he has always used (i.e. for 65 years) from the pump outside his house.

Botterills have their biggest single order yet, 20,000 pieces of sportswear from Norway worth £100,000.

Mabel Edwards, 69-year-old widow, rescued from her blazing terraced house at 12 Hope Street by neighbours Don Andrews (No. 22), Laurence Roberts (next door) and Arthur Warner (No. 8).

1970 Private estate built, mainly bungalows, in Queen's Street and Mill Road for an influx of people mainly from London, and the area became known as Diddyland or Diddyville, after comedian Ken Dodd, on account of the small size of the bungalows built there.

Vicar Norman Palmer initiated a major three-phase restoration programme: stage 1 replacing woodworm ridden timbers in roof and floor (completed 1970, cost £2,000), stage 2 restoration of stonework and windows, stage 3 overhaul of the 30-year-old electric organ. Overall £5,000 needed.

11th July: First Vicarage Garden Fête for 22 years. £150 raised for restoration work.

Church Sunday School re-established.

Miss Jennifer Drage (now Spencer) of 113 London Road realised her dream of driving a test car at the Aston Martin Works at Newport Pagnell. The *Evening Telegraph* has a headline 'Speed Girl is VIP in World of James Bond'. Today (1996) she owns a vintage Ford featured in an Anglia TV Village Programme of 1993, teaches lace making to children at Bozeat School and is currently chairperson of the Parish Council.

1971 Decimal currency introduced.

Concorde's first commercial flight from Heathrow.

Bozeat Bunny plus cash barometer sign set up in London Road, designed and made by Geoff Betts to help raise funds for the Playing Fields and Village Hall.

Complete rewiring of the Church by F. Mitton & Son, Northampton, £327.

1972 Private houses built in Fullwell Road and on and around Queen's Street. New estates double the size of village.

24th March: Recital by Roger Tivey (cousin of Fred Tivey) with John Bandy (tenor) after renewal of electric action and cleaning of pipes of the Yates Organ in St Mary's (built 1939) at a cost of £1,000.

Susanne Sinclair, Miss Netball 1972, visits Botterills, now the largest manufacturer of leather sportswear in U.K. (*Evening Telegraph*.)

August: Three-day flower festival in all three Anglican churches (St Mary's, Strixton and Easton Maudit), organised by Mrs Audrey Brook of Easton Maudit. Rushden Mission Band played on the vicarage lawn. Flower show in Working Men's Club. Songs of Praise on Saturday night.

27th August: Dedication of Leatherworkers' Banner depicting St Crispin & St Crispinian by Rt. Rev. A. R. Graham Campbell, assistant Bishop of Diocese of Peterborough at Feast Day Morning-sung Eucharist. The figures and lettering were traced from an identical banner in Higham Ferrers Parish Church by Rev. Norman Palmer. The leather for the background and figures were supplied by Botterill's Ltd. Mrs Floss Tivey, wife of Fred Tivey, Churchwarden, cut out the figures and Mrs F. A. Botterill had the lettering machined. The Bozeat Boot Company paid for the banner pole.

1973 Mother's Union ceases and church ladies join with Women's Fellowship at the Chapels.

Friday 23rd February: *Northants Advertiser* has an article, 'Giving the Ten Commandments a clean-up' describing how a group under Mr Pierson (see 1982) are working on Saturdays to 'Give St Mary's a Facelift', one of whom had the 'bright' idea of shifting the ingrained dirt on the Ten Commandments in St Mary's, in the sanctuary on the East wall, using car polish, causing them some serious damage! (but see 1997.)

1st May: Children move to new school in Harrold Road, having been in old one for exactly 100 years. Headmaster Barry James has 193 children on the school roll.

October: Linda Old marries Joseph Birke at St Mary's Church. Attending the service were sisters Jean and Kathy. Linda is a member of Bozeat Women's Netball Team for several years. Today (1996) Linda works in Clinic and helps in the Paper Shop, and her son Matthew (aged 18 in 1996) plays rugger for The Saints.

London Road in April 1974, showing Don Roberts' shop on the left, and on the right the old entrance to Easton Lane with the old Post Office behind and Ivy Mabbutt's haberdashery shop. (*Evening Telegraph*)

1974   Oil Crisis.
Botterills, along with The Bozeat Boot Company, were bought by Electronic Rentals Ltd and formed a new company, Gola Sports Limited.
John Houlford appointed head of Wollaston School (until Easter 1995).
Alan Knott, Kent and England wicketkeeper, promotes a new cricket boot made by Botterills for the 1974 cricket season.
Kenneth Moore (59) takes the lead in a new Father Brown series filmed by ITV at Easton Maudit. The old school is transformed into 'The Crusader' free house.

1975   Jan: Joyce Wesley's thatched cottage in Easton Lane caught fire and was reduced to a shell.
August: York Bros Bus Service from Bozeat to Northampton ceased operation.
Installation of Combat Oil Fired Warm Air Heater at NW end of Nave.

1976   P.C. Griffin comes to the Police House at Wollaston.
April: Topping out ceremony by Mayor Mick Holmes for new Commercial Centre for Wellingborough, the Arndale Centre, built between Sheep Street, Market Street and Midland Road.
May: Keith Badrick of Three Fields Farm, Hinwick Road, wins Norlington Cup for best herd in Northamptonshire Dairy Herd Competition. The farm has 94 acres. Keith and wife Anne moved here from Herefordshire two years ago (in 1974).
Drought. Pitsford reservoir almost empty.
Nov: Rachel Mallows (14), Janet Callaghan (15) and Christine Sarvy (16) receive the Queen's Guide Award, presented at St Mary's.

1977   Centenary Celebrations of Bozeat Methodist Church. Four previous ministers are present, Revds Allen, Smith, Godden, and Dawes.
June: The Browns of Manor Farm win 1st Prize in the Northampton Show

with their Friesian bull, 'Bozeat Jacobite'.

June: Freak storm drowns High Street (soon after 11 am) in three feet of water for more than two hours. The culvert carrying the brook through the village is just not big enough for an exceptionally heavy downpour. "I looked out of my window and saw the manhole covers in the street lift up and the water started surging through them at an astonishing rate," said Mrs Ann Tompkins of 42 High Street.

Dec: Keith Haggar (18) of Easton Maudit is voted Apprentice of the Year at Marriotts (builders) of Rushden. Voucher presented by the Company Chairman Eric Brook who lives at the Old Vicarage, Easton Maudit.

1978 New clinic built in Brookside.
Drage Shoe Co. closes in Hope Street and moves to Kettering.
March: Paul Cox (16) is the first Bozeat Scout to be presented with the Chief Scout Badge.
Oct: Bozeat Methodist 'Toyland' Bazaar raised £700.

1979 Margaret Thatcher becomes first women Prime Minister – a decade of what was to be known as 'Thatcherism' begins.
9th February: Keith and Carol Cullip come from Irchester, Keith to be Postmaster and together they run the Post Office and Spar Supermarket. They have two children, Andrew (9) and Stephen (6). Our post ladies are Stella Nye and Tricia Roach.
May: Christopher Allen, son of Dennis and Audrey Allen of 22 Fullwell Road, finishes his three-year Curacy at St Andrews, Wellingborough. He is now a vicar in Leicester.
July: Singer Cleo Laine and saxophonist John Dankworth support the Action Group fighting to prevent London's third airport being built at Yardley Hastings. "It seems silly building an airport which won't be used for many years because there will be no oil left to power jumbos." (MP Peter Fry reported in the *Evening Telegraph*.)
October: Old School in Camden Square up for sale by County Council for £40,000.
November: Derek Nimmo opened Church Christmas Bazaar which raised a record £385.
December: Brothers Derek and Michael Young take over Bozeat Service Station in London Road in Christmas week, after owning a car workshop in Luton. Mike is a mechanic, does MOTs, and Derek is a panel beater.
Corner at Easton Lane with London Road improved.

Bozeat today 1980-2000

1980 March: First edition of *About Bozeat* is published (editors: Penny Brannon and Sue Embleton).
Parish Councillors: Audrey Allen, Ted Caws, Bill Cleaton, Dennis Evans, David Higham, Mavis Holman, Elizabeth Mallows, Kate Morton, Ted Spicer, Violet Tebby, Tom Underwood, Diane West (Clerk).
Organisations:
Playgroup (Brenda Bould); Community Playgroup (Ann Turnbull); Brownies (Sue Evans, Caroline Darnell); Cubs (Brenda Bould, Sue Wagstaff); Guides (Janet Albury); Scouts (Dan Bould); Young Wives (Allison Botterill);

Women's Institute (Marjorie Stamford, Agnes Jones); Tea Pot Club (Sue Embleton and Penny Brannon); Over 60s (Miss Bettles); Youth Club (Pauline Drage); Playing Fields Association (Richard Holman); Women's Fellowship (Phyllis Silsby).

School Managers:

Parish Council Members: Dennis Evans, David Higham, Mavis Holman.

Four recommended by Northants County Council: Margaret James (chair), Fred Dilley (parent rep.), Geoff Smith (District Councillor), John Grose (County Councillor).

Co-opted members: Mary Clarke, Teacher Representative, Maureen Sowden, Headteacher Barry James, i.e. nine in all.

Teachers: Mrs Maureen Sowden (Reception), Mrs Patricia Finke (Middle Infants), Mrs Sheila James (Third Year Infants), Mrs Rosemary Bates (First Year Juniors), Mrs Jessie Dalton (Second Year Juniors), Mrs Madeleine Newton (Third Year Juniors), Jim Stopps (Fourth Year Juniors). (i.e. 8 staff including the Headteacher.)

Don Roberts' shop in London Road closes.

Bozeat Historical and Archaeological Society is formed (David Mallows, Barbara Scott, Vi Tebby).

Bozeat Girls Rangers Group is formed (ages 14 to 19) (Christine Corby, Betty Palmer, Lia Drury).

Introduction of Alternative Service Book Traditional Rite B Eucharist at St Mary's.

1981 Gola Shoe Factory (Bozeat Shoe Co.) closes. All workers are made redundant.

St Mary Christmas Bazaar raised £404.

Bozeat School Football Team win Wollaston District Cup.

29th July: Marriage of Prince Charles and Lady Diana Spencer. Street Party in Bull Close. Thirty of all ages take part with tea tables decorated in patriotic colours in garden of Graham and Mary Clarke. Floss Tivey recollected when Grandma Smart's family lived there and the garden was a small farmyard with outbuildings, a stable and a horse and cart, and Joe Smart fell off his penny-farthing bicycle on pebbles in Bull Close.

Wollaston Co-op merges with East Northants Co-op Society Ltd. Mr Neal, manager retires to Wollaston and Glenda Drage is promoted to manager.

4th December: Old school bell is presented to the School by Chairman of Parish Council, beautifully restored.

December: Tricia Roche's first coffee evening for the homeless in her house at 4 Brookside. Still going in 1998 when over £400 was raised!

1982 New Church Hall dedicated by Bishop Douglas Fever. It was opened by the Bishop's wife on 12th June. It is built on the site of the old church hall, but is 50% bigger and cost £1,000 for new chairs, tables and china for 100 people. The Hall was built and funded by the Marguerite Pierson Trust, a charity set up by Mr Wim Pierson (who lived at Greenwood, London Road) in his wife's memory.

Bigger water pipes installed to carry water from High Street into London Road.

Sept *About Bozeat*: Letter from County Surveyor with a promise of a bypass "within the next 10 years." A509 signed as part of M1 south route has

caused increase in traffic, especially lorries, through village.
Radio Northampton opened.
Mary Wallis of 43 Harrold Road wins £1,040 in groceries for a slogan for Bendix washing machines, Moffatt cookers, Kenwood mixers and Trinity freezers: "Cook, wash, or freeze – these are the goods that please."
Falklands War – Steven Nye, son of Stella Nye, the local post lady, is serving in Royal Navy on *HMS Arrow*.
Frank Gibson retires after 20 years as Cemetery caretaker and John Smith takes over.
Knapp Toolmakers takes over the Hope Street Factory.
Cavels take over Paper Shop.

1983 Kath Silsby appointed the first Lady Churchwarden.
24th January: Alan and Linda O'Connor become proprietors of Red Lion coming from large pub in Alperton, Wembley, London.
Carnival Day. Michelle Ward is voted queen out of 15 competitors.
Tom Partridge-Underwood voted Borough Councillor, and Kate Moreton chair of the Parish Council.
Jim and Maureen Lewis take over the Fish and Chip Shop in the High Street.
Wesley Guild alive and well with secretaries Marjorie Drage, Dolly Line, Flos Tivey, Miss G. Dunmore, Dolly Roberts. Open to all, it stands for Comradeship, Consecration, Culture and Christian Service.
Fred Dilley with Bob Lymn formed RAM Sportswear after being made redundant from Gola.

1984 March: *About Bozeat* has adverts for Keep Fit (ladies/retired), Yoga, Aerobics, Weight Training, Dance Exercise, reflecting interest in physical health!
Crimewatch Scheme proposed – established in 1985.
Mr James retires as Head of Bozeat School after 21 years.
Margaret Elliot takes over as Secretary of the Over Sixties from Mrs W. Partridge who resigns after six years.
Vicar Palmer starts appeal to restore Church Tower for £10,000.
Six Bozeat Queen Guides – 'Six of the Best' (*Evening Telegraph*) – Hayley Cobbald, Sharon Callaghan, Elizabeth James, Heather Badrick, Kirsty Webber and Tania Kingham. Guide Leader is Margaret Webber.
Burial Authority commend Bozeat on a tidy and well-kept cemetery (caretaker John Smith).
26th March: Public Meeting on bypass. Questionnaire distributed to all adults in the village. Voting is 45.7% for final scheme, 14.7% same but with roundabout connection to Easton Maudit, improve existing A509 6.3%, not returned 16.2%.
21st/23rd June: Second exhibition on bypass by NCC in Church Hall.
Phyllis Darnell, who started the Brownies in Bozeat, retires as District Commissioner.

1985 March: Richard Wilkins starts as new head of Bozeat School.
Sunday School at St Mary's restarted, organised by Alison Botterill and Debbie Elliott with six helpers.
Alan and Joy Wildman take over Paper Shop with help of Anne Simms, now called 'Family Afayre'.

6th July: Grand Fête in aid of St Mary's Restoration Fund opened by Peter Fry MP.

September: Robert and Pat Driver take over the Paper Shop (returned to its old name) in the High Street.

December: "There are new houses in the old school and others being built alongside it. There is another development near the Parish Church (which I believe is to be called Church Farm Close) and new houses in Wollaston Road. Am I alone in looking at these changes with mixed feelings?" Editorial by Penny Brannon in *About Bozeat*.

1986 Tidy Village Competition in Northants. Bozeat comes fifth out of 14 for the village award and 19th out of 73 for the cemetery.

Beaver Colony started at Methodist Church by Sue Wagstaff, which is dedicated at the Church Anniversary Weekend (18th May) by Rev. Bill Mason.

Fish & Chip shop is taken over by Pat (ex-midwife) and Roger Alderman.

Vera Askew retires and pulls down shutters on her London Road Stores after 30 years of service.

Matt Emberton who lived in Fullwell Road ran the London Marathon in 4½ hours raising £350 for Muscular Dystrophy and £150 for *About Bozeat*.

Arnold Dobbs, builder and stonemason retires 'officially'.

Bozeat Pantomime Society formed by John Burgess and others (Penny Brannon Sec.). *Sleeping Beauty* is to be their first production.

3rd May: Peter Fry MP meets Action Group and Parish Council re bypass.

15th May: AGM decides to close Wesley Guild after 59 years. Some members present were there when it began in 1927.

The 'Old Shed' where the painter Spencelayh worked, built in 1926 by Albert Partridge, had to be taken down – a little bit of Bozeat history disappears.

Community Neighbourhood Watch Scheme is up and running.

10th August: Rev. Bill Mason takes his last service at the Methodist Church and our new minister Rev. David Scott takes his first at Earls Barton on 5th September.

Responses to questionnaire, 'Why did you make your home in Bozeat' in *About Bozeat*. Replies included: "It was cheap and the only place we could afford." "We intended to move but we liked it so we stayed." "Because every single person spoke to us."

1987 20th January: Enquiry into Bypass Scheme in Church Hall conducted by Major-General J. M. Sawers.

Darren Laughton (grandson of Max Laughton) selected to play for County Under-11s Cricket.

During September/October four motor vehicles stolen, two thefts from motor vehicles and one house burglary – worrying increase in auto-crimes.

12 new families arrive in village and 10 babies born in months Sept-Nov.

1988 25th February: Bulldozers begin to carve out path of bypass this week. The County Council scheme is costed at £2.7m. Bozeat's oldest resident, Laura Bettles aged 92, former teacher, cuts the first turf of grass, aided by Parish Council Chairman, Mavis Holman.

February: Carpet Bowls Club started by Comsport in Church Hall. In

1989

November members start raising money to buy their own kit.

Youngest ever Chairman of Bozeat P.C. – Bernadette Woodford (née Roche).

31st January: Contractors give permission for torchlight procession along the completed bypass, the night before the official opening.

May: Tom (35) and Sue (29) Partridge-Underwood, are the youngest ever Mayor and Mayoress of Wellingborough, and only the second ever Mayor appointed from the rural area. They attended 382 social functions including Buckingham Palace and the Houses of Parliament during their year of office, the year in which Northants County Council celebrated 100 years, North-ampton 800 years since its charter, and Northampton Constabulary 150 years of service. There are 65,000 people in the Borough.

Lyndis Payne is new Clerk of Parish Council.

Youth Club five-a-side football team become Youth Club County Champions.

Tom Partridge-Underwood, Bozeat man and boy, made Mayor of Wellingborough, 1989-90, with his wife Sue.

The procession down Bozeat High Street to the Civic Service at the Methodist Church. Leading is Geoff Betts mace-bearer, followed by the Mayor and Mayoress, then the Chief Executive of the Council, Brian Veal, and borough councillors.

40th anniversary of Bozeat Women's Institute.

March: Residents of Sunny View vote to change its name back to the historic Pudding Bag Lane.

11th April: Council Meeting introduces free trial of wheeled bins for refuse. Radon in Homes. A free test is made available by NRPB as some houses in Wellingborough area are sufficiently high to warrant it. (Vicarage is tested, but not above average.)

June: Carpet Bowls equipment purchased and new club called 'Bozeat Bowling Club', for men and women aged 60-plus, meeting at the Church Hall.

27th August: Feast Day. The new Bishop of Brixworth, Paul Barber, preaches at Evensong. Garden Fête (in Church Hall) raises £345.

Vicar Palmer retires due to ill health, and retires to Bexhill-on-Sea.

Doctors David and Sheila Swan retire as GPs after 25 years.

End of rapid increase in property prices nationally (at least 20 houses empty in the village).

Mike from Sri Lanka takes over Bozeat Garage in London Road.

1990 According to *About Bozeat*, 14 babies are born in the village this year. School now has its own budget to manage, covering all aspects of the running of the school including salaries. 'The need for fund-raising takes on a new emphasis,' says Mr Wilkins, the Headteacher.

Stephen Cullip chosen by British Chess Foundation to be in the team of nine invited by the People's Sport Council of Kiev to play in Moscow in February.

Mrs Curtis leaves Bozeat School to become acting head of Irchester Junior School.

Bozeat to remain a restricted infill category village in County Structure Plan.

11th August: Re-opening and rededication of refurbished Independent Wesleyan Chapel.

Monday 2nd July: Doctors Sudhir and Sulabha Marathe have their first clinic as they start their medical practice in Bozeat and Wollaston.

July: Garrett's the butchers at the top of Allens Hill closes after about 100 years. Derek Taylor, their butcher's boy for 40 years finds a new job in Tesco's in the Wellingborough Arndale Centre.

Wednesday, 14th November 7.30 pm: Institution and induction of Philip Bligh as Vicar of Bozeat with Easton Maudit with his wife Audrey by the Bishop of Brixworth (Paul Barber). Churchwardens: Kath Silsby and Cliff Fenn, Tower Capt: Rex Line.

Mrs Finke retires from Bozeat School after 15 years.

November: Publication of *Pictorial History of Bozeat*.

December: Children in Need Appeal – Working Men's Club raises £1,504 and Red Lion £3,500.

British Gas £500,000 project begins in Bozeat. The first 50 houses will have gas by the middle of next January.

1991 Gulf War: Flight Lt. Richard Wesley (son of Joyce Wesley) serves as Tornado Navigator.

Mission Praise (first published in 1989) became the new hymn book for the church, (members buying and dedicating books) and the modern Rite A Eucharist was introduced on 4th and 5th Sundays for the first time.

The Secker Altar in the sanctuary was replaced by the fine imitation

Jacobean table given by Mr and Mrs J. H. Taylor in memory of their son Frank who fell in the Second World War, to be used at the celebration of the Eucharist from East End.

5th/6th April: Children and young people in a performance of *Oliver* in aid of the Church Restoration Fund, organised by Penny Brannon and Ruth Webb. Gas is first connected to the village.

21st July: Village Cricket on Playing Fields. Bozeat beat Abington Church.

August: Co-op store in London Road closes.

31st August: Welcome service for new Methodist Minister Rev. Philip Taylor.

1992   New kitchen/toilet installed in Church in Old Vestry (build in 1894 for installation of hot air heating system). Work done by local men, Gordon Brannon, Arnold Dobbs, George Line, Brian Taylor, George Sharratt, and Peter Collier. Cost £5,000.

Russell Line in his JCB dug a trench from the Church to the Vicarage to carry water and soil pipes.

First Series of Bozeat Lent Talks organised by combined churches and taking place at Independent Wesleyan Chapel entitled 'Contemporary Issues of Life and Faith'.

20-25th August: First Holiday Club for children of Primary School age held at Methodist Church using Scripture Union material, 'The J Team'. Some 80 children attended with leaders from all four churches, Catholic, Wesleyan, Methodist, and Anglican.

Upgrading and extension of electrical system. Floodlighting installed by Wellingborough Borough Council.

1993   Feb: Second Series Bozeat Lent Talks. Theme: 'This is My Story' including Bill Westwood, Bishop of Peterborough.

New gas-driven radiator heating system installed in St Mary's by Howsden's of Bedford. First switched on 3rd March.

Tuesday, 11th May: 2.30 pm meeting at Vicarage with John Gale from Age Concern to consider the possibility of a Lunch Club in the Church Hall. Also present, Pat Rothwell (Social Services), Audrey Bligh, Doug Browning, Wynne Threlfell, Lyndis Payne, Ellie Minney, Vicar.

8-9th April: *Jesus Christ Superstar* performed on Maundy Thursday and Good Friday in Church, producer Penny Brannon, Phil Ansell as Jesus and Debbie Ansell (née Silsby) as Mary. Church full for both performances.

Wednesday, 9th June: First Lunch Club in Church Hall for Senior Citizens in collaboration with Age Concern on Wednesdays.

New village choir called Windmill Singers begun in June under direction of Marian Brown of Manor Farm.

Anglia Television make a programme on the village in their series called 'The Village Show'.

Floodlighting of Church (installed by Wellingborough Council) and Lych Gate Lantern, made by Derek Cox and his son James, then the blacksmith at Castle Ashby.

Sound Enhancement System installed in Church cost £2,000 given in memory of Vicar's father.

Exact replica of crumbling 15th century Rose Window in north side of west wall made and fitted by Bowden & Ward.

1994 28th January: First Bozeat Men's Dinner in Church Hall. Guest Speaker Brenda Courtie. Chefs: Audrey Bligh, Sue Partridge-Underwood and helpers. 50 men attended.

New ringing platform and Vestry in Church Tower built by Robert Hollowell of Cogenhoe, cost £7,000 (Architect Donald Loe).

St Mary's: Rewiring and extension of electrical system with new trip/fuse system carried out by Richard Zang with help from team led by Gordon Brannon.

Rev. Gordon Chisnell becomes new Methodist Circuit Superintendent Minister.

St Mary's: New window installed in North Aisle dedicated to memory of Ernie and Amy Dilley, who had lived at 2 Pudding Bag Lane.

New Lych Gate Lantern installed.

Restoration of two plain glass windows in North Aisle.

1995 24th March 1330 hrs: casting of new Treble Bell at John Taylor's of Loughborough. Cost (including fittings) £4000. The inscription on the bell: *Thanks be to God EII R 1995 T. Hickling, K. Silsby – Church Wardens. R. Line – Captain.*

21st May: Licensing of our first Lay Reader at Peterborough, Penny Brannon.

26th November: First time at Bozeat Six Bells rung for Worship after being hung by Whites of Appleton. Total overall cost £10,000.

1996 Wednesday, 31st January, 7.30 pm: A Service of Thanksgiving to mark the Consecration of the new Treble Bell and re-dedication of the Bells and new Ringing Gallery by the Bishop of Brixworth in the presence of the Mayor and Mayoress of Wellingborough, Councillor and Mrs John Watts, and the Parish Council.

31st January: Mavis Holman retires from being practice manager at Brookside Medical Centre after 26 years.

January: Half the churchyard wall adjacent to the vicarage garden fell down.

6th February at 5 pm: Raiders wielding axes burst into Bozeat sub-Post Office but fled empty-handed. They smashed the security screen setting off the alarm. Sub-postmaster Keith Cullip, aged 50, said: "It happened very quickly. I didn't have time to panic. The police were on the scene within minutes."

March: Planting of four trees in SW Corner of Churchyard in memory of Andrew Brannon, the son of Gordon and Penny Brannon: two *Prunus Accalade* (pink flowering cherry), one *Acer Campestre* (field maple), and one *Pyrus Chanicleer* (pear family).

30th March: Commissioning of our first two Pastoral Assistants at Peterborough, Anne Hickling and Pat Smith.

Saturday 18 May: Waendel Walk. Bozeat won the Rutherford Shield, the 'Best Village Award'. One of the walkers (E. O. Pederson from Viborg, Denmark) wrote: "I will never forget the church with the resting place. I have never seen one like that before, and it would have been impossible in Denmark."

March: St Mary's: Dave Bryant of Bryant & Sons repaired the Ogee window in the tower, and one chancel window, and one in the North Aisle with

The Ten Commandments and the Lord's Prayer in St Mary's Church.

Polish glass of the sort he was using in the restoration of St George's Chapel, Windsor Castle after its great fire.

1997 27th January: Harriet Partridge died aged 99 (born 1887) Her husband Joshua Partridge (whose father was landlord first of the Lord Nelson, then of The Chequers) had been a 'carrier' and Captain of the Belfry. Harriet helped in the first church bazaar in the 'new' church hall in 1929 and then on until 1992, 63 bazaars in all! Married on Christmas Day 1922, she retired in 1977 aged 80 as a home help. Harriet came from Ibstock, Leicester and her father was a miner, breeding canaries for the mines.

23rd February: Coat of Arms taken down from the inside wall of the tower of St Mary's with the help of Rex Line, Tim Hickling, Gordon Brannon, Robert Hollowell, Mark Rudd, Ian Mapp, Eric Green and Mervin Chapman, and thanks to Barry Wagstaff of Griggs who provided a van to take it to the studio of Clifford Ellison (restorer of the Queen's paintings) at Long Buckby to be restored for £1,000. Mr Ellison also voluntarily cleaned and restored our Ten Commandments/Creed/Lord's Prayer in the sanctuary.

24th March: After years of debate, the huge sycamore leaning towards the church tower growing in churchyard wall was sawn down. A ring count showed it to be about 124 years old and half way down its trunk it had rotted inside leaving only five inches thickness of wood around a central hole! If left it would have crashed through the Ogee Window.

Sunday 6th April: Archdeacon Allan Huggins, Rector of Holy Cross, Canberra, Australia with his wife Jan starts a nine month exchange with our vicar and becomes the 69th Vicar of Bozeat.

31st August: Bozeat Feast with a live link with Holy Cross, Canberra.

Lady Diana Spencer, Princess of Wales, dies in a car crash in Paris with boyfriend Dodi Fayed whose father owns Harrods.

Dec: Stella Nye retires as post lady after 23½ years.

1998 6th January: Last Sunday for Allan and Jan Huggins before returning to Australia.

Paper Shop under new management as, after 14 years, Robert and Pat Driver hand over to Barry and Steph Strain. Robert and Pat have bought one of the new houses on the Triangle where Dolly Roberts played as a child 70 years ago!

April: The wettest since 1818 with widespread flooding along the River Nene, flooding many houses in Northampton.

April: New lantern at Hensmans Lane entrance to Churchyard given by Mary Clarke and family (20 Allens Hill) in memory of her husband Graham.

June: Village Garage opened for sales and repairs of Audi and VW cars by Mick Carroll, Peter Spence and Blaise Holman.

30th June: Salvaturi Bovenzi died aged 78 cutting his grass at the top of Hope Street. The father of eight children, he was a jovial and happy man. He married Sheila Drage, sister of Barry of Arch Villa, first cousin to the Drages of Red Gables Farm and second cousin to the Drages of 2 Hope Street! He came as an Italian Prisoner of War and worked for the Garretts on their farm at Dungee Corner.

June edition of *About Bozeat*: Penny Brannon resigns as editor of *About Bozeat* having been so since its first edition in March 1980, performing an invaluable service to the village.

6th July: Mrs Emily Walsh (1A Council Street) died today aged 100, a Londoner who came with her four children – Eddie, and Nora (who married John Drage) still live in Bozeat. They came as evacuees to Wollaston during World War II. Emily was cousin to Peg Price in Firtree Close. The oldest person in Bozeat is Mrs Blanche King (77 Queen Street) aged 104 who came from Guernsey and reads without glasses, clear-witted and still lively and mobile!

July: Knapp Toolmakers Ltd have put the Hope Street factory up for sale as they need larger premises and so are moving to Wellingborough.

Current members of the Parish Council are: Alan Brealey, Fred Dilley, Annette Hunt, John Smith, Marjory Stanford, Gloria Wallis, Colin Curtis, Doreen Dimmock, Tom Partridge-Underwood, Jennifer Spencer, and Andrew Underwood.

Out of 1,100 teams, a team of three boys from Wollaston School, including Philip Boswell of 2 Allens Hill, came eighth overall in the British Heart Foundation National Golf Junior Finals.

Nov: New village magazine begins – *Bozeat Matters* – editor Lynne Ward with David and Anne Brown.

1999 Some 20 new houses on Manor Farm opening into Dychurch at prices around £150,000 and 30 more modest ones at about £70,000 built behind the factory at the top of London Road are finished. Six of the latter are co-operative housing for folk associated with the village not currently able to afford to buy a home – a co-operative venture between the Council Housing Committee, East Midlands Housing Association and Northamptonshire Rural Housing Association whose chairman is the Bishop of Brixworth, Paul Barber. He officially opened these homes on Friday, 11th August 1999. The venture is the first of its kind in the Borough of Wellingborough.

Tuesday, 2nd March: Derek Nimmo the well-known actor who lived in Easton Maudit is buried in Easton Maudit churchyard after being unconscious for three months after falling down the steps of his London flat and striking his head against a stone wall. He was 68. He was an enthusiastic supporter of our benefice.

April: New lantern installed at entrance to churchyard from Hensmans Lane in memory of Graham Clarke, given by his family (see Chapters 18 and 19).

May: Waendel Walk. The village win the Rutherford Trophy Shield for the third time.

14th May: Oriana Singers in Concert in Easton Church raised £600 in aid of the Church and Oakfield Home, with a raffle that raised £200 for Kosovo.

31st May: Bill Silsby one of the great characters of the village (along with brother Harry who died 23rd October 1998 aged 87) dies at the age of 81.

2nd June: Bozeat Windmill Singers give concert in the Castle Theatre in Wellingborough in aid of Marie Curie Cancer Care for which it raised £2,000. It was a sell-out and a great personal achievement for their director Marian Brown of Manor Farm.

27th June: Philip Bligh resigns as vicar to take up Rectorship of Holy Cross Anglican Church, Canberra, Australia for two years starting October 1999.

Field Names

This list was compiled by Edgar Corby and Bill Silsby, who numbered and identified the fields with the help of local farmers in the 1980s, as members of the Bozeat Archaeological and Historical Society.

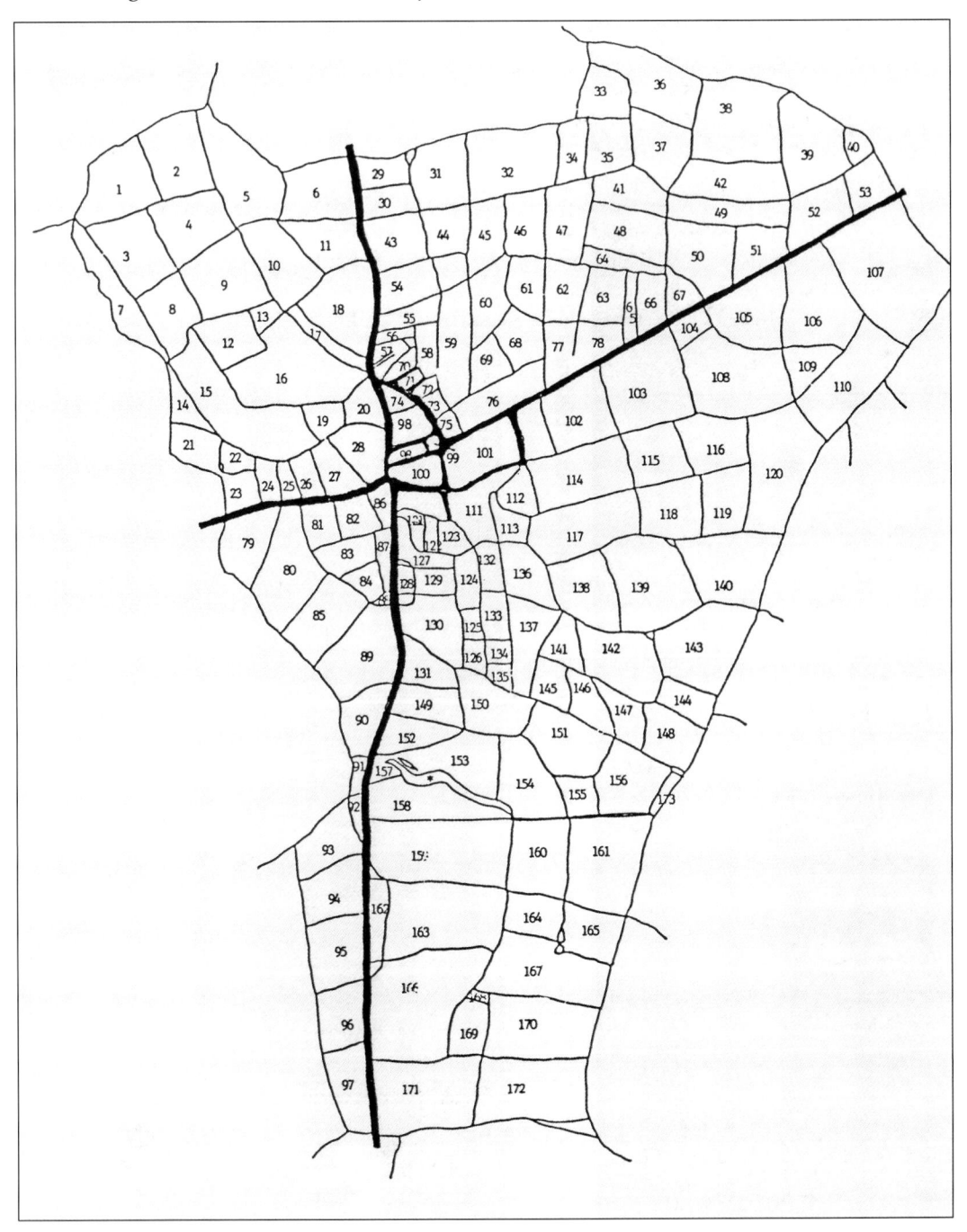

FIELD NAMES

1. Sandwell/Watsons Hole
2. Gripes Hole
3. Hovel Close
4. Dicks Hill
5. Great Close
6. Forthams (Strixton Lane End)
7. Long Meadow
8. Brick Yard Field
9. The Hooks
10. Wet Furrow
11. Rough Close
12. The Bogs
13. The Paddocks
14. Bottom Slype
15. The Meadow
16. Windmill Field
17. Paddock
18. Fulwell
19. Bottom Hopground
20. Top Hop Ground
21. Tor Slype
22. Sandpit Field
23. Home Close
24. Roses Span
25. Easton Glebe
26. Roses Span
27. White Wall
28. Bury Yard
29. Little Sandy
30. Shrives Field
31. Sandy
32. Thirty Acres
33. Bankey
34. The Slade
35. Little Fox
36. Big Fox
37. Top Fox
38. Fox Hill
39. Black Hedge Field
40. Voting Field
41. Linchills
42. Linchills
43. Top Close
44. Pye Corner
45. Ten Acres
46. Stubbs Close
47. 2nd Stubbs Close
48. Stare Hill
49. Linchilla
50. Chalk Hill
51. Home Close
52. Top Dungee
53. Little Dungee
54. Fulwell Close
55. Dock Hill Allotments
56. Dockhill Close
57. Hope Close
58. Bull Close
59. Lime Kiln Close
60. Twelve Acres
61. Nine Acres
62. Smith Hill West
63. Smith Hill East
64. The Slipe (Slade)
65. Town Well Acre
66. Church Lands
67. Three Corner Piece
68. Ten Acres
69. Eight Acres
70. Little Gains
71. Bull Close
72. Bradshaws Close
73. Lime Kiln
74. Chequers Field
75. Pit Field
76. 2nd Pit Field Close
77. Front Home Close
78. Back Home Close (Old Hilleys)
79. Bumper Hill Gate
80. Chalk Hill
81. 2nd Stoney Piece
82. Stoney Piece
83. Clayland
84. The Orchard
85. Stone Pit Close
86. The Stone Pit
87. 2nd Clayland
88. The Mill
89. Mill Field
90. Stocken Hill
91. Stocken
92. Wood Field
93. 1st Plain
94. 2nd Plain
95. 3rd Plain
96. Top Plain
97. Plain Gap
98. Glebe Land
99. Top Glebe
100. The Orchard
101. Rookery
102. Sunbury Land
103. Middle Close
104. Little Sandpit Slade
105. Dodsons Field
106. Kape Mere
107. Dungee Leys
108. Sand Pit Slade (Redland)
109. Bottom Kape
110. Pundle Close
111. Home Close
112. The Paddock
113. Hoam Field
114. Towns end
115. Rough Close
116. Tow Mowing
117. Big Home Close
118. Rough Field Close
119. The Paddock
120. Park Close
121. Canada
122. Fareys Land
123. Hovel Close
124. 2nd Close
125. Top Close
126. The Paddock
127. Home Close
128. Little Close
129. Home Close
130. Pebble Road
131. Mile Stone
132. Dag Lane Field
133. Dexters Close
134. Barn Field
135. Top Close
136. Bottom Willow Close
137. Top Home Close
138. French's Close
139. Larks Hill
140. Park Green
141. Little Meadow
142. Hungry Hill
143. Westwood Close
144. Stocken Leys
145. Bottom Close
146. Middle Close
147. Pond Close
148. Big Stocken Leys
149. Mile Stone
150. Barn Close
151. Bean Land
152. Skevington's Close
153. Top Skevington Close
154. The Baulk
155. Bull Way
156. Ox Ground
157. Home Field
158. The Stocken
159. Big Stocken
160. Moat Field
161. New Ground
162. The Pigin
163. Wood Hill
164. Moat Field
165. Barn Close
166. The Park
167. Wood Barn Field
168. Bozeat Wood
169. Bozeat Grange
170. Nun Wood Slype Close
171. Mitre Corner
172. Bottom Hole
173. Fir Tree Planting
* The Belt

Field Names

Arranged alphabetically by name. Numbers refer to map on page 404.

Name	No.	Name	No.	Name	No.	Name	No.
Back Home Close (Old Hilleys)	78	Dodsons Field	105	Middle Close	146	Shrives Field	30
Bankey	33	Dungee Leys	107	Mile Stone	131	Skevington's Close	152
Barn Close	150	Easton Glebe	25	Mile Stone	149	The Slade	34
Barn Close	165	Eight Acres	69	The Mill	88	The Slipe (Slade)	64
Barn Field	134	Fareys Land	122	Mill Field	89	Smith Hill East	63
The Baulk	154	Fir Tree Planting	173	Mitre Corner	171	Smith Hill West	62
Bean Land	151	Forthams (Strixton Lane End)	6	Moat Field	160	Stare Hill	48
The Belt	*	Fox Hill	38	Moat Field	164	Stocken Hill	90
Big Fox	36	French's Close	138	New Ground	161	Stocken Leys	144
Big Home Close	117	Front Home Close	77	Nine Acres	61	Stocken	91
Big Stocken	159	Fulwell	18	Nun Wood Slype Close	170	The Stocken	158
Big Stocken Leys	148	Fulwell Close	54	The Orchard	84	The Stone Pit	86
Black Hedge Field	39	Glebe Land	98	The Orchard	100	Stone Pit Close	85
The Bogs	12	Great Close	5	Ox Ground	156	Stoney Piece	82
Bottom Close	145	Gripes Hole	2	Paddock	17	2nd Stoney Piece	81
Bottom Hole	172	Home Close	23	The Paddock	112	Stubbs Close	46
Bottom Hopground	19	Home Close	51	The Paddock	119	2nd Stubbs Close	47
Bottom Kape	109	Home Close	111	The Paddock	126	Sunbury Land	102
Bottom Slype	14	Home Close	127	The Paddocks	13	Ten Acres	45
Bottom Willow Close	136	Home Close	129	The Park	166	Ten Acres	68
Bozeat Grange	169	Home Field	113	Park Close	120	Thirty Acres	32
Bozeat Wood	168	Home Field	157	Park Green	140	Three Corner Piece	67
Bradshaws Close	72	The Hooks	9	Pebble Road	130	Top Close	43
Brick Yard Field	8	Hope Close	57	The Pigin	162	Top Close	125
Bull Close	58	Hovel Close	123	Pit Field	75	Top Close	135
Bull Close	71	Hovel Close	3	2nd Pit Field Close	76	Top Dungee	52
Bull Way	155	Hungry Hill	142	1st Plain	93	Top Fox	37
Bumper Hill Gate	79	Kape Mere	106	2nd Plain	94	Top Glebe	99
Bury Yard	28	Larks Hill	139	3rd Plain	95	Top Home Close	137
Canada	121	Lime Kiln	73	Plain Gap	97	Top Hop Ground	29
Chalk Hill	50	Lime Kiln Close	59	Pond Close	147	Top Plain	96
Chalk Hill	80	Linchills	41	Pundle Close	110	Top Skevington Close	153
Chequers Field	74	Linchills	42	Pye Corner	44	Tor Slype	21
Church Lands	66	Linchills	49	Rookery	101	Tow Mowing	116
Clayland	83	Little Close	128	Roses Span	24	Town Well Acre	65
2nd Clayland	87	Little Dungee	53	Roses Span	26	Towns End	114
2nd Close	124	Little Fox	35	Rough Close	11	Twelve Acres	60
Dag Lane Field	132	Little Gains	70	Rough Close	115	Voting Field	40
Dexters Close	133	Little Meadow	141	Rough Field Close	118	Westwood Close	143
Dicks Hill	4	Little Sandpit Slade	104	Sand Pit Slade (Redland)	108	Wet Furrow	10
Dock Hill Allotments	55	Little Sandy	29	Sandpit Field	22	White Wall	27
Dockhill Close	56	Long Meadow	7	Sandwell/Watsons Hole	1	Windmill Field	16
		The Meadow	15	Wood Field	92	Wood Barn Field	167
		Middle Close	103	Sandy	31	Wood Hill	163

Place Names of the Past
Mavis Holman (adapted and expanded)

The author (left) standing with Bernard Line in The Bogs and looking over the Windmill Field towards the bypass and village beyond.

BACKSIDE	Allotment back of Lord Nelson Pub, High Street and back of 5 Dag Lane, now the new housing estate, St Mary's Road area.
BANKY	Hedge between Horn Wood and Easton Maudit known for blackberries. No.33 on the field name map is also called Banky.
THE BELT	Belt-shaped strip of land north of what is now Fir Tree Grove.
BENNES FIELD	Field on which Council Street was built.
THE BOGS	A piece of marshland west of Long Meadow (see field map) just beyond Windmill Field, going out of the village, now on the other side of the bypass, consisting of 5 acres of rush

	marsh and rough grassland, now drained. Previously a dangerous area, wet and treacherous. A nesting place for wagtails and snipe. (There is a snipe on the new Bozeat village sign.)
BRADSHAWS CLOSE	Allotment (presently used) at the top of Fullwell adjacent to Lime Kiln alongside Allens Hill. Bradshaw is the name of the man who donated the field to the village for use as allotments.
BRAITCH	The Gap – Braich being a 'Bozeat word'.
BRICKYARD	In 1860, Thomas Bignall was making bricks in his brickward. Here is probably the only brick kiln in the village. The large hole left by the dug-out clay was used as the village rubbish tip – see Tin Pits. Accessed by the footpath through The Bogs, on the other side of the bypass.
THE BRIDLE	Field north of what is now Fir Tree Grove.
BUMBLY	Field past York Cottage towards Easton Maudit.
BURY YARD	(Bury = fortified) Field west side of 'The Flat', London Road, below the cemetery and divided by the new road to Easton Maudit. Site of the mediaeval village where the original Bozeat Manor House once stood in the 14th century, and possibly earlier. The levelled area at the top of this sloping field where probably the manor stood is clearly visible – surrounded by a ditch around the lower sides.
THE CAKE WALK	The old name for Fish Alley, once an open brook, joining High Street to Mile Street.
CHEQUERS FIELD	Field up Allens Hill near the Windmill Field, where the Bozeat Feast was often held.
CHEQUERS COTTAGES	Two cottages in London Road demolished since the Second Word War.
CHURCH COTTAGES	Church Walk. The site where these stood is now the garage of 6 Church Walk.
CHURCH END ROAD	Original name for Allen's Hill.

CLAYLAND	A field now incorporated into Easton View Estate, recalled in the naming of Clayland Close. A house in London Road was once called 'The Clayland'.
COW LANE	From Shepherds Lodge (now demolished) going through to the Brickyard one way, and back to the village and London Road in the other.
CROSS KEYS VILLAGE GREEN	Village green named after the pub on the site which closed in 1931, demolished in the 1950s.
DAISY CASTLE	Situated near Harrold Park Farm, possibly one or two cottages (*About Bozeat*, March 84, p17).
DOCKHILL	Allotment incorporated into Fullwell Road.
DYCHURCH	Named as such since mediaeval times, meaning ditch.
FIR TREE PLANTIN	Field on the north of Fir Tree Grove, now with oak and ash trees.
THE FLAT	London Road between Mile Street and Allens Hill.
FORTY FOOT	A riding (bridleway) which is probably a Roman Road, leading from the top of Harrold Road, going right to Odell. It is now a picnic area, and is the start of a footpath across old Podington aerodrome to Sharnbrook via Yelnow Lane.
FULLWELL	Formerly Fullwell Close containing one of the many wells in the village – presumably usually full! The well is at the bottom of Fullwell Road, where it meets the old Wollaston Road. The present Fullwell Road is on the other side of Wollaston Road to the field of the same name.
THE GANNICK	*Marlow*, 1936 p90: "many of the present inhabitants of Bozeat went to the lace school kept by Mrs Belle Pettitt 'round the ganic' up Wheelrights Yard," meaning 'up the alley'. Dorothy Grimes, in her classic book on Northamptonshire dialect *Like Dew Before the Sun*, has the spelling as 'gannock'.

THE GOLD	Burleigh Terrace in Mile Street. *Marlow* (1936, p16) suggests originally 'The Guild' where members of the weaver's guild once lived. This was the site of the first Methodist Chapel in Bozeat.
GRIPE'S HOLE	Field next to Sandwell/Watsons Hole on the edge of the parish towards Grendon.
HORN WOOD	West side of London Road and north of the village, ancient woodland, probably mediaeval.
HUNGRY HILL	Field to the west of White House Farm.
LIME KILN	Part of the allotments at the top of Fullwell Road which continue through to Allens Hill, along the south side of Bull Close.
LINE PROP YARD	Easton Lane where Botterill's Factory (now Electrosite) stands. It was a square of houses which used the centre court to hang out washing.
LITTLE GAINS	Name of field where Council Street was built. Suggested as name when Council Street could have been re-named, but refused by residents.
LITTLE HELL	Top of Mile Street, now a building plot.
LONG MEADOW	Field along by the Bozeat Brook after it has gone along the London Road and then under the bypass on its way to Grendon. This low-lying land is very marshy (close to the Bogs and the Meadow).
MEETING YARD	This is an early name for Line-Prop Yard.
MILLERS CORNER	Junction of High Street and Church Lane on Camden Square.
NEW BARN	Now known as Newlands Farm.
NEW ROAD	The old name for Harrold Road.
THE PICLE	A small piece of land or garden associated with a building. Particularly, it could have been attached to the previous (pre-1729) vicarage, possibly in the vicinity of Lavender Cottage in Church Walk (the former Workhouse).

PIT FIELD	Field opposite the new school, used as a quarry for stone for many of the buildings in Bozeat, also known as Home Field. The unevenness of the field shows its origins.
POUND, THE	There were several fields known by this name, where stray animals were accommodated. The man in charge was called 'The Hayward', whose job it was to round up these animals before crops were damaged. The last Pound in Bozeat was on the corner of Church Lane and Harrold Road, and is remembered by Tom Partridge-Underwood as a very wide verge to Church Lane, which would have been enclosed, with a large stone in the middle, known as the Pound Stone. This vanished when the new houses were built.
PUDDING BAG LANE	Situated half way up Church Lane, the area covered being in the shape of a 'pudding bag nest' – that of a finch. An alternative derivation is that the bakehouse which was once on the left side on the lane would hang out suet bags on a line. In 1962, the residents voted to change the name to Sunny View, but in a re-run in 1989, its heritage was restored as the vote was to change the name back again. Until the 1980s, the lane continued as a footpath through to Mile Street.
PUNDLE WOOD	Top of Harrold Road, turn right to Odell – wood on right hand side.
REAR STREET	An old name for Burton Terrace.
RISELEY GARDENS (or Pychle)	House at the top of Allens Hill, where Mr Risely lived, had his shoe factory, and where the Methodists once met.
ROBERTS YARD	Where 7 Church Lane now is. Also called Wallaces Yard after the Wallaces who lived in Glebe Cottage.
ROCK VILLA	Impressive house at the Olney end of London Road, built by the Berrills in the 1860s. For many years the home of William Drage, and later Dr Selby. It is now known as 'Greenwood'.

THE ROOKERY	This was in the field between where the new school is now and Church Lane, near the Pound, now housing. The present conspicuous rookery is in Vicarage Field in the limes alongside Hensmans Lane.
ROSIE'S SPAN	Field along Easton Lane north of cemetery opposite York Cottage. It is presumed that Rosie was once the owner.
SHEPHERDS LODGE	Cottage in the Paddocks field, beyond Windmill Field. This is now demolished, but was Dolly Roberts' home until 1926. During the Second World War it was occupied by evacuees. It was demolished following vandalism in the 1980s.
THE SLADE	The road from Dungee Corner to Hinwick. Several fields around Bozeat are called this, taken from the Old English *slaed*, meaning a little valley or piece of low moist ground.
SLIBBER SLOBBER	By Dag Lane Brook, the area leading from Dag Lane to Garden Field/Backside.
SLYPE FARM	Changed from Slipe Farm by Roy and Vi Allen who owned it 1955-65. Then 30 acres including The Meadow (15 acres) which they had drained. Slipe is a common name meaning a long narrow strip (French) or (Old English) Slyppe – paste, slime – a muddy place, slipe – a slippery place especially a stream bank. The Brook ran through the bottom of the farm, where it was very boggy.
SPANGLE ROW	Now Spencer Gardens off St Mary's Road, behind the Nelson pub. Named from the glass beads on lace bobbins of lace makers.
THE SQUARE	Camden Square.
STINKEY BROOK	This is the name given by older villagers to the brook which runs from the high ground above Dychurch along (now under) Bozeat High Street (once called Brook Street) then turning right along the London Road and crossing under it at Spring Vale Farm. Thereafter it makes its way westwards to the River Nene – along the bottom of Bury yard, under the bypass and

Site of the Tin Pits west of the village, on the other side of the bypass beyond The Bogs.

	following the lowest furrow of the land along the bottom Windmill field, into the bogs and then on beside Long Meadow.
STOKEN HOLLOW	West side of London Road, the entrance to Horn Wood, meaning 'stock (cattle) in the hollow'.
STONEYPIECE	This was an allotment area, now incorporated in Easton View. The name is descriptive of the type of soil, and the new cul-de-sac, now on part of the site, is called Stoneypiece.
TIN PITS	A Victorian rubbish tip in the Bogs, filling the hole resulting from the removal of clay for the Brickyard field, used until the 1930s. It is still a hollow now overgrown with mature trees, visible as a spinney from the bypass.
THE TOP	The upper part of Allens Hill, possibly as opposed to 'The Flat'.

TOWN WELL	Up on the right of Dychurch Lane, coming off the land from Spring Hill Farm. An ancient historic spring providing water for the village and its animals.
THE TRIANGLE	Bottom of Allens Hill where it meets the London Road, the corner of Chequers Field. A new house has now been built on it.
VINEGAR	Allotment back of Line Prop Yard, now developed.
WARNERS FIELD	A field behind the Red Lion frequently used for 'tea drinking'. Now built over by Hewlett's Close.
WATSON'S HOLE	Part of the brook from London Road, Bozeat to Grendon and on to the Nene. It is a deep hole, used for sheep dipping, in the same field as Sandwell Spring.
WARRENS GARDEN FIELD	Field to the east of London Road where the Empire Day Sports took place each year. Now build over by the Hewlett's Close/St Mary's Road estate.
WHEELWRIGHTS YARD	Yard off Camden Square.
WHITEWALL	Field next to the cemetery by Easton Lane.
WINDMILL FIELD	This is to the north-west of the village, divided by the new bypass, and to the left as London Road joins it at the Wellingborough end. Before the bypass it was used for grazing cattle from Church Farm and at its south-east corner still stands the animal food production plant owned by Raymond Roberts. This is not the area where the well-known post-mill was blown over in 1949, which was in Mill Field to the south, but nevertheless, the Enclosure Map of 1799 shows a post-mill in this field, which is probably the same mill before it was moved. The windmill is believed to have stood at the top of Cow Lane, opposite the present junction of Allens Hill onto London Road. In the 1886 sale of the Bozeat Estate, this field is included with Church Farm, with a reference to "an excellent site for a mansion in the Windmill

PLACE NAMES OF THE PAST

	Field having a nice elevation". Mr Hensman, a previous owner of Church Farm at the end of the 19th century, planted a double line of elm trees across it in preparation for a mansion which he planned to build, but never did.
WORKHOUSE YARD	Mallows Yard, still housing what was once the Workhouse, now called Lavender Cottage.
YARMOUTH SANDS	Behind the Cross Keys, two cottages now demolished, coming out onto Fish Alley.
YELVERTON MANOR	Situated to the north of Easton Lane between Park House and Easton Maudit Church. This was a large manor house built in its own park to the north of Easton Maudit Church belonging to the Yelverton family from Elizabethan times, and finally to the Earls of Sussex. When it was demolished at the end of the 18th century, it was reputed to have one of the finest libraries in England.
ZINC SQUARE	Crown of hill of Mile Street. Houses had zinc roofs.

Marlow, in Sheet 21, lists some descriptive 18th century names which he was not able to trace:

> Millway
> The Farkeshook
> Thickhorn
> Midsummer meadow
> Semnery hedges
> Lingells
> Bonfire Hill

LUMLEY DEEDS (15th March 1343)
(Some of the names of lands are situated part in Bozeat and part in Easton)

The following names predate the Field Names which themselves are becoming obscured with the passage of time and building developments. Even at the time of *Marlow's History*, he admits the difficulty in tracing the locations of these 14th century, and earlier, land names. For our part, some can be presumed or guessed at, but they do provide a window on life and language from that era, and are worthy of inclusion here:

1 Toft [homestead] at the horsemulneyard, Land at: Holeweye, Waterlond, Foldelayn, Brerheg, le Eldedych, Flexlond, Clavergars, Oterwellebalke, Pitteswelle, Merschebrok [Marshbrook?], Hewerscroft, Hangindekul, le Stub, Garbedeland, le

Pittes, Godewells Sike, Stokewellemoor, the Hent, Abrickeswelle, Derneford, Appletrefurlong, the Windmill, le Bury, le nether Stub, le Rugwey, Sixstonelowe, Blakhegmulne near the King's highway, Waytingheg, 1 acre binetheburi [i.e. beneath the Bury], le Mulnedam, Thykhat, Foxhyll.

[From *Marlow*, 1936, p.53]

The Bogs, looking towards the Tin Pits.

HONEST JOHN

The Footwear with the Makers' GUARANTEE

JOHN DRAGE & SONS, LTD., BOZEAT, Northamptonshire

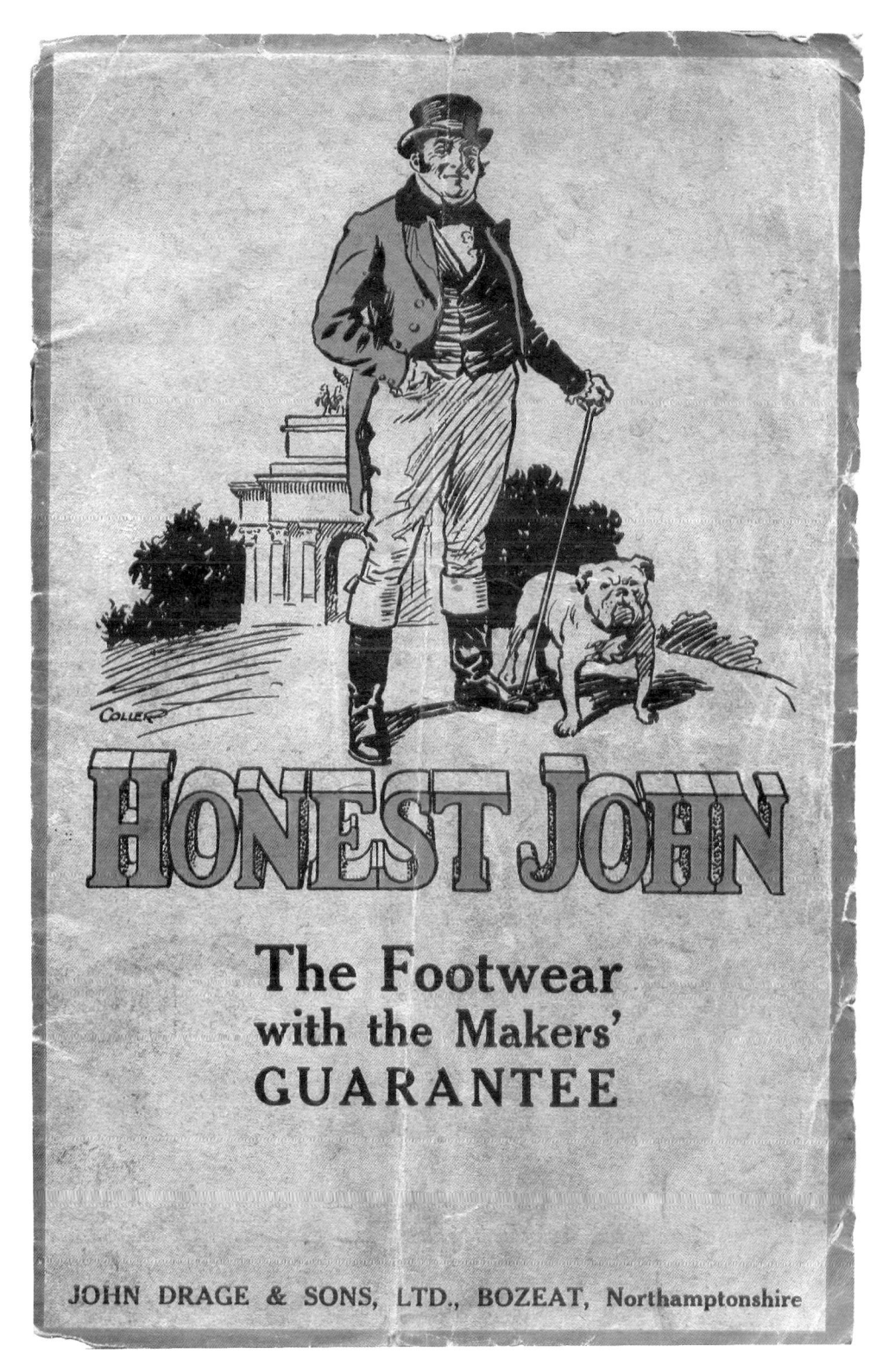

(Derek Edmunds collection)

A VIEW of our Factory at Bozeat, Northamptonshire, where "HONEST JOHN" Boots are manufactured, and whence they are posted direct to you.

This is our Correct Postal Address

Messrs John Drage & Sons Ltd
Bozeat,
Northamptonshire

JANUARY, 1921

"HONEST JOHN"
FOOTWEAR

The ALL-LEATHER Boots that are guaranteed to wear well and give you every satisfaction

MANUFACTURED BY

JOHN DRAGE & SONS, Ltd.
BOZEAT . NORTHAMPTONSHIRE

Established 1865

Why we can Guarantee "Honest John" Footwear

YOU have read the guarantee on the first page of this book. We hope that your first thought after reading it was: "Well, these people must believe pretty strongly in the boots they make, or they could never give a guarantee like *that*." Because we *do* believe in them. We know personally what leather they are cut from, how they are made from start to finish, and the way they are examined before they leave our factory. It is only because we *know* how good they are—all through, and every pair—that we pledge ourselves in this manner.

OUR GUARANTEE is not merely that we will return you your money if you don't like the boots when you receive them .. That, according to our ideas, is only common honesty. We go much further, and say that if the boots fail to give you satisfactory wear under fair conditions, we will repair them free of charge, or even replace them by a new pair.

Mr. Frank Drage
Our Managing Director is a Practical Bootmaker, with twenty years' experience and a thorough knowledge of the intricate technicalities of the trade.

Page 4

You will not get an assurance like that through any shop. We can only give it because we are the actual manufacturers.

That is also the reason why our prices compare so favourably with those of other firms. Of course, you will see cheaper boots—or rather, boots at a lower price—advertised in "catch-penny" advertisements. But you will know as well as we do that a sound, all-leather boot cannot be made, let alone sold, for a few shillings. For boots of really good quality—strong and hard wearing—our prices are exceptionally low. You save all intermediate profits by buying from us direct. The boots only leave our hands to come straight to you.

You will find it quite easy to order through the post, if you read the simple directions on page 7.

Our firm has been making boots since 1865. We claim, therefore, to know the essentials of a good boot, and we put that knowledge into every pair we make. Fifty years is a long time, but during that period our reputation for making thoroughly reliable footwear, and for straightforward dealing, has never been challenged. Mr. John Drage, who founded the firm, built up his business on these principles. We endeavour to carry on the same traditions.

That is the answer to our first sentence. We know we can supply a good article—we are proud of it—and we are prepared to back our statements by giving this binding guarantee.

Mr. Cecil Drage
is in charge of the Postal and Distributing side of the business. He sees that your order is executed to your satisfaction, and deals with all enquiries and correspondence personally.

Page 5

Do your Boots wear like this?

Castle Gresley
3 Nov. 1920

Town Drage & Sons

Dear Sirs,

The Brown Derby Boots which I had from you 6 years ago, have been in wear every winter since. They have now got their fifth sole on and the tops are still as good as ever. I have over a mile to walk 4 times a day across muddy fields so that they have had some very hard wear.

Yours faithfully,
B. J.

THE boots illustrated above are the actual pair referred to by our customer, after their fifth time of re-soleing. If you want boots as good as these, order a pair of "HONEST JOHN" by return.

The original of our customer's letter can be seen at our offices

HOW TO ORDER "HONEST JOHN" FOOTWEAR THROUGH THE POST

PLACE your stockinged foot firmly on a sheet of white paper. Then with a pencil, held upright, carefully trace the outline of your foot. Write down on the same sheet the size of boot you usually take, and whether you wish a medium or broad fitting.

Then add your full name and address.

Enclose a Cheque, Money Order, Postal Order or Treasury Notes for the amount of your purchase. It is advisable to cross Cheques and Postal Orders " & Co." and register all Treasury Notes.

Then post to us at Bozeat, Northamptonshire. You will get your boots by return of post—and we are confident that you will be so satisfied with them that we shall have made another regular customer for "HONEST JOHN" Footwear.

"HONEST JOHN" Footwear for Men is supplied in all sizes from 5 to 11. Size 12 is 2/- extra.

We pay postage.
We also supply suitable laces, leather or mohair with all footwear.
The prices given here are inclusive.

Page 7

JOHN DRAGE & SON LTD
Honest John Boot Factory
BOZEAT
NORTHANTS

This is an actual photograph of the boot

Strong Chrome Grain Derby

No. 22
Price **26/6**
POST FREE

THE man who wants real foot protection, but has to consider the question of price, will find this a wonderfully useful boot. A heavy, unlined, black Derby, it is made of good stout chrome grain leather. Its tough leather soles, $\frac{7}{16}$ in. thick, are screwed and stitched, so that they will give unequalled wear. A fine boot, *guaranteed* to be reliable, durable, and sound all through.

Sizes 5 to 11, in medium, broad and extra broad fittings

For Land Workers

A cheaper quality than No. 22, but a very hard-wearing, substantial boot all the same. A very popular boot with Cowmen, Gardeners and other workers on the land.

No. 303 PRICE **22/6** POST FREE

For Pitmen, etc.

Similar to No. 22, but made in strong, old-fashioned black English kip leather, with nailed bottoms and iron tips to heels. Heavy and durable, a splendid boot for Pitmen, Agricultural Workers, etc.

No. 304 PRICE **26/6** POST FREE

Sizes 5 to 11. Nos. 303 and 304 broad fitting only

Dozens of Friends want Boots like them

"A few weeks ago I obtained from you one pair of 'Honest John' (Brown). During my rounds visiting my Policy holders I have been asked by dozens to get them a similar pair of boots as the pair I got from you."

Original letter can be seen at our offices

Page 8

HONEST JOHN FOOTWEAR
Reg. No. 387175.

Selected Box Lace Boot

This is an actual photograph of the boot

No. 306

Price **25/-**
POST FREE

THIS is a very serviceable boot for ordinary wear. It is cut from a particularly supple and smooth Box, which takes a fine polish. The "whole-golosh" model is a favourite with many men because of its neat appearance, and you will find No. 306 an excellent specimen of this type of boot. It is strongly made, though of medium weight, and its $\frac{5}{16}$ in. soles, which are stitched and sewn, will beat many stouter models of other makes.

Also in superior quality leather a boot to be worn in town or country with equal comfort.

No. 307   PRICE **28/6**   POST FREE

Also in Derby style (similar superior quality to No. 307), with light double soles.

No. 314   PRICE **28/6**   POST FREE

Sizes 5 to 11 in medium and broad fittings.

"Honest John" Footwear comes direct from our factory to you

Cutting out the uppers from selected skins

Page 9

JOHN DRAGE & SON LTD.
Honest John Boot Factory
BOZEAT NORTHANTS

This is an actual photograph of the shoe

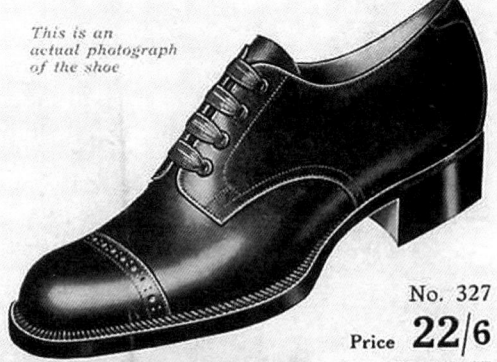

No. 327
Price **22/6**
POST FREE

A Good Choice in a Walking Shoe

A NEAT black Derby shoe is good style on most occasions when you don't need the protection of a boot. This is a medium-weight model, just right for walking, with good, hard-wearing soles and uppers cut from a selected Full Chrome Box. There is plenty of room across the joint, and it fits snugly and well round the ankle. A very fine shoe at a very moderate price.

Also made in Glace, a very nice, smart shoe, a little lighter, of course, than No. 327. In the medium fitting, we can also supply this shoe in half-sizes. No. 328. Price 22/6 post free.
No. 359. Superior quality Box Calf walking shoe, as illustration No. 327, 28/6

Three years' wear still good
"Messrs. J. Drage & Sons have made my shoes for over 20 years and they have given me every satisfaction. I generally walk from five to ten miles every day and the pair I am wearing now I have had three years."
Original letter can be seen at our offices

This is an actual photograph of the shoe

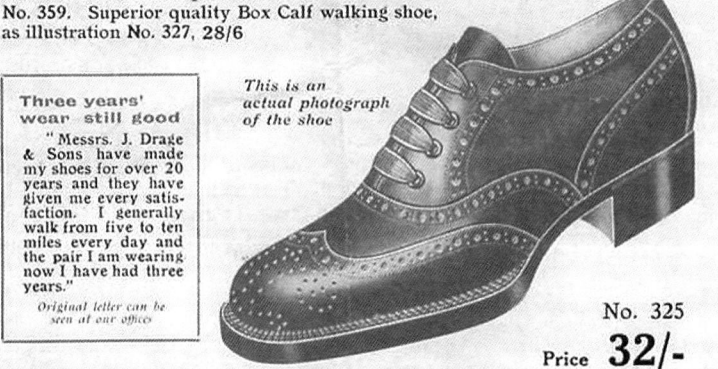

No. 325
Price **32/-**
POST FREE

Brown Willow Brogue Shoe

YOU will enjoy your game of Golf in this shoe. Or if you don't play the "royal and ancient game" you will find it very comfortable for ordinary walking. Its good stout soles, a full ⅜ inch in depth, are strong enough to stand any strain, being made of the best English tanned leather, and you won't find any of those weak spots that, in an inferior shoe, betray faulty materials or careless work.

Also in Toney Willow. No. 341. Price 25/-
Also in superior Black Box Calf. No. 326. Price 32/-
Also in Black Full Chrome Box, a slightly lighter shoe. No. 340. Price 25/-
Sizes 5 to 11, in medium and broad fittings

Page 20

No. 316
Price
38/-
POST FREE

HONEST JOHN FOOTWEAR
Reg. No. 387176.

This is an actual photograph of the boot

Ready Fitted with Rubber Soles

THERE is no doubt that rubber soles and heels do keep out the wet and lengthen the life of a boot—*if it is the right kind of boot.* You mustn't put them on to a light, welted model. That is why we are bringing out this boot already fitted with Wood-Milne Rubber Soles and Heels. It is made with ½ inch, *double* soles, which are screwed and stitched. This provides the necessary firm foundation for the rubbers, which are attached by short screws (not nails) and are very neat and inconspicuous.

Without exaggeration, this boot will last for a year before it wants re-soleing. It is a fine boot, of course, to start with—a solid, reliable, no-cap Derby, unlined, made of selected Box Calf. We can supply it in an extra broad as well as medium and broad fittings, and with toe-cap if desired.

Also a cheaper line, not quite such stout soles, or such fine quality uppers, but a fully-chromed leather and a boot carrying our guarantee. Made as above and same quality rubbers fitted.

No. 358. Price **32/-**
POST FREE

Sizes 5 to 11 in broad and extra broad fittings

In the Finishing Dept. Trimming round the soles

Page 21

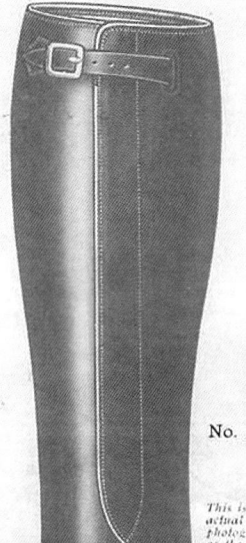

Smart, well-made Legging

A WHOLE-CUT Legging, nicely blocked to shape of leg, and made of the best smooth brown leather. It is easy to fasten with the patent spring, and there is an adjustable strap at the top. The height is 12½ inches. A favourite legging among country gentlemen, sportsmen and motorists, for it is very smart and workmanlike and thoroughly well-made.

No. 336

This is an actual photograph of the legging

No. 336, Calf measurement 13 to 17, in ½-sizes **13/-** Price Post free
(Also in Black, No. 337)

Very superior quality **19/6**
(Brown No. 338, Black No. 339)

Very satisfactory after a severe test
"The boots I have had from you have proved very satisfactory after giving them a severe test in all weathers. I find they keep the wet out better than any I have had before, they are just the thing for a farmer or sportsman."
Original letter can be seen at our offices.

Neat Brown Leather Slipper

"SLIPPER-SHOD" need not mean "slip-shod." After your day's work, you will appreciate the comfort and ease of this model, with its flexible sole, but you will also find it very neat and well-fitting. It is made of really good leather, and you will be entirely satisfied both with its wear and its appearance.

Also made in Black
No. 343, Price **18/6**
Post free

This is an actual photograph of the slipper

No. 342
Price **18/6** POST FREE

Whether you walk for business or pleasure you will find a pair of "Honest Johns" the best foot covering.

Page 24

A Beautiful Court Model

WHAT is smarter or more chic than a well-made Court Shoe for dressy occasions? The price of this shoe is no criterion of its quality. You could wear it anywhere with confidence, because it not only looks good, but *is* good. Its leather is a soft glacé, and it is made in sizes and half sizes. Though light in weight, you will find it a most durable shoe in wear.

Sizes 2½, 3, 3½, 4, 4½, 5, 5½, 6, 6½, 7, 7½

This is an actual photograph of the shoe

No. 402
Price
25/3
POST FREE

A Splendid Sample

"I have received boots which are a splendid sample but unfortunately just a little too large. Will you please forward me a pair of 5's as broad as you make them, when I think they will be quite satisfactory."

Original letter can be seen at our offices

Lady-like and Smart

THIS shoe is made on the hand-sewn principle. You get all the lightness and suppleness of the old-fashioned methods without having to pay the big price hand-work entails. You should try this model if you want a shoe that is both comfortable on the foot and smart in appearance. After all, a fine Glacé Derby with a Patent Toe-cap takes a lot of beating as a nice, lady-like shoe, doesn't it?

Sizes 3, 4, 5, 6, 7

This is an actual photograph of the shoe

No. 407
Price
31/-
POST FREE

A high standard is kept in all our footwear. No trash ever bears our Trade Mark.

Girls' High-leg Glace Lace Boot

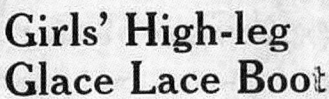

A BOOT for best wear. It is smartly cut, the leg being 8½ ins. high, and it is made from a beautifully fine Glace leather. Girlish requirements have by no means been overlooked, however, in getting this touch of smartness, for the heel is low and the medium weight soles are warranted to stand a big amount of real hard wear.

No. 416

Sizes	7 & 8	9 & 10	11 & 12	13 & 1
Prices	17/-	18/-	19/-	20/-

Sizes	2 & 3	4 & 5
Prices	21/-	22/-

POST FREE

Also made with 11 buttons instead of laced
No. 417. Same prices
POST FREE

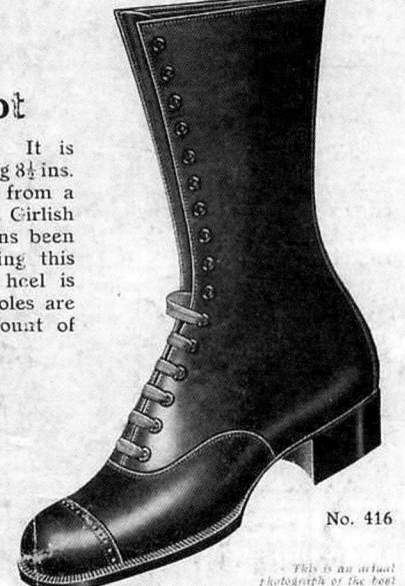

No. 416

This is an actual photograph of the boot

Another satisfied customer
"Very highly pleased with boots received; will recommend to friends. Many thanks for early attention to order."
Original letter can be seen at our offices

Girls' Strong Box Derby Boot

SCHOOLGIRLS, though not quite so hard on their boots as boys, want pretty strong, durable footwear in these days of sport and outdoor activities. This boot gives all the necessary protection, while it is neither clumsy nor heavy. It has good, stout, hard-wearing soles, and the uppers are cut from a sturdy but supple Box. The leg is 7½ ins. high, and it fits well and snugly round the ankle and calf. Made in all sizes.

No. 418

Sizes	7 & 8	9 & 10	11 & 12	13 & 1
Prices	14/-	15/-	16/-	17/-

Sizes	2 & 3	4 & 5
Prices	18/-	19/-

POST FREE

No. 419. Same quality and prices in button
POST FREE

No. 418

This is an actual photograph of the boot

Glace Derby Shoe with Patent Cap

A WALKING shoe of particularly smart and dressy design. It is light in weight, but will give you splendid wear, for there is nothing flimsy about its construction. It has a fashionable heel and the punching on the sides and counter gives it an extra touch of attractiveness. Altogether the kind of shoe that every lady likes to have in her wardrobe at all times of the year.

Sizes 2½, 3, 3½, 4, 4½, 5, 5½, 6, 6½, 7, 7½

This is an actual photograph of the shoe

No. 404
Price
26/-
POST FREE

Satisfactory in every way
3rd November, 1920
"The last pair of boots you sent me were satisfactory in every way. In quality, workmanship, appearance, price and fitting, they were all that could be desired."

Original letter can be seen at our offices

A Delightful Willow Calf Model

THE particularly deep and rich shade of the Willow Calf of this shoe will strike you first of all. Then you will note with appreciation the beautiful quality of the leather. It is a model made on the hand-sewn principle, and we cannot speak too highly of its refined, "good" looking appearance. It will wear splendidly, and is bound to be comfortable, because of its lightness and suppleness.

Sizes 3, 4, 5, 6, 7

This is an actual photograph of the shoe

No. 413
Price
31/-
POST FREE

"Honest John" Footwear comes direct from our factory to you.

Page 31

When your Boots want New Rubbers

FIXING Rubber Soles and Heels to a Boot is an expert job. You *can* do it at home, but naturally, as we have the right machinery and the experienced workmen, we can do it for you much more satisfactorily.

The next time you want Rubbers fixed, send the Boots to us. Provided they are still sound, we can give them a new lease of life. We will fix on Wood-Milne Rubber Soles and Heels in a skilful and workmanlike manner, iron up the sole edges, tree and clean the boots, and fit new laces. You will be delighted with the appearance of your old footwear when you get it back.

If, however, you prefer to fix on the Rubbers yourself, we can supply you with them separately.

	PRICES:		
	Men's	Youths'	Ladies'
Supplying and fixing Wood-Milne Rubber Soles and Heels, including Treeing, New Laces, etc. . post free	7/6	6/6	5/6
Supplying only . . post free	5/3	4/-	3/3

Our Assurance with Every Boot

This Indenture

Established 1865

Witnesseth that we, John Drage & Sons Ltd. guarantee the boots mentioned below to be sound and reliable in every respect; should the said Boots not give satisfaction under fair conditions of wear, we hereby undertake to repair them free of charge, or, if necessary, to replace them by a new pair.

John Drage & Sons Ltd

Bozeat. Northamptonshire.

THE above guarantee accompanies every pair of boots that bear the "Honest John" Trademark. You need have no hesitation, therefore, in ordering from this list, because you are protected to the fullest possible extent, and run no risk whatever.

BOZEAT IN SPRINGTIME

By Grendon pond and Easton brook
We'll wander in the Spring,
Where primrose, cowslip, violet
Their gentle fragrance bring.

On through the meadows' fresh green grass
Over the old white bridge
To the marshland where the rushes grow
And snipe and wagtail wing.

Then on again to Watson's Hole
Where minnows dart and gleam,
And soon to Sandwell's Spring we'll come
And rest awhile, and dream

There for awhile. All time stands still
As we hark back to the years
Of boyhood days – our little Spring –
Its childlike hopes and fears.

What memories of bygone days
And carefree happy hours
When, free as air, we roamed those ways
In sunshine or in showers.

But lets away from Sandwell's Spring
For we have still to go
To the Shepherd's Lodge, and the Windmill Field
Where the poplars used to grow.

So through the broom and the mushroom rings
Where fairies once danced by night,
By the tall old elms, to the gate which brings
Us out in the bright sunlight.

And when we come to Allens Hill
To stand on the brow, alone.
We'll gaze o'er the valley, so peaceful and still
– This bit of Olde England – Our Home.

William Harold Drage
1945

William Harold Drage was the son of George Alibone Drage and Lucy Emma Smart; brother of Florence Billing, Christine Maud Dickens and Mary (Dolly) Line. After the Second World War he moved to Leicester and married Margaret Tildesley, and lived there for the rest of his life, although it was always his ambition, after retirement from the City Council, that he would move back to Bozeat. He was born in 1892 and died in 1972.

Bibliography

Barley, M. W. *The English Farmhouse and Cottage*, Routledge, reissued by Sutton Publishing.
Barlow, Frank. *Thomas Becket*, Weidenfeld & Nicholson, 1985.
Bozeat Parish 2000 Produced by the Parish Council and first printed in April 1998 as part of the Millennium Celebrations.
Bozeat Pictorial History: Volumes 1 & 2. Published 1990/2 by Bozeat Methodist Church.
Bridges, John. *The History and Antiquities of Northamptonshire, 1762-1791*.
Brook, Rosalind and Christopher. *Popular Religion in the Middle Ages*, Thames & Hudson, 1984.
Duffy, Eamon. *The Stripping of the Altars*, Yale University Press, 1992.
Field, John. *English Field Names – a Dictionary*, David and Charles 1972, reissued by Alan Sutton, 1989.
Gover J. E. B., Mawer A. and Stenton F. M. *Place Names of Northamptonshire*, Cambridge University Press, 1933.
Hall, David. *Wollaston Portrait of a Village*, The Wollaston Society, 1977.
———. *Medieval Fields*, Shire Publications Ltd, 1982.
Hill, Christopher. *John Bunyan and His Church*, Oxford University Press, 1988.
Ireson, Tony. *Northamptonshire*, Robert Hale Ltd, 1954.
Marlow, Rev. J. H. *Bozeat – Your Village History*. Published in the Church Magazine of the 1930s – republished by Rachel Mallows in the 1990s.
———. *The History of Bozeat Village*, printed by J. Stevenson Holt, Northampton, 1936.
Noakes, Aubrey. *Charles Spencelayh and His Paintings*, Jupiter Books, London, 1978.
Neil, Stephen. *Anglicanism*, Penguin Books.
Stainwright, Trevor L. *Windmills of Northamptonshire*, W. D. Wharton, 1991.
Trevelyan, G. M. *History of England*, Longman, 1973.
Valee, Bert. *Scientific American*, June 1998.
Victorian History of the Counties of England (Northamptonshire), 1930 edition.

Index

[Page numbers in italics are illustrations]

Abbey Homesteads 72
Abbott, Arthur 57
Aberge Rofe 310
Abington Church 88
About Bozeat 7, 10, 15, 20, 22, 25, 27, 32, 34, 35, 36, 37, 47, 48, 235, 272, 359, 395
Abraham, Thomas 262
Abraham, William and Susannah 185-186
Adams, Rev. Stephan 88
advowson 12
Ahern, Lt. John 49, *50*, 58-60, 318, 334
Allebone, George 349
Allebone, John 164, 289, 291
Allebone, Mark and Pat 153
Allebone, Richard 13, 46, 48
Allen & Caswell 120
Allen, Christopher 336, 395
Allen, Dennis and Audrey 74
Allen, Rev. Michael 71
Allen, Richard and Ruth 237, 249, 348
Allens Hill 16, 17, 21, 26, 72, 86, *231*, 232, 262, *342*
Allin, George 153
allotments 72
Alston, Ted *90*
American pilots 45, 48, 49
Anglia Television 157
Anglo-Saxon hamlet 168
Ansell, Philip 348
Arch Villa 17, 18, 51, *191*
AYPA 53
Ayres, Elizabeth 249

Backside 72
Baddrick, Keith and Anne 77, 137, 394
Bailey, Rev. 294
bakehouse 34, 35
bakers 174-177
bakery 16
Ball, Lillian *361*
Band of Hope 16, 25, 163

Baptist Chapel 296
Barker, Jacqueline 244
Barlow, Vicar 325
Barnes, Mr J. 108
Baxter, Dr 25, 255, 257
Bayes, Alec 55
Bayes, Cecil *264*
Bayes, Daniel 299
Bayes, Dorothy *248*
Bayes, Ena *361*
Bayes, Evelyn *90*
Bayes, Gordon *241*
Bayes, Harry *92*
Bayes, Jack (Johnny 'Bundlehead') 55, *201*, *241*, *354*
Bayes, James 57, *166*, *217*
Bayes, Sam 160
Bayes, Sara 79
Bayes, Mrs Tom *290*
Beard, James *244*
Beard, Reg *290*
Beard, Win *290*
beer 161
Belcher, C. *379*
bell ringers (1948, 1950s) *316*, *317*
Belsher, Benjamin 104
Bennell, Mrs 23, 24, 238, 240, *383*
Bennes Field 26
Bennett, Dr 254
Bennett, PC 267
Berrill, Thomas 251
Berrills 89, 211-216, 219-220, 221, 222, 368
Bettle, John 251
Bettles, Laura 14, 24, *238*, *240*, 241, *242*, 273, *290*, *377*
Bettles, William 64, 159, 260
bicycles *46*, 265
Bird, Evelyn 26
Blackburn, PC 156
Blackmile Lane 36
blacksmith 23
Blanche, Mrs 89
Blenkharn, Linda *63*

Bligh, Audrey 6, 87, *313*, *338*, 363
Bligh, Marion 79, 82, *90*
Bligh, Norman 307
Bligh, Philip 6, *90*, 313, 337, *338*, 348, 409
Bloet, Robert 365
Bluet, Joan 168, 304, 310
Blundel, Margaret *241*
Blundell, Margaret *248*
Blunt, Mr 17
Blythe, Dr 254
Boddington, Samuel 175
Bogs, The 304, *409*
Bolton, Betty *384*
bombers B52 45
Boswell, Herbert and Jessie 108, 120, 121, 347, 381
Boswell, Philip 37, 40, 120-123, 244
Bosworth, Joe 289
Botterill, Alan *333*, *385*
Botterill, Alf 40
Botterill, Alison 51, 308, 313
Botterill, Dick 62, 77-78, 108
Botterill, Flo 40
Botterill, Frank 57
Botterill, William 25, 33, 38
Botterills 35, *38*, 39, 46, 61, 72, 74, 111-*113*, 112, 115-119, 392
Bovenzi, Salvadori 51, 89
Bowyer, Mr 64
Boy Scouts 21
Bozaid 46, 47, 71
Bozeat, aerial view *11*
Bozeat Ambulance Brigade 255-256
Bozeat Arch. and Hist. Soc. 7, 90
Bozeat Bands 16, 348
Bozeat Boot Co (BBC) 76, 78, 112
Bozeat Estate 72, 130-132, *133*
Bozeat Field Map 406-408
Bozeat football team 55

INDEX

Bozeat map (1835) *180*
Bozeat map (c.1930) *223*
Bozeat map (2000) *2*
Bozeat, name 10
Bozeat Parish Council 88
Bozeat Players 82, 92
Bozeat Playing Fields 77
Bozeat School 74, 89
  Board School (Camden Square) *160, 185, 188, 190*, 236-245, *239, 242*
  Board School elections 242-244
  Board School Staff *240*
  Harrold Road 245
  Parochial School 236
  School Class (c.1914) *248*
  School Class (1925) *241*
  School Class (1951) *244*
  School governors (1998) 249-250
  School Log 23, 53, 238, 239, 371, 377, 385
  School managers (1980) 245
  School Scrapbook *13, 16, 17, 19, 30, 31, 39, 233*
  Staff (1980) 245
  Staff (1998) 89, 245
Bozeat Scouts and Cubs 90, 282, 332, 381
Bozeat Village Sign *10*
Bradford, Vicar 324
Bradshaw's Close 340
Bradshaw, Doris *379*
Bradshaw, Frederick 57
Bradshaw, James 251
Bradshaw, Kathy *248*
Bradshaw, Mr 295
Bradshaw, William 108-109, 247, 292, *362*
Brannon, Gordon 88, 306, *313*
Brannon, Penny 7, 87, 88, 308, 338-339
Brearley, John *376*
Brearley, Miss Patty *376*
Bricks and tiles 219
Brightwell, Bill *244*
British Legion 75
Britten, Farmer 29
Britton, Vicar *331*
Brixworth, Bishop of 314, 422
Brook, Eric and Audrey (Easton Maudit) 78, 143, 166, 280, 336, 391, 393, 395
Brook Street 19, 374
Brooke, Rev. Donald 76
Brookside 73
Brotherston, George and Hilda 90, *383*, 384
Brown, Albert *384*
Brown, Cyril and Gwynneth 139-140
Brown, Eddie 45
Brown, Elsie *383*
Brown, Mrs Florence *391*
Brown, Hedley 139
Brown, Horace 158-159
Brown, John and Marian 89, 140, *343*, 348
Brown, John and Mary 152
Brown, Julie *244*
Brown, Mary *242*
Brown, Olive *383*
Brown, R. 327
Brown, Roy and Marion 76
Browning, Audrey and Doug 90, 249
Brownie Hall 33
Browns (farmers) 61-62, 394
Bryant & Sharman 306
Bryant, Annie 35, 335
Bryant, Wally *333*, 346, *385*
Brygg, J. 310
Buffalo Bus Company 269
building after Great War 223
building after the Second World War 224
building boom (1960s, 1970s) 224-225
building in 1980s, 1990s 226
building – numerical analysis 227-228
Bull Close 26, 77, 230-232
burials 15
Burnside, Ron and Christine 89
Burrows, Miss 196
Burton Terrace 15
buses *269, 270,* 271
butchers 174-177
bypass 85, 271-*274, 272, 273,* 297-399
Byrne, Mr R. 159

Cake Walk 20
Camden Square 19, 20, 21, 36, *188, 190*
'Canada' St Mary's Road *52*
Candy, Mabel 193
Candy, Roy 57
Cardington 56, 379
Carnival Queen (1938) *382-384*
Carpenter, Dr Ronald 143
carpet bowls club 56, 92
carriers 2
Carter, Drs Margaret and Cyril 255
Carter, Sue *343*
Carter-Locke, Dr 255
Cartwright, Peter 90, *343*, 348
Carvel, James 251
Carvel, Sandra 257, *353*
Castle Ashby 13
Caswells of Kettering 108
Cave, Bert 17, 61, 65, *385*
Cave, Dorothy 201
Cave, Jacqueline 167, *290*
Cave, Richard and Nancy 150, 156
Cave, Sarah (and Emma) 17, 35, 37, 375
Cave, Tom 17, 41
Cave, W. H. (CW) & Sons *134, 175,* 307, 332, *333*
cemetery 340, *341*
Census (1853) 103
Centin, Mr S. 335
Chamberlain, Neville 37
Chambers, John 289
Chapman, Mr 42
Chequers Field 21, 22
Chequers Inn 35, 151-153, *152*
Childs, Kenneth *333, 385*
Chisnell, Rev. Gordon 87
Choirs 28, 43, 45, 53
Christmas, Dr 255, *231,* 255, 257, 382
Church Cottages 213-*214*, 220-221
Church Farm *16,* 49, 55, 135, 153, 268
Church Hall 32, 33, 45, 242, 332, 396
Church Lane 185
Church School 12, 61, 236-237
Church, Maud 289
Church, Susannah 183-184, 192, 284-285,

INDEX

Church, Sydney 57
Church, William 183-184, 192, 260, 263
churchyard 340-341
cinema 33
Clapham, Arthur and Eileen 90
Clarke, Graham *231*, 232, 338
Clarke, Mary 90, 348, 391
Clarke, Spencer 112
Clements, Alan 244
coach travel 259
Coat of Arms *208*, 369, 403
Coe, Winnie 361
Cole, George 292
Cole, Mr J. H. 68
Colecloughs, John and Gertie 18, 68
Coleman, Carol 244
Coleman, Geoffrey 384
Coleman, Gladys *241*, 248
Coleman, Olive 361
Coles, Ann 244
Coles, Arthur 31
Coles, George 348
Coles, J. H. *379, 385*
Coles, Maurice 384
Coles, Ron 112
Collier, Lynne 90, *343*, 348
Collins, Irene 65
Collinson, Vicar 321
commercial travellers 70
Compton, Lord 13
Comsport 56
Confirmation Class 88
Constable's accounts 20
Co-op 18, 33, 42, 43, 44, 70, 85, 147, *195*-202, *197, 198, 199*
Cooper, Mr 51,53, 242
Corby 369
Corby, Charles 376
Corby, Dol *241*
Corby, Edward 348
Corby, Emma, Maud 382
Corby, Ena 379
Corby, Fred *261*, 265, 379
Corby, Freda 379
Corby, Gerald and Dorothy 72, 89, *343*, 348
Corby, Jack *241*
Corby, Kate 265
Corby, Keith 384
Corby, Laura 379
Corby, Maureen 352

Corby, Mick and Mary 33, 114, 352, 358
Corby, Miss Minnie 376
Corby, Nellie 289
Corby, Samuel 57
Corby, Ted 349
Corby, Thomas 103, 107, 108, 157-158, *159*, 247, 248
Corby, William 154
Corby, Winifred 15, 20, 22, 25, 32, 33, 34, 36
Coroner's Court 150
cottage, thatched *166*, *217, 261*
Cotton, Archdeacon 12
Council Street 26
Cox, Derek, James and Pat 307, 313, 336, 338
Craxton, Charles 57, 159
Craxton, 'Cody' *46*
Craxton, Joyce 384
Craxton, Stephen 378
Craxton, William 251
Cricket Club 57
Crofts, Josie 88
Cromwell 40
Cross Keys 20, 21, 25, 147, 149, *157*, *158*, *159*
Cubitt, Rev. George 286
Cullip, Keith and Carol *44*, 7
Cullip, Stephen 400
Curtis, Colin 85, 88, 91, *244*, 364
Curtis, Francis *317, 355*-356
Curtis, Mavis 244
Cutts, Paula 89

Daly, Dexter 349
Darnell, John 42, 347
Darnell, Newman 48, 49, *384*
Darnell, Nona 43, *90*
Darnell, Zena 244
David, King of Scotland 302, 321, 365
Davison, John Wykes *247, 327*
Daybell, Vicar *331*, 379
Deacon, Bruce 307
Denton, Mr 43
Denton, William 262
Depression, The 26
Deverill, A. 295
Deverill, Elsie 289
Deverill, Mr 61
Deviny, Barbara 88

Dexter, John 153, 175, 362
Dexter, Thomas 175
Dilley, Ernie and Amy *56*, 306
Dilley, Fred 79, 88, *244*
Dimmock, Doreen 86
Disney Bomb 46
Ditchfield 127
Dobbs, Miss Agnes 376
Dobbs, Arch 159
Dobbs, Arnold 24, 47, 52, 78, 153, 307, *384*
Dobbs, Esther (and Edith) 42, 196, *233*
Dobbs, Fred 'Poddy' 57, 265
Dobbs, George 159, 319
Dobbs, John 362, 367
Dobbs, Len 379
Dobbs, Mrs M. A. *233*
Dobbs, P. 317
Dobbs, Thomas 158, 291, 344
Dobbs, Tom Scott 349
Dobson, Mr 286
Doctors of Bozeat 254, 255
Doctors' practices 256-258
Dodson, Goody 20
Dodson, William 252, 368, 304
Dodson's Close 77
Dorrington, Sharon 88
Downey family 10, 86, 88, *313*
Dr. Martens 77, 121-123
Drage, Ada 24
Drage, Alison *45*, 51
Drage, Barry *48*, 68, 69
Drage, Bert *238*
Drage, Mrs Betsy Shep 187
Drage, Bill 248
Drage, Cecil *383, 386, 379*
Drage, Cephas 16, 24, 54
Drage, Charles 159, *209*
Drage, 'Clarry' 108, 110-111, 263, 265, 267
Drage, Cliff 42, 43
Drage, Clifton 57
Drage, Cyril 49, 57, 108, 141-143
Drage, Dick 17
Drage, Eddy *269*, 270, 398
Drage, Edna 290
Drage, Elwin 110
Drage, Ernest 25, 159
Drage, Evan 54
Drage, F. 327
Drage, Florence 242

440

INDEX

Drage, Floss 90
Drage, Frank 108, 120,
Drage, G. A. 292, 345
Drage, George 291, 348
Drage, 'Georgie' Dick 41
Drage, Gladys 361
Drage, Glenda 44, 197, 200
Drage, Graham 51, *244*
Drage, H. 156
Drage, H. Ernest 376
Drage, Hamilton 376
Drage, Harold 43, *241*
Drage, Harry 17, *241*, 379
Drage, Ian 45
Drage, J. 156
Drage, J. T. 295
Drage, Jack 'Tricky' *241*, *248*, 255-256
Drage, James, 158, 289
Drage, Jennifer 393
Drage, John 14, 18, 28, 247, 248, 291, 294
Drage, John (fruiterer) *186*, 187
Drage, John Henry 345
Drage, John 'Laddie' 35
Drage, Jonathan 295
Drage, Joseph 176, 291
Drage, Kath 45, *384*
Drave, Len 63
Drage, (née Line) Loreen 41, 64, *248*
Drage, Malcolm 45, 51, 53, 141-143, *384*
Drage, Margaret 248
Drage, Marion *241*, *248*
Drage, Marjorie 14, 17, 18, 19, 23, 29, 32, 33, 35, 36, 40, 41, 56, 57, *290*, 352, 355 358
Drage, Martin 244
Drage, Mrs 291
Drage, Nancy 289
Drage, Neil 349
Drage, Nora 54, 75
Drage, Paul *384*
Drage, Peggy 346
Drage, Percy 24
Drage, Peter and Rose (née Dunmore) 24, 46, *248*
Drage, Philip 43, *90, 333, 384-385*
Drage, Richard 384
Drage, Ron *333, 385*

Drage, S. 46
Drage, Samuel 27
Drage, Sarah 162, 251, 253
Drage, Seppy 64
Drage, Sheila *384*
Drage, Sidney 57
Drage, 'Spenny' *191*
Drage, Ted 17, 18, 64, *241, 248*, 307
Drage, Terry 24, *333, 385*
Drage, Thomas 237, 398
Drage, Tom Edgar 345
Drage, Tom 'Rocker' 54, 353
Drage, Thompson 349
Drage, W. 156
Drage, Walter 73, 73, 77
Drage, William 18
Drage, William C. 349
Drage, William Harold 419
Drage, William Hooton 247, 345
Drage, William Sidney 176
Drage Coach Co. 44, 69, 270
Drage's factory 17, 28, 35, 37, 39, 40
Drage's Shoe Co. 14, 33, 40, 103, 105, *106, 107*, 375
Drake, Vicar 275, 305, 324-325, 313
Driver, Robert and Pat 71, 177
Driver, Walter 248
drought 63-64
Dryberg Abbey 321
Duglas, Joseph 191
Dungee Corner 42, 51, 133
Dunmore, Arthur 57, 295
Dunmore, Em 333
Dunmore, Ernest 385
Dunmore, Fred 248
Dunmore, Miss G. 57
Dunmore, Rose 361
Dunmore, Stan 45
Dyches 62
Dychurch 19, 20, 27, 207

Eagles, Mrs 237, 240
Eaglesmere 53
Early, Thomas 57
East Farm 140
Easton Lane 49, *70*
Easton Lane Factory 52, 53, 112
Easton Maudit 13, 51
Eden, Bernard 57

Edmunds, Derek 30, 31, 221, 222, 242
Edmunds, Dick 31, 55, *267, 269, 270*, 316
Edmunds, Harry 12, 196, *221, 222*, 240, 349
Edmunds, Henry, *221, 222*
Edmunds, Ray and Jackie 75
Elderton, Peter 244
electricity 37
Electrosite 39, 53, 114
Elliot, Russell 316
Elliott, Arthur and Nancy 264
Elliott, Cissie 384
Elliott, Fred 159, *241*
Elliott, Harold 384
Elliott, Henry 349, 391-392
Elliott, Margaret 38
Elliott, Max *90*, 316
Elliott, Robert 349
Elliott, William 349
Elliotts, Messrs of Higham 55
Ellis, John 272
Empire Day 23, 29, *30*, 384
Enclosure Act 72, 128-129, 216-218
Engineer, The (pub) 35
epidemics 27
evacuees 52, *53*
Evans, Dennis and Sue 14, 85, 90, *343*, 348
Everest, Mr Cecil 378, 386
Everest, George 41
Everton, Agnes 310
Everton, Richard 310

Fairy, George 349
Farey, John 35, *46, 47, 48*, 68
Farey, Joy 47, 48, 243, 257, 351
farmers 19th and 20th century 132-136
Farrow, Cecil *343*, 348
Fayed, Dodi 12
Fayre 21
Feast Day 12, 21
Fenn, Cliff and Eileen 72
Fern, Mr 196
fire, Easton Maudit (1737) 276-277
fire, factory 278
fire, farm 279
Fire, Great (1729) 207-208, 275-276
Fire, House 280

INDEX

Firtree Grove 73
Fish Alley 20, 68
Fish & Chip Shop 18, 19
Flat, The *151, 261*
Fletcher, Barry and Anne 87-88, 90, 134, *343*
Flint, David 87
Flockton, Dr P Hebden 253
floods *19*, 20, 23, 47, 67-69
Flying Fortress 45
Ford, Jackie 90, 348
Forsythe, Dr 254
Forth, Mary 244
Forth, PC 35, 279, 389
Franklin, Olive 200-202
Freely, Pam and Peter 76-77, 279, 359
Frost, May *241, 333, 385*
Frost, Mr 38
Fry, Peter PC 279
Fullwell Road 72
Furn, Walter *384*
Furniss, Albert *384*
Furniss, Austin and Janet 79-80, 90, 354
Furniss, Jennifer *244*
Furr, Fred 57

Gaff, The 34
Gale, Olive *383*
Gall, Rene *361*
garage *46*, 71
Garbett, Cyril 27
Garrett, Sam 15, 41, 200-202, *201*
Garrett, William 196, 200-201, 286, 297, 375
Garretts 28, 45, 51, 365
Geeves, Edgar 43
Geeves, Paul and Julia 220-221, *244*
Gibbins, Brian & Terry 89
Gibbins, Jim 90
Gibson, Barry *244*
Gibson, Frank 397
Gilbert, Denton 181
Gilbert, Mr 297
Gillitt family 65-67
Girl Guides 21
Girls Life Brigade 56
Glebe Cottage 191-194, 285
Glebe Farm 52, 64, 72, 133, 143-144
Glover, William 169

Gluckstein, Dr 254
Goffs Yard 17
Gola Sports 77-78, 80, 112-113, 115, 117-119
Gold, The 108, 153, 167
Gooding, Connie *361*
Gooding, Phyllis *241*
Goodman F. & Sons 107
Goodman, H. Bryant 57
Goodman, Jack 57, *241*
Gough, John 251, 362
Grange, The 28
Grange Farm 35, 54, 134
Great War, the 23-25, 54
Green, Gladys *90*
Green, Kath 89
Green, Marion *343*, 348
Greens, White House Farm 17
Greenwood (Rock Villa) 24, 209
Gregory, Jim and Marjorie 73
Grendon 20, 43, 44
Griffin, PC 394
Griggs 77, 121-123
Guilds, the 165-166
Gulliford, Mr 242

Haggar, Peter 169, *317*
Haliday, Rev. 294
Hall, David 7, 139, 162, 201, 206, 228, 271
Harding, Vicar 322
Hardwick, Miss 13
Hardwick, Miss Maria 196
Hardwick, Rev. E. 49
Hargrave, Paynell 320-322
Harris, Edwin 57
Harris, Thomas 262
Harris, William 291
Harrison, Arthur 156
Harrison, Edward 57
Harrison, Mary 260
Harrison, Mr 293
Harrison, Mrs Susannah 186
Harrison, William 265
Harrold 9, 19
Harrold Road 20, 52, 72, 77, 262
Hawkins, William 192
Hayes, Norma (and Mabel) 56, 58, *248*
Hayes, W. J. 12, 14, 41, 295
Hayward, The 127
Healey, James 57

Hedges, Mr 28
Hensman, Thomas and Mary 27, 260, 362
Hensmans Lane 16
Hewlett, Miss Annie *376*
Hewlett, Em *333, 376*
Hewlett, Frank 31, 44, *333, 391, 376, 379, 385*
Hewlett, George 346
Hewlett, Mrs 35
Hewlett, Miss S. *376*
Hewlett, Miss Thora *385*
Hewlett, William 159
Hewletts Close 24
Hickling, Tim and Anne 86, 88-89, 91, 308, *313-314*, 339
Higginbotham, Phil and Mavis 89
High Street *18*, 19, 20, 147, 160, *161*, 372
Higham, David 76
Hill, W. F. 327
Hill, William 150,
Holiday Club 339
Hollowell, Robert 307
Holman, Mavis 52, 87, 243, 256-257, 257-258, 273
Holt, Len and Mac 88, 164, 213
Holy Cross, Canberra 12, 339
Home Guard 44, 46, 47
home life 36, 37
Honest John 18, *39*, *40*, 108, 120
Hooton & Barnes 35, 39
Hooton, Charles 57, *376*
Hooton, Daniel 167, 260
Hooton, Edward 167, 349
Hooton, Ernest 349
Hooton, Herbert 57
Hooton, Jonathan 260
Hooton, Mrs Louise *167*
Hooton, Thomas *349*
Hope Street 26, *221*
Horden, Mrs *290*
Horn, Peter 156
Houghton, Ian and Lynn 307
Houghton, Nicola *343*
Houghton, Thomas 154, 176
Housdens of Bedford 306
housing 27
Howard, Nancy *333, 385, 361*
Howarth, Arnold 90, 165-166, 298

INDEX

Howe, H. 327
Howkins, Grange Farm 54, 61, 87-89, 134
Hudson, James and William 289
Hudson, Mary 265
Huggins, Archdeacon Allan and Jan 12, 339
Hugh, Bishop 302, 365
Humphreys, Sara 160
Hungry Hill 33
Hunt, Annette 89
Hurdy-gurdy man 36
Hutchinson, Ernest *324*

Ingram, Helen 64
Ingram, Janet *244*
Inkly, Mr 286
Inoculation List (1789) 218, 252
intruders 321

Jakes, Nath and Mary 183
Jakes, William 313
James, Barry and Sheila 244-245
James, Gordon 29, 49, 137-137, 391
James, Margaret 88, 89, 249, 250
Jarvis, Jim 65
Jefferson, Carol *90*
Jeffs, Sydney 347
Jenner, Edward 252
Jennings, Vicar *330-331*
Johnson, Alfred 57
Johnson, Bert 33
Johnson, Dr 323, 369
Johnson, Miss Eadie *290*
Johnson, Ena *248*
Johnson, Ethel *167*
Johnson, George 292, 345
Johnson, Olive *242*, *254*, 265, 354
Jolley, William 195
Jolly, Jane *162*
Jones, Agnes 91, 130-132
Jones, Faith *343*
Jones, Miss Keziah 236
Jones, Lucy 35, 37
Jones, Peggy 346
Jones, Sid 20
Jones, W. Cuthbert 57
Jubilee 16, *30*, *31*, 373

Keech, Widow 276
Kendale, Isabella 310

Kimbolton 50
Kinch, Vicar *326*
King, Gertrude 9, *90*
King, Levi 349
King, William 349
Kirby, Mr J. W. 156, 238, 277, 327
Kirby, Mr 23, 29
Knapp Toolmakers 14, 91, 113-114
Knight, George 16, 21, 28 49, 268-269
Knight, Vicar 55, *317*, 334-335, 352, 358
Knightley, Jean *90*, *343*, 348

Lace School *166*
lacemaking 96, *167*-168
Lack, Ezra 297
Lack, Martin *298*
Lack, Mr 23, 29, 32, 53, 77, 238, *230-242*, 298
Lack, Mrs 40
Lancaster bomber 45
Lanyon, Gerald 129-130
Latimer family 365-367
Laud, Archbishop 322, 305, 322, 367
Laughton, Frank 68
Laughton, Joe 159, 349
Laughton, Max 45, 55
Laughton, Max and Eta 69, 358-359
Laughton, Sally *317*
Laughton's Shop *18*
Lawton, Graveley 175
Lawton, Hannah 101
Leach, Mr and Mrs 160
Lent Talks 339
Lee, Rev. Geoffrey 297
Lettice, Richard 162, 251-252, 254
Lettice, Vicar 322-324
lime kiln 26
Line, Bernard 14, 45, 181, *409*
Line, Bert 45
Line, Betty 45
Line, Christine 200
Line, Eileen *242*
Line, Ena *248*
Line, George 65, *384*
Line, Gladys 14
Line, Ivy 14
Line, Jack 57

Line, James 101, 261
Line, Janet *244*
Line, Judith 7, 143, 250
Line, Mabel 41, 358
Line, Norman *317*, *384*
Line, Rex 86, 88, 243, 308, *313*, 314, 315-319, *317*
Line, Ron 45
Line, Russell *244*
Line, William 45, *349*, 378-379
Linnell, Steve 40
Little Gains 21
Little, Mr and Miss 62, 181-182
Little Thatch 55
Lodge Plug Factory 80
London Road *18*, *20*, 68, *113*, 134, *209*, *210*, 261
Long Meadow 32
Lord Nelson 19, 35
Lovell, May *241*, *248*
Lovell, Edie *361*
Loveridge, Joyce *384*
Low Farm 28
Luatt, T. 366
Lucas, Baroness 72
Luck, A 57
Luck, Mary *241*, *248*
Luddington, William *376*
Lumley Deeds (1343) 128
Lunch Club 9, 90-91
Lymn, Bob 79, 80, 396

Mabbutt, Jack 391
Mabbutt, Matt and Charles 349
Mabbutt, Stanley 57
Macknis, Joseph (CW) 145-146, 304, 369
Magic Lantern 25
Mallows, Arch 39
Mallows, Bertie 57
Mallows, David and Elizabeth 18, 106, *244*
Mallows, John and family 102
Mallows, Ken *333*, *384*, 385
Mallows, Rachel 18, 79, 394
Mallows, Thomas 102, 291, 344
Mallows, William 102
Mallows Yard 65, *215*
Maltster 163-164
M&M Superstores 44
Mangle Ann Cottage *372*
Manktelow, Tony and Helen 90, *313*

INDEX

Manning, Vicar 322
Manor Estate 12
Manor Farm 17, 35, 139-140
Marathe, Drs 258
Marlow, Vicar 331-333, *332, 385*
Marriott, Grace 46
Marshes Manor 62
Mason, Paul and Fiona 17
Matchams 85
Matilda 302
Max 51
Maxwell, Alfred 349
Maxwell, Miss Annie 292
Maxwell, John Allebone 294
Maxwell, Eddy 349
Maxwell, Walter 247, 248, 293, 295
May Day *237, 242*
Maycock, John 262
Maycock, Sarah 352
Medieval buildings *205-206*
Mee, Arthur 62
Meeting Yard 102, 296
Memorial Board 25, 331
Methodist Church 16, 19, 35, 52, 84, 161, 163, *293*
   anniversary teas (1950s) *283, 290*
   Foundation Stone (1877) 293
   harmonium 292
   Love Feast 291
   revival 294
   Sunday School 41, 287, 287-288, *289, 295*
   Trustees (1877) 293
Mile Street 12, *153, 264*
Mile Street Beer House 153-154
Mill Road 6, 72
Millennium window 422
militia lists 175, 185, 218
Mines, Garry 159
Mines, Gordon and Julie 90, *343, 348*
Minney, Ellie 29, 87, 90, 298, *343, 348*
money 168-169
Monk, John 175, 248, 295
Monk, Miss 382
Monk, Sam and William 291, 344
Moore, 'Pepper' 35
Mooring, Betty 248

Morgan, Cyril *90*, 309, *313*
Mormons 41
Morton, Harold and Kate 272, 281
motorcycles 267
Moule, Vicar 329
Mount, The 65-67, 154, 176

Napoleonic Wars 101-102, 218, 259
National Grid 82
Neil, first shoemaker 100, 368
Neil, Bernard 42, 43, 44
Nellis, Jill 249
Nelson, Lord 88, 154-157, *155*
New Road 33
Newcombe, Bertha *167*
Newell, Margarite 359
Newlands Farm 35, *137-139*
Nichols, Henry 262, 286
Nichols, James 287
Nichols, John 263
Nichols, Lucy *248*
Nichols, Mr P. 176
Nichols, Paula 56
Nichols, Thomas 262, 286, 288
Nichols, William 349
Northampton Productive Society 121
Northey Farm 54, 260, 263
Nye, Stella 196

Oakfield Home 91
Oddfellows 72
Odell Leather 28
Old, Gary 26
Olney Galleries 38
Open (Three) Field System 126-127
Oram, John 296
organizations (1980-2000) 92-93
Ormsby, Bill 51
Orr, Dr 156, 372
Osbourne, J. P. 291
Osbourne, William 362
Overseers of Highways 261
Owen, Mrs 35

Packwood, William 156
Page, Alfred 57
Palmer, Vicar 7, 15, 16, 17, 22, 27, 166, 203, *336-337*

Paper Shop 18, 71
Parcel Fund 45
Park House 13
Parrott, John 90, *343*, 348
Partridge, Alan 316
Partridge, Albert and Lizzie (née Drage) 359, 360
Partridge, Bertram 57
Partridge, Cecelia *248*
Partridge, Dora *241, 248*
Partridge, Frances 102, *248*, 295
Partridge, Francis 27, 351, 360
Partridge, Frank 349
Partridge, George 156
Partridge, Harry 295, 304
Partridge, Heather *290*
Partridge, John 13, 14, 57, 360
Partridge, John Warren 164, 285
Partridge, Joshua 55, 264, *315-316*
Partridge, Joyce 56
Partridge, Len 349
Partridge, Mr 35
Partridge, Mrs *289*
Partridge, Ted 279
Partridge, William, John, Thomas, Frances 102, *248*, 295
Partridge-Underwood, Tom 8, 41, *63*, 68, 87-88, 164, 249, 273, 296-298, 397, 399
Partridge-Underwood, Sue 87, 90, 298, *343, 348, 399*
Patrick, Edward 57
Payne, Rev. Joseph 289
Payne, David and Lena *90*, 91, 116
Payne, Lyndis *63*, 87-88, 90, 298, *343*, 348
peace celebrations 24
Pearson, Robert 236
Peartree 26
pebble paths and pitching 219
Pell, John 260-261
Penn, Henry 313
Penn, William 26
Perkins, Dennis 39, 54, 55
Perkins, Ellen 64
Perkins, Frederick and Mary 158, 159
Perkins, John *133*
Perkins, Mrs *289*

INDEX

Pettit, Gladys *333*
Pettit, Johnny 'Hard Hat' *296*
Pettit, Richard and Mabel (née Tompkins) *86, 90, 262, 290, 348*
Pettit, William *57, 103, 295*
Pettitt, Miss Belle *166*
Pettitt, Jack *166*
Pettitt, Mr *269*
Pettitt, (née Bayes) Nancy *49, 51, 90, 264*
Phipps, Mr *28*
Pightle, Picle, Pykle, The *102, 135, 286*
Pioneer Sand & Gravel *42*
Pit Field *33*
Pitsford Reservoir *65*
Pitt, William *101, 163, 260*
Pizey, Vicar *236, 305, 326, 345*
Plough Monday *146*
Plowright *310*
Podington *15, 45, 46*
Podington Air Base *48, 49, 52*
Pollard, Mabel *248*
Pollard, Michael *11*
Pollard, Saunders William *247*
ponds *20, 64*
population *27, 73, 228-230*
Post Office *13, 23, 71*
Potato famine *15, 253*
Potman, the *35, 36*
Potter, Tara *90, 343, 348*
Pound, the *127*
Powell, Vicar *49, 121, 142, 316, 320, 333-334, 387*
Pratt, Ben *265*
Pratt, James *349*
Pratt, Kit and Peg *56, 73, 74-75*
Price, John and Jean *90*
Prisoners of War *51*
Pudding Bag Lane *413*

quarries *213*
Queen Mary *350, 356-357*

railway *266*
Ram Sportswear *79*
Razzle, Carol *90, 348*
Red Gables Farm *45, 49, 53, 73, 135, 141-143*
Red House Farm *35*
Red Lion *14, 21, 38, 39, 42, 146-151, 147, 149, 260*

Reeves, Heather *144*
Reeves, Snip *93, 245*
Religious Census (1671) *100*
Revis, Thomas *12, 22, 130, 150, 306, 308, 370*
Rice, Miss *21, 356, 376*
Rice, Mrs Lydia *167*
Risby, Viv *343*
Riseley, John *235, 362*
Riseley, Richard *102-103, 111, 286, 290, 291*
Riseley, Thomas *290*
Rivett, Mrs *42*
road repairs *261, 262*
roadman *20*
Roberts, Amos and Priscilla *14*
Roberts (née Tompkins), Dolly *12, 14-17, 25-29, 36, 42-45, 53, 54, 56-57, 70, 71, 83-87, 84, 290*
Roberts, Don *12, 14, 16, 22, 24, 25, 29, 39, 40, 42, 44, 51, 52, 61, 66, 69, 70-72, 83-84, 290, 389*
Roberts, Harold *248*
Roberts, Joan *237*
Roberts, Mr J. A. *279*
Roberts, Percy *14, 23-25, 31, 41, 76, 240, 248, 255, 295-296*
Roberts, Raymond *181*
Roberts, Richard *280, 287*
Robinson, Bob *352, 353, 357*
Robinson, Edwin *23*
Robinson, James *295*
Robinson, Mr *186-187*
Robinson, Mrs *23*
Robinson, R. *379*
Robinson, Thomas *159, 195, 248, 291*
Robinson, William *57, 159, 345, 349, 376*
Roche, Tony and Tricia *86, 129-139, 196*
Rookery, the *9, 20*
Roper, Jim *35*
Ross, Albert *57*
Ross, Catherine *246-247*
Ross, Florence *248*
Ross, Henry *57*
Ross, Lizzie *289*
Royal Antedeluvian Order of Buffaloes *298, 391*
Rudd, Mark and Linda *157*

Rushden Mission Band *92*
Ryan family *86*

St Andrew's Day *168*
St C(K)atherine *167*
St John Ambulance *21, 44, 296*
St Mary's Church *35, 43, 53, 86, 88, 203-205, 204, 299, 334-335, 403*
  belfry *307*
  coat of arms *208*
  choir (1923) *379*
  church chest *305*
  church clock *34, 55*
  organ *305, 332, 345, 346-347*
  plan *300-302*
  rood screen *304*
  tower/spire *308-309, 324-325, 328, 369, 371-372*
Sanders, Chris *55*
Sanders Yard *103*
Sandwell Field *127*
Sandwell Lodge *166*
Sandwell Springs *29*
Santa Pod *48*
Sargeaunt, Vicar *159, 248, 327, 376*
Sarrington, Mr *286*
Sarrington's, Mrs, Buildings *13*
Saving, Elizabeth *51*
Saving, John *160*
Saving, Peter *244*
Secker, Vicar *247, 326*
Second Field *33*
Selby, Dr *24, 25, 254, 256, 383*
Selby, Harold *358*
Selby, Mrs *40, 51*
Sellick, Mr *110*
sewage *62, 65*
Shaftoe, Robert *348*
Sharman, Peter *244*
Sharratt, Margaret *348*
Shaw, Dr Eric *255*
Sheldon Coaches *28*
Shepheard, Bill *90, 343, 348*
Shepherds Lodge *17*
Sheringham *24*
Shipton, Rex *241*
Shoe Co-operative *109*
shops *70-72*, 20th century *187-191*

INDEX

Shrive, William 288, 295
signposts 268-269
Silby, James 348
Silby, John 349
Silsby, Ada and Freda 41
Silsby, Albert 57
Silsby, Bill 26, 49, 57, 230, 241, 405
Silsby, Kath 308, *313*, 314, 397
Silsby, Harry 49
Silsby, John 349
Silsby, Mary *290*
Silsby, Neil 159, 348
Silsby, Stan 166, 349
Singh, Mohan and Mohinder 44
Skevington, Anne 196
Skevington, Edward 164, 175
Skevington, Miss M. *376*
Skevington, Samuel 153-154, 175
Skevington, Thomas Dexter 155-156, 176, 362, 370
Skevingtons 41
Skevington's Yard 175, 186
Skittrall, Brian 89, *343*, 348
Skivington, Mr E. 286
Skinners, Eric 384
Slindler, Frank *376*
Slype Farm 35, 134
Smart, Arthur 286
Smart, Haydn 6
Smart, John 264
Smart, Mrs *385*
Smart, Philip *384-385*
Smart, Richard 101
Smart, Rose *333*
Smart, Stella 196
Smart, Ted *316*
Smith, Miss Ada 23, 32
Smith, Charles 177
Smith, Dolly *290*
Smith, Frank 265
Smith, Gordon 248
Smith, Harold 90, *343*, 348
Smith, Henry *376*
Smith, Hollingsworth 24, 53-54, 244, *333*, 346, 347, *385*, 387
Smith, Mr J. Smith 156
Smith, John 264
Smith, John and Viv 157
Smith, Lynne 160
Smith, Max *241*

Smith, Mrs 35
Smith, Pat 339
Smith, Penny 249
Smith, Vera *333, 392-383*, 385
Smith, W. *379*
Smiths Buildings *46, 47, 161*
smithy 214
Somme, the 24
Sowden, Maureen 243, 249
Spakes, Harry 156
Spangle Row 27
Spar 71
Spencelayh House 19, 39, 46-47, 54-55
Spencer, Diana 12
Spencer, Earl 12, 130, 235, 242, 260
Spiers, Neville 38, 114
Spiritualism 25
Spring Hill Farm 133, 140
Spring Vale Farm 134
Squires, Benjamin 176, *261*, 376
Squires, Dick and Emily 34, *241, 248*
Squires, Joe *379*
Stanford, Marjorie 249, 298
Steele, John 272
Stein, Sharyn *343*
Stevens, Mr 297
Strixton 45
Stocken Hollow 28, 72
Stock(er), Edward and Margaret 184, 192
stocks 20
Stonebank 20
Stoneleigh 44
Stoneypiece 61, 70, 72
Strange, Dick 159
Strange, Peter *244*
Strange, Mr 35
Strudwick, Mr 22
Styles, Daniel 101
Styles, Samuel 101
Summerlin, Derek 49, 58, *264*
Summers, George and Pat 75, 88, 308, *343*, 348
Surridge, Thomas 162, 251
Surridge, William 264, 289, 304
Swann, Drs 75, 256-258
Swingler, Thomas and Anne 153-154, 158, 175
Swinn, Mrs 41

take-away 71
tanning 297
Tanyard Cottages 41, 286, 297
Taylor & Drage Co 111, *278-279*
Taylor, Derek 9, 15, 45, 48, 51, 88, 200-202, 339
Taylor, Frank 57
Taylor, J. H. *379*
Taylor, James 262
Taylor, Mr 44
Taylor, Pat *313*, 339
Taylor, Rev. William 287
Taylor, William 108, 110-111, 286
Tebbut, Jack 296
Temperance Movement 290
Terry, Mr John 242-*244*, 336
Terry, Nigel *317*, 336
Thorneycroft, Alex 46
Threadgold, Mr 17
Three Fields Farm 77, 137
Threlfall, Win *90, 91*, 339
Tin Pits 17, *415*
Tivey, Floss 21, 57, *290*
Tivey, Fred 43-44, 48, 197
Tivey, Len and Elsie 43
Tivey, Roger 336-337
Toc H 25, 389
Tombs, Tho 146-148, 368
Tomkins, Linda 90, *343*
Tompkins 384
Tompkins, Anne 76
Tompkins, Arthur *376*
Tompkins, Bert 16-17, 15-16, 19, *26, 28*, 44, daughters 86-87
Tompkins, Cyril 57
Tompkins, Miss E. *376*
Tompkins, Miss Elizabeth *376*
Tompkins, Emily 26, 53
Tompkins, Enid 43, *290*
Tompkins family (1918) *253*
Tompkins, Frank 'Wassy' 28, 267
Tompkins, Fred *15*-16, *26*-27, 349
Tompkins, Jim 76
Tompkins, John 68
Tompkins, Joyce 87
Tompkins (Higham), Laura 43, 76
Tompkins, Martha 36
Tompkins, Miss 'Mima' *167*

INDEX

Tompkins, Ralph and Sharon 76, 88, 103, 157
Tompkins, Sid 77
Tompkins, Trevor 76
Tompkins, W. 362, 376
Top Field 33
Torrance, Richard 317
Tots Group 88, 91
Town Farm 17, 35
Town Well 19, 29, 62-63, 212, 277
trades (1849, 1874, 1904, 1911) 170-174
trades (1980s) 177-178
trade directories 109-110
trade tokens 147, 148, 169-170
Triangle, The 29, 54
turnpikes 260, 262

undertaker 33
Underwood, Alan and Joan 90
Underwood, Alfie 37, 73-74
Underwood, Andrew 63, 88
Underwood, Dr 254
Underwood, Mary 376
Underwood, Mrs 68
Underwood, Olive 32, 354
United Counties Omnibus Co 270

Vicarage 323, 336
Vicars' Logbook 32
WAAF 45
Waendel Walk 402
Wagstaff, Barry 122-123
Wagstaff, Sue 122-123, 249
Walker, Jack 37, 40, 120
Walker, John 181
Wallace, Ada 193
Wallace, Mary 90
Wallace, Mr 23
Wallis, Elizabeth 298
Wallis, Frederick 57
Wallis, Gloria 87-88, 90, 298, 313
Wallis, Ted 164
Wallis, Thomas 184, 185-186, 192-193, 237, 247, 248, 205, 290-298
walls 214-215
Ward, J. 382
Ward, Lynne 7
Ward, Mr 38

Warner, Dick 241
Warner, Joseph 288
Warner, Mrs 'Mim' 156
Warner, Reuben 57
Warner's field 24, 25, 73
Warnford, Dr 254
Warren, Mr 176
Warren, Vicar 325, 329-330
Water diviner 64, 65
Watson, Joe and Betty 72, 90, 343, 348
Watsons Hole 32
weaving 96, 166-167
Weeds, John 285
Welch, Robert 391
Wellingborough 42, 52
  Mayor and Mayoress 307, 314
Wellingborough (Grammar) School 121, 235-236, 243, 258,
wells 19, 62, 63, 64
Welman, Len and Jean 193-194, 196
Wesley Guild 56-57
Wesley Institute 56
Wesley, John 284-285
Wesley, Joyce 58, 199-200, 243-244, 280-281
Wesleyan (Independent) Chapel 14, 35, 41, 68, 87, 190, 297-298
West, John and Diane 7, 92, 93, 191, 194, 395
Wharton, Robert 8
Wheelwrights Yard 23, 35, 166
whipping post 20
White House Farm 17, 35, 140
White, Mr A. 55
White Wall 32
Whites, Jack 54
Whites, John 28
Whittingham, William 72, 242
Wiggins, Gwyneth 90, 249, 343, 348
Wiggins, Louise 348
Wilkins, Richard 245 246, 249
Willey (ie), PC 35, 279
Williams, Julie 343, 348
Williams, Lil 54
Wilson, Horace 57
Wilson, Vicar 325
Windmill 62, 72, 128, 179-182, 180, 337-338

Windmill Field 21, 55, 57
Windmill Pond 21
Windmill Singers 89, 343, 348, 405
Wisemans 127, 130, 368-369
Wollaston 42, 43
Wollaston Co-op 42
Wollaston Road 14
Wollaston School 24, 53
Wollaston Silver Band 21
Women's Fellowship 91
Women's Institute 91
Woodfield 127
Woodford, Matthew 89, 348
Wooding, Robard 101
Woods, Sue 54
Woolley, Charles and Jane 148
Woolnough, Mr 44
Workhouse 215
Working Men's Club 14, 22-23, 33, 35, 46, 91-92, 159-160, 164, 327
Wright, Jack 336
Wright, James 101
Wright, Mr 42, 197
Wright, Tho 313
WVS 10
Wyant, Yvonne 244
Wykes Farm 136
Wykes, James 175, 192
Wykes, Mrs 291-292
Wyman Close 14
Wyman, Fred 31
Wyman, Olive 361
Wyman, Winnie 56

Yass, Australia 12
Yates, Robert 42, 305, 332, 346-347
Yelverton 13

Zang, Richard 45, 306, 309
zeppelin 24
Zinoviev letter 29

Millennium Window

On the back cover is a drawing by its designer Christopher Fiddes which became the stained glass Millennium Window of St Mary's Church, thanks to the skilled work of stained glass painter Nicholas Bechgaard. The journey from inception to installation was not easy and at times harrowing (the agricultural terminology is appropriate!). The proposal was rejected by the Diocesan Advisory Committee in conjunction with the Council for the Care of Churches more than once. I left for Australia in September 1999 believing that Faculty has been given only to hear it had been refused soon after my departure. Thanks to the sterling efforts and determination of the church leaders with the help of Chris Fiddes it finally gained its Faculty early in 2000, was installed by Nicholas on 2nd August 2000 and dedicated by the Bishop of Brixworth, Paul Barbour, on 3rd September of that year.

A major criticism by the advisory bodies was that the picture had 'nothing of God' in it. One specialist recommended that, if we insisted on having a window for the millennium, we should obtain a more appropriate one from one of the redundant London churches which were dispensing with some fine Victorian (his preference) windows.

But we wanted to celebrate the life of a village with a unique history of over 900 years. And if God is not present in 'our trivial round and common task' as the hymn has it – in the fabric of village life with its joys and sorrows, its laments and laughter, its labours and leisure – where is God to be found?

Initially we wanted the window to be in memory of Malcolm Drage, Bozeat farmer, man and boy, a church council member for over 50 years, and in memory of the village he loved. With money left in his memory together with generous gifts from others this splendid window now floods the hallowed precincts of its parish church with the warm light and rich memories of a remarkable village.

Philip Bligh